MW01092386

Praise for *Handbook of Military Social Work*

"This is an important book for anyone interested in providing care for our recent veterans and their loved ones. It provides a sophisticated, thoughtful orientation for nonmilitary clinicians. The discussion of military culture and diversity is especially comprehensive and brings together concepts that clinicians need to understand if they are to provide the best possible treatment for our military and their families. I highly recommend it!"

—Judith Broder, MD, Founder/Director, The Soldiers Project

"This handbook is a vital work for social work students as well as practitioners who are or plan to be engaged with veterans and their families. The chapters' authors represent a who's who of leading researchers and practitioners as they delve into the wide range of challenges, strengths, and interventions that social workers need to learn about. The text is also built around the Council on Social Work Education (CSWE)'s 2008 *Educational Policy and Accreditation Standards* while reflecting an evidence-based approach to practice. All social workers should become familiar with this important work. Rubin, Weiss, and Coll call us to stand firmly by our professional and civic responsibilities to these warriors and their families. To do otherwise would be the social work profession's shame."

—Ira C. Colby, DSW, LCSW, Dean and Professor of Social Work, University of Houston

"Wow, this is an extremely comprehensive and easy-to-read handbook regarding all aspects of military social work. The authors and editors have done a fantastic job of covering military life from the perspective of the serving members, veterans, and their families. This handbook will be of use to students and to experienced practitioners."

—Nicola T. Fear, PhD, Reader in Epidemiology, King's Centre for Military Health Research, King's College, London

"The editors of this handbook have literally written to meet Educational Policy and Accreditation Standards (EPAS) Core Competencies of the field of social work. The 26 chapters provide a comprehensive guide to understanding and helping within the military culture. This book fills a void in military social work and will become one of the most referenced handbooks of its kind."

—Professor Charles R. Figley, PhD, Paul Henry Kurzweg Distinguished Chair in Disaster Mental Health at Tulane University and School of Social Work Professor and Associate Dean for Research

"This handbook is a comprehensive and invaluable resource. It has relevance for all health professionals helping service members and families impacted by recent military operations."

—Colonel Rakesh Jetly, OMM, CO, MD, FRCPC, Psychiatrist and Mental Health Advisor to Surgeon General of Canada, Ottawa

"An excellent text that offers a lot of valuable information to social work students or professionals (especially nonveterans) who want to serve this population. Service members are a unique population because of their experience in war and the dramatic impact that can have on them and their families. An understanding of this culture is essential in order to provide them the services they need to reintegrate successfully."

—Stephen Peck, MSW, USMC, Vietnam Veteran, President/CEO, United States Veterans Initiative

"This book is a superb collection that will inform, educate, and inspire both social work students and practitioners in their commitment to provide the very best services to service members and their families. The challenges facing military personnel and their families are daunting. This volume meets a critical need in the preparation of practitioners who will meet those needs in the target population. I endorse it most highly."

—Julia M. Watkins, PhD, Executive Director Emerita, Council on Social Work Education, Alexandria, Virginia

Handbook of Military Social Work

Handbook of Military Social Work

Edited by
Allen Rubin
Eugenia L. Weiss
Jose E. Coll

WILEY
John Wiley & Sons, Inc.

Cover Design: Andrew Liefer

Cover Images; Backgound image: © Sava Alexandru/iStockphoto, Inset wheelchair image: © Mehmet Yunus Yesil/iStockphoto, Inset soldier image: © Daniel Bendjy/iStockphoto, Inset family counseling image: © Miodrag Gajic/iStockphoto, Inset father/daughter image: © Jason Swarr/iStockphoto, Inset family silhouette image: © kfotos/iStockphoto, Inset family image: © Blend Images/Alamy

This book is printed on acid-free paper. ♾

Copyright © 2013 by John Wiley & Sons, Inc. All rights reserved.

Published by John Wiley & Sons, Inc., Hoboken, New Jersey.
Published simultaneously in Canada.

No part of this publication may be reproduced, stored in a retrieval system, or transmitted in any form or by any means, electronic, mechanical, photocopying, recording, scanning, or otherwise, except as permitted under Section 107 or 108 of the 1976 United States Copyright Act, without either the prior written permission of the Publisher, or authorization through payment of the appropriate per-copy fee to the Copyright Clearance Center, Inc., 222 Rosewood Drive, Danvers, MA 01923, (978) 750-8400, fax (978) 646-8600, or on the web at www.copyright.com. Requests to the Publisher for permission should be addressed to the Permissions Department, John Wiley & Sons, Inc., 111 River Street, Hoboken, NJ 07030, (201) 748-6011, fax (201) 748-6008.

Limit of Liability/Disclaimer of Warranty: While the publisher and author have used their best efforts in preparing this book, they make no representations or warranties with respect to the accuracy or completeness of the contents of this book and specifically disclaim any implied warranties of merchantability or fitness for a particular purpose. No warranty may be created or extended by sales representatives or written sales materials. The advice and strategies contained herein may not be suitable for your situation. You should consult with a professional where appropriate. Neither the publisher nor author shall be liable for any loss of profit or any other commercial damages, including but not limited to special, incidental, consequential, or other damages.

This publication is designed to provide accurate and authoritative information in regard to the subject matter covered. It is sold with the understanding that the publisher is not engaged in rendering professional services. If legal, accounting, medical, psychological or any other expert assistance is required, the services of a competent professional person should be sought.

Designations used by companies to distinguish their products are often claimed as trademarks. In all instances where John Wiley & Sons, Inc. is aware of a claim, the product names appear in initial capital or all capital letters. Readers, however, should contact the appropriate companies for more complete information regarding trademarks and registration.

For general information on our other products and services please contact our Customer Care Department within the United States at (800) 762-2974, outside the United States at (317) 572-3993 or fax (317) 572-4002.
Wiley publishes in a variety of print and electronic formats and by print-on-demand. Some material included with standard print versions of this book may not be included in e-books or in print-on-demand. If this book refers to media such as a CD or DVD that is not included in the version you purchased, you may download this material at http://booksupport.wiley.com. For more information about Wiley products, visit www.wiley.com.

Library of Congress Cataloging-in-Publication Data:

Handbook of military social work / edited by Allen Rubin, Eugenia L. Weiss, Jose E. Coll.
p. cm.
Includes bibliographical references and index.
ISBN 978-1-118-06783-3 (cloth)
ISBN 978-1-118-33094-4 (e-bk)
ISBN 978-1-118-33022-7 (e-bk)
ISBN 978-1-118-33305-1 (e-bk)
1. Military social work—United States—Handbooks, manuals, etc. 2. United States. Armed Forces—Mental health services—Handbooks, manuals, etc. I. Rubin, Allen. II. Weiss, Eugenia L. III. Coll, Jose E.
UH755.H36 2013
362.8—dc23

2012020185

Printed in the United States of America

10 9 8 7 6 5 4 3 2 1

This book is dedicated to our brave men and women service members, veterans, and their families, who have unselfishly sacrificed so much for us to enjoy the freedoms provided by this great nation, and to social work faculty members, practitioners, and students dedicated to supporting the heroes of our past, present, and future generations.

Contents

Part II: Interventions for the Behavioral Health Problems of Service Members and Veterans

Part III: Veterans and Systems of Care

Foreword

It's about time! Finally, a book has been written to inform community social workers and other behavioral health providers about military culture, challenges, and clinical practices for military personnel, veterans, and their families. This type of book has been missing from our classrooms and professional bookshelves and is long overdue.

The wars in Iraq and Afghanistan are now the longest-running wars in U.S. history. Operation Enduring Freedom (OEF), Operation Iraqi Freedom (OIF), and Operation New Dawn (OND) are being fought with a small, all-volunteer military made up of less than 1% of the U.S. population. What motivates individuals to enlist? Many of the men and women who have been fighting these wars joined the military because they were inspired by a sense of patriotism or were continuing a family tradition of military service. Whatever the reason for joining, these individuals enter the ranks prepared to give their lives for their country. Nevertheless, they and their families have grown weary after a decade of war.

It is now apparent that the psychological and personal stress for service members, veterans, and their families is more prevalent and powerful than previously understood. The persistently high operational tempo, along with the development of invisible wounds and the challenges associated with reintegration, have clearly taken a toll. Evidence indicates that the key mental health issues affecting the approximately 2.4 million American troops deployed to Iraq and Afghanistan since 2001 are traumatic brain injury, posttraumatic stress disorder, substance abuse, depression, anxiety, marital discord, and suicide—and often these disorders overlap (Schell & Tanielian, 2011). As troops return from the war zones and contend with transitioning back into their communities, we expect to see an increase in these issues. This is a lesson we have learned all too well from the plight of Vietnam-era veterans. Health care workers and family members can be deceived by what seems to be a relatively smooth homecoming from deployment, and perceive that all is well among these service members. However, as the initial flush of homecoming fades and time stretches on, more and more people will come forward with their struggles. The influx of OEF/OIF/OND veterans into the U.S. mental health system has yet to peak, but it is clearly underway.

Many people are concerned that the mental health care system is not prepared to handle this inevitable wave of veterans. Recent reports indicate that there is a shortage of mental health professionals competent to meet the demands of those returning from war (Cameron, 2011). This is not from a lack of empathy or interest from the health care community. Although many civilian organizations and professionals are eager to work with service members and their families, the reality is that a cultural divide exists between military-impacted populations and their civilian counterparts—particularly regarding the warrior psyche and the experience of combat trauma. Civilian clinicians lack the means to fully comprehend these paradigms and the effect they have on the lives of service members and their families. As a result, military-impacted individuals, already reticent to seek services or mental health treatment, encounter well-meaning clinicians who are ill-prepared to accommodate them and their families with appropriate mental health and medical care, employment readjustment, training support, educational and financial guidance, and other critical services and transition supports.

The military, and the biopsychosocial challenges that arise from military involvement, have been a part of this country's history since its inception. So how did this cultural divide persist within the health fields between military and civilian populations? One factor has been that services for military personnel and veterans have historically been strictly segregated from their civilian counterparts. Compounded with the specialized and selective nature of professional military training in the United States, these factors have produced a distinctive "military culture" that is poorly understood by civilians. Drawing from my own experiences as an enlisted member and officer of both the Army and Air Force for 25 years, and having experienced deployment, I believe that to be truly effective, behavioral health professionals working with the military and veteran population need to be able to connect in a manner that says, "I understand you." If you do not connect with the military or veteran client during the first session, then he or she is not coming back.

Unfortunately, there has been little done within behavioral health education to increase the workforce supply in the area of military cultural competence and evidence-based treatment for this population. However, some steps have been taken in this direction with the Council of Social Work Education (CSWE) Task Force setting up educational and practice guidelines for a specialization in military social work. This task force was comprised of an array of military and veteran mental health experts who developed advance practice skills, behaviors and ethical conduct guidelines that define military social work today based on a set of core competencies that prepare professionals working with this population. (The Preface of this book links the CSWE approved core competencies for military social work to the chapters to which each competency pertains.) Additionally, the School of Social Work at the University of Southern California is one of the first to develop a military social work subconcentration (under the Master of Social Work), and includes curricula derived from the competencies and provides field training opportunities as well as a research center that is dedicated to studying military and veteran issues (and I am pleased to report that more and more of such educational, research, and training programs are coming to fruition around the country).

However, to fully address the behavioral health of military-impacted populations, the quality of care available, and the lack of qualified providers, there must be a concerted, coordinated effort between local, state, and federal agencies (as well as collaboration between educational institutions). We need to bring together a diverse set of resources, and ensure that access to these resources is not fragmented. We need to identify new opportunities in both the public and the private sectors that will support the range of services that this population needs. And we need to make sure that we lay a foundation that will last for many years to come—well beyond the wars in Iraq and Afghanistan.

The need for community behavioral health providers, programs and organizations to address the current and future behavioral health challenges facing our veterans and their families has never been more crucial. We need to increase our capacity to competently serve those who have so valiantly served us so that we can more effectively assist in the resolution of these hardships and in the restoration of human potential for veterans and their families. Our ability to meet these challenges will be enhanced by drawing from the valuable lessons in this timely and comprehensive handbook.

Anthony Hassan

REFERENCES

Cameron, P. (2011, July 20). Vets face shortage of therapists. *Chicago Tribune*. Retrieved from http://www.chicagotribune.com/health/ct-x-0720-vets-mental-health-20110720,0,66678.story

Schell T., & Tanielian, T. (Ed.). (2011). *A needs assessment of New York State veterans. A final report to the New York State health foundation*. Retrieved from http://www.rand.org/pubs/technical_reports/TR920.html

Preface

Allen Rubin

This book has been developed for use in the education and training of social work students and practitioners who are either currently or will in the future be working with our brave military personnel and their families. Social workers are uniquely poised to assist this population in dealing with the unprecedented and daunting challenges they face as active duty members, National Guard members, and reservists, or as veterans of today's ongoing Global War on Terrorism.

The book is directed not only to those who will work as uniformed military social workers, but also to those who will work with this target population as civilian social workers. Indeed, the vast numbers of service members returning from the wars in Iraq and Afghanistan likely will exceed the capacity of the Department of Veteran Affairs and affiliated programs such as the Vet Centers to serve them all adequately. These clients will be seeking services within the civilian sector, such as in community mental health agencies, HMOs, and private practices. It no longer will suffice for civilian social workers to just refer veterans to the VA on the grounds that they (the civilian social workers) lack sufficient expertise with such cases. Thus, one objective of this book is to help civilian social workers gain the knowledge they need to better serve this population. This book also helps students gain such expertise, including those students aspiring to become uniformed military social workers as well as those who—as civilian social workers—will be better prepared to work with active duty service members, National Guard and Reserve personnel, and veterans and their families.

ORGANIZATION

The chapters in this book address the wide range of challenges, strengths, and interventions that social workers need to learn about in working with this population. The chapters in Part I impart foundational knowledge about social work with service members and veterans, including the history of social work and the military; unique aspects of the military culture that practitioners must know to understand and be credible to military personnel, veterans, and their families; common ethical dilemmas confronting uniformed and civilian military social workers; the triumphs and challenges experienced by women in the military; and the secondary trauma practitioners often experience when working with veterans who have been physically or emotionally injured from traumatic combat experiences or from other types of trauma.

The chapters in Part II of the book cover behavioral health problems and related interventions with service members and veterans, including posttraumatic stress disorder (PTSD) and co-occurring disorders and their treatment; traumatic brain injury; substance use disorders; and preventing suicide. The chapters in Part III address the challenges social workers face in helping veterans transition to civilian life, including preventing homelessness and rehabilitating those who are homeless; helping veterans and their families navigate through complex systems of care; helping veterans secure employment, adequate housing, and veteran benefits related to education and health care; and helping transitioning service members offset the loss of camaraderie and cohesion by becoming involved in community activities and thus finding a new "mission."

The final section of this book, Part IV, contains chapters on families impacted by military service. These chapters discuss the impact of military service on families and its implications for the role of social workers, including content on family stress and resilience, such as the impact of multiple cycles of deployment on family well-being; domestic violence and its prevention and treatment; the unique circumstances of the families of National Guard and Reserve members and ways to support them; military families with children who have disabilities; grief, loss, and bereavement in military families—with a special focus on suicide loss; long-term family caregiving: the challenges faced by children and youth impacted by their parents' military service; empirically supported therapies for military couples and families; and a conceptual and historical overview of the impact of military service on families.

Most chapters provide case vignettes to illustrate the practice applications of the chapter topic, case vignette discussion questions, and/or end-of-chapter discussion questions for reflection on the chapter's main concepts—questions that might be particularly useful for instructors to employ in their teaching about those concepts. The book ends with a glossary that can help readers become familiar with military-related terms and an appendix that lists numerous resources relevant to helping service members, veterans, and their families.

EPAS CORE COMPETENCIES[1]

The contents of every chapter in this book pertain to core military social work competencies delineated in the Educational Policy and Accreditation Standards (EPAS) of the Council on Social Work Education (Council on Social Work Education [CSWE], 2010). For example **EP 2.1.1** regarding proper professional conduct pertains to Chapter 2 on military culture and the need for cultural sensitivity in serving this population as well as the ethical decision-making content in Chapter 4. Chapter 4 also addresses the ethical demands placed on social workers assisting military (active duty) versus veteran cultures and provides extensive content on ethics that also pertains to **EP 2.1.2**, which refers to ethical principles for guiding professional practice.

The critical thinking component of **EP 2.1.3** pertains to content in most of the chapters in Parts II, III, and IV of this book—particularly regarding (1) analyzing relationships among clients, families, the military, and veterans' organizations; and (2) considering various assessment, prevention, and intervention models being implemented in military social work.

---

[1]The military social work EPAS can be found online at www.cswe.org/File.aspx?id=42466.

The diversity component highlighted in **EP 2.1.4** pertains to most of the content in Chapter 2 on military culture and diverse groups, Chapter 3 on women in the military, Chapter 20 on families with children who have special needs, and the parts of Chapter 24 that discuss cultural responsiveness in connection to therapy with couples. Moreover, many of the case vignettes found in various other chapters involve culturally diverse cases.

The social and economic justice component in **EP 2.1.5** pertains to content found in all of the chapters in Parts I, II, and III of this book. Chapter 2, for example, discusses the stigma perceived by service members associated with seeking help for their psychosocial problems, and Chapters 12 and 13 discuss stigma in connection to seeking help for substance use disorders. Chapter 15 discusses poverty and financial hardship in connection to homelessness. Chapter 16 provides a "road map" for helping economically disadvantaged veterans access resources and benefits. Likewise, Chapter 17 discusses how social workers can help transitioning service members find employment, adequate housing, and veteran benefits. Chapter 21 discusses resources available to families of children with special needs. In addition, the Appendix provides an extensive list of resources that can enhance the lives of veterans and military families.

Virtually every chapter in this book that discusses interventions mentions the empirical support for those interventions, many of which are evidence-based. Thus, those chapters pertain to **EP 2.1.6** (engage in research-informed practice . . .). This is most evident in the chapters in Parts III and IV. For example, Chapter 3 applies the evidence-based intervention, cognitive behavioral therapy, to the case of a female veteran who was sexually harassed and who has PTSD. Chapter 6 discusses the evidentiary support for various theories of and interventions for PTSD. Chapter 8 describes exposure therapy, which is widely recognized as the most evidence-based treatment for PTSD. Chapters 12 and 13 describe motivational interviewing and seeking safety, two empirically supported interventions for substance abuse. Chapter 23 discusses the FOCUS model, which is empirically based. Chapter 25 describes empirically informed therapies being implemented with couples and families impacted by military service.

Virtually every chapter in this book contains extensive content pertaining to **EP 2.1.7** regarding human behavior and the social environment. The policy emphasis regarding advancing social and economic well-being in **EP 2.1.8** pertains to most of the chapters in this book, especially the chapters in Part III that contain content on preventing homelessness; helping veterans and their families navigate through complex systems of care; and helping veterans secure employment, adequate housing, and various veteran benefits.

EP 2.1.9 (respond to contexts that shape practice) is reflected in many of this book's chapters, especially the historical content in Chapter 1 and the cultural content in Chapter 2, which correspond to the CSWE recommendation that social work practitioners working with military clients should know about the history and current trends in service delivery to "service members, veterans, their families, and their communities" (p. 13). Additional content pertinent to **EP 2.1.9** can be found in the chapters in Part III, particularly Chapter 16, on helping veteran clients navigate through systems of care.

EP 2.1.10(a)–(d) refers to content regarding engaging, assessing, and intervening with clients at various levels of practice. This broad range of content pertains to almost every chapter in this book. To get a glimpse of the many ways our book reflects the extensive CSWE list of practice behaviors illustrating the **2.1.10** core competency, one need look no further than the Contents section that began on page ix. Providing examples of all of those ways would go beyond the scope of this preface, so I mention just a few. To begin, **EP 2.1.10** overlaps with **EP 2.1.6** regarding engaging in research-informed practice; thus, the examples provided above for that competency apply here, as well. Some other examples are as follows. Regarding engaging clients, Chapter 2 addresses how building a therapeutic alliance with military personnel, veterans, and their families requires knowledge of military culture. Chapter 5 identifies strategies for assessing, preventing, and treating secondary trauma among service providers working with combat veterans. Chapter 7 provides an overview of the cognitive processing therapy protocol, an empirically supported treatment for PTSD. Chapters 10 and 11 discuss the assessment and treatment of traumatic brain injury (TBI). Chapters 15 and 17 give considerable attention to organizational and community efforts to help veterans transition to civilian life. Chapters 18 and 19 discuss group and support system approaches for helping families cope with the cycle of deployment and other stressors.

The unique nature of the Global War on Terrorism has confronted military service members, veterans, and their families with unprecedented biopsychosocial issues. These include the widespread problems of traumatic brain injury (TBI) and PTSD, an increase in the number of suicide attempts and completed suicides, the devastating impact that multiple and lengthy deployments can have on service members and their families, difficulties in transitioning back into civilian life between deployments and after retiring from military service, as well as various other problems. Therefore, more than ever before social workers are needed to address the multifaceted issues faced by this population and assist in supporting our nation's warriors and their families. We hope this book spurs readers to have the desire to serve military personnel, veterans, and their families, and that it improves their effectiveness and confidence in working with this target population.

REFERENCE

Council on Social Work Education (CSWE). (2010). *Advanced social work practice in military social work*. Retrieved from www.cswe.org/File.aspx?id=42466

Acknowledgments

Special thanks go to four Wiley staff members who helped make this volume possible. Peggy Alexander, vice president and publisher, supported this project from the beginning. Rachel Livsey, senior editor, provided early inspiration for the book, and has been a solid source of support throughout the process. Amanda Orenstein, editorial assistant, has worked hard on this project from the start; we can't thank her enough for her valuable help. Thanks also go to this book's production editor, Kim Nir. We also thank our terrific chapter authors for their fine work and timely submissions. In addition, we would like to acknowledge the military and veteran clients and their families who have shared their stories of hardship and joy and taught us about sacrifice and honor. Finally, we want to acknowledge the veteran social work students who aspire to serve by giving back to the military community through their meaningful work. Their passion and commitment is an inspiration for the social work profession.

Allen Rubin
Eugenia L. Weiss
Jose E. Coll

Introduction
Understanding and Intervening With Military Personnel and Their Families: An Overview

Allen Rubin

Social workers have worked with military personnel, veterans, and their families throughout the history of the social work profession. In so doing, they have performed the full range of professional social work activities. With each new war, the value of military social workers became increasingly appreciated, and they have been increasingly employed by all of the branches of the armed forces. Today, the increased utilization of military social workers is seen not only among those in uniform, but also among those who work contractually on base, at the Veterans Administration (VA) and its centers, other departments of the federal government (such as the Department of Homeland Security), and in community agencies or private practice.

With each new war, the roles of military social workers expanded. Today, military social workers (including those in and not in uniform) perform work at all levels of social work practice, ranging from direct practice to administrative and policy-level roles. Some prominent examples of their varied services include case management; various modalities of psychotherapy; counseling; family psychoeducation and advocacy; medical social work and hospice care; and the development of community-level programs, policies, and procedures. Prominent examples of the types of problems that they deal with include posttraumatic stress disorder (PTSD), domestic violence and child maltreatment, traumatic brain injury (TBI), substance abuse, suicide prevention, family bereavement, combat stress, veteran homelessness, and readjustment to civilian life.

The expansion of social work roles in helping military personnel, veterans, and their families has escalated in the current Global War on Terrorism. Today's U.S. military service members, veterans, and their families have had to deal with unprecedented biopsychosocial problems. Biologically, there is the widespread problem of TBI from roadside bombs that imperil even noncombat service members in this war without a defined frontline. Psychologically, the constant danger posed by the lack of a defined frontline has contributed to a growing prevalence of PTSD among the service members. Military personnel are constantly vigilant, as the enemy is not another country, but rather segments of the populace that they are trying to help. Realizing that anybody could be an enemy amid a civilian population, service members know that attacks can come at any time or place, from indigenous enemies dressed in civilian clothes who often exploit women and children as a means of attack. This contributes to a state of hyperarousal that is an undesirable PTSD symptom after returning home, but is actually adaptive during deployment. It also means that the need to sometimes kill without being sure who the good guys and bad guys are can exacerbate feelings of guilt and self-blame on returning from war.

Treating combat-related PTSD, therefore, can be more challenging than treating most forms of civilian PTSD. For example, the levels of anger and aggression associated with combat PTSD tend to be greater than with most types of civilian PTSD. Also, comorbidity with other disorders is common with combat-related PTSD. Consequently, PTSD among military veterans tends to be complex and chronic and is likely to require a longer treatment regimen than with less complex forms of PTSD. Exposure therapy (an empirically supported treatment for PTSD to be discussed in Part II of this book) typically needs to be more flexible and titrated when provided to combat veterans than with civilians, and with combat vets it often needs to be preceded by or in conjunction with interventions targeting comorbid disorders, such as substance abuse, suicidality, and poor impulse control (Courtois & Ford, 2009; Moore & Penk, 2011; Rubin, 2003).

Today the ratio of wounded warriors who survive with devastating injuries is much greater than in the past. In Iraq, for example, 16 soldiers got wounded or sick for every fatality. The comparable ratios were 3 to 1 in Vietnam and Korea, and 2 to 1 in World War II (Hall, 2008). Thus, social work interventions of various modalities and at all levels of practice are needed to help veterans and their families deal with the long-term physical, psychological, and socioeconomic impact of polytraumatic injuries that can include not only TBI and PTSD, but also musculoskeletal and spinal cord injuries, amputations, burns and visual problems (Owens et al., 2008).

Also unprecedented is the number of military suicide attempts and completed suicides. As reported by Walker (2011), the number of suicide attempts by U.S. Marines is at an all time high, with the number of reported attempts during the first 11 months of 2011 more the doubling the number in all of 2002, the year that the Marine Corps first began recording and reporting suicide attempt statistics. A similar trend has been observed in the Army, where the suicide rate trended up every year between 2004 and 2009, with the rate in the latter year more than doubling the rate in 2001 (Ritchie et al., 2011). The rise in military suicides and attempted suicides has been attributed by mental health specialists to the nature of the current wars in Iraq and Afghanistan, including the stress of long and frequent deployments among other stressors. (Walker, 2011).

As discussed by Schwartz (2011), many of today's veterans have served multiple overseas deployments and return struggling to adapt to civilian life after knowing nothing but war for perhaps as long as a decade. No previous war has had such a drawn-out cycle of deployments. Although most service members in World Wars I and II served throughout the war, they were deployed just one time. In Vietnam, most service members served just a single 1-year tour of duty. Today, however, the churning cycle of being deployed, returning home for a couple of months, and then being redeployed can have a devastating effect on the psychosocial well-being of the service members and their families. This impact has been experienced not only by full-time service members and their families, but also by part-timers and their families in the Reserve Components and the National Guard being deployed over and over again in unprecedented numbers as part of the "Total Force."

A recent report by the Iraq and Afghanistan Veterans of America (2011) summarizes data that reflect the extraordinary burden shouldered courageously and with dignity by the more than 3 million military spouses, children, and adult dependents of military personnel who have served in the Global War on Terrorism. Included are the following data on the impact of multiple deployments on families—data that are particularly relevant to the need for social work intervention at all levels of social work practice:

- A prevalence of mental health disorders of 36.6% among military spouses
- A high likelihood of developing psychosocial problems among up to one third of children aged 5 to 12
- A higher rate of domestic violence than in civilian families (Marshall, Panuzio, & Taft, 2005)
- An unemployment rate of 26% among male and female military spouses and partners
- A 35% gap in full-time employment between military wives and their civilian counterparts
- Frequent moves (i.e., geographic relocation):
  - Create difficulties for almost 20% of military spouses in transferring licensure and credentials, making it hard to gain employment
  - Create obstacles in obtaining child care
  - Make it difficult for military spouses to earn an educational degree, with more than 30% taking at least 5 years to do so
  - Result in an average of six to nine educational transfers among military children
- Lower achievement test scores among children of parents deployed longer than 19 months cumulatively
- Increases in mortgage foreclosures, with more than 20,000 home foreclosures among military families in 2010
- Much higher levels of credit card debt than civilian families, with more than one third having trouble paying monthly bills and more than one fifth borrowing outside of banks
- A tendency of predatory lending companies to locate near military installations, making service members and their families vulnerable to fraud or exploitation

The burden service members and their families experience during deployment does not end after retirement or separation from military service. For example, certain psychological states that are desirable during deployment often linger and cause problems after returning home. One problem is the extreme sense of bonding and mutual support during deployment that cannot be matched in civilian life. Another is the adrenalin rush during combat that the vet may miss and seek to reexperience after returning home. Efforts to reexperience the adrenalin rush can involve risk taking ranging from pathological forms (such as substance abuse or gambling addiction) to more adaptive redirection, such as is reflected in the following quote from a retired Marine:

> The adrenaline is never shut off but instead redirected. For example, when I got out of the service, I was looking for the rush that I received when I would jump out at night at 25,000 feet with combat equipment. Many young retired Marines go out and purchase a very fast motorcycle, but I already had kids and could never figure out how to secure a car seat on the back of a Kawasaki. I found my rush Cave Diving. Yes, I would go into an underwater cave many times by myself at depths of 200+ feet and 2500 feet into the system. The isolation, challenge, and rush was as close as I could get to military skydiving.

These contrasts, coupled with other problems such as shame and guilt associated with the deaths of civilians, can, on returning home, contribute to interpersonal estrangement and detachment, reduced libido and sexual activity, a desire to reenlist, and other complications that result in a common complaint by spouses that the vet is not what he or she used to be.

Furthermore, as returning service members transition to civilian life—on top of the physical, psychological, and family challenges they experience—there can be a high rate of unemployment during an economic downturn. The aforementioned desire to reenlist, therefore, might be increased by reenlistment bonuses of up to $60,000 (U.S. General Accounting Office, 2003). Not all returning service members are in dire straits. Many, for example, return infused with a desire to use their abilities to help their communities or to help in the aftermath of natural disasters.

Nevertheless, the vast numbers of service members returning at roughly the same point in time from the wars in Iraq and Afghanistan likely will exceed the capacity of the Department of Veteran Affairs and affiliated programs such as the Vet Centers to serve them all adequately. Despite the admirable range of services provided by the VA, the sheer numbers of veterans returning likely will imply the need for greater reliance on civilian social workers to assist in the provision of services. It no longer will suffice for civilian social workers to just refer veterans to the VA on the grounds that they (the civilian social workers) lack sufficient expertise with such cases. Thus, an objective of this book is to help civilian social workers and other mental health professionals gain the necessary knowledge in better serving this population. It is also hoped that this book helps students gain such expertise, including those students aspiring to become uniformed military social workers as well as those who—as civilian social workers—will be better prepared to work with active duty service members, National Guard and Reserve personnel, and veterans and their families.

The chapters in this book address the wide range of problems and interventions that social workers need to learn about. The five chapters in Part I impart foundational knowledge about social work with service members and veterans. Chapter 1, for example, describes the history of social work and the military. Readers can learn about the earliest roots of military social work (dating back to the Civil War) and how it grew in subsequent wars, including the evolution of the roles of uniformed social workers in the Army, Navy, and Air Force.

Chapter 2 describes unique aspects of the military culture that practitioners must know to understand and be credible to military personnel, veterans, and their families. For example, building a therapeutic alliance with this population requires understanding the military's power and authority structure as part of military culture and its impact on their clients' lives. It also requires a sensitivity to ethnic, gender, and sexual identity diversity within the military culture, which is also presented in Chapter 2.

Chapter 3 focuses on the challenges of women in uniform, who continue to voluntarily enlist despite facing many challenges serving in masculine military culture. Although the opportunities for women to serve in the military are rising, and the opportunities for camaraderie and support systems for women are increasing, many women continue to be victims of military sexual trauma. The marriages of military women are much more likely to fail than those of their male counterparts. They face unique challenges in managing their biological feminine processes during field training and deployments. They are more likely than males to experience stressors related to family caregiving. And, like men, they are vulnerable to experience combat PTSD. After discussing those challenges, Chapter 3 describes a treatment approach for helping women with PTSD who also were victims of military sexual trauma.

Chapter 4 discusses common ethical dilemmas confronting uniformed and civilian military social workers. Among these are the conflict between the social workers' loyalty to the professional code of ethics and the clients they serve versus the needs of military mission preparedness. A related conflict is between protecting client confidentiality versus the commander's need to know about the service member's fitness for combat.

Chapter 5 discusses the secondary trauma practitioners often experience when working with veterans who have been physically or emotionally handicapped from traumatic combat experiences. After reading this chapter, students and civilian practitioners who have not yet worked with such clients may be somewhat inoculated against the impact that working with such clients is likely to have on them on a personal and professional level. The chapter also identifies strategies that they, as well as current military social workers, can employ to mitigate their own secondary trauma as well as to assess, prevent, and treat secondary trauma among other service providers working with combat veterans and those veterans who have experienced other types of trauma, such as military sexual trauma.

The eight chapters in Part II of the book cover behavioral health problems and related interventions with service members and veterans. Chapter 6 covers the history of PTSD in veterans and critically appraises the various models that have been postulated over time to define and explain it. The next three chapters discuss the treatment of PTSD. Chapter 7, for example, discusses the neurobiology of PTSD and its connection to cognitive processing therapy (CPT). CPT is an empirically supported treatment for PTSD, and Chapter 7 provides an overview of the 12-session CPT treatment protocol.

CPT is a form of exposure therapy, and Chapter 8 focuses on a promising new approach to exposure therapy that utilizes virtual reality as a means of improving the provision of the exposure component. Exposure therapy is widely recognized as the most evidence-based treatment for PTSD. Using virtual reality, the therapist controls what is presented so as to increase or decrease the degree of exposure to traumatic stimuli. The therapist can present cues that trigger client reactions, such as event-related odors that the client can smell during the treatment session. In addition, the therapist can monitor the client's physiological and mood reactions during the virtual reality presentation.

Chapter 9 provides basic information that social workers need to know about psychopharmacological interventions for PTSD and co-occurring disorders. Next, Chapter 10 imparts vital information that social workers need to know about TBI—the signature wound of recent warfare. The chapter discusses the prevalence, diagnosis, and treatment of TBI; its impact on psychosocial functioning and the family; and its implications regarding the treatment of and recovery from co-occurring disorders. Chapter 11 focuses on the social work practice implications of the information provided in Chapter 10 and thus builds on that chapter. It contains many specific suggestions for social work practitioners in working with clients with TBI, and organizes those suggestions according to five treatment phases, from contact to termination.

Chapters 12 and 13 both focus on the widespread problem of substance abuse disorders among service members and veterans. In Chapter 12, the focus is on assessing, preventing, and treating these disorders in active duty military settings. Two empirically supported outpatient treatment approaches are described, followed by a discussion of the need to provide such approaches within an ecosystemic context due to the impact of military culture and the current deployment schedules as well as considering the high prevalence of comorbidity of substance use disorders with other disorders, such as PTSD and TBI. The role that military chaplains can play in helping service members with substance use disorders is also discussed. In Chapter 13, the focus is on preventing and intervening with substance use disorders in veterans. The prevalence of these disorders among veterans and their co-occurrence with other disorders is covered in depth, followed by a discussion of best practices and prevention and treatment programs.

In the final chapter of Part II, Chapter 14 describes factors that contribute to military suicides, identifies potential military suicide risk factors, discusses programs to identify those at risk for suicide and how to prevent it, and identifies gaps in military suicide prevention efforts. Special attention is given to suicide prevention in the context of the Total Force Fitness concept, which is an overarching model for promoting resilience in all branches of military service.

The three chapters in Part III address the challenges social workers face in helping veterans transition to civilian life. Chapter 15, for example, focuses on the problem of homelessness among veterans. It describes its prevalence, its toll on communities, and the prevention, rehabilitation, and support systems that address that problem. Chapter 16 deals with helping veterans navigate through systems of care. It provides social workers with a road map to the daunting task of navigating complex systems such as the Department of Veteran Affairs and thus enables them to be better prepared to assist veterans with accessing and enrolling in needed services. Special attention is given to homeless veterans, women veterans, and military sexual trauma victims, suicide prevention efforts, and transition assistance.

Chapter 17 discusses the various experiences and tasks of transitioning to civilian life after full-time military service and how social workers can assist in that transition. For example, social workers can provide information relevant to securing employment, adequate housing, and veteran benefits related to education and health care. Chapter 17 also discusses ways to help transitioning service members offset the loss of camaraderie and cohesion by becoming involved in community activities and thus finding a new "mission."

The final section of this book, Part IV, contains nine chapters on families impacted by military service. It begins with a chapter that provides a conceptual and historical overview of the impact of military service on families and its implications for the role of social workers. Chapter 18 describes how recognition of the importance of families—both from the standpoint of stressors on the family and the family's impact on the military mission—has evolved throughout U.S. history, dating back to the Revolutionary War. It compares the current impact on military families and children to that of previous wars and portrays how families have made noble and significant contributions to each war effort.

Next, Chapter 19 focuses on the impact of the cycle of deployment on family well-being—especially regarding domestic violence and its prevention and treatment. It describes stages in the cycle of deployment—which include predeployment, deployment, sustainment, redeployment, and postdeployment. It shows how each stage can impact the family and describes support programs applicable to each stage.

Chapter 20 looks at the special needs of the families of National Guard and Reserve members and how to support them. It notes that guard and reservist families, unlike other military families, live in civilian communities where they experience a heightened sense of isolation and lack the support coming from being near other military families and from the support systems that are readily available on military installations.

Chapter 21 discusses military families with children who have special needs/disabilities. It provides an in-depth description of the Exceptional Family Member Program and the role of social workers and related personnel in the program, which is mandated by the Department of Defense for service members whose family members have special medical or educational needs.

Chapter 22 examines grief, loss, and bereavement in military families, with a focus on suicide loss. It discusses how the death of a loved one in the military involves complexities unlike the loss of a loved one in the civilian world. Among these unique complexities are the often violent nature of the death, the condition of the body remains, benefits and entitlements, and the loss of a (military) way of life. After delving into these, as well as other, unique circumstances, the chapter addresses clinician issues (such as countertransference) and suggested interventions.

Chapter 23 covers an approach geared to supporting long-term family caregiving: the Stress Process Model. This model offers a framework for considering the intersection of stress, appraisal, and coping connected to caregiving as well as other ongoing stressful life events. The chapter discusses how this model can be used by practitioners to mitigate burden and strain among caregivers of military service members and veterans.

Chapter 24 focuses on the children and youth impacted by their parents' military service. It describes the toll that ongoing cycles of multiple deployments take on children and their families, how military life experiences can positively or negatively impact the emotional and developmental growth of children, and programs and interventions that have been developed across a variety of settings to help them cope.

Chapter 25 presents an approach to couples therapy that is geared to the stressors of multiple deployments and reintegration after redeployment. The approach is based on contemporary attachment theory, secondary trauma, cultural responsiveness, and gendered responses to trauma.

Finally, Chapter 26 reviews the stressors, theoretical models, and assessment and intervention strategies regarding couples and families impacted by military service. In so doing, it provides some synthesis of material covered in earlier chapters regarding the stressors of military family life. It also describes empirically informed therapies that are currently being implemented with couples and families impacted by military service. In its concluding section it discusses why some service personnel and their families who need these therapies are not receiving them.

At the end of the book, an appendix lists numerous resources relevant to helping service members, veterans, and their families and a glossary of military terms.

As reflected in the foregoing chapter-by-chapter summaries, the emphasis in this book is on the *current* challenges faced by social workers and allied professionals who want to help military personnel and veterans and their families impacted by today's Global War on Terrorism. However, we recognize that their help also continues to be needed by veterans from earlier conflicts (such as in Vietnam, Somalia, the Gulf Wars, and others), and we have not forgotten these past heroes. Although many of the problems and interventions discussed in this book are also relevant to veterans of those previous conflicts, it is beyond the scope of this book to delve in depth into the unique issues faced by veterans of those conflicts. Nevertheless, the appendix identifies readings and resources for working with those veterans.

Most chapters in this book end with a list of relevant questions for reflection on the chapter's main concepts—questions that might be particularly useful for instructors to employ in their teaching about those concepts. Most chapters also provide case vignettes to illustrate the practice applications of the chapter topic. Most vignettes are followed by case vignette discussion questions.

Whether you are a current practitioner, student, or instructor, my co-editors and I hope you find this book useful. Most importantly, we hope it contributes to the improvement of your efforts to help our brave military personnel and their families deal with the unprecedented and daunting challenges they face as active duty members, National Guard members, and reservists, or as veterans of today's ongoing Global War on Terrorism.

REFERENCES

Courtois, C. A., & J. D. Ford (Eds.). (2009). *Treating complex traumatic stress disorders: An evidence-based guide*. New York, NY: Guilford Press.

Hall, L. K. (2008). *Counseling military families*. New York, NY: Routledge.

Iraq and Afghanistan Veterans of America. (2011). *Unsung heroes: Military families after ten years of war*. media.iava.org/reports/unsungheroes_quickfacts.pdf

Marshall, A. D., Panuzio, J., & Taft, C. T. (2005). Intimate partner violence among military veterans and active duty servicemen. *Clinical Psychology Review*, *25*, 7, 862–876.

Moore, B. A., & Penk, W. E. (2011). *Treating PTSD in military personnel: A clinical handbook*. New York, NY: Guilford Press.

Owens, B. D., Kragh, J. F. Jr., Wenke, J. C., Macaitis, J., Wade, C. E., & Holcomb, J. B. (2008). Combat wounds in operation Iraqi Freedom and operation Enduring Freedom. *Journal of Trauma*, *64*, 295–299.

Ritchie, E. C., Morales, W., Russell, M., Crow, B., Boyd, W., Forys, K., & Brewster, S. (2011). Suicide prevention in the US army: Lessons learned and future directions. In E. C. Ritchie (Ed.), *Combat and operational behavioral health. Textbooks of military medicine* (pp. 403–421). Washington DC: Borden Institute. Retrieved from http://www.bordeninstitute.army.mil/

Rubin, A. (2003). Unanswered questions about the empirical support for EMDR in the treatment of PTSD: A review of research. *Traumatology*, 9, 4–30.

Schwartz, J. (2011, November 6). After a decade of war, soldiers face a difficult transition. *Austin American-Statesman*, 1, 10, 11.

U.S. General Accounting Office. (2003, November). *Report to the subcommittee on defense, committee on appropriations, house of representatives*. Retrieved from http://www.gao.gov/new.items/d0486.pdf

Walker, M. (2011). *Military: Marine corps reports record number of suicide attempts*. mlwalker@nctimes.com/Posted: Wednesday, December 7, 2011, 7 p.m. Retrieved from http://m.nctimes.com/mobile/article_49c8abd1–520e-5fb5-b4ba-df0a02aba98b.html

About the Editors

Allen Rubin, PhD, is the Bert Kruger Smith Centennial Professor in the School of Social Work at the University of Texas at Austin, where he has been a faculty member since 1979. He is internationally known for his many publications pertaining to research and evidence-based practice. In 1997 he was a co-recipient of the Society for Social Work and Research Award for Outstanding Examples of Published Research. He has served as a consulting editor for seven professional journals. He was a founding member of the Society for Social Work and Research and served as its president from 1998 to 2000. In 1993 he received the University of Pittsburgh, School of Social Work's Distinguished Alumnus Award. In 2007 he received the Council on Social Work Education's Significant Lifetime Achievement in Social Work Education Award. In 2010 he was inducted as a Fellow of the American Academy of Social Work and Social Welfare.

Eugenia L. Weiss, PsyD, LCSW, is currently clinical assistant professor at the University of Southern California, School of Social Work, where she is lead instructor in the social work practice with military families class, the mental health concentration coordinator for USC's Virtual Academic Center (VAC), and the co-coordinator for the military social work subconcentration on the VAC. Dr. Weiss has maintained a private practice for 18 years with an emphasis on treating military personnel and their families. She is the co-recipient of the International Association of Health, Wellness, & Society Publication Award for the paper titled, *The Influence of Military Culture and Veteran Worldviews on Mental Health Treatment: Practice Implications for Combat Veteran Help-Seeking and Wellness*. She is the author and co-author of multiple peer-reviewed journal publications and is co-author of a book titled *A Civilian Counselor's Primer to Counseling Veterans* (2nd ed.), 2011. Dr. Weiss serves on the editorial board for the *Military Behavioral Health Journal.*

Jose E. Coll, PhD, is an associate professor in the Department of Social Work at Saint Leo University and director of Veteran Student Services, where he has been a faculty member since 2011. Prior to joining Saint Leo University Dr. Coll was a clinical associate professor at the University of Southern California, School of Social Work as director of the San Diego Academic Center and Chair of Military Social Work. In 2012 he was the co-recipient of the International Association of Health, Wellness, & Society Publication Award for the co-authored paper titled, *The Influence of Military Culture and Veteran Worldviews on Mental Health Treatment: Practice Implications for Combat Veteran Help-Seeking and Wellness*. Dr. Coll is the author and co-author of multiple peer-reviewed journal publications on military social work and is co-author of a book titled *A Civilian Counselor's Primer to Counseling Veterans* (2nd ed.), 2011. He is a graduate of Harvard's Management Development Program (MDP). Dr. Coll is a Marine Corps veteran.

About the Contributors

David L. Albright, PhD, MS, MSW, is an assistant professor of social work, coordinator of the Graduate Certificate in Military Social Work, and director of the Center for Education and Research for Veterans and Military Families at the University of Missouri at Columbia. He is a former Army infantry officer. His expertise is in military and veteran health care services and treatments of combat-related polytrauma. Dr. Albright is the managing editor for *Research on Social Work Practice* and is on the editorial boards of the *Journal of the Society for Social Work and Research* and the Campbell Collaboration's Social Welfare Group.

Sarah Asmussen, PhD, is the co-senior scientific director/neuropsychologist at the Defense and Veterans Brain Injury Center Camp Pendleton, serving active duty Marines. She is also a part-time lecturer at USC. She completed formal training at Palo Alto University, a Stanford Affiliate and specialized in treatment/assessment of various neurological conditions at the Palo Alto VA and James A. Haley VA. She also completed a 2-year fellowship at Barrow Neurological Institute specializing in neuropsychology with a focus on epilepsy, rehabilitation, and acute injury. She has presented at professional meetings nationally, lectured extensively in California, and trained providers regionally.

Willie G. Barnes has a doctorate degree in marriage and family systems. Colonel Barnes served 23 years as Chaplain in the Army National Guard. He served on the Functionality Advisory Council for the Joint Chaplaincy strategic goals for National Guard Bureau. He has presented on a national level on the subjects of spiritual resiliency, military culture, deployment dynamics, suicide prevention, and war-related injuries. Dr. Barnes is former associate professor of practical theology and visiting lecturer for universities in Peru and Jamaica. He is a clinical fellow and supervisor member of the American Association for Marriage and Family Therapy with 25 years of clinical, academic, and military experience.

Kathryn Basham, PhD, LICSW, professor, co-director of the PhD program and editor of the *Smith College Studies in Social Work*, engages in research, writing, practice, and education related to the reintegration of service members, veterans, and their families. She earned her MSW and PhD degrees in clinical social work. She has been appointed to three congressionally mandated committees with the Institute of Medicine, charged to evaluate approaches that enhance the mental health of military families. She was honored as a distinguished clinical practitioner with the National Academies of Practice, authored and co-authored several texts and papers, and presented nationally and internationally.

Cynthia Boyd, PhD, is a neuropsychologist and co-senior scientific director at the Defense and Veterans Brain Injury Center at Naval Medical Center San Diego. In this position, she evaluates military personnel returning from combat with traumatic brain injury and posttraumatic stress disorder. Dr. Boyd presents nationally on a variety of neuropsychological issues related to traumatic brain injury, PTSD, and malingering of cognitive and psychological symptoms. She also has an independent practice in forensic neuropsychology specializing in criminal and civil evaluations of brain injury, posttraumatic stress disorder, violent offenders, and stalking behavior.

Bruce Capehart, MD, MBA, is the OEF/OIF program medical director at the Durham VA Medical Center and an assistant professor of psychiatry at Duke University School of Medicine. His clinical interests are psychiatric evaluation and management of combat veterans with particular concern for neurologic conditions such as traumatic brain injury. His research interests include PTSD and the biomechanics and pathophysiology of blast injury. He has worked as a consultant to the U.S. Army on combat trauma and as an expert witness in civilian blast injury litigation. He is a veteran of the U.S. Army Reserve. In 2003 he completed a tour in Afghanistan.

Rachel Burda-Chmielewski, MSW, LISW, is a licensed clinical social worker at the Veterans Administration Medical Center in San Diego, California. She works with the Alcohol and Drug Treatment Program, specializing in assessment and treatment of veterans with co-occuring substance use disorders and PTSD. She has also worked with active duty service members and their families through internships with the Air Force as well as the Marine Corps Family Service Centers.

Edward V. Carrillo, MSW, LCSW, is a clinical social worker at the Department of Veterans Affairs, San Diego Health Care System. His expertise includes the treatment of persons with combat and crime victim PTSD and outreach to homeless veterans in the VA Health Care for Homeless Veterans Program. He is a part-time field instructor and community field immersion lecturer for the University of Southern California Graduate School of Social Work. He is a Vietnam combat veteran and he was recently ordained into the Order of Interbeing, a Zen Buddhist community.

Colanda Cato, PhD, MA, is a licensed clinical psychologist and PTSD and violence prevention subject matter expert at the Defense Centers of Excellence, Resilience and Prevention Directorate. She has developed and conducted briefings for senior military leaders on risk and prevention factors related to PTSD, suicide, and violence in the military and has presented at numerous conferences across the country. She currently oversees research on resilience and prevention factors and program evaluation. She serves as a chair, co-chair, and an active member of various military working groups and has served as an assistant professor of psychology. Dr. Cato has more than 11 years of military experience and is a distinguished Air Force veteran psychologist.

Allison N. Clark, PhD, is an assistant professor in the Department of Physical Medicine and Rehabilitation at Baylor College of Medicine. She is also a research scientist at the Brain Injury Research Center at TIRR Memorial Hermann. Her areas of interest include emotional functioning following acquired brain injury, knowledge translation, group interventions, and cognitive rehabilitation. Dr. Clark has presented at numerous national and regional conferences, and has co-authored more than 30 published articles and abstracts, including 16 peer-reviewed publications.

Joseph J. Costello, MA, MSW, is the team leader of the San Marcos, California Veterans Center. He has been employed at the Department of Veterans Affairs since

1994, focusing on readjustment concerns of returning combat veterans and their families. His expertise is in the treatment of combat-related PTSD and substance use disorders. Mr. Costello has lectured nationwide on readjustment and transition issues of Iraq and Afghanistan veterans. He also teaches continuing education courses on military culture at the University of Southern California Center for Innovation and Research. Mr. Costello is a veteran of the Afghanistan Campaign and retired from the Army Reserve in 2010.

Todd Creager, MSW, is an adjunct lecturer at the USC School of Social Work. He is a licensed clinical social worker and a licensed marriage and family therapist. He is known for his work with couples and sexual issues and is an author of *The Long, Hot Marriage*, which helps couples rekindle passion and aliveness. He has also been published in numerous articles on couples, communication, and sexuality. He has a private practice in Orange County, California, and has been on a variety of TV and radio shows as a relationship expert.

Judith Cukor, PhD, is an assistant professor of psychology in psychiatry at Weill Cornell Medical College. She has worked extensively in the treatment of posttraumatic stress disorder in diverse populations including military personnel, disaster workers, and burn survivors. Dr. Cukor provides training and supervision in specialized treatments for PTSD and has authored scientific articles and book chapters on trauma-related disorders. She is a consultant to the William Randolph Hearst Burn Center at New York–Presbyterian Hospital, and is a co-investigator on several studies concerned with developing treatments for PTSD in diverse trauma populations.

James G. Daley, PhD, MSW, LCSW, is an associate professor at the Indiana University School of Social Work. He has published and presented on international military social work, is co-editor of a special issue in spring 2012 on military social work in *Advances in Social Work*, was keynote speaker at the 2010 Uniformed Services Social Work Annual Conference, and served on the steering committee that developed the *Competencies in Military Social Work* guidelines for CSWE. He has served as a curricular consultant on military social work to several universities. He was editor of *Social Work Practice in the Military*.

Julie D'Amico, MA, is an intervention delivery support specialist for FOCUS at the UCLA Semel Institute for Neuroscience and Human Behavior. Ms. D'Amico is an experienced therapist and parent educator, with expertise working with children with developmental disabilities and behavioral challenges. Ms. D'Amico received her MA in counseling psychology. Prior to her work with FOCUS Ms. D'Amico also served as a volunteer at Mattel Children's Hospital UCLA to support children with severe medical illnesses and their families.

Tara DeBraber, MEd, MSW, is a social worker with the Veterans Homelessness Prevention Demonstration Program at the San Diego VA. She is a 2012 military spouse fellow with the FINRA foundation for the Accredited Financial Counselor Program. Ms. DeBraber is also a caseworker with Navy Marine Corps Relief Society.

JoAnn Difede, PhD, is a professor of psychology in psychiatry and director of the Program for Anxiety and Traumatic Stress Studies at Weill Cornell Medical College. Dr. Difede specializes in treating anxiety, mood, and trauma-related disorders, and has worked extensively with 9/11 World Trade Center survivors, burn patients, disaster workers, and military personnel. She has pioneered the application of virtual reality posttrauma and is the principal investigator of several studies of innovative treatments for PTSD. She serves on the scientific advisory board of the Anxiety Disorders Association of America, the advisory board of the Jericho Project, and supervises VR treatment at military medical centers around the country.

Keita Franklin, PhD, LCSW, is the branch head for behavioral health at headquarters, United States Marine Corps. She administers the programs Sexual Assault Prevention and Response, Family Advocacy, Suicide Prevention, Combat Operational Stress Control, and Substance Abuse. She directs the policy, future planning, training, technical assistance, resource management, and advocacy efforts for the branch. Her expertise centers on the impact of deployment and PTSD on military family members. She has published and lectured on numerous topics impacting military service members and their families, including deployment stress, secondary trauma, women's issues in the military, parenting in the military, and behavioral health needs of today's service members.

Ediza Garcia, PsyD, is a model supervisor for the Nathanson Family Resilience Center at the UCLA Semel Institute for Neuroscience and Human Behavior. She has specialized training in the prevention and treatment of child and family traumatic stress. Dr. Garcia is the co-developer of the FOCUS for Military Couples Resilience Training Manual. She serves as a consultant for the National Military Family Association's Operation Purple Family Retreat. Dr. Garcia is the clinical coordinator for the UCLA Child and Family Trauma Psychiatry Service, where she trains child psychiatry fellows in the facilitation of strength-based, trauma-informed therapeutic assessments.

Maryrose Gerardi, PhD, is an assistant professor in the Department of Psychiatry and Behavioral Sciences at Emory University School of Medicine. She provides cognitive behavior therapy services and supervision through the Trauma and Anxiety Recovery Program, and has therapist and supervisory roles in ongoing research studies examining virtual reality exposure therapy and prolonged exposure therapy for the treatment of military-related PTSD. She also trains professionals in the use of virtual reality exposure therapy.

Fran Goldfarb, MA, MCHES, is the director of family support at the USC UCEDD at Children's Hospital Los Angeles, one of 67 University Centers for Excellence in Developmental Disabilities nationwide. She is a master certified health education specialist but her role within the UCEDD is based on her life experience as the parent of a child on the autism spectrum—now a young adult. She has extensive experience in assisting systems to provide parent training and support, and in training professionals to work with parents as partners. She is the founder of the Los Angeles Asperger Syndrome Parent Support Group.

Christina Harnett, PhD, MBA, is a licensed psychologist and assistant professor at the Johns Hopkins University, School of Education. She has been active in the Maryland National Guard's deployment cycle support programs in both training and curriculum development and has published on the impact of reservist culture on military members and families and the challenges of reintegration for the veteran. She has participated on state and national committees focusing on military behavioral health issues and is actively engaged in building capacity among behavioral health providers in Maryland through outreach training. She is a major in the Maryland Defense Force/10th Medical Regiment and on the editorial board of the *International Journal of Emergency Mental Health.*

Jesse J. Harris, PhD, professor and dean emeritus, School of Social Work, University of Maryland, Baltimore is a retired U.S. Army colonel. His assignments included Walter

Reed Army Institute of Research where he was attached to the 82nd Airborne Division. His publications include experiences with Peacekeepers in the Sinai Desert as well as his State Department assignment to Mozambique to assess the condition of captured child soldiers. Dr. Harris has also written extensively on the history of military social work. He has lectured internationally and serves on civic and veterans agency boards.

Helena Harvie, MSSW, completed one internship with the Central Texas Veteran's Health Care System and another internship at Landstuhl Regional Medical Center in Germany, working with active duty service members suffering from severe PTSD. She has conducted research on working with military personnel and helped develop a course on social work with military personnel and families at the University of Texas at Austin.

Anthony M. Hassan, EdD, LCSW, is the director of the Center for Innovation and Research on Veterans and Military Families (CIR) at the University of Southern California. He is a retired Air Force officer who brings 25 years of experience in military social work and leadership. Dr. Hassan served during Operation Iraqi Freedom in 2004 on the first-ever Air Force combat stress control and prevention team embedded with an Army unit. His scholarship encompasses a diverse array of publications and presentations in social work, leadership, and higher education administration. Dr. Hassan led the CSWE Task Force for the development of national guidelines for military social work.

Matthew Jeffreys, MD, is associate professor of psychiatry at the UT Health Science Center in San Antonio, Texas. He has been PCT Medical Director for the South Texas Veterans Healthcare System since 1995 and has served as a PTSD mentor for VISN 17 through the National Center for PTSD (NCPTSD) since 2008. He consulted for the NCPTSD's Consultation Program from 2010 to 2011. Other service has included participation as a member of the working group revising the VA/DoD Clinical Practice Guideline for PTSD. Interests include ongoing educational and research projects related to the treatment of PTSD.

Jill Harrington-LaMorie, DSW, LCSW, is the senior field researcher at the Center for the Study of Traumatic Stress, National Military Family Bereavement Study and the former director of professional education at the Tragedy Assistance Program for Survivors (TAPS). She has extensive clinical experience working with individuals and families affected by trauma, grief, and loss. Dr. LaMorie is one of the first published authors on the subject of bereavement in U.S. military families. She has been an invited presenter for several universities, nonprofit organizations, the military, and hospices. Dr. LaMorie serves on the board of the Association for Death Education & Counseling; a peer reviewer for *Omega-Journal for Death and Dying* and is a member of the National Association of Social Workers. She is active with different charities that work with bereaved, veterans and military families.

Suzanne Leaman, PhD, is a research psychologist in the Department of Psychiatry at Emory University. She has worked with trauma survivors from diverse populations such as refugees, veterans, and active duty service members and has focused her research interests on the treatment and identification of PTSD and related disorders. Dr. Leaman has published multiple peer-reviewed journal articles and presented the results of studies on PTSD and interpersonal violence at international conferences and symposiums. She is currently a co-investigator on studies researching treatments for and early predictors of PTSD.

Gregory A. Leskin, PhD, serves as director, Military Families Initiatives at the UCLA National Center for Child Traumatic Stress and serves as liaison for FOCUS Project and the National Child Traumatic Stress Network (NCTSN). He has provided education, training, program development, evaluation and consultation on PTSD, TBI, anxiety disorders, resiliency training, child traumatic stress, and evidence-based interventions to the Department of Defense and Department of Veteran Affairs. He has published more than 30 scientific articles and book chapters on these topics.

Patricia Lester, MD, is the Jane and Marc Nathanson Family Professor of Psychiatry at UCLA Semel Institute. She directs the FOCUS (Families OverComing Under Stress) Project, a family resilience program for military families, and co-directs the UCLA Welcome Back Veterans Family Resilience Center. Dr. Lester's research and clinical work are dedicated to the development, evaluation, and implementation of family-centered interventions for families and children facing traumatic events, parental illness, and wartime deployments. She has published more than 40 research articles and book chapters on the foregoing topics.

James (Jim) Martin, PhD, BCD, is a professor of social work and social research at Bryn Mawr College. His scholarship, teaching, and public service focus on social and behavioral health issues; and his research and civic engagement address military and veteran populations. A retired Army colonel, Jim's 26-year career in the Army Medical Department included clinical, research, as well as senior management (command) and policy assignments. Jim was the senior social work officer in the Persian Gulf theater of operations during the first Gulf War and edited *The Gulf War and Mental Health: A Comprehensive Guide*.

Monica M. Matthieu, PhD, MSW, LCSW, is a research assistant professor at Washington University's Brown School of Social Work. She worked from 1995 until 2000 as a clinical social worker with the Department of Veterans Affairs, Readjustment Counseling Service's Veterans Resource Center in New Orleans. In 2008, she returned to work at the St. Louis VA Medical Center as a research social worker. With her joint appointment at the VA and the Brown School she continues to focus on veterans' issues and conduct research on the implementation of evidence-based practices, trauma treatment, and violence and injury prevention.

Deborah McGough, BA, is currently a manager of both the Exceptional Family Member Program and the School Liaison Program supporting a Marine corps base and multiple units at other armed forces installations in California and was the EFMP Manager for the Army for 4½ years. With formal training in psychology with special emphasis in children with disabilities and life experience as a foster parent of children with multiple disabilities, her expertise is in coordinating and leveraging civilian and military resources for and advocating on behalf of active duty EFMP families.

Michael Metal is an **MSW** candidate of 2013 and is a medically retired Navy veteran. He has a concentration on mental health with a focus on military social work. He is actively involved in multiple charitable endeavors with a focus on the above. Michael has presented nationwide on veteran worldviews and is published on the same subject.

Catherine E. Mogil, PsyD, is an assistant clinical professor at the UCLA Semel Institute for Neuroscience and Human Behavior in the David Geffen School of Medicine. She is a licensed clinical psychologist and serves as the director of training and intervention development for the Nathanson Family Resilience Center and the co-director of the Child and Family Trauma Service. Dr. Mogil is a co-developer of programs for military families and provides consultation and subject matter expertise for military family service organizations including National Military Family Association, Uniformed Services University, and Los Angeles County Department of Mental Health.

Aaron Nowlin, CADC 2, BA, is a drug and alcohol counselor at the Veterans Affairs hospital in La Jolla, California. His expertise is in treating those with the diagnoses of chemical abuse or chemical dependence, specifically with active duty military and veterans. He has been employed by the VA for the past 5 years and, prior to that spent his final 3½ years in the military employed at a residential treatment facility, Substance Abuse Rehabilitation Program (SARP) Point Loma. While at SARP, he provided treatment to active duty service members who were diagnosed with chemical dependence.

Caleb Yoon Ra, LCSW, is currently a senior social worker with the Healthcare for Homeless Veterans Clinic at the San Diego VA Healthcare Systems. He case manages chronically homeless veterans throughout the San Diego County.

Prior to his work with the Veterans Health Administration he served 8 years with the United States Marine Corp conducting combat engineering missions throughout the Syian Desert in Iraq. He completed two combat tours (2003, 2005) before being honorably discharged as a sergeant.

Albert "Skip" Rizzo, PhD, is an associate director at the USC Institute for Creative Technologies and a research professor in psychiatry and in gerontology. Skip's expertise is in the research and development of Virtual Reality systems for clinical assessment, treatment, and rehabilitation. His R&D group created the Virtual Iraq/Afghanistan VR exposure therapy system for treating PTSD in service members and veterans. Additionally, he has authored more than 200 scientific papers and chapters on his other work using VR across a range of psychological, cognitive, and motor clinical health conditions in both civilian and military populations.

Jennifer Roberts, MSW, LCSW, is a part-time adjunct professor of social work at the University of Southern California. She is the Women Veteran Program Manager at the VA San Diego Healthcare System. She has expertise on issues affecting women veterans. She presents throughout San Diego County on issues involving military families and women veterans.

Barbara Olasov Rothbaum, PhD, is a professor in psychiatry, associate vice chair of clinical research, and director of the Trauma and Anxiety Recovery Program at Emory. She specializes in research on the treatment of individuals with anxiety disorders, has authored more than 200 scientific papers and chapters and six books. She is a past president of the International Society of Traumatic Stress Studies, is on the Boards for the Anxiety Disorders Association of America and the Obsessive Compulsive Foundation, and is a pioneer in the application of virtual reality to the treatment of psychological disorders and co-founded Virtually Better (www.virtuallybetter.com).

Allison Santoyo, MSW, is a graduate of the University of Southern California School of Social Work. She is currently registered with the Board of Behavioral Sciences and obtaining hours toward licensure. She is employed at an acute hospital as a medical social worker serving a diverse population including medical surgical patients, maternal child health, and patients suffering from mental illness and substance abuse disorders.

Jimmy Stehberg, PhD, is an assistant professor at the Universidad Andres Bello of Chile. His expertise is in research of memory and psychiatric disorders, conducting research in both rodents and humans. He has published several research articles and book chapters on memory. Dr. Stehberg is the director of the Neurobiology Laboratory and associate researcher at the Institute for Biomedicine of the Universidad Andres Bello.

Margaret A. Struchen, PhD, is a clinical neuropsychologist and manager of psychology and neuropsychology services at TIRR Memorial Hermann Hospital. She is also assistant professor of physical medicine and rehabilitation at Baylor College of Medicine. She has extensive experience in providing psychological services to inpatients and outpatients with brain injury and other neurological injuries or illnesses. Dr. Struchen has served as principal investigator and co-investigator on numerous federally funded research and training projects regarding rehabilitation of persons with traumatic brain injury, including co-principal investigator for the Rehabilitation Research and Training Center on Community Integration of Persons with Traumatic Brain Injury.

Angela B. Swensen, BS, Ronald E. McNair Scholar (2010), is an MSW student in mental health services with a research specialization at the George Warren Brown School of Social Work at Washington University. She completed a research and development internship with the Department of Veterans Affairs in St. Louis and is currently completing her second VA internship with Veterans Justice Outreach.

Barbara Yoshioka Wheeler, PhD, RN, is an associate professor of clinical pediatrics, University of Southern California Keck School of Medicine and associate director, USC UCEDD at Children's Hospital Los Angeles—one of 67 University Centers for Excellence in Developmental Disabilities nationwide. She has 30 years of experience in graduate training and in building capacity in systems to serve individuals with developmental disabilities and their families. As the daughter of a career Army sergeant, the nation's interest in supporting military families refocused her academic work on the Exceptional Family Member Program. She served on the President's Committee on Mental Retardation 1995–2000.

LTC Jeffrey S. Yarvis, PhD, is the deputy commander for Behavioral Health at the Fort Belvoir Community Hospital and is an assistant professor of Family Medicine at the Uniformed Services University if the Health Sciences (USUHS) in Bethesda, Maryland and adjunct professor of social work at Virginia Commonwealth, the University of Windsor (Canada) and the University of Houston. Honored as the 2008 U.S. Army and Uniformed Services Social Worker of the Year, he has presented on, treated, and researched the mental health concerns of military beneficiaries worldwide for 24 years. He recently published a book on subthreshold PTSD in veterans.

PART

I

Foundations of Social Work With Service Members and Veterans

CHAPTER

1

A Brief History of Social Work With the Military and Veterans

ALLEN RUBIN AND HELENA HARVIE

Since World War II social workers have been playing an increasingly significant role in the provision of behavioral health services to military personnel, veterans, and military families in a variety of settings. Today, the military and the Veterans Administration (VA) continue to be prominent sources of employment for social workers. Licensed social workers can work full time as uniformed military officers or as civilians for the VA and vet centers. They also can serve on a part-time or on a full-time basis as civilians who are contracted by the armed forces or the VA. In addition, they can work with military families and the veteran population as private practitioners through the military's TRICARE health insurance plan or an Employee Assistance Program (EAP) that contracts for brief therapy services for active duty military personnel. Also, military service personnel and their families, including the National Guard and Reserve, are seen by civilian social workers in community mental health agencies that contract with the VA. If you Google keywords about social work in the armed forces, you can find websites from different armed forces branches that describe what military social workers do, the prerequisites for becoming a licensed social work officer, and so on. You can find similar information about serving as a social worker in the VA at its website at www.socialwork.va.gov. The VA employs more than 13,000 social workers (Partners for Public Service, 2010) and offers a clinical training program for social work students that trains approximately 900 students per year (Department of Veterans Affairs, 2010, p. 1).

In light of the extent to which military organizations currently value social workers, you might be surprised to learn that it was not until the end of World War II that social work was officially recognized by the U.S. armed forces as a military occupation. However, the historical roots of military social work date back to much earlier times, just as the roots of the social work profession predate its emergence as a profession, as concerns about charity and how to deal with poverty have existed throughout history. Likewise, the roots of military social work in the United States can be traced back as early as 1636, when the

Pilgrims of Plymouth County stated that the care of disabled veterans was the responsibility of the colony, and the first legislation about caring for veterans was enacted (Department of Veterans Affairs, n.d.).

The more recent roots of military social work in the United States are associated with the Civil War (1861–1865), when Clara Barton, the founder of the American Red Cross, not only helped wounded soldiers medically but also assisted soldiers with finding community resources and getting information to and from family members (American Red Cross, 2011). Volunteers also visited with Union soldiers to provide support and relief during the Civil War (Raiha, 2000). However, the American Red Cross would not become an official organization until after the Civil War.

It was not until the Spanish-American War of 1898, however, when the American Red Cross as an organization provided services to members of the American armed forces at war (American Red Cross, 2011). Although the Red Cross provided mostly medical care to service members, it also provided a nonmedical service—carrying on a limited means of communication services that handled inquiries from families. The year 1898 also witnessed the birth of professional social work education, as the first social work course was offered at Columbia University (National Association of Social Workers, n.d.). Many Red Cross services were provided by social workers during the Spanish-American War; consequently, the term military social work can be conceived as originating at that time. Before 1898, citizens might have been performing social work duties, but it was not until the profession emerged that professional social workers per se did so.

WORLD WAR I AND ITS AFTERMATH

Recognition of the need for psychiatric social workers grew during World War I, when nearly 100,000 service members and veterans were admitted with neuropsychiatric disorders to military hospitals (Harris, 2000). The first psychiatric social workers had been employed in neurological clinics in 1905 as part of interdisciplinary clinical teams. Their primary role was to obtain collateral information needed by psychiatrists, relative to family background and past life experiences. Later, psychiatric social workers were in charge of preparing families for the return home of mental patients (O'Keefe, 2009). The value of psychiatric social work to the military became showcased by the Red Cross in 1918 when the first social worker was employed at the special hospital for neuroses at the U.S. Army General Hospital #30 in Plattsburgh, New York. The social worker's duties were "to assist the medical officers by obtaining information regarding the personal, family, and community background of the soldiers under treatment, as an aid in diagnosis, treatment, and plans for aftercare" (O'Keefe, 2009, p. 1). The success of this project not only led to the increase of psychiatric social workers at this hospital, but also to the Red Cross assigning medical social workers (i.e., social workers who work in medical settings) to all hospitals.

After the war was over in March 1919, the Surgeon General asked the Red Cross to establish a social services program in federal hospitals similar to already existing psychiatric programs in civilian hospitals (Harris, 2000). While the U.S. Public Health Service had been made responsible for the care of veterans, the Red Cross assumed full responsibility for outlining the social service program, formulating policies, recruiting personnel, and assisting in the organization of the work. By January 1920, there were social service departments in 42 federal hospitals, which mostly served veterans and service members (O'Keefe, 2009).

The Red Cross continued to carry the full responsibility for these psychiatric social services until the Veterans Bureau established its own social work department on June 16, 1926. The Veterans Bureau General Order established the social work program and outlined its organization and functions (Department of Veterans Affairs, 2010). The first year staffing consisted of 14 social workers who were placed in psychiatric hospitals and 22 who were placed in regional offices throughout the country. The first director was Irene Grant Dalymple, a pioneer in providing social work in medical settings (Department of Veterans Affairs, 2010). The early stages of the program were centered on patients suffering from psychiatric disorders and tuberculosis. Eventually, Dalymple was instrumental in getting social work services incorporated into the Veterans Bureau instead of having social services contracted by an outside organization, as had been the practice following World War I (Department of Veterans Affairs, 2010).

WORLD WAR II AND ITS AFTERMATH

With the anticipation of World War II, the U.S. armed forces started to expand in 1940 and 1941. The contributions of social workers, however, had been mostly forgotten, and the social work specialty was not included in the expansion (O'Keefe, 2009). This was due to social work not being considered an integral part of the military medical organization.

> Some of the responsibility for this state of affairs must be placed on the field of social work which had established no working relations with any of the branches of the Armed Forces before Pearl Harbor. One indication of the situation was the fact that the National Roster of Scientific and Specialized Personnel of the National Resources Planning Board did not list social work as a profession. Since psychiatry at this time also did not receive adequate recognition within the Army, psychiatric social work had neither leadership nor high-level support in the mobilization period of World War II. (O'Keefe, 2009, p. 1)

Due to this lack of recognition, the Red Cross was tasked with supplying all social workers at the beginning of World War II. "Between 1942 and 1945 about 1,000 American Red Cross psychiatric social workers were assigned to named general and regional hospitals in the United States and overseas" (Harris, 2000, p. 3).

It was not until 1942 that the military allowed service members to work as psychiatric social workers. Six enlisted soldiers in the U.S. Army who were professionally qualified as psychiatric social workers were assigned to the newly formed Mental Hygiene Consultation service at Fort Monmouth, New Jersey. "This is the first time military personnel who were trained as psychiatric social workers were utilized as psychiatric social workers in a military unit" (Harris, 2000, p. 4). On October 18, 1943, the War Department published the

Military Occupational Specialty 263 for Psychiatric Social Work Technicians. This position was defined as:

- Under supervision of a psychiatrist, performs psychiatric casework to facilitate diagnosis and treatment of soldiers requiring psychiatrist guidance.
- Administers psychiatric intake interviews, and writes case histories emphasizing the factors pertinent to psychiatric diagnoses.
- Carries out mental-hygiene prescriptions and records progress to formulate a complete case history.
- May obtain additional information on soldier's home environment through Red Cross or other agencies to facilitate in possible discharge planning.
- Must have knowledge of dynamics of personality structure and development, and cause of emotional maladjustments. (Harris, 2000, p. 5)

Even though there was a great need for psychiatric social workers, professionally trained social workers who were already enlisted soldiers could not automatically expect to be awarded the psychiatric social work occupation specialty. Most of these soldiers were drafted into the U.S. Army and already were in positions that needed to be filled, which made receiving reclassification very hard (O'Keefe, 2009). However, a noncommissioned officer in the U.S. Army could apply for reclassification as a psychiatric social worker. Ironically, the memorandum also acknowledged that Army commissioned officers or any person in the Navy, Marines, Coast Guard, Seabees, or Women's Army Corps (WAC) could not apply for reclassification. "Between 1942 and 1945, 711 enlisted men and WACs served in the role of the psychiatric social worker. These service members were assigned to induction centers, named to general and regional hospitals, station and evacuation hospitals, and combat divisions" (Harris, 2000, p. 5).

Two major professional organizations were responsible for getting a social work branch established into the U.S. Army. These organizations were the Wartime Committee on Personnel of the American Association of Social Workers and the National Committee for Mental Hygiene. The latter organization worked on behalf of social workers during World War I in collaboration with the Surgeon General (Harris, 2000). On October 19, 1942, the War Service Office of the American Association of Psychiatric Social Workers was established and continued its operations until December 1, 1945 (O'Keefe, 2009). This office was under the direction of Elizabeth H. Ross, the former secretary of the association. Through her guidance and leadership, the War Service Office became the central contact point and source of information for social workers in the military services as well as the professional resource for the Surgeon General's Office. She would also be instrumental in developing an Army psychiatric social work program (O'Keefe, 2009).

Due to the impact of these three organizations, commissioned status in the U.S. Army for social workers was finally achieved in 1945; "Major Daniel E. O'Keefe assumed the position as the first Chief of the Army's Psychiatric Social Work Branch on July 1, 1945" (Harris, 2000, p. 6). However, with the war over at the end of August, almost all of the social workers were separated from the service. Major O'Keefe was in charge only 8 months before being separated from military duty; however, he was able to begin a centrally directed social work program. In February 1946, the Army granted the military occupational specialty for the professionally trained psychiatric social work officer (MOS 3506). Even though this was after many social workers had already separated, this assured the continuity of Army social work (Harris, 2000).

After Major O'Keefe left the service, the Surgeon General called on Elizabeth H. Ross to serve as the civilian psychiatric social work consultant until a qualified uniformed officer could be recruited and appointed (Harris, 2000). Ross was instrumental in getting social work into the military. She helped alert soldiers to possible reclassification as a psychiatric social worker and advocated on behalf of the profession to the Surgeon General. After the demobilization following World War II, there was an urgency to rebuild professional social work in the Army (Harris, 2000). There was an even greater thrust to recruit social workers with a master's degree. The Army training program was initiated for the purpose of training psychiatric social workers to work for the Army. "The selection would be made from male graduates, students of social casework who were enrolled in graduate schools of social work approved by the Secretary of the Army and who desired a career with the Regular Army Medical Service Corps" (Harris, 2000, p. 16).

Social Work in the Different Branches of the Armed Services

The growth of military social work during World War II and in its immediate aftermath was not the same in each branch of the armed services. As discussed earlier, that growth came primarily in the U.S. Army. The Air Force did not become its own military department until 1947. Many organizational characteristics of the Army were transitioned into the Air Force, including social work service. It was originally part of the medical service corps, but would eventually move into the Biomedical Science Corps.

> Initially, social workers were assigned to larger medical facilities with the senior social worker being designated as the Chief of Social Work Service. However, by the early 1970s, it was common for a single social worker to be assigned to a small medical facility, sometimes as a member of a multidisciplinary mental health team or, on occasion, as the only mental health provider. (Jenkins, 2000, p. 28)

Social work in the Air Force would grow from six initial commissioned social work officers in 1952 to 225 at the peak of expansion in 1988 (Jenkins, 2000).

In the Navy, a variety of medical and administrative personnel provided social work services in naval medical treatment facilities. The Navy Relief Society was one of the largest social services agencies to provide social support, and World War II was the first time that the Navy Relief Society provided social workers to assist Navy families. However, most professional social work activities were confined to training volunteers who provided the social services (United States Navy Medical Service Corps), and it was not until the Vietnam War era that military social work in the Navy burgeoned (as is discussed later).

THE KOREAN WAR AND THE START OF THE VIETNAM WAR: 1950–1970

During the 1950s and the 1960s a mix of long periods of conflict overseas led to the expansion of military social service provisions. The Korean and Vietnam Wars drew on the lessons learned in World Wars I and II, which led to an increase in social services to service members and their families. The growing field of social work found itself in many different areas of the military and the veteran community. From the stockades to family advocacy, social workers solidified their worth to the military.

During these two wars, social workers would be deployed with Mental Hygiene units to combat zones and continued to work in medical settings (Daley, 2000). Social workers would also work in mental health facilities and community service organizations (Daley, 2000). By the time the Vietnam War ended, the military community would forever be changed.

Stockades

Since the military is a microcosm of society, many of its systems mirror those in civilian society. During the 1950s and 1960s one such system became increasingly worrisome. The military penal system struggled with whether to punish or rehabilitate its offenders (Harris, 2000). Colonel William C. Menninger, MC, chief of the department of neuropsychiatry and neurology of the Surgeon General's office stated:

> Rehabilitation should be our first aim in dealing with military offenders, recognizing that some members who are potentially unsalvageable should be separated from the group. The first step on a man's arrival should be psychiatric and social evaluation to determine the nature of the problem and the most promising steps to take in his rehabilitation. To accomplish this mission, every member of the staff from the commander to guard must know and apply the principles of mental hygiene. (Harris, 2000, p. 12)

However, the treatment options for rehabilitation were slow to be integrated and implemented into the stockades. Mental hygiene units had always been a part of the stockades in some fashion, but they often lacked certain characteristics to make them successful. For instance, they rarely included the total prisoner population and they never represented a real, cooperative combined effort between the psychiatric personnel and the military commanders (Harris, 2000).

In September 1957, the first real effort to screen prison inmates took effect. Army Regulation 210–181 introduced the Army Stockade screening program, which made "provisions for the early identification of maladjusted soldiers and, if possible, the use of remedial efforts to render these individuals useful to the service" (Harris, 2000, p. 13). The psychiatric evaluations were conducted within the first few days of confinement and were most effectively conducted by social work personnel under the supervision of the psychiatrist (Harris, 2000). This screening program was hailed as a major achievement in military corrections, and was part of an organized effort to make the stockade a rehabilitation center rather than a place to isolate offenders—or what some had come to believe as a source of free labor (Harris, 2000).

However, there were several criticisms of these early rehabilitation efforts. One criticism pertained to the large variety of programs being implemented in the stockades facilities and whether these programs were effective. Most programs focused on the classical one-on-one psychotherapeutic relationship or a variety of group treatments. Another criticism was that social workers were being used to screen new inmates instead of being a larger part of the treatment process (Harris, 2000). Although they participated in individual treatment, many social workers felt the need to work on improving the military community as a whole (Harris, 2000).

In 1968, the Correctional Training Facility (CTF) was established in Fort Riley, Kansas. The purpose of this facility was to provide the training and assistance necessary to treat military offenders and return them to duty or to an honorable discharge (Harris, 2000). Social workers played a significant role in the development and implementation of the CTF and its programs.

Army Community Service (ACS): The Beginnings of the Family Advocacy Program

During the years between World War II and the Vietnam War, the demographics of the military changed dramatically.

> In 1940 there were 67,000 families in the Army. By 1965, there were about 450,000 families with over 1,300,000 million dependents. In 1940 enlisted men were required to obtain their superior's permission to marry. By 1965, 60% of the enlisted men were married and 80% of the officers. However, one consequence was that over 100,000 wives were separated from their husbands due to military duties. (Harris, 2000, p. 14)

Commanding officers were getting an increasing number of reports of problems from their troops in regard to family problems. These problems ranged from chronic financial problems to physical or mental health problems with children. These problems were leading to difficulties in retention of good soldiers and regular troop morale (Harris, 2000). A 2-year study was conducted to research these complaints and how the Army could aggressively address these problems. The study's findings led to the development of the Army Community Service (ACS) program, which was first started at Fort Dix in New Jersey, Fort Benning in Ohio, and Fort Lewis in Washington. The program later was established at all installations in which more than 500 military personnel were stationed.

The mission of the ACS program was to establish a centrally located service that would provide information, assistance, and guidance to members of the Army community in meeting personnel and family problems beyond the scope of the family's own resources. The program had to be recognizable and responsive to the needs of military personnel and their families. It was created with the intention of reducing hours consumed by command-personnel problems and soldiers seeking assistance for complex personal problems and domestic disputes. Another aim was to improve personnel retention by increasing career satisfaction. "Some of the services that were provided included information and referral for financial assistance, availability of housing, transportation, relocation of dependents, medical and dental care, legal assistance, and more complex family and personal issues" (Harris, 2000, p. 15).

In the beginning, 42 social work officers and 19 social work enlisted personnel were assigned. This assignment was the first time social workers, as a group, were called on to extend their knowledge and skills outside of the medical service. In addition to professional staff, the ACS relied heavily on volunteers. The concept of ACS started with the hope that its foundation would be a volunteer corps of Army wives who would support a small nucleus of military and civilian supervisors (Harris, 2000). Two wives who played a major role in the beginning of ACS were Beatrice Banning Ayer, the wife of General George S. Patton, and Dorothy Rennix, the wife of General Harold K. Johnston, the Army Chief of Staff from 1964 to 1968.

"By November 1966, over ninety ACS centers had been established worldwide, with over 132,000 individuals having received assistance at these centers" (Harris, 2000, p. 15). ACS centers were also established at major medical facilities, including Walter Reed Army Medical Center in Washington DC, Fitzsimmons General Hospital in Colorado, and Valley Forge General Hospital in Pennsylvania. Social workers played a major role in implementing and establishing ACS programs in medical centers across the globe (Harris, 2000). A major milestone was achieved on January 16, 1967, when an ACS branch was established in the Personnel Services Division of the Army Deputy Chief of Staff of Personnel. This achievement solidified the ACS program within the Army community, and the ACS program would become the foundation for the family advocacy program, an important development for military social work, as is discussed in more depth later in this chapter.

After the Vietnam War to the End of the Cold War

The end of the 1960s and early 1970s was a great period of change in society, and the military was no different. The Great Society carried out by President Lyndon B. Johnson increased awareness of poverty, racial tensions, and domestic issues including child abuse and domestic violence. This awareness brought a significant change in the military social services, including the creation of the Navy social work program.

The Red Cross decided to cease its contribution to the psychosocial services, due to the increasing need for professional trained mental health professionals during the Vietnam War. The magnitude of service members and family members that needed services also was too much for the organization to sustain on its own. When the Red Cross ceased its contribution in the 1970s, a temporary decline in social work services occurred in naval medical treatment facilities, and other health professionals had the burden of filling the void of social workers. However, before the Red Cross withdrew, several civilian psychiatric social workers had laid the foundation for an official social work program in the Navy. Eventually, the concern about the large number of prisoners of war (POWs) and personnel listed as missing in action (MIA) provided a catalyst for increasing the role of social work in the Navy (United States Navy Medical Service Corps, 2000). In 1972 a Center for Prisoner of War Studies was established at the Naval Health Research Center in San Diego, California. Its research concluded that strong outreach services, collaboration with other agencies, and mental health consultation were necessary to assist returning POWs and their families. This led to social workers being employed at several Navy treatment facilities. The social workers coordinated community services and facilitated the transition for repatriated POWs and their families. At these treatment facilities, programs were initiated to help families and children deal with service members returning home by providing individual and family counseling (U.S. Navy Medical Service Corps, 2000).

Other developments during the 1970s that increased the role of social services in the Navy included the establishment of Naval drug rehabilitation centers in 1971, family advocacy programs in 1976,and the Navy family service center system in 1978. At their start, however, these programs were created with few social workers. For example, only 29 civilian social workers were employed in naval hospitals. The other branches of the armed forces had comparatively robust social work programs, with a ratio of one military or civilian social worker for every 15 physicians. But the ratio in the Navy was only one civilian social worker to 170 physicians (U.S. Navy Medical Service Corps, 2000, p. 25). Those civilian social workers were responsible not only for caring for sailors in the Navy, but also for U.S. Marines.

This dearth of social workers led to increasing problems in caring for sailors and Marines, and the use of social workers in the Navy got a boost in 1979 when the Bureau of Medicine and Surgery approved a request to recruit and commission thirteen social workers in the Medical Service Corps. Consequently, in January 1980 the Navy's first uniformed social worker was commissioned as a lieutenant (junior grade) and was assigned to establish a department of social work at the Naval Regional Medical Center in San Diego (U.S. Navy Medical Service Corps, 2000). By the end of 1980, there would be 11 more uniformed social workers in the department. Another boost in 1979 occurred with the establishment of the Navy's first Family Service Center. Over the next 5 years, social work in the Navy would continue to grow in medical treatment facilities, drug and alcohol rehabilitation centers, family advocacy programs, and expanded clinical services with individuals, families, and groups (U.S. Navy Medical Service Corps, 2000).

Family Programs

As Jesse Harris discusses in Chapter 18 of this book, perhaps the most important factor contributing to the growth of military social work is the stress experienced by the families and children of active duty service members and veterans and the recognition by military commanders of the impact of family stress on the military mission. One of the largest programs to serve military families is the Family Advocacy Program (FAP), which, as mentioned earlier, emerged during the Vietnam War era. Its predecessors were family violence prevention programs, which concentrated primarily on child abuse. Although the initial focus of these programs was on the medical aspects of child maltreatment, the prevention and education foci soon followed (Nelson, 2000).

Many civilians believed that child abuse was an epidemic taking over the military community. However, at the time there was no central database to correlate that fact or deny it. Later studies would show that child abuse was actually less in the military than in the regular population during the 1970s (Nelson, 2000). However, this stigma continued to persist and led to passage of Public Law 93–247, "Child Abuse Prevention Treatment Act."

> This legislation authorized federal grants to states to develop and strengthen child abuse prevention and treatment programs, exclusively to states with an established system for reporting and investigation of incidents of suspected

> child abuse. The act also established the National Center on Child Abuse and Neglect (NCCAN), which was to become a strong advocate for programs in the DoD. (Nelson, 2000, p. 54)

Following the passage of this legislation, there was increased pressure on the Department of Defense (DoD) to create its own identification and treatment program. However, the DoD was reluctant and encouraged civilians that were working with the military to take charge of this program (Nelson, 2000).

In 1975, the Air Force became the first service to establish a child advocacy program (Nelson, 2000), and each service had its own child advocacy program by the end of 1976. In addition, the Navy included spouse abuse in its program (Nelson, 2000). However, none of these programs was directly funded or given high priority, because all staff assigned operated as additional or collateral duties (Government Accountability Office [GAO], 1979). Nelson (2000, p. 55) observed, "As such, the programs were little more than administrative mechanisms to formalize the existing structure. Any additional resources to fight child abuse or for prevention were not available at this time."

The catalyst that changed the direction of child advocacy in the military was a 1979 Government Accountability Office report, "Military Child Advocacy Programs: Victims of Neglect," which documented the need for overall DoD guidance in implementing military family violence programs. This report stated that child advocacy programs were inconsistent among the different services, were not properly funded, and were not in proper positions of the military installation level. This report also stated that the programs were understaffed and needed a unified and consistent DoD policy, greater resource allocation, and expanded education and training (Government Accountability Office, 1979). In response to this report, the DoD established the Military Family Resource Center. The first DoD directive on family violence was published, and funding was appropriated for the military family advocacy programs (Nelson, 2000).

The Military Family Resource Center (MFRC), established in October 1980, was the sole mission of the Armed Services YMCA (ASYMCA). It was created to "provide information and technical assistance to professionals serving military families, facilitate inter-service and inter-disciplinary cooperation, maintain liaison with other federal and civilian agencies serving families, and provide fiscal oversight to all of the military family violence programs" (Nelson, 2000, p. 56). Even though it was initially conceptualized as a place to share information, it became the vehicle to manage program development and training. It also acted as a catalyst for the development of prevention and family support programs (Nelson, 2000). By 1990, the ASYMCA relinquished control of the MFRC; however, it served a vital role in creating and implementing a place for family advocacy in the armed forces.

In 1981 the DoD issued a directive that expanded the scope of child advocacy programs to include spouse abuse and established a set of common definitions for each service. This directive shifted the focus from just child advocacy to family advocacy. It required each service to set up its own program for prevention, identification, reporting, treatment, and follow-up of child and spouse abuse. The Family Advocacy Program (FAP) initially was met with hesitation in the Department of Defense, because it was unclear how it could aid DoD's main mission of supporting active duty forces (Nelson, 2000). However, by fiscal year 1983, FAP funds were directly appropriated to DoD. "The centralization of family maltreatment funding was a key in consolidating individual and uncoordinated service activities into a coherent DoD program" (Nelson, 2000, p. 57), which was recommended in the GAO report of 1979. In 1987, the first standardized central registry reporting requirements for reporting child and spouse abuse was created (Nelson, 2000).

Currently, the FAP's mission is to prevent, identify, intervene, and treat all aspects of child abuse, neglect, and spouse abuse (Nelson, 2000). FAPs are also designed to support the integrity of the family unit without compromising the victim, and they collaborate with state and local civilian child protective services. They also work to make the family unit stronger by providing services and programs that include training and education and primary and secondary prevention programs that range from advocacy for nonviolent communities to programs targeted to at-risk populations (Nelson, 2000).

Social workers were instrumental in the creation and development of the FAP. Civilian social workers led the way, but control was quickly given to uniformed social workers. Early programs were managed by social workers, who were generally assigned as mental health officers. The role of the child advocacy officer was an additional duty, and workers consequently had to balance numerous competing demands. These demands included command-directed evaluations, counseling, and consulting, as well as the evaluation, treatment, and case management of child abuse cases. Unfortunately, this meant that child abuse cases were not always the highest priority (Nelson, 2000). It would not be until the late 1980s and early 1990s that child advocacy would be the sole job of a social worker.

Substance Abuse Programs

As discussed in Chapter 12 of this book, substance abuse became a large problem for the military during the Vietnam War, as service members were returning from Vietnam addicted to opiates, heroin, and/or marijuana. Consequently, Public Law 92–129 was enacted in 1971, which mandated a program for the identification and treatment of drug and alcohol dependent individuals in all branches of the armed services. Military substance abuse prevention programs parallel civilian Employee Assistance Programs (EAP), however, unlike civilian programs, which aim for economic benefits, military programs are aimed at assuring force readiness (Newsome, 2000).

The primary treatment model in the early stages was the 12-step model of Alcoholics Anonymous. Both inpatient and outpatient programs relied heavily on a 12-step treatment model, and the main criterion to be a provider was to be "in recovery" oneself. This criterion led to a paraprofessional work force, which continued into the 1980s. Each branch viewed the counselor role differently. Both the Army and Navy used individuals in recovery, but the Army established the counselor role as a specific duty, while the Navy had the counselor as an extra duty, with the individual maintaining their regular Navy position. All rehabilitative services were provided by paraprofessional counselors assigned to a multiservice agency called *Social Actions*. This agency also addressed employee relations, racial relations, and equal opportunity issues. The Air Force combined an initial assessment from a Social Actions counselor and then a medical consultant. Active duty social workers primarily filled the roles of the medical consultant, and they were mostly assigned to base mental health clinics (Newsome, 2000).

PTSD

In 1980 posttraumatic stress disorder (PTSD) was officially recognized as a diagnosis in the *DSM-III* (Lasiuk & Hegadoren, 2006). Although military trauma stress reactions were known by other names in earlier wars, as discussed in Chapter 6 of this book, it was not until the late 1960s and 1970s that veterans started to fight to have mental health viewed as an injury from combat. Before PTSD was an official diagnosis, veterans were unable to receive disability compensation for their PTSD symptoms (Lasiuk & Hegadoren, 2006). This new diagnosis led to an increase in mental health social workers at veterans hospitals and at mental health clinics in the military (Daley, 2000). However, this was also a period of decline for uniformed social workers working in mental health clinics in the military. Uniformed social workers were expanding their expertise to family advocacy and substance abuse programs, which caused them to lose their footing in mental health clinics (Daley, 2000).

The Veterans Administration

The Veterans Administration increased many of its services during this time period as well. After the passage of the Veterans Health Care Amendments Act of 1979, the VA set up a network of Vet Centers across the country, separate from other VA facilities. In response to Vietnam veterans' special needs, the Vet Centers at first were limited to just Vietnam veterans; however, they later expanded to serve all veterans (Department of Veterans Affairs, NA).

In 1975, in response to an increasing number of elderly veterans and their special needs, the VA began to train interdisciplinary teams of health care specialists. In the late 1980s, the VA began to take a special interest in helping homeless veterans and chronically mental ill patients (Department of Veterans Affairs, NA). Many of the professional staff positions for serving these new target populations were filled by social workers.

The Persian Gulf War Until 9/11

The 1990s was a period of expansion and a period of transition for military social work. After the end of the Cold War and the Gulf War of 1990–1991 (known as Operation Desert Shield/Desert Storm), many social work–led programs increased in funding and in size. The family advocacy program expanded greatly during this time period. So did the social work role within the military, in general, and in veterans hospitals. The Navy was an example of this expansion. "During Operation Desert Shield/Storm, social workers were deployed for the first time to a combat zone on board hospital ships Comfort and Mercy, and Fleet Hospital Five. They provided counseling and referral services, and mental health support" (U.S. Navy Medical Service Corps, 2000, p. 26).

Family Advocacy Programs

The family advocacy program's budget grew fourfold between 1988 and 1993—from $14.2 million to $62.2 million. The personnel in the FAP worked extensively to ensure standardization in reporting and training policies and extended prevention programs. All of these prevention programs were supported by funding including a New Parents Support Program, which was given $20 million in 1995 (Nelson, 2000).

Toward the end of the 1990s, increasing funding and resources were being taken away from the FAP. This was due to the drawdown of the military. By 1995 the DoD had approximately one third fewer active duty service members than just 5 years earlier, with the closing of numerous installations, particularly those that were overseas, and with the movement toward home basing. Even with this drawdown, however, by 1998 the FAP was a large, comprehensive, multidisciplinary operation funded at over $100 million per year and employing more than 2,000 staff, which provided a wide range of intervention and prevention services (Nelson, 2000).

Substance Abuse Programs

Substance abuse programs also experienced a change and growth in the 1990s. An increased focus on outpatient treatment instead of brief inpatient stays was becoming popular in the civilian society, which was affecting how the military treated substance abuse. The move to outpatient facilities led to a reduction of inpatient treatment facilities, which helped the DoD during a time when they were looking to make budget cuts (Newsome, 2000).

Due to the change from discretionary referral to mandated referral, service members were receiving treatment for alcohol abuse before they qualified for the *DSM* diagnosis. Military substance abuse prevention and treatment program managers, many of whom were social workers, were responsible for ensuring the lowest possible illegal drug use to maximize operational readiness in the armed forces. This responsibility meant that counselors had to develop skills for detecting early levels of alcohol abuse disorder. The use of screening instruments with well-established sensitivity and specificity, such as the World Health Organization's Alcohol Use Disorders Identification Test (AUDIT), would prove to be critical in the accuracy of early assessments (Newsome, 2000).

Illegal drug use also became a large focus in the 1990s. In the early 1980s, service members could be treated for illegal drug use under the Limited Privilege Communication Program; however, in the mid-1980s a "zero tolerance" policy was implemented, in which any report of illegal drug use—whether by self or by others—could result in administrative discharge and perhaps even criminal prosecution (Newsome, 2000).

In 1998 the Air Force implemented the Alcohol and Drug Abuse Prevention and Control (ADAPT) program, which allowed individuals who self-identified as using illegal drugs could be granted limited protection from criminal prosecution (Newsome, 2000). Treatment by the VA was granted to those individuals who came forward as long as they agreed to an administrative discharge. The establishment of ADAPT was the first time that efforts to assess outcomes were implemented. One of the requirements of the program included 3-, 6-, and 12-month follow-up assessments to evaluate behavior and duty performance (Newsome, 2000). Social workers and other behavioral health professionals were in charge of conducting these follow-up sessions, and in charge of treating service members addicted to illegal substances.

The Veterans Administration

In the 1990s the VA focused its attention on caring for veterans of the Persian Gulf War. Many Gulf War veterans were returning home with chronic illnesses that could not be linked to a specific cause. This unknown cause of their illnesses led the VA to conduct many research studies and to change its policy on how service connected compensation is determined (Department of Veterans Affairs, n.d.).

Female veterans were also becoming a large proportion of the veteran population during the 1990s. In response to this growth "the VA expanded medical facilities and services for women and increased efforts to inform them that they are equally entitled to veterans benefits. The Veterans Health Care Act of 1992 provided authority for a variety of gender-specific services and programs to care for women veterans" (Department of Veterans Affairs, n.d.).

The first VA center dedicated to women opened in November 1994. Its mission was to ensure that women veterans had the same access to VA health care and benefits as did male veterans and that the VA was responsive to the gender specific needs of women veterans. It also aimed to improve awareness of women veterans' benefits and eligibility criteria (Department of Veterans Affairs, n.d.).

The VA also made strides to protect women against sexual assaults. After the Tailhook scandal, which involved multiple midshipmen from the Navy assaulting multiple females, Congress began to take notice of how sexual harassment and sexual assaults were hurting female veterans. According to the VA website,

> In July 1992, a series of hearings on women veterans' issues by the Senate Veterans Affairs Committee first brought the problem of military sexual trauma to policy makers' attention. Congress responded to these hearings by passing Public Law 102–585, which was signed into law in November of 1992. Among other things, Public Law 102–805 authorized health care and counseling to women veterans to overcome psychological trauma resulting from experiences of sexual assault or sexual harassment during their military service. Later laws expanded this benefit to male veterans as well as female veterans, repealed limitations on the required duration of service, and extended the provision of these benefits until the year 2005. (Street & Stafford, 2004)

Military sexual trauma is a large focus in the VA, and the benefits for females and males that suffer from it continued to grow into the next decade. Social workers often work as sexual trauma counselors and military sexual trauma coordinators to help veterans suffering from military sexual trauma.

The Global War on Terrorism

On September 11, 2001, the United States was forever changed. Before 9/11, the military community believed it was going to increasingly drawdown its size and scope (Daley, 2000). However, after 9/11 the military increased in size to fight the Global War on Terrorism, which includes Operation Enduring Freedom in Afghanistan and Operation Iraqi Freedom in Iraq, which later became Operation New Dawn, (along with various counter terrorism operations in other countries). This was the first time since Vietnam that the U.S. military was in a prolonged war, and with a prolonged war comes changes in the social environment of the military. There were no "front lines" in these wars, so female service members were in combat situations that they had not been a part of in previous wars. This female equality shined a light on the abilities of women, but it also demonstrated how female service members could be in danger from their own colleagues through sexual harassment and assault (Hyun, Pavao, & Kimmerling, 2009).

Also during these wars, the military community took greater notice of suicides, when the amount of suicides began to outnumber the amount of combat casualties in a single year (Donnelly, 2009). The policy of Don't Ask, Don't Tell regarding open homosexuality in the service was overturned. In addition, the signature wound of these two wars, traumatic brain injury, was brought to the public's attention. All of these events have resulted in a period of increasing change within the military, and an increasing role for military social workers. Military social workers are now working in behavioral health units, combat operational stress control detachments, and warrior in transition units, which focus on injured returning troops and their transition into civilian society.

Sexual Assault

The 2000s saw the creation of the Sexual Assault Prevention and Response Office (SAPRO). Directive 6495.01 was created on October 5, 2005. This directive outlined the responsibilities of SAPRO and created the first agency to monitor and report on the sexual assault cases that take place in the military. This directive was DoD-wide and was created for each branch of the armed forces. The goal of this program was to eliminate sexual assaults that take place in the military (Department of Defense, 2005). Social workers and other behavioral health providers are often employed as sexual assault response coordinators and often volunteer as victim advocates in the military.

Another change was in how the military viewed the sexual assault of men. There is a much greater number of men in the military than women, yet, the number of reported military sexual traumas is about the same actual number for men as for women (1% of males reporting within the male military population versus 20 to 40% of female reports in the female military population) (Hyun et al., 2009; Kelly et al., 2011).

The VA took steps to combat the aftereffects of sexual assault. "A series of VA directives mandated universal screening of all veterans for a history of military sexual trauma and mandated that each facility identify a Military Sexual Trauma Coordinator to oversee the screening and treatment referral process" (Street & Stafford, 2004, p. 68). These positions were often filled with social workers.

Suicide Prevention

As mentioned earlier, during the Global War on Terrorism, suicides drew increased attention in the military. The vice chief of staff of the Army, General Peter Chiarelli, took a special interest in this problem, and he made it his personal mission to eliminate suicides in the military. One program that was implemented was a national call center for active duty service members and veterans, which was created in 2007. "Since its launch, the Veterans Crisis Line has answered more than 500,000 calls and made more than 18,000 life-saving rescues. In 2009, the VA added the anonymous online chat that has since helped more than 28,000 people" (Department of Veterans Affairs, 2011, p. 1). This call center is staffed with professionals specializing in crisis intervention and mental health techniques (Department of Veterans Affairs, 2011). Social workers often work as crisis intervention counselors at VA hospitals and in behavioral health departments at military medical treatment facilities.

Military Social Work Today

Social workers today are required to have at least a master's degree to work with veterans and to serve in the military. In recent years, the DoD has preferred that social workers have 2 years' postgraduate experience and/or a license to practice independent clinical social work before serving in the armed forces. However, each branch has created an internship for recent master-level social workers to help them obtain their clinical licensing while in the service (Department of Veterans Affairs, 2010).

The role of social work has evolved in the VA. It now has treatment responsibilities in all patient care areas. These include helping VA patients and families maximize their level of adjustment and coping, as well as promoting vocational and psychosocial rehabilitation (Department of Veterans Affairs, 2010). Social workers are part of multidisciplinary teams. They participate in the development and implementation of treatment approaches. They work with acute/chronic medical conditions and hospice patients, and are responsible for care through admission to follow-up services. They coordinate discharge planning and provide case management services (Department of Veterans Affairs, 2010). Social workers continue to be included in serving almost all VA target populations, including the veterans from the Global War on Terrorism, the homeless, the aged, the mentally ill, and the families that care for them.

The Department of Veterans Affairs is affiliated with more than 180 graduate schools of social work. As mentioned at the beginning of this chapter, it "operates the largest and most comprehensive clinical training program for social work students—training 900 students per year" (Department of Veterans Affairs, 2010, p. 1). In 2010, the VA employed more than 13,000 social workers, and it is increasing its numbers every year (Partners for Public Service, 2010).

CONCLUSION

This chapter presented a brief look at the historical roots and the growth of social work within the military and the Veterans Administration. From its early roots of medical social work in the Civil War to the Global War on Terrorism, social workers have been caring for America's wounded veterans. Social workers have been instrumental in implementing many different social reform programs in the military, including the family advocacy program, substance abuse programs, and the Sexual Assault Prevention and Response Office. Over the past 100 years, social workers have expanded the area of practice from purely mental health and medical fields of practice into many different areas, and will probably continue to do so long into the future.

REFERENCES

American Red Cross. (2011). *Military and Red Cross partnership*. Washington, DC. Retrieved from http://www.redcross.org/portal/site/en/menuitem.d8aaecf214c576bf971e4cfe43181aa0/?vgnextoid=b9681b655eb3b110VgnVCM10000089f0870aRCRD&vgnextfmt=d

Daley, J. (2000). Military social work practice in mental health programs. In J. Daley (Ed.), *Social work in the military* (pp. 123–136). Binghamton, NY: Haworth Press.

Department of Defense 6495.01. (2005). *Sexual assault prevention and response program.* Washington, DC.

Department of Veterans Affairs. (n.d.). *Veteran's affairs: A history in brief.* Washington, DC. Retrieved from www.va.gov/opa/publications/archives/docs/history_in_brief.pdf

Department of Veterans Affairs. (2010). *History of Veteran's Administration social work.* Washington, DC. Retrieved from http://www.socialwork.va.gov/about.asp

Department of Veterans Affairs. (2011). *Suicide prevention.* Washington, DC. Retrieved from http://www.mentalhealth.va.gov/suicide_prevention/index.asp

Donnelly, James. (2009). More troops lost to suicide. *Congressional Quarterly.* Retrieved from: <http://www.congress.org/news/2009/11/25/rising military_suicides?referrer=bk>

Government Accountability Office. (1979). *Military child advocacy programs: Victims of neglect.* Washington, DC: Author.

Harris, J. (2000). History of army social work. In J. Daley (Ed.), *Social work in the military* (pp. 3–22). Binghamton, NY: Haworth Press.

Hyun, J. K., Pavao, J., & Kimerling, R. (2009). Military sexual trauma. *PTSD Research Quarterly*, 20, 1–8.

Jenkins, J. (2000). History of air force social work. In J. Daley (Ed.), *Social work in the military* (pp. 27–48). Binghamton, NY: Haworth Press.

Kelly, V. A., Skelton, K., Meghna, P., & Bradley, B. (2011). More than military sexual trauma: Interpersonal violence, PTSD and mental health in women veterans. *Research in Nursing & Health* 34(6), 457–467.

Lasiuk, G., & Hegadoren, K. (2006). Posttraumatic stress disorder part I: Historical development of the concept. *Perspectives in Psychiatric Care*, *42*(1), 13–20.

National Association of Social Workers. (n.d.). *Social work history.* Washington, DC.

Nelson, J. (2000). Development and evolution of the family advocacy program in the departmet of defense. In J. Daley (Ed.), *Social work in the military* (pp. 51–66). Binghamton, NY: Haworth Press.

Newsome, R. (2000). Military social work practice in substance abuse programs. In J. Daley (Ed.), *Social work in the military* (pp. 91–106). Binghamton, NY: Haworth Press.

O'Keefe, D. (2009). Psychiatric social work. In *Neuropsychiatry in World War II.* Washington, DC. Retrieved from http://history.amedd.army.mil/booksdocs/wwii/NeuropsychiatryinWWIIVolI/default.htm

Partners for Public Service. (2010). *Social work jobs in the federal government.* Washington, DC. Retrieved from http://www.makingthedifference.org/federalcareers/socialwork.shtml

Raiha, N. (2000). Medical social work in the U.S. armed forces. In J. Daley (Ed.), *Social work in the military* (pp. 107–122). Binghamton, NY: Haworth Press.

Street, A., & Stafford, J. (2004). Military sexual trauma: Issues in caring for veterans. In *Department of Veterans Affairs & National Center for PTSD (2004) Iraq War Clinician's Guide.* Washington, DC.

United States Navy Medical Service Corps. (2000). History of navy social work. In J. Daley (Ed.), *Social work in the military* (pp. 23–26). Binghamton, NY: Haworth Press.

CHAPTER

2

Military Culture and Diversity

Jose E. Coll, Eugenia L. Weiss, and Michael Metal

INTRODUCTION

This chapter is written with the purpose of orienting the reader to what has been referred to as *military culture*. Culture in the military context is comprised of the values, beliefs, traditions, norms, perceptions, and behaviors that govern how members of the armed forces think, communicate, and interact with one another as well as with the outside world (Exum, Coll & Weiss, 2011). Mary Edwards Wertsch (1991), in her study of adults who grew up in military families post–World War II, described the military culture metaphorically as a "fortress" symbolizing the kind of separateness that military life entails from the rest of society. This brand of "culture" also determines how military personnel view their functioning in life, their status, and the role of the military in U.S. society.

A key tenet in the social work knowledge base today is the need for social workers to be culturally competent with regard to the target population they serve. However, most social work professionals who will be assisting military personnel, veterans and their families know little about this population (Freeman & Bicknell, 2008). This gap is particularly problematic today, given the increasing reliance on civilian practitioners to provide the needed behavioral health services to service members who are returning to their civilian lives. Among such returnees are members of the National Guard and Reserve Components who comprise almost half of the Total Force. These citizen soldiers are not full-time military personnel; that is, unless they are activated and deployed (Maxfield, 2008). Additionally, there will be veterans retiring from service or separating from active duty who may not access the traditional Veterans Affairs clinics but instead will be turning to community mental health agencies and private practitioners. Thus, it becomes essential for civilian practitioners to be familiar with the military lifestyle and its associated strengths and demands in order to offer culturally responsive services.

In addition to providing an introduction to military culture, this chapter also renders an overview of the various racial and ethnic groups that have served and continue to serve in the military, highlighting their sacrifices and their significant historical contributions to the security of our nation. The chapter also includes sections on aging veterans and on gay, lesbian, and bisexual military personnel and the unique occupational stressors and sacrifices they have endured.

MILITARY CULTURAL COMPETENCE AND COUNSELING

Clinical social workers and other mental health practitioners need to comprehend and take into account the client's worldviews (including culturally based worldviews), values, and experiences (Weiss, Coll, & Metal, 2011). This understanding is to "cultivate cross cultural understanding" and promote an "interpersonally close encounter" (Berg-Cross & Takushi-Chinen, 1995; as cited in Ponterotto, Gretchen, & Chauhan, 2001, p. 86). Achieving true cultural competence involves an ability to grasp the "broad worldviews of the cultural group" while examining the "individual expression of these views" (p. 87). Within the counseling professions cultural competence is brought to the forefront in the code of ethics by instructing mental health practitioners to understand the diverse backgrounds of the clients, and provide culturally competent services (American Psychological Association, 1992; National Association of Social Workers, 1999). Additionally, according to the Council on Social Work Education (2008), Educational Policy and Accreditation Standards, social work students are ethically obligated to identify, analyze and implement effective practice strategies with people from diverse cultures (CSWE, Educational Policy, 2.1.10[a]–[d]).

Borrowing from counseling diversity theories, concepts such as acculturation and ethnic identity development can be implemented to understand military service personnel and veterans as a distinct culture. For instance, acculturation models explore the degrees to which immigrants assimilate and adapt to their host cultures (D. W. Sue & Sue, 2008). Ethnic identity development models examine the degree to which people of color embrace their own heritage in the face of racism and discrimination experienced in a host or majority culture (D.W. Sue & Sue). Grieger and Ponterotto (1995) offer a framework that considers the client's level of acculturation as it applies to the counseling process. They posit that the more acculturated the client is to the host culture (i.e., in terms of holding middle-class Caucasian American societal values) the more likely the client will be at ease with the counseling process. Applying these notions to military personnel and veterans allows therapists to examine the levels of acculturation and cultural identity in service members who are transitioning from the military into the civilian world. It also offers a lens by which to ascertain veteran perceptions of the counseling process.

Both enlisted persons and officers in the armed forces are indoctrinated to believe that mental health issues and psychological problems are sources of weakness, and thus service member perceptions regarding counseling are ambivalent at best (although the military is currently attempting to destigmatize mental health services). This culturally driven value can serve as a potential obstacle in the therapeutic process. Clinicians need to address this issue with their clients on the first visit and validate the service member for attending therapy. According to Grieger and Ponterrotto (1995), a clinician should assess the client's level of psychological-mindedness (or capacity for insight) in comprehending, interpreting, and attributing individual problems. Within military culture, service personnel are dissuaded from considering individuality; instead, they are to follow orders from superiors and are to act as part of a group, whereby the unit takes precedence over the individual. This collectivistic standpoint may also present a challenge to mental health professionals working with veterans who highly identify with the military culture (Coll, Weiss, Draves, & Dyer, 2012). Many veterans even after separating from military service continue to lead their lives according to their military identity. Identity is defined as the process by which people define themselves, and this determines attitudes and behaviors and the manner in which they communicate that definition to others (Ashforth, Harrison, & Corley, 2008). This chapter's authors hypothesize that a veteran's overidentification with military culture could impact his or her ability to successfully transition into the civilian world and impinge on the ability to develop rapport in the therapeutic relationship (especially if the client's identity clashes with that of the civilian therapist). On the other hand, some veterans after completing military service choose not to adhere to the strict military identity. In other words, these individuals underidentify with the military, and for some this may be a way of easing their entry into new civilian roles (Kreiner & Ashforth, 2001). Thus, clinicians need to know that not all veterans are alike, just as intra-group variations exist within a given culture (D. W. Sue & Sue, 2008).

Cultural competence in general requires clinicians to consider their own cultural background and attitudes toward the client (Lonner & Ibrahim, 1996), and this is especially pertinent in working with military and veteran clients. For instance, the clinician may hold prejudices about military service or may harbor antiwar beliefs, and the expression of those beliefs could alienate the veteran client. Moreover, to do so would violate ethical practice in that the ethical foundation for the helping professions is formed on the premise of respect for client differences (Coll et al., 2012).

MILITARY CULTURE: VALUES AND BELIEFS

Military culture, as stated in the introductory paragraph, is comprised of values, beliefs, traditions, norms, perceptions, and behaviors that govern how members of the armed forces think, communicate, and interact. This notion of culture also determines how military personnel and veterans view their role in life. No matter the branch of service or era of service, the common threads shared by veterans are reflected in the indoctrination or socialization of the military core values, which include honor, courage, loyalty, integrity, and commitment. These core values guide service members in the highest ethical principles through creeds such as "I will bear true faith and allegiance," "I will obey my orders," "*Semper Fidelis*," ("*Always Faithful*") (U.S. Marine Corps values; as cited in Exum et al., 2011).

The values determine the behaviors that serve as the standards of conduct for military personnel. The standards of conduct apply regardless of whether the service member is in uniform. The military as a socializing institution believes that this pervasive application of standards of conduct is necessary because members of the armed forces must be "combat ready" (Exum et al., 2011). Additionally, Daley (1999) stated that over time service personnel develop a unique identity, which he termed an *ethnic* identity. This uniqueness forms as a result of shared commonalities that individuals and families encounter on entry into the military culture. For instance, the commonalities include the following aspects: the use of language that is unique to the military, a sense of exclusivity, status within command, branch of service, and military experience with or without combat. These are all factors that contribute to a sense of "we-ness," or a profound shared experience. Additionally, those who serve together in special operation forces can be deeply bonded to one another. This has been anecdotally referred to feel as a "tribal" experience.

DISTINCTIVE CHARACTERISTICS OF MILITARY CULTURE

When attempting to understand military culture we automatically think of our own culture as a form of comparison and measurement. For instance, for many U.S. civilians there is an emphasis on the individual or on individual achievements, personal freedoms and a striving for fluid social mobility. These typical civilian cultural characteristics stand in stark contrast to the military culture where there is an intrinsic hierarchical social structure and an emphasis on the mission, chain of command (direct report), and group solidarity (Exum et al., 2011). Social status in the military is clear, in that officers hold a higher status than enlisted personnel and both officers and enlisted personnel are further ordered in status according to rank. Duties, responsibilities, pay, living arrangements, and social interactions are all determined by rank structure (which is described in the next section). Military culture provides a clear understanding to its members that an individual's purpose is to support the mission through loyalty, obedience, and honor. Individual achievement is important to the degree that it supports efficient and effective completion of the assigned task (Exum et al., 2011).

Perhaps the most salient difference between civilian culture and military culture is that devotion to duty in the military includes being willing to sacrifice one's life for one's country, for one's comrades, and even for an unknown person or entity, as in the case of humanitarian missions. Thus, there is an implicit understanding among military personnel, that they follow lawful orders with the full recognition that they may die or be severely injured in fulfillment of those orders (Cook, 2004). Their commitment is profound and may impact their perspective toward and, their relationship with, those civilians who have not served. Service members develop a worldview that reflects the values of military culture, and for this reason they often feel out of place on returning to civilian life. Readjustment for military personnel to civilian culture is not as simple as civilians might think. It involves much more than taking off the uniform. For many veterans, transitioning means learning a new lifestyle, language, and adapting to a new culture (for additional information please see Chapter 17 by Coll and Weiss).

THE MILITARY AS AN ORGANIZATION

The U.S. military "is a hierarchical organization, with a system of military ranks to denote levels of authority within the organization" (Kadis & Walls, 2009, p. 1). The organizational rank structure includes three general categories: enlisted, warrant officers, and commissioned officers, each offering a unique career and leadership path that directly impacts earning potential, living environment, and military status (Daley, 1999).

The U.S. armed services are comprised of four branches (under the Department of Defense), each one with a unique mission, purpose, and subculture. The branches include the Army (which represents the main ground force of the United States); Navy (sea operations); Marine Corps (amphibious warfare); and the Air Force (air, space, and cyberspace). The Army is the oldest and largest branch and is comprised of Active Army, Army National Guard, and Army Reserves. The Navy (second largest branch), is comprised of an active and reserve component. The Marine Corps (smallest of the armed forces) has an active component and a reserve component. The Air Force is the youngest branch. It was established post–World War II and has an active and two reserve components, the Air Force Reserve and the Air National Guard. It is noteworthy that the United States Coast Guard is not part of the Department of Defense (DoD), but it falls under the Department of Homeland Security (DHS). The role of the Coast Guard is to ensure maritime safety, security, mobility, national defense, and protection of natural resources (Center for Deployment Psychology [CDP], n.d.; Exum et al., 2011).

The total number of individuals serving in the United States Armed Services is more than 3.6 million. This includes the DoD Active Duty, Department of Homeland Security Active Duty, and Ready Reserve Coast Guard; members of the Retired and Stand by Reserve; as well as DoD appropriated (funded) and nonappropriated civilian personnel. According to DoD (2011) statistics, Active Duty and Coast Guard Active Duty members comprise the largest portion of the military force (39.4%), followed by Ready Reserve members (29.2%), and DoD civilian personnel (24.9%). It is worth noting that there are also a variety of privatized military contract firms that provide support, technical assistance, and consultation services (see Singer, 2004).

Eligibility: Why Join?

The U.S. armed forces have typically been open to anyone who is a U.S. citizen or a U.S. resident (a green card holder), between the ages of 18 and 35. Requirements for joining include a high school diploma, absence of a criminal record, and relatively good health. However, there have been times when some of these requirements have been waived, specifically during times of war or shortage of enrollees (Exum et al., 2011).

Until recently, individuals who identified themselves as gay, lesbian, or bisexual were barred from military service. The official policy of the Department of Defense and Public Law 103–160, Section 654, Title 10, passed in 1993 was that homosexuals were excluded from military service. The Don't Ask Don't Tell Repeal Act of 2010 (H.R. 2965, S. 4023) was signed into law on December 22, 2010, repealing the ban on gays, lesbians, and bisexuals from serving in the U.S. Armed Services (additional information will be provided later in the chapter).

Those who serve in uniform join for a variety of reasons. Some may join because of the opportunities for travel. Others may join to satisfy a family tradition of forefathers who have served. Still others join out of a sense of patriotism or by being a high school graduate and viewing military service as a way to learn a professional skill while saving money for college through the Post–9/11 GI Bill. For many, the military is a guaranteed employer with equal opportunities for pay and advancement as well as offering excellent benefits for their families (Exum et al., 2011).

Women join the military for some of the same reasons that men join. The advent of the all-volunteer force removed the previous 2% quota, which had restricted the number of women who could serve on active duty ultimately increasing the number of career opportunities for women (see Chapter 3 on women in the military). Hall (2008) noted, "there are probably as many reasons to join the military as there are military service members" (p. 41). In addition to the above reasons, Hall included more psychological ones, such as desiring to have the identity of a warrior, wanting to flee from problems at home and in their personal lives, and so on. Hall urged civilian counselors to explore reasons for joining when working with service members and their families.

COMBAT READINESS: MISSION OF THE U.S. MILITARY

It is important for practitioners working with veterans to recognize the various conflicts or wars in which our veterans have served, to comprehend the historical, social, political, and cultural implications of military service, as veterans are not "a one size fits all." Historically, the U.S. military has provided four justifications for overriding the "noninterference clause" of international law (regarding the justifications for war). The first justification is the invitation to intervene in a state that has been besieged by another. The second justification is intervention by right of treaty in which case the United States would intervene based on a prior agreement for mutual defense of the state in question. The third justification is the protection of the lives and property of U.S. citizens in foreign states (as was the case during the invasion of Grenada in 1983). The final justification and the one that seems to best represent the principles of the "just war" doctrine is to engage in war as part of a humanitarian intervention (O'Brien, 1984).

The relevance for mental health practitioners has to do with how the military interprets the use of force to carry out its mission. The last congressionally declared war was World War II. Most U.S. military operations are not technically classified as "wars," and there are many veterans who have served in military operations that have received little or no media coverage. However, these "nonwar" operations were nevertheless dangerous and high risk, and probably involved loss life for both civilians and military personnel alike. Social workers need to understand that when troops are deployed to an "authorized military engagement" such as Operation Enduring Freedom (i.e., Afghanistan) they are being deployed to a war zone. The experience will change them. Accordingly, when they transition back to civilian society they will need to adapt or attenuate their combat responses to a "new normal." Hoge (2010) explained, "'transitioning' home from combat does not mean giving up being a warrior, but rather learning to dial up or down the warrior responses depending on the situation" (p. x). Hoge provided the LANDNAV acronym to assist veterans in this transition (we believe that most of the psychotherapies for combat stress are implicitly based on the elements provided in this model):

- L = **L**ife Survival Skills—Defines the veteran's need to understand how the body responds to stress and combat (as survival mechanisms).
- A = **A**ttend—Describes how veterans need to pay attention to and modulate their psychological (emotional and cognitive) and physiological reactions.
- N = **N**arrate—Emphasizes the need for combat veterans to narrate their war stories.
- D = (Learn to) **D**eal—Expresses the need for veterans to come up with alternative (positive) coping skills.

- N = **N**avigate—Where the veteran and his or her family members need to learn how to navigate the complex veteran health care and service systems.
- A = **A**cceptance—Relates to the importance of veterans reaching a point of acceptance in their lives with regards to their losses and experiences.
- V = **V**ision, **V**oice, **V**illage/Community and **V**ictory—Veterans should celebrate what is good in their lives within the context of community/family and have hope for the future.

MILITARY CULTURE AND CIVILIAN SOCIETY

As noted earlier, military life is fundamentally different from civilian life. Military society is characterized by its own laws, rules, customs and traditions—including numerous restrictions on personal behaviors, or the lack of personal freedoms, which would not be acceptable in the civilian world. Military culture does broadly conform to constitutional norms of individual rights and liberties, but "derives from the functional imperative [battlefield success] and . . . values collective over individual good" (Hooker, 2003, p. 6).

Therefore, the extraordinary responsibilities of the armed forces, the unique conditions of military service, and the critical role of unit cohesion require that the military community, while being subject to civilian control, exist as a separate specialized society (Davenport, 1987). Hence, as Davenport (1987) noted, it is civilian ambivalence about the military's power plus the military's obsession with unit cohesion that serves to keep both cultures in potential conflict. Hooker (2003), however, stated that the psychological distance and so-called estrangement between military culture and civilian society have been exaggerated. He suggested that the large number of veterans and reservists that live and comingle in civilian society have contributed to a greater understanding both from a psychological perspective and from physical proximity, between these two segments of the U.S. population. Although military culture embraces and imposes a set of values that more narrowly restricts individual behavior, civilians seem to accept the military's rationale for having a "conservative outlook that emphasizes the group over the individual and organizational success over personal validation" (Hooker, 2003, p. 16).

Although the dynamic tensions that teeter between civilian and military cultures may be suboptimal, "they are far from dangerous" (Hooker, 2003, p. 16). The relevance of this contrast (between the military and civilian worlds) for social workers and other mental health practitioners is that individuals are highly influenced by their environment; that is, every human being goes through some form of socialization. Therefore, helping professionals need to evaluate their own socialization via a self-assessment of their personal attitudes and views towards whichever diverse population they may be encountering (O'Neal, 2012)—in this case, the military and veteran populations. Furthermore, professionals need to expose themselves to various perspectives and multiple realities even within a particular population. Keeping this in mind, professionals need to familiarize themselves with historical and multicultural contexts and policies that have impacted individuals in their respective environments.

This leads us into the next segment of our chapter, which discusses ethnically and racially diverse groups in the military (as the military has long been used as an agent of social progression and change). The discussion provides a historical overview of the different ethnic groups and their contributions to the U.S. armed forces, to provide the context necessary for social workers delivering services to a multiethnic military population. We begin our discussion of diversity with Hispanics/Latinos.

Hispanics/Latinos

Hispanic/Latino(a) military personnel have served through every major conflict in the history of the United States, often receiving recognition for their achievements while their ethnicity has not always been noted. During the Mexican-American War, for example, Native Mexican descendants became contracted scouts for the U.S. Army. During World War I, although allowed to serve and given the opportunity to achieve the highest ranks, Hispanics were still mostly relegated to segregated units throughout the military. During World War II, Hispanics were integrated into most units; however, segregated units still existed that were predominately scattered across the globe, and most were tasked with defending the Caribbean islands from Japanese invasion. The war in Vietnam saw a host of changes and issues resulting from the conversion of the military from an all-volunteer force to a mandated draft. The draft affected Hispanics and African Americans disproportionately as compared to Whites, who were more likely to be able to afford college and avoid service. Forced service created undue hardships for Hispanics who served during Vietnam. Prevalent racism combined with a lack of community support from within the military is believed to be one of the reasons that Hispanics were so heavily affected by posttraumatic stress disorder during and after this conflict (Pole, Best, Metzler, & Marmar, 2005). During the initial invasion into Afghanistan, three of the first soldiers to be killed were Hispanics who were not yet citizens (e.g., Marine Lance Corporal Jose Gutierrez, a recent immigrant from Guatemala). President Bush recognized the efforts of documented as well as undocumented immigrants serving in the military and signed an executive order granting posthumous citizenship for those immigrants who were killed in action. This order, though hailed by some, was viewed by many as an insult to the sacrifices made by those men and women who gave their lives for a country that had not yet accepted them as their own (Estrada, 2009).

African Americans

African Americans served in the military during the Revolutionary War and the Civil War when the continental Army or Union recognized the need for service people and viewed freed slaves as an asset for service. Unlike White soldiers, Black soldiers were not permitted to remain in the Army after serving in combat during the Revolutionary War and after the Civil War were permitted to remain but typically were stationed in distant outposts isolated from the rest of civilian society. The treatment of African American soldiers was typically demeaning in nature by White military officers and enlisted soldiers, harboring racist and ethnocentric beliefs (Trudeau, 1998). During World War I African Americans were once again called to serve and allowed to serve worldwide given the scope of the conflict. As many as 350,000 served in uniform during World War I; however, many were placed in support roles, such as cooks and laundry personnel. The need for service people dictated the utilization of African Americans in combat operations in which they performed with valor and distinguished themselves in combat. One such soldier was Sergeant Henry Lincoln Johnson of the New York all-Black 369th Infantry Regiment, who was the first African American to receive the French Croix de Guerre. Johnson received posthumously the Purple Heart in 2003 and in 2004 was awarded the Distinguished Service Cross. Their performance served to help change the public opinion that supported the social movements to expand the rights and establish equal rights for Black minorities in the United States (Barbeau, Henri, & Nalty, 1996).

World War II brought significant changes for minorities in the military. Although African Americans were still mostly relegated to support roles, during World War II they served in the frontlines. By 1945 the U.S. Army integrated the Army Officer Candidate School. This marked the first time that African Americans and Whites were housed together. That summer, African-American troops were sent to reinforce White companies in Western Europe, and the positive experience served as a model which was supported by President Truman, who in 1948 signed Executive Order 9981, which led to the desegregation of the military (Evans, 2001).

Native Americans

Native Americans participated in the American Indian Wars and the Revolutionary War. From the beginning, the service of Native Americans in the military would coincide with their fight for equal rights (DoD, 1996: NHHC, 2012;). Having distinguished themselves throughout multiple conflicts in the young American nation, Native Americans were included in the development of the U.S. Army Indian Scouts in 1866. During the 1898 Spanish-American War these Indian Scouts would serve alongside Teddy Roosevelt, fighting as a part of his famed Rough Riders in Cuba (DoD; NHHC). During World War II Native Americans would again show their unbridled patriotism toward the United States. Though eligible for the draft, 99% of those Native Americans enlisted ahead of selection; this percentage qualified them as having been the highest represented ethnic/racial group in the war. At the onset of the Vietnam War, Native Americans were again called to arms. This time, along with being drafted in numbers disproportionate to Whites, they also volunteered in disproportionate numbers to serve in a war that was discriminatory toward them throughout the conflict (DoD; NHHC). More than 42,000 Native Americans served in Vietnam, of which 90% volunteered ahead of being drafted. It was noted that those of Native American descent were most likely to be sent on perilous scouting missions behind enemy lines because they were perceived to be inherently able to perform these duties in a more efficient manner. These incursions behind enemy lines were said to be trips into "Indian Country." Native Americans continued their established trend of honorable military service during Panama, Grenada, and Desert Shield and throughout the latter part of the 20th century (Cross, 2005).

Asians and Pacific Islanders

Asians and Pacific Islanders (API), like many identified racial and ethnic minorities, have played an integral role in the development of the United States and have served bravely in the U.S. military. Although their loyalties were questioned by the U.S. government through World War II, APIs have consistently demonstrated a willingness to serve in the military (DoD, 2012). Even from the beginning of their immigration into the United States, APIs have experienced racism and discrimination. By the middle of the 19th century APIs became the first ethnic group to be prohibited from being eligible for U.S. citizenship even if they had served in the military. As with other minority groups, it was the outbreak of a major world war, in this case World War I, which provided APIs an opportunity to serve in greater numbers and within a wider scope, but most importantly it established citizenship for APIs. The establishment of military bases in the Philippines and in other API countries would bring young U.S. service members into contact with APIs in their host countries and provide them with the opportunity to become familiar with their culture (Nash, 2010). Unfortunately, the United States again set discriminatory policies toward APIs post–World War I with laws such as the Tyding-McDuffie Act of 1934, which identified Filipinos as being ineligible for citizenship and with the continued support of the Alien Land Law Act of 1910, which dictated that anyone ineligible for citizenship could not own land (Wing, 2005).

With the threat of war looming across Europe in the 1930s President Roosevelt called for the covert observation of people of Japanese descent across the West Coast, primarily in Hawaii (DoD). General Patton also saw the Japanese in Hawaii as a threat and began compiling a list of prominent Japanese and Japanese-American community leaders and businesspeople in Hawaii during the same time frame. On December 7, 1941, Japan attacked Pearl Harbor, followed by the War Relocation Act of 1942, which identified resident Japanese and Japanese Americans as "enemy aliens" and established internment camps across the United States where Japanese and Japanese Americans were sent for the duration of the war (DoD, 2012).

However, more than 35,000 second generation Japanese Americans, or Nisei, chose to support the United States and entered the military and served in the European front. The dedication and patriotism displayed by APIs during World War II has been credited in tearing down the API exclusion efforts in the United States (Yenne, 2007). Ironically, with the end of World War II, Nisei soldiers who had fought so fiercely went back to life in an America that only months earlier had labeled them as the enemy.

President Clinton acknowledged the wrongs committed against APIs by way of a formal apology for the interment of the Japanese and Japanese Americans during World War II (Nash, 2010). President Clinton also identified APIs as an underserved population and directed the funding of programs aimed at developing resources for APIs in the United States. During the onset of the Global War on Terrorism in 2001, President Bush announced and recognized the various generations of Asian and Pacific Islander Americans who have proudly served the United States during times of conflict. In the next section, we will provide a case vignette of an Asian-American social work officer as an example of the generational influence of military service as well as the clashing of cultures (i.e., civilian versus military).

Case Vignette: Alice

Alice is a 31-year-old Asian American social work officer (Captain) in the United States Air Force. Her 33-year-old husband Robert, who is Caucasian, is currently unemployed. Alice describes Robert as a patient man with a good sense of humor who is generally supportive of Alice and her military career. Alice loves her job and is highly regarded by her superiors. However, Robert has been unhappy lately since their transfer to yet "another military base" (every 2 to 3 years), and he has not been able to find work due to the current lack of employment opportunities in the area. He enjoyed his engineering career and feels resentful that it has been so challenging for him as a military spouse with the constant moves and his not being able to remain in a steady job. Robert feels like he is "drowning" in the military culture and does not feel part of the military community.

Alice has experienced some issues in her military career. Her last assignment was supposed to be at a career-enhancing military base overseas but it was without spousal accompaniment, so she turned it down and instead she and her husband are at a military installation on the mainland. Alice is determined to stay in the military but also wants to salvage her marriage. Her family of origin includes a legacy of proud military veterans, many of whom have served honorably since World War II. She fears disappointing her family if she were to separate from the military (as her husband has asked her to do), and she has dreams of becoming the first Major General Social Worker in the U.S. military. She feels that her husband needs time to learn to love the military like she does.

Case Vignette Discussion Questions

This case exemplifies some of the notions expressed in this chapter with regard to the distinctiveness of military culture versus the civilian culture. Here we see the importance that honor and service represent in Alice's life. She comes from generations of veterans and thus is deeply connected to her military roots and identity—so much so that she does not envision herself not being part of the military. Yet, for her husband, the military is a foreign element in his life, and he cannot identify with what it means to be a service member. The questions provided below can serve as a point of discussion with regard to this vignette.

1. In what ways do Alice and Robert differ from each other regarding their views about living a military life?
2. What are their perceived strengths and challenges associated with the military lifestyle?
3. What are some of the ways that a social worker can help this couple understand each other's differing points of view?
4. How would you, as a civilian social worker, feel about working with this case? What aspects of this case may be difficult for you or other civilian social workers to relate to?
5. How do military culture and ethnicity (Asian American) intersect in the case scenario?

Gays in the Military

Little has been written about gays during the early development of the U.S. military (Ells, 1996). Prior to World War I there were no specific policies addressing homosexuality in military; instead, it was addressed at the lower command level by those in charge of specific units or vessels.

Homosexuality was targeted in 1942 as a means of screening out service members by the draft board. Service members being inducted were evaluated through a psychiatric examination, whereby those who were perceived to be homosexuals (i.e., demonstrating "feminine-like behaviors") would be deemed ineligible for military service.

Although the military was desegregated in 1948, an informal caste system based on racial/ethnic identity and sexual orientation developed among the ranks. The military stepped in to protect their last bastion of segregation in 1950 with the development of the Uniform Code of Military Justice, or UCMJ (Evans, 2001). Under the UCMJ, homosexuality was targeted in Article 125, which specifically prohibited sodomy, which included sexual contact between members of the same sex. This illegalization of homosexuality in the military would be used to discriminate against homosexuals, and anyone accused of being a homosexual would be penalized with a prison sentence and a dishonorable discharge.

In 1965, a rule was established by the DoD that allowed for the right of service members accused of homosexuality to defend themselves in front of a panel of superior officers (Evans, 2001). Prior to the passage of this rule a service member could be discharged based on allegations without a right to defend themselves against the accusation (Evans, 2001). Despite the 1971 development of the Defense Equal Opportunity Management Institute, which provided training on issues of equal opportunities, any steps taken toward acceptance of homosexuals in the military were erased in 1981 with the Department of Defense issuance of Directive 1332.14, which specifically outlawed homosexuality in any form (Evans, 2001). Prior to this policy a command had discretionary authority to discharge homosexuals, as it does with any other violation of the UCMJ. This policy led to the discharge of more than 17,000 homosexuals during the 1980s and created a spotlight on the military's exclusion of homosexuals (Evans, 2001).

Subsequently, in 1993 President Clinton, in an effort toward reaching a compromise, signed into law the "Don't Ask, Don't Tell, Don't Pursue" policy, which prohibited the military from screening for homosexual behaviors. Once in, service members could not be asked if they were homosexual, and anybody suspected of homosexuality could not be forced to reveal their orientation. This also meant that the person in question could not reveal him- or herself as homosexual under punishment by dishonorable discharge. This policy was implemented against the cries of both homosexuals and those who stood against them (Halley, 1998).

Recognized as an unfair policy, the U.S. public cried out for justice and the U.S. government listened, as finally demonstrated by the 2010 repeal of the Don't Ask Don't Tell policy (Public Law No. 111–321). Though it would not take effect until September 2011, the repeal of DADT was seen as a landmark achievement in the fight for equality for homosexuals. Initially intended for the repeal to take immediate effect, the military requested and received a 10-month grace period to develop, test, and implement policies designed to protect the newly included sexual minorities into their ranks.

Aging Veterans

In 2010, approximately 40% of veterans were 65 years old or older. Thus, it is important to recognize that those who served in earlier wars such as World War II, Korea, and Vietnam will face challenges that differ from those who have served in more recent conflicts (Chatterjee, Spiro, King, King, & Davison 2009).

As veterans age, we notice differences in their opinion regarding medical utilization. For instance, those veterans between the ages of 70 to 79 are less likely than younger veterans to ask for medicine and are willing to suffer in silence through pain caused by arthritis and other natural ailments associated with aging (Appelt, Burant, Siminoff, Kwoh, & Ibrahim, 2007).

A study conducted by the Department of Veterans Affairs noted physical and mental health issues among aging veterans that are not noticeable among the nonveteran aging population. However, among active veterans, or those who regularly exercise, physical health is reported to be substantially better than their civilian counterparts. On the other hand, sedentary veterans were found to be in significantly worse health than the civilians with whom they were compared (Peterson, Crowley, Sullivan, & Morey, 2004). Furthermore, those who served as officers were found to be in much better health both physically and mentally than their enlisted counterparts. Although this study did not identify the reasons for these differences, it did find that those who served four years or fewer as an enlisted service member had standards of living on par with their civilian counterparts (Peterson et al., 2004).

Aging veterans may find that they have either late-onset posttraumatic stress disorder (PTSD) or have been living with PTSD for the past 50 years postcombat. For many, the symptoms of PTSD may increase with age. The Veterans Administration has recognized the following four antecedent contributing factors (http://www.ptsd.va.gov/public/pages/ptsd-older-vets.asp):

1. Retirement, when the veteran has more time to think of the trauma and less time to keep him- or herself occupied or distracted from previous memories.
2. Multiple medical problems, which may contribute to the veterans perceptions of vulnerability or that they are not as strong as they use to be.
3. Watching bad news and current conflicts on television may bring back unwanted memories.
4. If a veteran has been suffering from chronic PTSD and there has been a major change in coping mechanisms; for instance, if a veteran had used alcohol to cope and if there is a sudden decrease in alcohol use or in the absence of an alternative coping mechanism, PTSD symptoms may heighten.

It is important to understand that no matter the age of the veteran, PTSD can stand in the way of allowing the veteran the opportunity to address other challenges in life or live life to its fullest (Veterans Administration [VA], 2012).

CONCLUSION

This chapter has attempted to provide civilian practitioners more insight into the culture and worldviews of their veteran clients and to enhance their historical understanding of the contributions of different ethnic groups to the U.S. armed forces. A case was depicted that exemplified an Asian American service member's commitment to the military as well as the influence of her family tradition and ethnic heritage in promulgating her desire to serve her country. The case was not of a deployed combat veteran suffering from posttraumatic stress disorder; instead, it offered a less dramatic depiction of the inculcated values of loyalty and sense of duty in a female social work officer who aspires to be a leader in her professional role to assist fellow service members in need and to continue to impart to others the values, the dignity, and the pride associated with serving in the U.S. military.

CHAPTER DISCUSSION QUESTIONS

1. How does the current organization that you work for (or attend school in) mirror or differ from a military structure?
2. Beyond what has been written in this chapter, can you identify other areas where the military culture is uniquely different than the civilian culture?

Military Culture	Civilian Culture

REFERENCES

American Psychological Association. (1992). *Ethical principles of psychologists and code of conduct.* Washington, DC: Author.

Appelt, C. J., Burant, C. J., Siminoff, L. A., Kwoh, C. K., & Ibrahim, S. A. (2007). Arthritis-specific health beliefs related to aging among older male patients with knee and or hip osteoarthritis. *Journal of Gerontology, 62*(2), 184–190.

Ashforth, B., Harrison, S., & Corley, K. (2008). Identification in organizations: An examination of four fundamental questions. *Journal of Management, 34*(3), 325–374. doi: 10.1177/0149206308316059

Barbeau, A. E., Henri, F., & Nalty, B. C. (1998). *The unknown soldiers: African American troops in World War I.* Philadelphia, PA: Temple University Press.

Berg-Cross, L., & Takushi-Chinen, R. (1995). Multicultural training models and the person-in-culture interview. In J. G. Ponterotto, J. M. Casas, L.A. Suzuki, & C. M. Alexander (Eds.), *Handbook of multicultural counseling* (pp. 333–356). Thousand Oaks, CA: Sage.

Chatterjee, S., Spiro, A., King, L., King, D., & Davison, E. (2009). Research on aging military veterans: Lifespan implications of military services. *National Center for PTSD Research Quarterly, 20*(3), 1–4.

Coll, J. E., Weiss, E. L., Draves, P., & Dyer, D. (2012). The impact of military cultural awareness, experience, attitudes, and education on clinician self-efficacy in the treatment of veterans. *Journal of International Continuing Social Work Education, 15*(1), 39–48.

Cook, M. (2004). *The moral warrior: Ethics and service in the U.S. military.* Albany: State University of New York Press.

Council on Social Work Education. (2008). *Educational policy and accreditation standards*. Retrieved from http://www.cswe.org/File.aspx?id=13780

Cross, M. J. (2005). Decisive battle and the Global War on Terror. *School of Advanced Military Studies*, *04–05*, 1–54.

Daley, J. G. (1999). Understanding the military as an ethnic identity. In J. G. Daley (Ed.), *Social work practice in the military* (pp. 291–303). New York, NY: Haworth Press.

Davenport, M. M. (1987). Professionals or hired guns? Loyalties are the difference. In M. M. Watkins, K. Wenker, & J. Kempf (Eds.), *Military ethics: Reflections on principles—The profession of arms, military leadership, ethical practices, war and morality, educating the citizen soldier* (pp. 5–12). Washington, DC: National Defense University Press.

Estrada, J. (2009, November 11). Veterans Day 2009: A tribute to the forgotten force. *La Prensa*, 14–15. Retrieved from http://search.proquest.com/docview/368604064?accountid=14749

Evans, R. (2001). *U.S. military policies concerning homosexuals: Development, implementation and outcomes*. Center for the Study of Sexual Minorities in the Military. Retrieved from http://escholarship.org/uc/item/2wv6s1qb

Exum, H., Coll, J. E., & Weiss, E. L. (2011). *A civilian counselor's primer for counseling veterans* (2nd ed.). Deerpark, NY: Linus.

Freeman, D., & Bicknell, G. (2008, September). The Army Master of Social Work Program. *Army Medical Department Journal*, 72–75.

Grieger, I., & Ponterotto, J. (1995). A framework for assessment in multicultural counseling. In J. G. Ponterotto, J. M. Casas, L. A. Suzuki, & C. M. Alexander (Eds.), *Handbook of multicultural counseling* (pp. 357–374). Thousand Oaks, CA: Sage.

Halley, J. (1998). *Don't: A reader's guide to the military anti-gay policy*. Durham, NC: Duke University Press.

Hoge, C. W. (2010). *Once a warrior always a warrior*. Guilford, CT: Globe Pequot Press.

Hooker, R. D. (2003). Soldiers of the state: Reconsidering American civil-military relations. Parameters. *U.S. Army War College Quarterly*. Winter 2003–2004, Vol. 33, 4, 4–18.

Kadis, J., & Walls, D. (2009). *Military facts: For non-military social workers*. [Handbook], VHA Directive.

Kreiner, G., & Ashforth, B. (2001). Evidence toward an expanded model of organizational identification. *Journal of Organizational Behavior*, *25*(1), 1–17. doi: 10.1002/job.234

Lonner, W., & Ibrahim, F. (1996). Appraisal and assessment in cross-cultural counseling. In P. B. Pedersen, J. G. Draguns, W. J. Lonner, & J. E. Trimble (Eds.), *Counseling across cultures* (4th ed., pp. 293–322). Thousand Oaks: CA: Sage.

Maxfield, B. (2008). *Army profile FY 2008*. Retrieved from http://www.armyg1.army.mil/hr/docs/demographics/FY08%20Army%20Profile.pdf

National Association of Social Workers. (1999). *Code of ethics*. Retrieved from http://www.socialworkers.org/pubs/code/code.asp

National History & Heritage Command. (2012). *Native Americans in the U.S. Military*. Retrived from http://www.history.navy.mil/faqs/faq61-1.htm

O'Brien, W. V. (1984). Special ops in the 1980s: American moral, legal, political and cultural constraints. In F. R. Bennett, B. H. Tovar, & R. H. Shultz (Eds.), *Special operations in U.S. strategy* (pp. 54–84). New York, NY: National Defense University Press.

O'Neal, G. S. (2012). Teaching note—Self-assessment and dialogue as tools for appreciating diversity. *Journal of Social Work Education, 48*(1), 159–166.

Peterson M. J., Crowley, G. M., Sullivan, R. J., & Morey, M. C.(2004). Physical function in sedentary and exercising older veterans as compared to national norms. *Journal of Rehabilitation Research and Development, 41*(5), 653–658.

Pole, N., Best, S. R., Metzler, T., & Marmar, C. R. (2005). Why are Hispanics at greater risk for PTSD. *Cultural Diversity and Ethnic Minority Psychology, 11*(2), 144–161. doi: 10.1037/1099- 9809.11.2.144

Ponterotto, J. G., Gretchen, D., & Chauhan, R. V. (2001). Cultural identity and multicultural assessment: Quantitative and qualitative tools for the clinician. In L. A. Suzuki, J. G. Ponterotto, & P. J. Meller (Eds.), *Handbook of multicultural assessment: Clinical, psychological and educational applications* (2nd ed., pp. 67–99). Hoboken, NJ: Jossey-Bass.

Singer, P. W. (2004). War, profits, and the vacuum of law: Privatized military firms and international law. *Columbia Journal of Transnational Law, 42*(2), 522–550.

Sue, D. W., & Sue, D. (2008). *Counseling the culturally different: Theory and practice* (3rd ed.). Hoboken, NJ: Wiley.

Trudeau, N. A. (1998). *Black troops in the Civil War, 1862-1865*. Boston, MA: Little Brown Co.

U.S. Department of Defense. (2012). *Asian American Pacific Islanders*. Washington, DC: Department of Defense. Retrieved from http://www.defense.gov/pubs/

U.S. Department of Defense. (1996). *20th century warriors: Native American participation in the United States military*. Washington, DC: Department of Defense.

U.S. Department of Defense. (2011). *Reserve components: Noble Eagle/Enduring Freedom/Iraqi Freedom*. Washington DC: Department of Defense.

Van Ells, M. D. (1996). The story the soldiers wouldn't tell: Sex in the civil war. *Journal of American Culture, 19*(2), 140–141. Retrieved from http://search.proquest.com/docview/2006 07761?accountid=14749

Veterans Administration. (2012). *Aging veterans and posttraumatic stress symptom*. Retrieved from http://www.ptsd.va.gov/public/pages/ptsd-older

Weiss, E. L., Coll, J. E., & Metal, M. (2011). The influence of military culture and veteran worldviews on mental health treatment: Implications for veteran help seeking and wellness. *International Journal of Health, Wellness and Society, 1*(2), 75–86.

Wertsch, M. E. (1991). *Military brats: Legacies of childhood inside the fortress*. New York, NY: Harmony Books.

Yenne, B. (2007). *Rising sons: The Japanese American GI who fought for the U.S. in World War II*. New York, NY: Thomas Dunne Books.

CHAPTER

3

Women in the Military

Eugenia L. Weiss and Tara DeBraber

INTRODUCTION

Today, women occupy more than 80% of all military occupational specialties (MOS) and 90% of careers in the military (Pierce, 2006). In fact, the U.S. military asserts that "today's military has no gender" (Schading, 2007, p. 4). According to Moore and Kennedy (2011), 15% of the total active force is comprised of women, and it is estimated that this figure will continue to grow. Even though women are allowed into more occupations within the military and ranks, direct combat-related positions still remain closed to women; however, women serve in combat support roles and often face war-related risks (Smith, Jacobson, Smith, Hooper, & Ryan, 2007). Although military policy states that women are *technically* prohibited from serving in combat, in practice, a growing number of women end up being deployed and engaging in combat through support positions (Pierce, 2006). Additionally, even with the combat restrictions for women the current war efforts in Iraq and Afghanistan have made it difficult to determine combat lines. Moore and Kennedy (2011) posited that the restriction associated with combat roles for women is a moot point in the current wars because the "front lines are ill defined and women are in places where they are becoming involved in combat action" (p. 71).

The traditional rationale for maintaining women out of the active fighting units include: "the possibility of inappropriate interactions ranging from distraction to romance to rape between men and women in both friendly and enemy forces; risk taking by men on behalf of women soldiers; sexual harassment; the inherent "weaker" physical nature of women; and religious objections" (Schading, 2007, pp. 4–5). Whether these arguments are valid, this is where the limitations associated with women's service originate.

Even with the increase of eligible positions for women, as a whole, women are underrepresented in the military (Grube-Farrell, 2002). Women are effectively performing in a traditionally hypermasculine culture and are overcoming challenges associated with gender discrimination. Women are slowly achieving equality, as demonstrated in the year 2008 when General Ann E. Dunwoody became the first female four-star general

(Clemmitt, 2009). Silva (2008) portrays women as defying the military and society's image of women as "weak, passive and sexual" (p. 954). Women are demonstrating their achievements through successful leadership of battalions, physical fitness, and competent use of weaponry. This chapter discusses the triumphs and challenges faced by women serving in the military. A case study illustrating a female veteran who suffered from military sexual harassment in addition to combat posttraumatic stress is covered in this chapter along with the application of two therapeutic interventions. (For a historical account of women's participation in the U.S. Armed Services the reader is referred to Cooke, 1993, and Hoiberg, 1991).

We begin the chapter with an examination of gender stereotypes. The authors then address the following areas that could impact women in the military: military sexual trauma and harassment; the role of marital status; the challenges associated with menses and pregnancy; sexual orientation; and female veteran health concerns.

GENDER

Women often have to struggle with negative stereotypical images as compared to their male counterparts. In addition to having to engage in the daily struggle for inclusion, women can be negatively affected by stereotypes that impact their job performance and career paths. Looney, Robinson-Kurpius, and Lucart (2004) found that when comparing male and female leadership in the military, "more emotion-based characteristics were attributed to the women" (as cited in Pierce, 2006, p. 101). An emotion-based characteristic such as empathy is not always prioritized in military culture. Thus, this type of attribute can have a negative impact on a woman's military career trajectory and could account for the limited role of women in higher ranking positions. Negative gender stereotypes can go so far as to say women in uniform are "unsuitable for the work," which can create a hostile work climate (Grube-Farrell, 2002, p. 341). This less-than-friendly work environment was described by Riley (1999) as sometimes encompassing "filthy or nonexistent bathrooms, spiteful coworkers who create horrifying unsafe working conditions, isolation, lack of respect and sexual harassment" (p. 7). Threats or acts of physical violence toward women are also included in this definition.

Women in the military often find themselves isolated and have few women leaders as role models and mentors (Moore & Kennedy, 2011). Even though women were legally allowed admission to military academies and to voluntarily serve in the military since the 1970s, it took 30 years for a woman to become a four-star general (Clemmitt, 2009). A U.S. Department of Defense report found that only 2% of female military officers were a "brigadier general, rear admiral or higher" (Eagly & Karau, 2002, p. 573). The shortage of women in top leadership positions has been hypothesized as stemming from women exhibiting fewer "leadership" and "motivational" traits that are needed to achieve leadership positions, which are stereotypically male traits that tend to be emphasized in military culture (Browne, 1999; Eagly & Karau, 2002; Goldberg, 1993).

Another reason given for why women hold few leadership positions in both the civilian and military sectors is what has been termed as the "glass ceiling effect." The glass ceiling effect as defined by Eagly and Karau (2002) is "a barrier of prejudice and discrimination that excludes women from higher level leadership positions" (p. 573). These authors stated that women are more likely to be viewed and evaluated by others as well as by their superiors on "communal" characteristics, which are defined as a concern for the welfare of others. Communal characteristics are traditional female gender-based traits, where women demonstrate acts of affection, kindness, sympathy, and nurturance toward others, which makes attaining leadership roles in the military especially difficult.

Boldry, Wood, and Kashy (2001) posited that women "threaten the established male [military] culture" (p. 691). Herbert (1998) described some women as behaving in stereotypically masculine ways to gain acceptance within the military culture (as cited in Pierce, 2006). Some of the stereotypical masculine qualities that women demonstrate for gaining acceptance in the military are self-control and stoicism (Silva, 2008). Some argue that if women successfully assimilate into the male dominated military culture (i.e., conform to masculine gender traits), then women may be perceived by others as being competent and capable of attaining leadership positions (Carli & Eagly 2001). Assuming male qualities can be problematic for some women because behaving in masculine ways to gain acceptance and inclusion requires rejecting their feminine qualities and identity (Boldry, Wood, & Kashy, 2001). In spite of what women undertake to feel as though they fit into the military, the military culture and environment can be empowering to women. Silva (2008) noted that the military "demands physically and mentally tough, goal-oriented, aggressive soldiers with skills of violence, weaponry and, ultimately, death" (pp. 937–938). Although women appear to respond to stressors differently than men, more systematic research is needed in the area of gender-based response to trauma—specifically regarding deployment and combat related stress (Pierce, 2006).

MILITARY-RELATED SEXUAL HARASSMENT AND ASSAULT

Military sexual trauma (MST) is defined as sexual violence "from verbal pressure for contact to homicide, and includes forced sexual intercourse" (Skinner et al., 2000, p. 292). Although MST occurs in both men and women, the focus here is on the occupational, psychological, and physical impact of MST on females.

The military workplace can be a risky environment, especially for those women in junior ranks (Campbell, Lichty, Sturza, & Raja, 2006; Pierce, 2006). Women may be reluctant to report sexual harassment or assault for a variety of reasons including fear of revenge, scorn, and negative work repercussions (Pierce, 2006). Occupational issues can also include lowered morale and a decrease in job satisfaction and performance (Skinner et al., 2000).

As previously stated, women now serve in supportive combat-related roles, which expose women to "multiple deployments, extended tours of duty, environmental hazards, loss of friends, and mental and physical traumas" (Gregg & Miah, 2011, p. 136). Additionally, while serving overseas 23% to 30% of females report being victims of actual or attempted MST (Gregg & Miah, 2011). Women serving overseas can develop combat stress from a multitude of environmental and psychological conditions such as being shot at, witnessing injuries and death, and poor living arrangements (Gregg & Miah, 2011). Although combat stress is diagnosed in both men and women, the combination of combat stress and MST can result in an increased risk for the development of posttraumatic stress disorder (PTSD) as well as "impaired functioning, chronic unemployment, poor interpersonal relationships, divorce and homelessness" (Gregg & Miah, 2011, p. 137).

Female victims of MST can also suffer long-term emotional effects and experience a violation of trust. Hoppen (2006) cited a U.S. Department of Defense (DoD; 2002) report that indicated that 30% of female veterans reported rape or attempted rape by their fellow male service members while on duty. Hoppen (2006) described this as a devastation of basic trust because "camaraderie becomes cruel captivity" as a result of serving with the attacker (p. 14).

Female veterans who experienced MST also have a higher frequency of reporting gynecological symptoms (Campbell et al., 2006). The trauma related with MST can increase women's stress levels that can trigger an inflammatory body response resulting in chronic pain conditions (Campbell et al., 2006). Physical trauma as a result of forced sex may explain the amount of gynecological health problems found in women veterans (as cited in Campbell et al., 2006). In addition to gynecological symptoms, Suris and Lind (2008) found that female veterans also report "pelvic pain, menstrual problems, back pain, headaches, gastrointestinal symptoms, and chronic fatigue" (p. 262). In addition to the risk of pregnancy as a result of rape, VA medical centers report that 20% of MST victims also suffer from closed head injuries as a result of the assault (Matsakis, 2007).

A sense of community or belonging is necessary for some women to recover from sexual trauma (Skinner et al., 2000). The military has its own sense of community, or unit cohesion, so female service members who are victims of sexual assault may be denied community support. Since the attacker could be a co-worker or someone from a higher rank, female service members who have been victims of sexual assault may not able to leave their workplace to seek help or attend medical appointments without permission from the supervisor, who may be the perpetrator. Female service members who defy orders to remain at the workplace could be subject to punishment if they leave without approval (Suris, Lind, Kashner, Borman, & Petty, 2004). In addition, the female service member may have to work in close quarters with her attacker and may not have other females to turn to for support. Female service members who have been victimized are also more likely than other service members to rate their overall experience in the military as negative (Skinner et al., 2000). In addition to the aforementioned potential consequences and incidence of mental disorders (i.e., depression, anxiety, substance abuse), female military members and veterans who experienced MST seek out health care at a higher rate than other female military members and civilian women (Suris et al., 2004).

Military Response to MST

Even though education and prevention of MST is increasing in the military, research shows that consistent reports of rape in the military demonstrate that violence toward women service members is an "unresolved problem" (Sadler, Booth, Cook, & Doebbeling, 2003, p. 270).

Turchik and Wilson (2010) pointed out that certain aspects of military culture can be a hindrance to preventing sexual violence, such as the use of sexualized and violent language that has been traditionally associated with military service as well as the acceptability of violence. To address the high rates of MST, the DoD implemented a Sexual Assault Prevention and Response Office (SAPRO), which "serves as a single point of accountability for sexual violence" in the military (Turchik & Wilson, 2010, p. 273). Although commanding officers and law enforcement are still responsible for reporting assaults, SAPRO also provides care and support to victims and works to prevent MST through training, education, and prevention throughout the DoD (Turchik & Wilson, 2010). In addition to the services offered, SAPRO operates under a confidential reporting system where victims can retain their privacy. Although SAPRO is a positive response to MST, military members need "to be taught to discriminate when the use of violence is appropriate [i.e., combat] and when it is not" (Turchik & Wilson, 2010, p. 275).

MARRIED WOMEN IN THE MILITARY

Married military women face many challenges balancing their workplace demands with their home environment. They face the occupational challenges of having to work long hours, being on call, and always adhering to the mission first. In addition to preparing for lengthy trainings and deployments, a military service member must also plan to keep the household running in her absence. Vinokur, Pierce, and Buck (1999) added that the extensive preparation calls for "extraordinary planning and multiple sources of support" (p. 866). Women in the military can be affected by PTSD, traumatic brain injury (TBI), MST, pregnancy, lengthy and extended deployments, combat exposure, as well as having their spouse in the military (i.e., dual military marriages). Gregg and Miah (2011) found that the marriages of military women are three times as likely to fail in contrast to their male counterparts.

Other stressors facing married female service members can include issues of domestic violence perpetrated by the civilian or military male spouse. One study found that enlisted females were three times more likely to be victims of "unilateral severe violence than their male civilian spouses" (Forgey & Badger, 2006, p. 369). Another study (Helmkamp, 1995) found that active duty females had a higher risk for being homicide victims in comparison to civilian females (as cited in Forgey & Badger, 2006). Forgey and Badger suggested that women in the military are at risk for being victims of domestic violence as well as for perpetrating violence against their civilian spouses (i.e., bidirectional violence). However, as in community samples, women often report more negative physical and emotional consequences resulting from being victims of intimate partner violence. These authors noted that more research is needed on intimate partner violence involving women in the military.

MENSES AND PREGNANCY

Women in the military face unique challenges in managing their military obligations and their menstrual cycle. They must develop unique coping skills to manage biological feminine processes during field trainings and deployments. Wardell and Czerwinski (2001) reported that in addition to the use of oral contraceptives to hormonally manage menstrual flow, at least one female service member had a hysterectomy to better manage her menses and eliminate the risk for pregnancy. In fact, women in the military report several challenges in managing their menses. These challenges include mood fluctuations associated with hormonal changes and lack of time for "obtaining, changing, and disposing of menstrual supplies" (Trego, 2007, p. 343). In addition, Thomson and Nielsen (2006) noted that most women do not receive information or training on how to manage their menstrual cycle while they are in the field.

In addition to the biological effects of menses on the female body, women also face many environmental challenges. When training in the field or on a deployment, there is limited access to restroom facilities and clean water or showers. The predominantly male environment of the military can make it difficult for engaging in timely hygiene during the menstrual cycle. One female service member noted that convoys were especially difficult on deployment because the driver could drive for 8 hours before stopping (Trego, 2007). In addition, the extreme temperatures in deployment areas can also negatively affect women. For instance, the temperature fluctuation can increase the physical and psychological symptoms associated with menses.

Pregnancy can present as a significant stressor to both civilian and military women. Active-duty women are exposed to a high number of environmental risk factors, such as heavy lifting, small workspaces, loud noises, as well as toxins (Magann & Nolan, 1991). This can result in preterm births, which can be seen in women in the lower pay grades (Magann & Nolan, 1991). Although pregnancy requires the participation of two individuals, women in the military often face the burden of pregnancy alone (Christopher & Miller, 2007). Additionally, pregnant women are not able to deploy, whereas the male who participated in the pregnancy has his career unaffected. Crowley, Bender, Chatigny, Trudel, and Ritchie (n.d.) added that if a female service member is prematurely taken home from a deployment due to pregnancy, "this can be seen by other soldiers as an abandonment of duty and obligation, regardless of the true intent of the pregnancy" (p. 706). Pregnant women in the military also can be stigmatized by the negative perception that pregnant service members leave more work for others in the unit to complete. Olson and Stumpf (1978) found that in spite of the negative perceptions regarding pregnant women in the military, women missed fewer workdays than their male counterparts even with hospitalization for childbirth (as cited in Pierce, 2006).

Pregnancy and childbirth raise another set of issues for women in the military. These issues include the ability to breastfeed, finding adequate child care, and the impact of separation on the mother-child bond. Many studies have found that breastfeeding is advantageous to infants over bottle feeding. Bell and Ritchie (2003) claimed that successful breastfeeding after returning to the workplace requires four elements, as follows: "space, time, support, and gatekeepers" (p. 813). Gatekeepers are the individuals who control the "time, space, and support needed" for successful nursing (Bell & Ritchie, 2003, p. 814). In the military, the gatekeeper is the commander of the unit.

The above four elements can be impacted by military service. Military mothers who have field training may have to pump and dump their milk to maintain their milk supply while away from the infant. In addition, the mother will need to be able to express her milk every 3 to 6 hours to maintain her supply and prevent infection, which could interrupt field exercises (Bell & Ritchie, 2003). Higher-ranking females and officers have more control over their work environments and schedule, which can lessen the stress related to breastfeeding; however, the lower-rank enlisted mothers benefit more from the cost savings associated with breastfeeding over formula (Bell & Ritchie, 2003). In addition, breastfeeding could potentially create a readiness issue for women in uniform. Vaccinations are discouraged for breastfeeding mothers; however, military members who are overdue or missing vaccinations are not deployable (Bell & Ritchie, 2003).

Returning to work while balancing the roles of military member, mother, and spouse can result in "role-specific stress and role overload" (Pierce, 2006, p. 108). Women must arrange for child care for their normal working hours, field trainings, and deployments, which can result in increased stress. Military mothers can also experience a paradox of emotions between not wanting to let their unit down and not wanting to leave their child or children. Once deployed, mothers reported more mental, emotional, and physical problems as a result of having to separate from their infant (Crowley et al., n.d.). As with all childbearing women, military mothers can also experience postpartum depression (Crowley et al., n.d.).

BISEXUAL AND LESBIAN SERVICE MEMBERS

Women who identify as lesbian or bisexual have had to historically remain closeted about their identity while serving in the military under the Don't Ask Don't Tell (DADT) policy. Craig (2007) stated that under DADT "simply the perception that a person is outside the normative gender or sexual orientation is considered enough evidence to be legally dismissed" (p. 3). This type of workplace environment, which has been found in the military until DADT was repealed in 2011, increased job anxiety for homosexual and bisexual service members (Craig, 2007). Although women make up a small percentage of the total military force, a "disproportionate number of women service members [were] discharged compared to men" under DADT (Glauser, 2011). Prior to the repeal of DADT, sexual stigma was openly seen in the military through antigay statements, violence, and witch hunts to have individuals discharged (Burks, 2011). Although there are limited data about rates of MST and mental health consequences for lesbian and bisexual service members while DADT was in effect, Burks (2011) found that women in the military who identify as lesbians or bisexual are at risk for increased victimization from MST and that lesbian service members who experienced MST under DADT felt more hindered to report their attacks because they feared that they could draw attention to their sexual identity or increase their chance for revictimization.

HEALTH IN WOMEN VETERANS

There is little research on the health effects of female service members despite the increasing numbers of women being deployed to combat zones. Although deployment length has shown to increase distress in male service members, females perceive, respond, and cope with stressors differently than males (Pierce, 2006). It is important to understand the different ways in which each gender responds to stressors. Taylor et al. (2000) posited that this difference may be attributed to the "tend-and-befriend model," which states that women are better protected and better able to positively cope with chronic stressors from long deployments because they seek social supports (as cited in Pierce, 2006). In Chapter 25 (this volume) Basham further explains gender related responses to trauma. Although women respond to stressors differently than men, more systematic research appears to be needed in the area of gender-based responses to trauma—especially regarding deployment and combat related stress (Pierce, 2006). Women veterans are the "fastest-growing segment of the veteran population" and will be in need of appropriate health care responses by Veterans Affairs (Pierce, 2006).

TREATMENT IMPLICATIONS AND CASE APPLICATION

Although there are differences in the way men and women respond to trauma, there are also commonalities. One commonality is risk of developing PTSD. As readers will see in various subsequent chapters in this book, one of the most empirically supported psychotherapeutic interventions for PTSD is cognitive behavioral therapy (CBT). This treatment approach is comprised of four components: psychoeducation, exposure, cognitive restructuring, and anxiety management techniques (Harvey, Bryant, & Tarrier, 2003). Psychoeducation involves explaining responses to trauma and describing symptoms of PTSD (Williams & Bernstein, 2011). This process can help to build rapport and normalizes the client's experiences. During this process, the therapist can also help the client to identify and access her internal and external resources that can assist her in the recovery process. Prior to beginning the trauma work, the therapist can also educate and teach the client positive coping skills such as breathing exercises, mindfulness, and progressive relaxation (Williams & Bernstein, 2011).

In the second phase of CBT treatment, the therapist helps the client remember and process her trauma memory. During this process, referred to as exposure, the client identifies the memories and the associated smells, sights, and sounds of the traumatic experience. For greater effectiveness, the therapist asks the client to recount the trauma in the "present tense, speak in the first person, and ensure that there is focus on the most distressing aspects" (Harvey et al., 2003, p. 502).

It is important to find a way to both monitor and control the level of the emotional activation that the client may experience while still providing enough exposure to the traumatic memories for an effective therapeutic process to occur (Briere & Scott, 2006). Without the monitoring and controlling aspects, the memories may overwhelm the client and increase her use of avoidant behaviors. The therapeutic relationship provides an environment in which the clinician can "adjust or *titrate* the level of memory exposure . . . to accommodate the reduced emotional capacities or excessively upsetting memories" [italics in original] (Briere & Scott, 2006, p. 124). During this component of the treatment the client must also complete homework assigned by the therapist; for example, she could work on identifying triggers relating to her traumatic memories.

The third phase of CBT is cognitive restructuring. During this phase of the treatment, the client identifies the negative thoughts she believes about herself and the world. Negative thoughts or memories from the traumatic experience can also be identified during the exposure phase. Once the negative thoughts are delineated, the therapist and client examine the evidence for the negative and often distorted thoughts. During the evaluation of negative thoughts, the therapist will help the client to evaluate "beliefs about the trauma, the self, the world, and the future" (Marks, Lovell, Noshirvani, Livanou, & Thrasher, 1998; as cited in Harvey et al., 2003, p. 503).

The last phase of CBT is anxiety management training. During this component of therapy, the therapist helps the client work on identifying and practicing positive coping skills. Positive coping skills can help the client to master fears and manage triggers of painful memories that are activated by a dysregulation of the body's stress response system. Positive coping skills include self-talk, relaxation, meditation, and mindfulness (Cukor, Spitalnick, Difede, Rizzo, & Rothbaum, 2009). Additionally, during this phase of treatment the therapist provides a structured approach to engage the client in social activities in an effort to decrease her avoidant and isolative behaviors (Cukor et al., 2009). A study by Bleiberg and Markowitz (2005) found that CBT for PTSD "was successful in improving social relationships and in reducing symptoms" (Cukor et al., 2009, p. 717).

"Case Vignette: Sally" provides an example of a female veteran (prior enlisted) who experienced military sexual harassment in addition to post combat stress.

Case Vignette: Sally

Sally began her Army services as a Private (E-1). Her military occupational specialty (MOS) was a radar repairer. While Sally served in the Army, her company Sergeant (E-5) sexually harassed her. In 2005, Sally deployed to Iraq for a 12-month deployment. While on a mission, Sally was engaged in a firefight. Sally provided defensive fire, but three of the other soldiers on her convoy were killed.

When Sally returned to the States after her deployment, she went to a medical doctor and reported that she had trouble sleeping. Her physician prescribed her a mild sleeping aid. Although Sally took her prescription, she still had difficulty going to and staying asleep. At night, when she closed her eyes, she saw the three soldiers who were killed in the firefight. Sally began to isolate herself from her Army friends and became hypervigilant every time she left the post or was in any kind of social situation. Sally started to avoid social situations and began to show up late to work. Her commanding officer referred her to the Army mental health social worker. After Sally served for 4 years, she was honorably discharged as a Corporal (E-4).

Sally returned to her hometown in the Midwest with plans to enroll in college. When Sally returned home, she had a difficult time managing her fears and refused to leave her room. She had difficulty finding employment. Sally also became socially isolated as she refused to reconnect with her high school friends since she felt she would no longer fit in with them. Sally was referred to the local VA for mental health treatment.

Prior to enlisting in the Army, Sally grew up as the youngest child of three. She was raised by both of her parents. Her father worked in a factory and her mother worked part time as a housekeeper. Sally was a quiet child and she earned average grades throughout her public school education. Between the ages of 10 and 14 Sally was sexually molested by her maternal uncle. Sally never told her parents, siblings, or friends because her uncle threatened her if she told anyone and thus this was never reported to the authorities. As soon as Sally graduated from high school she enlisted in the Army to have a "fresh start" in life.

Chapter Discussion Questions (based on vignette)

1. What additional information is needed in order to assess Sally and devise a treatment plan?
2. Develop a treatment plan based on CBT.
3. What are Sally's risk factors and strengths? How would you utilize her strengths in therapy?
4. What veteran and/or civilian resources would you recommend for Sally?

In light of its empirical base, CBT would be an appropriate treatment to try to reduce Sally's isolative behaviors and negative thoughts. In the psychoeducation phase, the manifestation and effects of Sally's trauma symptoms would be explained and normalized. During the second phase, Sally would develop a narrative of her trauma memory starting with her experience of being molested as a teenager. She would also include her experience of being sexually harassed in the military and her memory of the firefight. In the third phase, following the development of her trauma narrative, the therapist would work with Sally to restructure her negative thoughts and beliefs of herself and of others. Reconstructing Sally's negative thoughts could also reduce her isolative behavior. In the final stage of treatment, the therapist and Sally would develop positive and behavioral coping skills to help Sally manage her anxiety so she is able to reengage in her social world.

CONCLUSION

Although women face many challenges serving in a masculine military culture, they continue to voluntarily enlist and are commissioned to fight for U.S. freedoms. As more military occupations open up to women, more females may decide to join the military, thus providing an opportunity for increased female camaraderie as well as positive support systems. Although women have made gains in military service and have significantly contributed to the Armed Forces, some could be vulnerable to MST and combat-related PTSD. Psychotherapeutic treatments such as CBT can be effective in reducing trauma symptoms; however, further studies are needed to understand gender differences in the military organization as well as in devising health care responses to the many consequences of stress.

REFERENCES

Bell, M. R., & Ritchie, E. C. (2003). Breastfeeding in the military: Part II. Resource and policy considerations. *Military Medicine*, *168*, 813–816.

Bleiberg, K. L., & Markowitz, J. C. (2005). A pilot study of interpersonal psychotherapy for posttraumatic stress disorder. *American Journal of Psychiatry*, *162*(1), 181–183.

Boldry, J., Wood, W., & Kashy, D. A. (2001). Gender stereotypes and the evaluation of men and women in military training. *Journal of Social Issues*, *57*, 689–705.

Briere, J., & Scott, C. (2006). *Principles of trauma therapy. A guide to symptoms, evaluation, and treatment*. Thousand Oaks, CA: Sage.

Browne, K. (1999). *Divided labours: An evolutionary view of women at work*. New Haven, CT: Yale University Press.

Burks, D. J. (2011). Lesbian, gay, and bisexual victimization in the military. *American Psychologist*, *66*, 604–613.

Campbell, R., Lichty, L. F., Sturza, M., & Raja. S. (2006). Gynecological health impact of sexual assault. *Research in Nursing and Health*, *29*, 399–413. doi: 10.1002/nur.20155

Carli, L. L., & Eagly, A. H. (2001). Gender, hierarchy, and leadership: An introduction. *Journal of Social Issues*, *57*(4), 629–636.

Christopher, L. A., & Miller, L. (2007). Women in war: Operational issues of menstruation and unintended pregnancy. *Military Medicine, 172*, 9–16.

Clemmitt, M. (2009). Women in the military: Should combat roles be fully opened to women? *CQ Researcher, 19*(40).

Cooke, M. (1993). Woman, retelling the war myth. In M. Cooke & A. Woollacott (Eds.), *Gendering war talk*. Princeton, NJ: Princeton University Press.

Craig, T. Y. (2007). Don't ask, don't tell: Lesbian women and work-relationship conflict. *Forum on Public Policy*, 1–19.

Crowley, D., Bender, T., Chatigny, A., Trudel, T., & Ritchie, E. C. (n.d.). Women, mental health, and the military. *Combat and Operational Behavioral Health*, 703–716.

Cukor, J., Spitalnick, J., Difede, J., Rizzo, A., & Rothbaum, B. O. (2009). Emerging treatments for PTSD. *Clinical Psychology Review, 29*, 715–726.

Eagly, A. H., & Karau, S. J. (2002). Role congruity theory of prejudice towards female leaders. *Psychological Review, 109*, 73–598.

Forgey, M. A., & Badger, L. (2006). Patterns of intimate partner violence among married women in the military: Type, level, directionality and consequences. *Journal of Family Violence, 21*, 369–380.

Glauser, S. (2011). The end of "don't ask, don't tell." *Hinckley Journal of Politics*, 37–45.

Goldberg, S. (1993). *Why men rule: A theory of male dominance*. Chicago, IL: Open Court.

Gregg, G., & Miah, J. S. (2011). Tragedy, loss, and triumph after combat: A portrait of young women veteran survivors of sexual and combat trauma. In D. C. Kelly, S. Howe-Barksdale, & D. Gitelson (Eds.), *Treating young veterans: Promoting resilience through practice and advocacy* (pp. 135–151). New York, NY: Springer.

Grube-Farrell, B. (2002). Women, work, and occupational segregation in the uniformed services. *Affilia, 17*, 332–353. doi: 10.1177/0886109902173005

Harvey, A. G., Bryant, R. A., & Tarrier, N. (2003). Cognitive behavior therapy for posttraumatic stress disorder. *Clinical Psychology Review, 23*, 501–522. doi: 10.1016/S0272–7358 (03)00035–7

Helmkamp, J. C. (1995). Homicide victims in the military: 1980-1992. *Military Medicine, 160*, 51–56.

Herbert, M. S. (1998). *Camouflage isn't only for combat*. New York, NY: University Press.

Hoiberg, A. (1991). Military psychology and women's role in the military. In R. Gal & A. D. Mangelsdorff (Eds.), *Handbook of military psychology* (pp. 725–739). New York, NY: Wiley.

Hoppen, J. (2006). Women in the military: Who's got your back? *Off Our Backs, 36*(2), 14–16.

Looney, J., Robinson-Surpius, S., & Lucart, L. (2004). Military leadership evaluations: Effects of evaluator sex, leader sex, and gender role attitudes. *Consulting Psychology Journal: Practice and Research, 56*(2), 104–118. doi: 10.1037/1061-4087.56.2.104

Magann, E. F., & Nolan, T. E. (1991). Pregnancy outcome in an active-duty population. *Obstetrics and Gynecology, 78*, 391–393.

Marks, I., Lovell, K., Noshirvani, H., Livanou, M., & Thrasher, S. (1998). Treatment of posttraumatic stress disorder by exposure and/or cognitive restructuring: A controlled study. *Archives of General Psychiatry, 55*, 317–325.

Matsakis, A. (2007). *Back from the front: Combat trauma, love, and the family*. Baltimore, MD: Sidran Institute Press.

Moore, B. A., & Kennedy, C. H. (2011). *Wheels down: Adjusting to life after deployment*. Washington, DC: APA Lifetools.

Olson, M. S., & Stumpf, S. S. (1978). *Pregnancy in the Navy: Impact on absenteeism, attrition, and work group morale*. TR 78-35. San Diego, CA: Navy Personnel Research and Development Center.

Pierce, P. E. (2006). The role of women in the military. In T. W. Britt, A. B. Adler, & C. A. Castro (Eds.), *Military life: The psychology of serving in peace and combat* (pp. 97–118). Westport, CT: Greenwood.

Riley, J. (1999). Women on the (mostly male) jobsite: Still struggling. *Feminist Collections: A quarterly collection of women studies research*, *20*(2), 5–21.

Sadler, A. G., Booth, B. M., Cook, B. L., & Doebbeling, B. N. (2003). Factors associated with women's risk of rape in the military environment. *American Journal of Industrial Medicine*, *43*, 262–273. doi: 10.1002/ajim.10202

Schading, B. (2007). *A civilian's guide to the U.S. military: A comprehensive reference to the customs, language and structure of the armed forces*. Cincinnati, OH: Writer's Digest Books.

Silva, J. M. (2008). A new generation of women? How female ROTC cadets negotiate the tension between masculine military culture and traditional femininity. *Social Forces*, *87*, 937–960.

Skinner, K. M., Kressin, N., Frayne, S., Tripp, T. J., Hankin, C. S., Miller, D. S., & Sullivan, L. M. (2000). The prevalence of military sexual assault among female veterans' administration outpatients. *Journal of Interpersonal Violence*, *15*, 291–310. doi: 10.1177/088626000015003005

Smith, T. C., Jacobson, I. G., Smith, B., Hooper, T. I., & Ryan, M. (2007). The occupational role of women in military service: Validation of occupation and prevalence of exposures in the millennium cohort study. *International Journal of Environmental Health Research*, *17*, 271–284. doi: 10.1080/09603120701372243.

Suris, A., & Lind, L. (2008). Military sexual trauma: A review of prevalence and associated health consequences in veterans. *Trauma Violence Abuse*, 9, 250–269. doi: 10.1177/1524838008324419

Suris, A., Lind, L., Kashner, M., Borman, P. D., & Petty, F. (2004). Sexual assault in women veterans: An examination of PTSD risk, health care utilization, and cost of care. *Psychosomatic Medicine*, 66, 749–756.

Taylor, S. E., Klein, L. C., Lewis, B. P., Gruenewald, T. L., Gurung, R. A. R., & Updegraff, J. A. (2000). *Biobehavioral responses to stress in females: Tend-and-befriend, not fight-or-flight*. Psychological Review, 107, 411–429.

Thomson, B. A., & Nielsen, P. E. (2006). Women's health care in operation Iraqi freedom: A survey of camps with echelon I or II facilities. *Military Medicine*, *171*, 216–219.

Trego, L. L. (2007). Military women's menstrual experiences and interest in menstrual suppression during deployment. *Association of Women's Health, Obstetric and Neonatal Nurses*, 342–347.

Turchik, J. A., & Wilson, S. M. (2010). Sexual assault in the US military: A review of the literature and recommendations for the future. *Aggression and Violent Behavior*, 267–277.

U.S. Department of Defense. (2002). *Armed forces 2002 sexual harassment survey*. Washington, DC: Defense Manpower Data Center.

Vinokur, A. D., Pierce, P. F., & Buck, C. L. (1999). Work-family conflicts of women in the air force: Their influence on mental health and functioning. *Journal of Organizational Behavior*, *20*, 865–878.

Wardell, D. W., & Czerwinski, B. (2001). A military challenge to managing feminine and personal hygiene. *Journal of the American Academy of Nurse Practitioners*, *13*, 187–194.

Williams, I., & Bernstein, K. (2011). Military sexual trauma among U.S. female veterans. *Archives of Psychiatric Nursing*, *25*(2), 138–147.

CHAPTER

4

Ethical Decision Making in Military Social Work

James G. Daley

Ethical practice for and with the military is complex, conflicted, and occurs within legal and moral contexts that often battle with each other. There are common ethical dilemmas facing uniformed and civilian social workers across the continuum of care from soldier to wounded warrior to veteran. There are unique dilemmas that clash with the National Association of Social Workers Code of Ethics, and many dilemmas that have no clear answer. Is the client the service member or the Air Force? Do we have an obligation to ensure that the Marine is ready for combat and, if cleared, can we handle his or her subsequent combat death because we sent him or her back to duty? Do commanders have the authority to order our clinical decisions to slant the "desirable" way? Should a civilian social worker who opposes the war work with a veteran who has gone to war? These dilemmas and many more are faced by military social workers. The key question is whether there are models of ethical decision making that may aid in sorting through these dilemmas. This chapter strives to address these thorny issues and offer the reader a succinct summary of the literature that has sought to offer sound ethical decision making.

THE MILITARY CONTEXT AS THE DOMINANT PARADIGM

Becoming part of the military involves immersion into a unique culture (Daley, 1999). The military culture demands that there be a full adaptation to its rules, mannerisms, and requirements. The uniform is to be worn a certain way, a salute is done in a precise manner, and superiors are to be obeyed regardless of the sailor's desire. Further, there are dominant themes within the military culture. Image is crucial and self-control is expected. The military takes care of its own. Mission is first: Military needs take priority. Mobility exists within an unchanging world. Hierarchy dictates social convention (Daley, 1999).

These dominant themes are particularly striking in combat situations. War is ugly and unforgiving, and soldiers strive to achieve the impossible—making sense of it. The military mission is first priority, over life, comfort, or reason. Leaders lead, followers die. In Sebastian Junger's powerful narrative *War*, a returning veteran of intense combat visits an injured buddy in the Walter Reed Army Medical Center. The veteran was injured in an ambush as they were on patrol. "Did anyone bring up the issue of walking at night?" "No," the lieutenant said, "We're leaving now. What are you going to say to him?" The visiting veteran retorts: "Fuck off?" The wounded veteran smiles but they both know they couldn't change the events that led to his injuries (Junger, 2010, p. 8). Both veterans knew the military culture, even when it causes unnecessary injury and death. The officers give commands, the troops comply. The structure is hierarchical and authoritarian. Commanders are not questioned and decisions are obeyed.

Military members, especially officers, are taught and expected to abide by "military ethics." The ethics include "good behavior" in military combat situations and abiding by laws such as the Geneva Convention. Baumann (2007) outlines four levels of military ethics: when is military force justified, what limiting norms govern military action, what is a good military leader, and what should a soldier be (p. 35)? Sustaining that continuum of "good behavior" through the rank structure can be challenging. Breakdown of military ethics has resulted in incidents such as interrogation at Guantanamo Bay and tortures at Abu Ghraib (Clark, 2006; Wynia, 2007). The intense operational tempo and revolving deployments involved in the wars in Iraq and Afghanistan put much strain on military members, producing a significant and growing number of casualties of war, and a future cohort of veterans with chronic mental health and family needs (Helmick et al., 2010; Khaylis et al., 2011; Pascrell, 2009; Peterson, Baker, & McCarthy, 2008).

Though military mental health response in wartime has a long history (Pois & Oak, 2007), there continue to be ethical dilemmas when the mental health professions connect with the military professions. The military profession embraces the military culture with mission completion as the dominant premise. The helping professions bring their own ethical standards and culture to the joint effort. There is an interesting merger of the minds where each side respects the other—the war machine and the therapy machine. The military wants our help and expertise but expects compliance with military customs and priorities. The classic argument erupts between "line officers" and "medical officers"—are you a military officer first or a social worker first? This clash is the first of the ethical dilemmas to discuss.

ETHICAL DILEMMA: DUAL LOYALTY ISSUES

Military social workers, like other military mental health providers, are caught in "dual-role," "dual loyalty," or "multiple-role" dilemmas that are most overt in combat but are also subtly present in all settings (Atac, Guven, Ucar, & Kir, 2005; Benatar & Upshur, 2008; Gross, 2010; Jeffrey, Rankin, Jeffrey, 1992; Johnson, Bacho, Heim, & Ralph, 2006; Johnson, Grasso, & Maslowski, 2010; Kelly, 2010; London, Rubenstein, Baldwin-Ragaven, & Van Es, 2006; Ritchie, 2007; Robertson & Walter, 2008; Sessums, Collen, O'Malley, Jackson, Roy, 2009; Simmons, & Rycraft, 2010; Staal & King, 2000). The basic theme of this ethical quandary is: "Are we loyal to our profession or to the military environment that we service?" This dilemma is not unique to social work. Johnson and colleagues (2010) describe a case where a psychiatrist deployed to Afghanistan recommends that several soldiers are unfit for duty due to posttraumatic stress disorder (PTSD) but the commanding officer rejects the findings, orders the soldiers back to duty, and pressures the therapist as he needs "every soldier in the fight." Another case described by Johnson et al. (2010) describes a Navy psychologist on board an aircraft carrier who successfully treats a self-referred military client. The client is promoted and requires a security clearance; the psychologist is required to complete the clearance as the only mental health provider available. The report is read by the executive officer who denies the clearance due to the mental health diagnoses revealed in the report. The incident may violate several ethical standards.

Robertson and Walter (2008) point out that dual-role dilemmas exist beyond the military and can include forensic settings, child therapy, involuntary treatment, distributive justice, and research projects. "In each domain where the dual-role dilemma occurs, the psychiatrist finds him or herself the servant of two masters: the patient and a third party. This third party, whether it be the courts, the family, employers or society itself, is usually in a position of power over the patient" (p. 233). The authors conclude with an assertion that "there is a moral equivalence between psychiatrists serving the collective good and serving the good of the patient" (p. 234). In other words, it is the responsibility of the therapist to juggle both issues and strive for a just balance of outcomes.

In a qualitative study of deployed social workers by Simmons and Rycraft (2010) some of the narratives reflected the balancing act suggested by Robertson and Walter. For example, an Air Force major stated, "I truly believe that (with some exceptions) it is not good for the troop or for the mission to send them back. All of the research I have read tells me that having the troop stay and complete their mission helps them in the long term while sending them home has negative implications for their mental health, long term. As for the mission, if we send them home, someone else has to take their place. The cost of sending them home is greater for both the individual and the unit than keeping them in place" (p. 13). Clearly this major, who is a social worker, is juggling both issues.

Tallant and Ryberg (1999) comment on the dual-role dilemma as follows: "It is obvious that role conflict will develop for the military social worker. The military social worker is both a professional social worker and professional officer. Each profession has its own set of morals, values, and ethics. Each has its own purpose or mission. This role conflict will create core ethical dilemmas for the military social worker" (pp. 184–185).

Civilian social workers helping veterans in the Veterans Affairs agencies have a similar dual-role ethical dilemma. The VA programs offer care but within a strict accountability culture of "service connected disability." The first step of acceptance is determining eligibility. Veterans with service-connected disabilities are provided disability income, free health care, and ancillary services including caregiver salaries if applicable. The Veterans Administration (VA) becomes the monitor of disability status. There are two key dual-role issues that arise. First, the hand-off from the military medicine process of mission readiness to the VA process of benefit delivery can be problematic. What happens if an active duty person wants to seek counseling for PTSD with the VA but does not want the military to know as it would affect deployability? I have talked to VA social workers who have advised soldiers that the records will not be released to the military. What happens if treatment of veterans with PTSD improves their symptoms, but they do not want the results recorded as the findings would reduce their disability pay? I attended a workshop by a prominent PTSD therapist who got great results but the VA clients begged the therapist not to report improvements as their disability pay would be reduced. The therapist did not record in the medical record the improvement, including some clients with no symptoms remaining.

ETHICAL DILEMMA: CONFIDENTIALITY AND PRIVACY ISSUES

A second ethical dilemma is the lack of confidentiality for mental health providers when working with military personnel and their families. In essence, mission readiness and national security trumps all therapist-client privacy or confidentiality. An Air Force captain commented, "There's very little privacy. A patient's issues are quickly known to his unit and to the base. It's a fine line between protecting the client's right to privacy and the 'need to know' for commanders" (Simmons & Rycraft, 2010, p. 14). Jeffrey et al. (1992) described a case where an officer was referred to a military psychologist after expressing suicidal ideation. The officer requested that no record be kept due to the potential impact on his career, but the psychologist refused the request. The client was then offered a choice to see a civilian therapist, which the client declined due to financial concerns. The military psychologist then saw the client for eight successful sessions but was then transferred overseas. After the military psychologist was transferred overseas, the client's supervisor requested a report on the client's ability to do his duties. The supervisor of the military psychologist completed the report expressing some concerns about the duties, the client's stress issues, and suicidal potential. The client's supervisor was concerned after reading the report, the client decided that his career was damaged, resigned from the service, and filed an ethics violation (confidentiality) complaint with the American Psychological Association (APA) against the original psychologist (perhaps unaware that it was the psychologist's supervisor who was responsible for completing the report?). Jeffrey et al. provided a detailed discussion of the ethical issues and concluded "DOD (Department of Defense) directives and Army regulations provide authority to release health care information (without patient consent) to officials within DOD with a 'need to know'" (p. 92). However the APA ethics review found the military psychologist had violated ethical standards (perhaps unaware that it was his supervisor who completed the report?). "In the opinion of the APA Ethics Committee, the psychologist should have obtained a signed statement from the patient before any release of information to the commanding officer" (p. 92). Jeffrey et al. succinctly summarize the issue—"the psychologist adhered to DOD regulations but was reprimanded for failing to *concurrently* attend to guidelines and ethical principles of the APA" (p. 92). Further they assert "this case demonstrates the importance of patient advisement of limits of confidentiality and careful documentation of such in patient charts" (p. 93). Unfortunately, the psychologist was overseas and had no knowledge of the report being done until he received the ethics violation complaint. It is unclear to this author why the supervisor was not the source of the ethics complaint instead of the initial psychologist as the aggrieved actions were the supervisor's.

Confidentiality and privacy issues can evolve due to the small community on base or ship and ways to be sensitive to colleagues. Johnson et al. (2006) described two illustrative cases. In one case, the only psychologist on an aircraft carrier had a friend of equal rank who began chatting about his marital issues. As the concerns got more frequent and complex the therapist finally confronted him about his depression and the need for formal documented sessions. The officer refused to go into therapy and stopped contact with the therapist.

The other case illustrated a complex dynamic in which the only psychologist in a small command provided therapy for midlife issues for the executive officer who wrote his fitness reports, completed inspections on the therapist's clinic, and gave him a mild letter of reprimand on an incident. The clinical relationship, though completed 6 months earlier, became an issue when the executive officer was charged with fraternization. The attorneys wanted copies of all mental health records. As the notes would not help the client (the executive officer), the psychologist expressed reservations about releasing "all records." However, his commanding officer ordered him to release the records as a "need to know" requirement. The psychologist released the records but not his notes, which satisfied the attorneys but infuriated the commanding officer who interpreted the act as disobeying a direct order. The psychologist's final performance report was negatively impacted by this tug of war on client privacy.

An illustrative case from my own career involved an Air Force social work officer who created a confidential space by playing racket ball games with pilots who would share concerns and issues that the therapist would process on the racket ball court. No records were kept, but the therapist felt he could help many military officers who would not otherwise get help. I kept holding my breath fearing that a serious incident would erupt that exposed this unofficial intervention but it never did to my knowledge.

Johnson et al. (2006, p. 314) included nine recommendations for navigating these stormy ethical waters:

1. "Strive for a neutral posture in the community" as it can infer that you are "available and nonpartisan."
2. "Assume that every member of the community is a future patient."
3. "Provide immediate informed consent information to all patients."
4. "Use stringent interpretations of 'need to know' policies" and especially "be conservative when determining what information is crucial to the question posed by a command."
5. "Avoid significant self-disclosure" due to the multiple role relationships and not knowing what might make future clients hesitate to reach out.
6. "Consider alternative mental health resources" when complicated or awkward situations occur.
7. "Increase tolerance for boundary crossings" due to the small military community and multiple role relationships inherent in the fishbowl settings.
8. "Actively collaborate with patients regarding management of nonclinical interactions" so you and client know how to respond in informal contact.
9. "Carefully document uncomfortable multiple relationships" and your efforts to "carefully document awareness of the problem, ethical reasoning, and clear efforts to resolve the dilemmas in the most expeditious and elegant fashion possible."

(Many of the above nine recommendations are strikingly similar to common practice guidelines for rural social workers who struggle with small communities with multiple role relationships, ambiguous boundaries, and limited resources or referral sources.)

ETHICAL DILEMMA: HIERARCHY AND POWER ISSUES

The third ethical dilemma is inherent in living within an authoritarian closed society. Line officers, who come through Reserve Officer Training Corps (ROTC) or Officer Candidate School (OCS) and select a field where they will be trained in a specialty, are expected to have total devotion to the military culture. From day one, they are trained to be decision makers and to be strictly obedient to the chain of command. If a higher ranking officer tells them to do something, they will do their utmost to comply. They have some wiggle room if they can prove that the order is not lawful, but the expectation is that they will give their life, their full commitment, and the soldiers under their command to the orders of a superior. Mission completion is paramount. Medical officers (doctors, nurses, social workers, etc.) take a different path. The military wants a skill set already achieved before the medical officers come on active duty. They do not seek to shape medical officers from clay to a military product, they just want to not have the medical officers "embarrass the military," as was explained to me in the 2-week crash course on adapting to the military that I went to when joining the Air Force as a social work officer. Medical schools, nursing schools, and social work schools are the core preparation arenas with a military polish added. Therefore, there are often moments of culture clash between the professional culture and the military culture. I heard often the saying "You are an officer first and a social worker second." None of us believed it for a minute. We are social workers who learn to navigate the military system well, using rank and power to help our clients, and identifying career-lethal potholes of custom or expectation to avoid or circumvent.

Simmons and Rycraft (2010) share a narrative of an Air Force major whose view was as follows: "Working with commanders who did not (do not) follow my advice. Although I tried to work with some of the commanders, I found there is no recourse for this. We are merely advisers. The commander is the one who makes the final decision about the troop" (p. 15). Johnson et al. (2010) describe an Army psychiatrist's quandary when he is stationed in Afghanistan, determines that a soldier needs to be medically evacuated, and the commanding officer "rejected these recommendations and ordered the service member back into action" and chastised the therapist saying "you can diagnose them all with PTSD if you want to but your job is to shore them up and return them to duty whenever possible; this is a combat zone captain, our threshold for 'crazy' is a bit higher out here. The reasons should be obvious to you, we're at war" (p. 551). The clear inference in both of these cases is that, despite bringing mental health providers into the military for our expertise, the commander can and is the hierarchical authority on clinical issues. Unfortunately, it is a rare commander who has any training in clinical assessment. The reality is that commanders see soldiers as building blocks to victory. The clinician is a means to an end, and any expertise given is filtered through mission requirements.

The ethical dilemma is how to utilize power in the situations to neutralize the hierarchical structure preventing appropriate care. This process is complex, but is at times achievable. A powerful principle in the military is that you fight rank with higher rank. If the commander is shutting down your clinical judgment, you go up your chain of command until you can have a higher ranking medical officer discuss the importance of clinical input. When I was a family advocacy officer, I would routinely ensure that a medical officer with higher ranking than the unit commander was in our family advocacy management meetings so that treatment recommendations were considered. There is a power struggle within the military setting, and we social workers need to know how to maximize it for our clients.

LEGAL AND MORAL CONTEXTS FOR ETHICAL DILEMMAS

The above ethical dilemmas are common occurrences and often imply a delicate balance between compliance to military demands and honoring our profession's ethical standards. Kelly (2010) described the struggle nurses go through as follows: "achieving operational effectiveness is a feature that every military nurse must accept and anything after that, such as nurse autonomy or patients' self-determination, is secondary" (p. 640). She emphasizes that soldiers in combat "must be fit to fight and win the battle" and therefore are "more of a commodity rather than individual persons with distinct health care needs" (p. 636). She gives the example of a soldier injured by a bomb, and the nurse wants to help the amputated and dying soldier but is ordered to wait until the bomb crew can clear the area of explosives. The moral act is to save the soldier, but the legal act is to obey the lawful order. Kelly asserts that there is no comparable civilian environment to the battlefield and that ethical negligence should not be applicable. The tug of war between moral and legal actions remains, regardless of the uniqueness of combat.

Figure 4.1 illustrates the challenge of ethical process when deciding on an issue with a client. The overt issue is helping the client through the trusting relationship that is essential to effective interventions. However, an event occurs that demands a decision on what is possible or appropriate related to the client. The event can be a commander demanding sensitive information or refusing to honor your recommendation to pull a soldier out of combat. The event can be watching a soldier die while waiting for bomb-clearing equipment. The event can be subtle, such as being encouraged not to advocate for a spouse of a high-ranking officer who has been abused and needs to be reported. The essence of an ethical dilemma is the tug of war between the moral side and the legal side. Moral stance

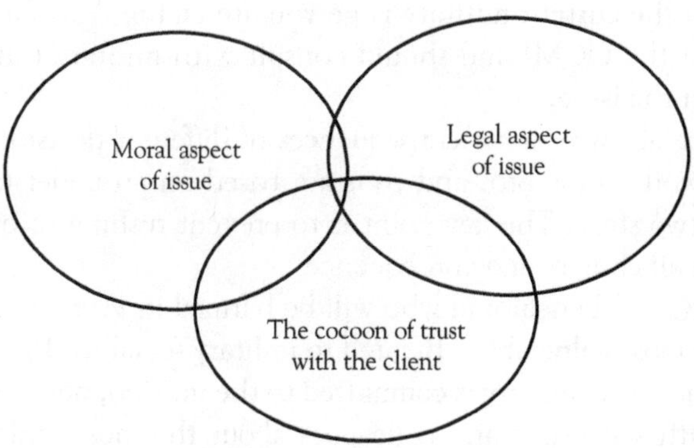

Figure 4.1 Triad model of ethical dilemmas

centers on the humanitarian actions, the best way to help the client, and the efforts in the best interest of the client. The legal stance is what the laws, most often the Uniformed Code of Military Justice (UCMJ), dictate that you do. Though legal protections are available to individual service members, the primary thrust is protecting and reinforcing the military enterprise. The code of ethics primarily is a way to codify the moral standards expected in the behavior of social work, but the code also reflects a legal expectation that the social worker will abide by the code of ethics to maintain licensure or avoid ethics violations. The therapist struggles to decide what is the "right thing" to do. No matter which professional actions are chosen, the relationship with the client can be damaged. The obligations of the UCMJ and protecting the military mission can result in a social worker recommending that a service member is not cleared for duty. The client (the service member) will likely be angry at the social worker even though the social worker did "the right thing."

MODELS FOR ETHICAL DECISION MAKING

In this complex and confusing social dynamic of ethical dilemmas, it would be ideal if there were clear models of ethical decision making. Unfortunately, that is not the case. However, several models have been proposed, some specific to the military, and some others generic.

The ETHIC Model

A classic model for ethical decision making is by Elaine Congress (2000). Her ETHIC model outlined a 5-step process:

1. "**E**xamine relevant personal, societal, agency, client and professional values." Related to military social work, this step implies the social worker needs a clear understanding of the military context, cultures, and chain of command and an in-depth awareness of the client's rights to appeal or negotiate decisions directly impacting the client's best interest.
2. "**T**hink about what ethical standard of the NASW code of ethics applies, as well as relevant laws and case decisions." Related to military social work, this step implies the need for a thorough understanding of the code of ethics and when it clashes with the current military issue you are facing. You should have a detailed awareness of the UCMJ and should consult with military (and possibly civilian) attorneys on the issue.
3. "**H**ypothesize about possible consequences of different decisions." Related to military social work, these pros and cons are based on an understanding of the issues in the first two steps. The key point is to prevent rushing to one decision without working out all choices and consequences.
4. "**I**dentify who will benefit and who will be harmed in view of social work's commitment to the most vulnerable." Related to military social work, this step is most challenging because the military is committed to the mission, not to the most vulnerable.
5. "**C**onsult with supervisor and colleagues about the most ethical choice." Related to military social work, consultation is sound advice and can include going up the

chain of command and seeking legal advice from Judge Advocate General (JAG) officers. The complex issue could be not being able to share sensitive military information when consulting with civilian counterparts who could be naive to the military context.

Congress's model strives to process the pros and cons, consequences, and effects of any legal dilemma that a social worker faces. The five steps can help slow down the decision-making process and build a consensus of advice on what should be the final decision. However, a solo provider in a combat situation with immediate results demanded by a unit commander can be a challenging scenario to manage. If the military social worker is on a stateside base, a VA clinic, or a hospital setting, the ETHIC model can be processed. In the heat of battle, the best option is to process after the event with your chain of command and colleagues, preparing for the next round of events. The brusque unit commander will surely have another round of challenges to the social worker. It is also feasible that running the issue up your chain of command can create a discrete chat between your commander and the unit commander's commander and subtle pressure can be applied back to the unit commander. My point is simply that the ETHIC model may have to be adapted dependent on the setting.

Loewenberg and Dolgoff's Ethical Decision-Making Questions and Ethical Principles Screen

Loewenberg and Dolgoff (1992) assert that "ethical decision making does not involve the automatic application of arbitrary rules" (p. 41). Rather, "the skilled social worker must assess and weigh all options and outcomes and then select the one that appears to be the most ethical" (pp. 41–42). They propose seven key ethical questions to consider in making the best decision (p. 55):

1. "What principles, rights, and obligations have an impact on these ethical issues?"
2. "What additional information is needed to properly identify the ethical implications?"
3. "What are the relevant ethical rules and principles that can be applied? Which ethical criteria are relevant in this situation?"
4. "If there is a conflict of interests, who should be the principal beneficiary?"
5. "How would you rank order the ethical issues, rules, and principles that you have identified?"
6. "What are the possible consequences that result from utilizing different ethical rules and principles?"
7. "Who should make the ethical decision? When is it justified to shift the ethical decision making to another person (not the social worker)? To whom should it be shifted?"

Similar to the ETHIC model, Loewenberg and Dolgoff emphasize careful gathering of information about rights, rules, any conflict of interests, and consequences. Related to military social work, the important rights and rules would include the NASW Code of Ethics and the UCMJ, which clash at times (i.e., privacy versus mission). They propose some interesting points. Does the military always have to be "the primary beneficiary" in a conflict of interest? Is it appropriate for a military social worker to shift the ethical decision to someone who isn't a social worker, and does it absolve them of the responsibility? For example, if a Judge Advocate General (JAG) officer tells you the legal decision, do you accept it? What happens to your moral obligation to protect the client?

Further, Loewenberg and Dolgoff (1992, p. 60) asserted a ranking of ethical principles which they called the Ethical Principles Screen (EPS), as follows:

Ethical Principle 1: Protection of life
Ethical Principle 2: Equality and inequality
Ethical Principle 3: Autonomy and freedom
Ethical Principle 4: Least harm
Ethical Principle 5: Quality of life
Ethical Principle 6: Privacy and confidentiality
Ethical Principle 7: Truthfulness and full disclosure

The main point of the principles was that the first principles trumped the later principles. For example, protection of life supersedes full disclosure or privacy. A client stating he will kill himself negates the client's right to privacy. Tallant and Ryberg (1999), in a discussion of the ethical dilemmas of military social work, proposed that Ethical Principle 1 should be amended for military social work to read "***Ethical Principle 1: Protection of life/military mission.***" They felt that protection of the military mission is on the same priority as protection of life. Frankly, when military missions fail, lives can be lost, national security priorities can be thwarted, and morale can be shattered. Tallant and Ryberg's recommendations were an innovative effort to merge the dual-loyalties debate and support the ethical quandaries often faced by military social workers.

Gottlieb's Decision-Making Model

Gottlieb (1993) described an ethical decision-making model primarily focused on multiple relationship issues. Staal and King (2000) applied the model to military psychology settings. The Gottlieb model emphasizes three key factors to consider: power, duration, and termination. *Power* reflects how much influence the social worker would have over the client (i.e., a social work officer and an enlisted client would have a large power differential). *Duration* indicates how much time the relationship has. *Termination* refers to the expectation that the client and social worker will continue to meet. These three factors can interact (i.e., as duration increases, power often increases and termination (which to me would be better termed *desire to continue*) will increase. From an ethical decision-making standpoint, a key issue is to watch for power having a negative impact on the relationship (i.e., when an enlisted client is ordered to be evaluated by a social worker there is much power imbalance). The longer the duration (i.e., number of sessions client has attended) means the more complicated the multiple relationships are, and the better the termination contract is defined (i.e., clear mutual expectations of what your continued client-provider relationship will continue to be).

Gottlieb prioritizes these three factors as important screening tools when facing dual or multiple relationships (such as when being deployed with a client or having a VA client who also volunteers at the VA hospital in a role that connects to your role). Degree of power, time investment as a client so far, and motivation to continue therapy should be weighed when facing multiple relationship issues. A startling example is described by an Army major social worker deployed to a war zone who stated, "If you'll pardon the blunt report . . . it was entirely odd to work on a mental health issue with a client and then find yourself standing right next to the guy an hour later . . . with both of you naked and showering" (Simmons & Rycraft, 2010, p. 17). Most multiple relationships are not that dramatic, but this example illustrates that anything can happen in the military!

Johnson, Grasso, and Maslowski's Strategies for Managing Ethical-Legal Conflicts

Johnson, Grasso, and Maslowski (2010) described the conflicts between law and ethics faced by military mental health providers and recommend six strategies for managing the conflict (pp. 551–552):

1. "Determine whether the dilemma constitutes a tension or a conflict." Social workers should use negotiation skills and chain of command to reduce the tension and clarify the concern so the issue can be navigated legally and ethically. For example, a lawful order to release mental health records can be clarified to see what specific issue (i.e., security concerns) may be complied with without releasing the whole record.
2. "Know your ethical code and relevant federal laws." The NASW Code of Ethics is well known. The primary legal document to familiarize yourself with is the Uniformed Code of Military Justice (http://www.ucmj.us/). The best way to understand the UCMJ is to chat with a Judge Advocate General (JAG) officer about possible situations that you are likely to face.
3. "Develop a process for ethical decision making." The authors do not detail the process but do emphasize a slow process of researching your options and rights and avoiding impulsive or naive reactions to legal requests.
4. "Recognize that military service does not overrule or negate one's identity and obligations as a health professional." The authors reaffirm our allegiance to our code of ethics and warn against "'drift' in the direction of primary allegiance to military tradition and regulations at the expense of adherence to professional ethics" (p. 552).
5. "Seek to balance client best interests with DOD regulations." Basically, the authors advocate to carefully minimize harm to the client if feasible and be sure to discuss the options with the client at each step. Document what steps you are taking and the client's involvement.
6. "Work to reduce conflicts between ethical guidelines and federal law." Advocate for legal changes to laws and policies and educate people in power about the conflicts when they occur.

Johnson and colleagues (2010) have offered some useful ideas that help military social workers keep focused on minimizing the damage done to clients in the complex military environment. The basic message is to be prepared, knowledgeable, and savvy about navigating the military culture. When possible, change the military laws and policies.

You may want to keep the above models for ethical decision making in mind as you examine the three case vignettes and consider how you would answer their discussion questions.

Case Vignette: Captain John Doe, MSW

In the military, there are regulations that allow a military member with a personality disorder and administrative conflict to be discharged quickly from the military. A recent recruit who is unhappy with the military demands and culture came to John Doe, MSW (a military social worker) seeking a personality disorder (PD) diagnosis so that he could be quickly discharged. His first sergeant strongly hinted to the soldier that a PD diagnosis is the easiest way to get discharged quickly. However, based on his assessment, John concludes that the soldier does not meet the criteria for a PD. Instead, John believes that the soldier meets the criteria for an adjustment disorder, which will not qualify the soldier to get the discharge papers.

Case Vignette Discussion Questions

1. Some military social workers have made a PD diagnosis for the benefit of clients so the clients don't feel trapped to escalate their symptoms to escape the military. What would you do if you were in John Doe's place? Help the client or be accurate on your diagnosis?
2. By contrast there are military people who meet the diagnostic criteria for more serious mental illness issues (depression, anxiety) but are insistent that they will only work with you if you give them a more benign diagnosis like adjustment disorder. If they have the accurate diagnosis, they may be grounded as a pilot, designated as nondeployable (a career killer), or be discharged from the military. Do you protect their privacy by lying?

Case Vignette: Carl

Carl is a veteran who has a 100% service-connected disability for severe PTSD, for which he has received a monthly check for $2,000 from the government for the past 6 years. He enrolls in a treatment program for PTSD that you run. After 3 months of treatment, Carl reports significant improvement with minimal symptoms and no longer meets the criteria of active or severe PTSD. Carl is delighted with the results but begs you not to document any results as he will lose his disability check.

Case Vignette Discussion Question

1. Do you protect Carl or accurately document the findings?

Case Vignette: The Jones Family

Jack and Jill Jones have a child with autism. Jack, a military service member gets an assignment in Korea that is fantastic for his career, but he needs to get prior clearance from family advocacy staff that the new base will have services for the autistic child. The base staff indicate that they have minimal services for the child. As the social worker, your judgment is that the child should not go. Jack argues with you that the needs of his child are minimal and the base can handle the child's needs. Jill states she will not work at the new location and will be home to care for the child. You pass on this information to the family advocacy staff at the new base, but they are still concerned about the child's adjustment overseas. You choose to not approve the family going overseas to Korea. The commander chooses to send Jack unaccompanied for 2 years to Korea. The Jones family has to leave the base and return to their hometown while Jack is in Korea. The hometown has minimal services for autistic children. The Jones family is furious at you, and Jack berates the family advocacy program to everyone in his unit. The commander is unhappy because Jack is unhappy.

Case Vignette Discussion Question

1. Should you have sent the Jones family to Korea?

CONCLUSION

As promised at the beginning of the chapter, there are more questions than clear answers. The ethical dilemmas, whether dual loyalty, confidentiality, or hierarchy and power, confirm that there are clashes between the laws and wishes of the military and the protection of the clinical relationship with the client. No studies were found that offered an annual or even systematic survey of the volume of or results from ethical decision making by social workers working with the military or Veterans Affairs. The Simmons and Rycraft (2010) qualitative study of military social workers in combat was commendable, but a more systematic mechanism of data collection is needed. The Tallant and Ryberg (1999) chapter was a nice conceptual piece with case examples. Case examples were given for different mental health professions (Jeffrey et al., 1992; Johnson et al., 2006; Johnson et al., 2010; Staal & King, 2000) and deployed physicians (Hollon & Hickey, 2010; Sessums et al., 2009). One noteworthy study (Atac et al., 2005) included a survey of 51 physicians on their opinions on informed consent and refusing treatment. There remains a need to develop systematic evidence of legal-ethical conflict and practical solutions for the conflicts. Policy and legal evolution are better with data to guide the changes.

The models of ethical decision making were informative and often duplicative of intent. Synthesizing the content from the different authors results in a model targeted for military social workers struggling with the ethical decisions—the PSPIDD Model. This model highlights 5 steps:

1. **Prepare:** Each of the authors emphasized learning the laws, policies, and military UCMJ. This step is needed before the ethical-legal conflict occurs. Read the

articles that have case examples to sensitize yourself to different events that can happen and ways to respond to the conflict. Review the NASW Code of Ethics and determine the portions of the Code that would be likely to clash with the military demands.
2. **Slow down**: When the conflict occurs, every model that I described in the earlier section suggested to slow down the process of your response to the conflict so you do not react before you have your choices. There will be much pressure and efforts to plow past you, because the military is an action profession. Take a deep breath and remind yourself that you have the right to know your choices.
3. **Pros and cons**: Gather your pros and cons on the requested action, and gather facts on your rights. Talk to your supervisor, the JAG office or agency attorney, and the ombudsman's office. Get the request in writing.
4. **Involve**: Ensure that your client is involved and understands the pros and cons of the choice you are going to make.
5. **Decide and document**: Select the wisest choice, and document your actions with the client and your decision. Build case material for advocating for changes in policy or law. Pursue the chain of command to correct the conflict if you lose. Remember that your anguish is likely being repeated throughout the military. Issues such as the lack of confidentiality of records, pressure to change diagnoses or ignore our opinions are going to occur until the context allows a better outcome.

The above model strives to remind the military social workers what steps to take to prepare for and react to the next ethical-legal conflict that lands in their laps. Remember to also use stress management skills to manage your own anxiety as these events often create knotted stomach, fear of the force of the military bearing down on you, and uncertainty about what to do. Each event takes its toll. So be sure to take care of yourself, too!

CHAPTER DISCUSSION QUESTIONS

1. Do you believe that you can balance the military as a client and the service member as a client? Which would you choose as your "primary client"? Can you see a situation where the military needs to be your primary client? Can you see a situation where the service member needs to be your primary client?
2. Do you believe that the situation is ethical if a service member wants you to support the military family's request for approval of an overseas assignment if the services for their autistic child are not adequate in your judgment? What would you do?
3. Do you believe the situation is ethical if the veteran with posttraumatic stress disorder makes significant improvement but wants you to not record the improvement as the veteran would have his service-connected disability check reduced? What would you do?
4. Using the PSPIDD model of ethical decision making, what ways can you think of to "slow down" the decision making and allow you to work out your options? Often you will receive pressure from the commander or designee to act the way they desire. How do you take the time needed?

REFERENCES

Atac, A., Guven, T., Ucar, M., & Kir, T. (2005). A study of the opinions and behaviors of physicians with regard to informed consent and refusing treatment. *Military Medicine, 170*(7), 566–571.

Baumann, D. (2007). Military ethics: A task for armies. *Military Medicine, 172* (12 suppl), 34–38.

Benatar, S. R., & Upshur, R. E. G. (2008). Dual loyalty of physicians in the military and in civilian life. *American Journal of Public Health, 98*(12), 2161–2167.

Clark, P. A. (2006, Fall). Medical ethics at Guantanamo Bay and Abu Ghraib: The problem of dual loyalty. *Journal of Law, Medicine & Ethics*, 570–580.

Congress, E. P. (2000). What social workers should know about ethics: Understanding and resolving practice dilemmas. *Advances in Social Work, 1*(1), 1–25.

Daley, J. G. (1999). Understanding the military as an ethnic identity. In J. G. Daley (Ed.), *Social work practice in the military* (pp. 291–303). New York, NY: Haworth Press.

Gottlieb, M. C. (1993). Avoiding exploitive dual relationships: A decision making model. *Psychotherapy, 30*, 41–48.

Gross, M. L. (2010). Teaching military medical ethics: Another look at dual loyalty and triage. *Cambridge Quarterly of Healthcare Ethics, 19*, 458–464.

Helmick, K., and members of consensus conference (2010). Cognitive rehabilitation for military personnel with mild traumatic brain injury and chronic post-concussional disorder: Results of April 2009 consensus conference. *NeuroRehabilitation, 26*, 239–255.

Hollon, J. R., & Hickey, P. W. (2010). Select clinician recommendations for military medical practitioners conducting humanitarian and civil assistance activities. *Military Medicine, 175*(9), 647–654.

Jeffrey, T. B., Rankin, R. J., & Jeffrey, L. K. (1992). In service of two masters: The ethical-legal dilemma faced by military psychologists. *Professional Psychology: Research and Practice, 23*(2), 91–95.

Johnson, W. B., Bacho, R., Heim, M., & Ralph, J. (2006). Multiple-role dilemmas for military mental health care providers. *Military Medicine, 171*(4), 311–315.

Johnson, W. B., Grasso, I., & Maslowski, K. (2010). Conflicts between ethics and law for military mental health providers. *Military Medicine, 175*(8), 548–553.

Junger, S. (2010). *War*. New York, NY: Twelve Hachette.

Kelly, J. (2010). Battlefield conditions: Different environment but the same duty of care. *Nursing Ethics, 17*(5), 636–645.

Khaylis, A., Polusny, M. A., Erbes, C. R., Gewirtz, A., & Rath, M. (2011). Posttraumatic stress, family adjustment, and treatment preferences among National Guard soldiers deployed to OEF/OIF. *Military Medicine, 176*, 126–131.

London, L., Rubenstein, L. S., Baldwin-Ragaven, L., & Van Es, A. (2006). Dual loyalty among military health professionals: Human rights and ethics in times of armed conflict. *Cambridge Quarterly of Healthcare Ethics, 15*, 381–391.

Loewenberg, F. M., & Dolgoff, R. (1992). *Ethical decisions for social work practice* (4th ed.). Itasca, IL: Peacock.

Pascrell, B. (2009). Introduction to the report of the international conference on behavioral health and traumatic brain injury. *Clinical Neuropsychologist, 23*, 1281–1290.

Peterson, A. L., Baker, M. T., & McCarthy, K. R. (2008). Combat stress casualties in Iraq. Part 1: Behavioral health consultation at an expeditionary medical group. *Perspectives in Psychiatric Care, 44*(3), 146–158.

Pois, H., & Oak, S. (2007). War & military mental health: The US psychiatric response in the 20th century. *American Journal of Public Health, 97*(12), 2132–2142.

Ritchie, E. C. (2007). Update on combat psychiatry: From the battlefront to the home front and back again. *Military Medicine, 172*(12), 11–14.

Robertson, M. D., & Walter, G. (2008). Many faces of the dual-role dilemma in psychiatric ethics. *Australian and New Zealand Journal of Psychiatry, 42*, 228–235.

Sessums, L. L., Collen, J. F., O'Malley, P. G., Jackson, J. L., & Roy, M. J. (2009). Ethical practice under fire: Deployed physicians in the global war on terrorism. *Military Medicine, 174*(5), 441–447.

Simmons, C. A., & Rycraft, J. R. (2010). Ethical challenges of military social workers serving in a combat zone. *Social Work, 55*(1), 9–18.

Staal, M. A., & King, R. E. (2000). Managing a multiple relationship environment: The ethics of military psychology. *Professional Psychology: Research and Practice, 31*(6), 698–705.

Tallant, S. H., & Ryberg, R. A. (1999). Common and unique ethical dilemmas encountered by military social workers. In J. G. Daley (Ed.), *Social work practice in the military* (pp. 179–204). New York, NY: Haworth Press.

Wynia, M. K. (2007). Breaching confidentiality to protect the public: Evolving standards of medical confidentiality for military detainees. *American Journal of Bioethics, 7*(8), 1–5.

CHAPTER

5

Secondary Trauma in Military Social Work

ALLEN RUBIN AND EUGENIA L. WEISS

Imagine yourself as a recently graduated and newly hired social worker in a community-based mental health clinic that serves large numbers of returning military combat veterans who served in Iraq and Afghanistan. Before long, your caseload is comprised mainly of such veterans, and each has a different horrific tale to tell of his or her tragic, traumatic combat experiences and other challenges relating to military life. Having learned about empirically supported interventions for psychological trauma, you understand the importance of encouraging these clients to narrate the vivid details of their traumatic experiences and to do so repeatedly.

One veteran of the war in Iraq, let's call him Joe, an Army specialist, during Operation Iraqi Freedom, narrates a graphic account of seeing his buddy blown to pieces by a roadside bomb that hit the vehicle (Humvee) that Joe was driving. Joe blames himself for the incident, thus exhibiting survivor guilt, and you need to try to help him reframe his self-blame cognitions while at the same time trying to help him readjust to civilian life. The latter is no easy task in light of Joe's own physical and psychological handicaps resulting from the explosion and the deterioration of his relationship with his wife since his return from Iraq.

Another veteran, attached to the Marine Corps Infantry Battalion, Michael, who served in Afghanistan during Operation Enduring Freedom, describes in great detail an experience in which he accidentally shot Afghani civilians in a security mission during a home sweep that was also housing enemy combatants. The details that he narrates about what happened to the children and their families are gruesome and heartbreaking.

The third veteran that you begin to see as part of your caseload is Jeff, a private in the Army. Jeff lost his right arm and both legs from detonating an intermittent or improvised explosive device (IED) while driving. You can only begin to imagine the depth of his emotional pain as he contrasts his life now with his earlier life as an all-around athletic star in high school who was quite popular with his peers and whose dating life was the envy of the other guys. You also treat a female Marine, Sgt. Cheryl, who was sexually assaulted by her peers while deployed in Iraq during Operation New Dawn and who has become suicidal and severely depressed as a result of the attack.

As your caseload fills up with additional veterans who vividly narrate different but equally tragic and horrifying traumatic experiences, imagine how hearing repeatedly about all of that might affect your own thoughts and emotions—both during your work day as well as after you go home. As an empathic mental health practitioner, chances are that it would be hard not to have your own functioning—both at work and at home—impacted both by what you keep hearing and by the difficulty of the task of trying to help your clients cope with and alleviate the suffering associated with combat and deployment experiences. Later in this chapter we identify some things you can do to try to minimize the negative psychological repercussions that can accompany this line of work. First, however, let's examine some of the ways in which you might be impacted.

You might find yourself experiencing various troubling thoughts and emotions both at work and after you go home each day. You might have difficulty not thinking about and feeling emotional pain about the tragic details you hear at work even when you are engaging in normally enjoyable activities. These intrusive thoughts and emotions might disturb your sleep patterns, and you might start having nightmares. You might start engaging in dysfunctional behaviors, such as excessive drinking, just to try to avoid the intrusive thoughts and painful emotions.

The difficulty you are experiencing might start harming your professional work. You might become irritable with other staff members. You might start trying to rescue clients or experience difficulty in maintaining professional boundaries with them. You might start pushing your clients too soon to overcome their difficulties (to alleviate your own distress about their lack of progress). Your own worldview might be hampered, losing hope and developing a bleak view of the world. Over time, you might become so overwhelmed by all of this and so discouraged that you find it hard to maintain enthusiasm for your work, and your clients may sense your own pessimism and despair. At the other extreme, you might feel the need to deny the tragic client experiences about which you are hearing.

And who could blame you! Hearing about trauma can be contagious (Herman, 1992). All of these unfortunate effects of treating trauma survivors are quite common among mental health professionals specializing in trauma treatment and who therefore repeatedly hear horrific tales of extreme human suffering. These effects on the practitioner parallel the effects that the actual traumas have had on their clients—effects that are known as trauma symptoms (such as reexperiencing, avoidance, and hyperarousal) and that are associated with posttraumatic stress disorder (PTSD), as discussed in the next section of this handbook. When the practitioner (or even others close to the client) has these symptoms, a term that is commonly used for this phenomenon is *secondary trauma*; other commonly used terms that are virtually synonymous with secondary trauma are *vicarious trauma* and *compassion fatigue* (Figley, 1995; McCann & Pearlman, 1990; Stamm, 1995).

DEFINING SECONDARY TRAUMA AND RELATED TERMS

Secondary trauma (or secondary traumatization) among mental health professionals is defined as being indirectly exposed to trauma by hearing a firsthand and vivid recounting of the trauma by the trauma survivor and the practitioner's subsequent cognitions and emotions related to the trauma that might lead to a set of symptoms that are associated with PTSD (Zimering, Munroe, & Gulliver, 2003).

Another term that is often used synonymously with secondary trauma is *vicarious trauma.* Pearlman and Caringi (2009, pp. 202–203) define vicarious trauma (or *vicarious traumatization*) as "the negative transformation in the helper that results from empathic engagement with trauma survivors and their trauma material, combined with a commitment or responsibility to help them." Although the terms *secondary trauma* and *vicarious trauma* are typically used interchangeably, one way to think about the subtle distinction between them is that vicarious trauma puts more emphasis on *cumulative* effects on practitioners working with multiple survivors. However, the distinction between the two terms is a bit like splitting hairs, so to keep things simple *secondary trauma* will be the primary term used in this chapter. Regardless of which of the two terms one uses, the implications are the same regarding the deleterious impact it has on the practitioner's life and work and the ways to try to prevent it, minimize it or treat it.

Other terms related to secondary trauma are *compassion fatigue* and *traumatic countertransference* (Herman, 1992). Some define compassion fatigue as just another word for secondary trauma and its related trauma symptoms. Others define it more like the concept of burnout or apathy, referring to physical, emotional and spiritual exhaustion, and a diminished capacity to feel joy or feel empathy for and care for others. The latter conception of compassion fatigue is viewed as a result of either or both of two causal influences: (1) becoming worn down from constantly providing so much care and compassion; and (2) experiencing a gap between the expectations you have, or others have of you, regarding what you should do or accomplish and the realities that limit what you can do or accomplish (Figley, 1995; Pearlman & Caringi, 2009).

Traumatic countertransference has been defined in various ways, all of which refer to clinicians' responding to their own personal reaction to what an individual client says or does. The client's problem or trauma might resemble the clinician's troubling past or current experiences or personal issues with which they are trying to cope (Pearlman & Caringi, 2009; Rubin & Springer, 2009). Noting the virtual interchangeability of these terms, Salston and Figley (2003, p. 167) define them as follows:

> The debilitating mental health effects that may be experienced by clinicians who treat the trauma of crime victims has been referred to as secondary traumatic stress (STS). The research and practice literature reflects the use of various terms that are or are nearly synonymous with STS. These include burnout, compassion fatigue, vicarious traumatization (VT), and traumatic countertransference. "Burnout" may be manifested in the emotional responses of depression, anxiety, and emotional exhaustion; the physiological responses of headaches and hypertension; and the behavioral responses of insomnia, increased addiction or dependencies, interpersonal difficulties, and general disillusionment.

"Compassion fatigue" parallels the diagnosis of posttraumatic stress disorder (PTSD), except the traumatic event is the client's traumatic experience that has been shared in the process of therapy or interaction with the survivor. Vicarious traumatization occurs as the clinician's exposure to the client's trauma begins to affect the clinician's worldview, emotional and psychological needs, the belief system, and cognitions. "Traumatic countertransference" occurs as the clinician has a spontaneous or evoked response to information provided by the client, as well as the client's behaviors and emotions. Countertransference reactions inhibit the clinician from correctly diagnosing and treating the effects of trauma.

In light of the essential interchangeability of these terms, you might well wonder why this chapter went to the trouble of defining them all. Why not just define secondary trauma and leave it at that? The rationale is that in your future clinical work and reading, you are almost certain to encounter some colleagues or authors using one of these terms while other colleagues or authors use a different one of these terms, despite the fact that they are all referring to phenomena and clinical implications that are basically the same. Rather than allow the different terminology to perplex you, there are at least three important things to remember:

- First of all, if you begin to experience any of these reactions in your practice with military personnel or veterans, it does not mean that there is something wrong with you or that you are a poor clinician. These reactions are normal in light of the horrific traumas with which you are dealing; they are occupational hazards.
- Second, you need to remember that these reactions can hinder your ability to help your clients; therefore, you should recognize and deal with them early on, before they take too much of a toll on you.
- Third, there are things you can do to alleviate and better cope with these reactions and prevent them from getting to the point where they hinder your work with clients, not to mention sapping the joy you get from life in general.

All of the foregoing terms—*secondary trauma*, *vicarious trauma*, *compassion fatigue*, and *traumatic countertransference* are evident in the "Case Vignette: Donna," which describes a composite case example of a clinician working with combat survivors, derived and adapted from Tyson (2007).

Case Vignette: Donna

Donna, age 40, suffers from compassion fatigue. She grew up in New York City as a first-generation American whose parents experienced trauma as war immigrants and who felt safe and patriotic to be in America. Shortly after starting her career as a clinical social worker in a VA outpatient clinic located near New York City, the 9/11 terrorist attacks on the twin towers occurred. This impacted her profoundly, having watched the towers being constructed as a child and knowing people who were killed or displaced by the attacks. Several years later her caseload doubled to 80 cases of combat veterans suffering with PTSD and comorbid issues, whom she treats in individual and group therapy. One of her cases involves providing bereavement counseling to the wife of a soldier who was killed as part of the same National Guard unit in which other of her clients served. Another of her clients graphically describes his blast injuries and limb amputation. Donna keeps getting intrusive mental images of the blast and amputation while in session with the bereaved wife, who keeps inquiring about how her husband died. Donna begins to feel like a helpless bystander. She finds herself struggling to remain neutral when her clients discuss their conflict between fearing inevitable redeployment to Iraq or Afghanistan versus their identity as a soldier and their sense of duty to return to combat. Some of her clients show her photos of dead combatants or video footage of beheadings of Americans. She recently learned that some of her redeployed clients whom she had treated for a year had been severely wounded or killed in combat. Lately, some of Donna's friends and family have been telling her that she has been changing. She has been avoiding intimate contact with her husband, becoming overprotective of her children, and losing her usual sense of dark humor. She has noted her own increased feelings of rage without knowing the source of the rage. She now spends less time with friends. Having always been very patriotic and proud to be an American, she has become disillusioned with the government. She no longer can tolerate watching TV news reports regarding the wars. She has difficulty resisting the urge to overidentify with her clients and try to rescue them. Once very optimistic, she has become cynical about the world and pessimistic about the world her children will inherit. She is losing sleep and having nightmares. She is having difficulty remaining empathic with her clients without becoming overwhelmed. She has lost confidence in her clinical skills and the interventions she employs. She is experiencing increased difficulty in not letting her mind wander when her clients recount the details of their traumas. She no longer has the same sense of great meaning and purpose in her work. In light of all of this, including her exhaustion and diminished sense of self-esteem, she is considering a career change.

ASSESSING SECONDARY TRAUMA

As with any other clinical problem, the assessment of secondary trauma can be done in a clinical interview and/or by administering a self-report scale. Although no standardized clinical interview protocol has yet been developed for assessing secondary trauma per se, other such protocols can be used to assess PTSD symptoms among people experiencing secondary trauma. The gold standard clinical interview scale for measuring PTSD in general is the Clinician Administered PTSD Scale (CAPS), which has had extensive research supporting its reliability and validity (Briere & Spinazzola, 2009). However, Zimering, Munroe, and Keane (2006) found the CAPS to be useful in a study of secondary trauma in disaster relief clinicians. One practical problem with the CAPS is its length. Its administration requires a 90-minute interview. There is a shorter version, the PTSD Symptom Scale-Interview Version (PSS-I), which takes about half that amount of time. The CAPS measures the frequency, intensity, and severity of each symptom; the PSS-I measures only the severity of each symptom.

Four reliable and valid self-report scales have been developed for assessing secondary trauma per se:

1. Compassion Fatigue Self-Test (CFST) for Psychotherapists (Figley, 1995)
2. TSI Belief Scale (TSI-BLS) (Pearlman, 1996)
3. Secondary Trauma Questionnaire (STQ) (Motta, Hafeez, Sciancalepore, & Diaz, 2001)
4. Secondary Traumatic Stress Scale (STSS) (Bride, Robinson, Yegidis, & Figley, 2004)

Three of the above instruments were developed to assess secondary trauma experienced by practitioners. The exception is the STQ scale, which was designed for anyone who has had ongoing and close exposure to someone who has been traumatized.

The most recently developed of the above scales—the STSS scale—was designed for and tested out on social workers per se (although it also can be used with other helping professionals). It contains 17 items that are followed by a 1 (never) to 5 (very often) response format. Five items (Bride et al., 2004, p. 33) measure intrusion symptoms, such as Item 10, which reads as follows: "I thought about my work with clients when I didn't intend to." Seven items assess avoidance symptoms, such as Item 14, which reads as follows: "I wanted to avoid working with some clients." Five items measure arousal symptoms, such as, Item 15, which reads as follows: "I was easily annoyed."

Military mental health practitioners (i.e., those clinicians serving in uniform) are thought to be at a greater risk than civilian mental health professionals for developing secondary stress reactions due to both being exposed to the suffering of those they are treating and to the demands associated with military operational stress. Military operational stress involves providing services to military personnel while in dangerous zones, having to participate in multiple deployments, lack of reprieve time and competing demands for the ethical treatment of the client versus the provider (the military as the employer) (Pechacek, Bicknell, & Landry, 2011). The U.S. Army Medical (AMEDD) Command uses the Professional Quality of Life Scale (ProQOL) to assess secondary stress in clinicians in uniform, which is a revised version of the CFST (Stamm, 2005). This is a 30-item instrument consisting of three scales: (1) compassion fatigue or secondary stress scale; (2) burnout scale; and (3) compassion satisfaction scale. Compassion fatigue is measured with 10 statements ranging from 0 (never) to 5 (very often), containing such items as "I feel as though I am experiencing the trauma of someone I have helped" and "I think I may have been 'infected' by the traumatic stress of those I help." The reader can refer to Stamm (2005) for further details regarding the scale as well as information on reliability scores.

TREATING SECONDARY TRAUMA

Pechacek devised the EAT model to instruct military leaders and military mental health clinicians in the management of provider fatigue in the Army Medical Department Center and School (Pechacek et al., 2011) based on a resilience building plan. This model can also be applied in the civilian sector. EAT is an acronym. The letter E stands for "Educate" yourself (i.e., Who is affected? What is provider fatigue? What is resiliency?). The letter A stands for "Assess" your level of provider fatigue (What is the provider fatigue severity level? What is the resiliency level? How might resiliency be increased?). The letter T represents, "Take Action" (i.e., build up your resilience, create a self-care plan, and seek professional help if needed) (Pechacek et al., 2011, p. 385).

Although the level of provider fatigue can be measured in part by the ProQOL, clinicians should also monitor symptom "markers" in themselves and in fellow coworkers (through self-report and self-observation). The symptom markers fall into six categories:

1. *Emotional* markers involve the clinician experiencing feelings of powerlessness, anger, and survivor guilt.
2. *Cognitive* markers entail lowered concentration, intrusive thoughts, and preoccupation with trauma.
3. *Behavioral* markers include symptoms such as being jumpy or on edge, suffering from sleep disturbances, and experiencing changes in appetite.
4. *Spiritual* markers typically involve a provider feeling hopeless and questioning previously held religious beliefs.
5. *Somatic* markers include physical exhaustion, having aches and pains, suffering from an impaired immune system and gastrointestinal problems.
6. *Social* markers entail a clinician experiencing a general mistrust of others, becoming socially isolative, and having interpersonal conflicts in addition to becoming overprotective as a parent or as a leader.

According to this model, to build resilience in the mental health practitioner, a practitioner needs to be able to self-soothe and self-confront. Examples of self-soothing techniques can be found in Figure 5.1 on ideas for self-care. Self-confrontation involves a practitioner assessing his or her own anxieties as well as assessing the personal and professional growth that can result from the stressful situation. For instance, practitioners are encouraged to ask themselves:

- Why am I anxious?
- What am I trying to prove?
- Who am I trying to impress?
- What I am trying to fix?
- Am I depending on someone else to validate my sense of self-worth?
- What is the growth potential in this situation?

(Taken from Pechacek et al., 2011, p. 386)

Clinicians are also encouraged to combat secondary stress through a holistic (i.e., physical, mental, emotional, spiritual, and social) renewal approach that involves many of the elements already presented in Figure 5.1 covering ideas for self-care.

Exercise
Good nutrition and eat slowly
Get enough sleep
Spend time with friends
Vacation trips
Develop a hobby
Remind yourself to leave work at work
Remind yourself that your reactions are normal
Soothing relaxation activities

- Meditation
- Yoga
- Listening to music
- Getting a massage
- Taking long baths or showers
- Walking your dog
- Doing artwork
- Dancing

Seek self-nourishing spiritual renewal

- Prayer and religion (if applicable)
- Enjoying nature
- Remind yourself of the importance and challenging nature of your work and take pride in your mere efforts to help our traumatized heroes, regardless of the outcome

Figure 5.1 Ideas for self-care

PREVENTING SECONDARY TRAUMA: POLICY, ORGANIZATIONAL, AND PERSONAL STRATEGIES

A variety of recommendations have been made for preventing secondary trauma. Some are at the policy or organizational level; others refer to the clinician's personal strategies (Perlman & Caring, 2009; Zimering et al., 2003).

Policy and Organizational Recommendations in the Civilian Sector

Adequate agency funding is needed to reduce the likelihood of secondary trauma among service providers. It should permit the hiring of well-trained and experienced professionals to treat the most traumatized clients. (In addition to being less likely to becoming overwhelmed by secondary trauma symptoms, such professionals will be more likely provide better services in general.) The funding should enable organizations to avoid burdening any practitioners with caseloads that are too heavy or that are overloaded with too many traumatized clients, especially regarding traumas that are particularly intense or horrific. The office environment should be comfortable, private, and safe. Ample breaks and vacation time should be provided, along with flexible work schedules. The agency should make sure that practitioners are adequately trained for the type of trauma work that they will be doing before they start doing it. Likewise, the organization should ensure that the practitioner receives sufficient, accessible supervision, along with peer-support teams. Supervisors should remember to normalize supervisee reactions to trauma as an occupational hazard (as discussed earlier). They should remind the practitioner that the practitioner's job is to empower the client to heal, not to rescue the client or feel responsible for whether or not the client changes.

Policy and Organizational Recommendations in the Military

According to Colonel Joseph Pecko, former chief of the Army's Soldier and Family Support Branch of the AMEDD Center and School, the most important organizational element is the role and function of military leadership (cited in Pechacek et al., 2011). According to Col. Pecko, military leadership should make the care of military mental health providers a priority and allow providers sufficient dwell time in between deployments or while on duty in order to recover from mentally and or physically arduous tasks. Leaders should embrace an open-door and a "back-door" policy (anonymity) where providers can more comfortably approach their leaders with issues and concerns. Additionally, providers should be treated with respect and dignity and feel a sense of appreciation. Ultimately, leaders set the tone for provider self-care and resiliency by exemplifying a positive attitude and resilience in the face of adversity.

Personal Strategies

The practitioner should remember to respect his or her own limits and to maintain time for self-care activities. Likewise, the practitioner should employ coping strategies for self-nurturing and being socially connected including developing a support system with colleagues who also conduct trauma work. The practitioner should remember to seek professional help if these strategies do not succeed in preventing secondary trauma symptoms from becoming too severe, and they should be alerted to that possibility in their educational training and supervision.

Figure 5.1 lists various ideas for self-care that have been proposed for preventing secondary trauma (Greenwald, 2005; Meichenbaum, 2003; Pearlman & Caringi, 2009; Tyson, 2007; Zimering et al., 2003). The last item in Figure 5.1 is of special importance. It pertains to a concept that is the antithesis of compassion fatigue, and is called *compassion satisfaction*. Tyson (2007, p. 185) defined compassion satisfaction as the clinician's ability "to derive a great sense of meaning and purpose from their work." Compassion satisfaction can serve as a buffer against compassion fatigue among clinicians working with military personnel, especially if the clinicians can keep reminding themselves that there is "a great sense of purpose and meaning working with . . . combatants and their families" (Tyson, 2007, p. 185).

Finally, because stress reactions are thought to occur when emotional demands exceed internal and external resources (Lazarus & Folkman, 1984), ongoing support is therefore needed to bolster compassion satisfaction and decrease the risk for compassion fatigue. Supporting mental health providers can assume many forms: through the organization (or workplace), through peer support, and through individual supervision and/or individual therapy. These forms of external support are crucial (Pardess, 2005). Findings from Israeli trauma volunteer workers at the Selah-Israel Crisis Management Center suggest that the method of minimizing compassion fatigue and maximizing posttraumatic growth (Tedeschi, Park, & Calhoun, 1998) (or we could call it compassion satisfaction) in volunteer trauma workers has to do with nurturing a sense of belonging and connectedness (within the volunteer network) and helping the workers with meaning making as well as providing them with ongoing support. Pardess states, "when volunteers feel part of the team, receive recognition for their efforts, and are involved in decision making, their initial motivation is enhanced and the risk of burnout and secondary trauma is reduced" (p. 617). Although the Selah model is based on volunteer workers, we believe that these tenets are applicable to all professionals working with traumatized clients and that our agencies and our organizations have some lessons to learn from this model.

CONCLUSION

This chapter defines and provides examples of secondary trauma. It also discusses ways to assess, prevent, and treat it. Recommendations are provided at the micro- and macro level of practice, including ideas for the practitioner's own self-care. The chapter notes that it is normal to experience some of the symptoms of secondary trauma when working with returning military combat veterans. So, if you experience *some* such symptoms you should not feel that this reflects negatively on your capability as a practitioner to serve this population or on your emotional stability. The trick, however, is to recognize the symptoms of secondary trauma early and follow the recommendations of this chapter to alleviate the problem and prevent it from hindering your ability to help your clients.

CHAPTER DISCUSSION QUESTIONS

1. What sort of self-care strategies would you employ in working with difficult and or traumatized client populations?
2. In anticipation of working with traumatized veterans, what sort of client problems would you find most difficult to work with? Why?
3. What would you do to prevent compassion fatigue? And how would you recognize it in yourself?
4. How is your organization suited to assisting you in preventing or treating compassion fatigue? Are there systemic risk factors in your place of work? (If you are a student, you can discuss these questions in reference to the settings where you or your classmates have had their field internships.)

REFERENCES

Bride, B. E., Robinson, M. M., Yegidis, B., & Figley, C. R. (2004). Development and validation of the secondary traumatic stress scale. *Research on Social Work Practice, 14*(1), 27–35.

Briere, J., & Spinazzola, J. (2009). Assessment of the sequelae of complex trauma: Evidence-based measures. In C. A. Courtois & J. D. Ford (Eds.), *Treating complex traumatic stress disorders* (pp. 104–123). New York, NY: Guilford Press.

Figley, C. R. (1995). Compassion fatigue as secondary traumatic stress disorder: An overview. In C. R. Figley (Ed.), *Compassion fatigue: Coping with secondary traumatic stress disorder in those who treat the traumatized.* New York, NY: Brunner/Mazel.

Greenwald, R. (2005). *Child trauma handbook.* New York, NY: Haworth Press.

Herman, J. L. (1992). *Trauma and recovery: The aftermath of violence from domestic abuse to political terror.* New York, NY: Basic Books.

Lazarus, R. S., & Folkman, S. (1984). *Stress, appraisal and coping.* New York, NY: Springer.

McCann, I. L., & Pearlman, L. A. (1990). Vicarious traumatization: A framework for understanding the psychological effects of working with victims. *Journal of Traumatic Stress, 3*(2), 131–149.

Meichenbaum, D. (2003). *A clinical handbook/practical therapist manual for assessing and treating adults with PTSD.* Ontario, Canada: Institute Press.

Motta, R. W., Hafeez, S., Sciancalepore, R., & Diaz, A. B. (2001). Discriminant validation of the modified secondary trauma questionnaire. *Journal of Psychotherapy in Independent Practice, 2*(4), 17–25.

Pardess, E. (2005). Training and mobilizing volunteers for emergency response and long-term support. *Journal of Aggression, Maltreatment and Trauma, 10*(1/2), 609–620.

Pearlman, L. A. (1996). Psychometric review of TSI belief scale revision L. In B. H. Stamm (Ed.), *Measurement of stress, trauma and adaptation.* Lutherville, MD: Sidran Press.

Pearlman, L. A., & Caringi, J. (2009). Living and working self-reflectively to address vicarious trauma. In C. A. Courtois & J. D. Ford (Eds.), *Treating complex traumatic stress disorders* (pp. 202–224). New York, NY: Guilford Press.

Pechacek, M. A., Bicknell, G. C., & Landry, L. (2011). *Provider fatigue and provider resiliency training.* In Combat and Operational Health. U.S. Army Medical Department, Borden Institute (pp. 375–389). Retrieved from http://www.bordeninstitute.army.mil/published_volumes/combat_operational/combat.html

Rubin, A., & Springer, D. W. (2009). *Treatment of traumatized adults and children.* Hoboken, NJ: Wiley.

Salston, M. D., & Figley, C. R. (2003). Secondary traumatic stress effects of working with survivors of criminal victimization. *Journal of Traumatic Stress, 16*(2), 167–174.

Stamm, B. H. (1995). *Secondary traumatic stress: Self-care issues for clinicians, researchers and educators.* Lutherville, MD: Sidan Press.

Stamm, B. H. (2005). *The ProQOL manual. The professional quality of life scale: Compassion satisfaction, burnout and compassion fatigue/secondary trauma scales.* Baltimore, MD: Sidran. Available at http://www.proqol.org/ProQOL_Test_Manuals.html

Tedeschi, R., Park, C., & Calhoun, L. (Eds.). (1998). *Posttraumatic growth: Positive changes in the aftermath of crisis*. Mahwah, NJ: Erlbaum.

Tyson, J. (2007). Compassion fatigue in the treatment of combat-related trauma during wartime. *Clinical Social Work Journal, 35*, 183–192.

Zimering, R., Munroe, J., & Gulliver, S. B. (2003). Secondary traumatization in mental health care providers. *Psychiatric Times, 20*(4), 43.

Zimering, R., Munroe, J., & Keane, T. M. (2006). Post traumatic stress disorder in disaster relief workers following direct and indirect trauma exposure to Ground Zero. *Journal of Traumatic Stress, 19*(4), 553–557.

PART

II

Interventions for the Behavioral Health Problems of Service Members and Veterans

CHAPTER

6

Posttraumatic Stress Disorder (PTSD) in Veterans

Jeffrey S. Yarvis

INTRODUCTION

Since the introduction of posttraumatic stress disorder (PTSD) to the psychiatric nomenclature, most research has focused on methods to define, assess, and treat it. However, defining the disorder has been difficult and remains the subject of debate despite the fact that there is a current definition used for diagnosis and classification by the *Diagnostic and Statistical Manual of Mental Disorders*, 4th Edition (*DSM-IV-TR*; American Psychiatric Association [APA], 2000) and by the International Statistical Classification of Diseases and Related Health Problems, 10th Revision (ICD-10; World Health Organization [WHO], 1992). The identification threshold of PTSD is hard to pinpoint and has created a gap in the literature. Research on proper and specific treatments has proved difficult, particularly in combat and in peacekeeping veterans afflicted with PTSD (Shalev, Bonne, & Eth, 1996). According to Forbes, Creamer, Hawthorne, Allen, and McHugh (2003), many studies have reported significant residual symptomatology after treatment and considerable heterogeneity of response to treatment, with the majority of trauma victims (i.e., veterans) gaining little from most models of intervention.

Recent studies by Zlotnick, Franklin, and Zimmerman (2002) and Marshall et al. (2001), suggest a similar problem for using universal diagnoses to conceptualize operational definitions of stressors, stress reactions, and stress-related disorders. The varying qualities of the criteria and the symptoms that make up those criteria expose a "labile, polymorphic" disorder (Solomon, 1993, p. 104). This polymorphic disorder is characterized by high variability when defined in empirical studies and demonstrates rapid changes in temporal manifestations from one period to the next. The heart of the threshold debate lies in the true difficulty of establishing a one-size-fits-all diagnostic yardstick. As with most clinical settings, clinical social workers and military mental health professionals in most armed forces use the standard functional gauge established by the *DSM-IV-TR* (APA, 2000) for the diagnosis and treatment of PTSD.

In this chapter the current *DSM* criteria for PTSD is discussed, followed by a history of the taxonomic evolution of the disorder. This is followed by a discussion of the debate concerning thresholds for diagnosis. Finally, a case example is provided that illustrates a combat veteran suffering from PTSD.

POSTTRAUMATIC STRESS: *DSM* DIAGNOSTIC CRITERIA

The inclusion of PTSD in the third edition of the *Diagnostic and Statistical Manual of Mental Disorders* (*DSM-III*; APA, 1980) marked the formal recognition of a specific syndrome etiologically linked to traumatic events. The diagnostic criteria for PTSD provided a standardized means for assessing the effects of trauma and were initially validated with Vietnam veterans (Zimering, Caddell, Fairbank, & Keane, 1993). With the publication of the *DSM-III* (APA, 1980), the common symptoms experienced by a wide variety of persons were first grouped under a single diagnostic category (van der Kolk, 1996). The *DSM-III* has since undergone three revisions (*DSM-III-R*, *DSM-IV*, and *DSM-IV-TR*). The version of PTSD in the *DSM-IV-TR* (APA, 2000) came about from various sources; first, from a review of the available literature relative to clinical phenomenology, epidemiology, and in relationship to other disorders. That version of the diagnosis was also derived from a series of multisite clinical and community trials (Saigh & Bremner, 1999).

As defined in the *DSV-IV-TR*, PTSD typically develops following exposure to an occurrence that is threatening or is perceived to be threatening to the well-being of oneself or another person; where symptoms are grouped into the following three clusters: reexperiencing the event (e.g., intrusive thoughts), avoidance and emotional numbing (e.g., restricted affect), and hyperarousal (e.g., marked sleep disturbance and hypervigilance). Additionally, to satisfy criteria for diagnosis, a person must have the following symptoms or experiences:

- Exposure to an actual or perceived threat.
- Feelings of intense fear or helplessness.
- At least one reexperiencing symptom.
- At least three avoidance and numbing symptoms.
- At least two hyperarousal symptoms.
- Symptoms must be present for more than one month.
- There must be significant distress or impairment in social, occupational, or other functioning.

(Asmundson, Coons, Taylor, & Katz, 2002)

Recent findings indicate that lifetime PTSD prevalence rates for the general U.S. population are 9.2%; having met criteria for full PTSD and 2.2% having subthreshold PTSD (not meeting the full criteria and defined as having the reexperiencing cluster (B criterion) plus another symptom cluster (C or D symptom criteria) per *DSM IV* (Yarvis, Bordnick, Spivey, & Pedlar, 2005). Thus, the overall rate exceeds 11% (Manzer, 2003), and in certain at-risk groups (e.g., survivors of sexual assault, motor vehicle accidents, and combat), the rates can be substantially higher (APA, 2000). At this writing, veteran PTSD rates from the conflicts in Iraq and Afghanistan are thought to be 12.5% and are somewhat consistent with previous conflicts such as Vietnam at 15% and Desert Storm at 9% to 24% (Hoge et al., 2004; Kulka et al., 1990; Stretch et al., 1996). However, some studies show that two or more deployments could increase rates of PTSD in veterans (Yarvis et al., 2005; Yarvis & Schiess, 2008).

PTSD is unique among psychiatric diagnoses because of the great importance placed upon the etiological agent, that is, the traumatic stressor. In fact, one cannot make a PTSD diagnosis unless the client has actually met the "stressor criterion," which means that he or she has been exposed to a historical event that is considered traumatic. Clinical experience with the PTSD diagnosis has shown, however, that there are individual differences regarding the capacity to cope with catastrophic stress. Therefore, although some people exposed to traumatic events do not develop PTSD, others go on to develop the full-blown syndrome. Such observations have prompted the recognition that trauma, like pain, is not an external phenomenon that can be completely objectified. Like pain, the traumatic experience is filtered through cognitive and emotional processes before it can be appraised as an extreme threat. Because of individual differences in this appraisal process, different people appear to have different trauma thresholds, some more protected from and some more vulnerable to developing clinical symptoms after exposure to extremely stressful situations. Although there is currently a renewed interest in subjective aspects of traumatic exposure, it must be emphasized that events such as rape, torture, genocide, and severe war zone stress can be experienced as traumatic events by nearly everyone. However there are some unique features of PTSD in warrior populations.

PTSD in Combat Veterans

There is growing evidence that physical injury during deployment is associated with a higher prevalence of mental health issues postdeployment. Military personnel are returning from combat with different levels and types of injuries than in previous wars. This is partially due to more rapid and sophisticated medical response on the battlefield and to improved protective equipment such as Kevlar vests. These protect soldiers from mortal internal injuries but not from extremity trauma or concussive brain injuries. Recent studies detailing the most common injuries have found that approximately one half involved the head or neck. The great majority of injuries were due to explosions, and many involve more than one area of the body (polytrauma). Several studies from the Defense and Veteran's Brain Injury Center (DVBIC) of soldiers returning from Afghanistan or Iraq document the occurrence of traumatic brain injury (TBI) in many service personnel. Chapter 10 of this handbook discusses traumatic brain injury in the military in further detail.

A history of experiencing physical injury during deployment is associated with a higher prevalence of PTSD postdeployment. Taber and Hurley (2009) note a recent survey of soldiers following their return from deployment with findings showing that 9% of military personnel who had not been injured while deployed screened positive for PTSD. The rate was almost doubled (16%) in those reporting bodily injury during deployment. This rate is similar to that of past veteran studies assessing the increased risk for PTSD due to combat-related injury, and others report an increased incidence of PTSD per number of injury mechanisms: 14% for one injury, 29% for two, and 51% for three or more (Yarvis et al., 2005). These results are consistent with the incidence of PTSD symptoms following significant orthopedic trauma in civilians. However, what is unique about veterans experiencing TBI is that blast-related loss of consciousness and memory deficits can also contribute to combat-related PTSD (Taber & Hurley, 2009) The nosological boundary between PTSD and TBI is at times elusive; however, studies continue to support current definitions of PTSD.

PTSD now exists as a formalized and clearly defined psychiatric diagnosis. The evolution of the diagnosis highlights the historical, political, and social momentum to normalize an individual's symptoms following adversity. During the formative years of PTSD as a diagnosis many theorists created models to explain stress and embarked on empirical studies that would explore the neurobiology of stress. The following is a terse look at the history and conceptualization of PTSD.

History of PTSD

The diagnosis of PTSD was created to fill a gap in the prevailing psychiatric understanding by acknowledging that extremely traumatic events could produce chronic clinical disorders in normal individuals. The idea that stress could contribute to psychiatric symptoms has its roots in the early disaster literature, and the notion that stress stimulates psychiatric illness in normal individuals predates formal nosologic classifications systems (Kaplan & Sadock, 1998). A chronology of the history behind PTSD is summarized in Figure 6.1.

The Evolution of Contemporary Theories of PTSD

Modern theories of PTSD began with the 19th-century concept of traumatic neurosis. From the middle of the century, railway accidents resulted in increased litigation by injured persons suffering from chronic pain and paralysis. The development of the specialty of neurology initially attributed these apparent neurological deficits to spinal cord injury. However, clinical and autopsy evidence began to accumulate, revealing little correspondence between tissue destruction (usually absent) and degree of disability. By 1885 it was recognized that "railway spine" was a functional or accepted medical disorder (Jones, 1995).

Charcot, a French neurologist, who demonstrated the onset of paralysis and other symptoms in "hysterical" women, suggested to Freud in 1893 a psychological etiology of hysteria (Laughlin, 1967). Charcot retained his belief in the prevailing idea of a neurological cause of hysteria and its manifestations. In 1889, Charcot's student, Oppenheim, coined the term *traumatic neurosis* to describe what he believed was a "molecular derangement" of nerve tissue (Robitscher, 1971). Initially Freud accepted this notion, postulating with Breuer in their work, *Studies in Hysteria*, an organic hypnoid state that made a person vulnerable to hysterical symptoms when stimulated by a traumatic event (Strachey & Freud, 1957). Freud held that the traumatic event in hysteria was sexual trauma. Later, he postulated that fantasized sexual trauma could produce hysteria (Freud, 1955a). Additionally, Freud attributed war neurosis to conflicts in ego structures (i.e., id, ego, and superego) and instinctual drives (libido and destrudo; the urges to create and destroy, respectively) (Freud, 1955b).

1666	Diary of Samuel Pepys captures his posttraumatic reactions to the Great Fire of London.
1812	Combat stress reactions among Swiss soldiers documented by Napoleon's field surgeons.
1865	Military surgeons document combat trauma as Da Costa's syndrome, nostalgia, or soldier's irritable heart.
1885	Charcot recognizes that "railway spine" was a functional disorder characterized by paralysis and chronic pain after railway accidents.
1889	Oppenheim coins the term "traumatic neurosis" to describe a "molecular derangement of nerve tissue."
1893	Freud suggests that paralysis and other neurotic symptoms in women were antecedents to "hysteria."
1919	Frederick Mott and Ernest Southard document the neurological and psychological effects of war. "Shell shock" described by T.W. Salmon.
1943	Adler describes "post-traumatic mental complications" in the survivors of the Boston Cocoanut Grove Fire.
1945	Grinker and Spiegel enumerates symptoms of "combat neuroses" in "returnees" from World War II.
1952	*DSM-I* with diagnosis of Gross Stress Reaction addressed the "severe physical demands or extreme stress such as in combat or in civilian catastrophe" (p. 40) in response to problems observed in survivors of World War II.
1962	Buchenwald Syndrome documented in concentration camp survivors.
1968	The APA's Committee on Nomenclature and Statistics omits gross stress reaction and introduces "transient situational disturbance" in the *DSM-II*.
1974	Burgess and Holmstrom introduce the idea of Rape Trauma Syndrome.
1975	Delayed Stress Syndrome introduced by Horowitz and Solomon after study of veterans who had served in Southeast Asia.
1980	Posttraumatic stress disorder established in the *DSM-III*.
1987	*DSM-III-R*.
1992	ICD 10 establishes different criteria for posttraumatic reaction than *DSM-III-R*.
1994	Acute stress disorder established along with *DSM-IV*.
2000	DESNOS—Disorder of Extreme Stress Not Otherwise Specified established in *DSM-IV-TR*.

Figure 6.1 Chronology of the historical roots of posttraumatic stress disorder

The idea that psychological trauma could produce apparent physical disabilities became generally recognized, especially with the appearance of numerous "shell shock" casualties during World War I (Salmon, 1929). The pendulum swung from considering traumatic neuroses as neurologically based to considering them to be of purely psychological causation. Eventually traumatic neurosis was mostly subsumed under conversion or somatoform disorders, but many individuals whose symptoms took the form of mood and behavioral disturbances did not fit this categorization (Jones, 1995).

Investigators who studied psychiatric casualties in World War II combat veterans variously labeled the constellation of symptoms they saw as "traumatic war neurosis" (Kardiner & Spiegel, 1947), "combat exhaustion" (Swank, 1949), and "operational fatigue" (Grinker et al., 1946, I., II.). Whatever the label, it is clear that these investigators were seeing a condition much like what we now recognize as PTSD. For example, Kardiner and Spiegel described a chronic syndrome that included preoccupation with the traumatic stressor, nightmares, irritability, increased startle responsiveness, a tendency to angry outbursts, and general impairment of functioning. Many investigators attempted to determine the etiology of the syndrome by asking veterans about their premilitary home life and postwar adjustment as well as their experiences in combat. Grinker et al. (1946) found that air crew officers with "operational fatigue" were more likely than combat controls to report premilitary anxieties and neurotic trends and reported having experienced more symptoms while in combat. Similar findings were seen in enlisted flying personnel (Grinker et al., 1946, II.). In addition, parental discord, broken homes, and parental alcoholism (factors not assessed in the officers) were more likely in the enlisted men with operational fatigue. Swank (1949) found some evidence of premilitary personality disturbance in his study of more than 2,000 cases of "combat exhaustion," but also found that amount of combat exposure (e.g., unit casualty rate) predicted symptoms. He counseled against viewing cases of combat exhaustion as resulting entirely from either premilitary personality instability or combat stressors.

Follow-up studies of World War II veterans continued into the 1950s, when veterans of the Korean conflict were included as a comparison group in some investigations; they rarely have been studied on their own. A theme of chronicity began to emerge. Futterman and Pumpian-Mindlin (1951) reported a 10% prevalence of traumatic war neurosis in a series of 200 psychiatric patients in 1950. They noted as significant the fact that many of the men had not sought treatment even 5 years after the war. Brill and Beebe (1955) reported continuing impairment of functioning in a sample of almost 1,500 veterans who had been discharged for "psychoneurosis" in World War II, almost half of whom were combat casualties. Archibald et al. (1962) found World War II combat veterans with "gross stress syndrome" to have severe problems such as increased startle, sleep disturbance, and avoidance of activities reminiscent of combat. A follow-up of these men (Archibald & Tuddenham, 1965) that included Korean conflict veterans showed the same symptom profile and relatively more symptoms than in noncombat psychiatric patients or in combat controls. The Archibald studies are notable for their use of the Minnesota Multiphasic Personality Inventory, MMPI (www.ptsdsupport.net/ptsd_MMPI-2-test.html), which showed combat veterans to be elevated on the depression, hysteria, and hypochondriasis scales and to differ from noncombat psychiatric patients on 47 items.

Dobbs and Wilson (1960) reported an interesting experiment that foreshadowed current laboratory studies on the psychophysiological correlates of PTSD. They exposed World War II veterans with combat-related psychiatric symptoms, healthy combat controls from World War II and the Korean conflict, and nonveterans to audiotapes of combat sounds. Combat controls showed greater pulse, respiration, and EEG responsiveness to the stimuli than did nonveterans. The combat-symptoms group was so unable to tolerate the sounds that physiological recordings could not be made. Dobbs and Wilson commented on the chronicity of combat fatigue and discussed its similarity to animal models of neurosis.

Few studies of World War II or Korean conflict veterans were performed in the 1970s, when articles about Vietnam veterans began to emerge. The exceptions seemed to focus on prisoners of war (POW). For example, Klonoff et al. (1976) reported on the MMPI profiles of POWs and Beebe (1975) reported on POWs physical and mental health. Most studies indicated that prisoners interned by the Japanese or Koreans were more symptomatic than those interned by the Germans.

After the formalization of PTSD as a diagnosis, isolated case studies began calling attention to the fact that some veterans of wars prior to Vietnam had PTSD. Van Dyke, Zilberg, & Mckinnon (1985) reported on a World War II combat veteran who had been well functioning until a medically necessary retirement at age 53, when he began to experience combat nightmares for the first time. Subsequent to further medical problems, the man developed PTSD.

For veterans of World War II, PTSD would have been viewed as traumatic war neurosis. It was seen as occurring among combatants in a combat area with a relatively high degree of frequency. Focal points would be on guilt about killing or assailing defenseless enemy personnel, either military or civilian, as an important factor in the precipitation of a traumatic war neurosis. Traumatic war neurosis was also seen as occurring in conjunction with physical injury. An overidealization of the pretraumatic history was viewed as occurring in cases of traumatic war neurosis. The monotonous repetition of the traumatic war experiences and combat dreams in cases of traumatic war neurosis was seen as being caused by the transformation of the world into a threatening place.

Veterans of Vietnam were often pathologized for both psychological and sociological reasons. PTSD was coined during that war, and it was noticed that its veterans exhibited more severe PTSD symptoms and higher scores on measures of depression, hostility, and psychoticism than veterans of the past. They also had more survivor guilt, impairment of work and response, derealization, and suicidal tendencies. Vietnam veterans had a greater lifetime frequency of panic disorder and an earlier age of onset for alcoholism. Like World War II veterans, Vietnam veterans experienced an emergence of psychiatric diagnoses after the war. Today the signs and symptoms of PTSD are described in terms of an anxiety disorder (APA, 1980, 1987, 1994, 2000).

PSYCHOSOCIAL MODELS OF POSTTRAUMATIC STRESS

Change in the conceptualization of PTSD has created research barriers. One notable discrepancy pertains to the nature and sources of normal and traumatic stress; specifically, how the construct of stress is conceptualized and operationalized (Bride, 2001; Danieli, 1998; Danieli, Rodley, & Weisaeth, 1996; Lamerson & Kelloway, 1996; Lewis, 2003). The following section provides a brief, general overview of explanatory theories or psychosocial models that are frequently associated with posttraumatic stress.

Traditional psychodynamic models of posttraumatic stress have been used to explain the process of stress transmission and traumatization. Psychodynamic theory examines the extent to which a traumatic incident influences a person's perception of self or others. This model seeks to characterize environmental factors that influence subsequent stress response, such as the importance of early childhood trauma and early psychological conflicts (Krystal, 1988). Affective responses result when conscious or unconscious representations of oneself or others are altered by trauma, resulting in conflict ridden representations of self and others. Traumatized individuals then mobilize their psychological defenses to cope with these discrepant meanings and emotions. With time, trauma responses continue, and the individual may regress to using primitive defenses, including splitting (e.g., either thinking people are good or bad) and dissociation (Marmar et al., 1994). The trauma victim will lose control of the sense of self and have affective instability. Unresolved early conflicts may evoke traumas from earlier developmental periods associated with attachment and protection issues, thereby reactivating the traumatic effects. Consequently, maladaptive coping pushes the trauma victim to repeat maladaptive relationship patterns, resulting in unstable interpersonal relationships (Resick, 2001).

A variety of psychodynamically oriented treatment approaches have been provided to clients with PTSD, including individual and group therapy in different institutional settings. The problem with this model and its associated therapies is that no obvious thread ties together the different psychodynamic interventions, and no systematic rationale connects the type of therapy to PTSD (Rothbaum & Foa, 1996).

In the 20th century one of the most important influences in the study of stress was the work of Hans Seyle, a physiologist and physician. Seyle introduced the General Adaptation Syndrome model in 1936 showing in three phases what the alleged effects of stress has on the body. The earliest conception of stress was defined as a response. Response-based theories of stress stem from Seyle's early medical research, which noted that stress was a "nonspecific response of the body to any demand placed on it" (Seyle, 1956, p. 1). Seyle observed that any adverse event could trigger a biological response. Seyle's definition was guided by his medical research in which he categorized common responses to a variety of events termed *stressors*. The stress response, which he described as a general adaptation syndrome, was characterized by many of the precursors to the vegetative symptoms of affective disorders, such as melancholy, loss of motivation, loss of appetite, and loss of energy. Underlying his presuppositions was the assumption that stress symptoms were somewhat universal and could therefore be generalized to the nature of the stressor (Lewis, 2003). Seyle described the general adaptation syndrome as being comprised of three stages: alarm and mobilization, resistance, and exhaustion. In the first stage, the autonomic nervous system (ANS) and the endocrine system are engaged as a sympathetic reaction to the "fight-or-flight" response (Cannon, 1914). This sympathetic response causes muscle groups and respiratory and circulatory systems to give the body additional energy to respond under acute stress situations. During the second stage, the body's physiological responses continue as long as necessary to combat the effects of the stressors. In the third stage, the body is fatigued from operating at this sustained high-energy level and comes down from this level as stressors subside. Seyle's conceptualization of stress was a foundation for the incorporation of the biological model, the transactional theory of stress, and learning theories associated with stress as applied to models of posttraumatic stress. The evolution of these models will be described in the following section.

The biological model is not a new concept in the study of trauma. In 1918, Meakins and Wilson studied the physiological responses of shell-shocked veterans. Kardiner (1941) labeled traumatic stress as *physioneurosis*, identifying a connection between psychological and physiological responses to stress. When researchers began studying traumatic stress and PTSD, they made the assumption that the biological processes would reflect normal responses to stress as later conceptualized in Seyle's (1956) General Adaptation Syndrome. However, while the normal stress response is an acute reaction that rapidly reverts to homeostasis, the biological responses to PTSD reflect chronic or potentially permanent changes with increasing reactivity over time.

Studies utilizing the biological model of PTSD made such conclusions possible. Biological studies have allowed for independent tests of the distinctness of the disorder and its similarity to neurobiological changes observed following traumatic events. For example, one of the major symptom clusters of PTSD is associated with physiological reactivity (i.e., hypervigilance). Thus, a number of studies have been conducted using arousal as a marker for PTSD, with research targeting automatic nervous system (ANS) activity, heart rate, respiration, and blood pressure in traumatized groups (mostly Vietnam veterans) and nontraumatized (control) groups. In early studies, a number of investigations did find that PTSD subjects had higher heart rates and states of arousal than non-PTSD groups (Adler, 1943; Meakins & Wilson, 1918; Salmon, 1929). However, more recent studies have found this not to be the case (Pittman, Orr, Forgue, Altman, & deJong, 1990; Prins, Kaloupek, & Keane, 1995; Shalev, Freedman, & Peri, 1998).

In reviewing studies of baseline arousal, Prins et al. (1995), observed that there were a number of methodological differences that could account for these findings. Further comparisons to other anxiety disorders found that there were no differences (Pittman et al., 1990). Other shortcomings of the biological model were noted. Prins et al. (1995) suggested that rather than a biological difference, these investigations were picking up greater anticipatory anxiety in subjects with PTSD or other forms of anxiety than healthy comparison subjects. Shalev et al. (1998) looked at several variables associated with PTSD in a controlled study. They confirmed Seyle's idea about increased heart rate; however, they observed that other biological responses to acute stress might condition an individual to adapt to the alarm response and that coronary responses did not serve to maintain the PTSD symptoms over time in the majority of PTSD cases.

Numerous transactional theories challenge Seyle's assumptions. For example, Lazarus and Folkman (1984) assert that response-based conceptualizations do not provide a theoretical foundation to derive potential stressors or describe PTSD, observing a lack of systematic ways to prospectively identify stressors. Cooper, Dewe, and O'Driscoll (2001) argued that theories emphasizing the stress response ignore important contextual and environmental factors, such as intensity, frequency, and duration of the stimulus, often discussed in the PTSD literature (Lerner, 1976, 1991; Robinson & Lee, 2000). Lazarus and Folkman (1984) believed that there is no objective way to predict psychological stress without reference to properties of the individual in their context. To date, however, there is no empirical investigation that supports the transactional stress model. Despite the lack of empirical evidence, Lazarus and Folkman's response-based definitions of stress do have heuristic value in the overall traumatic stress literature by describing taxonomies of common physiological (van der Kolk, 1996), psychological (Solomon, 1993), and behavioral stress reactions (Rothbaum & Foa, 1996).

The diathesis-stress model is an amalgam of all the models discussed. In the strictest sense, it purports that individuals are genetically vulnerable (diathesis), or have had early childhood experiences or brain abnormalities that render them vulnerable to psychological trauma (stress) (Deykin & Buka, 1997). The attraction to genetic investigations of PTSD is compelling. This research attempts to explain individual predispositions to traumatization and different patterns of stress response. Although there is increasing genetic evidence that parents that suffer from PTSD render children vulnerable to PTSD (Danieli, 1998), without evidentiary support for intergenerational transmission there should be concerns about overestimating genetic factors associated with PTSD.

Although there are numerous psychosocial theories advancing and explaining the etiology of PTSD, behavioral models have the strongest evidentiary support and are more widely accepted in the scientific community than the other models (Bisson, Jenkins, Alexander & Bannister, 1997; Devilly & Spence, 1999). The behavioral model of PTSD, as posited by Keane, Zimering, and Caddell (1985), puts forth that traumatized individuals acquire conditioned fears of a wide variety of trauma-related stimuli. Subsequently, they avoid these stimuli. Through the processes of higher-order conditioning and stimulus generalization, the number of feared stimuli continues to increase even after the trauma has occurred. For example, if a veteran witnessed and smelled burning bodies after a firefight, they might experience a trauma reaction to grilled chicken at a barbeque and begin to fear or avoid previously unconditioned stimuli such as barbeques.

The cognitive model of PTSD articulated by Foa, Steketee, and Rothbaum (1989) suggests that PTSD occurs when the traumatic incident reinforces negative beliefs concerning a client's safety and competence. Individuals with PTSD subscribe to the cognitive distortion that the world is a dangerous place and therefore live their lives in constant fear. These individuals may also perceive themselves as incompetent and are unlikely to confront challenging situations. According to this model, PTSD progresses and/or is maintained when actual trauma or threat-related material receives preferential information processing by an individual over less-threatening information. Maladaptive processing of this kind leads to distorted ways of perceiving and comprehending their environment (Lilienfeld, Lynn, & Lohr, 2003).

Scientific research has revealed a number of efficacious treatment procedures for the amelioration of PTSD symptoms. Most are based on behavioral models and involve procedures that have withstood rigorous scientific experimentation. By the same token, there are a number of models that possess terminology associated with science, but are not based on empirically supported scientific theory. These models failed to withstand empirical scrutiny and determine the results of their effects. As a result, poorly supported models pose a threat to the understanding of the classification of PTSD and cloud understanding of the extent of impairment caused by PTSD.

Case Vignette: SSG Brown

SSG Brown is a 27-year-old male who has been honorably discharged from the U.S. Army after serving in active combat in Iraq. SSG Brown is Latino, married, has two children, and is employed by a leading national retailer and he attends college classes. He joined the Army 2 days after 9/11. He was a soldier for nearly 9 years and served in the initial ground invasion of Baghdad in 2003, when the military still had much to learn about the signature injuries of the war, PTSD and TBI.

In Iraq, he sustained head and shoulder wounds in combat, ending his service as a highly decorated member of a scout platoon. SSG Brown has received outpatient treatment for the symptoms of PTSD. Like many returning warriors, SSG Brown faced an uncertain future regarding work and lifestyle after separating from the military. He said, "I had no idea of what I was going to do or how I was going to fit in or live in the general population." This uncertainty extended to core values, such as family, with SSG Brown stating "my kids didn't even know who I was." There was, however, clearly a sense of vocational duty in that his military training and experience were exemplary and had application in such disciplines as police work. Yet, this opportunity of interest was elusive, if not impossible, due to physical injuries incurred in combat. In fact, today's warriors experience much higher survival rates (more than 90% in OIF/OEF versus 80% in the Persian Gulf and 67% in Vietnam), but SSG Brown was left with the existential question of competency in the world postinjury and wondering if he should have survived.

SSG Brown desired to return to the familiar in Iraq. He missed the strong sense of meaning and purpose found in the war zone, the ability to protect his battle buddies, and the excitement associated with combat environments. The absence of the combat rush led SSG Brown to attempt to create a similar reaction by, for example, riding motorcycles with fellow veterans at speeds in excess of 165 mph on deserted stretches of highway, or by numbing the desire through excessive alcohol consumption. Regardless, with SSG Brown there always existed a sense of responsibility and propriety, where, for example, he and his group adhered to posted speed limits in school zones "[We] didn't want to hurt any kids." With Brown one can see the complex interplay of rules adapted for combat that do not readily work in U.S. society upon return.

SSG Brown was treated for PTSD. His symptoms included flashbacks, night sweats, insomnia, agitation, and hypervigilance. Other conditions stemming from PTSD include drinking or drug problems, feelings of hopelessness, employment problems, and relationship problems. SSG Brown was at risk for developing a drinking problem and was having difficulty adjusting to his home life in the "new normal." Recent returnees show increased risks of new-onset heavy drinking and other alcohol-related problems among personnel deployed with combat exposures as compared to those non-deployed. These behaviors are often explained as efforts to self-soothe or self-medicate to offset the hypervigilance symptoms such as anger, increased startle response, and marked sleep disturbance.

Additionally, Latinos may be greater risk of PTSD and readjustment compounded by traditional ethnic issues. As a consequence this population may subsequently have greater readjustment concerns.

Reintegration is a process, not a single event. Carter and McGoldrick (2005) discuss family systems moving through time rather than in cycles so as a member of the family's trajectory of experience changes, so does the family's life course. Returning warriors often have difficulty being around children as can be seen in SSG Brown's situation. Veterans with PTSD symptoms have greater interpersonal problems (e.g., difficulties expressing intimacy, lack of sociability), and poorer marital and family relationships as well. SSG Brown described engaging in other risk behaviors such as driving fast. It is important to note that hypervigilance causes adaptations that might be functional in the combat zone but not in one's civilian life. SSG Brown described missing the "rush" associated with combat. In addition to combat-driving on the highway at home he also was engaging in fast-driving cars and motorcycles that had more to do with missing the rush than the response generalization of combat adaptations. Soldiers returning to garrison life after extended combat deployments may have difficulty adjusting, and may seek the adrenaline "rush" they have grown accustomed to in combat environments. Social workers must be cognizant of the need to help warriors like SSG Brown adjust back to duties in the "rear" on post or base as well as manage the symptoms of PTSD. In addition the provider must address the complex interplay of the warrior ethos and sense of duty, with the warrior's role in the family and sense of purpose.

Case Vignette Discussion Questions:

1. Discuss what you know about the case and possible resources for SSG Brown and his family.
2. What are the societal, cultural, and community contexts of the case?
3. What are elements of SSG Brown's world that could serve to maintain his problems?
4. How would you address the maintenance of problems?
5. What else would you want to know about the case and about SSG Brown's situation to develop a better understanding of him?

CONCLUSION

In the simplest terms, PTSD is discussed through each model as a stress response. When evaluating each model's conceptualization of how symptoms move from the abstract to the observable, consider that PTSD includes processes that: (a) attenuate and perpetuate maladaptive and prolonged psychological stress responses within the individual, observed as anxiety, tension, and levels of distress; and (b) appear to maintain maladaptive psychobiological processes. These processes include hyperarousal, hypervigilance, startle responses, sleep disturbance, cognitive distortions, and affective instability ranging on a continuum from anger to depression to varied forms of anxiety. For each of the models pertaining to PTSD, it is important that the processes can be both observed and measured.

Studies relying on unproven models of traumatic stress and dependence on the current diagnostic classification of posttraumatic stress disorder led to neglected study of posttraumatic sequelae that fall short of full criteria for PTSD. In a military population it is important to look at the full continuum of trauma-related care. Recent research demonstrates in military samples that PTSD may be best understood as a war-induced trauma spectrum disorder where all aspects of trauma to include so-called subthreshold posttraumatic disorders should be considered when educating, treating, and researching veterans (Yarvis et al., 2005; Yarvis & Schiess, 2008).

This chapter reviews the history of how PTSD has been defined, which models of PTSD best capture the construct, and the prevalence of PTSD. This review focuses on empirically supported studies of PTSD in various populations and empirically supported models that best describe it. As detailed in this chapter, numerous models of stress attempted to capture the process of PTSD and define the boundary between normal and pathological trauma responses, including, but not limited to, psychodynamic, general adaptation syndrome, biological, transactional, and behavioral, and various combinations of these models. Despite past and current research, empirical support for clear definitions of PTSD is still lacking

(Lilienfeld et al., 2003). Currently, there appears to be more pseudoscience than science with regard to conceptualizing PTSD and the diagnostic cutoffs separating normal stress responses from maladaptive stress responses (Lewis, 2003; Lilienfeld et al., 2003; Yarvis et al., 2005; Yarvis & Schiess, 2008; Yarvis & Spivey, 2003). Indeed, there is no consensus on a model, and many models exist to explain PTSD in only one particular population, such as veterans (Bartone & Asler, 1998; Goodwin, 1987; Lamerson & Kelloway, 1996; Weisaeth, 1994). Solomon (1993) called PTSD a labile-polymorphic disorder because the diagnostic yardstick and reliance on categorical models of PTSD do not fully explain the experience of the veteran. In an extensive review of the trauma literature, no one explanatory model or classification of PTSD has been scientifically proven to be predictive of clinical impairment in veterans.

This chapter also explores the history of views of the etiology of PTSD. It presents several models that served to explain how PTSD evolves and affects warriors.

CHAPTER DISCUSSION QUESTIONS

1. What beliefs and perceptions did you have about PTSD and about veterans before reading this chapter, and how did they change after reading this chapter?
2. How does the veteran experience compare and contrast to the civilian experience in general and with trauma?
3. In what ways is PTSD considered to be unique among psychiatric diagnoses?

REFERENCES

Adler, A. (1943). Neuropsychiatric complications in victims of Boston's Coconut Grove disaster. *Journal of the American Medical Association, 123*, 1098–1101.

American Psychiatric Association. (1980). *Diagnostic and statistical manual of mental disorders* (3rd ed.). Washington, DC: Author.

American Psychiatric Association. (1987). *Diagnostic and statistical manual of mental disorders* (3rd ed., rev.). Washington, DC: Author.

American Psychiatric Association. (1994). *Diagnostic and statistical manual of mental disorders* (4th ed.). Washington, DC: Author.

American Psychiatric Association. (2000). *Diagnostic and statistical manual of mental disorders* (4th ed., text rev.). Washington, DC: Author.

Archibald, H. C., Long, D. M., Miller, C., Tuddenham, R. D. (1962). Gross stress reaction in combat: A 15-year follow-up. *American Journal of Psychiatry, 119*(18), 317–322.

Archibald, H. C., & Tuddenham, R. D. (1965). Persistent stress reaction after combat. *Archives of General Psychiatry, 12*, 475–481.

Asmundson, G. J. G., Coons, M. J., Taylor, S., & Katz, J. (2002). PTSD and the experience of pain: Research and clinical implications of shared vulnerability and mutual maintenance models. *Canadian Journal of Psychiatry, 47*(10), 930–937.

Bartone, M. P. T., & Asler, A. B. (1998). Dimensions of psychological stress in peacekeeping operations. *Military Medicine, 163*(9), 587–593.

Bisson, J. I., Jenkins, P. L., Alexander, J., & Bannister, C. (1997). A randomized controlled trial of psychological debriefing for victims of acute harm. *British Journal of Psychiatry, 171*, 78–81.

Beebe, G.W. (1975). Follow-up studies of World War II and Korean War prisoners, II: Morbidity, disability, and maladjustments. *American Journal of Epidemiology, 101*, 400–422.

Bride, B. E. (2001). *Psychometric properties of the secondary traumatic stress scale.* Unpublished doctoral dissertation, University of Georgia, Athens, Georgia.

Brill, N. Q., & Beebe, G. W. (1995). *A follow-up study of war neuroses.* Washington, DC: U.S. Government Printing office, xviii, 410 (pp. 26–55).

Cannon, W. B. (1914) The emergency function of the adrenal medulla in pain and the major emotions. *American Journal of Physiology, 33*, 356–372.

Carter, B., & McGoldrick, M. (2005). *The expanded family life cycle: Individual, family, and social perspectives* (3rd ed.). Columbus, OH: Allyn & Bacon.

Cooper, C. L., Dewe, P. J., & O'Driscoll, M. P. (2001). *Organizational stress: A review and critique of theory, research, and applications.* Thousand Oaks, CA: Sage.

Danieli, Y. (Ed.). (1998). *International handbook of multigenerational legacies of trauma.* New York, NY: Plenum Press.

Danieli, Y., Rodley, N., & Weisaeth, L. (Eds.). (1996). *International responses to traumatic stress.* Amityville, NY: Baywood.

Devilly, G. J., & Spence, S. H. (1999). The relative efficacy and treatment distress of EMDR and a cognitive behavioral trauma treatment protocol in the amelioration of posttraumatic stress disorder. *Journal of Anxiety Disorders, 13*, 131–157.

Deykin, E. Y., & Buka, S. L. (1997). Prevalence and risk factors for posttraumatic stress disorder among chemically dependent adolescents. *American Journal of Psychiatry, 154*, 752–757.

Dobbs, D. & Wilson, W. P. (1960). Observations on persistence of war neurosis. *Diseases of the Nervous System*, 21,686–691.

Foa, E. B., Rothbaum, B. O., & Furr, J. M. (2003). Augmenting exposure therapy with other CBT procedures. *Psychiatric Annals, 33*(1), 47–53.

Foa, E. B., Steketee, G., & Rothbaum, (1989). Behavioral cognitive conceptualizations of post-traumatic stress disorder. *Behavior Therapy*, 20, 155–176.

Forbes, D., Creamer, M., Hawthorne, G., Allen, N., & McHugh, T. (2003). Comorbidity as a predictor of symptoms change after treatment in combat-related posttraumatic stress disorder. *Journal of Nervous and Mental Disease, 191*(2), 93–99.

Freud, S. (1955a). Beyond the pleasure principle. In J. Strachey (Ed.), *Beyond the pleasure principle, group psychology, and other works (1920–1922)* (Vol. 18, pp. 3–64). London, UK: Hogarth Press.

Freud, S. (1955b). The war neurosis. In J. Strachey (Ed.), *An infantile neurosis and other works (1917–1919)* (Vol. 17, pp. 3–64). London, UK: Hogarth Press.

Friedman M., Resick. P., Bryant, R., & Brewin, C. (2011). Considering PTSD for DSM-5. *Depression & Anxiety, 28*, 750–769.

Futterman, S., & Pumpian-Mindlan, E. (1951). Traumatic war neuroses five year later. *American Journal of psychiatry*, *108*, 401–408.

Goodwin, J. (1987). The etiology of combat-related traumatic stress disorders. In T. Williams (Ed.), *Post-traumatic stress disorders: A handbook for clinicians* (pp. 1–18). Cincinnati, OH: Disabled American Veterans.

Grinker, R.R., Willerman, B., Bradley, A.D. & Fastovsky, A. (1946). A study of psychological predisposition to the development of operational fatigue: II. In enlisted flying personnel. *American Journal of Orthopsychiatry*, 16, 207–214.

Hoge, C. W., Castro, C. A., Messer, S. C., McGurk, D., Cotting, D. I., & Koffman, R. L. (2004). Combat duty in Iraq and Afghanistan, mental health problems, and barriers to care. *New England Journal of Medicine*, *351*, 13–22.

Jones, F. D. (1995). Chronic post-traumatic stress disorder. In F. D. Jones, L. R. Sparacino, V. L. Wilcox, J. M. Rothberg, & J. W. Stokes (Eds.), *War psychiatry* (Part I, pp. 411–430). Bethesda, MD: Office of the Surgeon General of the United States Army.

Kaplan, H. I., & Sadock, B. J. (Eds.). (1998). *Synopsis of psychiatry* (8th ed.). Baltimore, MD: Williams & Wilkins.

Kardiner, A. (1941). The traumatic neuroses of war. *Psychosomatic medicine monographs*, *1*(2 & 3).

Kardiner, Abram: and Spiegel, Herbert. (1947). *War, stress and neurotic illness*. New York, NY: Paul Hoeber.

Keane, T. M., Zimering, R. T., & Caddell, J. M. (1985). A behavioral formulation of posttraumatic stress disorder in Vietnam combat veterans. *Behavior Therapy*, *20*, 245–260.

Klkonoff, H. Clark, C., Horgan, J., Kramer, P., & McDougall, G. (1976). The MMPI profile of prisoners of war. *Journal of Clinical Psychology*, *32*(3), 623–627.

Krystal, H. (1988). *Integration and self-healing: Affect, trauma, alexithymia*. Hillsdale, NJ: Analytic Press.

Kulka, R. A., Schlenger, W. E., Fairbank, J. A., Hough, R. L., Jordan, B. K., Marmar, C. R., & Weiss, D. S. (1990). *Trauma and the Vietnam war generation: Report of findings from the national Vietnam veterans readjustment study*. New York, NY: Brunner/Mazel.

Lamerson, C. D., & Kelloway, E. K. (1996). Towards a model of peacekeeping stress: Traumatic and contextual influences. *Canadian Psychology*, *37*(4), 195–204.

Laughlin, H. P. (1967). *The neuroses*. Baltimore, MD: Butterfield Press.

Lazarus, R. S., & Folkman, S. (1984). *Stress, appraisal and coping*. New York, NY: Springer.

Lerner, R. M. (1976). *Concepts and theories of human development*. Reading, MA: Addison-Wesley.

Lerner, R. M. (1991). Changing organism-content relations as the basic process of development: A developmental contextual perspective. *Developmental Psychology*, *27*, 27–32.

Lewis, S. J. (2003). *A multi-level, longitudinal study of strain reducing effects of group efficacy, group cohesion, and leader behaviors on military personnel performing peacekeeping operations*. Unpublished Doctoral dissertation, Florida State University, Tallahassee, Florida.

Lewis, S. J. (2003). Do one-shot preventive interventions for PTSD work: A systematic research synthesis of psychological debriefings. *Aggression and Violent Behavior*, *8*(3), 329–343.

Lilienfeld, S. O., Lynn, S. J., & Lohr, J. M. (Eds.). (2003). *Science and pseudoscience in clinical psychology*. New York, NY: Guilford Press.

Litz, B. T., & Keane, T. M. (1989). Information processing in anxiety disorders: Application to the understanding of post-traumatic stress disorder. *Clinical Psychology Review, 9*, 243–257.

Manzer, J. (2003). APA: Post-traumatic stress plaguing Canadians. Study reveals prevalence higher than in U.S. *Medical Post, 39*(22).

Marmar, C. R., Weiss, D. S., Schlenger, W. E., Fairbank, J. A., Jordan, B. K., Kulka, R. A., Hough, R. L. (1994). Peritraumatic dissociation and post-traumatic stress in male Vietnam theater veterans. *American Journal of Psychiatry, 151*, 902–907.

Marshall, R. D., Olfson, M., Hellman, F., Blanco, C., Guardino, M., & Struening, E. L. (2001). Comorbidity, impairment and suicidality in subthreshold PTSD. *American Journal of Psychiatry, 158*, 1467–1473.

Meakins, J. C., & Wilson, R. M. (1918). The effect of certain sensory stimulation on the respiratory rate in case of so-called "irritable heart." *Heart, 7*, 17–22.

Pittman, R., Orr, S., Forgue, D., Altman, B., & deJong, J. (1990). Psychophysiologic responses to combat imagery of Vietnam veterans with posttraumatic stress disorder versus other anxiety disorders. *Journal of Abnormal Psychology, 99*, 49–54.

Prins, A., Kaloupek, D. G., & Keane, T. M. (1995). Psychophysiological evidence for autonomic arousal and startle in traumatized adult populations. In M. J. Friedman, D. S. Charney, & A. Y. Deutch (Eds.), *Neurobiological and clinical consequences of stress: From normal adaptation to post-traumatic stress disorder*. Philadelphia, PA: Lippincott-Raven.

Resick, P. A. (2001). *Stress and trauma*. East Essex, UK: Psychology Press.

Robinson, M., & Lee, H. (2000). Developmental contextualism. *International Journal of Welfare for the Aged, 3*, 44–60.

Robitscher, J. (1971). Mental suffering and traumatic neurosis. In J. J. Leedy (Ed.), *Compensation in psychiatric disability and rehabilitation* (p. 233). Springfield, IL: Thomas.

Rothbaum, B. O., & Foa, E. B. (1996). Cognitive-behavioral therapy for posttraumatic stress disorder. In B. A. van der Kolk, A. C. McFarlane, & L. Weisaeth (Eds.), *Traumatic stress: The effects of overwhelming experience on mind, body, and society* (pp. 491–509). New York, NY: Guilford Press.

Saigh, P. A., & Bremner, D. J. (Eds.). (1999). *Posttraumatic stress disorder: A comprehensive reference*. Boston, MA: Allyn & Bacon.

Salmon, T. W. (1929). The care and treatment of mental diseases and war neurosis ("shell shock") in the British Army. In P. Bailey, F. E. Williams, P. A. Komora, T. W. Salmon, & N. Fenton (Eds.), *Neuropsychiatry* (Vol. 10, Appendix pp. 497–523). Washington, DC: Office of the Surgeon General of the United States Army.

Seyle, H. (1956). *The stress of life*. (Vol. 2nd ed.). New York, NY: McGraw-Hill.

Shalev, A. Y., Bonne, O., & Eth, S. (1996). Treatment of posttraumatic stress disorder: A review. *Psychosomatic Medicine, 58*, 165–182.

Shalev, A. Y., Freedman, S., & Peri, T. (1998). Prospective study of posttraumatic stress disorder and depression following trauma. *American Journal of Psychiatry, 155*, 630–637.

Solomon, Z. (1993). *Combat stress reaction: The enduring toll of war*. New York, NY: Plenum Press.

Strachey, J., & Freud, A. (Eds.). (1957). *Studies on hysteria*. New York, NY: Basic Books.

Stretch, R. H., Marlowe, D. H., Wright, K. M., Bliese, P. D., Knudson, K. H., & Hoover, C. H. (1996). Post-traumatic stress disorder symptoms among Gulf War veterans. *Military Medicine, 161*, 407–410.

Swank, R.L. (1949). Combat exhaustion: A descriptive and statistical analysis of causes, symptoms, and signs. *Journal of Nervous and Mental Disease*, 109, 475–508.

Taber, K., & Hurley, R. (2009). PTSD and combat-related injuries: Functional neuroanatomy. *Journal of Neuropsychiatry and Clinical Neurosciences, 21*, iv–4.

van der Kolk, B. A. (1996). The body keeps score: Approaches to the psychobiology of posttraumatic stress disorder. In B. A. van der Kolk, A. C. McFarlane, & L. Weisaeth (Eds.), *Traumatic stress: The effects of overwhelming experience on mind, body, and society* (pp. 214–241). New York, NY: Guilford Press.

Van Dyke, C., Zilberg, N.J. & Mckinnon, J.A. (1985). Posttraumatic stress disorder: A thirty-year delay in a World War II veteran. *American Journal of Psychiatry*, 142, 1070–1073.

Weisaeth, L. (1994). *Preventive intervention*. Paper presented at the North American Treaty Organization Conference. Bonas, France.

World Health Organization (WHO). (1992). *ICD-10: International statistical classification of diseases and related health problems* (10th rev.). Geneva, Switzerland: Author.

Yarvis, J., Bordnick, P., Spivey, C., & Pedlar, D. (2005). Subthreshold PTSD: A comparison of alcohol, depression, and health problems in Canadian peacekeepers with different levels of traumatic stress. *Stress, Trauma and Crisis: An International Journal*, 8(2–3), 195–213.

Yarvis, J. S., & Schiess, L. (2008). Subthreshold PTSD as a predictor of depression, alcohol use, and health problems in soldiers. *Journal of Workplace Behavioral Health, 23*(4).

Yarvis, J. S., & Spivey, C. A. (2003). Eye movement desensitization and reprocessing: Ethical considerations of EMDR marketing, training, and research procedures. *Scientific Review of Mental Health Practice*, 2(2), 4.

Yarvis, J. S., Vonk, M. E., & Bordnick, P. S. (under review). PREPS, pre-disaster required equipment package for social workers: A comprehensive guide to disaster social work. *Journal of Social Work.*

Zimering, R. T., Caddell, J. M., Fairbank, J. A., & Keane, T. M. (1993). Post-traumatic stress disorder in Vietnam veterans: An experimental validation of the DSM-III diagnostic criteria. *Journal of Traumatic Stress*, 6, 327–342.

Zlotnick, C., Franklin, C. L., & Zimmerman, M. (2002). Does "subthreshold" posttraumatic stress disorder have any clinical relevance? *Comprehensive Psychiatry*, 43(6), 413–419.

CHAPTER

7

The Neurobiology of PTSD and Cognitive Processing Therapy (CPT)

Jimmy Stehberg, David L. Albright, and Eugenia L. Weiss

Posttraumatic stress disorder (PTSD) symptoms can be part of a normal reaction to a traumatic event (Rothbaum, Foa, Riggs, Murdock, & Walsh, 1992) and typically extinguish without external intervention. According to the *Diagnostic and Statistical Manual of Mental Disorders* (*DSM-IV-TR*; American Psychiatric Association [APA], 2000), PTSD is an Axis I anxiety disorder requiring exposure to a traumatic event (Criterion A) resulting in fear, helplessness, or horror. Symptom clusters are characterized as reexperiencing (Criterion B), avoidance (Criterion C), and arousal (Criterion D) that must last longer than 1 month (Criterion E) and result in loss of day-to-day functioning (Criterion F).

The development and maintenance of PTSD can be understood as a cycle. An individual is exposed to a traumatic event. The traumatic event elicits fear and anxiety. Co-occurring stimuli can also be associated with the traumatic event and elicit fear and anxiety. The interpretation of both the stimulus and response can lead to "stuck points" (rigid patterns in the flow of information processing associated with traumatic experiences) that are resistant to change and continue despite the fact that the original traumatic event is no longer present.

This chapter highlights—from a physiological perspective—the neurobiological mechanisms that help explain how PTSD occurs and how PTSD is maintained by an individual who has been exposed to traumatic events, such as combat. The chapter aims to help clinical social workers become versed in the neurobiological underpinnings of trauma to inform psychotherapeutic practice with traumatized veterans.

We thank Rodrigo Moraga-Amaro and Adolfo Villalón Sandoval for their helpful contributions.

Those neurobiological mechanisms are consistent with the prevailing view in the literature that sees unresolved trauma as an information-processing deficit. The consistency of the two perspectives is reflected in Siegel's (2003) eloquent depiction of an information processing deficit as "an impairment in the innate capacity of the mind to balance the differentiation and integration of energy and information flow" (p. 43). Siegel added that it is through the "contingent communication" (i.e., therapeutic relationship and rapport) as well as through the newly created narratives (meaning making and cognitions associated with alternative explanations) of the traumatic events, where the neural integration of newly created synaptic linkages of emotion, memory, learning, and associations combine to resolve the "stuck points." This chapter also provides a case that exemplifies the use of cognitive processing therapy with a traumatized veteran as a method of mitigating PTSD associated symptoms and how the clinician can work through the "stuck points" in order to help with the client's resolution of the trauma.

THE NEUROBIOLOGY OF PTSD

When faced with a stressful situation we first experience a rush of adrenaline. This release of adrenaline is mediated by the autonomic nervous system through the hypothalamus-pituitary-adrenal (HPA) axis and is designed to prepare the body to survive the stressor. Muscles need increased oxygenation and blood glucose, heart rate and breathing increase, and pupils dilate all in preparation for the individual to physically respond to a potential threat. Yet the brain needs not only to prepare the body for the incoming stress; it also needs to deal with the situation and determine the best way to proceed. Immediately, several processes begin inside the brain, primarily mediated by a group of neurotransmitters known as monoamines released throughout the cortex (for a review see Joëls & Baram, 2009). These processes include a shift from focused processing of sensory information to a general scanning of the environment (believed to be mediated by the neurotransmitter, noradrenalin) along with increased risk assessment and decision making (believed to be mediated by dopamine) and an increase in post-stress anxiety (thought to be mediated by serotonin). It is suggested that the importance of each of these neurotransmitters may depend on the type and length of the stressor (Joëls, Fernandez, & Roozendaal, 2011). Human and animal studies suggest that PTSD is characterized by an exacerbated stress response and concomitant dysfunction of the stress associated pathways in the brain.

PTSD AS A MEMORY DISORDER

PTSD can be considered a paradoxical disorder of memory functioning. PTSD includes, on the one hand, an increased recollection of certain aspects of the event (i.e., hypermnesia) standing in stark contrast with an inconsistent, patchy amnesia (i.e., dysmnesia) of the actual event (Elzinga & Bremner, 2002). Often in PTSD the traumatic event may be intrusively and repeatedly reexperienced when an individual is awake and in the form of nightmares when asleep. These intrusive images are characteristically very vivid and may contain somatosensory, audiovisual, and affective components.

Our present knowledge on the neurobiology of PTSD comes from evidence suggesting that PTSD may be similar to a conditioned response, where such somatosensory, audiovisual, or affective aspects of the traumatic event are associated with the traumatic emotion to the event (e.g., life-threatening feeling of fear or insecurity). This can be supported by the fact that the most common PTSD symptoms include exaggerated responses to cues and persistent avoidance of stimuli associated with the trauma, which may even be generalized to other stimuli. Further support comes from studies with PTSD patients that find that the probability of developing PTSD increases as a response to the magnitude of the traumatic event. For example, prisoners of war (POWs) who have been tortured will exhibit a higher incidence of PTSD than those POWs who have not been tortured. Similar findings apply to earthquake victims, where those who are more proximal to the epicenter of the earthquake will more likely suffer from PTSD than those who are farther away from the epicenter (reviewed in McNally, 2003). Pavlovian classical conditioning paradigms in animals (e.g., conditioned fear responses) have been paralleled to PTSD, and shape our current understanding of the brain substrates affected in PTSD.

THE AMYGDALA AND PREFRONTAL CORTEX

Fear conditioning has been widely studied in rodents. The involvement of several brain regions have been identified, such as the amygdala (or amygdalae), hippocampus, prefrontal, and cingulate cortices. These areas are part of the limbic system and are crucial for most memory systems (LeDoux, 2000). Studies from PTSD patients suggest that these same brain areas show abnormal activity as a result of trauma retrieval. In PTSD patients, retrieval of the traumatic event induces increased activity in the amygdala (reviewed by Bremner, 2002; Tanev, 2003). Such increases in amygdala activity have been shown in human fear conditioning in response to a stimulus when it is paired with a negative reinforcer. Interestingly, the magnitude of amygdala activation is correlated with the strength of the conditioned response (Phelps, Delgado, Nearing, & LeDoux, 2004). Increased amygdala activity is a hallmark of strong emotional responses and traumatic memory retrieval in PTSD patients.

Trauma retrieval also induces decreased activity in the prefrontal cortex (PFC), particularly of the ventromedial part of the prefrontal cortex (vmPFC), hippocampus, and posterior cingulate cortex in PTSD patients (reviewed by Bremner, 2002; Tanev, 2003). The vmPFC is believed to regulate the activity of the amygdala (Bechara, Damasio, Damasio, & Lee, 1999). Functional neuroimaging studies in PTSD patients indicate a hyperresponsive amygdala accompanied by hypoactivation of the vmPFC. In studies where subjects were asked to "reappraise" the emotional significance of a negative scene by interpreting the event in a nonemotional way, a decrease in amygdala activation was found to be correlated to an increased activation of the right PFC (reviewed in Phelps, 2004). Moreover, further studies in PTSD patients showed that symptom severity is positively correlated to right amygdala activation and negatively correlated to vmPFC activation (Shin et al., 2004).

Taken together, current evidence suggests that PTSD patients have an overactivation of the amygdala and a hypoactivation of the vmPFC, and that the vmPFC modulates amygdala activity and the expression of the conditioned response. Recent studies have reported that the vmPFC can also directly inhibit stress responses through inhibiting the release of corticotrophin-releasing factor (CRF), which is crucial for the activation of the hypothalamus-pituitary-adrenal axis during stress (Radley, Gosselink, & Sawchenko, 2009). Thus, decreased vmPFC activity as seen in PTSD could induce increased CRF levels in PTSD patients (Baker et al., 1999; Bremner et al., 1997) producing exacerbated stress responses. Consequently, the vmPFC appears as a major regulator of amygdala activity and emotionally arousing stress responses.

EMOTIONAL VERSUS EPISODIC MEMORY

Both animal and human studies have suggested that temporal lobe structures, such as the hippocampus and amygdala, are linked to two independent memory systems. In emotional situations, these two systems act in concert, that is, where emotions meet memory. The amygdala modulates the encoding and storage of hippocampal-dependent memories with emotional significance, while the hippocampus forms episodic representations of those events, and can influence the amygdala to respond when emotional stimuli are encountered (reviewed by Phelps, 2004).

Evidence that these two memory systems are independent comes from patients with lesions to the hippocampus or amygdala and from several imaging studies. Patients with amygdala lesions show marked deficits in recognition of emotionally relevant stimuli and emotional attention, but have an unaffected recollection of the event (i.e., episodic memory). For example, in human fear conditioning studies, patients with amygdala damage fail to show normal physiological fear responses, though they are able to report that a neutral stimulus (tone) predicts an electric shock (LaBar, LeDoux, Spencer, & Phelps, 1995). Patients with hippocampal damage, on the other hand, respond normally with fear to the neutral stimulus when predicting the electric shock, but have no conscious recollection of the event (Bechara et al., 1995). Imaging studies also show that verbal recognition of emotionally arousing words activates the amygdala but not the hippocampus (Strange & Dolan, 2004).

The above evidence is part of a large bulk of data that indicates that the amygdala is critical in the acquisition and retention of emotional memories associated with an event, while the hippocampal system is critical in the acquisition of the episodic representations of the event.

MEMORY CONSOLIDATION AND RECONSOLIDATION

After we engage in learning, the new relevant memory turns from short-term memory into a more stable long-term form. Memory consolidation is the period in which this process takes place. Consolidation is marked by fragility, which means that any interference with the brain areas serving the memory can lead to amnesia. For example, a strong emotion may induce amnesia of memories that were being consolidated prior to the emotional event. Substances can also induce loss of memory during memory consolidation and are known as amnesic agents.

Misanin and colleagues (1968) reported that electroconvulsive shock therapy (ECT), a known amnestic procedure, leads to memory loss if administered immediately after retrieval of a seemingly consolidated, long-term memory. This implies that every time we retrieve a previously consolidated memory, it suffers from a brief period of fragility, now known as *reconsolidation* (reviewed in Dudai, 2004). During this period, chemical or behavioral interference could lead to loss of that particular memory. Memory blockade during reconsolidation has been achieved in almost all types of memory using amnesic agents targeting different brain areas in animals (reviewed in Dudai, 2004) and using behavioral interference in humans (for a review see Schiller & Phelps, 2011).

Thus, these findings suggest that every time we learn or remember something those memories may become temporarily fragile, and the memories could be susceptible to interference, which may have great potential for PTSD prevention and treatment. Unfortunately, to date, no attempts have been made to use memory reconsolidation as a means to treat PTSD, except for some isolated clinical trials involving the oral use of beta-blockers (Brunet et al., 2008) or low doses of cortisol (Aerni et al., 2004; Weis et al., 2006) after memory retrieval in PTSD patients. Future advances in novel PTSD therapies based on this concept could affect amygdala-dependent emotional memory of the trauma, leaving hippocampus-dependent episodic memory unaffected.

It is suggested that reconsolidation itself is the process by which already consolidated memories are updated (Forcato, Rodríguez, Pedreira, & Maldonado, 2010; Rodriguez-Ortiz & Bermudez-Rattoni, 2007). As an example, every time we look at our parents, we constantly update their image instead of retrieving the image of the first time we saw them. Only recently, Schiller and colleagues (2010) reported that consolidated fearful memories in humans can be updated with nonfearful information during reconsolidation (Schiller et al., 2010), opening new vistas into using memory reconsolidation as a means for therapy.

Memory Extinction

Memory reconsolidation stands in stark contrast with memory extinction, which is the decrease in conditioned response when presented with a nonreinforced conditioned stimulus previously associated to a negative reinforcer. Simply stated, whereas reconsolidation would be a process by which we update a stable memory, extinction would be the process by which two different memories compete: one of a stimulus conditioned to aversion, and a second memory created later where the same stimulus now appears either void of emotional valence, or associated with a positive reinforcer. Extinction learning is also closely related to amygdala function and vmPFC regulation (Phelps et al., 2004).

PTSD-RELATED PSYCHOTHERAPIES

The main focus of current psychotherapies involves the extinction of the conditioned memory. This is accomplished by teaching the patient that those cues initially conditioned to the trauma are no longer negative, thereby resulting in a reduction of anxiety (Milad, Rauch, Pitman, & Quirk, 2006). The two major strategies to treat PTSD in patients are prolonged exposure therapy (PET) and trauma-focused cognitive behavioral therapies, including cognitive processing therapy (CPT). Although their methods are somewhat different, both are based on inducing extinction learning. In exposure types of therapies, the subject is confronted with the trauma-associated cues via imaginal-exposure, in vivo exposure, or through the use of virtual reality exposure therapy (which is discussed in Chapter 8). CBT therapies use a form of extinction learning in which conditioned fear responses are ameliorated by learning that associated cues are no longer signals of threat (Bryant, Moulds, et al., 2008) and by correcting distortions of cognition and memory associated with the traumatic event (Bryant et al., 2006; Foa et al., 1999; Hackmann, Ehlers, Speckens, & Clark, 2004; Resick & Schnicke, 1992). In response to treatment, a reduction of amygdala hyperactivity has been documented (Bryant, Felmingham, et al., 2008). There is current evidence that suggests that exposure based therapies and cognitive behavioral therapies are effective in relieving PTSD symptoms (Bisson & Andrew, 2007; Harvey, Bryant, & Tarrier, 2003; Powers, Halpern, Ferenschak, Gillihan, & Foa, 2010). However, there seem to be no significant differences in effectiveness between the two approaches (Bisson & Andrew, 2007; Ougrin, 2011).

In cognitive behavioral therapy, a clinician can use a combination of exposure and cognitive techniques. Exposure therapies include the process of presenting to the individual a feared stimulus until the fear and anxiety are reduced. The individual is asked to confront stimuli associated with the memories of his or her traumatic experiences while simultaneously acknowledging and resisting any avoidant behavior that emerges. In this way, the fear and anxiety are experienced and slowly habituated or extinguished. Cognitive therapies attempt to challenge distorted beliefs that result in maladaptive behaviors. The individual is asked to question these beliefs by examining whether or not the underlying assumptions are rational and valid. In this way, dysfunctional thinking can be changed by identifying the trauma, the consequences of the trauma, and the beliefs about the trauma.

COGNITIVE PROCESSING THERAPY (CPT)

Cognitive processing therapy (CPT) is a type of cognitive behavioral therapy that can be used by clinicians to treat PTSD symptomology (Resick & Schnicke, 1992). It appears promising in reducing PTSD in veterans (Monson et al., 2006; Monson, Price, & Ranslow, 2005).

CPT is based on cognitive theory. As such, PTSD is considered to result from an activating event (i.e., exposure to a traumatic event; Criterion A) that leads to fear, helplessness, or horror. These emotional consequences manifest as reexperiencing, avoidance, and arousal symptoms. Reexperiencing (Criterion B) symptoms generally involve memories that trigger feelings of fear, helplessness, or horror. Avoidance (Criterion C) symptoms can manifest as behaviors (e.g., substance abuse) that serve to distract individuals from situations and experiences that trigger memories of the traumatic event. Arousal (Criterion D) symptoms can include increased anger and difficulty sleeping. Rothbaum, Foa, and colleagues (1992) suggest that symptom clusters potentially result from someone holding overly rigid core beliefs, which is another way of saying that individuals are unable to reconcile their respective belief systems with the activating events and thus may experience posttraumatic stress symptoms.

The primary goal of cognitive processing therapy is to reconcile pretrauma beliefs and posttrauma information by way of a manualized treatment delivered over 12 sessions (Resick, Monson, Price, & Chard, 2007). Briefly stated, the first five sessions focus on a discussion of the traumatic memories. The remaining sessions focus on the identification and the challenging of maladaptive beliefs associated with the traumatic memories. The VA social work clinician uses cognitive processing therapy to reduce PTSD in the veteran over the course of 12 sessions. A brief overview is provided for each session. We provide this overview in connection to the Case Vignette: Sgt. Hernandez. (For a comprehensive explanation of the sessions refer to Resick, Monson, and Chard's [2008] manual on cognitive processing therapy for military and veteran clients.)

Case Vignette: Sgt. Hernandez

While serving in Iraq, Sgt. Hernandez, a motor transport operator, is assigned as a driver of an armored vehicle in a convoy along the Ar Ramadi-Baghdad corridor. Sgt. Hernandez's vehicle detonates an improvised explosive device (IED) deployed by an insurgent's vehicle. Although she survives, during the next several convoys along the corridor she experiences psychological distress and exhibits a startle response to approaching vehicles. Sgt. Hernandez observes her peers inebriated after the completion of every convoy. She begins to overindulge in alcohol as well. On returning to the continental United States, Sgt. Hernandez continues to recollect the detonation of the IED. She avoids driving as much as she can. When she rides with other people she sometimes becomes irritable or angry when they get too close to other vehicles. She continues to overindulge in alcohol use. Sgt. Hernandez's spouse convinces her to seek treatment at the local Veteran's Affairs (VA) outpatient clinic.

In the case of Sgt. Hernandez, driving a vehicle along the Ar Ramadi-Baghdad corridor is the neutral stimulus. The detonation of the IED is the unconditioned stimulus that produces the unconditioned response of fear and anxiety. Associating driving and approaching vehicles along the corridor with the detonation of the IED produces the conditioned response of fear and anxiety, with driving and approaching vehicles becoming the conditioned stimuli. Imitating the drinking behavior of her peers (observational learning) results in a temporary reduction of psychological distress (negative reinforcement); this is avoidant behavior (Criterion C for PTSD diagnosis). Back in the United States, driving and approaching vehicles are generalized stimuli resulting in fear and anxiety. These conditioned stimuli lead to recurrent memories of the IED (Criterion B) and outburst of anger when vehicles approach (Criterion D).

Session 1

The primary goals of the initial session are to provide psychoeducation on the cognitive model of PTSD, the symptom clusters of PTSD, introduce the idea of "stuck points," and to explain the importance of working to overcome avoidance.

The primary assumption of cognitive theory is that activating events result in consequences that are filtered by an individual's belief systems. Activating events can be situations, thoughts, or memories. These events result in emotional consequences (i.e., feelings). Individuals' feelings and emotions are filtered by belief systems that might include attitudes, perceptions, expectations, and thoughts. It is important to note that beliefs can be positive and negative.

Applying cognitive theory, the activating event for Sgt. Hernandez is the IED explosion that occurred along the Ar Ramadi-Baghdad corridor. The emotional consequences include the subsequent fear, horror, helplessness, and anger. The patient's belief system is what cognitive processing therapy directly targets, so the VA clinician helps Sgt. Hernandez identify and challenge her maladaptive thoughts that are resulting in the emotional consequences.

The VA clinician explains that associations between the stimulus, the response, and the interpretation of both the stimulus and response lead to the creation of stuck points in memory. The clinician explains that these stuck points are resistant to change and continue despite the lack of an ongoing traumatic event. It is important that the clinician introduce the idea that identifying and challenging stuck points is a fundamental component of therapy.

The VA clinician also explains the importance of working to overcome avoidance. Avoidant behaviors within the context of the session can manifest in a variety of ways, including a patient's difficulty in completing and submitting therapy homework assignments. Overcoming avoidance is aided by the development of rapport. Research also suggests that the quality of the therapeutic relationship is an important measure of success in clinical encounters (Kolden, Howard, & Maling, 1994; Martin, Garske, & Davis, 2000). Siegel (2003) posited that effective psychotherapy (at an interpersonal neurobiological level) includes the "Cs" of therapy, which include compassion, connection, and contingent communication (where contingent communication is defined as "the ability of one person to perceive, make sense of and respond to the signals of the other person in a timely fashion," which creates a sense of communion, joining and attunement) (p. 6).

The clinician also assigns the client an Impact Statement and Stuck Point Log. The Impact Statement focuses on why the client thinks the traumatic event occurred and how it is affecting him or her. It does not focus on the actual traumatic event. The Stuck Point Log is used by the client to note reoccurring thoughts that make him or her feel bad.

Session 2

The primary goals of the second session include beginning to identify stuck points with the client and reinforcing the use of the Stuck Point Log. The session begins by having Sgt. Hernandez read her impact statement. While she is reading the statement, the VA clinician begins to identify stuck points. For example, Sgt. Hernandez might share that she had always been safe during prior convoys and that she must have done something wrong to have detonated the IED. She now irrationally believes that she is never safe when driving a vehicle. The VA clinician identifies this as a distorted sense of responsibility and might use Socratic dialogue to evaluate this line of thinking with her to guide Sgt. Hernandez in explaining the differences between driving and riding in vehicles in the United States and Iraq; thus, helping her to identify and replace a generalized thought with a functional, differentiated thought. Using Socratic dialogue, for example, the clinician might ask questions like the following: "How many prior convoys were you on, and how many times was an IED detonated? I have read that many other service members have experienced IED detonations in Iraq; do you think most of them occurred because your comrades did something wrong?" Near the end of the session the clinician introduces the ABC (i.e., activating event, beliefs, and consequences) worksheet and directs Sgt. Hernandez to complete it every day. The worksheet will aid her by asking her to connect the emotional consequences she is experiencing with the beliefs she has about the activating event. It is an important tool because it encourages Sgt. Hernandez to think critically about whether her cognitions are realistic, and if not, what are the possible substitutions for those irrational thoughts.

Session 3

The primary goals of the third session include reviewing the ABC worksheets, helping Sgt. Hernandez recognize differences between thoughts and feelings, and asking her to write a Trauma Account. The Trauma Account focuses on the traumatic event and should include as many sensory details as possible.

Session 4

The primary goals of the fourth session include having Sgt. Hernandez read her trauma account to the clinician, identifying stuck points, and challenging her thoughts of self-blame using Socratic dialogue. As exemplified briefly in the second session, Socratic dialogue challenges irrational belief systems by asking clarification questions that probe her beliefs, assist in exploring alternative perspectives, and aid in explaining how maladaptive beliefs lead to negative emotional consequences. It teaches critical thinking and is a tool that clients will be able to continue to use beyond the sessions. It is nondirective, which means the role of the therapist is not to interpret but to help the client come to her own understanding of the maladaptive beliefs. At the end of the session, the VA clinician asks her to complete a second Trauma Account adding more details and anything that was previously left out.

Session 5

The primary goals of the fifth session include having Sgt. Hernandez read the second Trauma Account out loud, helping her to identify differences between the first and second accounts, and confronting maladaptive thoughts and stuck points. The VA clinician also asks her to complete the Challenging Questions worksheet that focuses on several previously identified stuck points. The worksheet includes questions asking Sgt. Hernandez to provide evidence for and against her stuck points and other questions that force her to challenge the rationality of her thoughts. This is important for her to understand because it aids in changing her thinking patterns and strengthens her ability to critically challenge her beliefs.

Session 6

The primary goals of the sixth session include reviewing the Challenging worksheet, continuing to work on identifying and challenging stuck points using Socratic dialogue, and introducing the Patterns of Problematic Thinking worksheet. This worksheet challenges

Sgt. Hernandez to identify patterns that she can identify among the previously identified stuck points. Some of these patterns include jumping to conclusions when there is no evidence, overgeneralizing an event, and emotional reasoning, which assumes that because you have a feeling there must be a reason for it.

Session 7

The primary goals of the seventh session include helping Sgt. Hernandez continue to identify and challenge problematic patterns in her beliefs, helping her to generate adaptive beliefs for the maladaptive ones, and introducing the Challenging Beliefs worksheet.

Sessions 8 Through 12

The primary goals of the remaining sessions include focusing on one of five core themes (i.e., safety, trust, power/control, esteem, and intimacy) during each remaining session and helping Sgt. Hernandez come to see how these areas were likely disrupted after the traumatic event. The clinician uses the final session to have the veteran review and recap what tools are available to facilitate cognitive change and the practical gains made during treatment.

CONCLUSION

This chapter examines how neurobiological research indicates that traumatic stress presents a complexity of interrelated brain mechanisms and neuronal functions that cognitive neuroscience is beginning to grasp. One of the consequences of severe or chronic stress is the deleterious effects on the brain and how elevated levels of stress hormone can damage the limbic system, which is the system that is involved in learning and memory (Bremner, 2002). Although many studies point to the effectiveness of several cognitive behavioral types of therapies in ameliorating posttraumatic stress symptoms, the one examined in depth in this chapter is cognitive processing therapy (CPT). This application of CPT was illustrated through the use of a case vignette involving a veteran suffering from PTSD after detonating an IED. The authors demonstrated how through psychotherapy clinicians can utilize learning and conditioning paradigms to assist clients in their cognitive and emotional response to traumatic memories.

CHAPTER DISCUSSION QUESTIONS

1. What are other potential avoidant behaviors that Sgt. Hernandez might manifest?
2. What are additional potential stuck points that Sgt. Hernandez and her clinician might identify?
3. Using Socratic dialogue, what are some Socratic questions that could be posed to challenge the stuck points identified in Question 2?
4. Apply the ABC model to the three stuck points identified in Question 2.
5. Provide adaptive beliefs for the maladaptive ones identified in Question 4.

REFERENCES

Aerni, A., Traber, R., Hock, C., Roozendaal, B., Schelling, G., Papassotiropoulos, A., . . . de Quervain, D. J. (2004). Low-dose cortisol for symptoms of posttraumatic stress disorder. *American Journal of Psychiatry, 161*(8), 1488–1490.

American Psychiatric Association. (2000). *Diagnostic and statistical manual of mental disorders* (4th ed., text rev.). Washington, DC: Author.

Baker, D. G., West, S. A., Nicholson, W. E., Ekhator, N. N., Kasckow, J. W., Hill, K. K., . . . Geracioti Jr., T. D. (1999). Serial CSF corticotrophin-releasing hormone levels and adrenocortical activity in combat veterans with posttraumatic stress disorder. *American Journal of Psychiatry, 156*(4), 585–588.

Bechara, A., Damasio, H., Damasio, A. R., & Lee, G. P. (1999). Different contributions of the human amygdala and ventromedial prefrontal cortex to decision-making. *Journal of Neuroscience, 19*(13), 5473–5481.

Bechara, A., Tranel, D., Damasio, H., Adolphs, R., Rockland, C., & Damasio, A. R. (1995). Double dissociation of conditioning and declarative knowledge relative to the amygdala and hippocampus in humans. *Science, 269*(5227), 1115–1118.

Bisson J., & Andrew, M. (2007). *Psychological treatment of post-traumatic stress disorder (PTSD). Cochrane Database of Systematic Reviews, 2007*(3), Article CD003388. doi: 10.1002/14651858.CD003388.pub3

Bremner, J. D. (2002). *Does stress damage the brain?* New York, NY: Norton.

Bremner, J. D. (2002). Neuroimaging studies in post-traumatic stress disorder. *Current Psychiatry Reports, 4*(4), 254–263.

Bremner, J. D., Licinio, J., Darnell, A., Krystall, J. H., Owens, M. J., Southwick, S. M., . . . Charney, D. S. (1997). Elevated CSF corticotropin-releasing factor concentrations in posttraumatic stress disorder. *American Journal of Psychiatry, 154*(5), 624–629.

Brunet, A., Orr, S. P., Tremblay, J., Robertson, K., Nader, K., & Pitman, R. K. (2008). Effect of post-retrieval propranolol on psychophysiologic responding during subsequent script-driven traumatic imagery in post-traumatic stress disorder. *Journal of Psychiatric Research, 42*(6), 503–506.

Bryant, R. A., Felmingham, K., Kemp, A., Das, P., Hughes, G., Peduto, A., & Williams, L. (2008). Amygdala and ventral anterior cingulate activation predicts treatment response to cognitive behaviour therapy for post-traumatic stress disorder. *Psychological Medicine, 38*(4), 555–561.

Bryant, R. A., Moulds, M. L., Guthrie, R. M., Dang, S. T., Mastrodomenico, J., Nixon, R. D., . . . Creamer, M. (2008). A randomized controlled trial of exposure therapy and cognitive restructuring for posttraumatic stress disorder. *Journal of Consulting and Clinical Psychology, 76*(4), 695–703.

Bryant, R. A., Moulds, M. L., Nixon, R. D., Mastrodomenico, J., Felmingham, K., & Hopwood, S. (2006). Hypnotherapy and cognitive behaviour therapy of acute stress disorder: A 3-year follow-up. *Behaviour Research and Therapy, 44*(9), 1331–1335.

Dudai, Y. (2004). The neurobiology of consolidations, or, how stable is the engram? *Annual Review of Psychology, 55*, 51–86.

Elzinga, B. M., & Bremner, J. D. (2002). Are the neural substrates of memory the final common pathway in posttraumatic stress disorder (PTSD)? *Journal of Affective Disorders*, *70*(1), 1–17.

Foa, E. B., Dancu, C. V., Hembree, E. A., Jaycox, L. H., Meadows, E. A., & Street, G. P. (1999). A comparison of exposure therapy, stress inoculation training, and their combination for reducing posttraumatic stress disorder in female assault victims. *Journal of Consulting and Clinical Psychology*, *67*, 194–200.

Foa, E. B., Davidson, J. R. T., & Frances, A. (1990). Expert consensus guideline series: Treatment of posttraumatic stress disorder. *Journal of Clinical Psychiatry*, *60*(Suppl. 16), 1–76.

Forcato, C., Rodríguez, M. L., Pedreira, M. E., & Maldonado, H. (2010). Reconsolidation in humans opens up declarative memory to the entrance of new information. *Neurobiology of Learning and Memory*, *93*(1), 77–84.

Hackmann, A., Ehlers, A., Speckens, A., & Clark, D. M. (2004). Characteristics and content of intrusive memories in PTSD and their changes with treatment. *Journal of Trauma and Stress*, *17*(3), 231–240.

Harvey, A. G., Bryant, R. A., & Tarrier, N. (2003). Cognitive behaviour therapy for posttraumatic stress disorder. *Clinical Psychology Review*, *23*(3), 501–522.

Joëls, M., & Baram, T. Z. (2009). The neuro-symphony of stress. *Nature Reviews Neuroscience*, *10*(6), 459–466.

Joëls, M., Fernandez, G., & Roozendaal, B. (2011). Stress and emotional memory: A matter of timing. *Trends in Cognition Science*, *15*(6), 280–288.

Kolden, R. G., Howard, K. I., & Maling, M. S. (1994). The counseling relationship and treatment process and outcome. *The Counseling Psychologist*, *22*, 82–89.

LaBar, K. S., LeDoux, J. E., Spencer, D. D., & Phelps, E. A. (1995). Impaired fear conditioning following unilateral temporal lobectomy in humans. *Journal of Neuroscience*, *15*(10), 6846–6855.

LeDoux, J. E. (2000). Emotion circuits in the brain. *Annual Review of Neuroscience*, *23*, 155–184.

Martin, D. J., Garske, J. P., & Davis, M. K. (2000). Relation of the therapeutic alliance with outcome and other variables: A meta-analytic review. *Journal of Consulting and Clinical Psychology*, *68*, 438–450.

McNally, R. J. (2003). Progress and controversy in the study of posttraumatic stress disorder *Annual Review of Psychology* *54*, 229–252.

Milad, M. R., Rauch, S. L., Pitman, R. K., & Quirk, G. J. (2006). Fear extinction in rats: Implications for human brain imaging and anxiety disorders. *Biological Psychology*, *73*(1), 61–71.

Misanin, J. R., Miller, R. R., & Lewis, D. J. (1968). Retrograde amnesia produced by electroconvulsive shock after reactivation of a consolidated memory trace. *Science*, *160*(827), 554–555.

Monson, C. M., Price, J. L., & Ranslow, E. (2005). Lessons learned in researching an evidence-based PTSD treatment in the VA: The case of cognitive processing therapy. *Federal Practitioner*, *22*, 75–83.

Monson, C. M., Schnurr, P. P., Resick, P. A., Friedman, M., Young-Xu, Y., & Stevens, S. P. (2006). Cognitive processing therapy for veterans with military-related posttraumatic stress disorder. *Journal of Consulting and Clinical Psychology*, *74*, 898–907.

Ougrin, D. (2011). Efficacy of exposure versus cognitive therapy in anxiety disorders: Systematic review and meta-analysis. *BMC Psychiatry*, *11*(1), 200.

Phelps, E. A. (2004). Human emotion and memory: Interactions of the amygdala and hippocampal complex. *Current Opinion in Neurobiology*, *14*(2), 198–202.

Phelps, E. A., Delgado, M. R., Nearing, K. I., & LeDoux, J. E. (2004). Extinction learning in humans: Role of the amygdala and vmPFC. *Neuron*, *43*(6), 897–905.

Powers, M. B., Halpern, J. M., Ferenschak, M. P., Gillihan, S. J., & Foa, E. B. (2010). A meta-analytic review of prolonged exposure for posttraumatic stress disorder. *Clinical Psychology Review*, *30*(6), 635–641.

Radley, J. J., Gosselink, K. L., & Sawchenko, P. E. (2009). A discrete GABAergic relay mediates medial prefrontal cortical inhibition of the neuroendocrine stress response. *Journal of Neuroscience*, *29*(22), 7330–7340.

Resick, P. A., Monson, C. M., Price, J. L., & Chard, K. M. (2007). *Cognitive processing therapy: Veteran/military version: Trainer's manual.* Washington, DC: Department of Veterans' Affairs.

Resick, P. A., & Schnicke, M. K. (1992). Cognitive processing therapy for sexual assault survivors. *Journal of Consulting and Clinical Psychology*, *60*, 748–756.

Rodriguez-Ortiz, C. J., & Bermúdez-Rattoni, F. (2007). *Neural plasticity and memory: From genes to brain imaging*. Boca Raton, FL: CRC Press.

Rothbaum, B. O., Foa, E. B., Riggs, D., Murdock, T., & Walsh, W. (1992). A prospective examination of post-traumatic stress disorder in rape victims. *Journal of Traumatic Stress*, *5*, 455–475.

Schiller, D., Monfils, M. H., Raio, C. M., Johnson, D. C., Ledoux, J. E., & Phelps, E. A. (2010). Preventing the return of fear in humans using reconsolidation update mechanisms. *Nature*, *463*(7277), 49–53.

Schiller, D., & Phelps, E. A. (2011). Does reconsolidation occur in humans? *Front Behavioural Neuroscience*, *5*, 24.

Shin, L. M., Orr, S. P., Carson, M. A., Rauch, S. L., Macklin, M. L., Lasko, N. B., . . . Pitman, R. K. (2004). Regional cerebral blood flow in the amygdala and medial prefrontal cortex during traumatic imagery in male and female Vietnam veterans with PTSD. *Archives of General Psychiatry*, *61*, 168–176

Siegel, D. J. (2003). An interpersonal neurobiology of psychotherapy: The developing mind and the resolution of trauma. In M. F. Solomon & D. Siegel (Eds.), *Healing trauma: Attachment, mind, body and brain* (pp. 1–56). New York, NY: Norton.

Strange, B. A., & Dolan, R. J. (2004). Beta-adrenergic modulation of emotional memory-evoked human amygdala and hippocampal responses. *Proceedings of the National Academy of Science in the United States of America*, *101*(31), 11454–11458.

Tanev, K. (2003). Neuroimaging and neurocircuitry in post-traumatic stress disorder: What is currently known? *Current Psychiatry Report*, *5*(5), 369–383.

Weis, F., Kilger, E., Roozendaal, B., de Quervain, D. J., Lamm, P., Schmidt, M., . . . Schelling, G. (2006). Stress doses of hydrocortisone reduce chronic stress symptoms and improve health-related quality of life in high-risk patients after cardiac surgery: A randomized study. *Journal of Thoracic and Cardiovascular Surgery*, *131*, 277–282.

CHAPTER

8

Treating Combat-Related PTSD With Virtual Reality Exposure Therapy

Suzanne Leaman, Barbara Olasov Rothbaum, JoAnn Difede, Judith Cukor, Maryrose Gerardi, and Albert "Skip" Rizzo

Posttraumatic stress disorder (PTSD) is a chronic condition that occurs in a significant minority of persons who experience life-threatening traumatic events. It is characterized by reexperiencing, avoidance, and hyperarousal symptoms (American Psychiatric Association, 1994). PTSD has been estimated to affect up to 18% of returning Operation Iraqi Freedom (OIF) Veterans (Hoge et al., 2004). In addition to the specific conditions in Iraq and Afghanistan, an unprecedented number are now surviving serious wounds (Blimes, 2007). The stigma of treatment often prevents service members (SMs) and veterans from seeking help (Hoge et al., 2004), so finding an acceptable form of treatment for military personnel is a priority. The current generation of military personnel may be more comfortable participating in a virtual reality treatment approach than in traditional talk therapy, as they are likely familiar with gaming and training simulation technology. This chapter provides information on the development of and research on virtual reality (VR) as well as the application of VR to mental health treatments, including a protocol of virtual reality exposure (VRE) utilizing a virtual Iraq/Afghanistan system for combat-related PTSD.

THE MILITARY HEALTH CARE CHALLENGE

War is perhaps one of the most challenging situations that a human being can experience. The physical, emotional, cognitive, and psychological demands of a combat environment place enormous stress on even the best-prepared military personnel. Since the start of the Operation Iraqi Freedom/Operation Enduring Freedom (OEF/OIF) conflicts in Iraq and Afghanistan, approximately 1.9 million troops have been deployed (Department of Defense [DoD], 2010a). As of December 2010, there have been 5,836 deaths and 41,583 SMs wounded in action (DoD, 2010b; Fischer, 2010). Of the wounded in action (WIA), the total includes 1,222 major limb amputations and 399 minor amputations and as of 2010, traumatic brain injury (TBI) has been diagnosed in 178,876 patients (many of which are not included in the WIA statistics because mild TBI is often reported retrospectively, on redeployment home). The stressful experiences that are characteristic of the OIF/OEF war-fighting environments have produced significant numbers of returning SMs at risk for developing PTSD. In the first systematic study of OIF/OEF mental health problems, the results indicated that "the percentage of study subjects whose responses met the screening criteria for major depression, generalized anxiety, or PTSD was significantly higher after duty in Iraq (15.6 to 17.1 percent) than after duty in Afghanistan (11.2 percent) or before deployment to Iraq (9.3 percent)" (Hoge et al., 2004, p. 13). Reports since that time on OIF/OEF PTSD and psychosocial disorder rates suggest even higher incidence statistics (Fischer, 2010; Seal, Bertenthal, Nuber, Sen, & Marmar, 2007; Tanielian et al., 2008). For example, as of 2010, the Military Health System has recorded 66,934 active duty patients who have been diagnosed with PTSD (Fischer, 2010) and the Rand Analysis (Tanielian et al., 2008) estimated that at a 1.5-million deployment level, more than 300,000 active duty and discharged veterans will suffer from the symptoms of PTSD and major depression. These findings make a compelling case for continued focus on developing and enhancing the availability of evidence-based treatments to address a mental health care challenge that has had a significant impact on the lives of our SMs, veterans, and their families, who deserve our best efforts to provide optimal care.

At the same time a virtual revolution has taken place in the use of VR simulation technology for clinical purposes. Technological advances in the areas of computation speed and power, graphics and image rendering, display systems, body tracking, interface technology, haptic devices, authoring software and artificial intelligence have supported the creation of low-cost and usable VR systems capable of running on a commodity level personal computer. The unique match between VR technology assets and the needs of various clinical treatment approaches has been recognized by a number of scientists and clinicians, and an encouraging body of research has emerged that documents the many clinical targets where VR can add value to clinical assessment and intervention (Glantz, Rizzo, & Graap, 2003; Holden, 2005; Parsons & Rizzo, 2008; Powers & Emmelkamp, 2008; Riva, 2011; Rizzo, Lange, Suma, & Bolas, 2011; Rizzo, Schultheis, Kerns, & Mateer, 2004; Rose, Brooks, & Rizzo, 2005). This convergence of the exponential advances in underlying VR enabling technologies with a growing body of clinical research and experience has fueled the evolution of the discipline of *Clinical Virtual Reality*.

INTRODUCTION TO CLINICAL VIRTUAL REALITY

In its basic form, VR can be viewed as an advanced form of human-computer interface that allows the user to "interact" with and become "immersed" within a computer generated simulated environment (Rizzo, Buckwalter, & Neumann, 1997). VR sensory stimuli can be delivered by using various forms of visual display technology that integrates real-time computer graphics and/or photographic images/video with a variety of other sensory output devices that can present audio, "force-feedback" haptic/touch sensations and even olfactory content to the user. An engaged interaction with a virtual experience can be supported by employing specialized tracking technology that senses the user's position and movement and uses that information to update the visual, audio and haptic/touch stimuli presented to users to create the illusion of being immersed "in" a virtual space in which they can interact. One common configuration employs a combination of a head-mounted display (HMD), which consists of separate display screens for each eye, display optics, stereo earphones, and a head-tracking device that allows delivery of computer-generated images and sounds of a simulated virtual scene that corresponds to what the individual would see and hear if the scene were real. Other methods employ 3D displays that project on a single wall or on a multiple wall space (multiwall projection rooms are known as CAVES). As well, basic flat-screen display monitors have been used to deliver interactive VR scenarios that, although not immersive, are sometimes sufficient, cost-effective options for delivering testing, training, treatment, and rehabilitative applications using VR. With the capacity of VR technology to create controllable, multisensory, interactive 3-dimensional stimulus environments, it is well suited to simulate the challenges that people face in naturalistic environments, and consequently can provide objective simulations that can be useful for clinical assessment and treatment purposes.

A short list of areas where clinical VR has been usefully applied includes fear reduction in persons with simple phobias (Parsons & Rizzo, 2008; Powers & Emmelkamp, 2008), treatment for PTSD (Difede et al., 2007; Difede & Hoffman, 2002; Rizzo et al., 2011b; Rizzo, Difede, Rothbaum, & Reger, 2010; Rothbaum, Hodges, Ready, Graap, & Alarcon, 2001), stress management in cancer patients (Schneider, Kisby, & Flint, 2010), acute pain reduction during wound care and physical therapy with burn patients (Hoffman et al., 2011), body image disturbances in patients with eating disorders (Riva, 2011), navigation and spatial training in children and adults with motor impairments (Rizzo et al., 2004; Stanton, Foreman, & Wilson, 1998), functional skill training and motor rehabilitation with patients having central nervous system dysfunction (e.g., stroke, TBI, SCI, cerebral palsy, multiple sclerosis), (Holden, 2005; Merians et al., 2010), and for the assessment and rehabilitation of attention, memory, spatial skills and other cognitive functions in both clinical and unimpaired populations (Parsons & Rizzo, 2008; Rizzo et al., 2006; Rose et al., 2005). To do this, VR scientists have constructed virtual airplanes, skyscrapers, spiders, battlefields, social settings, beaches, fantasy worlds, and the mundane (but highly relevant) functional environments of the schoolroom, office, home, street, and supermarket. In essence, clinicians can now create simulated environments that mimic the outside world and use them in the clinical setting to immerse patients in simulations that support the aims and mechanics of a specific therapeutic approach.

VIRTUAL REALITY EXPOSURE

Among the many approaches that have been used to treat PTSD, cognitive-behavioral treatment (CBT) with prolonged exposure (PE) appears to have the best-documented therapeutic efficacy (Cahill, Rothbaum, Resick, & Follette, 2009; Institute of Medicine

[IOM], 2008). PE is a program of exposure therapy based on Foa and Kozak's (1986) emotional processing theory, which posits that PTSD involves pathological fear structures that are activated when information represented in the structures is encountered. These fear structures are composed of harmless stimuli that have been associated with danger. Successful treatment requires emotional processing of the fear structures to modify their pathological elements so that the stimuli no longer evoke fear. Imaginal exposure entails engaging mentally with the fear structure through repeatedly revisiting the traumatic event in a safe environment. In practice, a person with PTSD typically is guided and encouraged by the clinician gradually to *imagine*, *narrate*, and *emotionally process* the traumatic event within the safe and supportive environment of the clinician's office. This approach is believed to provide a low-threat context where the patient can begin to process therapeutically the emotions that are relevant to the traumatic event as well as decondition the avoidance learning cycle of the disorder via a habituation/extinction process. Expert treatment guidelines for PTSD published for the first time in 1999 recommended that CBT with exposure should be the first-line therapy for PTSD (Foa, Davidson, & Frances, 1999). The comparative empirical support for exposure therapy was documented in a review by the IOM at the National Academies of Science of 53 studies of pharmaceuticals and 37 studies of psychotherapies used in PTSD treatment (IOM, 2008). The report concluded that although there is not enough reliable evidence to draw conclusions about the effectiveness of most PTSD treatments, there is sufficient evidence to conclude that exposure therapies are effective in treating people with PTSD.

Although the efficacy of imaginal exposure has been established in multiple studies with diverse trauma populations, many patients are unwilling or unable to effectively visualize the traumatic event. This is a crucial concern because avoidance of cues and reminders of the trauma is one of the cardinal symptoms of PTSD. In fact, research on this aspect of PTSD treatment suggests that the inability to emotionally engage (*in imagination*) is a predictor for negative treatment outcomes (Jaycox, Foa, & Morral, 1998). To address this problem, researchers have recently turned to the use of VR to deliver exposure (VRE) by immersing clients in simulations of trauma-relevant environments in which the emotional intensity of the scenes can be precisely controlled by the clinician in collaboration with the patients' wishes. In this fashion, VRE offers a way to circumvent the natural avoidance tendency by directly delivering multisensory and context-relevant cues that evoke the trauma without demanding that the patient actively try to access his or her experience through effortful memory retrieval. Within a VR environment, the hidden world of the patient's imagination is not exclusively relied upon.

The first use of VRE for a Vietnam veteran with PTSD was reported in a case study of a 50-year-old, Caucasian male veteran who met *DSM-IV* criteria for PTSD (Rothbaum et al., 1999). Results indicated posttreatment improvement on all measures of PTSD, and maintenance of these gains were seen at a 6-month follow-up. This case study was followed by an open clinical trial of VRE for Vietnam veterans (Rothbaum et al., 2001). In this study, 16 male Vietnam veterans with PTSD were exposed to two virtual environments delivered in a head-mounted display, a virtual clearing surrounded by jungle and a virtual Huey helicopter, in which the therapist controlled various visual and auditory effects (e.g., helicopter flybys, explosions, day/night effects, men yelling). After an average of 13 exposure therapy sessions over 5 to 7 weeks, there was a significant reduction in PTSD and related symptoms in the treatment completers. Similar findings were discovered 6 months later, suggesting that VRE could be a promising component of a comprehensive treatment approach for veterans with combat-related PTSD.

In the aftermath of the 9/11 terrorist attacks on New York City, many thousands of World Trade Center (WTC) survivors, including first responders and disaster recovery workers as well as civilians, were deemed to be at high risk for developing PTSD. In response to this, Difede and Hoffman (2002) developed a virtual WTC for treating survivors that gradually, yet systematically, exposes the client to a simulated attack on the WTC. A wait-list-controlled study, comprised of firefighters, disaster recovery workers and civilians, some of whom were not successful in previous imaginal therapy, found positive results from VRE (Difede et al., 2007). The VRE group showed both statistically and clinically significant improvement in the Clinician Administered PTSD Scale (CAPS) compared to the wait-list comparison group.

VR environments have been used worldwide to facilitate PTSD treatment in civilians. In Portugal, Gamito and colleagues (2007) developed a VR application in response to the estimated 25,000 survivors with PTSD from their 1961 to 1974 wars in Mozambique, Angola, and Guiné. This research group constructed a single virtual reality "ambush" scenario by modifying a common PC-based combat game. They reported having recently conducted an initial user-centered test with one PTSD patient who provided feedback suggesting the need for a system that provides more graduated delivery of anxiety provoking trigger stimuli. Josman and colleagues (2006) are currently implementing a virtual bus bombing PTSD treatment scenario for civilian survivors of terrorist attacks in Israel.

VIRTUAL REALITY EXPOSURE THERAPY USING VIRTUAL IRAQ/AFGHANISTAN

In response to the growing numbers of veterans returning with combat-related PTSD from Operation Iraqi Freedom, development of a Virtual Iraq scenario was commenced in 2005 at the University of Southern California (Rizzo, Reger, Gahm, Difede, & Rothbaum, 2009) Institute for Creative Technologies (ICT). The *Virtual Iraq* application (and the new *Virtual Afghanistan* scenario) consists of a series of virtual scenarios designed to represent relevant contexts for VRE, including Middle Eastern–theme city and desert road environments (see Figure 8.1). In addition to the visual stimuli presented in the VR HMD, directional 3D audio, vibrotactile and olfactory stimuli of relevance can be delivered. The presentation of additive, combat-relevant stimuli in the VR scenarios can be controlled by a therapist via a separate "wizard of oz" clinical interface, while in full audio contact with the patient. The clinical interface is a key feature in that it provides a clinician with the capacity to customize the therapy experience to the individual needs of the patient. The clinician can place the patient in VR scenario locations that resemble the setting in which the traumatic events initially occurred and can gradually introduce and control real time "trigger" stimuli (visual, auditory, olfactory, and tactile) as is required to foster the anxiety modulation needed for therapeutic processing and habituation. Initial usability studies and case reports were published with positive findings in terms of SMs acceptance, interest in the treatment, and clinical successes (Gerardi, Rothbaum, Ressler, Heekin, & Rizzo, 2008;

Figure 8.1 Latest version of *Virtual Iraq/Afghanistan* scenarios
Source: Courtesy of USC Institute for Creative Technologies.

Reger et al., 2007, 2011; Reger, Gahm, Rizzo, Swanson, & Duma, 2009; Wilson, Onorati, Mishkind, Reger, & Gahm, 2008).

An open clinical trial to evaluate the feasibility of using VRE with active duty participants who had previously engaged in PTSD treatments (e.g., group counseling, EMDR, medication) without benefit was conducted at the Naval Medical Center San Diego and at Camp Pendleton (Rizzo et al., 2011b). The standard treatment protocol consisted of two-times weekly, 90- to 120-minute sessions over 5 weeks. The VRE exposure exercises followed the principles of prolonged exposure (PE) therapy (Foa et al., 1999) and a manual developed for that study (Rothbaum, Difede, & Rizzo, 2008). Self-report measures were obtained at baseline and prior to sessions 3, 5, 7, 9, 10, and 1 week and 3 months posttreatment to assess in-treatment and follow-up symptom status. The measures used were the PTSD Checklist-Military Version (PCL-M) (Blanchard, Jones-Alexander, Buckley, & Forneris, 1996), Beck Anxiety Inventory (BAI) (Beck, Epstein, Brown, & Steer, 1988) and Patient Health Questionnaire-Depression (PHQ-9) (Kroenke & Spitzer, 2002).

Analyses of the first 20 active duty service members to complete treatment (19 male, 1 female, Mean Age = 28, Age Range: 21–51) indicated positive clinical outcomes. The average number of sessions for the sample was just under 11. Two of the successful treatment completers had documented mild and moderate TBIs, which provide an early indication that this form of exposure therapy can be useful (and beneficial) for this population. Results from uncontrolled open trials are difficult to generalize and should be interpreted with caution. However, using accepted diagnostic measures, 80% of the treatment completers in the VRE sample showed both statistically and clinically meaningful reductions in PTSD, anxiety and depression symptoms that were maintained 3 months posttreatment. Also, anecdotal evidence from patient reports suggested that they saw improvements in their everyday life.

Other studies have also reported positive outcomes. Two early case studies have been published that reported positive results using VRE (Gerardi et al., 2008; Reger & Gahm, 2008). Following those studies, an open clinical trial with active duty soldiers ($n = 24$) indicated significant pre- and postreductions in PCL-M scores and a large treatment effect size (Cohen's $d = 1.17$). After an average of 7 sessions, 45% of those treated no longer screened positive for PTSD and 62% had reliably improved (Reger et al., 2011).

Currently three randomized controlled trials (RCT) are ongoing with the *Virtual Iraq/Afghanistan* system with active duty and veteran populations. Two RCTs are focusing on comparisons of treatment efficacy between VRE and imaginal PE, while the third RCT investigates the additive value of supplementing VRE and imaginal PE with a cognitive enhancer called *D-Cycloserine* (DCS). DCS, a N-methyl-d-aspartate partial agonist, has been shown to facilitate extinction learning in laboratory animals when infused bilaterally within the bilateral amygdala prior to extinction training (Walker, Ressler, Lu, & Davis, 2002). The first clinical test in humans that combined DCS with VRE was performed by Ressler et al. (2004) with participants diagnosed with acrophobia ($n = 28$). Participants who received DCS + VRE had significantly enhanced decreases in fear within the virtual environment 1 week and 3 months posttreatment, and reported significantly more improvement than the placebo group in their overall acrophobic symptoms at 3-month follow-up and on a psychophysiological measure of anxiety.

The research on VRE has been supported by the relatively quick adoption of the VRE approach by approximately 55 Military, VA, and university clinic sites over the past 3 years.

SUGGESTIONS FOR THE USE OF *VIRTUAL IRAQ/AFGHANISTAN* FOR VRE

Research on VRE has led to the development of standardized treatment protocols for clinicians using VRE. These protocols provide important instructions and suggestions to clinicians for conducting VRE, as well as key considerations for clinicians before they engage patients in the treatment.

Prior to Initiating Treatment With *Virtual Iraq/Afghanistan*

When a possible referral for VRE is received, the following information should be elicited to make sure this is an appropriate treatment modality for this individual:

- Referral source (how they heard about the program) and why specifically they are seeking treatment.
- The basic nature of their symptomatology, that is, elicit whether a doctor diagnosed them with PTSD or do a basic screen to identify whether they may have symptoms of PTSD.
- The nature of their exposure to the traumatic event. It is important before scheduling treatment to ascertain if the nature of their trauma seems appropriate for the virtual reality environment; however, one should not elicit their entire experience over the phone before the initial appointment. Currently, there are three virtual Iraq/Afghanistan environments: a virtual Humvee driving down a desert highway alone; a virtual Humvee driving down a desert highway in a convoy; and a Middle Eastern city foot patrol scene. If one of these environments would not be appropriate given the nature of the patient's traumatic event, you may want to consider prolonged imaginal exposure without the VR.

Components of Treatment

Most treatment sessions will include:

- Review of patient's reactions and functioning (approximately 15 minutes)
- Virtual reality exposure therapy (45 minutes)
- Processing of material that emerged during exposure (20 to 30 minutes)
- Assignment of homework for next session or conclusion of session (5 to 10 minutes)

Other components that may be used include:

- Breathing relaxation
- In vivo exposure
- Cognitive restructuring
- Pleasant events scheduling

Options for Treatment

There are slight variations on the exact protocols being used currently, and all seem to be effective at this time. We recommend VRE alone as the primary treatment component, matching the virtual reality to what the patient describes as the most traumatic memories in exposure from the start of treatment. Others have preferred to begin with imaginal exposure only for the first one to two sessions, followed by gradual exposure to the virtual environments allowing the patient to "wander" and explore the virtual environment while describing aloud any memories triggered by the virtual reality environment for one to two sessions. Then, finally, imaginal exposure to the most traumatic memories matching what the patient describes with the virtual reality. Still others prefer to start with imaginal exposure first to the most traumatic memories for one or two sessions prior to initiating VRE. All of the current studies begin with VRE.

VR Assessment

This chapter is written for clinicians using VRE with OIF or OEF veterans. At a minimum, we suggest administering the CAPS, the PTSD Symptom Scale (PSS) (interview or self-report version), or similar measures such as the PCL-M to assess the patient's PTSD symptoms as well as the Beck Depression Inventory (BDI) or similar measures to assess depression before and after treatment. We also recommend administering the PSS self-report before every session to plot the patient's progress. Other assessment instruments may be useful depending on the setting.

OVERVIEW OF VRE USING *VIRTUAL IRAQ/AFGHANISTAN*

The following is part of a current protocol of VRE utilizing *Virtual Iraq* or *Virtual Afghanistan* (Difede, Rothbaum, & Rizzo, 2011). This description focuses on using VR during sessions but does not include imaginal or in vivo exposure homework assignments, which should be used when conducting a full protocol of VRE and can be found in other texts (e.g., Foa, Hembree, & Rothbaum, 2007; Rothbaum et al., 2008). Much of the treatment is presented here in the voice of the clinician making the text user-friendly for clinical application. When presenting the text to the patient, the clinician should "talk it" rather than read it or lecture it to the patient.

Session 1

Overview

1. Present session agenda (5 minutes)
2. Provide overview of treatment (30 minutes)
3. Gather information from patient (35 minutes)
4. Breathing retraining (15 minutes)
5. Assign homework and end session (5 minutes)

Present Session Agenda

"Today's session will be an introduction to our treatment. I'll tell you a bit about what to expect, some basic information about our treatment, and an overview of the interventions we will use and how they will target the symptoms and problems you are having. Then I'll ask you to tell me more about your symptoms, your experience, and yourself in general. Finally, we'll introduce and practice our first skill, a breathing technique, which should be helpful for you. This entire treatment is collaborative, so feel free to ask questions and express any concerns you might have. It's best we talk about everything openly to get the most from our time together, so please feel free at all times to discuss honestly any problems, concerns, etc. that may arise. Before I begin, do you have any questions?"

Provide Overview of Treatment

Introduction: "Based on our assessment, we found that you have posttraumatic stress disorder, which we call PTSD for short, as well as . . ." (*List other diagnoses/problems*). "This treatment is designed to treat all of the symptoms of PTSD, but many of the interventions we will use are effective in reducing feelings of depression and generalized anxiety as well.

"The good news is that PTSD is a disorder for which there are effective treatments, and our treatment program includes several interventions that have been shown to be very helpful in reducing symptoms and helping people recover from trauma. I will review the treatment plan and interventions now, and we will discuss them in detail when they are introduced in later sessions."

Treatment Duration: "This treatment involves our meeting weekly for eight more sessions after today, nine total, and each session will be approximately 90 minutes long."

Goals of Treatment: "The goal of this treatment is to help you deal with what happened in Iraq [or Afghanistan] and to hopefully decrease the posttraumatic stress symptoms that you have been experiencing. The way we view PTSD is that someone is haunted by something that happened in their past. What we want to do in treatment is to help them process the traumatic experience and come to some peace with it. **To that end, several techniques will be utilized to address two of the primary factors that maintain post-trauma symptoms: avoidance and unhelpful thoughts and beliefs**. We know that avoiding thinking about the trauma can lead to symptoms of PTSD becoming chronic. When you allow yourself to think about the trauma in a safe environment, you are able to challenge some of the unhelpful thoughts and beliefs. The core of the treatment will be exposure therapy, not exposure as in wartime, but helping you confront the memory of what happened in a therapeutic manner so it gets easier. In trauma research, exposure therapy has been found to be the most effective technique for helping PTSD.

"Imaginal exposure requires a person to retell his or her trauma experience repeatedly in the present tense as if it is happening now. Therefore, the person is instructed to narrate the experience in the present tense, describing out loud everything that s/he sees, smells and hears. In order to enhance the reliving component, we are building on the traditional exposure technique by using the virtual reality as a tool for the exposure. The virtual reality helps to engage your senses, thereby enabling you to reexperience the memory of the trauma more realistically. You will use the virtual reality to aid in the retelling of your experience repeatedly over the course of treatment. Though this may seem daunting and may indeed be a difficult task, it is a very important part of treatment that works to help you process what happened. By going through it repeatedly, it does get easier." (*Allow patient here to voice any concerns about treatment.*)

Breathing: Following a trauma, people often find that their bodies are at a constant state of alertness. Symptoms such as irritability, difficulty sleeping and trouble concentrating are common. Relaxation and breathing exercises are instrumental in addressing these symptoms. In this treatment, we use a brief breathing relaxation method to help our bodies relax and decrease these symptoms at times when it's not the right time to do exposure, like going to sleep, at work or while driving."

Cognitive distortions (unhelpful thoughts): A traumatic event can also change a person's view and perspective about him- or herself, about other people and about the world in general. Sometimes, these thoughts are inaccurate. During treatment, we will discuss whether your views about yourself, and about the world in general, have changed and evaluate the accuracy and helpfulness of these beliefs and thoughts."

Treatment adherence: "As you may have already guessed, this treatment can be intense, and at times distressing. The reason that we do it, however, is because it is the treatment that has the most success. You might find yourself thinking of cancelling sessions or not showing up since you know the sessions might be tough. But this is a short-term treatment for only nine sessions. Your symptoms have been distressing and causing problems in your life for [length of time]. If you can bear with at the most, eight more appointments, hopefully you can have some relief from the problems that have been bothering you.

"If you experience urges to not come to your session, it is *very* important that we talk about it. I will *not* be offended. We know that it can be challenging for people to confront their worst fears, but we also know that the interventions included in this treatment, especially the exposure, are the most effective PTSD treatments out there and our experience is that most people who stick with the treatment find it worthwhile.

"These interventions really do work best if you come each week. This is really important once we start the exposure exercises. If for some reason your schedule changes or things happen in your life that makes regular attendance difficult, it is very important for us to talk about it and I will be as flexible as possible in scheduling the sessions to be convenient for you."

Elicit any questions: "I know that was a lot of information I just provided. Do you have any questions about anything at this point?" If the patient says he or she is nervous or not sure that he or she wants to do this, the therapist can respond, "That's exactly why you need to do this. If it were easy or didn't bother you, we wouldn't need to do this. It does take courage and we don't use that word lightly. We define courage as being scared and doing it anyway because it's the right thing to do."

Gather Information From Patient

"Now that I've told you about the treatment, I'm going to ask you a bit about yourself. I'd like to learn about why you're seeking treatment, what problems you find most distressing, and a bit about yourself in general."

Information to elicit from patient:

- Why did he or she seeks treatment.
- What symptoms are most distressing.
- Describe his or her deployment(s).

- Some information on the most distressing trauma. If there is a close second, it can be noted and will be the focus of exposure if there's time for an adequate response.
- Other trauma history.
- Social situation and any current social stressors.
- Occupational situation and any occupational or financial stressors.
- Social support and resources he or she can rely on during this treatment.
- Suicidal ideation and contracting for safety.

Breathing Retraining

The clinician will explain to the patient the association between anxiety and quick breathing demonstrating the usefulness of breathing slowly and calmly to reduce tension or stress. The clinician then takes the patient through a breathing exercise, teaching the patient a technique for engaging in slow, calming breaths. The patient will be given a recording of the breathing exercise made during the session to practice at home and develop the skill. For an example text, please refer to Foa, Hembree, and Rothbaum, (2007).

Assign Homework and End Session

The clinician assigns the following homework: (a) Practice breathing retraining three times per day, and (b) read "Rationale for Treatment by Prolonged Exposure" handout (see Foa et al., 2007). Remind patients that the more they practice the breathing, the better trained their body will be to relax and to use it when they really need it.

At the conclusion of the session, (a) elicit any questions, doubts, or concerns; (b) instill hope and excitement for starting this work together; (c) make sure that the next session time is scheduled, it is okay also to schedule all eight sessions and write them down for patient; (d) give therapist's card with contact information; and (e) give patient rationale for treatment by prolonged exposure handout.

Session 2

Overview

1. Review homework (5 minutes)
2. Present session agenda (5 minutes)
3. Discuss common reactions to trauma and normalize patient's reactions (45 minutes)
4. Present detailed rationale for exposure (20 minutes)
5. Introduce SUDS Scale (10 minutes)
6. Assign homework and end session (5 minutes)

Review Homework

The clinician will check in on the patient's week in general as well as check in on specific homework assignments. The clinician should also ask about the patient's perceptions regarding treatment.

Present Session Agenda

"This session we will focus in detail on common reactions to traumatic events, and see how your symptoms may or may not be similar to what we discuss. Then I will present a more detailed rationale for the exposure therapy that we will begin next week."

Discuss Common Reactions to Trauma and Normalize Patient's Reactions

The clinician should provide the patient with psychoeducation on PTSD while normalizing and validating the patient's symptoms. The clinician should discuss common reactions to a traumatic event (e.g., depressed mood, guilt, substance abuse) and give the patient a detailed handout on this information to review during the week. To review the "Common Reactions to Trauma" handout, please refer to Foa et al., 2007. It is important to make this a conversation rather than a lecture. This can be done best by asking the patient about his or her experience, saying "Is that something you've been experiencing?" after each cluster of symptoms. At the end of the discussion, revisit the most distressing symptoms and/or suicidality as needed.

Present Detailed Rationale for Exposure

"As we have mentioned previously, exposure is the first line of treatment for PTSD because of its proven effectiveness. You may remember that during the exposure, you will relate your traumatic experience in as much detail as possible, repeatedly, in a structured way. I am going to take some time now to explain the mechanism by which exposure works."

The clinician may use different methods for explaining the rationale for exposure. Often using a metaphor is useful, for an example of a file cabinet metaphor, please refer to Foa et al. (2007).

"This technique may seem counterintuitive, as our natural reaction is not to dwell on disturbing memories; however, it has been shown to work. I have faith in this technique because I have seen it work with many patients, though I know you may doubt it because you have not seen it work as I have. But I am going to walk you through it and we'll work at a pace that you can manage. It is certainly not an easy task and takes courage to face these memories head on. However, avoiding the memories simply doesn't work. **Although avoidance may help reduce the anxiety for the moment (i.e., work in the short run), in the long run it maintains PTSD symptoms and prevents new learning.** This may be difficult, but it is the path to proper healing. It is also a short-term treatment. You have been living with these symptoms for an extended period of time. This treatment is only seven more sessions. Although it may be painful initially, it becomes less painful as exposure is repeated."

Distinguishing between exposure and intrusive thoughts: "Some people tell us that they think about it all the time anyway, so how is this different? The way most people with PTSD think about the traumatic event is not therapeutic. It's like if the event were a book, the book falls open and they read a line, and they hate it and slam the book shut. Then something opens up the book again, they read a line, and they hate it and slam the book shut again. In contrast, this treatment consists of therapeutic exposure. We will open the book and read it all the way through over and over again to try to make some sense of it and to help you feel in control if and when you want to read it.

"So the central idea behind this type of treatment is that the trauma needs to be emotionally processed, or digested and organized, so that it can become less painful. The process is similar to the grief process: When a loved one dies, it is extremely painful, but by experiencing and expressing that pain like through crying and by spending the time focused on it at the funeral, it gradually becomes less painful. Eventually, we can think about that person without crying, although the loss will always be sad."

Distinguishing between event and memory: "Your body is reacting to reminders of the event as if the event was happening again. Exposure to the memories helps the body to distinguish the memories from the event itself, recognize the memory is upsetting but not dangerous, and importantly, realize that you can handle the memories. Then, as you do the exposure repeatedly, the overwhelming emotion that accompanies it will decrease. So the memory will always be sad or upsetting, but not something overwhelming that controls your life.

"So to summarize, by confronting the memories through exposure, it helps to: (a) block avoidance; (b) process and organize the trauma; (c) discriminate the memories from the trauma itself; (d) make you realize that memories are not dangerous and that you can handle them giving you mastery over this experience; (e) decrease anxiety and distress as you repeatedly confront the memory through a process known as habituation; and (f) give you back a feeling of control and competence. Facing the exposure gives you control over the memories that feel like they are controlling you.

"In this process, you'll need to try to confront the memories and any emotions they bring up. Any attempts to distance yourself from those emotions can negatively impact the treatment. This is true both during the session, and for the day or so afterward when your brain is still processing the exposure. So for the duration of this treatment, feeling bad emotions isn't the enemy, but avoiding them is. For that reason, as much as possible you'll need to avoid taking medications or substances that you don't take on a regular basis that will interfere with this process. That includes benzodiazepenes like Xanax, Klonopin, Valium, and Ativan and pain medication that you take prn. If you take any of these medications, they should be taken on a regular schedule, and not in response to anxiety or distress that might come up from the session. If you don't take them on a regular schedule, you should not take them on the day of the session before the start of the session, or for about 24 hours after the session. This also includes alcohol or illegal drugs, which you should not take for the day or so prior to the session, since we don't want you coming in hung over, and for at least 24 hours following the session, or in response to distress that comes up from these memories. Do you have any concerns about that?"

Introduce SUDS Scale

"For your account of the trauma, we will be evaluating your discomfort at the time by using a SUDS scale. The acronym SUDS stands for subjective units of distress and the scale ranges from 0 to 100. Distress may mean feelings of anxiety, anger, fear or whatever emotion it may evoke. A SUDS rating of 100 informs me that you are highly distressed and 0 indicates no distress at all. I will be asking you for your SUDS before you begin the exposure, and then after it's completed I'll ask for your SUDS, and, at the end, I'll ask you to report the highest SUDS you reached during the exposure. You'll just give a number indicating how you are feeling right now, sitting in the room with me, not how you were feeling at that point in Iraq [or Afghanistan]." Elicit anchors from the patient of a "0"-rated time in his or her life and a "100"-rated time in his or her life.

Assign Homework and End Session

The clinician assigns the following homework: (a) continue to practice breathing retraining, and (b) read common reactions handout several times (see Foa et al., 2007) and discuss it with family and friends as desired.

Session 3

Overview

1. Review homework (10 minutes)
2. Present session agenda (5 minutes)
3. Present brief review of rationale for exposure (5 minutes)
4. Instructions for exposure (10 minutes)
5. Conduct exposure (30 to 40 minutes)
6. Process exposure and end session (15 to 20 minutes)

Review Homework

The clinician will check in on the patient's week in general as well as check in on specific homework assignments (breathing practice and reading common reactions to traumatic events). The clinician should also ask about the patient's perceptions regarding treatment.

Present Session Agenda

"This session we will start by briefly reviewing the rationale for the exposure. Then I will give you the specific instructions on how to do the exposure, and we'll conduct our first exposure session. After the exposure, we'll spend some time processing it before the end of the session. Do you have any questions about the agenda?"

Brief Review of Rationale for Exposure

"Just to review from last time, in the long run, avoidance maintains PTSD symptoms. The goal of the exposure is to revisit the memory in a controlled and structured environment, to help you to process and organize this trauma memory so that it will no longer feel overwhelming to think about, nor will it intrude on your life. By repeatedly confronting your fear, and connecting the feelings about the event with the memory where it belongs, you will learn that the memories are not dangerous, and that you can handle the emotions associated with the memory, and be more in control of it. The repetition of the memory will facilitate habituation and decrease anxiety and other symptoms of PTSD. The memory and experience will remain a part of you, but you will be able to choose to think about it if/when you desire to do so." Elicit any questions or doubts about the rationale.

Instructions for Exposure

Relating narrative details: "I'm going to ask you to start at a point just prior to the incident and recount, in full detail, a narrative of the trauma. It is key to the exposure to really immerse yourself in the memory so that it feels almost like you're back there, even while you know that you are really here safe in this room and it is just a memory. We say it's like keeping one foot here (in the present) and one foot there (in the past). It is very important to try and experience all the feelings and emotions that are connected to this event, and that you not try to hold back the emotions though it might be your inclination to do so.

"In order to increase your engagement in the memory, you should tell it in the present tense as though it were currently happening, for example, 'I get my orders and find I am suppose to go to . . . I am driving down . . . I see. . . .' As you relate the event, add every detail you can think of, using all of your senses to describe what you are seeing, hearing, smelling, thinking, and feeling throughout every aspect of the experience. As you relate the details, focus on putting yourself there and letting yourself feel any emotions that arise. Remember that avoidance is the enemy, not emotions, so if you feel negative emotions we don't want to avoid them, and in fact that means we are doing what we need to do. We are going to aim for a target time of 30 to 40 minutes for the exposure, since it has to be long enough for the habituation process to start occurring. That means that when you're done, I'll ask you to start again right back at the beginning without taking yourself out of the memory. I may also ask some questions or clarifications, but I'll try to minimize that since I don't want to disrupt your immersion in the memory."

The patient will recount the most traumatic memories while immersed in the virtual world. The patient will recount his or her memories with eyes open and the therapist will match the virtual reality environment to the patient's recounting as much as possible. Though one of the clinician's goals is to re-create a virtual scenario with as much content as possible that matches the patient's reported traumatic memories, it is not likely, nor necessary, that the clinician match the scenario exactly to the trauma. In this first session, the therapist should minimize the amount of VR sensory elements that are added, and may utilize less intense elements; for example, a small explosion instead of full IED stimuli or keeping the volume low. Depending on the patient's engagement, he or she may just stay in the environment without many added elements.

"We will be using virtual reality to aid in the exposure exercise. You will focus on your own experience and tell it while immersed in a virtual environment. Let me explain the function of each piece of equipment. You will be wearing headphones and a head mounted display (HMD) that will allow you to view 3-dimensional computerized images. The virtual world is programmed such that I control what you experience in VR by touching preprogrammed keys on the keyboard and you can control your movements by looking around and moving with a joystick. As you view the scenes through the HMD, I will be watching the same images simultaneously on the computer screen. I will speak into a microphone that will allow you to hear me through your headphones, and I can hear when you speak to me. In addition to the sights and sounds, you will be sitting on a platform that may vibrate in conjunction with certain sounds to add a tactile element. The sensory elements will be added gradually throughout the sessions, at a pace individualized for you. The elements and environment may not be a perfect match for what you experienced, but our experience has shown us that a match is not necessary, and an approximate environment or cues that trigger your memory are sufficient. We are using virtual reality to help you engage with the memory. If certain aspects aren't a great match, try not to let yourself get distracted by them. Do you have any questions before we begin?" (The clinician should direct the patient to sit in the appropriate chair and put on the headphones and HMD while introducing the patient to the HMD and other VR components.)

"Okay, so as we discussed, you'll begin describing the events leading up to the incident on that day, describing the sights, sounds, smells, your thoughts and feelings, and as many details of the experience as possible, speaking in the first person and the present tense. Before we start, can you tell me your SUDS score right now sitting in the room?" Record the patient's response on a SUDS rating form. "Okay, let's get started. Its [date] and you are [location]. Tell me what's happening now."

Conduct Exposure

During the exposure, prompt for present tense if necessary by repeating patient's last phrase back to them in the present tense, for example, "I am driving back to the FOB." Offer periodic encouragement such as: "You're doing great," "Stay with it," "What happens next," "This is exactly what you need to be doing; keep going," "You're safe here, go on," or "I know this is very painful for you to talk about, but you're doing a good job."

At the end of the exposure ask for a final SUDS score and an estimate of the peak SUDS that was reached during the exposure. Record these numbers into the SUDS form. The target time for an exposure exercise is 30 to 40 minutes.

Process Exposure and End Session

Instructions for clinician: In addition to fear extinction, which occurs during exposure therapy, you are attempting to help the patient to emotionally and cognitively process the event by placing it in a broader context, allowing it to be examined from different vantage points, to eventually gain a sense of peace with the experience. You are trying to make certain experiences explicit, for example, that by staying with the memory repeatedly, it becomes less distressing. You will try to identify unhelpful thoughts and help the patient challenge them and identify paths that he or she needs to take to think about them differently.

Following completion of the imaginal exposure, ask the patient for his or her reactions, using an open-ended query such as, "How was that experience for you?" Often they may express surprise at the intensity of the feelings experienced, or about some of the details that were recalled during the exposure. Allow them to sit with how they are feeling and validate these reactions. Always acknowledge the difficulty of the task and reinforce the effort to complete the exposure exercise and tolerate the affect. Remind them again that this processing of emotions is what could not happen at the time of the trauma, but needs to happen now.

It is also helpful to then share some of your observations, such as noting increasing amount of detail present in the narration over consecutive recountings, noting how much was going on (thoughts and feelings) in a short amount of time, noting changes in levels of distress, or noting particular areas of difficulty. It also may be helpful to assist the individual in labeling some of his/her feelings.

Approach areas of difficulty with a Socratic questioning approach: For example, if the patient is questioning whether he or she might have done something to prevent a given outcome, ask specifically about what that might be, how he or she might have anticipated the event, or what other factors might have been relevant to the outcome. Another important query might be regarding the patient's assessment of his/her own and others' performance in doing their jobs and making decisions under such stressful conditions which may lead to the acknowledgment of being in a position in which there was often no good choice to make. With this approach, your goal is to have the patient begin to entertain other interpretations of the way the events transpired, and to begin to challenge some assumptions or judgments that may be inaccurate.

Sometimes an obvious topic will emerge, and you may judge that the patient is not yet ready to discuss it or hear alternative approaches; in which case you may choose not to raise it until a later session. You can acknowledge it and bookmark it, for example, "It sounds like you are really struggling with. . . . I think that is going to be an important part for us to work on and we will come back to it."

Common themes to explore include feelings of guilt or blame, anger and grief related to the incident, as well as generalizations drawn from the incident to current behavior like hatred of an ethnic group or questions of own or command competency.

Session 4

Overview

1. Check-in (10 to 15 minutes)
2. Present session agenda (5 minutes)
3. Conduct exposure (30 to 40 minutes)
4. Process exposure (30 minutes)
5. End session (5 minutes)

Check-In

The clinician will check in on the patient's week in general as well as check in on any changes in symptoms in the past week, including more frequent thoughts of trauma. The clinician will normalize any changes, telling the patient that symptoms may increase logically since the patient is facing something he/she has tried to avoid but that indicates the treatment is working. The clinician should also check-in on the patient's perceptions regarding treatment.

Present Session Agenda

"This session we will get right into the exposure and focus on the exposure and processing pieces. You did a great job last time. This time we're going to dig even deeper, and I want you to include everything in your memory and all sensory elements." As needed, the clinician will ask more questions to flesh out details or evoke emotion.

Conduct Exposure

Conduct exposure to entire trauma memory, the same as last time. Add more sensory elements using VR as needed. The target time for the exposure session is 30 to 40 minutes. At the end of the exposure ask for a final SUDS score and an estimate of peak SUDS that was reached during the exposure, while recording the numbers.

Process Exposure

Following the exposure session, ask the patient, "How was that for you? Did you notice anything in particular?" In addition, you may check in on discussions from previous weeks and/or you may raise themes that you have noticed.

End Session

Schedule next session.

Session 5

Overview

1. Check-in (10 minutes)
2. Present session agenda (5 minutes)
3. Introduce and identify hot spots (10 to 15 minutes)
4. Conduct exposure (30 to 40 minutes)
5. Process exposure and end session (20 minutes)

Check-In

The clinician will check in on the patient's week in general as well as check in on any changes in symptoms in the past week, including more frequent thoughts of trauma. The clinician will normalize any changes, telling the patient that symptoms may increase logically since the patient is facing something he or she has tried to avoid but that indicates the treatment is working. The clinician should also ask about the patient's perceptions regarding treatment. Lastly, the clinician should identify potential hot spots, such as by asking, "Have you noticed any parts of the memory bothering you more than others?"

Present Session Agenda

"This session we are going to move to the next step in the exposure, where we focus on hot spots. We'll spend a bit of time discussing hot spots, and then we will do the exposure and processing." The clinician should only start with hot spots once the patient is ready.

Introduce and Identify Hot Spots

Hot spots are the specific moments in the trauma memory that cause more anxiety than the rest of the narrative. It is often the moment the explosion occurred, or gunfire started, or when the patient or a comrade was injured or thought he or she would die. There are usually several hot spots in any trauma narrative. The therapist should make notes during exposure about which moments seem to be the hardest for the patient, and talk to the patient about what bits of the memory trigger more anxiety during the exposure in session.

Explanation for patient: "We've spent a couple of sessions going over the entire memory from start to finish. Now we'll start focusing on smaller pieces of the experience, which we call hot spots. I'm going to ask you to identify two to three parts of the trauma that were the most intense emotionally. This could be a 10-minute segment or a 10-second segment. Then we will choose one to begin with, and you will conduct the exposure on just that one segment of the experience. You'll try to uncover every detail of that hot spot, and retell it repeatedly, possibly retelling it eight times in one session. By focusing on the most intense pieces of the trauma, you can really facilitate habituation to that part. It has been shown that as you habituate to the hot spots your arousal to the less intense parts of the memory decreases as well.

"We think about it a bit like getting a massage. If you're having back discomfort and go for a massage, the massage therapist may work on your whole back, but if she finds a knot, she will focus on that knot and go over and over it in order to work it out. We're going to do the same thing—we'll focus on the area which is the most distressing and go over and over it to address it. Does that make sense to you? Can you tell me what those hot spots might be for you?"

Have the patient identify his or her hot spots and rate them from least to most intense. Start with the worst and repeatedly expose the patient to that in minute detail, as if in slow motion, over and over until it gets easier. At that point, move on to the next highest hot spot and repeat as above.

Conduct Exposure

Conduct exposure to the specified hot spot. Allow patient to tell it once through, and then help them to flesh it out in subsequent retellings, leaving no stone unturned, by asking questions like: "What thoughts are going through your head at that moment?," "What kinds of feelings are you having at that moment?," "What is your body feeling at that moment?," "What other sounds do you notice?," and/or "Describe the details of . . ." (may be clothing, person's face, dead body, wreckage, etc). The discussion should be focused on the hot spot. VR sensory elements should be used to match the hot spot. At the end of the exposure ask for a final SUDS score and an estimate of peak SUDS that was reached during the exposure, and record the numbers into the SUDS form. The target time for the exposure is 30 to 40 minutes.

Process Exposure and End Session

Ask the patient "How was that for you? Did you notice anything in particular?" You may check in on discussions from previous weeks and/or raise themes that you have noticed. Schedule next session.

Sessions 6–8

Overview

1. Check-in (10 to 15 minutes)
2. Present session agenda (5 minutes)

3. Conduct exposure to hot spot (30 to 40 minutes)
4. Process exposure (30 minutes)
5. End session (5 minutes)

Check-In

The clinician will check in on the patient's week in general as well as check in on any changes in symptoms in the past week, including more frequent thoughts of trauma. The clinician will normalize any changes, and ask about the patient's perceptions regarding treatment.

Present Session Agenda

"This session we will continue with the hot spots and try to really engage in everything which is there. Do you have any questions before we begin?"

Conduct Exposure to Hot Spots

Conduct exposure to hot spot. If patient has shown habituation to the last hot spot, then continue with the next one. If not, repeat the last hot spot, with goal of completing all hot spots by end of Session 8. By end of Session 8, aim for description of all details and habituation to all sensory elements. If habituation is not occurring, troubleshoot with consultants or supervisors to facilitate habituation. At the end of the exposure ask for a final SUDS score and an estimate of peak SUDS that was reached during the exposure, and record the numbers into the SUDS form. The target time for the exposure session is 30 to 40 minutes.

Process Exposure

Ask the patient "How was that for you? Did you notice anything in particular?" You may check in on discussion from previous week and/or raise themes that you have noticed. Process all themes that have emerged.

End Session

Schedule next session.

Session 9

Overview

1. Check-in (10 minutes)
2. Present session agenda (5 minutes)
3. Conduct exposure to entire trauma memory (25 to 30 minutes)
4. Process exposure (15 minutes)
5. Review treatment program and patient's progress (20 to 30 minutes)
6. Termination (10 minutes)

Check-In

Check in on the week in general.

Present Session Agenda

"This session is our final one. We will conduct our final exposure to wrap up the whole exposure exercise and note the differences between the first time you did the exposure and this time. Then we will review the skills we introduced in treatment, your progress over the course of therapy, and how to continue working for further improvement. Do you have any questions before we begin?"

Conduct Exposure

Conduct exposure to entire trauma memory, from start to finish for the last time, as many times as time allows up to 30 minutes. (Note: This may be one time through, or may be more than once depending on the length of the trauma.) The target time for this exposure session is 30 minutes.

Process Exposure

Ask the patient: "How was that for you? Did you notice anything in particular?" Ask the patient: "How was that different than your first exposure? And how was it different after working on the hot spots?"

Review Treatment Program and Patient's Progress

Review of skills: "We introduced a couple of skills in this protocol. We began by describing what PTSD is and how it manifests itself. We spent a long time describing the rationale behind the exposure therapy. We utilized a breathing exercise to help induce a relaxation response when necessary. Then we focused on the exposure exercises, and implemented processing to evaluate themes, emotions, and changes in cognitions that were due to the trauma. Were any of those in particular helpful or not helpful for you?"

Review of progress in treatment: "There were some major changes that occurred over the course of treatment." Review any changes here, including: PTSD symptom changes, comorbid disorder symptom changes, relationship/quality of life changes, and habituation to exposure. If applicable, say, "I know there is more you would like to improve. There is evidence that in many cases symptoms continue to improve after the end of treatment."

Symptom exacerbation: "It is not uncommon for people to have periods of time when a flare up of symptoms occurs again. It may be due to a certain trigger like an anniversary or meeting someone connected to the event, or come out of the blue. It is important in those situations to remember you are able to handle the emotions related to the event. Make sure not to avoid or isolate. Make sure to use breathing skills, and process your own reactions."

Positive feedback about work: "This was a very difficult treatment, and you should give yourself a lot of credit for facing this head on and giving it your all. I enjoyed working with you and wish you the best of luck."

Termination

Discuss future goals and make referrals if applicable.

Case Vignette: Ann

A similar protocol of VRE was conducted with a patient (we'll call her Ann) who was part of the ONR study discussed earlier. Ann was a 22-year-old, female Army private who met *DSM-IV* criteria for PTSD and major depressive disorder, recurrent (MDD). Her service in Iraq typically involved direct evaluation of locations immediately following suicide and/or IED bombings, and she was exposed to significant human carnage during the course of her 1-year deployment. On returning stateside, following an evaluation, Ann was diagnosed with PTSD and agreed to participate in a standardized clinical research protocol. The protocol employed a 10-session treatment model that includes components of psychoeducation, initial imaginal exposure transitioning to prolonged VRE, and exposure-based homework exercises between sessions. Psychological assessment instruments administered were the PCL-M, PHQ-9, and BAI. Subjective Units of Distress (SUDs; 0 to 100 scale) were gathered every 5 minutes during the virtual reality exposure. The homework included listening to the audiotapes of Ann's self-generated verbal narrative of her trauma-relevant experiences while participating in VRE.

Ann showed a gradual and progressive improvement over the course of the VRE sessions. Scores on the PCL-M, PHQ-9, and BAI, prior to treatment were 42, 20, and 12, respectively. Posttreatment scores on these measures decreased to 22, 3, and 0. At follow-up, Ann did not meet *DSM-IV* diagnostic criteria for PTSD, and met remission status for MDD. She displayed signs of habituation across VRE sessions and self-reported a concomitant decline across homework sessions while listening to the audiotape of her trauma narrative recorded during treatment sessions. For example, initial SUDs ratings while doing audiotape listening of exposure at home fell in the 30 to 35 range and declined to the 10 to 15 range at the end of treatment. Following completion of treatment, Ann was able to return to her unit and, at 3-month follow-up, she continued to maintain the therapeutic gains observed at the end of treatment with scores on the PCL-M, PHQ-9, and BAI, at 18, 1, and 1, respectively.

Case Vignette Discussion Questions

1. Why would the use of virtual reality enhance and speed up the effectiveness of exposure therapy with this case?
2. What assessment issues should have been considered in this case to ensure that using virtual reality was safe and appropriate for Ann? For example, what if Ann's PTSD were comorbid with suicidality?

CONCLUSION

A recent report noted that among Iraq/Afghanistan War veterans, "those whose responses were positive for a mental disorder, only 23% to 40% sought mental health care. Those whose responses were positive for a mental disorder were twice as likely as those whose responses were negative to report concern about possible stigmatization and other barriers to seeking mental health care" (Hoge et al., 2004, p. 13). Although military training methodology has better prepared soldiers for combat in recent years, such hesitancy to seek treatment for difficulties that emerge on return from combat, especially by those who may need it most, suggests an area of military mental health care that is in need of attention. VRE may be an appealing option and promote treatment seeking by certain demographic groups in need of care. The current generation of young military personnel, having grown up with digital gaming technology, may actually be more attracted to and comfortable with participation in a VR application approach as an alternative to what is viewed as traditional "talk therapy" (even though such talk therapy would obviously occur in the course of a recommended multi-component approach for this disorder). It has been generally reported by practitioners who use VR to treat civilians with simple phobias that patients who have avoided therapy for years will sometimes choose to seek VRE, perhaps due to a reduced perception of stigma. Reger et al. (2007) has recently reported a similar attitudinal propensity in military personnel; among those who reported a disinclination to seek standard mental health treatment, 19% rated a VR approach more favorably.

Of note, VRE is not intended to be an automated treatment protocol that is administered in a "self-help" format. The presentation of such emotionally evocative VR combat-related scenarios, while providing treatment options not possible until recently, will most likely produce therapeutic benefits when administered within the context of appropriate care via a thoughtful professional appreciation of the complexity and impact of this disorder.

CHAPTER DISCUSSION QUESTIONS

1. What are the signs and symptoms of PTSD?
2. Which class of psychotherapeutic techniques have received the strongest evidence to date for PTSD?
3. What is the efficacy of prolonged imaginal exposure for PTSD?
4. What is the efficacy of virtual reality exposure for PTSD?
5. How are virtual reality exposure and prolonged imaginal exposure for PTSD similar and different?

REFERENCES

American Psychiatric Association. (1994). *Diagnostic and statistical manual for mental disorders* (4th ed.). Washington, DC: American Psychiatric Publishing.

Beck, A. T., Epstein, N., Brown, G., & Steer, R. A. (1988). An inventory for measuring clinical anxiety psychometric properties. *Journal of Consulting and Clinical Psychology, 56*, 893–897.

Blanchard, E. B., Jones-Alexander, J., Buckley, T. C., & Forneris, C. A. (1996). Psychometric properties of the PTSD Checklist (PCL). *Behavior Research and Therapy, 34*(8), 669–673.

Blimes, L. (2007). *Soldiers returning from Iraq and Afghanistan: The long-term costs of providing veterans medical care and disability benefits*. John F. Kennedy School of Government Faculty Research Working Paper Series, No. RWP07–001.

Cahill, S., Rothbaum, B., Resick, P., & Follette, V. (2009). Cognitive-behavioral therapy for adults. In E. Foa, T. Keane, M. Friedman, & J. Cohen (Eds.), *Effective treatments for PTSD* (pp. 139–223). New York, NY: Guilford Press.

Difede, J., Cukor, J., Jayasinghe, N., Patt, I., Jedel, S., Spielman, L., . . . Hoffman, H. (2007). Virtual reality exposure therapy for the treatment of posttraumatic stress disorder following September 11, 2001. *Journal of Clinical Psychiatry, 68*, 1639–1647.

Difede, J., & Hoffman, H. G. (2002). Virtual reality exposure therapy for World Trade Center post-traumatic stress disorder: A case report. *Cyberpsychology and Behavior, 5*, 529–535.

Difede, J., Rothbaum, B. O., & Rizzo, A. A. (2011). *Enhancing exposure therapy for PTSD: Virtual reality and imaginal exposure with a cognitive enhancer.* USAMRAA: W81XWH-10–1-1045. Retrieved from http://weill.cornell.edu/news/releases/wcmc/wcmc_2011/12_12_11.shtml

Department of Defense. (2010a, December 4). Retrieved from http://www.defense.gov/news/

Department of Defense. (2010b, December 4). Retrieved from http://www.defenselink.mil/news/casuality.pdf

Fischer, H. (2010, December 4). *United States military casualty statistics: Operation New Dawn, Operation Iraqi Freedom, and Operation Enduring Freedom, Congressional Research Service 7–5700:RS22452.* Retrieved from http://opencrs.com/document /RS22452/

Foa, E. B., Davidson, R. T., & Frances, A. (1999). Expert consensus guideline series: Treatment of posttraumatic stress disorder. *American Journal of Clinical Psychiatry, 60*, 5–76.

Foa, E. B., Hembree, E. A., & Rothbaum, B. O. (2007). *Prolonged exposure therapy for PTSD: Emotional processing of traumatic experiences, therapist guide.* New York, NY: Oxford University Press.

Foa, E. B., & Kozak, M. J. (1986). Emotional processing of fear: Exposure to corrective information. *Psychological Bulletin, 99*, 20–35.

Gamito, P., Ribeiro, C., Gamito, L., Pacheco, J., Pablo, C., & Saraiva, T. (2007, June). *Virtual war PTSD: A methodological thread.* Paper presented at the 10th Annual Cybertherapy Conference, Basel, Switzerland.

Gerardi, M., Rothbaum, B. O., Ressler, K., Heekin, M., & Rizzo, A. A. (2008). Virtual reality exposure therapy using a virtual Iraq: Case report. *Journal of Traumatic Stress, 21*(2), 209–213.

Glantz, K., Rizzo, A. A., & Graap, K. (2003). Virtual reality for psychotherapy: Current reality and future possibilities. *Psychotherapy: Theory, Research, Practice, Training, 40*(1), 55–67.

Hoffman, H. G., Chambers, G. T., Meyer, W. J., Araceneaux, L. L., Russell, W. J., Seibel, E. J., . . . Sharar, S. R. (2011). Virtual reality as an adjunctive non-pharmacologic analgesic for acute burn pain during medical procedures. *Annals of Behavioral Medicine, 41*(2), 183–191.

Hoge, C. W., Castro, C. A., Messer, S. C., McGurk, D., Cotting, D. I., & Koffman, R. L. (2004) Combat duty in Iraq and Afghanistan, mental health problems, and barriers to care. *New England Journal of Medicine, 351*(1), 13–22.

Holden, M. K. (2005). Virtual environments for motor rehabilitation: Review. *CyberPsych and Behavior, 8*(3), 187–211.

Institute of Medicine Committee on Treatment of Posttraumatic Stress Disorder. (2008). *Treatment of posttraumatic stress disorder: An assessment of the evidence*. ISBN: 0–309–10925–6. Retrieved from http://www.nap.edu/catalog/ 11955.html

Jaycox, L. H., Foa, E. B., & Morral, A. R. (1998). Influence of emotional engagement and habituation on exposure therapy for PTSD. *Journal of Consulting and Clinical Psychology*, 66, 186–192.

Josman, N., Somer, E., Reisberg, A., Weiss, P., Garcia-Palacios, A., & Hoffman. H. (2006). BusWorld: Designing a virtual environment for post-traumatic stress disorder in Israel: A protocol. *CyberPsychology & Behavior*, 9(2), 241–244.

Kroenke, K., & Spitzer, R. L. (2002). The PHQ-9: A new depression and diagnostic severity measure. *Psychiatric Annals*, *32*, 509–521.

Merians, A. S., Fluet, G. G., Qiu, Q., Saleh, S., Lafond, I., & Adamovich, S. V. (2010). *Integrated arm and hand training using adaptive robotics and virtual reality simulations*. Proceedings of the 2010 International Conference on Disability, Virtual Reality and Associated Technology, Chile.

Parsons, T. D., & Rizzo, A. A. (2008). Affective outcomes of virtual reality exposure therapy for anxiety and specific phobias: A meta-analysis. *Journal of Behavior Therapy and Experimental Psychiatry*, *39*, 250–261.

Powers, M., & Emmelkamp, P. M. G. (2008). Virtual reality exposure therapy for anxiety disorders: A meta-analysis. *Journal of Anxiety Disorders*, *22*, 561–569.

Reger, G., & Gahm, G. (2008). Virtual reality exposure therapy for active duty soldiers. *Journal of Clinical Psychology*, *64*, 940–946.

Reger, G., Gahm, G., Rizzo, A., Swanson, R., Etherage, J., & Reger, M. (2007, June). *Virtual reality in operational and garrison psychology: A review of the applications of the VR Iraq at Fort Lewis*. Presented at the Cybertherapy 2007 Conference, Washington, DC.

Reger, G. M., Gahm, G. A., Rizzo, A. A., Swanson, R. A., & Duma, S. (2009). Soldier evaluation of the virtual reality Iraq. *Telemedicine and e-Health Journal*, *15*, 100–103.

Reger, G. M., Holloway, K. M., Rothbaum, B. O., Difede, J., Rizzo, A. A., & Gahm, G. A. (2011). Effectiveness of virtual reality exposure therapy for active duty soldiers in a military mental health clinic. *Journal of Traumatic Stress*, *24*(1), 93–96.

Ressler, K. J., Rothbaum, B. O., Tannenbaum, L., Anderson, P., Zimand, E., Hodges, L., & Davis, M. (2004). Facilitation of psychotherapy with d-cycloserine, a putative cognitive enhancer. *Archives of General Psychiatry*, *61*, 1136–1144.

Riva, G. (2011). The key to unlocking the virtual body: Virtual reality in the treatment of obesity and eating disorders. *Journal of Diabetes Science and Technology*, 5(2), 283–292.

Rizzo, A. (2010). *Virtual Iraq/Afghanistan and how it is helping some troops and vets with PTSD*. Retrieved from: http://www.veteranstoday.com/2010/07/29/virtualiraqafghanistan-and-how-it-is-helping-some-troops-and-vets-with-ptsd/

Rizzo, A. A., Bowerly, T., Buckwater, J. G., Klimchuk, D., Mitura, R., & Parsons, R. D. (2006). A virtual reality scenario for all seasons: The virtual classroom. *CNS Spectrums*, *11*(1), 35–44.

Rizzo, A. A., Buckwalter, J. G., & Neumann, U. (1997). Virtual reality and cognitive rehabilitation: A brief review of the future. *Journal of Head Trauma Rehabilitation, 12*(6), 1–15.

Rizzo, A., Difede, J., Rothbaum, B. O., & Reger, G. (2010). Virtual Iraq/Afghanistan: Development and early evaluation of a virtual reality exposure therapy system for combat-related PTSD. *Annals of the New York Academy of Sciences (NYAS), 1208*, 114–125.

Rizzo, A. A., Lange, B., Suma, E. A., & Bolas, M. (2011). Virtual reality and interactive digital game technology: New tools to address obesity and diabetes. *Journal of Diabetes Science and Technology, 5*(2), 256–264.

Rizzo, A., Parsons, T. D., Lange, B., Kenny, P., Buckwalter, J. G., Rothbaum, B. O., . . . Reger, G. (2011b). Virtual reality goes to war: A brief review of the future of military behavioral healthcare. *Journal of Clinical Psychology in Medical Settings, 18*, 176–187.

Rizzo, A. A., Reger, G., Gahm G., Difede, J., & Rothbaum, B. O. (2009). Virtual reality exposure therapy for combat related PTSD. In P. Shiromani, T. Keane, & J. LeDoux (Eds.), *Post-traumatic stress disorder: Basic science and clinical practice* (pp. 375–399). New York, NY: Humana Press.

Rizzo, A. A., Schultheis, M. T., Kerns, K., & Mateer, C. (2004). Analysis of assets for virtual reality applications in neuropsychology. *Neuropsychological Rehabilitation, 14*(1/2), 207–239.

Rose, F. D., Brooks, B. M., & Rizzo, A. A. (2005). Virtual reality in brain damage rehabilitation: Review. *CyberPsychology and Behavior, 8*(3), 241–262.

Rothbaum, B., Difede, J., & Rizzo, A. (2008). *Therapist treatment manual for virtual reality exposure therapy: Posttraumatic stress disorder in Iraq combat veterans*. Atlanta, GA: Virtually Better.

Rothbaum, B. O., Hodges, L., Ready, D., Graap, K., & Alarcon, R. (2001). Virtual reality exposure therapy for Vietnam veterans with posttraumatic stress disorder. *Journal of Clinical Psychiatry, 62*, 617–622.

Rothbaum, B. O., Hodges, L. F., & Smith, S. (1999). Virtual reality exposure therapy abbreviated treatment manual: Fear of flying application. *Cognitive and Behavioral Practice, 6*, 234–244.

Schneider, S. M., Kisby, C. K., & Flint, E. P. (2010, December 10). *Effect of virtual reality on time perception in patients receiving chemotherapy*. Supportive Care in Cancer. Retrieved from http://www.springerlink.com/content/?k=(au%3a(Susan+Schneider)+OR+ed%3a(Susan+Schneider))+pub%3a(Supportive+Cancer+Care)

Seal, K. H., Bertenthal, D., Nuber, C. R., Sen, S., & Marmar, C. (2007). Bringing the war back home: Mental health disorders among 103,788 US veterans returning from Iraq and Afghanistan seen at Department of Veterans Affairs facilities. *Archives of Internal Medicine, 167*, 476–482.

Stanton, D., Foreman, N., & Wilson, P. (1998). Uses of virtual reality in clinical training: Developing the spatial skills of children with mobility impairments. In G. Riva, B. Weiderhold, & E. Molinari (Eds.), *Virtual reality in clinical psychology and neuroscience* (pp. 219–232). Amsterdam, The Netherlands: IOS Press.

Tanielian, T., Jaycox, L. H., Schell, T. L., Marshall, G. N., Burnam, M. A., Eibner, C., . . . the Invisible Wounds Study Team. (2008). *Invisible wounds of war: Summary and recommendations for addressing psychological and cognitive injuries*. Rand Report. Retrieved from http://veterans.rand.org/

Walker, D. L., Ressler, K. J., Lu, K. T., & Davis, M. (2002). Facilitation of conditioned fear extinction by systemic administration or intra-amygdala infusions of d-cycloserine as assessed with fear-potentiated startle in rats. *Journal of Neuroscience, 22*, 2343–2351.

Wilson, J., Onorati, K., Mishkind, M., Reger, M., & Gahm, G.A. (2008). Soldier attitudes about technology-based approaches to mental healthcare. *Cyberpsychology and Behavior, 11*, 767–769.

CHAPTER

9

Psychopharmacology for PTSD and Co-Occurring Disorders

Bruce Capehart and Matt Jeffreys

INTRODUCTION

The preferred treatment for Posttraumatic Stress Disorder (PTSD) is psychotherapy (Management of Post-Traumatic Stress Working Group, 2010). Although there are few direct comparisons between medications and psychotherapy, the effect sizes for psychotherapy studies are usually larger than for medication studies (Shalev, 2009). Medications can be a useful adjunct to the evidence-based psychotherapies but are not a substitute or a shortcut to improvement.

A working knowledge of pharmacotherapy is important to the social worker or psychotherapist for many reasons. In modern health care, therapists and prescribers often work with the same patient in collaboration as part of a multidisciplinary treatment team. It is important to understand the medication options and to share the same language as the prescribing physician. Patients often have legitimate questions about medications and side effects that they expect their therapist to be able to answer. Knowing about potential benefits and risks of medications can help the therapist and the patient make an informed decision about referral to a psychiatrist or primary care physician for further discussion of psychiatric medication.

Medications work through a variety of neurotransmitters affecting mood and anxiety states. In general, these neurotransmitters originate in the mid-brain and brainstem and project to cortical regions giving emotional valence to thoughts and experiences. Serotonergic neurons located in the raphe nuclei are important in regulating mood and anxiety. Neurons containing norepinephrine are present in the locus ceruleus of the brainstem and are responsible for excitatory impulses to the brain and the rest of the body,

Opinions expressed in this chapter belong solely to the authors and do not necessarily represent those of the Department of Veterans Affairs.

causing increased alertness and the "fight or flight" response. Peripherally, norepinephrine (noradrenaline) stimulates release of epinephrine (adrenalin) from the adrenal glands, contributing to further arousal. Neurons releasing gaba-aminobutyric acid (GABA), an inhibitory neurotransmitter that contributes to a state of relaxation, are present throughout the brain. Dopaminergic neurons in the mid-brain and ventral tegmental area regulate the reward and pleasure centers of the brain and play an important role in addiction and psychosis. Although there is still much that is not known about the individual role of each neurotransmitter and their interactions of each of these neurotransmitters in PTSD, there appears to be a direct link between the pharmacological effects of medications and PTSD symptoms.

Currently, the only two medications approved by the U.S. Food and Drug Administration (FDA) for treatment of PTSD are two serotonin-specific reuptake inhibitors (SSRI), namely, sertraline and paroxetine.[1] All other medications mentioned in this chapter are discussed for "off-label use," meaning that there is some scientific merit to suggest that the medication is effective in treating PTSD even though there is no official FDA approval for that particular purpose. Both sertraline and paroxetine have been shown to reduce PTSD symptoms of hyperarousal, reexperiencing, and avoidance in large clinical trials. Venlafaxine, a serotonin-norepinephrine reuptake inhibitor (SNRI), affects serotonin at lower dosages and both serotonin and norepinephrine at higher dosages. SSRIs and venlafaxine are considered first-line agents for treatment of PTSD according to the current Department of Defense (DoD)/Veterans Affairs VA PTSD Practice Guidelines (Management of Post-Traumatic Stress Working Group, 2010).

A number of other antidepressants have some evidence to support their use in PTSD. Nefazodone and mirtazapine are primarily serotonergic agents acting upon serotonergic neurons through different mechanisms than the SSRIs. Both have some evidence of being effective in PTSD. Older antidepressants such as the tricyclic antidepressants (TCAs) and monoamine oxidase inhibitors (MAOIs) have some evidence that supports their use as well. Both the TCAs and MAOIs are limited in their use because of potentially serious side effects. For example, TCAs may cause cardiac arrhythmias at higher doses, and MAOIs may cause hypertensive crisis if taken along with certain medications or foods containing tyramine (e.g., an amino acid contained in dry, aged cheeses and sausages).

Selected agents may be used to treat targeted symptoms of PTSD. Prazosin has been useful in decreasing nightmares in PTSD. Atypical antipsychotics are not recommended as monotherapy (i.e., as the only treatment) for PTSD, and the 2010 revision to the VA/DoD Clinical Practice Guideline for PTSD recommends against the use of risperidone as adjunctive treatment. The usefulness of other antipsychotics as adjunctive treatment remains unknown. These agents typically target hyperarousal and reexperiencing symptoms. The atypical antipsychotics can produce serious side effects and are not used as first-line treatments in PTSD.

It is important to discuss with patients that medications are not recommended as the only therapeutic response to PTSD. Although medication can make important treatment contributions for many patients, the best clinical response requires psychotherapy to work through the painful experience that led to PTSD. The authors of this chapter are

[1] Medication names are given as generic names. Inclusion of a trade name does not imply the endorsement of any particular brand of generic medication.

experienced VA psychiatrists who firmly believe that while medications can reduce PTSD symptoms, psychotherapy is the single most effective method for creating long-term symptom remission. Further, all medications come with potential side effects that need to be discussed prior to initiating psychotropic treatment. Certain medications such as the benzodiazepines including alprazolam, lorazepam, clonazepam, and others may lead to increased avoidance and disinhibition. Benzodiazepines also carry a risk of substance use disorders and they also may interfere with the optimal arousal needed for effective trauma-focused therapy. Patients receive the most benefit from medication as a means of managing symptoms that may interfere with effective psychotherapy and daily functioning in their lives.

ANTIDEPRESSANTS

Antidepressants were suggested as a treatment for posttraumatic psychiatric symptoms even before the *Diagnostic and Statistical Manual of Mental Disorders* (*DSM-III*) introduced the diagnosis of PTSD in the early 1980s. A 1971 report on traumatic neurosis in patients after burn injury, recommended amitriptyline, a tricyclic antidepressant (TCA), for depressive symptoms but did not explicitly address reduction in anxiety from the use of this medication (Andreasen, Norris, & Hartford, 1971). After the *DSM-III* publication in 1980, one of the earliest PTSD treatment reports documented clinical improvements in traumatic war neurosis with the monoamine oxidase inhibitor (MAOI) phenelzine (Hogben & Cornfield, 1981). In 1985, a clinical trial showed a reduction in PTSD symptoms among veterans following treatment with a TCA (Falcon, Ryan, Chamberlain, & Curtis, 1985). Since that time, clinical trials established the efficacy of TCAs (e.g., imipramine, amitriptyline) and MAOIs, but these medications were not a cure for PTSD. Further, although TCAs and MAOIs remained effective for reducing PTSD symptoms, patients often experienced medication side effects.

The TCAs cause anticholinergic and antihistaminic side effects. The anticholinergic effects include dry mouth, constipation, and urinary retention. The antihistaminic effects commonly reported are sedation, slowed cognition, and weight gain; and may additionally cause dizziness from low blood pressure. The MAO inhibitors require careful adherence to a special diet to prevent stroke or heart attack from abrupt and marked elevations in blood pressure. More concerning, both MAOIs and TCA demonstrate a narrow therapeutic index, meaning that there only is a small difference between therapeutic and toxic doses. The narrow therapeutic index causes both TCA and MAOIs to be highly dangerous when taken in an accidental or intentional overdose. As a general rule, a fatal overdose can occur if a patient ingests an entire 30-day supply of a TCA prescribed for PTSD or major depression. Although these medications were useful for treating PTSD in the 1980s, there was an obvious need for pharmacotherapy that was effective, safe, and caused fewer side effects. This need was underscored by Friedman's 1988 observation that medication is only partially effective against PTSD and must be combined with psychotherapy (Friedman, 1988).

First-Line Antidepressants

When the selective serotonergic reuptake inhibitors (SSRI) agents were introduced in the late 1980s, psychiatrists were intrigued by the possibility of an effective new treatment for PTSD without the adverse side effects or overdose risk associated with the TCA and

MAOI antidepressants. Numerous studies with SSRIs confirmed their efficacy in treating PTSD, major depression, and other conditions. Relative to TCA and MAOI antidepressants, the SSRIs have a wider therapeutic index and fewer side effects. Clinical experience, comparative studies, and FDA indications all support the recommendation of SSRI agents as first-line treatment for PTSD (Brady et al., 2000), major depression, panic disorder, and obsessive-compulsive disorder.

The Food and Drug Administration has approved two SSRI antidepressants, sertraline and paroxetine, for pharmacologic treatment of PTSD. Other SSRIs such as fluoxetine and the closely related serotonin-norepinephrine reuptake inhibitor, venlafaxine, are believed effective for treating PTSD although the supporting evidence varies by medication.

The strongest support for any pharmacologic treatment is a placebo-controlled, randomized clinical trial (RCT). Excellent clinical outcomes data from multiple RCTs support SSRI treatment of PTSD by sertraline or paroxetine. There are some RCT data showing good efficacy for the SNRI antidepressant venlafaxine.

Other antidepressants are commonly prescribed "off-label" for the treatment of PTSD. Off-label use of antidepressant medication is a common clinical practice and in the years 2005 to 2007, approximately 17% of prescriptions for six common antidepressants were written for off-label indications (Walton et al., 2008). In the treatment of PTSD, there are some data from placebo-controlled RCTs showing efficacy for off-label use of fluoxetine, a SSRI antidepressant, and venlafaxine. Venlafaxine, often ordered as a sustained-release form (SR) to obtain the convenience of once-daily dosing, was found superior to placebo in a 6-month trial for treating PTSD (Davidson et al., 2006).

The evidence to date for other SSRIs is less convincing but there are open-label trials indicating they may be helpful. In an open-label trial, both the prescriber and patient are aware if the prescribed treatment is a medication or placebo, thus possibly introducing bias into the clinical outcome measures. The SSRI antidepressants citalopram, escitalopram, and fluvoxamine, and the SNRI antidepressant duloxetine, have been reported effective in open-label trials. Although several open-label trials suggest that citalopram, escitalopram, fluvoxamine, or duloxetine may be effective in treating PTSD, the available scientific evidence indicates greater likelihood of treatment response with sertraline, paroxetine, or venlafaxine.

Second-Line Antidepressants

The older tricyclic and monoamine oxidase inhibitor antidepressants mentioned above can be useful treatments for PTSD. Their efficacy often is tempered by medication side effects and a narrow therapeutic index as described earlier. Important side effects of the TCAs include dry mouth, constipation, urinary retention, drowsiness, and the potential to cause alterations in cardiac functioning. The cardiac effects are typically seen only in overdose, but they can emerge at normal therapeutic doses in patients with certain types of heart conditions; the cardiac effects can be lethal with overdose on a typical 30-day supply of TCA. The TCAs can slow the entry of sodium into cardiac muscle cells, thus prolonging the time for the electrical signal causing a heart contraction. This side effect is, however, one of the reasons for using low-dose TCAs in neuropathic pain because decreasing sodium channel activity will decrease a damaged neuron's tendency to send a pain signal.

Mirtazapine, a novel antidepressant with mixed serotonergic and noradrenergic activity, may be effective for PTSD based on several small pilot studies. Weight gain is a common side effect with mirtazapine. For this reason, patients with an existing weight problem, diabetes, or elevated cholesterol, or chronic pain from overuse orthopedic injuries may not be the best candidates for mirtazapine. For the Vietnam veteran population, prior exposure to Agent Orange is a known risk factor for diabetes (Henriksen, Ketchum, Michalek, & Swaby, 1997). Thus, Mirtazapine may be useful in selected clinical situations for certain patients.

Nefazodone is a highly useful second-line treatment for PTSD. However, given the small number of subjects in nefazodone clinical trials, the possible hepatoxicity (i.e., chemical liver damage) risk from nefazodone, and given the significantly larger amount of high-quality RCT data for first-line antidepressant choices (e.g., sertraline, paroxetine, or venlafaxine), we continue to recommend the three first-line antidepressants prior to starting nefazodone.

Either mirtazapine or nefazodone are viable treatment options following either the second failed trial of a SSRI or/and venlafaxine. Although hepatotoxicity is a specific risk of nefazodone and this side effect occurs only rarely, liver function should be checked periodically.

Bupropion was tested in a placebo-controlled RCT as an additional medication to existing PTSD therapies in a group of 30 veterans with PTSD (Becker et al., 2007). It was no more effective than placebo. However, as a treatment for smoking cessation in veterans diagnosed with PTSD, 4 of 10 veterans receiving bupropion were tobacco-free at 6 months compared to only one of five veterans given placebo (Hertzberg, Moore, Feldman, & Beckham, 2001). Given the known efficacy in augmenting citalopram in the STAR*D trial for major depression (Trivedi et al., 2006), it would be reasonable to augment a SSRI or SNRI antidepressant with bupropion when treating major depression, either alone or as a comorbid condition with PTSD. These data suggest a role for bupropion in treating nicotine dependence or major depression associated with PTSD, but not for bupropion as monotherapy for PTSD. Buspirone, a nonbenzodiazepine agent with modest anxiolytic effects, has been reported useful in an open-label trial for veterans with PTSD and comorbid major depression (M. Hamner, Ulmer, & Horne, 1997).

Antidepressants: Conclusion

It is important for psychotherapists to remain aware of medication issues when treating patients suffering from PTSD. Patients must take medication as prescribed and should not become discouraged if the medication does not appear to be working within the first 8 weeks of treatment. We recommend encouraging the patient to speak with the psychiatrist or prescribing physician. Alternatively, the psychotherapist could directly contact the psychiatrist. This latter option is often more practical when working in an organized group practice setting such as a military or VA facility.

When compared to their use for major depression, the SSRI and SNRI antidepressants prescribed for treating PTSD may require dosages at the upper end of those recommended for treatment of depression and additional time to exert maximum clinical benefit. We anticipate veterans who have been refractory (not responding) to antidepressant treatment to not respond as readily, and similarly, it is reasonable to expect treatment-naive patients to show a greater probability of responding to medications. In our clinical practice, we commonly encounter situations where primary care physicians may start a SSRI antidepressant for PTSD and then refer the patient to psychiatry as a medication "nonresponder." Increasing the SSRI dosage often induces a good clinical response. A similar occurrence is noted for the time course of treatment. Allowing the patient to take medication for 12 weeks can demonstrate a good clinical response even when there was no response at 6 to 8 weeks.

One intriguing result is a time-based response of PTSD symptoms to sertraline (Davidson, Landerman, & Clary, 2004) and extended-release venlafaxine (Stein et al., 2009). The sertraline study demonstrated a relationship between reduced anger after 1 week of SSRI treatment and an overall good response to medication at 12 weeks. The venlafaxine study sought to extend these findings beyond anger, and it showed that decreased activation to trauma reminders (i.e., reduced irritability, decreased physical reactivity) by the second week of medication predicted additional reduction in other PTSD symptoms over the next 6 to 8 weeks. The early reduction in anger and irritability persisted throughout the 12-week study. Although these results can reassure patients that an early response likely predicts an overall good response at 12 weeks, it is not necessarily true that no early response indicates a treatment failure.

Our clinical experience, published studies, and clinical treatment guidelines can be summarized as an overall guide on antidepressant selection in PTSD pharmacotherapy. We recommend initial medical treatment with a SSRI antidepressant, preferably paroxetine or sertraline, the two SSRI for which there are placebo-controlled RCT data. If necessary, a next step can be switching from an SSRI to the SNRI venlafaxine, another medication for which there is good placebo-controlled RCT data. When prescribing an SSRI or SNRI antidepressant, the required dose may be higher than doses typically used to treat major depression. An early decrease in anger or early reduction in the activation response to trauma reminders may predict a good medication response at 12 weeks. Other antidepressant options if the SSRI or SNRI are ineffective or not tolerated include switching to mirtazapine, augmenting venlafaxine with mirtazapine, augmenting an SSRI or SNRI with buspirone, or switching to nefazodone. We also recommend awareness of bipolar disorder and serotonin syndrome, two conditions that may mimic increased anxiety and could be mistaken for medication failure. The veteran with bipolar disorder may experience hypomania from an SSRI or SNRI antidepressant. Serotonin syndrome can result from any serotonergic antidepressant combined with another serotonergic agent, and it will cause increased anxiety with fever, tremor, and diarrhea (Boyer & Shannon, 2005). Awareness of these possible complications will facilitate appropriate and timely treatment for PTSD.

BENZODIAZEPINES

Although it seems intuitive that benzodiazepines would be useful in treatment of PTSD, these medications are not recommended for the pharmacotherapy of PTSD. The benzodiazepines act on GABA receptors,[2] which lower the arousal level of the nervous system.

[2] Gamma-amino butyric acid (GABA) is an inhibitory neurotransmitter in the brain. Other substances that act at the GABA receptor include alcohol and barbiturates.

Benzodiazepines have been effective in treating panic disorder and other anxiety conditions. Yet, there is little support in the scientific literature regarding the use of benzodiazepines for PTSD, and the available clinical trials show benzodiazepines are not effective in treating or preventing PTSD.

There is evidence that chronic stress increases the risk of substance abuse and dependence and that those with PTSD are 2 to 4 times more likely to have substance use problems (Kessler, Sonnega, Bromet, Hughes, & Nelson, 1995; Sinha, 2008). Given the high comorbidity of substance use disorders in persons diagnosed with PTSD, benzodiazepines add an increased risk for abuse in patients with PTSD. Although the benzodiazepines may lower hyperarousal, they also can lead to disinhibition and create more difficulty with anger control. The current VA/DoD PTSD Practice Guidelines advise against the use of benzodiazepines in the treatment of PTSD (Management of Post-Traumatic Stress Working Group, 2010).

Benzodiazepines might be used for the short-term treatment of insomnia or for augmenting SSRI treatment of co-occurring anxiety disorders such as panic disorder with PTSD. Whatever the indication for starting a benzodiazepine in a patient diagnosed with PTSD, a careful history of comorbid substance problems should be taken before starting a benzodiazepine, and their use should be kept to the shortest duration and minimal dosage possible. Benzodiazepines are best avoided entirely in PTSD, and if a benzodiazepine must be prescribed, short-acting agents such as alprazolam should be avoided.

ANTIPSYCHOTICS

The atypical antipsychotics are not recommended as first-line treatments for PTSD. They may be used as adjunctive therapy in patients refractory to SSRIs. Two recent VA studies raised questions about off-label use of the atypical antipsychotics. These studies estimated that $4 billion to $5 billion of antipsychotic expenditures in 2007 within the VA system may have been for off-label use of these medications for PTSD and several other diagnoses (Leslie, Mohamed, & Rosenheck, 2009; Mohamed & Rosenheck, 2008). Risperidone and olanzapine are currently the only atypical antipsychotics with published RCT data supporting their use in PTSD. Older data on risperidone are mixed with some results supporting its use and other results arguing against it. However, in 2011, a large VA cooperative study reported risperidone did not show any benefit as an adjunctive medication in a group of treatment-resistant veterans with PTSD (Krystal et al., 2011). Olanzapine trials show similar mixed results on its efficacy. Overall, there are few data to support first- or second-line use of atypical antipsychotic medications for PTSD, especially when their modest benefits are weighed against the high rates of metabolic side effects discussed further on.

All remaining published studies of the atypical antipsychotics risperidone, olanzapine, and quetiapine have been open trials (Ahearn, Mussey, Johnson, Krohn & Krahn, 2006; Hamner, Deitsch, Brodrick, Ulmer, & Lorberbaum, 2003; Hamner et al., 2003; Petty et al., 2001; Pivac, Kozaric-Kovacic, & Muck-Seler, 2004) There have been some case reports but no controlled trials with aripiprazole. There is no information currently available on other atypical antipsychotics in the treatment of PTSD. Additionally, little information is available regarding the first generation of typical antipsychotics in the treatment of PTSD. There was one case report in 1993 regarding thioridazine for PTSD (Dillard, Bendfeldt, & Jernigan, 1993). Another study showed olanzapine appeared superior to fluphenazine treating PTSD symptoms and had fewer extrapyramidal side effects (e.g., muscle rigidity, restlessness, tremors), but there was no placebo control group (Pivac et al., 2004).

Although the atypical antipsychotics are associated with fewer neurological side effects than the typical antipsychotic agents, the atypicals are linked to other problematic side effects including weight gain, elevated blood lipids, hyperglycemia, and sedation. The higher cost of these newer antipsychotic medications can be an issue for patients as well. Extrapyramidal side effects and tardive dyskinesia may occur, though less frequently than with the first generation agents. One study estimated an annualized rate for tardive dyskinesia (i.e., disorder resulting in involuntary repetitive body movements) of 3.9% for the atypical antipsychotics as compared to 5.5% for the typical agents (Correll & Schenk, 2008). Neuroleptic malignant syndrome, a life-threatening neurological disorder, is a rare but potentially dangerous side effect of treatment with any antipsychotic medication.

MEDICATION ADHERENCE

Medications will not be helpful if patients do not take them as prescribed. Adherence is a complex issue related to a number of issues, and the most important factors include patient and clinician beliefs, medication tolerability, and medication cost. A recent study on medication adherence with veterans new to VA care showed no differences between veterans with a traumatic brain injury (TBI) and a matched group without TBI. Both groups showed the poorest compliance with SSRI medications. Although we know factors differ for each individual patient, the factors improving adherence in this study included taking multiple medications, living with a spouse, owning memory-assistance devices such as a personal digital assistant or advanced cell phone, and a comorbid diagnosis of PTSD (Huggins et al., 2011). Another study found a wide range of treatment adherence for veterans with various medical conditions (Neugaard, Priest, Burch, Cantrell, & Foulis, 2011). With the importance of medication as a contributor to recovery from PTSD, it is useful to examine some helpful approaches to improved medication compliance.

Communication between patient and a medical practitioner is the key to any successful treatment, including medical treatment. It is unreasonable to expect a patient to take medication as prescribed "just because the doctor told you to do so." Patients need and deserve information about the benefits and potential side effects of taking medications, including the benefits and possible harm of not taking medication. Examples of the potential harm from not taking medication might include substance use from self-medication, continued difficulty with relationships or occupational problems, and difficulty performing assigned military duties. Issues regarding readiness to take medications, concerns about side effects, and other barriers must be discussed. Cost of medications should be disclosed along with options for lower-cost alternatives; this recommendation is especially important if the patient does not have health insurance with prescription drug coverage. In the examples below, potential strategies taken from the authors' clinical experience will illustrate approaches to improve medication adherence.

High-Cost Medication

A medical practitioner should discuss lower-cost alternatives if present and social workers could assist patients in applying for financial assistance. A prescriber should be made aware of any patient financial constraints so that less-expensive generic medications can be ordered first. For the veteran population, if the PTSD is due to events during military service and the veteran is eligible, a social worker could encourage application for a VA service-related disability or referral to a veteran service officer to assist with applying for VA disability benefits. The presence of a service-connected disability for PTSD allows veterans to receive medications and psychotherapy for PTSD at no charge. Also within the VA system, veterans returning from Afghanistan and Iraq receive care for any deployment-related health issue at no cost for the first 5 years after the most recent military discharge date.

Negative Beliefs About Medications

A clinician (both medical and nonmedical professionals) should discuss all treatment options with his or her patients, including psychotherapy, which is the preferred treatment for PTSD. Often, the best option for reducing or eliminating psychiatric medications is completing a course of psychotherapy for PTSD. Practitioners should discuss risks and benefits and respect patient autonomy in decisions. If it is the prescribing doctor's judgment that there is a compelling need for medication, such as a patient with a comorbid severe major depression or a psychotic disorder, then obtaining consultation and a second opinion may help the patient understand the need for medication. Social workers should also refer their clients for medication evaluation.

Difficulty Staying Organized

For patients who take multiple medications, lead busy lives, or suffer cognitive impairments, the inclusion of trusted family members in treatment can facilitate medication compliance. For instance, family members can help by creating a weekly pill organizer with the patients so that they have their medication organized and know when to take it. Having memory aids such as a chart or list can be helpful also. If a traumatic brain injury (TBI) is present, a useful referral is occupational therapy or speech pathology for cognitive rehabilitation.

Medications Side Effects

Prescribing physicians should start low and go slow on the dosage for patients with a history of medication side effects or any patient with a history of TBI. Physicians should be supportive and address side effects frequently. Many patients with PTSD and other anxiety disorders have a high sensitivity to bodily sensations and may be afraid they are having a serious medical problem when it is just a minor side effect. The open communication between patient and prescribing physician is essential and can promote medication adherence through the patient's experience of having questions answered. Thus, social workers can promote the communication between the patient and his or her treating physician as well as regularly consult with the physician.

COMBINING PSYCHOTHERAPY AND MEDICATIONS

There are few studies directly comparing psychotherapy to pharmacotherapy for PTSD. Extended-release paroxetine versus placebo was studied in 23 randomly assigned patients who had completed prolonged exposure (PE) therapy but whose symptoms had not remitted. There was no significant difference between the groups treated with paroxetine as compared to the placebo group (Simon et al., 2008). Two studies compared PE to sertraline in women with PTSD. Women with concurrent major depressive disorder and lower education were more likely to choose sertraline. The overall preference for PE was 82% and 74.2% in the two studies. Both sertraline and PE showed benefit, with PE showing an advantage over sertraline in adjusted analyses (Feeny, Zoellner, Mavissakalian, & Roy-Byrne, 2009).

Successful PE requires the ability to reach a certain level of anxiety for the therapy to be effective. Certain medications such as benzodiazepines, or significant daily alcohol intake, may interfere with reaching the required level of anxiety required for successful PE treatment. The benzodiazepines and alcohol block the beneficial impact of integrating the emotional and cognitive responses induced by the imaginal and in vivo exposure. It is recommended that patients referred for PE not be started on benzodiazepines or that they be tapered off these medications prior to beginning PE. The authors have anecdotal experience with combining PE and clonazepam, a long-acting benzodiazepine that has a slow onset of action, on an as-needed basis for veterans with comorbid panic disorder and PTSD. The PE and clonazepam combination requires close collaboration between psychotherapist and psychiatrist, accompanied by clear instructions for the patient, including education on how benzodiazepines can prevent successful PE treatment. Educating the patient about benzodiazepine effects on anxiety and the resulting ineffectiveness of PE can be a helpful step.

One study compared eye-movement desensitization and reprocessing (EMDR) to fluoxetine and a placebo medication in 88 trauma survivors over an 8-week period. Study participants were rated on PTSD symptoms immediately following treatment and at 6 months. There was a large placebo response in the study with fluoxetine being no more effective than placebo immediately following the 8-week period. At 6 months, 57% of the EMDR group was asymptomatic as compared to none of those in the fluoxetine group (van der Kolk et al., 2007).

Where does all of this leave the clinician treating PTSD patients? Based on what we know currently, psychotherapy with an evidence-based treatment is the optimal way to address PTSD. Medications may be helpful for patients without access to evidence-based psychotherapies, for patients who decline psychotherapy, and for concurrent symptomatic relief such as improvement in sleep. Antidepressant medication may reduce PTSD symptoms enough to facilitate the patient's entry into an evidence-based psychotherapy or as a temporizing measure pending the start of psychotherapy. The best treatment for PTSD is an adequate trial of evidence-based psychotherapy from a therapist competent in providing this type of treatment.

MANAGING COMORBID MEDICAL AND PSYCHIATRIC ISSUES

Several comorbid medical and psychiatric conditions can complicate the pharmacologic management of PTSD, including pain, bipolar disorder, depression, and substance use disorder. The patient with chronic pain requires a careful medical evaluation by a primary care physician or a specialist physician skilled in chronic pain management. Chronic pain can be caused by various conditions, and these conditions may respond differently to different types of medication. Three types of chronic pain examined next include neuropathic pain, pain from overuse injuries, and headache.

Neuropathic pain occurs after illness or injury affects a nerve. When managing chronic pain with PTSD, the underlying cause of the pain can guide treatment. For neuropathic pain (e.g., pain from diabetic neuropathy or a nerve injury), the combination of SSRI + low-dose nortriptyline at bedtime can be highly effective. Finally, the monthly cost of this SSRI + TCA combination is lower than the cost of a SNRI.

The pain from an overuse injury is common among combat veterans, veterans of airborne units, and persons with obesity. In wartime, carrying even a small rucksack plus body armor, helmet, weapon, ammunition, and water can lead to chronic stress in the back, hips, knees, and ankles. Similar overuse injuries occur in obese persons whose joints are carrying significantly more weight when compared to the person's ideal body weight. Veterans of airborne units commonly report lower extremity injuries from parachute landing falls and the intense physical conditioning common to airborne units. In general, psychiatric medications neither help nor hinder pain management from overuse injuries.

Headache can be a frustrating topic for clinicians and patients. In our experience, the best first intervention for headache that occurs three to four times per week is a TCA. The TCAs are useful for preventing chronic headaches in the same doses as shown above for neuropathic pain treatment. Topiramate, an anticonvulsant medication, may be helpful in certain pain conditions such as migraine headache, but does not appear to be effective for PTSD. These recommendations for headache apply equally to postconcussive headache (e.g., after traumatic brain injury) or migraine.

The management of comorbid PTSD and bipolar disorder is one of the most complicated challenges in psychopharmacology. We urge psychotherapists to include a psychiatrist in their management of patients with these two conditions. For comorbid bipolar I disorder and PTSD, the recommended approach combines a mood stabilizer for bipolar disorder with psychotherapy for PTSD. If a medication must be used for PTSD, a small dose of an SSRI is a reasonable step, although the SSRI may worsen the bipolar disorder (Ghaemi, 2008). The use of antidepressants in the patient with bipolar disorder can cause irritability (El-Mallakh et al., 2008), and if the bipolar disorder is not recognized, increasing the antidepressant dose to manage irritability that is mistakenly attributed to PTSD will further worsen the irritability. If a patient with comorbid bipolar disorder and PTSD enters a manic episode while taking an antidepressant for PTSD, the antidepressant must be stopped. The psychotherapist can greatly assist in this complex management problem by reinforcing the need to abstain from alcohol and illicit substances, obtain regular and consistent sleep each night, and regularly communicate any changes in symptoms with the patient's psychiatrist. Evidence-based psychotherapy for PTSD is absolutely crucial in this patient population.

Some bipolar disorder symptoms are revealed after treatment with an SSRI/SNRI for PTSD. In these situations, a lower antidepressant dose may be sufficient to treat the anxiety without further aggravating the bipolar disorder. The patient should be started in an evidence-based psychotherapy for PTSD, and on completion of the psychotherapy, every effort should be made to reduce and ultimately stop the SSRI/SNRI. If the antidepressant is necessary for managing PTSD symptoms and the patient continues to have some bipolar disorder symptoms, adding a mood stabilizing medication may be a useful intervention.

For treating comorbid major depression, we have found that as a general rule, antidepressants that treat depression also treat anxiety. In many situations, the antidepressant prescribed for PTSD will alleviate depressive symptoms. For the situations of depressive symptoms that do not respond to initial antidepressant medication, the STAR*D trial offers solid guidance on next steps. In the setting of comorbid PTSD and major depression that doesn't respond to an initial trial of an SSRI or SNRI, we like mirtazapine as an augmenting agent for the SSRI/SNRI, particularly for patients with sleep problems. For patients who are trying to stop tobacco use and treat comorbid PTSD and major depression, the prescription of an SSRI or SNRI with bupropion is a good choice. Bupropion should be used only cautiously, if at all, among persons with elevated seizure risk. Buspirone may have some benefit in augmenting an SSRI or SNRI for PTSD and depression, though placebo-controlled evidence is lacking. Two open-label trials reported a meaningful improvement with buspirone for combined PTSD and major depression (Duffy & Malloy, 1994; Hamner et al., 1997). Buspirone has a short half-life and must be taken two to three times daily, a challenge for some patients.

Substance abuse presents a significant challenge to the psychopharmacologic and psychotherapeutic treatment of PTSD. In 1980, alcohol dependence was reported as a complication of PTSD among Vietnam veterans with the recommendation that treatment should address both alcohol use and the underlying trauma (Lacoursiere, Godfrey, & Ruby, 1980). More recently, a VA study found more than 11% of all veterans of Afghanistan and Iraq were diagnosed with at least one substance use disorder (Seal et al., 2011). This same study found that 55% to 75% of veterans with a substance use diagnosis also were diagnosed with depression or PTSD. Another VA study compared veterans of Afghanistan or Iraq who did or did not screen positive for depression or PTSD and found that the veterans with positive screens were twice as likely to report problematic alcohol use (Jakupcak et al., 2010). Although naltrexone is established as a safe and effective treatment for alcohol dependence (Anton, 2008), the treatment of alcohol dependence and PTSD requires further study. There was one double-blind RCT of persons with PTSD and alcohol dependence compared placebo to naltrexone, disulfiram, and the combination of disulfiram and naltrexone (Petrakis et al., 2006). Results showed a significant reduction in alcohol use for either active treatment. Disulfiram was slightly more effective than naltrexone, perhaps due to its effect on alcohol use or perhaps due to a direct effect on PTSD symptoms. As neither treatment worsened PTSD symptoms and disulfiram can be associated with prominent side effects, we recommend naltrexone for comorbid PTSD and alcohol dependence. Patients taking opiate medication for chronic pain cannot take naltrexone; the primary care physician should be involved in the management of patients with pain, PTSD, and a substance use disorder to prevent inadvertent overuse of prescription pain medications.

Smoking cessation is a particularly prominent issue among veterans and military personnel, and the combination of smoking with PTSD presents a difficult clinical problem. A comprehensive literature review found 40% to 85% of persons diagnosed with PTSD are regular tobacco users (Fu et al., 2007). Failed attempts to quit smoking are associated with greater emotional reactivity to trauma reminders (Calhoun, Dennis, & Beckham, 2007). The best available program for comorbid PTSD and smoking is integrated care, a program that combines PTSD treatment with counseling and medications for smoking cessation (McFall et al., 2010). In the integrated care study, approximately 85% of participants received at least one medication for smoking cessation. These medications included nicotine replacement (transdermal nicotine patch; nicotine gum or lozenge), bupropion, and varenicline. All of these medical interventions are known to be effective for stopping smoking (Eisenberg et al., 2008).

In our experience, the most effective intervention for smoking is one that the patient will use in an attempt to stop smoking. Further, it is acceptable to combine nicotine replacement with bupropion. One study of persons with schizophrenia, major depression, bipolar disorder, or an anxiety disorder did not report greater psychiatric distress with either varenicline or bupropion plus nicotine replacement compared to a single smoking cessation medication (Steinberg et al., 2011). Despite the success of the integrated care program above, approximately 70% of study participants relapsed with tobacco use within 18 months. The large public health burden from tobacco use underscores the need for further research into smoking cessation strategies among persons with PTSD.

GENDER ISSUES

Several studies have examined gender factors in antidepressant response for PTSD, and there are no known gender differences attributed to venlafaxine SR, paroxetine, or sertraline (Rothbaum et al., 2008; Tucker et al., 2001). Many psychiatric medications are not known as to whether these are completely safe during pregnancy or are associated with birth defect risks. For these reasons, we recommend female patients of childbearing age use effective contraception when taking medication for PTSD. We also recommend psychotherapy as an alternative to pharmacotherapy for female patients who plan to become pregnant.

If a female patient states her plan is to become pregnant, the psychiatric medication should be stopped 4 or more weeks prior to attempts at conception. The risk of fetal harm is greatest in the first trimester and many women may not be aware of pregnancy until after approximately one month after conception. Limited use of psychiatric medications during pregnancy may be considered on a case-by-case basis with careful attention to maternal benefit and fetal risks. The benefits from medication may include fewer psychiatric symptoms and an enhanced maternal ability for self-care (e.g., appropriate diet, exercise, abstention from alcohol and tobacco, maintaining appropriate weight, and adherence with prenatal care visits). The potential risks from medication include birth defects, preterm labor, and delivery complications.

Mood stabilizing medication should be avoided for female patients who are pregnant or are trying to become pregnant. Many of these medications are known to cause birth defects (e.g., lithium, valproic acid). Although initial reports may show some newer mood-stabilizing medications to appear safe in pregnancy, it is best to inform patients that absence of known birth defect risk is not the same conclusion as absence of birth defect risk. As a general rule, women who wish to become pregnant should not take mood-stabilizing medication during attempts to become pregnant. Antipsychotics are best avoided so as to not increase the risk of gestational diabetes and excessive weight gain.

We recommend avoiding antidepressants prior to attempts to become pregnant and during the first trimester. The SSRI/SNRI antidepressants appear reasonable to take in second and third trimester but should be stopped 2 weeks prior to anticipated delivery to avoid neonatal SSRI discontinuation syndrome (i.e., newborns exhibiting convulsions or withdrawal symptoms from SSRI medications). During this time, avoid fluoxetine due to its long half-life (half-life is defined as the time that it takes for half of the substance to be eliminated from the body). Benzodiazepines are not to be taken during first trimester because of the risk for adverse effects on fetal development. Finally, many psychiatric medications are secreted in breast milk and can be transferred from mother to child. As a general rule, we strongly encourage females who are or plan to become pregnant to treat their psychiatric issues with maximal use of psychotherapy in an attempt to minimize, if not entirely avoid, pharmacotherapy.

CASES

Two cases are presented to illustrate important concepts from this chapter. These cases represent clinical challenges and real-world scenarios facing military service members and veterans. These cases are entirely fictional and any resemblance to living persons, either deceased or alive, is purely coincidental.

Case Vignette: Staff Sergeant Jones

SSG Jones is a 26-year-old African American male who serves on active military duty with the U.S. Army. He joined the Army after high school graduation. He intends to serve the 20 years required for military retirement, and thus when presenting for an initial mental health evaluation, he admitted to some reluctance in seeking help, for fear of negative work repercussions. However, after his second combat zone deployment in the past 4 years, his wife urged him to seek counseling. After SSG Jones spoke with his battalion chaplain, a fellow devout Baptist, he decided to seek medical intervention in addition to pastoral counseling.

SSG Jones states his chief complaint as "I can't seem to get anything done unless I'm in a combat zone, and I feel like an alien around my wife and kids." SSG Jones reported numerous symptoms of PTSD and met the *DSM-IV* criteria for the diagnosis. His Criterion A stressor was seeing his former squad leader killed during combat. He denied any lifetime history of seeking mental health care and his medical history is positive only for mild injuries of soldiers in an airborne infantry regiment. He denied any combat wounds and specifically denied any blunt or blast head trauma that caused altered level of consciousness or loss of consciousness. He does not take any prescription medications and has never taken psychiatric medications. His family history is negative for mental illness or substance use disorders. He is married to his first wife and they have two young children together. She works as a teaching assistant at an elementary school on the Army base. SSG Jones does not drink alcohol because of his religious faith. He does not use illicit drugs. He smokes cigarettes and would like to quit. He attends weekly religious services when he does not have conflicting military obligations and said his faith is very important to him. His Army career has been very positive to date, and he anticipates promotion to Sergeant First Class (E-7) within the year. His current assignment is acting Platoon Sergeant for an infantry platoon and it is likely his unit will return to a combat zone within the next 6 to 9 months.

SSG Jones's mental status examination shows a youthful, athletic male who appears his stated age. He is dressed in the Army combat uniform with parachutist and combat infantry badges. He makes good eye contact with the examiner and answers most questions with "Yes, Ma'am" or "No, Ma'am" but elaborates freely when asked to. Mood is stated as "Okay, but not really right, ma'am" and affect is appropriate yet restricted in range. His speech demonstrates a normal rate, rhythm, volume, and latency. His thought processes are logical, goal-directed, and without evidence of flight of ideas or loose associations. He denies auditory or visual hallucinations, paranoia, and thoughts of harming others. He admits to thoughts of suicide three to five times weekly, mostly when reminded of his former squad leader's death, but denied any intent or plan to harm himself.

Case Vignette: Ms. Lopez

Ms. Lopez is a veteran of the U.S. Marine Corps. She is a Latina female who is 26 years of age. She resigned her commission as a Captain after completing her statutory service obligation and now seeks mental health care from a VA outpatient clinic. Ms. Lopez joined the Marines after graduating from college and currently plans to start law school later in the calendar year. She is ambivalent about returning to military duty and noted that her private law school tuition is expensive, and returning to active or reserve military duty might be a reasonable option to repay her loans. She decided to seek counseling after she told her grandfather about her disturbing nightmares. He is a Vietnam veteran who is rated 50% disabled by the VA for PTSD, and his account of VA mental health care encouraged her to seek help.

Ms. Lopez states her chief complaint as, "My sleep is all jacked up, I'm arguing with my boyfriend, and I used to read all the time. I love football and I can't even finish the sports page now." Ms. Lopez reported numerous symptoms of major depression and PTSD, meeting the *DSM-IV* criteria for both diagnoses. Her PTSD Criterion A stressor was believing that she would die during a firefight that occurred when insurgents ambushed her motor transport unit. She reported seeking counseling during college to cope with anxiety after an attempted sexual assault but otherwise denied any history of mental health care. Her medical history is positive for a possible traumatic brain injury (TBI) that occurred during the firefight. A roadside improvised explosive device (IED) detonated approximately 15 feet from her nonarmored truck, causing the driver to lose control and run off the road. Ms. Lopez's first memory after the explosion was a firefight in her immediate vicinity, and then checking to ensure that her driver was not wounded. She then exited the vehicle to assume leadership of her marines, and in the ensuing firefight, she personally killed two enemy combatants with small arms fire. She denied any combat wounds. Her only prescription medications are oral contraceptives prescribed years ago by a Navy gynecologist for endometriosis. She also takes over-the-counter ibuprofen 2 to 4 days per week for migraine-like headaches that developed after the IED explosion. Her family history is negative for mental illness or substance use disorders. She has never been married, however she has been involved in a steady romantic relationship for approximately one year. She supports herself by funds saved from overseas deployment but plans to take out loans for law school. Ms. Lopez drinks fewer than three alcoholic drinks per week and does not drink more than two per occasion. She does not use tobacco products or illicit substances, but she does drink four to six cups of caffeinated coffee daily. She attends religious services sporadically. She described Marine Corps service as "a good experience." She denied any incidents of actual or threatened sexual assault or any sexual harassment or intimidation during military service. She said she initiated disciplinary action within her platoon when a Marine attempted to assault a fellow female Marine, and she reported feeling angry and frustrated when the battalion commander declined to investigate further.

Ms. Lopez's mental status examination shows an age-apparent Hispanic female dressed appropriately in civilian clothes. She makes good eye contact except when discussing her battalion commander's decision to not pursue disciplinary action in the alleged sexual assault case. Her speech demonstrates a normal rhythm and tone, a slight decrease in volume, and a slight increase in latency. Thought processes are logical, goal-directed, and without evidence of flight of ideas or loose associations. She denies auditory or visual hallucinations, paranoia, and thoughts of harming self or others.

Case Vignette Discussion Questions

1. Assume SSG Jones starts an SSRI antidepressant and is referred for evidence-based psychotherapy. If he reports inability to obtain an erection 3 weeks later, what is an appropriate response from his psychotherapist?
2. SSG Jones has only a partial response to the SSRI after 12 weeks. He is interested in stopping smoking. What psychopharmacologic options are available to treat the combination of PTSD and smoking cessation?
3. Ms. Lopez wants to begin prolonged exposure therapy for her PTSD. She is taking lorazepam from a non-VA primary care physician for sleep. How should this situation be addressed?

CONCLUSION

The pharmacologic management of PTSD presents a challenge to military, VA, and civilian clinicians. Although the present conflicts in Afghanistan and Iraq have focused public and professional attention on these younger veterans, there are other veterans who suffer from PTSD. For example, there are those veterans who served in combat operations in Vietnam, Desert Shield/Storm, and other conflicts, including deployment on peacekeeping or humanitarian relief operations. There are also veterans who have PTSD resulting from military sexual trauma; motor vehicle accidents; and military training accidents. All of these patients deserve the highest quality health care for optimal mental health and wellness.

We join other clinicians, physicians, and researchers in heartily recommending the evidence-based psychotherapies as the single most effective intervention for PTSD. We recognize that many persons with PTSD do not begin one of these therapies for a variety of reasons: work or school obligations may interfere with weekly psychotherapy visits; a pressing need to treat a comorbid substance use disorder; availability of a suitably trained psychotherapist to provide evidence-based psychotherapy; or patient preference. Under these circumstances, starting an SSRI antidepressant, preferentially paroxetine or sertraline is the recommended first-line intervention. Treatment may require doses that exceed those commonly used for major depression and up to 12 weeks may be required for a full therapeutic response. Switching to an SNRI antidepressant, preferentially venlafaxine is the recommended second-line intervention. Further psychopharmacologic intervention may include a switch to mirtazapine or nefazodone for side effects or for those who do not respond to other antidepressants. We recommend including a psychiatrist on the treatment team after the patient does not respond to the first two SSRIs or SNRI antidepressants because the psychopharmacologic decision making can be complex.

The value of an interdisciplinary team cannot be overstated. We believe an interdisciplinary team delivers optimal PTSD care. Our clinical practices include psychiatry, psychology, and social work based on the VA model for a PTSD Clinical Team (PCT). This team can coordinate efforts to manage any preexisting or emerging comorbid conditions such as substance abuse, other psychiatric diagnoses, or medical issues that may affect psychiatric care. Communication and cooperation among team members will enhance the adherence to pharmacotherapy and improve its effect on the patient. This same cooperation and communication will encourage the patient to enter evidence-based psychotherapy, thus providing the best chance at optimal recovery from PTSD.

CHAPTER DISCUSSION QUESTIONS

1. Your client thinks that her ability to read would improve if she could sleep better at night. She reports difficulty falling asleep most nights and nightmares about the firefight wake her from sleep 3 to 5 nights per week. What three pharmacologic interventions might be mentioned by her psychiatrist?
2. A veteran begins taking an SSRI for depression and PTSD. After 12 weeks, it is only partially effective. She is concerned about taking "too many medications: this one for PTSD, that one for headaches, and I'm afraid my psychiatrist will want to add another medicine because my PTSD isn't much better." What pharmacologic option might help both PTSD and migraine-like headaches? How does the answer change if she reports a family history of bipolar disorder?

REFERENCES

Ahearn, E. P., Mussey, M., Johnson, C., Krohn, A., & Krahn, D. (2006). Quetiapine as an adjunctive treatment for post-traumatic stress disorder: An 8-week open-label study. *International clinical psychopharmacology, 21*, 29–33.

Andreasen, N. J., Norris, A. S., & Hartford, C. E. (1971). Incidence of long-term psychiatric complications in severely burned adults. *Annals of Surgery, 174*, 785–793.

Anton, R. F. (2008). Naltrexone for the management of alcohol dependence. *New England Journal of Medicine, 359*, 715–721.

Becker, M. E., Hertzberg, M. A., Moore, S. D., Dennis, M. F., Bukenya, D. S., & Beckham, J. C. (2007). A placebo-controlled trial of bupropion SR in the treatment of chronic posttraumatic stress disorder. *Journal of Clinical Psychopharmacology, 27*, 193–197.

Boyer, E., & Shannon, M. (2005). The serotonin syndrome. *New England Journal of Medicine, 352*, 1112–1120.

Brady, K., Pearlstein, T., Asnis, G. M., Baker, D., Rothbaum, B., Sikes, C. R., & Farfel, G. M. (2000). Efficacy and safety of sertraline treatment of posttraumatic stress disorder: A randomized controlled trial. *JAMA: The Journal of the American Medical Association, 283*, 1837–1844.

Calhoun, P. S., Dennis, M. F., Beckham, J. C. (2007). Emotional reactivity to trauma stimuli and duration of past smoking cessation attempts in smokers with posttraumatic stress disorder. *Experimental and Clinical Psychopharmacology, 15*, 256–263.

Correll, C. U., & Schenk, E. M. (2008).Tardive dyskinesia and new antipsychotics. *Current Opinion in Psychiatry*, 21, 151–156.

Davidson, J., Baldwin, D., Stein, D. J., Kuper, E., Benattia, I., Ahmed, S., . . . Musgnung, J. (2006). Treatment of posttraumatic stress disorder with venlafaxine extended release: A 6-month randomized controlled trial. *Archives of General Psychiatry*, 63, 1158–1165.

Davidson, J., Landerman, L. R., & Clary, C. M. (2004). Improvement of anger at one week predicts the effects of sertraline and placebo in PTSD. *Journal of Psychiatric Research, 38*, 497–502.

Dillard, M. L., Bendfeldt, F., & Jernigan, P. (1993). Use of thioridazine in post-traumatic stress disorder. *Southern Medical Journal*, 86, 1276–1278.

Duffy, J. D., Malloy, P. F. (1994). Efficacy of buspirone in the treatment of posttraumatic stress disorder: An open trial. *Annals of Clinical Psychiatry: Official Journal of the American Academy of Clinical Psychiatrists*, 6, 33–37.

Eisenberg, M. J., Filion, K. B., Yavin, D., Belisle, P., Mottillo, S., Joseph, L., . . . & Pilote, L. (2008). Pharmacotherapies for smoking cessation: A meta-analysis of randomized controlled trials. *Canadian Medical Association Journal, 179*, 135–144.

El-Mallakh, R. S., Ghaemi, S. N., Sagduyu, K., Thase, M. E., Wisniewski, S. R., Nierenberg, A. A., . . . STEP-BD Investigators. (2008). Antidepressant-associated chronic irritable dysphoria (ACID) in STEP-BD patients. *Journal of Affective Disorders, 11*, 372–377.

Falcon, S., Ryan, C., Chamberlain, K. & Curtis, G. (1985). Tricyclics: Possible treatment for posttraumatic stress disorder. *Journal of Clinical Psychiatry*, 46, 385–388.

Feeny, N. C., Zoellner, L. A., Mavissakalian, M. R., & Roy-Byrne, P. P. (2009). What would you choose? Sertraline or prolonged exposure in community and PTSD treatment seeking women. *Depression and Anxiety, 26*, 724–731.

Friedman, M. J. (1988). Toward rational pharmacotherapy for posttraumatic stress disorder: An interim report. *American Journal of Psychiatry*, 145, 281–285.

Fu, S. S., McFall, M., Saxon, A. J., Beckham, J. C., Carmody, T. P., Baker, D. G. & Joseph, A. M. (2007). Post-traumatic stress disorder and smoking: A systematic review. *Nicotine & Tobacco Research: Official Journal of the Society for Research on Nicotine and Tobacco, 9*, 1071–1084.

Ghaemi, S. N. (2008). Why antidepressants are not antidepressants: STEP-BD, STAR*D, and the return of neurotic depression. *Bipolar Disorders, 10*, 957–968.

Hamner, M., Ulmer, H., & Horne, D. (1997). Buspirone potentiation of antidepressants in the treatment of PTSD. *Depression and Anxiety 5*, 137–139.

Hamner, M. B., Deitsch, S. E., Brodrick, P. S., Ulmer, H. G., & Lorberbaum, J. P. (2003). Quetiapine treatment in patients with posttraumatic stress disorder: An open trial of adjunctive therapy. *Journal of Clinical Psychopharmacology, 23*, 15–20.

Hamner, M. B., Faldowski, R. A., Ulmer, H. G., Frueh, B. C., Huber, M. G., & Arana, G. W. (2003). Adjunctive risperidone treatment in post-traumatic stress disorder: A preliminary controlled trial of effects on comorbid psychotic symptoms. *International Clinical Psychopharmacology, 18*, 1–8.

Henriksen, G. L., Ketchum, N. S., Michalek, J. E., & Swaby J. A. (1997). Serum dioxin and diabetes mellitus in veterans of operation ranch hand. *Epidemiology, 8*, 252–258.

Hertzberg, M. A., Moore, S. D., Feldman, M. E., & Beckham, J. C. (2001). A preliminary study of bupropion sustained-release for smoking cessation in patients with chronic posttraumatic stress disorder. *Journal of Clinical Psychopharmacology, 21*, 94–98.

Hogben, G. L., & Cornfield, R. B. (1981). Treatment of traumatic war neurosis with phenelzine. *Archives of General Psychiatry, 38*, 440–445.

Huggins, J. M., Brown, J. N., Capehart, B., Townsend, M. L., Legge, J., & Melnyk S. D. (2011). Medication adherence in combat veterans with traumatic brain injury. *American Journal of Health-System Pharmacy: AJHP: Official Journal of the American Society of Health-System Pharmacists, 68*, 254–258,

Jakupcak, M., Tull, M. T., McDermott, M. J., Kaysen, D., Hunt, S. & Simpson, T. (2010). PTSD symptom clusters in relationship to alcohol misuse among Iraq and Afghanistan war veterans seeking post-deployment VA health care. *Addictive Behaviors, 35*, 840–843.

Kessler, R. C., Sonnega, A., Bromet, E., Hughes, M. & Nelson, C. B..(1995). Posttraumatic stress disorder in the national comorbidity survey. *Archives of General Psychiatry, 52*, 1048–1060.

Krystal, J. H., Rosenheck, R. A., Cramer, J. A., Krystal, J. H., Rosenheck, R. A., Cramer, J. A., . . . & Stock C. (2011). Adjunctive risperidone treatment for antidepressant-resistant symptoms of chronic military service-related PTSD: A randomized trial. *Journal of the American Medical Association, 306*, 493–502.

Lacoursiere, R. B., Godfrey, K. E., & Ruby, L. M. (1980). Traumatic neurosis in the etiology of alcoholism: Viet Nam combat and other trauma. *American Journal of Psychiatry, 137*, 966–968.

Leslie, D. L., Mohamed, S., & Rosenheck, R. A. (2009). Off-label use of antipsychotic medications in the Department of Veterans Affairs health care system. *Psychiatric Services, 60*, 1175–1181.

Management of Post-Traumatic Stress Working Group, Departments of Veterans Affairs and Defense. (2010). *VA/DoD Clinical Practice Guideline for Management of Post-Traumatic Stress*. Washington, DC: Office of Quality and Performance, Department of Veterans Affairs.

McFall, M., Saxon, A. J., Malte, C. A., Chow, B., Bailey, S., Baker, D. G., . . . Lavori, P. W. (2010). Integrating tobacco cessation into mental health care for posttraumatic stress disorder: A randomized controlled trial. *JAMA: The Journal of the American Medical Association, 304*, 2485–2493.

Mohamed, S., & Rosenheck, R. A. (2008). Pharmacotherapy of PTSD in the U.S. Department of Veterans Affairs: Diagnostic- and symptom-guided drug selection. *Journal of Clinical Psychiatry, 69*, 959–965.

Neugaard, B. I., Priest, J. L., Burch, S. P., Cantrell, C. R., & Foulis, P. R. (2011). Quality of care for veterans with chronic diseases: Performance on quality indicators, medication use and adherence, and health care utilization. *Population Health Management, 14*, 99–106.

Petrakis, I. L., Poling, J., Levinson, C., Nich, C., Carroll, K., Ralevski, E., & Rounsaville, B. (2006). Naltrexone and disulfiram in patients with alcohol dependence and comorbid posttraumatic stress disorder. *Biological Psychiatry, 60*(7), 777–783.

Petty, F., Brannan, S., Casada, J., Davis, L. L., Gajewski, V., Kramer, G. L., . . . Young, K. A. (2001). Olanzapine treatment for post-traumatic stress disorder: An open-label study. *International Clinical Psychopharmacology, 16*, 331–337.

Pivac, N., Kozaric-Kovacic, D., & Muck-Seler, D. (2004). Olanzapine versus fluphenazine in an open trial in patients with psychotic combat-related post-traumatic stress disorder. *Psychopharmacology, 175*, 451–456.

Rothbaum, B. O., Davidson, J. R., Stein, D. J., Pedersen, R., Musgnung, J., Tian, X. W., . . . Baldwin, D. S. (2008). A pooled analysis of gender and trauma-type effects on responsiveness to treatment of PTSD with venlafaxine extended release or placebo. *Journal of Clinical Psychiatry, 6*, 1529–1539.

Seal, K. H., Cohen, G., Waldrop, A., Cohen, B. E., Maguen, S., & Ren, L. (2011). Substance use disorders in Iraq and Afghanistan veterans in VA healthcare, 2001–2010: Implications for screening, diagnosis and treatment. *Drug and Alcohol Dependence, 116*, 93–101.

Shalev, A. Y. (2009). Posttraumatic stress disorder and stress-related disorders. *Psychiatric Clinics of North America, 32*, 687–704.

Simon, N. M., Connor, K. M., Lang, A. J., Rauch, S., Krulewicz, S., LeBeau, R. T., . . . Pollack, M. H. (2008). Paroxetine CR augmentation for posttraumatic stress disorder refractory to prolonged exposure therapy. *Journal of Clinical Psychiatry, 69*, 400–405.

Sinha, R. (2008). Chronic stress, drug use, and vulnerability to addiction. *Annals of the New York Academy of Sciences, 1141*, 105–130.

Stein, D. J., Pedersen, R., Rothbaum, B. O., Baldwin, D. S., Ahmed, S., Musgnung, J. & Davidson, J. (2009). Onset of activity and time to response on individual CAPS-SX17 items in patients treated for post-traumatic stress disorder with venlafaxine ER: A pooled analysis. *International Journal of Neuropsychopharmacology/Official Scientific Journal of the Collegium Internationale Neuropsychopharmacologicum, 12*, 23–31.

Steinberg, M. B., Bover, M. T., Richardson, D. L., Schmelzer, A. C., Williams, J. M., & Foulds, J. (2011). Abstinence and psychological distress in co-morbid smokers using various pharmacotherapies. *Drug and Alcohol Dependence, 114*, 77–81.

Trivedi, M. H., Fava, M., Wisniewski, S. R., Thase, M. E., Quitkin, F., Warden, D., . . . STAR*D Study Team. (2006). Medication augmentation after the failure of SSRIs for depression. *New England Journal of Medicine*, *354*, 1243–1252.

Tucker, P., Zaninelli, R., Yehuda, R., Ruggiero, L., Dillingham, K., & Pitts, C. D. (2001). Paroxetine in the treatment of chronic posttraumatic stress disorder: Results of a placebo-controlled, flexible-dosage trial. *Journal of Clinical Psychiatry*, *62*, 860–868.

van der Kolk, B. A., Spinazzola, J., Blaustein, M. E., Hopper, J. W., Hopper, E. K., Korn, D. L., & Simpson, W. B. (2007). A randomized clinical trial of eye movement desensitization and reprocessing (EMDR), fluoxetine, and pill placebo in the treatment of posttraumatic stress disorder: Treatment effects and long-term maintenance. *Journal of Clinical Psychiatry*, *68*, 37–46.

Walton, S. M., Schumock, G. T., Lee, K. V., Alexander, G. C., Meltzer, D., & Stafford, R. S. (2008). Prioritizing future research on off-label prescribing: Results of a quantitative evaluation. *Pharmacotherapy*, *28*, 1443–1452.

CHAPTER

10

Traumatic Brain Injury (TBI) and the Military

Cynthia Boyd and Sarah Asmussen

OVERVIEW

Traumatic brain injury (TBI) is a significant cause of death and disability worldwide. In the United States it is estimated that 1.5 million to 3 million individuals experience a brain injury every year; likely an underestimate given data is primarily derived from those who seek medical attention (Comper, Bisschop, Carniden, & Tricco, 2005; Langlois et al., 2003; McCrea, 2008; World Health Organization, 1992). Men aged 15 to 24 are the largest population affected (American Psychological Association, 1994; Jennett, 1996; Kraus et al., 1996). The mechanisms of injury vary, but include motor vehicle accidents and occupational, that is, on-the-job injuries. In the active duty military population, the majority of brain injuries are caused by explosive devices used by insurgents. This type of warfare is quite effective in causing mass injuries and casualties.

Traumatic brain injury (TBI) remains the signature wound of Operation Iraqi Freedom (OIF) and Operation Enduring Freedom (OEF). Since 2000, it is estimated that more than 195,000 service members have been screened for a suspected brain injury (Department of Defense, 2009). In the civilian and military population, an estimated 70% to 90% of brain injuries are diagnosed as mild in severity (Kraus et al., 1996; Thornhill et al., 2000; World Health Organization, 1992). This chapter provides an overview of TBI, with a focus on mild TBI (mTBI) in the military including: diagnostic considerations, complicating factors, treatment considerations, and case examples.

Changes in combat warfare, coupled with advances in military medicine, have resulted in an overall higher rate of survival from war-related injuries. Traumatic brain injury (TBI), the primary wound of modern day combat, ranges in severity from mild to severe. Injuries

We would like to thank Dr. Leslie Baxter for assisting in obtaining MRI examples for this chapter.

caused from blast exposure include both penetrating (e.g., shrapnel) and nonpenetrating (e.g., blast wave, blunt force) brain injuries. It is important to be familiar with the most common perpetrator of military TBI, which is blast exposure. Improvised explosive devices (IEDs), rocket-propelled grenades (RPGs), and mortar rounds are the "faceless" enemies responsible for moderate to severe TBI and the "invisible wound": mild TBI (mTBI).

In a combat zone, more than one injury can occur from a single blast wave. A service member can feel the pressure of the blast wave (e.g., head, ear, and lung pressure) and also be thrown or hit by flying debris. Blast caused by explosive devices tends to move in a wave like motion. The physical force of the blast wave can move objects and people, causing penetrating injuries or blunt trauma to the brain. Effects of an explosion are likely to be intensified in a confined space, which could lead to more severe injury (Brenner et al., 2010), such as when an enclosed vehicle drives over an explosive device or a rocket-propelled grenade is launched into a building.

A myriad of physical injuries can occur from a blast exposure, with TBI being the most common. The pathophysiology of blast-related TBI is complex and not fully understood; it may be similar to civilian mechanical injuries caused by motor vehicle accidents and falls. Rapid pressure changes create shear and stress forces that lead to trauma such as mTBI/concussion, or more severe TBI. When an individual sustains a moderate to severe brain injury, symptoms are usually detected early and appropriate treatment decisions follow rapidly (e.g., computed tomography or brain imaging findings may lead neurosurgery). In mild traumatic brain injury (mTBI) secondary to blast exposure, it remains unclear and controversial whether the brain is injured by the primary blast force, as it has been demonstrated in animal studies (Warden, 2006). In a combat setting, service members who sustain an mTBI/concussion following a blast exposure often present with a multitude of complex symptoms. Social work and mental health providers need to understand the basics of TBI to assist with recovery and treatment recommendations.

DIAGNOSTIC CONSIDERATIONS AND SEVERITY

Conventionally, TBI severity has been established by diagnostic criteria including: any period of loss of consciousness (LOC), posttraumatic amnesia (PTA), and a rating on the Glasgow Coma Scale (GCS). The *VA/DoD Clinical Practice Guideline* (2009) defines LOC and PTA as:

- **LOC** (loss of consciousness)—Any period of loss of consciousness or a decreased level of consciousness.
- **PTA** (posttraumatic amnesia)—Any loss of memory for events immediately before or after the injury.

The **GCS** (Glasgow Coma Scale) is an assessment technique typically used by emergency medical technicians in the field and by combat trauma medical personnel to determine severity of injury in patients whose consciousness is compromised. The scale, ranging from 3 to 15, measures a patient's ability to respond to commands verbally, with motor functions, and eye opening (Lezak, Howieson, & Loring, 2004). Remember that a limitation of GCS is that it is affected by anything that would preclude the patient from responding verbally. If the patient had an obstructed airway, verbal response would not be possible; thus, the GCS score would be lowered, and would not be an accurate measure of brain functioning at the scene. Additionally, significant alcohol intoxication and effects from drugs have an impact on GCS. For example, one of this chapter's authors (Boyd) worked on a forensic case that involved an individual who was described as having "severe brain injury based on his low GCS score." With further investigation she found that his low GCS score was the result of alcohol-induced intoxication; he was so intoxicated, he could not respond verbally or physically to commands.

Table 10.1 illustrates general guidelines on how to use LOC, PTA, and GCS information to rate TBI severity. The severity of TBI must be assessed by the acute injury characteristics as defined in Table 10.1, and not by the severity of symptoms reported by the patient either acutely or over time. Symptom presentation can vary individually and can also be influenced by other factors not relevant to a TBI diagnosis (e.g., effects of medication, physical injury, or psychiatric illness). If patients meet the criteria described in Table 10.1, then their TBI can be classified as mild/moderate/severe. If more than one criterion is met, the higher severity level should be assigned. For example, if the patient had a loss of consciousness (LOC) of 20 minutes and posttraumatic amnesia (PTA) extended to 36 hours (without sedating medication) the severity rating would increase from a mild to a moderate brain injury. In addition to being familiar with the diagnostic criteria of LOC, PTA, and GCS, other assessment tools can also include the Rancho Los Amigos Scale (2006) and category of concussions measurements (Grade I-III) (Cantu, 1998).

Traumatic brain injury is a "historical" event; that is, an event that meets the minimum threshold of an *alteration of consciousness*. Symptom onset closely follows the event, and in most cases, the majority of symptoms resolve overtime, see Figure 10.1. TBI is not a

Table 10.1 Guidelines on TBI Severity Ratings for the GCS, LOC, and PTA

	TBI Severity Rating		
Severity	GCS	LOC	PTA
Mild*	13–15	<30 min	<24 hr
Moderate	9–12	>30 min to 24 hr	24 hr to 7 days
Severe	3–8	>24 hr	>7 days +

*Includes alteration in consciousness (AOC).

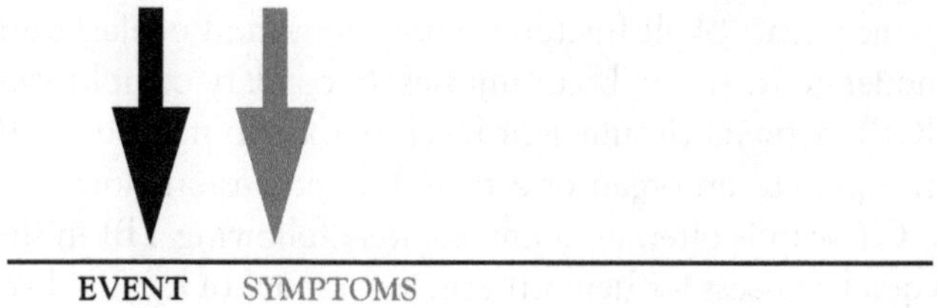

Figure 10.1 Brain injury symptom onset timeline

progressive disorder; that is to say, symptoms do not worsen over time as one would expect in a progressive disorder like dementia. When the brain is injured, there is a course of recovery based on the severity of the injury. Following a mild to moderate brain injury, individuals begin to return to pre-injury level of functioning over weeks to months. An exception to this rule is when there are other complications in functioning such as psychiatric illness, substance abuse, and/or chronic pain.

This image (Figure 10.1) represents the time of injury (event) and close proximity of symptom presentation.

Neuroimaging can assist with assessing the severity of TBI and potential outcome. MRI and CT are commonly used. An MRI (magnetic resonance imaging) uses magnetic signals to generate images that create a structural map of the brain. A CT (computerized tomography) generates computerized pictures of the brain that are produced from multiple X-ray images.

Abnormal neuroimaging, found on a MRI or CT, following TBI will result in the patient being classified in the range of moderate to severe. For example, if a patient sustained a mild TBI as classified above and there was evidence of abnormal MRI or CT findings (e.g., hemorrhage), the injury severity would be classified as moderate.

It is important to be familiar with different types of neuroimaging. To review the basics, a CT of the brain is often completed immediately after a suspected brain injury to assess for potential bleeding. An MRI of the brain may be used to generate a structural map of the brain to assess what areas are injured in more detail. The MRIs in Figure 10.2 are of a 19-year-old female who was in a motor vehicle accident and sustained a severe traumatic brain injury. As you can see, the MRI demonstrates shearing to the frontal and temporal lobe (left image), and lower in the brain there is evidence of a countercoup injury (right image) or brain injury suffered by tissue at the end of the skull opposite the trauma site.) For comparison, below the two images of the 19-year-old female, the reader will find a MRI of the brain in a normal healthy adolescent.

MODERATE TO SEVERE TBI IN THE MILITARY

Moderate to severe TBI is noted in the military population. Typically there is evidence of abnormal neuroimaging at this level of severity. Acceleration/deceleration injuries such as a vast fall from a building or a high-speed motor vehicle accident affect the brain with such force that it causes shearing and tearing of axons, resulting in diffuse axonal injury (DAI) (Morgan & Ricker, 2008). This type of finding can be detected on an MRI. As seen in Figure 10.2, the 19-year-old sustained shearing as a result of a severe brain injury secondary to a motor vehicle accident. Skull fractures, contusions, and ocular/eye injuries are commonly found in moderate to severe brain injuries. Secondary complications such as intracranial pressure (ICP), hypoxia (insufficient levels of oxygen in blood or tissue) anoxia (an absence of oxygen supply to an organ or a tissue), hypotension (low blood pressure), and seizures can occur. CT scan is often used immediately following TBI in suspected moderate to severe cases to quickly assess for hemorrhage, hematoma (a localized swelling filled with blood resulting from a break in a blood vessel) and/or edema (a condition of abnormally

MRI (T2) of Brain with Shearing in Frontal and Temporal Lobes and Countrecoup

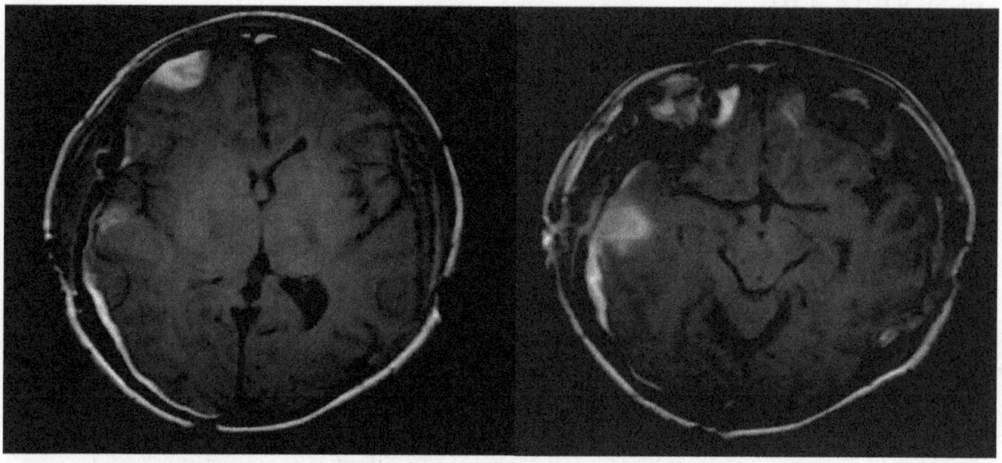

Normal MRI (T2) of Brain

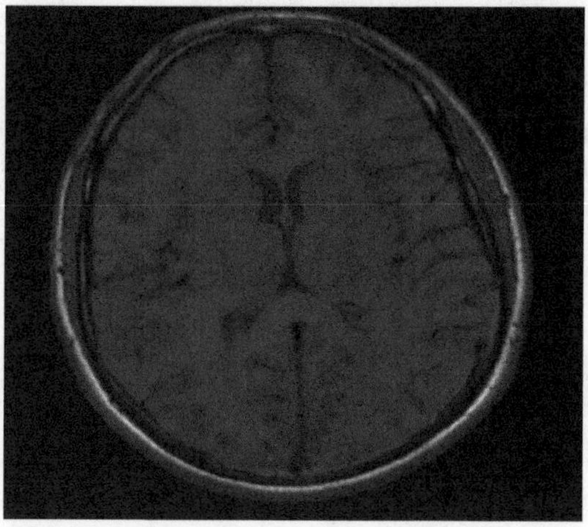

Figure 10.2 An MRI of a severe traumatic brain injury (top) compared to an MRI of a healthy brain (bottom)

large fluid volume in the circulatory system or in tissues between the body's cells), which can lead to death.

Acute symptoms following a moderate to severe TBI can include: severe headache with progressive worsening, dizziness, pain, fatigue, sleep difficulties, repeated vomiting or nausea, convulsions or seizures, the inability to wake up from sleep, dilation of one or both pupils of the eyes, problems speaking, limb weakness or numbness, loss of coordination, confusion, restlessness, and agitation. In the military, symptoms such as severe headache and vomiting are considered "red flags" and warrant immediate medical attention.

TREATMENT AND RECOVERY FOLLOWING MODERATE TO SEVERE TBI

Immediate, intermediate, rehabilitation, and transitional treatment are the four stages targeted in the recovery process following moderate to severe TBI. Treatment in each stage will generally vary depending on the severity of the injury and physical and emotional condition of the patient at each stage. In the military following a severe TBI, service members are medically evacuated out of theater. They require intensive rehabilitation, and are unlikely to return to full-duty status. They generally will have persistent impairments in functioning. Following a moderate TBI, the service member is typically evacuated out of theater. They generally require less intensive rehabilitation services and their return to duty rates are variable. Due to changes in behavior and in cognitive processes resulting from TBI, they may be at risk for disciplinary issues, work performance problems, and family discord.

In moderate to severe TBI, the vast amount of cognitive recovery (e.g., attention, memory, and processing speed) occurs primarily during the first 2 years following the event (Schretlen & Shapiro, 2003). The patient's severity of brain injuries will often dictate the pace and degree of injury recovery. Additionally, recovering from multiple physical injuries may complicate TBI recovery. The damage to the brain resulting from a moderate to severe TBI may lead to lifelong disabilities, including a loss of physical or mental functioning. Activities of daily living are often more challenging, even in those who appear to have fully recovered. Physical and mental changes can affect the service member's personal life, family relationships, career goals, and future. Moderate to severe TBI is often a life-changing experience in patients. As a part of the recovery and transitional processes following a TBI, it is crucial that the social work provider assist in offering early education, intervention, and continued support to both the patient and his or her family members.

Case Vignette: Albert

Albert presented to the clinic with the following history. He sustained a severe traumatic brain injury secondary to an explosion from a grenade launcher. He also sustained a serious injury to his left eye. Neuroimaging showed a frontal contusion, subdural hematoma, and complex depressed skull fracture (primarily to the left frontal region). LOC was estimated at 30 to 60 minutes. PTA was estimated at approximately two weeks, although not an accurate estimate of TBI severity because Albert was partially sedated during this period, which interfered with his memory. A few years after the TBI, he began having seizures, which appeared to occur largely in the left frontal region, consistent with the injury site. He was referred for a neuropsychological evaluation to assess current cognitive functioning and to provide treatment recommendations.

At the time of the evaluation, Albert continued to have headaches, disrupted sleep, and balance difficulties. His serious eye injury ultimately resulted in left eye blindness. Cognitively, he described difficulties with memory and attention/concentration, which began following the accident. Since the onset of seizures his wife noted that he had slowed down (physically and cognitively) and was more easily frustrated. His functioning appeared to be worsening. Following seizure onset he began having symptoms of anxiety and depression, including fleeting suicidal thoughts. Albert described some symptoms of PTSD related to the accident and postsurgical left eye changes.

Results from the neuropsychological evaluation revealed largely intact functioning in all cognitive domains assessed, with isolated difficulties on tasks correlated to left frontal brain regions. Findings were consistent with the patient's TBI history, neuroimaging, and seizure onset. Additionally, head pain, adjustment to permanent physical disability, and psychological symptoms (e.g., depression, irritability) contributed to the clinical picture.

Albert's clinical presentation, medical history, and cognitive testing results were consistent. He sustained a severe TBI following a grenade blast. He received immediate, intermediate, and rehabilitation treatment during the course of his recovery. Left eye surgeries and blindness slowed the pace of his recovery. Seizures, which began several years following the TBI, complicated the picture and essentially changed the course and pace of his recovery. With the support of Albert's wife and the VA, he was medically retired, and is transitioning to his new civilian life.

Albert's case represents a severe TBI with associated injuries that affected the course and timeline of his recovery. In contrast with Albert, in the next case vignette Robert has a more complex differential diagnosis. His case illustrates that in addition to being familiar with moderate and severe TBI, a working knowledge of repeated head injuries is important. A series of minor head injuries, in a short duration of time, can lead to a slower rate of recovery (Cifu & Drake, 2006). Thus, when working with the moderate to severe TBI population it is important to be familiar with all of the nuances that accompany the injury and recovery process.

Case Vignette: Robert

A more complex differential diagnosis was presented by Robert who was referred to the clinic in the early days of the Iraqi war. He had been part of the Marine infantry unit that encountered brutal insurgent activity in Fallujah. Robert sustained five concussions within a 72-hour period. Each concussion was documented by the award of a Purple Heart.

On formal neuropsychological testing, Robert's cognitive deficits were widespread. He also had significant vestibular-balance problems that interfered with his daily functioning. He could not drive a vehicle due to dizziness. Even as a passenger he suffered motion sickness, to the degree that he preferred to walk if at all possible, despite having challenges with balance. Robert also endorsed symptoms of hyperarousal, increased startle response, and intrusive thoughts; all consistent with a diagnosis of PTSD. On reevaluation 3 years later, Robert continued to demonstrate cognitive impairment. He was unable to maintain a job due to his deficits. Robert's clinical presentation was similar to "Repetitive Head Injury Syndrome," a condition where after a series of minor head injuries, an individual experiences a slow decline in cognitive abilities (Cifu & Drake, 2006). After the series of concussions in such a brief span, Robert's profile would not fit succinctly in the TBI severity classification table presented earlier in this chapter. Robert's deficits were persistent and debilitating; thus, more consistent with those seen in a brain injury of moderate, rather than mild severity.

MILD TBI IN THE MILITARY

In the civilian and military population, an estimated 70% to 90% of brain injuries are diagnosed as mild (Kraus et al., 1996; Thornhill et al., 2000; World Health Organization, 1992). The term *mild* is a descriptor used for diagnostic classification in the acute phase of injury, and is not based on an individual's reported symptoms. The term *mild TBI* and concussion are synonymous and used interchangeably in a clinical setting. There is not a consistent set criterion that all providers follow to define mTBI, therefore it is important to become familiar with the basics.

ADDITIONAL MTBI DIAGNOSTIC CONSIDERATIONS

A relatively new term has emerged in the literature over the past few years. Recent research suggests that an *alteration of consciousness* (AOC) or alteration in mental status should be considered as the minimum threshold for a diagnosis of TBI. This is contrary to the previously held belief that loss of consciousness was the hallmark diagnostic symptom (McCrea, 2008). AOC encompasses acute changes in mental state such as confusion, disorientation, slowed thinking, feeling "dazed" or a sense of having one's "bell rung." Clinically, AOC has become a relevant marker for diagnosis of mTBI in the military from blast exposure. It is not uncommon for service members to experience multiple blast exposures in the course of combat

Following a head injury, an individual with a GCS between 13 and 15, with an LOC of less than 30 minutes, and PTA of less than 24 hours, would be considered to have sustained a mild TBI (Table 10.1). This would also include those with an alteration of consciousness (AOC). For those with mTBI, neuroimaging, including MRI and CT, are unremarkable. The American Congress of Rehabilitative Medicine (ACRM) established the following guidelines in 1993 (Kay, Harrington, & Adams, 1993, pp. 86–87).

> A mild traumatic brain injury is a traumatically induced physiologic disruption of brain function, as manifested by at least one of the following: (1) Any period of loss of consciousness (LOC); (2) Any loss of memory for events immediately before or after the accident; (3) Any alteration in mental state at the time of the accident; (4) Focal neurologic deficit that may or may not be transient but where the severity does not exceed the following: (1) LOC of approximately 30 minutes or less, (2) An initial Glascow Coma Scale (GCS) of 13–15 after 30 minutes; and (3) Post-traumatic amnesia (PTA) of no more than 24 hours duration.

Symptoms Associated With mTBI

Symptoms will manifest immediately following a concussive event and can be categorized in three domains:

1. Physical: Headaches, nausea, vomiting, fatigue, blurred vision, sensitivity to light/noise, dizziness, balance problems, and sleep disturbance

2. Cognitive: Changes in attention, concentration, short-term memory, speed of processing information, judgment and executive functioning
3. Behavioral/emotional: Irritability, agitation, depression, anxiety, impulsivity and aggression

The symptoms may occur alone or in combinations. They can only be attributed to the TBI if they follow the injury *acutely*, and are not better explained by a preexisting condition, or other medical or psychological causes. As the reader may have noticed, the above listed symptoms are not unique to TBI. In fact, they frequently appear among healthy individuals, and those with other conditions such as depression or chronic pain, as described in the contributing factors section (Department of Veterans Affairs, 2009).

Postconcussion Syndrome Following mTBI

When the symptoms following a concussion persist for at least 3 months, the diagnosis of Postconcussion Syndrome (PCS) is given (American Psychological Association, 1994). PCS is a long-standing and controversial diagnosis in the realm of litigated civilian mild brain injury. Historically, concussion has been viewed as a transitory alteration of consciousness without associated pathological changes in the brain. Any change in cognitive or behavioral functioning was expected to be brief in duration. In the past, organic basis for persistent complaints was dismissed in favor of psychological or motivational reasons (Snyder & Nussbaum, 1998).

The debate lingers about the nonspecificity of PCS symptoms, and whether they are truly part of neurological phenomena, or rather maintained by psychological or noninjury-related factors. The constellation of symptoms that make up PCS are based exclusively on the patient's self-report. Several studies have demonstrated relatively high rates of post-concussion symptoms in many populations without a documented brain injury, including patients with chronic pain, mood disorders, personal injury claimants, and normal, healthy adults (Howe, 2009; Lippa, Patorek, Benge, & Thornton, 2010; McCrea, 2008). Following mTBI, the expectation is recovery with resolution of PCS symptoms.

TREATMENT AND RECOVERY FOLLOWING MTBI

Current evidence suggests that the pathophysiology of concussion involves a period of metabolic dysfunction, commonly known as a *neurometabolic cascade* that occurs at the time of injury. What follows is a rapid reversal and return to normal metabolic functions within several days of injury in most cases of concussion (McCrea, 2008). The expectation following mTBI is generally a full resolution of symptoms and recovery. A review of published research suggests that in the mTBI population cognitive functioning improves rapidly during the first few weeks, essentially returning to cognitive baseline within 1 to 3 months (Schretlen & Shapiro, 2003). However, in the military, trauma recovery may vary depending on the complexity of comorbid symptoms that often accompany the mTBI. For example, recovery of cognitive functioning can be hindered by chronic headaches, medication, substance abuse, PTSD, and other contributing factors.

Similar to a sports concussion that is managed without prolonged medical care, concussion sustained in theater is frequently medically managed in theater. Safety of the service member is the foremost priority. In a combat zone, acute symptoms following a concussion are likely to put a service member at risk. Concussion can affect a service member's ability to handle a weapon, operate heavy machinery, and to follow safety procedures. Following concussion, the service member is generally given a period of rest (e.g., 24 hours behind the wire), reevaluated, and then returned to duty as soon as they are asymptomatic. They typically do not require rehabilitation. However, even the effects of mTBI can cause changes in behavior and cognitive problems (e.g., attentional difficulties, slowed processing speed) that put service members at risk for disciplinary issues and changes in work performance. Comorbid factors including physical symptoms such as headache and lack of sleep can heighten symptoms. Due to the demands of a combat environment, subtle changes caused by a mild TBI may not be evident in theater. Once the service member returns from deployment, they may notice changes that may or may not be attributable to brain injury.

Interventions for mTBI vary. Much like the lack of consensus in criteria for the definition of mTBI, research and treatment of mTBI varies with limited empirically supported interventions. Early psychoeducation on recovery is important. Interventions for mTBI often target the presenting symptoms. Headache, depression, impaired cognitive performance, psychological distress, functional disability, and general PCS have been the focus of many known interventions (Comper et al., 2005). Group-based interventions, including compensatory strategy training, have shown a decrease in symptoms of depression and cognitive dysfunction (Huckans et al., 2010).

With early education, and intervention, most mTBI patients recover successfully. The following Case Vignette: Michael demonstrates a successful recovery following mTBI. Not all patients are as straightforward as Michael's case. As a mental health provider it is important to be aware of co-occurring factors when assessing treatment options for patients who have sustained an mTBI.

Case Vignette: Michael

Michael came to the clinic after completing two combat tours (2007 and 2008). He had a history of two blast exposures resulting in feeling "dazed" briefly with return to normal within seconds to minutes. He did not receive medical treatment following the events. He was on full duty with plans to deploy to Afghanistan in the near future as a videographer. He reported that he was able to complete his duties without difficulty at the time of the clinical interview and the command agreed.

He was seen at the command's request to assess duty status for future deployment given his history of likely AOC and mild concussion. He denied changes in mood or increased irritability. He was not involved in mental health services. He denied a history of illicit drug usage, and past or present substance abuse issues. He denied any physical complaints or cognitive difficulties.

Overall, results of neuropsychological evaluation revealed intact functioning in all cognitive domains. His pattern of performance was not consistent with a TBI. Given the patient's history of a mild concussion was greater than 2 years ago and he was functionally asymptomatic, he was considered fit for full duty including redeployment.

CO-OCCURRING RECOVERY CONSIDERATIONS

Although symptoms of PTSD and postconcussion syndrome do overlap and can be difficult to differentiate, some symptoms are characteristic of each. PTSD and symptoms of combat stress are driven by an overaroused limbic system that results in flashbacks, intrusive thoughts, and reexperiencing phenomena. These symptoms are not pathonomonic indicators of TBI.

Postconcussion symptoms have a physiological basis such as headaches, dizziness, and nausea or vomiting. Concussion/mTBI is not the same condition as PTSD. Concussion is the historical event. PTSD refers to a specific set or symptoms following trauma exposure. As illustrated in Figure 10.3, where the two disorders overlap, commonly shared symptoms include cognitive deficits, irritability, insomnia, depression, fatigue, and anxiety.

The overlap of shared symptoms, and the nonspecificity of postconcussion symptoms, complicates the diagnosis of concussion, particularly when the concussion occurred in a combat setting. Subtle changes in cognitive functions and behavior (e.g., increased irritability) may be overlooked because the environment warrants complete attention to imminent danger. In the clinic, service members frequently report that they did not notice changes until returning from deployment and were no longer in a combat zone. Adjustment to life postcombat can increase symptoms. Changes in mood and behavior are often first noticed by family members.

Differential diagnosis is challenging when the service member has had multiple deployments coupled with multiple blast exposure. However, as mentioned previously, concussion is a historical event, with symptom presentation following acutely. The only exception is when a service member has been engaged in a manner where the symptoms might not be realized early on and thus not attributed to a concussion. For example, if the service member was engaged in firefights for several hours and neglected to notice headaches or other physical symptoms because adrenalin was high and they were vigilant to survive. Another example is the polytrauma patient who sustains injury in theater and is aggressively treated with narcotics for pain control. Frequently, those patients will not even be aware that they sustained a concussion until sedation and pain issues are under control. At that time, often cognitive and/or behavioral changes emerge. Even in this scenario, we expect recovery of brain functions, quickly. PTSD symptoms are known to wax

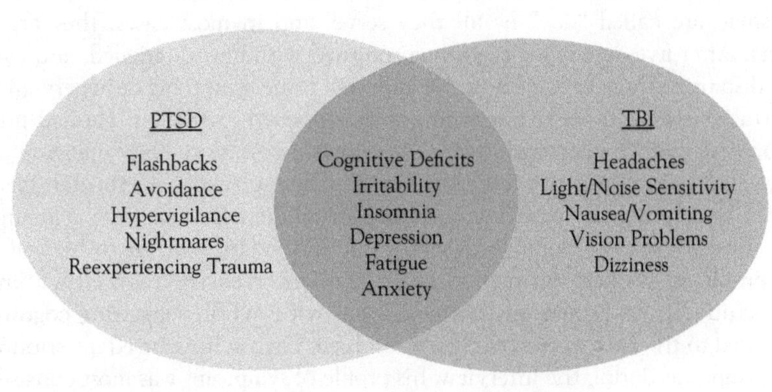

Figure 10.3 Illustration of overlapping PTSD and TBI symptoms

and wane over the course of many years or a lifetime, as found in the national Vietnam Veterans' Readjustment Study (Kulka et al., 1990).

As clinicians, we often ask ourselves if we are too quick to diagnose or label a service member with a "disorder," when what they may be experiencing are symptoms of "adjustment" from deployment versus changes in brain physiology. In addition to understanding the overlap between PTSD and TBI, it is imperative that you also consider other contributing factors that can cause impairment in daily functioning. Medical complications that may affect both physical and psychological well-being include complications from chronic pain, headache, substance abuse, mood disorders, and sleep deprivation.

As illustrated in Case Vignette: Joshua, neuropsychological testing can be beneficial in determining the level of cognitive functioning and severity of symptoms. It is also important to understand the history of the event and knowledge about TBI. Providing early psychoeducation including recovery expectations is essential. Patients who sustain an mTBI highly benefit from focused psychoeducation on positive recovery and addressing and treating symptoms (e.g., headaches). For mTBI, the presenting physical and cognitive symptoms can be managed with medication and if necessary with auxiliary services such as physical therapy, occupational therapy, and speech therapy. Mental health interventions are used to address combat stress symptoms, accompanying mood disorders, suicidal and/or homicidal ideation, irritability, and aggression.

Case Vignette: Joshua

A corpsman was referred to our clinic for evaluation of suspected concussion in theater. He was accompanied by his wife who described "significant changes in his behavior since returning home." *Joshua* had just returned from his fifth deployment to Iraq and Afghanistan. He reported being in close proximity to blasts that briefly "rocked his world" and caused moments of feeling "dazed." It was interesting because Joshua posed a question that we in the concussion field have frequently contemplated. He asked, "Do you think I was physically dazed by the blast, or in shock?" Good point. It is difficult to know at the time what is a physical response by the brain reacting to the force of the blast wave, or emotional shock; another type of physiological response.

Joshua went on to describe his deployments and his work as a corpsman. In theater, the corpsman are called "doc" by all they serve, and in most cases, they are the first responders. After five deployments, Joshua returned withdrawn, fatigued, and by his own account, distant to those around him. He reported some symptoms of hypervigilance and vague intrusive thoughts replaying events that happened in theater. He had mild headaches that were easily treated with over-the-counter medication. Neuroimaging was unremarkable. He began to notice the headaches after he returned from theater. His greatest complaints were problems with memory and irritability. Results from a neuropsychological evaluation showed variable deficits in attention. In contrast to his self-reported memory problems, his performance on tasks involving memory was well within normal limits. Cognitively, his profile was not consistent with mTBI, suggesting cognitive difficulties related to the blast event had likely resolved. On a self-reported questionnaire and report of symptoms during the interview, his profile of symptoms was most consistent with a diagnosis of PTSD.

A couple of weeks later, Joshua and his wife returned for feedback from the neuropsychological evaluation. They were very solemn at the initially greeting. Joshua explained that he had recently been arrested for disorderly conduct. His wife felt it was her fault because she was anxious for them to return to a routine as a young couple. She insisted he accompany her to a club nearby. He had not had any alcohol since before his last deployment. However, once inside, he had a couple of drinks. The music started with a rhythmic beat reminiscent of "gun fire." Ceiling lights swirled. Alcohol and the changes in the environment confused Joshua. He thought he was in Iraq. According to his wife, he began shouting: "Get down!" He tackled patrons on the dance floor, screaming for them to take safety. Bouncers came and removed him. His wife explained he had just returned from his fifth combat deployment. As Joshua climbed into the back seat of the waiting taxi, the driver turned and asked where he was going. The driver appeared to be Middle Eastern, and Joshua reacted badly. He assaulted the driver and was subsequently taken into custody.

In reviewing the historical elements of this case, there are several factors to consider when making a diagnosis. Joshua did have blast exposure, with possibly an "alteration of consciousness" that would suggest he had sustained a concussion. He did not have any lasting symptoms. He was able to complete all of his deployments without medical treatment. When he returned from theater he began to notice mild headaches. His headaches were not considered associated with the concussion because the onset was long after the blast exposure.

His greatest complaints at the time of the evaluation were problems with memory and irritability. On formal testing, the deficits found were attentional. This is often confused by patients as problems with memory. Joshua's testing showed he was able to learn material over time and remember it with good efficiency. Joshua had difficulty on tasks of sustained attention. The hyperarousal associated with PTSD has been shown to interfere with one's ability to sustain attention over time (Vasterling & Brewin, 2005). Irritability can be associated with both concussion and PTSD.

If there was any doubt about the effects of combat stress on this corpsman, his reaction in the bar leading up to an arrest was a distinct display of his active symptoms of PTSD (e.g., flashbacks, reliving traumatic events). Unfortunately, this scenario occurred prior to the opening of a Veteran's court in his area, which would have offered treatment in lieu of a criminal sentence or record.

CONCLUSIONS AND FUTURE CONSIDERATIONS

Traumatic brain injury (TBI), specifically mTBI caused by blast exposure, is the signature wound of recent warfare. As we emerge from OIF/OEF to Operation New Dawn, combat continues. Exposure to combat alone is a life-altering experience, affected by one's level of resilience and vulnerability. MTBI complicates the picture. The aftermath includes adjustment to civilian life. From physical limitations to emotional bondage, warriors return in some way altered by the experience. In war, there are no unwounded soldiers (José Narosky, 2011).

As a clinician it is critical to be knowledgeable of current medical standards that suggest that blast exposure does not equal brain injury, and at minimum an alteration of consciousness is the threshold to assess for brain injury. The full effects of blast exposure to the human brain is still in the infancy of study. As research unfolds it is likely that neuroimaging such as SPECT, DTI, and MEG will provide answers to lingering questions regarding brain recovery. Based on our current knowledge, treatment protocol for mTBI in the military population is similar to that in the sports injury population. There is an emphasis on education to normalize symptoms and protect against further injury. A positive expectation for recovery is expected. It is important to remember that, given the myriad of symptoms that often accompany mTBI, no two patients are alike. Understanding the severity of injury, the expectations for recovery, and co-occurring factors will help guide you in making the right treatment recommendations.

CHAPTER DISCUSSION QUESTIONS

1. A veteran comes into your office and tells you that during the weekend he was playing baseball and was struck in the head with a bat. He fell to the ground, blacked out for 20 seconds, and can't remember the hour prior to the baseball game. He tells you he is feeling "dizzy." What was the severity level of his concussion?
2. You see a sailor in your clinic on a regular basis. During the last visit he told you that he was having dizziness, irritability, thinking difficulties, headaches, depression. He has a recent history of concussion or mTBI and combat stress. Which of his symptoms could be related to combat stress? Which of his symptoms could be related to his concussion or mTBI? Which symptoms overlap?
3. You are completing a clinical interview with a Marine when she tells you she sustained a mild concussion, with 10 minutes of LOC, 1 hour of PTA, and minimal symptoms. While reading through her medical record, you discover that she was assaulted and has positive brain imaging findings. Her report of LOC and PTA is consistent with medical records. What is the severity level of her TBI?
4. What conditions other than a TBI can affect a Glasgow Coma Scale score?
5. What are the possible implications of a second concussion before the first concussion has resolved?

REFERENCES

American Psychological Association. (1994). *Diagnostic and statistical manual of mental disorder* (4th ed.). Washington, DC: Author.

Brenner, L. A., Homaifar, B. Y., Gutierrez, P. M., Harwood, J. E. F., Adler, L. E., Terrio, H., . . . Warden, D. (2010). Neuropsychological test performance in soldiers with blast-related mild TBI. *Neuropsychology, 24*(2), 160–167.

Cantu, R. C. (1998). Return to play guidelines after a head injury. *Clinics in Sports Medicine, 17*, 45–61.

Cifu, D., & Drake, A. (2006, August 17). Repetitive head injury syndrome. *eMedicine.com*. Retrieved from http://www.emedicine.com/sports/topic/113htm

Comper, P., Bisschop, S. M., Carniden, N., & Tricco, A. (2005, October). A systematic review of treatments for mild traumatic brain injury. *Brain Injury, 19*(11), 863–880.

Department of Defense Numbers for Traumatic Brain Injury. (2009). DVBIC.org

Department of Veterans Affairs. (2009). *VA/DoD clinical practice guideline for the management of concussion/mild traumatic brain injury* (Version 1.0). Department of Veterans Affairs, Department of Defense.

Howe, L. L. S. (2009). Giving context to post deployment post concussive-like symptoms: Blast related potential mild traumatic braining injury and co-morbidities. *Clinical Neuropsychologist, 23*(8), 1315–1337.

Huckans, M., Pavawallan, S., Demadura, T., Kolessar, M., Seelye, A., Roost, N., . . . Storzbach, D. (2010). A pilot study examining the effects of cognitive strategy training treatment on self-reported cognitive problems, psychiatric symptoms, functioning, and compensatory strategy use in OIF/OEF combat veterans with persistent mild cognitive disorder and history of traumatic brain injury. *Journal of Rehabilitation Research & Development, 1*(41), 43–60.

Jennett, B. (1996). Epidemiology of head injury. *Journal of Neurology, Neurosurgery, & Psychiatry, 60*, 362–369.

"Jose Narosky." (2011, June). Quote, n.d. http://www.quotationspage.com/quotes/Jose_Narosky/

Kay, T., Harrington, D. E. Adams, R., Anderson, T., Berrol, S., Cicerone, K., . . . Malec, J. (1993). Definition of mild traumatic brain injury. *Journal of Head Trauma Rehabilitation,* 8(3), 86–87.

Kraus, J., McArthur, J., Silberman, T., & Jayaraman M. (1996). Epidemiology of brain injury. In R. K. Narayan , J. E. Wilberger Jr., J. T. Povlishock (Eds.), *Neurotrauma* (pp. 13–30). New York, NY: McGraw-Hill.

Kulka, R. A., Schlenger, W. E., Fairbank, J. A., Hough, R. L., Jordan, B. K., Marmar, C. R., & Weiss, D. S. (1990). *Trauma and the Vietnam war generation: Report of findings from the national Vietnam veterans readjustment study* (p. 322) New York, NY: Brunner/Mazel.

Langlois, J. A., Keglar, S. R., Butler, K. E., Gotsch, R. L., Johnson, A. A., Reichard K. W., . . . Thurman, D. J. (2003, June 27). Traumatic brain injury discharges. Results for a 14-state surveillance system. *Morbidity and Mortality Weekly Report (MMWR) Surveillance Summaries,* 52(4), 1–18.

Lezak, M. D., Howieson, D. B., & Loring, D. W. (2004). *Neuropsychological assessment* (4th ed.). New York, NY: Oxford University Press.

Lippa, S. M., Patorek, N. J., Benge, J. F., & Thornton, G. M. (2010). Postconcussive symptoms after blast and nonblast-related mild traumatic brain injuries in Afghanistan and Iraq war veterans. *Journal of the International Neuropsychological Society, 16*(5), 856–866.

McCrea, M. A. (2008). *Mild traumatic brain injury and postconcussion syndrome.* New York, NY: Oxford University Press.

Morgan, J. E., & Ricker, J. H. (2008). *Textbook of clinical neuropsychology.* New York, NY: Taylor & Francis.

Rancho Los Amigos National Rehabilitation Center website. (2006). http://www.rancho.org/gi_history.htm

Schretlen, D. J., & Shapiro, A. M. (2003, November). A quantitative review of the effects of traumatic brain injury on cognitive functioning. *International Review of Psychiatry, 15,* 341–349.

Snyder, P. J., & Nussbaum, P. D. (1998). *Clinical neuropsychology: A pocket handbook for assessment*. Washington, DC: American Psychological Association.

Thornhill, S., Teasdale, G. M., Murray, G. D., McEwen, J., Roy, C. W., & Penny, K. I. (2000). Disability in young people and adults one year after head injury: Prospective cohort study. *British Medical Journal, 320*, 1631–1635.

Vasterling, J. J., & Brewin, C. R. (2005). *Neuropsychology of PTSD: Biological, cognitive, and clinical perspectives*. New York, NY: Guilford Press.

Warden, D. (2006). Military TBI during the Iraq and Afghanistan wars. *Journal of Head Trauma Rehabilitation, 21*(5), 398–402.

World Health Organization. (1992). *International statistical classification of diseases and related health problems* (10th ed.). Geneva, Switzerland: Author.

CHAPTER

11

TBI and Social Work Practice

MARGARET A. STRUCHEN, ALLISON N. CLARK, AND ALLEN RUBIN

In light of the high incidence of TBI as the signature wound of Operation Iraqi Freedom and Operation Enduring Freedom and the known high incidence of TBI in civilian populations in the United States and internationally (Finkelstein, Corso, & Miller, 2006; Kraus & McArthur, 1999; Selassie et al., 2003; Zaloshnja et al., 2005), social workers employed in health care settings or in other settings that treat service members or veterans are likely to have some clients with TBI included in their caseload. The previous chapter provided such social workers with the knowledge of the physical aspects of TBI, its assessment, and its implications for psychosocial functioning. The current chapter builds on that information by elaborating about the social work practice implications of that knowledge. Much of the information presented in this chapter is based on a manual entitled *Systematic Approach to Social Work Practice: Working with Clients with Traumatic Brain Injury* (Struchen & Clark, 2007) that was developed to serve as a resource for social workers who may not specialize in working with persons with TBI, but are likely to encounter such individuals in their practice setting.

Roles involved in social work practice with clients with TBI may include advocating on behalf of clients; serving as a liaison between the treatment team and the family; resource referral; counseling clients and/or their family or support system; discharge planning; advocating for public policies relevant to TBI; informing clients and families of sources of financial and social assistance; and helping clients and families apply for such assistance. The extent to which an individual social worker performs each of these roles depends to a large degree on the setting in which he or she practices. In performing these roles, this chapter describes a practical approach for working with clients with TBI according to a problem-focused model that outlines the knowledge, attitudes, and skills that social workers are likely to consider when working through each of the six phases of intervention identified by Compton and Gallaway (1989). The six phases are:

1. Contact
2. Problem identification, data collection, and assessment

3. Case planning
4. Intervention
5. Evaluation
6. Termination

Furthermore, information is presented with respect to both the severity and chronicity of the injury, as presenting issues and treatment needs may vary widely depending on these factors. The rest of this chapter is organized according to the above six phases and highlights several attitudinal issues, knowledge needs, and specific skill recommendations for each phase of intervention. For readers interested in a more thorough discussion of these issues, the manual referenced earlier is available as a free downloadable publication at www.tbicommunity.org

CONTACT

The contact phase involves the initial approach to the client and his or her support system, with the aim being to establish rapport and to build the groundwork for problem identification and definition, as well as goal identification. In the initial phase of contact with service members or veterans with moderate or severe TBI, the social worker should consider any preconceived ideas that he or she may hold regarding traumatic brain injury, as well as his or her comfort level with various sensory, motor, cognitive, and emotional/behavioral difficulties. For those working in more acute medical settings, evaluation of comfort level in approaching and interacting with clients who may be intubated, have tracheostomy tubes, have skull defects, or the like may be a consideration. Social workers in these settings should be aware of the need to be able to tolerate the sights, smells, and sounds of acute trauma care settings. Comfort level might also be an issue in working with clients with TBI in virtually all settings if the social worker is ill at ease when interacting with individuals who have sensorimotor, cognitive, or behavioral impairments. Finally, social workers should have an awareness of any barriers that may exist because of preconceived notions about the client's motivations for seeking help, such as a focus on litigation or secondary gain issues.

The knowledge that social workers will need during the contact stage includes the information discussed by Boyd and Asmussen in Chapter 10, such as knowing about the different problems typically experienced by clients with mild versus moderate or severe TBI. In light of such knowledge, social workers should examine the client's medical chart or talk with medical personnel to learn how well the client may be able to respond to them. With clients who have moderate or severe TBI, it is especially important to gain such information before approaching the client. Particularly in acute care settings, such clients might have limited or no ability to respond to the social worker. With these clients, social workers may need to make initial contacts with a family member or legal representative.

Within the acute phase, individuals from all TBI severity levels should be evaluated with regard to the level of orientation and confusion that is present, either through chart review or through a brief assessment of orientation, as some individuals may be capable of having conversations with the social worker, but may not be accurate historians and may have little or no recall of the interaction. The previous chapter on TBI provided some assessment tools that can be used in this regard. A brief evaluation of orientation can also be conducted informally in only a few minutes; for example, by asking the client about their name; their date of birth; their age; the current day, month, or year; what city they are in; what type of facility they are in; what happened yesterday; what led to their hospitalization; and if they have had recent visitors. If clients have difficulty with many of these questions, seeking out a family member or other decision maker would be appropriate.

Throughout the course of working with such clients, the social worker should continue to keep apprised of medical information to learn when the client is sufficiently responsive and oriented to engage in interaction with the social worker.

Appraisal of medical information will also inform social workers about sensory or motor functioning impairments that will affect how they should interact with the client. For example, clients might have vision impairments that preclude handing them a form to read, or they might have motor impairments that preclude a handshake. In appraising the medical information, it will be helpful to be familiar with medical terminology relevant to TBI. If you Google the search term *TBI glossary*, you can find several useful online TBI glossaries. One that pertains to military TBI per se is at: http://www.military.com/benefits/content/veterans-health-care/tbi-glossary.html

Also important during the contact phase is knowing how to interact with clients with cognitive difficulties such as slow cognitive processing, attention difficulties, memory difficulties, visuospatial difficulties, or problem-solving difficulties; and with clients who have behavioral/emotional issues, such as poor initiation, disinhibition/impulsivity, or emotional lability. Tips for interacting with clients with such difficulties are summarized in Table 11.1.

Table 11.1 Tips for Interacting With Clients Who Have Cognitive Difficulties or Behavioral/Emotional Issues

Cognitive Difficulties	Slowed Processing Speed	Use short sentences. Express only one idea at a time. Encourage only one speaker at a time to talk. Use patience in waiting for a client's response. Encourage client to paraphrase information to ensure that the message has been understood. Repeat information as necessary. Provide a written summary of information that can supplement your verbal communication.
	Attention Difficulties	Schedule a few short sessions, rather than one longer session. Limit other sources of distraction (e.g., turn off television, close door to limit hallway noise). Use short sentences and express only one idea at a time. Ask questions and/or gently prompt client to attend.

(*Continued*)

Table 11.1 (continued)

	Memory Difficulties	Remind the client of appointment the day before, and perhaps the morning of the appointment as well. Inform a family member or friend about the appointment time. Prepare a written summary of information presented to the client who can refer to it over time. Provide written instructions of requests for future appointments.
	Visuospatial Difficulties	Approach the client on the side of space to which he or she attends. This will avoid startling the client. Place materials that you would like the client to see or read in the side of space to which he or she attends. Use a red pen to draw a line along the edge of the paper for written material that you present. The red line should be on the side of the paper that corresponds to the side that the client neglects. This line can serve as an "anchor" to help the client scan the material fully.
	Problem-Solving Difficulties	Consider: • Providing a written list of steps that need to be taken to complete a given task. • Including a family member or friend in the discussion, so the client will have "back-up" to assist him or her in getting the job done.
Behavioral/ Emotional Issues	Poor Initiation	Provide prompts to clients to determine if they have questions. Engage a family member or friend to help cue the individual to begin and complete task requirements. Develop a cueing system that may work to help the client follow through with tasks (e.g., having office staff phone with reminders, having nursing and therapy staff use calendar or memory book, using Yahoo! calendars to prompt client over email).
	Disinhibition/ Impulsivity	In your initial contact with a client with TBI, you can attempt to address impulsivity issues by: • Gently redirecting client to current topic of conversation. • Keeping your voice tone calm and steady. • When safety is not a concern, ignoring problem behaviors and reinforcing desired behaviors with attention and praise.
	Emotional Lability	When lability of mood exists, you can try: • Gently redirect the client. Often, distracting the client with another topic will extinguish the affective response. • Try not to overattend to such affective displays, as this may actually exacerbate the response.

PROBLEM IDENTIFICATION, DATA COLLECTION, AND ASSESSMENT

In this phase, social workers begin to develop a therapeutic relationship with clients, collect information about the client perceptions of their problems, and identify targets for intervention. As with the contact phase, the social worker's comfort level is important. The social worker needs to feel comfortable obtaining medical information (as discussed earlier), asking about the problems identified in Table 11.1, and in dealing with a host of other potential comorbid problems such as substance abuse and mental illness. Likewise, social workers need to know about the kinds of symptoms that clients commonly experience following mild versus moderate to severe TBI, as discussed in the previous chapter.

The client's medical record is an initial source of information, especially for clients with moderate to severe TBI. Relevant areas of information to examine in the medical record include the date of the injury; its severity; presence and type(s) of neurological surgery, where applicable; physical, cognitive, emotional, and behavioral changes; treatment received and progress; assistive devices; and limitations and recommendations regarding activities. It will be important to remain mindful about when the information was obtained in relation to the time of injury and to the time of your contact with the client. For example, if you are reviewing results of a neuropsychological evaluation that was conducted 2 months after the person's severe TBI and you are seeing the client 3 years after injury, the results may be of limited utility. The relatively acute nature of that initial evaluation means that the person will likely have improved since that time. You will want to look for a more recent evaluation, or you may want to request a reevaluation. If this is not possible, you'll need to rely more on your clinical interview to have an idea about the client's current status.

Because medical records might not be obtainable, might have outdated information, or might lack some relevant information, your clinical interview will likely be of great importance in gathering information on the current problems being experienced. Because some clients will have relative problems with awareness of their difficulties or may have difficulty in self-generating a list of problems, it is useful to employ a strategy of questioning first in a general manner (for example, "Have you noticed any changes in your thinking abilities since your injury?"), and then to ask a series of more specific questions, (such as, "Any difficulties with your memory?"). In addition to obtaining information regarding physical, cognitive, and emotional/behavioral changes since injury, it will be important to enquire about whether the client has noted improvements or deterioration in functioning over time since injury.

Because of the importance of the family and other members of the support system in helping clients maximize their potential and transition to the community, social workers need to assess family stressors and emotional distress, changes in family roles and role expectations, as well as the availability of material and social resources that can help the family, such as needs for practical assistance with transportation and child care, for stress management techniques and/or supportive counseling or therapy services, and needs for education and educational resources regarding TBI.

Important areas of information to gain from the family during assessment pertain to pre-injury family roles and family expectations about these roles following injury. For example, will the person who formerly was the primary child caretaker now have to work full time? What emotional distress is likely to be experienced as such roles change? What resources are available within the family system to take on various roles needed to fulfill necessary family functions? This information should be obtained from multiple household members, who might have different viewpoints about these issues, including the client with brain injury.

It is also important to learn about the client's pre-injury psychosocial functioning in general. For example, a continued substance abuse problem can interfere with the client's recovery from TBI. Likewise, an understanding about pre-injury history regarding education, employment, medical problems, mental health/illness, legal issues, and so on will assist in identifying potential resources, facilitators, and barriers that may affect the client's functioning.

In working with clients with TBI, it is vital to explore your client's strengths as well as identifying problem areas. Categories of strengths to assess include sensory/motor, cognitive, and emotional/behavioral functions. For example, if the TBI has caused memory problems in clients who have organizational strengths, the social worker can help them come up with a way to use their organizational strengths to keep track of needed information. Likewise, supporting such emotional strengths as calmness, friendliness, or a sense of humor can help clients with their social functioning. In addition to learning about the client's internal strengths, the social worker should learn about external strengths, including such resources as the number of friends and relatives the client has in his or her support system (as well as the quality of and frequency of contact with these relationships), financial resources, and transportation availability, for example.

Finally, it is important to note that every brain injury is different. For example, some persons who suffer a severe injury may experience significant problems with memory, while other persons with a severe injury may have only mild memory problems. The consequences that people experience will depend on the severity of the injury, the location of the injury (what part of the brain was injured), the mechanism of injury, as well as other factors. Although some problems are more common following moderate to severe injuries, it is certainly possible that a person diagnosed with a milder injury could experience a symptom that is more common for those with moderate to severe injury. Thus, a thorough assessment of all areas of functioning, regardless of injury severity, will be the key for effective case planning and intervention.

CASE PLANNING

In this phase, social workers develop an intervention plan based on the information gathered in the previous stages and in light of client decisions and preferences. This process involves integrating information obtained from the medical records and from the client with TBI and his or her family support system regarding current status, resources, and eventual goals in the context of the realities of the clinical setting or agency functions where the social worker encounters the client. Awareness of the extent to which the social worker feels comfortable balancing the client's goal with family goals and the social worker's own assessment of service needs is important. Comfort level with seeking assistance or consultation with other professionals when needed should also be considered, especially for social workers who are employed in settings where relevant health care disciplines may not be present. In other settings, ongoing collaboration with other health care professionals working with the client is critically important, and a self-evaluation with one's comfort level in working within an interdisciplinary or multidisciplinary team is suggested.

The first part of the intervention plan involves developing realistic treatment goals. The social worker's notions about what is realistic will involve integrating the assessment information gathered with their knowledge from the previous TBI chapter regarding the limitations and capabilities associated with mild, moderate, and severe levels of TBI. A challenging aspect of this process is to maintain a "client-centered" focus, balancing client and family expectations with data gathered from other sources, such as evaluations of cognitive and behavioral strengths and weaknesses.

The social worker should aim to help clients and their families identify treatment goals that are realistic and achievable in light of the client's current level of functioning. The contrast between what is currently realistic versus perceptions of the client's pre-injury capacities can be quite distressful for clients and their families. Social workers consequently will need to employ their empathy and therapeutic relationship skills and be sensitive to grief and loss issues as well as to the possibility of the client's lowered self-esteem. Thus, helping the client formulate realistic goals needs to be done with great sensitivity and in ways that do not invalidate the client's unrealistic desire to achieve long-term goals too soon. Instead of ruling out such client hopes, the social worker should validate them as long-term goals while formulating short-term and intermediate steps toward attaining them. For example, clients who are eager to immediately resume managerial jobs might be encouraged to start out with work that involves some similar tasks, perhaps (but not necessarily) as a volunteer. Thus, the social worker can support the client's hope while helping them take initial, realistic steps toward meeting that long-term goal. It is imperative for the social worker to avoid making statements that suggest that the clients will never meet their goals. Discouraging such hope can be countertherapeutic and harmful to the therapeutic relationship, and the latter is a necessary precondition for any social work intervention to be effective.

In conceptualizing goals, it is important to consider the time point at which you are working with the client with regard to the typical recovery course after injury. For clients with a single mild TBI, most will be functioning at near pre-injury levels after the first few months following injury. Although it is important to recognize that not everyone will get better at the same rate, and factors may slow recovery (such as older age, substance use, subsequent injuries, or having a history of additional mild TBIs in the past), this guideline can help you determine current goals. If you are seeing such clients early after injury, you can help set expectations of the normality of symptoms and likelihood of improvement. Although medical prognoses are the responsibility of the medical profession, you can give guidance to help the client understand and manage current symptoms, while setting expectations of recovery and reinforcing the principle of gradual resumption of activities. If a client with mild injury presents at a later time point postinjury, it may be that problems are of a more chronic nature. In these cases, prolonged difficulties are thought to be multifactorial and may reflect aspects of the injury itself, pre-injury functioning, psychological reactions related to changes experienced as a result of injury, as well as environmental factors (such as stress related to loss of income if client is not working).

For clients with moderate to severe injuries, the most rapid improvements occur in the first 6 months after injury, and continued improvements between 6 months and 1 year after injury are typical. However, these improvements are usually not as dramatic or rapid as those seen in the early recovery period. The time period between 1 and 2 years after injury varies across individuals, with some individuals continuing to show slow, gradual improvements and others showing little improvement. After 2 years postinjury, impairments tend to stabilize, although functional changes are still possible, often through use of compensatory strategies.

If a social worker is referred a client within the first few months after a moderate to severe TBI, it is important to recognize that functioning is likely to improve significantly over the year after injury. Therefore, goal setting will need to consider both short-term needs to address current functional status and longer-term needs where functioning may be much improved. Goals may need to be adapted over time and/or a follow-up or referral for reevaluation of goals will need to be made so that goals can be adjusted to the client's current ability levels and functional needs. For clients seen several years postinjury, goals are likely to be more stable and your recommendations will likely be relevant for longer periods of time.

Another important part of case planning involves knowing about community, state, and national resources where clients and families can learn more about TBI and obtain additional support services. In this regard, there are three important national organizations and their websites:

1. Brain Injury Association of America, at www.biausa.org
2. North American Brain Injury Society, at www.nabis.org
3. Defense and Veterans Brain Injury Center (DVBIC), at www.dvbic.org DVBIC also funds a comprehensive website on TBI-related information and resources, at www.brainline.org

To help with intervention planning, social workers should attempt to maintain an updated list relevant to helping clients and families connect to the following local and regional resources, as shown in Table 11.2.

Table 11.2 Key Resource List Elements for Clients With TBI

The nearest VA medical center	The Social Security Administration
Local substance abuse facilities	Medicaid and Medicare
Goodwill Industries or other supportive employment or vocational agencies	Meals on Wheels
Food Stamps	Rehabilitation and specific brain injury support groups
Disability provisions offered by public utility organizations, telephone companies, transportation systems, and recreational organizations and facilities	Local health care professionals, such as: • Psychiatrists • Neuropsychologists
Advocacy and Legal Aid organizations	• Speech language pathologists
Drivers rehabilitation services	• Occupational therapists
Vocational rehabilitation services	• Physical therapists
Local mental health agencies and family service centers	• Rehabilitation counselors • Recreational therapists

INTERVENTION

Intervention involves the implementation of the plan that has been developed. It is important to recognize that interventions can be affected by:

- Attitudes that may be held about clients who may appear unmotivated due to initiation deficits.
- Perceptions regarding a client's compliance with the treatment plan that might be affected by his or her cognitive impairments.
- Beliefs about the role of family members' involvement in interventions.
- The willingness an individual social worker may have to be flexible and creative in adapting established practices to address client needs.

In this phase the social worker might perform several roles to help clients and families reach their goals. These roles might include acting as a client advocate, helping clients connect with and navigate the resources listed in Table 11.2, and supporting the use of clients' and family members' personal coping skills. In all these roles, it is imperative that the social worker perform them in a way that fits the client's level of impairment and functioning, as discussed in the previous chapter. For example, for clients with memory problems, extra time will be needed to learn new things, and those things may need to be repeated several times for the client. For clients with attention problems, potential distractions present in the client's room, or the consultation room where the social worker is meeting with the client, may need to be minimized, such as by turning off computer monitors, muting the telephone, and maintaining an organized work space. For clients with speech and/or language problems, the social worker should be patient and allow extra time for clients to speak. Clients should know that it is okay for them to speak slowly or struggle with finding the right words. Several practical suggestions can be offered to clients with TBI and their family members to help them address various sensory, motor, cognitive, emotional, and behavioral issues. These suggestions are outlined in detail in the referenced Struchen and Clark manual. Specific practice adaptations that may assist the social worker in communicating with their clients with TBI were presented in Table 11.1.

Additionally, social workers can ensure that the client with TBI has a more satisfying clinical experience by conducting training with ancillary staff that may have contact with clients (such as receptionists, billing clerks, etc.), so that clients with various physical, cognitive, and behavioral challenges are treated with courtesy and flexibility. Training should include all staff members who might interact with clients. Increased understanding of the potential difficulties that clients with TBI may experience may help prevent negative interactions from occurring. For example, some individuals with TBI may experience slurred speech or what is referred to as *dysarthria*, which can be misinterpreted as sounding like intoxication, whereby clients may be perceived over the phone as being "drunk." Awareness of this possible presentation can prevent a potential negative client experience from occurring. Perhaps the most common difficulty that may impact staff members' communications with clients with TBI may relate to memory difficulties, which can result in missed appointments and errors in compliance with readiness for appointments (e.g., failing to bring needed paperwork). Encourage office or clinic staff to provide information in writing and to provide reminder phone calls to enhance client participation and follow through with appointments and other instructions.

EVALUATION

In this phase the social worker assesses the extent to which the formulated goals in the treatment plan were achieved. Readers familiar with the evidence-based practice process will recognize this phase as the final phase of that process. Adequately covering what social workers need to know in this phase is beyond the scope of this chapter. Readers are encouraged to examine Rubin (2008) for that information as well as pages 102 to 111 of the Struchen and Clark manual (the latter in connection to applying research and evaluation efforts to the evaluation of TBI interventions per se).

TERMINATION

As with the earlier phases, when the time comes for the clinician-client relationship to end, the termination phase must be carried out with the same knowledge and sensitivities discussed above and in keeping with the material discussed in the previous chapter. Given that clients with TBI may have ongoing needs that continue after their relationship with the social worker ends, it is critical that the social worker be prepared to make needed referrals to other resources, such as those listed above in the case planning phase as well as extended case management services for clients with long-term needs.

Although this chapter provides some highlights to consider when working with clients with TBI, the interested reader may wish to review a more extensive coverage of the attitudes, knowledge, and skills that social workers will need to maximize their effectiveness while working with this population. Such information is presented in the practice manual referenced throughout this chapter. The manual was developed as part of the National Institute on Disability and Rehabilitation Research–funded Rehabilitation Research and Training Center on Community Integration for Persons with Traumatic Brain Injury (H133B031117), with the goal of improving health care for persons with TBI by providing education to nonspecialist practitioners in the fields of social work, psychology, and primary medical care.

Case Vignette: David

David is a 24-year-old right-handed male who enrolled in the Marine Corps shortly after his 19th birthday. He sustained a severe TBI approximately 12 months ago as a result of an IED explosion in Iraq. According to your review of medical records, a neuropsychological evaluation conducted 3 weeks ago reported impairments in several cognitive domains, including attention, learning and memory, problem solving, reasoning, and processing speed. The report also described problems with conversation skills, and an inability to manipulate test materials with his right hand. Review of medical records shows that he currently attends physical and occupational therapy 2 times per week. On presentation to your office, you observe that he walks with the use of a cane, and has limited use of his right arm and hand. During the course of your interview, he expressed a strong desire to return to his unit.

Case Vignette Discussion Questions

1. David has problems learning and remembering new information. What practice modifications would help David remember important information that was discussed in session?
2. David has expressed a strong desire to return to his unit. Do you think this is a realistic goal for David? How would you discuss this goal with him?
3. How would your problem identification, data collection, and assessment change if the only neuropsychological evaluation was conducted 2 months after his injury?
4. You have given David several forms to complete and return to you, but he has been unable to complete this task. What factors could contribute to his inability to complete these forms? What additional supports may David need in order to complete these forms in a timely manner?

CONCLUSION

The purpose of this chapter was to highlight the knowledge and skills that are useful in working with clients with traumatic brain injury throughout each of the six phases of intervention, and to feature important resources so that social workers can feel more comfortable and confident in their clinical interactions. A self-assessment of attitudes, knowledge, and skills can be a useful step in increasing the effectiveness of your clinical interactions. Furthermore, a willingness to be flexible and to implement modifications for persons with cognitive and behavioral deficits after injury can help you adapt your established clinical practice to fit the unique needs of your client with traumatic brain injury.

CHAPTER DISCUSSION QUESTIONS

1. What are your attitudes regarding those who are involved in litigation or are seeking disability compensation as a result of a mild traumatic brain injury?
2. How could a client's pre-injury psychosocial functioning impact your problem identification and case planning?
3. How could a client's poor attention, memory, and problem-solving skills affect your work together?
4. How can you address a client's unrealistic treatment goals while maintaining a client-centered focus?

REFERENCES

Compton, B., & Galaway, B. (1989). *Social work processes*. Homewood, IL: Dorsey Press.

Finkelstein, E., Corso, P., & Miller, T. (2006). *The incidence and economic burden of injuries in the United States*. New York, NY: Oxford University Press.

Kraus, J. F., & McArthur, D. L. (1999). Incidence and prevalence of, and costs associated with traumatic brain injury. In M. Rosenthal, E. R. Griffith, J. S. Kreutzer, & B. Pentland (Eds.), *Rehabilitation of the adult and child with traumatic brain injury*. Philadelphia, PA: Davis.

Rubin, A. (2008). *Practitioner's guide to using research for evidence-based practice*. Hoboken, NJ: Wiley.

Selassie, A. W., Zaloshnja, E., Langlois, J. A., Miller, T., Jones, P., & Steiner, C. (2008). Incidence of long-term disability following traumatic brain injury hospitalization, United States, 2003. *Journal of Head Trauma Rehabilitation*, *23*(2), 123–131.

Struchen, M., & Clark, A. (2007). *Systematic approach to social work practice: Working with clients with traumatic brain injury*. Waco, TX: Baylor College of Medicine. Available at www.tbicommunity.org/resources/publications/SW_Manual2009.pdf

Zaloshnja, E., Miller, T., Langlois, J. A., & Selassie, A. W. (2005). Prevalence of long-term disability from traumatic brain injury in the civilian population of the United States. *Journal of Head Trauma Rehabilitation*, *23*(6), 394–400.

CHAPTER

12

Assessing, Preventing, and Treating Substance Use Disorders in Active Duty Military Settings

Allen Rubin and Willie G. Barnes

Throughout history substance use has been a problem in U.S. military settings. Efforts to minimize the harmful effects of alcohol consumption have been noted as early as 1770, and a formalized substance abuse prevention effort in the U.S. military was enacted by congress in 1794 (Kennedy, Jones, & Grayson, 2006). During the American Civil War alcohol was used medically, and daily consumption of rum was common in part because it was thought to enhance coping skills before engaging in battle. During that war, the Army and Navy took actions to limit the availability of alcohol and prevent excessive drinking. Also during the Civil War, opiates (sometimes mixed with whiskey) were used when limbs were amputated, and an estimated 120,000 Civil War veterans developed significant opiate dependency (Freeman & Hurst, 2009).

During the Vietnam War, the pattern of substance abuse changed. Although alcohol continued to be prominent, the use of marijuana increased, coinciding with its increased consumption throughout civilian society. Marijuana was surpassed by heroin in prevalence of use later in the war. In 1971, the Army began urine testing for opiates, barbiturates, and amphetamines. Active service members returning from Vietnam who tested positive were required to undergo a 30-day treatment program (Freeman & Hurst, 2009).

Although active duty military personnel have always viewed substance use as a way to deal with boredom or to cope with or to numb themselves from the traumatic stress of combat, substance use impairs the soldier's ability to function in battle. (The term *soldier* here and elsewhere in this chapter is being used in a generic sense, interchangeably with *service member*, and applies to all military branches.) Even a small amount of alcohol, for example, can dangerously impair mental agility and visual tracking. Soldiers who are deployed in the immediate aftermath of significant alcohol consumption may experience a dangerous decline in cognitive abilities during battle. In addition, chronic alcohol abuse impairs memory (Lande, Marin, Staudenmaier, & Hawkins, 2011).

Placing a weapon into the hands of someone who might be under the influence of a mind- or mood-altering substance can have devastating consequences. For example, today there are service members whose duties include handling hazardous materials, nuclear weapons, tanks, airplanes, and protecting the lives of other service members. It is therefore understandable that the military has a robust drug-testing program and a zero tolerance for substance use, as it threatens training and mission; military security; military fitness; unit order and discipline; and safety.

Although these threats have been a problem in previous wars, concern about substance use has never been as great as it is today—especially regarding alcohol. In light of the increases in combat technology, "even modest amounts of alcohol can impair crucial decision-making abilities and negatively affect military operations" (Lande et al., 2011, p. 483). The exact prevalence of substance use in today's military is difficult to quantify in light of the stigma regarding seeking treatment. However, we do know that the unique stressors associated with the demands of protracted conflict in the Global War on Terrorism led to a near doubling of Army soldiers diagnosed with alcoholism or alcohol abuse between 2003 and 2009, and similar increases were observed among Marines (Zoroya, 2006). Members of those two branches of the Armed Forces may be particularly vulnerable to increases in alcohol abuse in light of their relatively greater number of combat tours and deployment cycles. These stressors are discussed in other chapters of this book, so to avoid redundancy we won't repeat them here. Instead, this chapter focuses on approaches to assess, prevent, and treat substance use disorders among active duty, Reserve, and National Guard military personnel. A separate chapter covers the special needs of veterans and their substance use concerns.

PREVENTION

In response to the increased substance abuse problems during the Vietnam War, in 1971 Congress enacted a law that mandated that the Secretary of Defense develop programs to identify, treat, and rehabilitate drug dependent persons in the Armed Forces. In response, the Secretary required each branch of the Armed Forces to develop programs to prevent substance abuse. The early prevention efforts emphasized detection and education. During and after the 1980s standardized prevention programs were developed in each branch of the military and are currently mandated for all troops. Specialized training is provided to the chain of command and to prevention specialists assigned to various units. Examples of prevention efforts include (Kennedy et al., 2006):

- A public website to support local commands regarding best practices to prevent substance abuse, with links to each branch of the armed forces: http://www.defense.gov/specials/drugawareness/usanews.html
- On-site substance screenings and prevention education by substance abuse counselors for all branches of the Armed Forces.
- Dissemination of prevention information and program availability via Armed Forces print, radio, and TV media.

- Provision of prevention briefs to educate the chain of command on deployment regarding the availability of local illegal and/or addictive substances in the area to which they are heading.
- After an alcohol-related incident, referral of the offending service member to an early intervention program usually consisting of 15 to 20 hours of education and discussion to improve awareness of the harmful effects of alcohol abuse.

Today, substance use disorder prevention efforts have been created based on a community-based model. This model is particularly applicable to National Guard members and Reservists who live some distance from an installation and who therefore often feel quite removed from the sense of military community. Required prevention programs include a variety of community members on an installation. Campaigns are tied to trends or prevalence rates of substances used. National prevention campaigns like Red Ribbon week (a week dedicated to celebrating living a drug-free lifestyle) in October are mandated to be carried out by all service branches.

An example of a community-based model is the Community Capacity model, which is used by the Air Force. As described by Huebner, Mancini, Bowen, and Orthner (2009), the community capacity approach contains two key components: "*shared responsibility* for the general welfare of the community and its members and *collective competence*, demonstrating an ability to take advantage of opportunities for addressing community needs and for confronting situations that threaten the safety and well-being of community members" (p. 219). The shared responsibility component pertains to a "collective sentiment of concern," whereas the collective competence component involves taking action. The model builds community capacity by activating formal and informal support networks.

Formal networks include military leadership as well as military and civilian organizations that support the needs of individuals and families through community participation activities that help build a sense of community. Informal networks include less-organized and voluntarily formed personal relationships among co-workers, neighbors, and friends. The synergy of these two types of networks is emphasized in the model; for example, by engaging in formal organizational activities community residents can meet new people and make friends who can then provide mutual support during stressful times. Thus, this model intentionally uses formal systems to build informal support systems. During stressful times experts in the formal systems can help individuals and families navigate needed services, and informal systems can help them access formal services. Huebner et al., after describing the community capacity model, cite various studies that supported its beneficial impact on reducing service member depression, suicide, and other adverse outcomes.

On the other hand, the Army is moving toward a public health model. Akhter and Levinson (2009) list five main steps to applying the model to a population: (1) collect prevalence data, (2) offer primary prevention strategies, (3) identify those who might benefit from secondary prevention efforts, (4) provide adequate treatment resources, including a variety of levels of care, and (5) challenge environmental obstacles that might increase risky choices. At most Army installations there are prevention coordinators, risk-reduction specialists, and employee assistance professionals who work together to improve the health and wellness of the total force.

ASSESSMENT

As mentioned earlier, toward the end of the Vietnam War laws were passed requiring the Armed Forces to identify, treat, and rehabilitate its members who are drug or alcohol dependent. There are five ways that someone can be identified as needing treatment: (1) medical referral, (2) legal investigation/apprehension, (3) command-driven, (4) biochemical testing (which includes alcohol breath testing), and (5) self-referral. Unless the identification was made by self-referral to a civilian provider off-base, the commander must be informed that the service member is in need of treatment. Consequently, the uniformed military clinician who conducts the assessment faces a balancing act. The need of the commander to know if the service member is fit to perform his or her military duties, combined with the needs of the individual who is being assessed can present a dilemma for the treating clinician. Regardless of the branch of the Armed Forces, the interests of national defense and safety are paramount. Service members do provide informed consent and are informed of the limits of confidentiality as well as privacy act statements. They are made aware of the potential for an alcohol- or drug-related offense or incident to impact their careers. Failure to participate in treatment or a lack of compliance can result in discharge from the military.

According to the *Iraq War Clinician Guide* (Lande, Marin, & Ruzek, 2004), screening for substance abuse should occur before, during, and on evacuation from the combat zone. The clinician conducting the predeployment screening should begin by asking about the individual's predeployment emotions and coping styles.

> For the vast majority of individuals the notice of impending deployment unleashes a myriad of cognitive and behavioral reactions. These reactions are generally mild and transient as the individuals' healthy coping mechanisms respond to the news. In a minority of cases the fear and uncertainty of the looming deployment precipitates a maladaptive response. Among this group, a fairly significant number will turn to substance abuse as a means of quelling the troubled pre-deployment emotions.
>
> (p. 79)

After assessing for emotions and coping styles, the clinician is advised to focus specifically on substance use with a comment such as the following: "Some people find that drinking a bit more alcohol, smoking a few more cigarettes, or pouring some extra java helps relieve the stress—have you noticed this in yourself?" (Lande et al., 2004, p. 79). If the answer suggests the possibility of a substance abuse tendency, the clinician should conduct a more formalized screening regarding the quantity and frequency of substance use. If the answers suggest a problematic amount of use, the clinician should next ask four "CAGE" questions, such as the following for drinking (p. 79):

C—Have you ever felt that you should CUT down on your drinking?
A—Have people ANNOYED you by criticizing your drinking?
G—Have you ever felt bad or GUILTY about your drinking?
E—Have you ever had a drink first thing in the morning to steady your nerves or get rid of a hangover (i.e., as an EYE-OPENER)?

The reliability of the CAGE questions has been empirically supported and shown to accurately predict 70% to 80% of soldiers who have a substance dependency problem (Freeman & Hurst, 2009).

Depending on the frequency and quantity of use indicated in the answers to the CAGE questions, a more in-depth clinical assessment may be required, including evaluating for diagnoses based on the *Diagnostic and Statistical Manual of Mental Disorders* (*DSM-IV*; American Psychiatric Association, 2000). Because of the frequency with which substance use disorders are comorbid with posttraumatic stress disorder (PTSD) among today's military personnel, the PTSD CheckList (Military Version, PCL–M) is also recommended as part of the substance use assessment. The PCL–M has good psychometric support and can be accessed online at www.pdhealth.mil/guidelines/appendices.asp

The foregoing predeployment screening procedure can also be applied during deployment in the combat zone as well as after deployment. If during deployment the findings from the assessment indicate the need to evacuate the individual from theater of operations, the clinician should advise the individual of the likely negative impact on his or her military career. The clinician should also offer helpful information about treatment options and about the possibility of redeployment after recovery. The military clinician is also required to inform the commander of any substance use problems. The Iraq War Clinician Guide states:

> A standing order prohibiting the use of any alcohol or illegal drugs exists in deployed environments. As a result, the military commander usually becomes involved when a soldier is identified in an alcohol or drug related incident. Commanders vary in their biases as how to handle these situations, but in general try to balance their concerns for the individual soldier's medical/treatment needs with the need for unit discipline. Commanders often look for direction in balancing these legitimate concerns and usually appreciate input from mental health providers in making such decisions. At times, an inappropriately high level of tolerance of substance use or abuse occurs in some units. This may be more likely in National Guard or Reserve units. Some mental health clinicians in Iraq report that alcohol use in some units was prevalent to the degree that officers, NCOs and junior enlisted drink together. Though rare, such circumstances create significant challenges for proper unit functioning and for the effectiveness of mental health interventions.
>
> (Lande, Marin, & Ruzek, 2004, p. 81)

Related to screening for substance use problems is a much more comprehensive health assessment screening procedure, the Deployment Health Assessment Model, which is currently implemented by all branches of the Armed Forces at predeployment, on postdeployment, and in a reassessment 90 to 100 days after returning home postdeployment. The assessment instrument is completed by the service member electronically and it is lengthy. For example, the postdeployment version—the Post-Deployment Health Assessment (PDHA)—is 7 pages long and contains items covering a wide range of physical and mental health issues (including many symptoms such as muscle aches, irritability, and skin rashes), whether traumatic events were experienced during deployment and related PTSD symptoms, exposure during deployment to physical pathogens ranging from animal bites to toxic chemicals and the like, vaccinations received, and so on. Only one item on the instrument pertains to substance use. It asks about the service member's frequency and amount of alcohol use prior to or during deployment as well as desire to alter drinking habits.

ARMED FORCES TREATMENT PROGRAMS

As discussed by Lande et al. (2004), in each branch of the Armed Forces the substance use disorder treatment program in large part conceptually follows an employee assistance program model. Treatment is mandatory, and focuses on military preparedness and maintaining personnel. Command staff and clinical staff members comprise a rehabilitation team, chaired by a clinician. This approach combines coercion with treatment. The soldier being treated, who is also part of the team, is offered a positive outlook and learns the expectations and benefits of successful treatment completion, while at the same time learning the consequences of failing to comply with treatment guidelines. The soldier also learns about patient rights and receives assurances of support to alleviate his or her fears.

The responsibilities of command and clinical staff are separated, with professional clinical staff being responsible for clinical decision making. The clinical staff members are required to be professionally licensed and to be certified in substance abuse rehabilitation. The clinical staff members complete a comprehensive biopsychosocial and substance abuse assessment and make treatment recommendations based on the degree of impairment. Individuals diagnosed with substance use disorders generally are required to enroll in treatment for at least 3 months and perhaps up to 1 year. Program intensity can range from a 12-hour instructional program to outpatient treatment. For individuals needing more intensive care the treatment plan might include detoxification, partial hospitalization, intensive outpatient programs, or residential treatment. The treatment plan is based on the principle of requiring the least intrusive, least restrictive treatment environment needed according to therapeutic needs. Treatment is provided by a multidisciplinary team that "emphasizes motivational enhancement over confrontational drama" (Lande et al., 2004, p. 481). More detailed information about the treatment programs can be found at the following websites:

Army: http://armypubs.army.mil/epubs/pdf/R
Navy: www.public.navy.mil/bupers-npc/support/nadap/Pages/default2aspx
Air Force: www.af.mil/shared/medical/epubs/AFI44–121.pdf

TWO EMPIRICALLY SUPPORTED OUTPATIENT TREATMENT APPROACHES

Although the extent of well-controlled outcome studies on the effectiveness of outpatient treatment approaches with military personnel is sparse, two evidence-based approaches have been applied with active duty soldiers. These two approaches are Seeking Safety and Motivational Interviewing. Each of these approaches is described later. These descriptions are drawn from chapters on each approach that appear in a compendium on substance abuse treatment by Springer and Rubin (2009). Readers are referred to that book for much lengthier, much more detailed guides regarding how to provide each approach.

Seeking Safety (Seeking Strength)

As discussed by Najavits (2009), Seeking Safety is a cognitive behavioral therapy (CBT) with the core goal of encouraging clients to surmount the chaos and destruction of substance abuse and attain greater safety. The term *safety* in this context pertains to seeking safety not only from substances, but also from dangerous relationships (such as substance-using friends) and from extreme symptoms like suicidality and dissociation. Seeking Safety addresses the link between substance use and trauma, but without the features of exposure therapy that could destabilize early recovery by delving into the details of traumatic events. One of the advantages of Seeking Safety is its applicability to treating individuals with comorbid substance use disorders and mental illness, including PTSD. (Other CBT approaches are contraindicated for these comorbid disorders.)

Seeking Safety sessions begin with check-in questions about how clients are doing. Next, a quotation is read aloud by the client to foster client emotional engagement in the session. The clinician then asks about the meaning of the quotation and links it to the session topic. Most of the session then involves clients reading a handout on a new coping skill, followed by the clinician summarizing the key points of the handout and then asking the client how those points relate to them. The rest of the session is devoted to discussing how the topic relates to the client's life and to rehearsing the new coping skill. The session ends with a check-out period in which clients identify what they got out of the session and whether there are any problems with it, and then answering the clinician's question, "What is your new commitment?" (Najavits, 2009, p. 318).

Najavits notes that Seeking Safety has been used in VA settings as well as active duty military settings. She recommends that when used in those settings that the name *Seeking Strength* should be used instead of *Seeking Safety* because "military personnel must go into harm's way, and thus the term *Seeking Safety* may be inaccurate for them. Most military and veterans are men, and the term *strength* may be more appealing than 'safety'" (p. 336). She also recommends substituting the term *training* for the term *treatment*, as the latter term may be stigmatizing. Other suggestions are (pp. 336–337):

- Use examples that emphasize the bonding that occurs in military settings (e.g., bonding like warriors or teams).
- Address prominent concerns for military and veterans: difficulty with feelings (which are often devalued or "trained out" in military contexts); issues with perpetration of violence (feeling "like a monster"); betrayal, such as when they are not supported on their return; difficulty readjusting to civilian life; and issues with authority and control. Women in the military also have major challenges such as having experienced high rates of military sexual trauma, being vastly outnumbered by men, and trying to function in a highly male-oriented culture.
- Understand how trauma and substance abuse may occur in the military. Traumatic experiences that are typical in military settings include military sexual trauma; handling bodies or body parts; watching buddies die; and traumatic brain injury. Substance abuse may be either encouraged (as in the Vietnam era) or discouraged (in the current era).

More details about implementing Seeking Safety (Seeking Strength) can be found in the Najavits chapter in Springer and Rubin (2009).

Motivational Interviewing

As discussed by Sampson, Stephens, and Valesquez (2009), motivational interviewing (MI) is a counseling style that aims to strengthen and reinforce the client's motivation and commitment to change. As was originally developed by Miller and Rollnick (1991), the counseling style is strategically paradoxical in that it is directive in a client-centered manner that relies on active listening and gentle feedback techniques. When applied to soldiers with substance use disorders, for example, the clinician elicits the soldier's own concerns about the disorder and helps the soldier articulate reasons to change the problematic behavior. Although the fundamentals of nondirective counseling are employed, the MI counselor selects appropriate moments to intervene with directive strategies while at the same time avoiding argumentative persuasion.

The direct approach of MI is not what most clinicians imagine when they hear that word. Instead, according to Sampson et al. (2009, p. 6):

> First, MI is not directive in the traditional sense which implies confrontation, persuasion, and indoctrination. Instead, the directiveness of MI is exemplified by sessions that are goal-focused as client and counselor explore specific behavioral goals together such as increased sobriety ... MI is not "just" being "warm and fuzzy," empathic, accepting and genuine. While empathy and acceptance are essential to the practice of MI, this approach also incorporates directive (in the sense of goal-oriented) strategies and methods that are applied in the service of change.
>
> MI is not something that is done to a client; rather it is both an art and a craft that integrate relational processes with a set of skills and strategies.
>
> In addition, although numerous studies have documented significant behavior changes after a single MI session, MI is not a "snap your fingers" method that is always instantly transformative; instead we have learned that MI sessions may simply plant a seed that facilitates more distal behavior changes.
>
> MI is also not a hierarchical, top-down approach in which counselors are viewed as experts who dispense wisdom, advice, and solutions. [It is] an egalitarian exchange that acknowledges and respects the right to socially responsible self-determination. In MI, counselors set aside their own goals and timetables and begin where their clients are, by inviting them to explore and set their own goals . . . the client is seen as a powerful agent who possesses an inherent will and ability to set meaningful goals and work toward their accomplishment. Therefore, rather than giving incentives, setting goals, and providing solutions for a client, the counselor's task is to elicit and foster those elements from the client [in the context of] a strong working alliance with the client.

MI can be provided in two phases. The first phase is most applicable to soldiers who have little or no commitment to change. In this Phase 1 stage the focus is on building rapport, exploring the soldier's reluctance or ambivalence about changing, and increasing his or her readiness to change. The counselor does this by using an OARS approach, which refers to:

- Asking **O**pen questions
- **A**ffirming
- **R**eflecting
- **S**ummarizing

The OARS strategy also is employed in Phase 2, but with a focus on strengthening a growing commitment to change and developing action plans for achieving specific change goals.

Sampson et al. (2009) provide the following dialogue to illustrate asking open questions (p. 13):

> **Counselor:** What concerns, if any, do you have about your alcohol use? (*as opposed to: "Are you concerned about your alcohol use?"*)
>
> **Client:** Well, I'm really doing just fine. My wife nags me a lot about my beer drinking, and my boss is really fed up—he says he may have to let me go if I don't get back on the wagon.
>
> **Counselor:** In some ways things are going really well for you, and at the same time you are a little concerned about how alcohol may be affecting your marriage and your job.

Sampson et al. (2009) provide the following dialogue to illustrate affirming statements (p. 13):

> **Client:** I really want to be sober. My kids deserve it.
>
> **Counselor:** Your children are really important to you. You want to be the kind of father they can look up to.
>
> **Client:** You know, I did stay away from the booze all last week, and I think they really were glad about that.
>
> **Counselor:** Staying away from liquor really made a difference. What a gift to your children!

Sampson et al. (2009) provide the following dialogue to illustrate reflective listening (p. 16):

> **Client:** I just wish everyone would quit nagging me about my drinking, it really bothers me. (*sagging shoulders, subdued voice, indications of sadness in facial expression*)
>
> **Counselor:** Everyone's worried. It makes you sad.
>
> **Client:** I feel like I've let them all down again and again and again.
>
> **Counselor:** You'd like them to be proud of you.
>
> **Client:** Yeah, I'd feel like an eagle, proud and soaring the skies, looking down and seeing them proud of me.
>
> **Counselor:** That will be wonderful—flying with pride.
>
> **Client:** It's a great picture in my mind. Making them proud.

Sampson et al. (2009) provide the following dialogue to illustrate summarizing (pp. 17–18):

Client: I was surprised, but the urges are getting less these days. But when I go around the old neighborhood, it's really hard not to drink. I'll confess. I did slip a little last week. I just couldn't resist.

Counselor: Some of the urges have lessened, which surprised you a little.

Client: Yeah, I just hadn't expected that—it was kind of a relief.

Counselor: A welcomed surprise.

Client: For sure! But that slip worries me. I hate the thought of not being in control of what I do.

Counselor: Being in charge of your life is really important—something you highly value. And the slip gives you some concern. Tell me about that.

Client: It makes me mad. And worries me because if I don't get back on the right track, I'll lose custody of my kids again. I couldn't stand that. They are the most important thing in the world to me. Really the only thing that matters.

Counselor: Your children are everything to you. Alcohol will mean you will lose them. That would be unbearable.

Client: Yes! (*tearful*) Next time I'm staying away from that place—there's nothing good there for me.

Counselor: Let us see if I've got it right. The urges are starting to calm down, which really surprises and pleases you. Part of you found it hard to resist when you got back to your old neighborhood, and at the same time part of you is really worried about the slippery slope—about how alcohol can interfere with the most important thing in your life, your children. You are determined to get back on track and that track won't go through your old neighborhood. What did I leave out?

Client: That says it all. I want to be on the right track to take me to my children.

Four principles that guide MI are:

1. Express empathy
2. Develop discrepancy
3. Roll with resistance
4. Support self-efficacy

The first principle, expressing empathy, involves active listening and reflecting the meanings and feelings conveyed by the client. The second principle, developing discrepancy, involves helping clients examine the pros and cons of changing their behavior. Sampson et al. (2009, p. 10) provide the following dialogue to illustrate developing discrepancy:

Client: I feel two ways about this whole thing. I want to quit drinking, but I'd feel lost without it . . . it's like a friend I can count on.

Counselor: You would feel at a loss if you gave up alcohol, and at the same time you really want a change. What are some of the good things for you about drinking?

Client: Hmmm. Well, I guess it helps me put aside the troubles of this life . . . it helps me escape.

Counselor: It helps you deal with a lot of difficulties. What might be some of the not so good things for you about drinking?

Client: Wow. My wife is about to take off, and I can't see my kids right now. That hurts.

Counselor: So while alcohol helps you take some "time off," your wife and children are important and you might lose them.

Client: Yeah. That'd be terrible.

The third principle, rolling with resistance, means reacting to client resistance in a manner that is not defensive and avoiding confrontation or argumentation. Sampson et al. (2009, p. 11) provide the following dialogue to illustrate this principle:

Client: It's *my* life. Nobody has the right to tell me how to live it! You've never been in this position of having everybody boss you around.

Counselor: You're exactly right. You are in charge of your life. You are really the expert on your life, and you are the only one who can decide the next steps. What would be helpful for us to talk about in this time we have?

The fourth principle, supporting self-efficacy, entails conveying support and optimism about the client's capacity for change and asking the client about previous successes. Sampson et al. (2009, p. 11) provide the following dialogue to illustrate this principle:

Client: This has been so hard. I've tried so many times to make this work—to quit drinking once and for all.

Counselor: You have really wanted things to be different—not drinking was terribly important to you. You kept trying. Tell me, what worked a while for you before—when you were successful for a period of time in terms of not drinking?

Client: Well, I stayed away from bars and old friends who drank day and night.

Counselor: So staying away from temptation helped you be successful. What else?

Client: I also got the liquor out of the house. I just threw it away.

Counselor: What a great strategy—sounds like it helped you meet your goal.

The OARS strategy and the four guiding principles are employed with the aim of eliciting from the client statements about changing their substance use. For more details and tools about how this is done, readers are referred to the comprehensive Sampson et al. (2009) chapter in Springer and Rubin (2009).

AN ECOSYSTEM PERSPECTIVE FOR TREATING VETERANS WITH COMORBID SUBSTANCE ABUSE DISORDERS AND OTHER DISORDERS

The two foregoing empirically supported treatment approaches, while having been applied in military contexts, were not developed specifically for treating active duty service members or veterans. Weiss et al. (2012) identify special challenges associated with engaging and maintaining this population in treatment due to military training and deployment schedules and the distinct nature of the military lifestyle and culture that emphasizes its own unique values, codes of conduct, emotional restraint, and a warrior ethos. Consequently, Weiss et al. (2012) recommend that to be effective with military personnel or veterans, the foregoing empirically supported approaches need to be provided in the context of a systems-ecological approach. Another reason for such an approach is the high prevalence of comorbidity of substance use disorders with other disorders among active duty personnel and veterans. For example, substance use disorders are not only commonly comorbid with PTSD, and not only commonly comorbid with TBI, but among today's service members and veterans there is often a triple threat of comorbidity in which many individuals suffer from all three disorders.

Weiss et al. (2012) propose that whatever clinical intervention used "encompass both individual/systemic variables as well as cultural/worldview variables" (p. 8). The Case Vignette: Joe and the ensuing discussion illustrate how the systems-ecological approach takes into account the foregoing variables in a holistic, systematic manner. It also illustrates the application of motivational interviewing and Seeking Strength (Seeking Safety) in the context of the systems-ecological approach. The case and case discussion that follow are taken from Weiss et al., (2012, p. 155–157).

Case Vignette: Joe

Joe is a 23-year-old enlisted active duty Marine Corps Corporal (E-4) who comes for counseling with a licensed social work practitioner in the civilian sector. He is self-referred through a Department of Defense contract for brief counseling/crisis intervention services for a maximum of 11 sessions. He states that he is not comfortable seeking services on the military installation for fear of negative work repercussions and he is anxious about attending counseling out of fear his command will find out about it. Joe reports that his wife has threatened to leave him because of his drinking. He tells the social worker that he is "not an alcoholic" in that he only drinks on the weekends and he doesn't understand why his wife is reacting this way. He did state that he crashed his vehicle last weekend (lost control of the car and ran into a pole) after visiting the local bar. He reports that he has never been in a significant motor vehicle accident and that he has no legal history of driving under the influence (DUIs). In a subsequent visit, Joe's wife Mary (age 23), comes in with Joe, and reveals that their children (ages 4 and 5) don't want to have much to do with their father. She further elaborates that the children don't seem to be bonded with their father. There is no reported history of domestic violence in the home, or incidents of child abuse. Joe's military occupational specialty (MOS) is a 0311, an infantry Marine. He has been on two combat tours to Afghanistan.

His wife feels that his drinking has become progressively worse with each deployment. During his first deployment 3 years ago, he was shot in the arm and exposed to an IED (improvised or intermittent explosive device) and she suspected he suffered a mild traumatic brain injury (TBI) because he exhibited problems with his attention and memory, but Joe never followed up for a formal neurological evaluation or for treatment. During his second deployment 1 year ago, he lost his best friend in a firefight, and Joe felt that this loss could have been avoided with better leadership and air support. He acknowledges that combat has changed him. Joe was awarded two combat action awards and a purple heart. Joe states that he once loved the Marine Corps, and wanted to make a career of it. After his last deployment, he reported losing his confidence in the Corps and stated that he did not plan to reenlist. He also reports feeling disturbed over an incident that occurred on the last deployment where, according to the client, the team leader deliberately stabbed himself in the leg so he would be sent home early. Joe's wife at the time was five months pregnant and miscarried and he was not permitted to return home until the end of the deployment. Joe feels resentment toward the Marine Corps and is angry at having lost fellow marines and the manner in which the Marine Corps handled the situation of the sergeant who stabbed himself. Joe reports having trouble sleeping and is having recurring nightmares of people shooting at him.

Joe is of Salvadoran descent and was born in Texas. Joe reported that his mother abandoned the family when he was 10 years old, and according to Joe, she suffered from "nervios" (nerves) leaving him and his younger brother in the care of their father who worked two factory jobs to provide for the family. His mother died a few years later due to cirrhosis of the liver, associated with her alcoholism. Joe's father died last year from lung cancer that may have been related to his workplace environment (asbestos exposure). Joe has sporadic contact with his younger brother, who has also joined the service. Joe's parents were undocumented immigrants from El Salvador who escaped a violent civil war where many of their family members (especially on his mother's side) had been tortured and killed. He has a few living aunts and uncles in the United States, whom he has regular phone and Internet contact with, but has not been able to visit them due to his deployments, busy work schedule, and lack of finances. Joe grew up in an observant Catholic home, and although he believes in God he questions his faith since losing his battle buddy, but feels that reconnecting with his religion may be helpful to him.

Discussion of the Case Vignette: Joe

In the first session, Joe must be assured of treatment confidentiality and the limits to confidentiality. In a civilian context Joe's treatment record would not be a part of his military medical record and his commanding officer would not have access to his record, unless the client provides written authorization. His motive for seeking treatment should be explored. His concern about being labeled an alcoholic would be addressed by the social worker. The social worker would clarify that without an official diagnosis, only Joe can label himself an alcoholic. Motivational interviewing could be utilized to prepare Joe for change by pointing out the costs of his using alcohol, such as the compromised relationships with his wife and children, their safety, his safety, legal consequences, work-related consequences, and financial impact. The motive to reduce his drinking or abstain from alcohol must be internally driven (e.g., internal locus of control and responsibility) for it to be meaningful and lasting. In addition, Joe's success would be enhanced by having him explicitly state what he most values through values clarification such as his relationships with his wife and children and his ability to support his family. Values can also be explored in terms of his cultural and ethnic heritage, specifically the value of "familismo" (family values) that was passed down from his father. Joe also values his extended family and longs to visit them. Additionally, his family of origin struggled to survive through a war-torn country and they risked their lives as undocumented immigrants crossing into the U.S. border. The intergenerational transmission of trauma can also be explored with Joe, as it seems both of his parents may have been trauma survivors themselves, especially his mother and how this could have made him vulnerable to secondary stress and later to combat related PTSD. In addition, his mother's alcoholism could also present as a genetic risk factor for Joe becoming an addict. On the other hand, his father, whom he strongly identifies with, held negative views regarding drinking and so alcohol was not glorified or used in his home while he was growing up, which could also be discussed with Joe. His devotion to the Marine Corps (especially prior to his second combat tour) and his sense of duty to his comrades and to his country could also be emphasized as strength factors in addition to his strong family values.

Seeking Strength (SS) techniques can also be applied individually with Joe in the private practice setting, such as ways of promoting safety and providing education about how many individuals turn to addictive substances or behaviors to numb their overwhelming feelings. Here, it would be explained that the use of alcohol is numbing and serves to thin the repression barrier, thus causing strong feelings to be easily expressed seemingly without accountability or consequence. It would be pointed out that he is experiencing real and serious consequences of his behavior and he has power over these behaviors. Perhaps the clinician could bring to light the potential powerlessness he may have felt during combat and in the war-riddled life of his family of origin; yet how he was able to overcome many obstacles as his father and extended family did. The connection between the method of expression of strong feelings and consequences would be highlighted while helping the client gain more adaptive coping mechanisms. SS is an effective model to use as the thrust of the intervention is only on the earliest phase of recovery. Activities of SS are used to assist Joe to be more present, to identify the circumstances in which he is experiencing strong feelings and/or memories of combat, and to learn more adaptable coping skills to manage these feelings resulting in less-distressing consequences and an increase in his quality of life and relationships.

Additionally, the social worker would encourage Mary to participate in couple's counseling with Joe to recognize the interactional/reciprocal effect of PTSD/SUD on the family members and on the veteran. Mary could participate in the SS model with Joe in covering such topics such as "Respecting Time," "Healthy Relationships," "Creating Meaning," "Red and Green Flags," "Triggers," and "Grounding" (Najavits, 2001). In fact the entire family could be included in the grounding topic as a way of giving the entire family relaxation exercises and coping skills for stress reduction. An exploration into family life-cycle transitions and stressors would also need to be taken into account. A few sessions of family therapy with the children could also be implemented to enhance attachment and resilience (Rutter, 1999). Additionally, Joe's multiple losses; his mother and father, the loss of his friend in battle, his unborn child, the loss of identity with the military, and the losses associated with trauma, could also be addressed in individual therapy as part of the deeper grief work that Herman (1992) recommends in terms of the mourning that is necessary for trauma recovery. Part of his grief work could be addressed through faith-based practices. Thus, the social worker could encourage Joe to seek out the assistance of the Navy chaplain on base and/or attend services at a church of his choosing.

Due to the strong military value of group cohesion, Joe would benefit from group work in which he can access the needed validation, support, and accountability from his male veteran peers. If the client is reluctant to attend mental health and/or substance abuse services on base, once he completed the brief therapy with the private practitioner he could be referred to a local Vet Center, where his treatment could continue beyond the private practice setting where he could receive ongoing individual and/or group therapy. Additionally, once he separated from the military, he would be eligible to participate in services through the VA with an honorable discharge. The VA also has a new mandate to assist family members. SS also has a case-management component that should be utilized in assisting this veteran and his family with other adjunctive resources as needed. The point to this approach is that if we want to engage veteran clients and maintain them in treatment, we must utilize the client's own narrative, set of belief systems including culturally derived worldviews, and an ecosystemic perspective that informs and guides our practice. The ecosystemic model speaks to the complexity of human beings in a relational world, and that there are multiple factors to consider when treating the whole human being and the systems that interact with that being. It is about examining the combination and interaction of factors beyond a minimalist and linear model of therapy, and this holistic approach entails a helper who is willing to venture outside of the box and travel with clients in their multifaceted worlds.

THE ROLE OF THE CHAPLAIN

Social workers and other professional service providers should be aware of the help that chaplains can provide to service members with substance use disorders. The chaplain is a member of the commander's personal staff and has direct access to the commander without having to address the chain of command. The chaplain is protected as a "religious officer" as related to privileged and confidential information and is protected by regulations and law in hearing the "confessional words" of any person to whom he/she may provide religious support and care. The role of the chaplain has evolved throughout history from a nonsalaried staff member to the commander's advisor with broad knowledge of a variety of services and resources. Chaplains can provide referrals and resources to the following military support systems: Resource Management, Family Life Counselor, Casualty Assistance Team, Religious Liaison, Religious Christian, Pastoral Care and Crisis Intervention, Traumatic Specialist, writers, musicians, sacramental support, hospital chaplain, and much more. Multiple testimonies from war veterans returning home recount the remarkable work of pastoral care, spiritual mentoring, spiritual fitness, and compassion exhibited on the part of hundreds of chaplains in the war zones whether they were Catholic, Jew, Presbyterian, Baptist, Pentecostal, Methodist, Lutheran, or Seventh-Day Adventist.

It is vital that first responders such as chaplains have the knowledge and ability to walk alongside the warrior in their journey for healing and well-being. Healing is a lifelong process and requires much patience, understanding, forgiveness, hope, and renewal. Chaplains can provide spiritual support, encouragement and understanding to our wounded warriors. They are able to offer interventions for forgiveness, restoration, and healing to the wounded memories of the warrior. The challenge of the warrior is to work through the processes of detachment, attachment, restoration, reconnection, forgiveness, and renewal.

This process invites the chaplain to journey patiently and compassionately with the warrior and their family as it relates to using the basic assumptions of the Solution-Focused Brief Therapy Model (de Shazer, 1985) to engage the major process themes mentioned earlier.

Five basic assumptions of the model are:

1. If we concentrate on successes, changes can take place, so the focus should be on what is right and working, rather than on what is wrong and troublesome.
2. Every problem has identifiable exceptions that can be transformed into solutions, so it is important for counselors to listen for hints as to when, where, and how exceptions occur to help clients develop solutions.
3. Small changes have a ripple effect, and as clients begin to adjust to a minor change, the chain reaction expands into major changes.
4. All clients have what it takes to resolve their difficulties, so focusing on the clients' expertise and strengths rather than on deficits is important.
5. The client's goals are seen as positive, pointing toward what clients want to do, rather than as negative or reflecting the absence of something. (Hall, 2008)

Regardless of the discipline of the helping professional, various studies (as reviewed by Duncan, Miller, Wampold, & Hubble, 2009) have identified the common attributes of the helping relationship, and some studies have suggested that the strength of the helping relationship has a much greater impact on treatment outcome than does the specific intervention approach selected. Specific techniques that facilitate the development of a therapeutic or working alliance are:

- Maintaining a respectful, welcoming, accepting, warm, empathic, hope-inspiring, confident, nonjudgmental, trustworthy, and open stance.
- Setting appropriately frequent and consistent appointments/sessions.
- Listening reflectively [active listening skills].
- Proving accurate feedback and interpretations.
- Expressing interest, empathy, and understanding.
- Actively addressing a misstep or conflict.
- Setting appropriate limits and boundaries.
- Being sensitive to the client's ethnic identity, cultural values, and beliefs.
- Being a good role model.

Chaplains (as well as social workers) are likely to possess these relationship skills and thus can provide an environment where the soldier can begin to share and better understand their ambivalence toward their substance issues.

CONCLUSION

Due to the unique stressors associated with the demands of protracted conflict in the Global War on Terrorism, concern about substance use disorders in active duty military settings is at an all time high. Although ample empirical support exists regarding the effectiveness of some approaches for preventing and treating substance use disorders among civilians, special challenges confront social workers and other practitioners who seek to prevent or treat these disorders in military settings, and more research is needed as to the effectiveness of these approaches with this unique population. This chapter has described some of the more promising approaches and addressed ways in which they may need to be adapted to fit the military lifestyle and culture.

CHAPTER DISCUSSION QUESTIONS

1. What are some factors that explain the high prevalence of substance use disorders in active duty military settings?
2. Why is substance use so dangerous in those settings?
3. Which prevention or treatment strategies or approaches described in this chapter seem to have the best chances for being effective in active duty military settings? Why?
4. Based on the insights discovered in this chapter, what new applications will enhance your work, as a mental health professional in working with military members and their families?

REFERENCES

Akhter, M. N., & Levinson, R. A. (2009). Social immunization: A public health approach for the management of substance abuse. *Journal of the National Medical Association, 101*, 1176–1179.

American Psychiatric Association. (2000). *Diagnostic and statistical manual of mental disorders* (4th ed., text rev.). Washington, DC: Author.

de Shazer, S. (1985). *Keys to solution in brief therapy*. New York, NY: Norton.

Duncan, B. L., Miller, S. D., Wampold, B. E., & Hubble, M. A. (2009). *The heart and soul of change, second edition: Delivering what works in therapy*. Washington, DC: American Psychological Association.

Freeman, S. M., & Hurst, M. R. (2009). Substance use, misuse, and abuse: Impaired problem solving and coping. In S. M. Freeman, B. A. Moore, & A. Freeman (Eds.), *Living and surviving in harm's way: A psychological treatment handbook for pre- and post-deployment of military personnel* (pp. 259–280). New York, NY: Routledge/Taylor & Francis Group.

Hall, L. K. (2008). *Counseling military families* (pp. 218–219). New York, NY: Routledge.

Herman, J. H. (1992). *Trauma and recovery: The aftermath of violence—From domestic abuse to political terror*. New York, NY: Basic Books.

Huebner, A. J., Mancini, J. A., Bowen, G. L., & Orthner, D. K. (2009). Shadowed by war: Building community capacity to support military families. *Family Relations*, 58, 216–228.

Kennedy, C. H., Jones, D. E., & Grayson, R. (2006). Substance abuse services and gambling treatment in the military. In C. H. Kennedy & E. A. (Eds.), *Military psychology: Clinical and operational applications* (pp. 163–190). New York, NY: Guilford Press.

Lande, R. G., Marin, B. A., & Ruzek, J. I. (2004). *Substance abuse in the deployment environment. Iraq war clinician guide* (2nd ed., pp. 79–82). White River Station, VT: National Center for Post-Traumatic Stress Disorder, Department of Veterans Affairs. Retrieved from http://www.ncptsd.va.gov/ncmain/ncdocs/manuals/iraq_clinician_guide_ch_12.pdf

Lande, R. G., Marin, B. A., Staudenmaier, J. J., & Hawkins, D. (2011). Substance use and abuse in the military. In E. C. Ritchie (Ed.), *Combat and operational behavioral health. Textbooks of military medicine* (pp. 473–484). Washington, DC: Borden Institute. Retrieved from http://www.bordeninstitute.army.mil/

Miller, W. R., & Rollnick, S. (1991). *Motivational interviewing: Preparing people to change addictive behavior*. New York, NY: Guilford Press.

Najavits, L. M. (2001). *Seeking safety: A treatment manual for PTSD and substance abuse*. New York, NY: Guilford Press.

Najavits, L. M. (2009). Seeking safety: An implementation guide. In D. W. Springer & A. Rubin (Eds.), *Substance abuse treatment for youth and adults: Clinician's guide to evidence-based practice* (pp. 311–347). Hoboken, NJ: Wiley.

Rutter, M. (1999). Resilience concepts and findings: Implications for family therapy. *Journal of Family Therapy*, *21*, 119–144.

Sampson, M., Stephens, N. S., & Velasquez, M. M. (2009). Motivational interviewing. In D. W. Springer & A. Rubin (Eds.), *Substance abuse treatment for youth and adults: Clinician's guide to evidence-based practice* (pp. 3–53). Hoboken, NJ: Wiley.

Springer, D. W., & Rubin, A. (Eds.). (2009). *Substance abuse treatment for youth and adults: Clinician's guide to evidence-based practice*. Hoboken, NJ: Wiley.

Weiss, E. L., Coll, J. E., Mayeda, S., Mascarenas, J., Krill, K., & DeBraber, T. (2012). An eco-systemic perspective in the treatment of Posttraumatic Stress Disorder and substance use in veterans. *Journal of Social Work Practice in Addictions*, *12*(2), 143–162.

Zoroya, G. (2006, November 2). Troubled troops in no-win plight. *USA Today*. Retrieved from http://www.usatoday.com/news/nation/2006-11-01-troubled-troops_x.htm

CHAPTER

13

Preventing and Intervening With Substance Use Disorders in Veterans

Rachel Burda-Chmielewski and Aaron Nowlin

This chapter discusses substance use disorders among this country's veterans. A study by Kulka et al. (1990) that assessed the prevalence of co-occurring PTSD and substance use disorders (SUD) in Vietnam veterans found that 73% of male Vietnam veterans met the criteria for comorbid PTSD and chronic diagnosis of alcohol dependency. More recently, the Veterans Affairs Gulf War Era Report (released in February 2011) reported that in 2009 out of an estimated total number of 110,487 Gulf War veterans receiving VA treatment, 8,298 received treatment for alcohol dependency and 10,359 were being treated for drug abuse. These statistics were increased from 2005 when there were an estimated 70,273 Gulf War veterans receiving care through the VA, with 5,466 of those being treated for alcohol dependency and 5,927 for drug abuse.

These veterans, much like with Vietnam-era veterans, are presenting for substance abuse treatment in increasing numbers as the years go on. This can be attributed to the fact that it often can take an individual a long time to reach the point where they feel treatment is necessary, commonly referred to as "*hitting bottom.*" This "*bottom*" is different for each person and can be at varying degrees of severity, but those with addictions often try to manage the disease on their own or don't even recognize it as a real problem for some time before treatment is even considered. However, there is also the factor of court-mandated treatment, which can be required of someone due to being charged with an offense that is related to drug or alcohol use. This population often goes through some type of alcohol and drug treatment more than once, and has a lower rate of success due to the motivation for treatment being external rather than internal.

Current Prevalence in Iraq and Afghanistan Veterans

Service members from the United States will have been deployed to the Middle East, specifically Iraq and Afghanistan, for about a decade (at this writing). Many of the members have gone on multiple deployments ranging from 3 to 17 months in length, and the majority of them have also experienced combat during these tours. Because this population of veterans is newly separated from the military, they are still just finding their way into the VA health care system and just beginning to come forward with the problems that they are facing or possibly have been facing for a while. The main barrier to helping this population has been the stigma attached to seeking help, especially for mental health–related issues. The culture within the military, although there have been initiatives taking place to try to change it, is saturated by mantras of "suck it up" and "show no weakness." These attitudes make it difficult for service members to feel comfortable enough to seek help for problems they may be having. This problem is compounded by the fact that they feel their job and ability to deploy with their unit may be compromised should any type of problem be documented in their record. Once out of the military it still may take some veterans a while to enroll with the VA for health care, although this is being dealt with by having transition assistance events and assessments through the Department of Defense where service members who are about to be discharged (as well as reservists) are given the opportunity to enroll right there on the spot. As of 2010, roughly 48% of the more than 1 million returned combat OIF/OEF (Operation Iraqi Freedom/Operation Enduring Freedom) veterans were enrolled in the VA health care system (Department of Veterans Affairs, 2010).

Seal et al. (2011) reported that the prevalence of mental health disorders among OIF/OEF Veterans continues to rise—particularly with the co-occurring diagnosis of PTSD. Seal et al. (2011) also stated that of those veterans undergoing screening through the VA, 22% to 40% screened positive for high-risk drinking, and 7% screened positive for cocaine and marijuana use disorders. It is believed that the rates of drug use disorders (DUD) may be higher than what is reported because disclosure of drug use normally presents a higher risk of negative work repercussions for those disclosing. A 2008 survey of roughly 28,500 active duty military personnel found that 12% reported illicit drug use, which was an increase from the 5% reported in 2005 (Bray et al., 2006).

Another substance use issue that is prevalent not only with today's veterans, but also with active duty military personnel, is that of prescription drug abuse. The military regularly prescribes medications for service members for a variety of reasons, including alleviating their physical pain, helping them with psychological stress, and keeping them awake and alert in training or combat situations (Winkel, 2009). These medications can become addicting, and the problem is increasing. A study released by the National Institute on Drug Abuse reported that among military personnel there has been an increase in prescription drug abuse and heavy alcohol use, and that although alcohol abuse is the most prevalent problem in this population, prescription drug abuse tripled from 2005 to 2008 (National Institute on Drug Abuse [NIDA], 2011). According to Seal et al. (2011), it is important to note that at this time there are no national level studies of prevalence of substance use disorders for the OIF/OEF veteran population as a whole.

CO-OCCURRING DISORDERS

Alcohol and drug abuse along with mental illness are commonly comorbid conditions, with a reported 6 out of 10 people who have a substance use disorder also having another form of mental illness (NIDA, 2007).

What Does Co-Occurring Mean?

The presence of a psychiatric disorder in an individual significantly increases the risk of comorbid substance abuse. According to the National Institute on Drug Abuse (NIDA), there are four main reasons that drug abuse and mental disorders commonly co-occur. One reason is overlapping genetic vulnerabilities to mental disorders and addiction. The same types of genetic factors that can predispose someone to having a mental illness can also predispose someone to have an addiction, or to be at an increased risk of developing one if they have developed the other.

Another reason is overlapping environmental triggers. The term '*environmental triggers*' refers to occurrences in someone's immediate environment that can cause them distress, either triggering drug and alcohol use or causing enough distress to exacerbate a mental illness. Things like stress, experiencing a trauma, or early exposure to drugs are common factors that can lead to mental illness and addiction problems, especially if the individual already has the genetic vulnerabilities discussed previously.

A third reason is the fact that similar regions of the brain have been found to be affected by both substance abuse and mental disorders. More specifically, the area of the brain that is involved in processing reward and pleasure perception is directly impacted when substances are abused, and it is impacted similarly in certain mental disorders (NIDA, 2007).

The fourth reason is that drug abuse and mental illness are both developmental disorders, which means that they often occur in either childhood or early adolescence. Because these are times in development when the brain is undergoing dramatic change, it has been shown that early exposure to drugs can alter the brain in certain ways that can increase the risk for mental illness. Similarly, early symptoms of a mental disorder can also increase the vulnerability of someone to abuse drugs and develop addiction (NIDA, 2007).

Petrakis et al. (2011) looked at rates of comorbidity among veterans and found that males were significantly more likely to be diagnosed with co-occurring disorders, as were minorities, single veterans, and those with a non service-connected disability. (Substance use disorders are not seen as service-connected disabilities.) Petrakis also found that the rates of these disorders were higher than what was found in the general population.

Most Common Comorbid Disorders

According to an article released by the Substance Abuse and Mental Health Services Administration (SAMHSA), mental health and substance use disorders were the leading causes of hospitalizations for U.S. troops in 2009. Also reported in that article; "Approximately 18.5% of service members returning from Iraq or Afghanistan have post traumatic stress disorder (PTSD) or depression" (Power, 2011, p. 39). Petrakis (2011) found that of a total of 1,001,996 veterans who were diagnosed with one of the six specified mental health disorders, the rate of substance use disorders was 21% to 35%. According to this study, "affective disorders, in comparison to PTSD, are most strongly associated with dual diagnosis among post-Vietnam and OIF/OEF Veterans, while anxiety disorders are most strongly associated with dual diagnosis among Persian Gulf Veterans. Bipolar disorder and Schizophrenia are both most strongly associated with dual diagnosis in OIF/OEF Veterans, compared to those with PTSD" (p. 188).

It is not surprising that the highest rates of comorbidity occur in those with severe mental illnesses such as bipolar disorder and schizophrenia, as these disorders also have a lower rate of medication compliance and the people who are inflicted with these diagnoses have more significant and life-interfering symptoms than those who suffer from less severe mental illness. These high rates are consistent with what is found in the general civilian population as well. These findings were also supported by a report by the Substance Abuse and Mental Health Services Administration. The National Survey on Drug Use and Health's most recent report regarding co-occurring disorders documented the prevalence of substance use disorders among adults with a comorbid mental health diagnosis. The findings show that the likelihood of a substance use disorder is directly related to the level of mental illness.

According to Petrakis (2011), clinical experience and research evidence have shown that among those veterans who suffer from PTSD, there are high rates of substance abuse, and those suffering from both disorders have a worse clinical prognosis than those who have PTSD alone. Petrakis found that PTSD occurs more commonly than do other serious psychiatric disorders, and that veterans who served in the post-Vietnam era (1973 to 1991) had the highest rates of comorbidity. For this reason, veterans are screened for PTSD as well as for depression, substance abuse, and suicide risk upon return from deployment and prior to discharge from the military. All OIF/OEF veterans are also screened for these disorders when they first present to the VA to enroll for health care benefits to identify their needs, and are given the appropriate referrals if they screen positive.

Best Treatment Practices for Co-Occurring Disorders

Treatment of co-occurring disorders has been challenging because people have historically had a difficult time accessing services for both mental health and substance use disorders, and the services that are available rarely address the common elements of these issues. Also, within the VA health care system until recently there was no program for veterans to be able to receive care for these comorbid issues. Someone could seek substance abuse treatment, or seek treatment for a mental health disorder, but it was common practice for a clinic to not accept a patient for mental health treatment if they were actively using substances. This created a problem because commonly in co-occurring disorders the symptoms of the mental health disorder would serve to maintain the substance use disorder, just as a substance use disorder would quite often limit a patient's ability to receive treatment for a co-occurring mental health disorder.

It is an important part of treatment to determine whether a substance use disorder is serving to maintain mental health symptoms. For example, the symptoms in a mood disorder might have been created by the abuse of a substance or might be present even if the person was not abusing a substance. If someone has been using drugs and/or alcohol to self-medicate the symptoms of a mental health disorder, and they enter treatment for substance use to become clean and sober, the substance use may be removed temporarily but the cause of those symptoms is not being treated and therefore chronic relapsing would occur. Substance use disorders and mood and anxiety disorders that develop independently of intoxication and withdrawal are among the most prevalent psychiatric disorders in the civilian population of the United States. As found by Grant et al. (2004), statistical associations between most substance use disorders and independent mood and anxiety disorders were overwhelmingly positive and significant, suggesting that treatment for a comorbid mood or anxiety disorder should not be withheld from individuals with substance use disorders. This also implies that pharmacological interventions (medications) for people with diagnosed co-occurring mental disorders should be continued, and specific medications that are meant for patients with substance dependencies should also be considered. Some of these medications are naltrexone, suboxone/methadone, acamprosate, and antabuse.

The hole in dual diagnosis patient care was filled with the VA's creation of Dual Diagnosis programs that serve veterans who have co-occurring psychiatric illness as well as a substance use disorder. These programs, such as the SAMI (Substance Abuse and Mental Illness) program at the VA Medical Center in San Diego, California, aim to serve the dually diagnosed veteran population through concurrently treating both the substance use disorder as well as the mental health disorder. A veteran who is screened and accepted into the SAMI program would be placed in a group with other clients who have the same or similar mental health diagnosis, such as an anxiety disorder or a mood disorder, and receive therapy in a group setting as well as being given an individualized treatment plan that targets his or her specific substance abuse and mental health needs. If clients are not receiving the care necessary through group therapy, they also can be assigned to an individual therapist to be provided with one-on-one therapy.

The interventions used for these clients include working with each client in whichever stage of treatment they are in; providing patient-centered treatment goal setting for each stage as well as case management and resource referrals; the application of cognitive behavioral techniques for behavior modification; pharmacological interventions managed by a primary psychiatrist; relapse prevention interventions, and skill building (among others). The goal of the dual diagnosis program is for the client to stay under outpatient care for anywhere from 3 months to 1 year, after which the client hopefully will have stabilized his or her symptoms and no longer need regular therapy services or would be referred to a different specialty clinic within the VA that deals more in depth with specific needs—such as a clinic that provides alcohol and drug treatment alone, an anxiety disorders clinic; a mood clinic; a military sexual trauma clinic; a PTSD clinic.

PREVENTION AND TREATMENT PROGRAMS

Both active duty military personnel and veterans are at risk due to the factors that have been discussed in the previous two parts. In addition to the impact on service members and veterans themselves, the impact on the labor force is staggering. This impact on the military and civilian community is difficult to quantify—due to the progressive nature of the illness and the many co-occurring factors. Additionally, those who develop a substance use disorder (SUD) while in the military carry this with them when they discharge, much like a major depressive disorder or a posttraumatic stress disorder. Because of the aforementioned factors, a significant amount of energy and resources has gone into the development and application of both prevention and treatment programs. This chapter now examines options available and brief evaluation of the efficacy of these programs.

As was discussed in the co-morbid section, accurate assessment is equally as important as the type of treatment prescribed so that appropriate measures can be taken rather than a one-size-fits-all approach. Consequently, motivational enhancement has been found to be an important part of both early intervention and treatment. This is due to its appropriateness of meeting the person where they are at and allowing them to dictate the course of their prevention and/or treatment. Motivational interviewing is especially important to patients being treated for an SUD because many of those who are considering treatment are doing so primarily due to extrinsic motivation. By exploring their motivation and what is important to them, they often improve their desire to change. Research has supported the cost-effectiveness of motivational interviewing (Garner, 2009).

When discussing prevention and treatment, it is important to keep two points in mind. One is that prevention requires honesty from the client. Many active duty service members have a fear of self-disclosure of SUD symptoms for fear of reprisal. Because of this, substance use–related problems often progress to the point of abuse and dependence, and prevention programs become ineffective and treatment is then more appropriate. The other key point is that many veterans who arrive at the VA and are being assessed for SUD symptoms have already passed the point of prevention due to already developing an SUD. Therefore, they are now more appropriate for treatment rather than prevention. Although early intervention is still appropriate, it would now be in the form of treatment, not prevention. Because of this, prevention efforts are particularly needed while the service member is still on active duty. This is not to assert that civilian and veteran related service organizations (primarily the VA) have no responsibility for prevention; it is only to explain why the primary focus for veterans organizations has been treatment rather than prevention.

PREVENTION FOR ACTIVE DUTY PERSONNEL

The prevalence of substance-related problems within the active duty ranks warrant that every command have a member and often multiple members, responsible for the development and coordination of awareness and prevention of substance-related problems. In addition to this, each service within the active duty ranks has a zero-tolerance policy associated with any positive test for illicit drugs resulting in administrative action, which 99% of the time results in either a "dishonorable" or an "other than honorable" discharge. Either one of these types of discharge strip a veteran of important privileges such as treatment at the VA health care centers, GI Bill benefits, and other entitlements. This awareness, which is made known to all service members multiple times through their first year of indoctrination, is perhaps the primary preventative measure at deterring drug use behavior. Additionally, fear that an alcohol-related problem could affect promotion and/or work status is a prevention measure to limit abuse. However, punishment itself has often been shown to be an ineffective method of modifying high-risk behaviors in service members and as a result illicit drug offenses continue to occur at most military installations.

Each command provides a service that uses substance abuse awareness coordinators to initiate and employ prevention measures intended to deter the onset of substance use disorders. These measures often include advertisements that cast a negative light on substance abuse and a positive light on being responsible. They also include education classes that highlight at-risk groups as well as high-risk behaviors. Education for the ranks is provided regarding how to spot early warning signs in an effort to catch a behavior before it develops into abuse or dependence (e.g., service members become preoccupied with discussions about partying/drinking, arriving to work late, decline in work production).

When service members are seen at a clinic or hospital for any type of treatment, they are often screened about the frequency and amount of alcohol consumption. Service members who screen positive are given information and are directed to communicate with a substance use disorder specialist. (This is not an actual title; it could be a physician, psychologist, social worker, or drug and alcohol counselor. The title varies in the different branches of the armed services.) A primary difference between active duty service members and veterans is that while on active duty, command may be informed if the service member has screened positive for an SUD depending on their job requirements and as a result they are given additional pressure to seek out early intervention or treatment before the substance use progresses.

TRANSITION TO VETERAN STATUS

Prior to discharge from active duty all service members are given a physical examination and a review of their illnesses and their medical history. This is an opportunity prior to a service member transitioning out of the military to receive appropriate counseling. In most cases this assessment is brief and more of a formality, whereas in others it is more thorough. Too often it is left up to the service members themselves to advocate or initiate a more comprehensive assessment. Because of this, potential signs or warning signs of a SUD are difficult to detect in an assessment.

In addition to the final physical, service members are given the opportunity to attend an education class focused on preparing them for the transition out of the military. This class is intended to prepare veterans for becoming civilians: The focus of the military on preparing its service members for transition has progressively improved. In the past, facilitating this transition received much less attention. However, despite this improvement, little time is spent explaining how separation from the military places one at special risk for either onset of substance use problems or symptoms that can be a catalyst for the onset of substance-related problems. Although service members are made aware of the myriad potential stressors that may beset them during transition (as discussed in other chapters of this book), the connection between these stressors and substance use problems are rarely highlighted by this transition class. Outside of this transition class, the responsibility rests solely on the veteran until he or she is seen at a veteran service organization or in the VA itself.

PREVENTION WITHIN THE VA

The impact of substance use disorders on one's mental and physical health, as was discussed in the section on co-occurring disorders, is both difficult to treat and is a reason why the VA emphasizes early intervention. (For reasons noted earlier, within the VA "prevention" is primarily in the form of early intervention.) The services begin the first time veterans are treated by a health care provider, which usually occurs shortly after they enroll (often they meet with a provider that same day if timely and available).

The first time veterans are seen by a health care professional they are given a questionnaire asking them about their alcohol use (in addition to other various screenings for physical and mental health). This standard form is called the AUDIT-C and it asks three or more questions about amount and frequency of alcohol use. The higher the score, the more questions are asked, and in turn they are asked if they are willing to be referred to a provider. Due to the influence of military culture and stigma, there is a general tendency to underreport symptoms, and thus most of these questionnaires are not accurately completed by veterans. However, if accurately completed and a substance use problem is identified, then a brief counseling session is conducted where clients are encouraged to either address their misuse or they are referred to more comprehensive counseling.

This brief counseling session by itself has been shown to have positive outcomes once the veterans become aware they are at risk for the development of a substance use disorder. The AUDIT-C is the primary early intervention and prevention tool available to the VA for assessing early signs of an SUD. However, there are other screening tools that are mandated by the VA. These tools assess for suicide risk; PTSD; symptoms of depression; sexual trauma; and traumatic brain injury. If an individual screens positive for any of these, he or she is seen by a mental health provider for an intake or assessment, and at this assessment they are screened more in-depth for potential substance use disorders or other behavioral health problems. As was pointed out earlier, the climate within the VA has become one of early intervention, and although the screening tools are limited, there are many opportunities for early intervention beyond the screenings. These opportunities involve sessions with providers who are trained to notice warning signs of misuse, abuse, and dependence. These providers often work within the mental health/psychiatric field but may also be in areas of the social work service, such as homeless outreach and transition assistance.

The longer that substance abuse or dependence is allowed to progress, the more difficult it becomes to treat (primarily tolerance- and withdrawal-related, but also due to increased habituation and dependence on self-medication properties). Because of this, early intervention is geared to addressing misuse before it becomes abuse (associated with legal, health, and relationship problems, to name a few), or abuse before it becomes dependence (associated with onset of withdrawal and/or tolerance, using more than intended, inability to quit or cut back, excessive time investment in drug- or alcohol-seeking behaviors, negative lifestyle change, exacerbation of physical or mental health problems).

Veterans are educated about their symptoms and other treatment options available to them (AA meetings, etc.). Because early intervention often entails (hence *early*) that a severe problem with their substance use has not yet occurred, or they do not endorse a problem as serious although other people associated with the veteran do, a focus of early intervention is often on enhancing their motivation to change. This approach has been called motivational interviewing (MI) (Miller & Rollnick, 2002). MI is a humanistic approach that assumes that if a person improves their motivation to change, they dramatically enhance their ability to change. It also assumes that those people who continue to use substance(s) in the face of mounting problems—rather than resisting abstinence—are often ambivalent about abstaining (i.e., conflicted about the desire to quit/cut back and a desire to continue using). As discussed in the previous chapter, MI has been shown to be effective when working with those affected by substance use disorders (Cook, Wasler, Kane, Ruzek, & Woody, 2006). (The previous chapter also provided more detail about how MI interviews are conducted.)

Also as discussed in the previous chapter, an evidence-based treatment program, which simultaneously treats both PTSD and substance use disorders, is Seeking Safety. It does so by using MI techniques in conjunction with a curriculum exploring current behaviors in a nonthreatening manner. Abstinence from a given behavior is not mandated, but as the treatment progresses the act of making commitments becomes more focused and related to the client's PTSD or substance use. An example of this would be committing to not drink at their regular time of the day, or taking a shower when feeling angry instead of playing video games. These little commitments improve the client's self-efficacy and overall ability to make and keep commitments.

A core concept within MI is that people must recognize that the priorities in their life are in conflict with their harmful behavior (e.g., substance use) and despite their ambivalence to change, their priorities and behaviors are not congruent. The clients are encouraged to identify this for themselves, and a common example of this would be to use a rating scale. On a scale of 1 to 10, assume they rate their substance use at a 5 (10 being the highest and 0 representing the lowest). If they rate their marriage at a 9, then it is clear that they feel their marriage is more important than their drinking. If their substance use is harming their marriage, and they are allowed to see this on their own, versus a provider or person telling them that they are harming their marriage, it becomes invaluable toward improving motivation to change.

Although most providers of early intervention techniques would assert that MI (as well as some other therapeutic tools) is a part of the process of treatment, it is designed to be more of a jumpstart to treatment and by itself should not be considered a complete treatment protocol.

Once a person has been assessed as being at risk or having met criteria that constitutes a probable substance use disorder they are then referred to the program within the VA for independent assessment of a substance use disorder. To gain a more complete picture of an individual's functioning and determine if treatment is indicated, these initial intake screenings—which occur at the VA—assess other areas of a person's life in addition to substance use disorders. These areas include such things as living arrangements, support networks, past treatment attempts, and physical/mental health. These intakes combine comprehensive screening tools with feedback geared to empowering the person to take responsibility for their diagnoses (if these include more than misuse) and options for treatment should they choose it. In addition to establishing criteria for abuse, it is important to assess how severe the substance use disorder is. If they do choose to engage in treatment the options are fairly simple—Outpatient, Intensive-Outpatient, Residential, or a combination of the three. The client is typically collaborated with on identifying which is the most appropriate method of treatment. There is then a recommendation made by the program, which typically entails an interdisciplinary team assessment of the client's case.

TREATMENT AT THE VA AND OTHER PROGRAMS

Since the mid-1990s the VA has undergone a transition from providing more inpatient care to more outpatient care for the treatment of clients with an SUD. Cognitive behavioral treatment (CBT) is the most common treatment modality for the treatment of substance use disorders at the VA, partly because of its strong empirical support. Almost all CBT models-group, psychoeducation, individual therapy exploring discrepancies in the thoughts, feelings and behaviors of clients, are used in conjunction with individual or group therapy sessions designed to assist the client with improving honesty as well as support. CBT is essentially geared to assisting clients with identifying how various parts of their thought processes are affecting their behavior. Once these problems are detected, the clients are then given education and support to change the faulty cognitions.

A veteran who first presents to the VA with no history of treatment (either at the VA, or in military or civilian programs) and with a minimal to moderate severity index of abuse or addiction will typically be referred to an outpatient treatment program within the VA. However, if the client is homeless, the treatment recommendation could include residential placement within the VA or if the VA is unable to provide this then it is typically contracted to a civilian organization. This element of SUD treatment is commonly underappreciated. It is highly difficult to address physical or psychological abuse/dependence if one's basic needs are not met. It would be incorrect to conclude that if people address their basic needs they then have the necessary elements to change, however, because they could have low-motivation, a severe co-occurring disorder, or other psychopathology that is inhibiting their attempts at change.

The treatment recommendation comes with the assumption that the veteran is motivated to attend treatment. Veterans who meet the criteria for abuse/dependence but are past the early intervention point and lack the motivation to attend treatment are, to some degree, at a crossroads. Their decision to either attend and participate in care or decline the option may impact their eligibility for other types of care, such as CBT for an anxiety disorder or a vocational rehabilitation program. Their eligibility might be delayed until they are able to maintain abstinence for a prescribed number of days and/or enter into SUD treatment. If they continue to decline SUD treatment despite these stipulations, an option that remains available is for either continuing or beginning motivational interviewing. Aside from MI, which is generally noninvasive/nonthreatening to veterans, there is little else a provider can do aside from informing them that if they change their mind, treatment is available.

Most VAs offer brief detoxification treatment, which offers medically managed support while a client withdraws from a given chemical. This is managed through prescribed medication and can be done either as an outpatient or inpatient. A common misconception is that detoxification is provided only as an inpatient modality. The reality is that outpatient detoxification can be just as effective as inpatient detoxification if the client is appropriate and at low enough risk for withdrawals, health concerns, mental health concerns, and relapse potential.

In the case of opioid dependence, either street or prescription opioids, opioid substitution treatment is often prescribed alone or as an adjunct to outpatient therapy. Buprenorphine and methadone are the two primary examples of this. The medications used to assist with cravings for alcohol and/or deterrents are acamprosate and naltrexone. These medications are intended to reduce cravings for alcohol or reduce the positive reinforcement that alcohol use provides. Additionally there is antabuse, which creates a negative physical reaction when one uses it and then consumes alcohol.

Outpatient treatment is typically delivered once weekly, usually being comprised of a 60- to 120-minute group therapy session with a mix of talk therapy/interaction with group members as well as an introduction of CBT concepts. This group therapy may be especially helpful for veterans due to a feeling of dislocation since discharge and a lack of identification with nonveterans over their individualized concerns. In addition to this therapy, their intake is complimented by a fully integrated assessment that explores the whole person for problems related to the substance use and unrelated issues, which left untreated place a veteran at risk for relapse, progression of the illness, or other problems. Examples of the areas explored in an integrated assessment are history of abuse, employment problems, educational background, sexual dysfunction, spirituality, as well as many others. In addition to group therapy and comprehensive assessment, veterans collaborate on a treatment plan intended to highlight their significant SUD problems as well as to create goals for change intended to address these problems.

In cases where veterans have a comorbid mental illness, in addition to an SUD, they often have the option to attend a treatment program to treat both diagnoses. This treatment is similar to outpatient treatment, except that it entails treatment focused on both their disorders (e.g., major depression or PTSD) and their SUD. Because it is highly difficult to treat mental illness without being abstinent from substance use, abstinence is often a prerequisite for this type of combined treatment. An exception to this is Seeking Safety (also called Seeking Strength, which was discussed earlier and is illustrated further in the previous chapter). In cases where clients are continuing to use chemicals but are appropriate for comorbid treatment, it is often appropriate to first focus solely on the SUD, and then once stabilized they can then receive appropriate treatment for their comorbid diagnoses. Once clients achieve abstinence they are often transferred to this comorbid treatment program or referred to a program that treats their mental health independently while they engage in aftercare or follow an abstinence-related recovery program.

When veterans exhibit a more severe progression of chemical dependence, multiple substances of abuse/dependence, or history of failed treatment attempts they will be referred to either an intensive outpatient (IOP) or residential program—explained earlier. IOP and residential programs offer essentially the same treatment as OP or Dual Diagnoses OP programs except that they are more intensive for the first 30 to 90 days. IOP typically requires 20 to 30 hours of treatment-related functions per week, and residential requirements are even greater. These treatment-related functions usually include CBT, or can include rehabilitative interventions (such as employment counseling, exercise therapy, and recreational therapy).

Residential treatment has become more commonly used in the VA since 1995 (Humphreys & Horst, 2006). The primary difference between an inpatient and a residential treatment program is the amount of 24-hour nursing services available, but aside from this the difference is negligible when the service is being provided by the VA. In many cases residential care is contracted out by the VA and provided by an outside agency. In such cases, nursing services are usually limited. The specifics of residential treatment are similar to that of IOP, but even more programming is available and required if a client commits to the program. The need for a person to have shelter is not the only reason for residential treatment, but the intensive 24-hour setting fosters almost complete immersion into a positive setting, which can prevent or limit lapsing or relapsing while in treatment. This can allow for more focus on a person's individual treatment plan. When patients have completed their initial treatment plan and have success while in treatment, they have improved their ability to stay sober afterward.

Examples of specific areas of treatment plan foci include teaching how to cope with cravings (which are expected and normal), changing recreational habits, improving/incorporating refusal skills, coping skill improvement for emotions and/or pain, and addressing complacency (Marlatt & Donovan, 2005). By addressing these, as well as other topics with a CBT approach, the client is enabled to make improved decisions intended to support abstinence or other change associated with addressing problem areas.

CONTINUING CARE

Treatment through outpatient, IOP or residential modalities is only the initial step required toward addressing SUD. This is because SUD(s) are progressive and have no known cure. Often when people have achieved some level of success and they are faced with a challenging life situation like unemployment, spousal separation, or declining health, they become more prone to lapse. Lapse (Marlatt & Donovan, 2005) is defined as a short-term return to use of a chemical when the person has achieved some period of abstinence. A lapse often leads to a return to previous use behavior or a relapse. Because of this risk to lapse and relapse, continuing care involves creation of a long-term recovery or relapse-prevention plan. Realistically, there is no plan that can assure 100% success at being sober; however, within the VA treatment paradigms are created for those motivated for long-term sobriety and or relapse-prevention. In many cases continuing care would involve treatment of the veteran's co-occurring disorder (which includes follow up with psychiatrist and/or therapist).

Within the SUD prevention and treatment community it is difficult to gauge the success of a program because of a variety of factors. One research flaw in evaluating the success of a program is the lack of a sufficiently lengthy longitudinal follow-up posttreatment. Typically, at most, cases are followed up as far as 1 year following treatment, and because recovery from chemical dependence is a lifelong process this follow-up is limited.

The Case Vignette: Craig provides an example of an OIF/OEF veteran who presented to the VA Medical Center for treatment and assistance. Utilizing some of the concepts discussed in this chapter, the case illustrates the transition from active duty service member to veteran, and the steps that would be taken to provide clients with the benefits and services they may need or want.

Case Vignette: Craig

The veteran, Craig, is a 24-year-old Caucasian male who was discharged from the Army 3 years ago at the rank of E-4. During his 3 years enlisted he served one 12-month deployment in Iraq and one 14-month deployment in Afghanistan. He began seeking services from the VA 2 years ago when he was mandated to complete a drug and alcohol treatment program following a DUI and an assault charge he received when he was intoxicated and got into a fight, where he badly injured someone to the point of hospitalization and he served time in prison.

Craig was born and raised in Los Angeles, California, and grew up in what he called a "normal home environment" with his older brother and was primarily raised by their mother after their parents got a divorce when he was 10 years old. He began to drink alcohol and smoke cigarettes socially in high school when he was 16 years old. Throughout the next few years his drinking increased to the point that by the time he graduated high school at 18 years old he was drinking to intoxication 3 days a week, and smoking marijuana before and after school 2 to 3 times a week as well. He was suspended from school once for marijuana possession, and graduated with a low GPA because his grades were poor and he had poor attendance. He enlisted in the Army immediately after high school, and began basic training 4 months after graduation.

While in the Army Craig's drinking increased further. He lived in the barracks at his first duty station and would drink with his roommates and others who lived near them mostly every night. He also would drink to blackout intoxication both nights most weekends, and began attracting attention from his command due to coming into work hung over some mornings. He was put on warning for this and for his decreased productivity.

During Craig's two deployments he was involved in regular foot patrols and direct combat. He was involved in an improvised explosive device (IED) explosion that hit his convoy in Iraq, and although not seriously injured he sustained a concussion and some memory loss. He also witnessed a few of his unit members being killed during an ambush on his deployment to Afghanistan a year later. He began to experience symptoms of PTSD soon after his return from Iraq but did not want to call attention to himself regarding that, as he wanted to be able to deploy again with his unit.

After his discharge from the Army he moved home and enrolled in college, planning to use his GI Bill to obtain a bachelor degree. He began experiencing worsening PTSD symptoms including anger outbursts, hyper vigilance, avoidance of large crowds and crowded places, and nightmares. He began to increase his marijuana smoking as he found it calmed him down and lowered the anxious feeling he normally had all the time. He also was drinking heavily, consuming a six-pack of beer and several shots of liquor a day, usually in one sitting at night after his classes. He began missing class and getting low grades, got a DUI, and ultimately dropped out of college after a semester. One night he was out at a bar drinking with his friends and got into an altercation with another person while he was extremely intoxicated. He went into a rage and physically assaulted the person to the point that the man had to be hospitalized for his injuries. Craig was arrested and put into prison for 9 months, where he underwent some alcohol and drug education. After his release, as part of his probation, he was required to complete a residential rehabilitation program. He presented to the San Diego VA Medical Center located in Southern California and requested treatment through the Alcohol & Drug Treatment Program (ADTP).

Case Disposition

When Craig presented to the VA ADTP he was immediately seen by an addiction therapist for an initial screening and intake assessments. The addiction therapist (AT) went through his whole psychosocial history, gathering relevant information and obtaining a history of his alcohol and drug use, any past treatment history, and gauging his motivation for treatment as well as determining what level of treatment his problem warranted. At the end of this assessment the therapist came to the conclusion that a 28-day inpatient rehabilitation would be most beneficial for the client, followed by at least 3 months in a residential recovery home. Craig agreed to this and was admitted a week later into the medical center's inpatient ADTP program.

During his 28-day stay he completed a full schedule of daily classes and groups, group therapy, weekly meetings with a primary contact, and attendance of 12-step meetings. He was also screened by the Operation Iraqi Freedom/Operation Enduring Freedom (OIF/OEF) care management team and began to be followed by a case manager, who was a licensed social worker, and monitored his treatment as well as provided any resource referrals or case management needs he had or would continue to have.

Post discharge he was assigned a weekly aftercare group to attend, which was an AT-facilitated group therapy session each week to help veterans like himself through their early recovery and reinforce the skills they learned on the inpatient unit. He also was accepted into Veterans Village of San Diego, which is a highly structured year-long recovery home program in the area. During his stay there he received further case management, weekly individual therapy, group substance abuse therapy and classes, PTSD group therapy, and continued to attend his aftercare group at the medical center. He remained at this facility for 3 months until he was transferred to the VA Palo Alto's inpatient PTSD program in Northern California, which required he have some sustained sobriety prior to admission, to receive more structured treatment for his PTSD.

CONCLUSION

This chapter has examined substance use disorders among veterans. After discussing prevalence rates for veterans of the Vietnam War and of more recent wars, it discussed the problem of co-occurring disorders and their impact in increasing the risk of substance abuse and in worsening the veteran's prognosis. Treatment and prevention programs were then described, and the need for long-term continuing care was emphasized. A case vignette illustrated the transition from active duty service member to veteran, and the steps that can be taken to provide clients with the benefits and services they may need or want.

CHAPTER DISCUSSION QUESTIONS

1. What are the unique challenges of the military culture that place veterans at an increased risk of developing a substance use disorder?
2. What type of treatment approach has been found to be the most effective for veterans with co-occurring substance use and mental health disorders?
3. What are the purposes and benefits of early intervention in substance use treatment?
4. What is the concept of motivational interviewing, and how is it used with the veteran population in treatment?

REFERENCES

Beck, J. S. (1995). *Cognitive therapy: Basics and beyond*. New York, NY: Guilford Press.

Bray, R. M., Hourani, L. L., Olmstead, K. L. R., Witt, M., Brown, J. M., Pemberton, M. R., . . . Hayden, D. (2006). *Department of veterans defense survey of health related behaviors among military personnel*. Research Triangle, NC: Research Triangle Institute.

Cook, J. M., Wasler, R. D., Kane, V., Ruzek, J. I., & Woody, G. (2006). Dissemination and feasibility of a cognitive behavioral treatment for substance use disorders and posttraumatic stress disorder in the veterans administration. *Journal of Psychoactive Drugs*, *38*, 89–92.

Department of Veterans Affairs. (2010, December). *Veteran Population Projections: FY2000 to FY2036*. Washington, DC: National Center for Veterans Analysis and Statistics.

Fisher, A. H. Jr., Nelson, K., & Panzarealla, J. (1972). *Patterns of drug usage among Vietnam veterans*. Washington, DC: Office of the Chief of Research and Development (Army).

Garner, B. R. (2009, June). Research on the diffusion of evidence-based treatments within substance abuse treatment: A systematic review. *Journal of Substance Abuse Treatment*, *36*(4), 376–399.

Grant, B. F., Stinson, F. S., Dawson, D. A., Chou, S. P., Dufour, M. C., Compton, W., . . . Kaplan, K. (2004). Prevalence and co-occurrence of substance use disorders and independent mood and anxiety disorders: Results from the national epidemiologic survey on alcohol and related conditions. *Archives of General Psychiatry*, *61*, 807–816.

Humphreys, K., & Horst, D. (2006). *Moving from inpatient to residential substance abuse treatment in the VA*, *5*(8). http://psychservices.psychiatryonline.org

Kulka, R. A., Schlenger, W. E., Fairbank, J. A., Hough, R. I., Jordan, B. K., Marmar, C. R., & Weiss, D. S. (1990). *Trauma and the Vietnam War generation: Report of findings from the national Vietnam veterans readjustment study*. New York, NY: Brunner/Mazel.

Marlatt, G. A., & Donovan, D. V. (2005). *Relapse prevention: Maintenance strategies in the treatment of addictive behaviors* (2nd ed). New York, NY: Guilford Press.

McDevitt-Murphy, M. E., Williams, J. L., Bracken, K. L., Fields, J. A., Monahan, C. J., & Murphy, J. G. (2010). PTSD symptoms, hazardous drinking, and health functioning among U.S.OEF and OIF veterans presenting to primary care. *Journal of Traumatic Stress*, *23*, 108–111.

Miller, W. R, & Rollnick, S. (2002). *Motivational interviewing: Preparing people for change* (2nd ed.). New York, NY: Guilford Press.

Najavitis, L. M. (2002). *Seeking safety: A treatment manual for PTSD and substance abuse*. New York, NY: Guilford Press.

National Institute on Drug Abuse (2007). *Addiction and co-occurring mental disorders*. Retrieved from http://www.drugabuse.gov/news-events/nida-notes/2007/02/addiction-co-occurring-mental-disorders

National Institute on Drug Abuse (2011). *Topics in brief: Substance abuse among the military, veterans, and their families*. Retrieved from: http://www.drugabuse.gov/publications/topics-in-brief/substance-abuse-among-military-veterans-their-families

Petrakis, I., L., Rosenheck, R., & Desai, R. (2011). Substance use comorbidity among veterans with posttraumatic stress disorder and other psychiatric illness. *American Journal on Addictions*, *20*(3), 185–189.

Power, K. (2011). *Strategic initiative #3: Military families*. Rockville, MD: Substance Abuse and Mental Health Services Administration. Retrieved from www.smhsa.gov/militaryfamilies/

Robins, L. N., Helzer, J. E., & Davis, D. H. (1975). Narcotic use in Southeast Asia and afterward: An interview study of 898 Vietnam returnees. *Archives of General Psychiatry*, *32*(8), 955–961.

Rosen, C. S., Kuhn, E., Greenbaum, M. A., & Drescher, K. D. (2008). Substance abuse-related mortality among middle aged male VA psychiatric patients. *Psychiatric Services*, *59*(3).

Seal, K. H., Cohen, G., Waldrop, A., Cohen, B. E., Maquen, S., & Ren, L. (2011). Substance use disorders in Iraq and Afghanistan veterans in VA healthcare, 2001–2010: Implications for screening, diagnosis and treatment. *Drug and Alcohol Dependence*, *116*(1–3), 93–101.

Substance Abuse and Mental Health Services Administration, Office of Applied Studies. (2004, November 11). *The NSDUH report: Male veterans with co-occurring serious mental illness and a substance use disorder*. Rockville, Maryland: Author.

Substance Abuse and Mental Health Services Administration, Office of Applied Studies. (2007, November 1). *The NSDUH report: Serious psychological distress and substance use disorder among veterans*. Rockville, Maryland: Author.

Winkel, B. (2009). *The military and substance abuse*. Retrieved from www.treatmentsolutionsnetwork.com/blog/index.php/2009/08/04/the-military-and-substance-abuse

CHAPTER

14

Suicide in the Military

COLANDA CATO

This chapter focuses on self-directed violence in the military with a particular emphasis on prevention through the promotion of resilience.[1] Specifically, the chapter covers theoretical applications of military prevention efforts within a Total Force Fitness Framework, which relies heavily on evidence-based, cognitive-behavioral strategies.

The number of suicide deaths in the military has been growing. At the time of this writing, the most recent military suicide data are from 2010, when 295 service members died by suicide, with 269 occurring in the Active Component across all services and 26 in the Reserve Component. Nearly half of those who died by suicide (48%) visited military treatment facilities within 3 months of the suicide death.

Many people have speculated that the increase in suicides among military personnel is related to the number, length, or operational tempo of military deployments. At present, however, studies have found no direct relationship between the number of times an individual service member has deployed and suicide deaths. For 2009, the majority of suicides did *not* occur in theater (Luxton et al., 2009). In fact, only about 13% of military suicides (n = 39) occurred during an OEF/OIF deployment (Luxton et al., 2009), with the majority of military suicides occurring in the United States (79%, n = 234). Moreover, many suicides occur among service members who have never deployed.

One notable study, the Army *Study to Assess Risk and Resilience in Service members* (STARRS), contradicts the earlier finding, noting that women and men experienced an increased risk for suicide while deployed. Specifically, data from 2004 to 2008 show that deployed female soldiers were three times more likely to die by suicide than those who had never deployed (males also showed a similar disparity 14.8 versus. 21.1 per 100,000 soldier; Robins, 2011). Although one might conclude that this represents an elevated risk associated with military deployments, the relatively small number of deaths by suicides among women does not provide reliable or stable estimates of suicide risk/rates.

[1]The views expressed in this chapter are the views of the author and do not reflect the official position of the Department of Defense, the Defense Center of Excellence, or any individual military service.

Thus, one should not draw firm conclusions from such limited data regarding female suicides. What it does suggest, however, is that further research is needed to examine more thoroughly suicide rates among female and male service members during deployment and on their return home.

POTENTIAL MILITARY SUICIDE RISK FACTORS

Suicide data in the military indicate three primary risk factors associated with those who died by suicide: *relationship*, *legal*, and *financial troubles* (U.S. Department of Defense [DoD], 2010).

The Centers for Disease Control (CDC) has identified potential risk factors associated with civilian suicides. These factors focus on family history and social situations, as well as access to care and lethal weapons. Such risk factors include prior suicide attempts, a family history of suicide or child maltreatment, history of mental health disorders (especially depression) or substance abuse, feelings of hopelessness, aggressive tendencies, other local suicides, isolation from others, social/occupational/financial losses, physical illness, access to lethal weapons, and failure to seek help (Centers for Disease Control [CDC], 2007). Social workers and providers conducting suicide risk assessments among service members should have a thorough understanding of civilian suicide risk factors as well as those associated with military suicides. Moreover, suicide assessments with service members should include a thorough examination of both civilian and military-specific risk factors.

Potential suicide protective factors have also been identified in the civilian population and are believed to be promising for the military community (see Figure 14.1). Comparison of military and civilian protective factors indicates that family and community support are potentially key aspects that might help prevent suicide deaths. As such, social workers working with suicidal service members should aim to provide family members with necessary information about utilizing self-care strategies (e.g., integrated health strategies such as deep breathing, meditation, or guided imagery) to

- Effective clinical care for mental, physical, and substance abuse disorders
- Easy access to a variety of clinical interventions and support for help seeking
- Family and community support (connectedness)
- Support from ongoing medical and mental health care relationships
- Skills in problem solving, conflict resolution, and nonviolent ways of handling disputes
- Cultural and religious beliefs that discourage suicide and support instincts for self-preservation
- Restricted access to lethal means
- Frustration tolerance and ability to regulate emotions

Figure 14.1 Suicide protective factors
Source: U.S. Public Health Service (1999).

help manage and regulate their own emotions and be better prepared to assist an at-risk service member. Social workers should also engage in psychoeducation strategies with family members to provide information about recognizing potential suicide warning signs, restricting access to weapons, and intervening and assisting service members with obtaining help from trained, mental health providers. Such action will not only equip individual family members with self-help tools, but also provide tools to potentially help service members and prevent suicide deaths.

MILITARY SUICIDE PREVENTION GAPS

The breadth of military suicide prevention programs, efforts, and initiatives is vast. Identifying and understanding key prevention gaps within these programs can critically inform how social workers engage in clinical practice with military members. Such knowledge of military prevention efforts and gaps provides a rich, contextual background for providing clinical care to service members. Summarized below are key gaps recent review efforts have identified within the Department of Defense (DoD) suicide programs. The brief summary provided here is based on three major reviews: (1) *The DoD Task Force Report on the Prevention of Suicide by Members of the Armed Forces* (U.S. DoD, 2010), (2) RAND's recent publication, *The War Within: Preventing Suicide in the U.S. Military* (RAND, 2011); and (3) the *Army Health Promotion, Risk Reduction, and Suicide Prevention Report 2010* (U.S. Army, 2010). The gaps identified in these reports focus on four main areas for improvement: (1) leadership involvement, (2) surveillance and research, (3) program access and quality of care, and (4) resilience and skill building. Knowledge of these gaps can help social workers understand how to better interact with military leadership, the importance of tracking key suicide risk variables in the event of a suicide death, which will help inform possible postsuicide review efforts, and the critical role that risk reduction and resilience building efforts play in preventing suicide deaths.

Leadership Focus

All of the earlier reports emphasize the role of military leaders in preventing suicide and their role in supporting service-specific and DoD-level prevention oversight programs. This commonality among the reports recognizes the importance that military leadership plays in suicide prevention and acknowledges that suicide prevention efforts in the military do not occur in a vacuum. Military leaders play a critical role in effecting culture change within their units and surrounding communities by encouraging and modeling help-seeking behaviors. When working with service members, it is necessary to take into account the larger military community in which the service member works to better understand the context of their behaviors. As such, working with military service members who are exhibiting suicidal behaviors, thoughts, or plans, social workers may want to reach out to the service members' unit leadership. Connecting with a key military unit leader, with the service member's permission, could allow the exchange of critical information about specific unit stressors and demands that might inform treatment planning and specific interventions. Such action can also inform military leadership about significant stressors that might be impacting other service members in the unit.

Surveillance and Research Focus

The DoD, Army, and RAND reports also recognize a clear need to improve and standardize surveillance and research efforts related to service member suicides. This would include the adoption and utilization of common nomenclature and reporting policies to allow for better tracking of military suicides and associated risk and protective factors. Social workers treating suicidal service members can play a critical role in advancing suicide surveillance and research efforts within the military. Identifying and tracking key risk factors discussed in this chapter, such as relationship, financial, and legal problems, as a routine part of clinical interventions could help inform military suicide review processes in the event of a suicide death.

Program Access and Quality of Care Focus

Access to quality care and reducing barriers to care were noted in all three reports as areas that are lacking within DoD-wide prevention efforts. The reports cite both insufficient quantity and quality of behavioral health providers, including social workers (U.S. Army, 2010; U.S. Public Health Service [PHS], 2009), noting that there are not enough providers available, nor are providers adequately trained in recognizing and responding appropriately to service members who are at risk for suicide (RAND, 2011; U.S. DoD, 2010). Social workers can play a critical role in closing this gap by working to continually improve their knowledge about risk and protective factors as well as military-specific demands and culture. Such action will further expand the existing provider base, potentially improving access to care and reducing the number of suicides.

Resilience and Skill-Building Focus

In each of the reports, resilience and skill-building efforts were recognized as potential means for preventing military suicides. Such a focus acknowledges that unique military-specific demands, which might potentially increase suicide risk among individual service members, could perhaps be mitigated by improving and fostering resiliency and coping skills or strategies (e.g., cognitive reframing). To this end, the reports recommend adopting a holistic approach to overall wellness, one which promotes the utilization of healthful behaviors (e.g., reduced alcohol intake, sleep hygiene, and exercise), and the development of life skills (e.g., problem solving, decision making, and money management skills).

Outlined in the next section of this chapter are specific steps that social workers can take to help build service member resilience within or outside of traditional clinical settings. Relying solely on traditional means of identifying and "treating" individuals who may be at risk for suicide limits one's reach to only those who present in a medical treatment facility. As indicated earlier, nearly half of those who die by suicide have not been seen by a mental health provider, suggesting that further outreach in the community to build resilience and skills is critically necessary in order to help prevent suicide deaths. Social workers who are trained to work within community settings are uniquely positioned to assist the military community in building resilience in service members in nontraditional settings.

BUILDING RESILIENCE: SUICIDE PREVENTION IN THE CONTEXT OF TOTAL FORCE FITNESS

This section focuses on the concepts and definitions of resilience and Total Force Fitness (TFF). Suicide prevention in the context of TFF is addressed from both theoretical and practical perspectives. Specific examples within each of the TFF domains are provided to highlight key steps social workers and other mental health professionals can take to help build resilience and potentially prevent suicides in the military.

What Is Resilience and Why Focus on It?

Traditionally, mental health care systems have focused on a deficits-based model as the primary method of identifying, assessing, and treating those in need. However, concepts such as competency, well-being, psychological fitness, and resilience have gained significant ground not just as theoretical psychological concepts, but as a mechanism to promote mental health. Accordingly, these concepts are increasingly being applied in general prevention efforts, which focus on a strengths-based approach to address a variety of psychological health conditions, including suicidal behaviors.

It is important to note that resilience is not a new concept. Rather, it has received considerable attention over the years (Garmezy, 1983; Masten, 2001, 2009). It has been defined as "positive mental health" (Jahoda, 1958), "effectance motivation" (White, 1955), "social competence" (Gladwin, 1967), "individual psychosocial competence" (Tyler, 1978), a personality trait such as hardiness (Kobasa, 1979), general "coping skills" (Pearlin & Schooler, 1982; see also Blechman & Culhane, 1983) and as "competence" (Gearon & Coursey, 1996), and "learned optimism" (Seligman, 1991). Despite the absence of a common definition or concrete measures of resilience, resilience-building has become a critical concept of mental health promotion and an emerging construct being applied by military researchers and leaders to better understand and prevent negative mental health outcomes. As mentioned previously, three recent reports from the DoD, the Army, and RAND note that well-being, skill building, and resilience are critical aspects of suicide prevention (RAND, 2011; PDUSD, 2008; U.S. Army, 2009, 2010; U.S. DoD, 2007, 2010). By identifying significant periods of stress and taking steps to bolster resilience beforehand, social workers can take a proactive role in preventing suicides.

What Is TFF and How Does It Relate to Resilience and Suicide Prevention?

Researchers and clinicians from military and civilian academic institutions developed the concept of TFF at the request of the Chairman of the Joint Chiefs of Staff (CJCS; Admiral Michael Mullen). The goal was to create an overarching model, applicable to all branches of military service, for developing a fit and ready force of service members who are resilient and less likely to experience adverse psychological outcomes, including suicide. TFF is comprised of eight domains within a mind-body framework, and leverages resources or skills within the individual, family, and organization (see Figure 14.2). Walter et al. (2010) have defined TFF as:

> A state in which the individual service member, family, and organization can sustain optimal well-being and performance under all conditions. It encompasses the whole person and is not merely the absence of disease or infirmity. (p. 103)

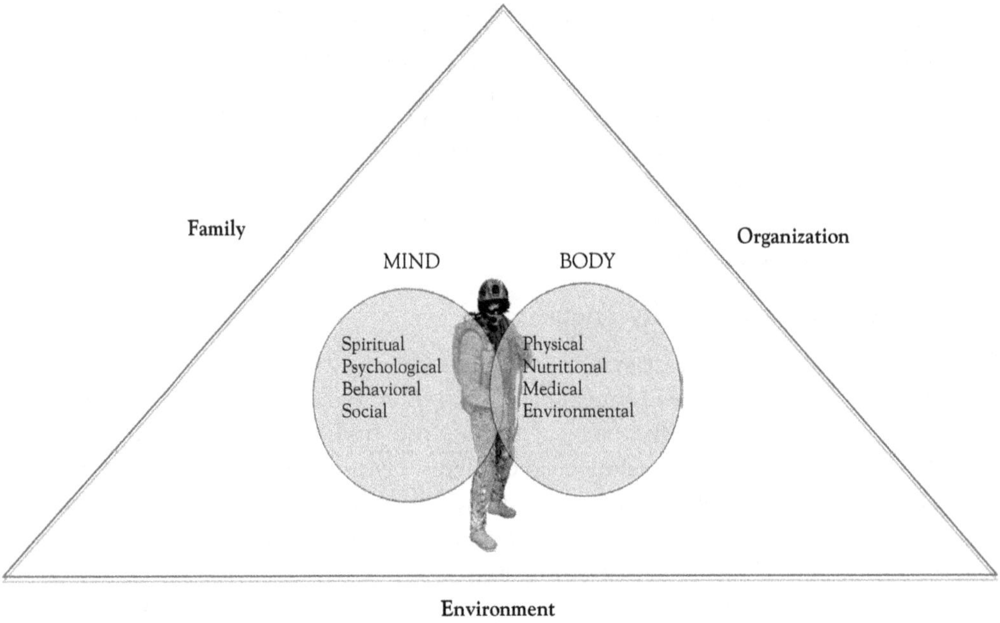

Figure 14.2 Total force fitness mind-body domains within the family, organization, and environment framework
Source: Jonas et al. (2010).

TFF has clear applications to promoting resilience among service members and can be used to inform clinical interventions by social workers. Recent guidance from the CJCS Admiral Mullen noted that TFF is a methodology for changing the way well-being is understood, assessed, and maintained. It represents a new way of approaching mental health for service members, family members, and civilians (Mullen, 2011) to improve mission readiness (CJCS Guidance, 2011) and overall health. Specifically, this concept recognizes the importance of focusing on healthful behaviors, practices, and interventions, and decreasing vulnerability to negative outcomes. The success of TFF in the military relies upon the belief that resilience (or well-being) *can be built or developed and that individuals can independently or with the assistance of social workers and other providers learn key skills that promote well-being.* As such, TFF is not an inherent, static characteristic. Rather, it is a malleable construct that can be enhanced with proper resources and support or threatened by excessive unmitigated demands and stressors. Each of the eight TFF domains has been described elsewhere in great detail (see Jonas et al., 2010). A brief description of each domain is provided below, along with relevant supporting research. Specific examples of how social workers and other providers can assist service members with learning specific skills within each domain to prevent suicide are discussed.

Medical Fitness

"Medical fitness is defined as a condition of mental and physical well-being as determined by medical metrics that establish prerequisites for individual mission accomplishment and worldwide deployability" (O'Connor Deuster, DeGroot, & White, 2010, p. 57).

Regulations are in place within each of the services that generally assess medical readiness for deployment, such as the Medical Profile system. Typically, service members are rated on a 1 to 4 scale across a number of variables, including psychological conditions, which determine a service member's deployment eligibility. Such a system could be expanded in military medical treatment facilities and outpatient clinics through the increased use of screenings for a variety of conditions, including population-wide screenings for suicidal ideation and known risk factors. This could be accomplished through existing programs, such as the Air Force's Behavioral Health Optimization Program (BHOP; see U.S. Air Force, 2002), in which service members are referred by their medical provider to receive further attention and intervention from behavioral health specialists (such as psychologists and social workers) who are embedded in the primary care setting. Moreover, social workers in their assessment of service members would do well to continually conduct suicide screenings as part of routine consultations to medical providers or incorporate this as a routine part of traditional treatment plans.

Other programs, such as Respect-Mil, could also be extended beyond screenings for PTSD and depression and include specific suicide screenings for known risk factors as well as protective factors. Service members scoring high on specific risk factors would then be provided with additional self-care information and referral and follow-up care. Such an effort could not only serve to reach service members who may not otherwise seek or be referred to a traditional mental health clinic, but also serve to destigmatize and normalize mental health interventions. These screenings would occur with all service members visiting a primary care setting at various known windows of risk, such as pre- and postdeployment. The screenings should not rely solely on self-reported information, but social workers and psychologists should also take into account observed objective criteria such as relationship/marital status, age, sex, weight, other medical conditions/illness, overall medical fitness, and associated risk taking behaviors.

Environmental Fitness

Environmental fitness has been defined as "the ability to perform mission-specific duties in any environment and withstand the multiple stressors of deployment and war" (O'Connor et al., 2010, p. 57). O'Connor et al. (2010) note that multiple deployment-specific stressors, such as changes in temperature and harsh living conditions, compound already extensive burdens on service members. Social workers providing care to service members who are about to deploy could provide educational materials about how to handle harsh environmental conditions and the importance of regular fluid intake and eating balanced, nutritional meals in counteracting the impact of extreme heat or cold. Such actions taken predeployment could potentially enhance the fitness of individual service members (as well as that of their overall unit) during deployment by preventing dehydration and maintaining optimal energy levels despite adverse conditions.

Psychological Fitness

Bates et al. (2010) defined psychological fitness as "the integration and optimization of mental, emotional, and behavioral abilities and capacities to optimize performance and strengthen the resilience of warfighters" (p. 21). To understand how psychological fitness is developed, they propose a Military Demand-Resource Model, which focuses on three main components: (1) demands placed on the service members, (2) a resource environment comprised of internal and external aspects, and (3) outcomes. Psychological fitness outcomes can be either positive or negative, resulting in resilience or in the development of mental health problems, as well as significant difficulty dealing with the deployment challenges that could result in suicidal behaviors or a suicide death.

To better understand how psychological fitness is developed or sustained, Bates et al. (2010) propose a "Military Demand-Resource Model," comprised of internal factors such as coping skills, awareness/appraisals/beliefs, and engagement. (Engagement involves being fully involved with activities with a sense of purpose.) Such factors have been associated with having a positive impact of reducing or eliminating feelings of hopelessness, where hopelessness has been associated with higher rates of depression and suicide rates among civilians (see Defilippis et al., 2008). In fact, Bates et al. (2010) propose that one of the key operational outcomes to examine as an indicator of psychological fitness is the number of suicide deaths in the military services. This connection highlights a strong theoretical association between improved psychological fitness (i.e., resilience) and the reduction in vulnerability to die by suicide. The extent to which existing and future military programs focus on aspects that increase psychological fitness may determine the military's success in lowering suicide deaths among service members.

Social workers and other providers working with service members at risk for suicide have a clear role in helping to promote individual psychological fitness. Whether through direct patient care or population-based educational classes, providing information about what cognitive skills are, as well as how and when to use such skills, could help build psychological fitness within service members. Specifically, social workers could educate service members on cognitive skills such as reframing or cognitive restructuring, which are cognitive behavioral techniques that help individuals refocus negative, maladaptive, and unhelpful thoughts and responses to adaptive realistic, and more positive cognitions. Individuals could be taught to (1) become aware of and recognize distorted or faulty cognitions (see Burns, 1980), (2) to understand the importance of challenging such negative thoughts, and (3) to replace such unhelpful thoughts with ones that are more adaptive and realistic. The extent to which service members effectively learn and utilize such techniques on a regular basis will better prepare them to cope when problematic situations arise.

Nutritional Fitness

As defined by Montain et al. (2010), nutritional fitness is comprised of three components: (1) dietary quality, (2) specific nutritional requirements, and (3) healthy food choices. Such components are identified as being key elements to physical health and the prevention of health problems. Maintaining weight by engaging in healthful eating practices and not overusing dietary supplements can be influenced by unit leaders serving as role models in eating balanced meals, providing adequate time to eat meals during training, and providing educational opportunities about healthful eating habits outside what is offered in military-mandated weight management programs. Research has long shown that maintaining a healthy weight and proper food intake are related to overall improvements in physical health (Blair & Morris, 2009). Research also shows that positive mental health outcomes, such as decreases in depressive symptoms, are linked to healthy weight management through proper eating habits, nutrition, and exercise (Conn, 2010; Deslandes et al., 2009; Donnelly et al., 2009; Goldberg & King, 2007).

Behavioral Fitness

Bray, Spira, Olmsted, and Hout (2010) defined behavioral fitness as "the relationship between one's behaviors and their positive or negative health outcomes" (p. 39). Behavioral components related to this TFF domain include sleep hygiene, proper substance use, and coping behaviors. Bray et al. (2010) note that the Army and Marine Corps had the highest rates of heavy alcohol users as defined by five or more drinks, per occasion, on a weekly basis, in the 30 days prior to being surveyed, according to the 2008 DoD Survey of Health Related Behaviors Among Active Duty Personnel. Substance abuse has also been noted as a potential risk factor in the Army Report (U.S. Army, 2010) on suicide. Thus, reducing alcohol use represents a direct way to promote healthful behaviors and an indirect way of potentially preventing a factor believed to be associated with suicide and potentially suicide related deaths. As such, identifying and providing support to service members engaging in high-risk behaviors (e.g., substance misuse) by applying targeted substance abuse reduction strategies can help reduce vulnerabilities and improve soldier resilience (U.S. Army, 2010).

Social Fitness

Social fitness refers to social support, task and social cohesion, and a sense of belonging (Coulter, Lester, & Yarvis, 2010). Although social support and social cohesion are self-explanatory, MacCoun (1993) defines task cohesion "as the shared commitment among members to achieving a goal that requires the collective efforts of the group" (p. 291). The concept of social fitness is probably one of the most critical components of TFF, as research shows that the majority of active duty service members rely on family or friends to cope with stress (Bray et al., 2006).

A number of studies in the civilian population have also highlighted the importance of social support, showing that social support reduces the likelihood of developing mental health problems (Bonanno, Galea, Bucciarelli, & Vlahove, 2007; Resick, 2001), improves positive behavior changes (Groh, Jason, & Keys, 2008), prevents negative outcomes (Grenier, Darte, Heber, & Richardson, 2007), and promotes wellness and overall quality of life (Solomon, 2004). Similar results have been found for service members with PTSD (Brewin, Andrews, & Valentine, 2000). Theoretical models of competency and resilience have shown that social support or supportive networks are key factors to developing and maintaining competency (Blechman & Culhane, 1993; Gladwin, 1967; Tyler, 1978), as well as serving as protective factors against mental health problems. A reasonable conclusion in terms of suicide prevention in the military services is to ensure that military members have a sense of belonging and have an active social network within and outside the military in which information, resources, and advice can be exchanged in times of distress or calm.

Two examples of existing social support concepts that can be leveraged by social workers and others working with service members are the "Battle Buddy" and "Wingman" constructs in the Army and Air Force, respectively. These concepts focus on encouraging service members to partner with a fellow service member as a means of "looking out" for each other during their initial military training and during deployment. Social workers can use these concepts to appeal to service members and emphasize the importance of reaching out to a Battle Buddy or Wingman in times of stress not only during initial military training or deployments, but also throughout their time in service to engage social activities.

Physical Fitness

The physical fitness domain of TFF refers to the strength, endurance, flexibility, and physical mobility of service members (Roy, Springer, McNulty, & Butler, 2010). Regular exercise or other means of physical activity is not only related to improved overall physical health, but also improved mental health. Specifically, within the behavioral health arena, physical activity has long been recognized and recommended as an effective nonmedical means of preventing and treating depression (Craighead, Craighead, & Ilardi, 1998; Mazzucchelli, Kane, & Rees, 2010). Clinical research has shown that physical exercise helps to balance mood, maintain healthy weight, improve self-image and self-esteem, reduce depressive symptoms (Dunn et al., 2005) and reduce anxiety. As such, social workers who are working with service members who may be at risk for suicide could incorporate into their treatment plans routine physical exercise schedules or recommend the use of personal trainers to help develop more in-depth exercise plans.

Spiritual Fitness

Although Hufford, Fritts, and Rhodes (2010) define spiritual fitness as a complex concept comprised of seven (somewhat overlapping) components: (1) spiritual beliefs that focus on the nonphysical aspects of life such as belief in the human spirit; (2) spiritual values that focus on morality and ethics; (3) spiritual practices that include mind-body techniques; (4) core beliefs about purpose and meaning; (5) self-awareness that focuses on reflection and introspection; (6) transcendence of relationships beyond the self, which focus on connections to a larger purpose and meaning in life; and (7) exceptional spiritual experiences. Key aspects of spiritual fitness appear to be directly related to suicide prevention (Koenig, McCullough, & Larson, 2001, as cited in Hufford et al., 2010). Components of spiritual fitness such as core beliefs about an individual's purpose and transcendence beyond the self, with a focus on connectedness to others and to a larger purpose (CDC, 2010b), could be emphasized in suicide prevention training and in family interventions with service members.

To build spiritual fitness among service members, social workers could use existing service-specific concepts, such as the "Soldier's Creed" and the "Airman's Creed" to help service members relate specific military job duties to a larger purpose and develop a specific mission-related focus. These concepts incorporate aspects related to spiritual fitness by emphasizing the need for service members to focus on "service before self," being "a member of team" and "placing the mission first." Fostering a greater sense of belonging and helping service members identify a higher purpose of their routine military activities during deployments and redeployments (i.e., returning home) is a potential method of reducing feelings of hopelessness, isolation, and helplessness, which are associated with suicide deaths.

Family Fitness

Military family fitness is an emerging construct associated with TFF (Westphal & Woodward, 2010). The Military Family Fitness Model (MFFM), being developed by Bowles, Moore, Cato, and Pollock (2011), is a "process oriented, multi-level systems model for service members, families, leaders, policy makers, and program managers to see how family fitness can be achieved/maintained" (p. 8). Drawing on the Military Demand-Resource Model (Bates et al., 2010), the MFFM rests on the assumption that families have individual, family, and organizational resources available to draw on in response to military-specific and other family demands. As such, social workers could help service members and their families develop and utilize a variety of resources in the individual domain (e.g., coping skills), the family domain (e.g., communication and decision-making skills), and the community domain (e.g., family-readiness groups). The purpose of building skills within these areas is to improve the overall fitness of the family, which in turn strengthens the fitness of the service member. Expected outcomes, as proposed in the MFFM, are reduced adverse impacts such as family violence, psychological health problems, and suicide.

Examples of Resilience and Family Fitness Programs in the Military

The Army, Air Force, Navy, and Marine Corps have policies in place that appear to support a holistic view of preventing suicide and are consistent with the concept of TFF. Each service-specific program is briefly described later. These programs provide excellent examples of community prevention efforts that social workers and other health care providers could refer to as concrete models or examples of comprehensive approaches to help prevent suicide deaths among service members.

The Army's "Comprehensive Soldier Fitness" (CSF) program was launched in 2009. CSF is key example of a military-specific program that addresses several TFF domains: physical, social emotional, spiritual, and family well-being. The goals of the programs are to enhance both soldier and family fitness and build resilience (Land, 2010; http://csf.army.mil/index.html). CSF uses the Global Assessment Tool, an index developed specifically for the Army to assess functioning in soldiers as well as their families. Although the program's intent is to build resilience, it is also likely to have an indirect effect on preventing suicide. Although, additional research is needed to examine the exact impact of this effort within the Army in preventing suicide deaths, its emphasis on building resilience within service members represents a new wave of thought within the Army (as well as other services) that focuses on prevention.

Similar to the Army's CSF program is the Air Force's "Comprehensive Airman Fitness" program. This program, which was launched within the Air Combat Command in 2010 and later expanded to the Air Mobility Command, focuses on helping Air Force members and their families engage in self-care and encouraging Air Force members to reach out to others for help. The program focuses on four key areas: (1) physical, (2) social, (3) mental, and (4) spiritual wellness. It relies upon educating Air Force members and family members about connecting and communicating with leaders, peers, and immediate and extended family members; celebrating large or small accomplishments or successes; committing to a mission that is either personal or work-related; and caring for yourself and others, as well as subordinates.

Military Suicide Prevention Programs

Although there are number of suicide prevention guides within the military, one notable guide is that of the Air Force, *U.S. Air Force Guide for Managing Suicidal Behaviors: Strategies, Resources, and Tools* (U.S. Air Force, 2004). This evidence-based guide provides information to psychologists, social workers, related professionals, and leaders for managing suicidal service members. The Air Force guide has been recognized by the American Association of Suicidologists as an outstanding contribution in preventing suicide, as it provides details about specific risk factors, information sharing and tracking, suicide risk assessment and management, key recommendations for managing suicidal behaviors, and addresses issues related to continuity of care and coordination are listed in Figure 14.3. Such key features in the Air Force guide are consistent with the RAND (2011), U.S. DoD (2010), and U.S. Army (2010) reports on suicide in the military, which all call for improved training and guidance on risk assessment, surveillance, and management. Social workers working with military personnel should familiarize themselves with key concepts from this guide to become of aware of key approaches the Air Force is taking to address suicide risk.

For the Navy and the Marine Corps, the Operations Stress Control (OSC) and Combat Operational Control (COSC) programs (http://www.usmc-mccs.org/cosc/) are largely aligned with the TFF framework. Key components of COSC focus on psychological health and building resilience among sailors and Marines, as well as their families. COSC (http://navynavstress.com) is a leader-led initiative with support from sailors and Marines, peers and health care providers, such as social workers, psychologists, and paraprofessionals. COSC is designed to assist with preventing, identifying, and treating combat-related stress reactions and is offered before, during, and after deployment. While COSC focuses largely on combat stress, suicide prevention is also generally addressed in that the program encourages sailors and Marines to seek help when needed in the face of significant stressors. Help-seeking behavior for suicidal ideations is a consistent theme across the services that social workers can capitalize on even after a service member is engaged in treatment.

Two hallmark features of COSC program are the Operational Stress Control and Readiness (OSCAR) program and the Marine Operational Stress Training (MOST) program. The OSCAR program provides three key supports: (1) structured peer support and senior mentors, which provide information about COSC as well as where to seek help; (2) trained behavioral health and medical providers as well as chaplains, who are embedded in the units and provide basic counseling and spiritual guidance; and (3) credentialed mental health providers, who are trained to provide more in-depth support in cases of significant stress or dysfunction. MOST training is provided for leaders, family members, and Marines and focuses on family reintegration, information about potential postdeployment stressors, and ways in which to cope with such issues or be a supportive leader or family member.

COSC, OSCAR, and MOST emphasize concepts consistent with the TFF domains of social, family, behavioral, psychological, and spiritual fitness. For example, these programs stress peer and family support, proper sleep habits/hygiene, "adaptive coping" to promote "optimal functioning and personal well-being" (United States Marine Corps, 2010, pp. 1–9). Existing elements of these programs could be leveraged further to educate sailors and Marines about suicide risk factors in addition to the psychoeducation components already

Category	Recommendation
Assessment of Suicide Risk	Formally assess suicide at every initial evaluation, and as clinically indicated at follow-up contacts. Use appropriate measures to assess suicidality.
A Decision-Making Framework	Determine suicide risk level based on assessment information and match to appropriate suicide-specific interventions.
Outpatient Management Strategies	Specifically target suicidal symptoms and risk factors in the formal outpatient treatment plan. Take steps to safeguard the environment; limit accessibility to means of self-harm. Establish processes for ongoing monitoring of suicide risk. Use management strategies that are uniquely applicable to active duty members.
Documentation Strategies	When documenting a suicide risk assessment, include both current and historical risk factors, observations from the session, rationale for actions taken or considered but not taken, and follow-up plans, including a response plan when there is evidence of increased suicidality.
Coordinating with Inpatient Care	Establish a process for coordination when patients are hospitalized. Reassess a patient's needs (including suicidality) following inpatient or partial hospitalization before assuming or reassuming responsibility for outpatient care.
Clinic Support and Peer Consultation	Use a high-interest log as a clinic tracking procedure for suicidality and share information between relevant specialty mental health clinics. Consult professional peers regularly regarding suicidal patients and document the consultation.
Ensuring Continuity of Care	Use a standardized follow-up and referral procedure for all previously suicidal patients dropping out of treatment prematurely. Ensure clinical coverage when the primary provider is unavailable. Establish a procedure for ensuring continuity of care during provider and patient transitions.
Links With the Community	Establish a written plan for after-hours evaluations. Ensure other relevant agencies and individuals (i.e., Security Forces, First Sergeants, etc.) are aware of the plan. Mental health providers and staff are the primary resource within the base community regarding mental health issues; as such, they should serve as consultants to unit leadership regarding the management of at-risk personnel. Use community support resources in managing suicidal behavior.

Figure 14.3 U.S. Air Force suicide management recommendations
Source: U.S. Air Force Guide for Managing Suicidal Behaviors: Strategies, Resources, and Tools (2004).

embedded into the programs, which provide information on healthy coping strategies and behaviors. In short, programs such as COSC, OSCAR, and MOST highlight the importance of mitigating psychological health problems by enhancing components related to TFF. Additional research is critically needed to empirically determine which, if any, of the key COSC components are associated with reduced suicide risks and greater resilience.

One of the most promising evidenced-based examples of a family-oriented resilience curriculum is "Families OverComing Under Stress" (FOCUS; www.focusproject.org/home). FOCUS (which is described further in Chapter 24) aims to mitigate stressors of deployment and improve family reintegration and reunion postdeployment. The extent to which these outcomes are born out will likely have a significant impact on suicide deaths among service members and families. As such, FOCUS represents a key opportunity to educate family members about suicide risk and resilience factors and incorporate additional resilience components based on the TFF concepts directly into existing training modules.

DISCUSSION

To better understand the content presented in this chapter, the following discussion highlights a two-pronged approach to potentially prevent suicide. This approach involves (1) identifying suicide risk factors, which have been described in this chapter, and (2) addressing known risk factors by focusing on TFF domains and key interventions. The suicide prevention strategies in this approach are not exhaustive. Instead, they supplement existing best practices in suicide prevention interviewing and intervention strategies (e.g., properly and thoroughly assessing family history of suicidal behavior, limiting or addressing access to lethal weapons when suicidal ideation is present, and inquiring about past suicide attempts).

Case Vignette: Airman First Class Jones

Airman First Class Jones was in a 4-month relationship with his supervisor's spouse. On his supervisor's return from deployment, the supervisor learned of the relationship and threatened to expose the Airman "for adultery" and "ruin his career." Distraught and believing that his career was over and that he would be "kicked out of the military," he began drinking heavily to lessen his worries. He began worrying more, became depressed, and eating less because "he didn't feel like eating." He was withdrawn from family members, friends, and co-workers, and eventually stopped altogether "hanging out" with his friends. He felt overwhelming guilt for having begun an affair with the spouse of a man who was deployed "risking his life for his country." He feared that if his unit found out, "he would never live down the guilt and shame" of his actions. He was sleeping only 4 to 5 hours a night, was showing up late for work, having extreme difficulty concentrating on routine tasks, and he appeared sad and despondent nearly all the time. After drinking heavily over a long holiday weekend, the Airman took his personal side arm and fatally shot himself in the head.

Identify Risk Factors

As shown in the Case Vignette: Airman First Class Jones, a number of critical risk factors are portrayed. For example, the Airman was experiencing a number of depressive symptoms (such as depressed mood, decreased sleep, poor appetite, trouble concentrating, difficulties at work, and withdrawing from activities with friends). He was also engaged in several high-risk behaviors and was exposed to a number of potential stressors, to include drinking heavily, and being engaged in a relationship with another service member's spouse, who also happened to be his supervisor in his chain of command. Additionally, the Airman had access to a personal firearm, which was apparently not registered or stored in the base armory.

Bolster Protective Factors

The second part of this approach involves addressing known risk factors by bolstering protective factors. Using a number of TFF concepts such as *medical, psychological, behavioral,* and *social fitness*, specific protective factors are identified, which could be addressed and bolstered by providers, commanders, and family members to potentially help reduce suicides. The TFF concepts, along with specific prevention efforts, are described below.

TFF Domains and Possible Intervention/Prevention Recommendations

Medical fitness. The excessive alcohol use depicted in this vignette may have been noticed by someone in the Airman's chain of command or at home by family or friends. During routine medical appointments or on the recommendation of a commander, routine screening at a medical treatment facility regarding the Airman's alcohol use may have indicated the need for follow-up or referral for additional services or potential immediate intervention. For social workers and other providers, inquiring about service members' alcohol intake (as well as other substances) should be a routine part of ongoing treatment or assessments.

Psychological fitness. The Airman began worrying and drinking more, to reduce his anxiety and worry and cope with his depressive symptoms. Such worries, along with the excessive guilt and shame he was experiencing, were likely related to his fears about others in his unit learning of his relationship with his supervisor's spouse and what fellow Airmen would think about him if they found out that he began the affair while his boss was deployed. Moreover, he was worried that he would be "kicked out" out of the military for his actions, believing that he had violated military law or code of conduct. Psychological fitness, as described earlier in this chapter involves being aware of unreasonable cognitions, and having the skills and abilities to challenge distorted thoughts.

Providing service members with cognitive tools, such as cognitive reframing, either before or after negative events such as this occur, could help individuals accurately appraise situations and circumstances and prevent extreme adverse behaviors such as a suicide attempt or death. Rather than jumping to unreasonable or extreme conclusions and believing irrational, unwarranted, negative thoughts (i.e., "my career is over" or "the other Airmen in my unit will despise me if they find out what I've done"), cognitive reframing skills could have helped this Airman potentially appraise his situation entirely differently. Instead of believing that he had done something shameful that warranted death, reframing skills might have helped him understand that, although his actions were not necessarily respectful of his boss or terribly beneficial to him in the long run, other less severe outcomes were possible. Although it is likely that his chain of command might speak with him about poor judgment for engaging in a relationship with his supervisor's spouse, as a junior person in the situation and having no legal relationship to his boss or his boss's spouse, it would be extremely unlikely that the military would have taken any steps to "end his career." This simple realization that his career would not be ended prematurely or that others in his unit might not even care about his actions with his supervisor's wife might have made a difference in preventing the Airman from taking his life.

Behavioral fitness. Difficulty sleeping, decreased appetite, and excessive alcohol intake are three key behaviors in the vignette the Airman displayed. The Army Report (U.S. Army, 2009) and the DoD TFR (U.S. DoD, 2010) note that alcohol misuse is a key risky behavior associated with many military suicides. Observation of daily behaviors is one of the benefits afforded to many military commanders as well as family members and friends. Whether leaders (or others) in his chain of command noted the Airman in this vignette was arriving late to work, having difficulty concentrating on routine tasks, or that he appeared fatigued at work is unknown. However, taking note of significant changes in behavioral patterns at work or home such as alcohol consumption, or changes in eating and sleeping habits and encouraging individuals to practice good sleep hygiene, moderate alcohol intake (or seek medical intervention), and eat healthy meals represent simple, but potentially critical steps in reducing one's risk for suicide.

Social fitness. The Airman in this example had become withdrawn from family, friends, and co-workers. Eventually he stopped "hanging out with friends" altogether. Someone may have noticed this and perhaps asked if everything was okay, thus providing an opportunity for the Airman to talk about what was going on and providing an opportunity to discuss the Airman's behaviors, thoughts, and feelings. Moreover, engaging in regular social activities with friends or family members might also be a way to not only provide opportunities for the Airman to focus on other events besides the negative interaction he had with his supervisor, but also an opportunity for someone to notice the various risk factors he was experiencing and for the Airman to talk about his experiences and receive support from his social network.

CONCLUSION

In conclusion, social workers need to be aware of military-specific and other factors that might increase a service member's risk for suicide. It is even more important to be aware of skills that service members can engage in to help reduce known risk factors associated with suicide deaths. The extent to which social workers and other mental health providers are aware of these risk factors and preventative resilience building skills, such as those outlined in the TFF model, could potentially save a service member's life. Addressing these risk factors through the promotion of TFF concepts that build resilience can further enhance existing suicide prevention efforts

CHAPTER DISCUSSION QUESTIONS

1. What military-specific risk factors should be considered when working with service members who might be at risk for suicide?
2. What are some of the shared suicide risk factors for civilians and military service members?
3. How could Total Force Fitness concepts be applied to individuals who might be at risk for suicide?

REFERENCES

Bates, M. J., Bowles, S., Hammermeister, J., Stokes, C., Pinder, E., Moore, M., . . . Burbelo, G. (2010). Psychological fitness. *Military Medicine, 175*(8), 21–38.

Blair, S. N., & Morris, J. N. (2009). Healthy hearts—And the universal benefits of being physically active: Physical activity and health. *Annals of Epidemiology, 19*(4), 253–256.

Blechman, E., & Culhane, S. (1983). Aggressive, depressive and prosocial coping with affective challenges in early adolescence. *Journal of Early Adolescence, 13*(4), 361–382.

Bonanno, G. A., Galea, S., Bucciarelli, A., & Vlahov, D. (2007). What predicts psychological resilience after disaster? The role of demographics, resources, and life stress. *Journal of Consulting and Clinical Psychology, 75*(5), 671–682.

Bowles, S., Moore, M., Cato, C., & Pollock, E. (2011, April 27). *Military family fitness model.* Presented at Forging the Partnership: 2011 DoD/USDA Family Resilience Conference, Chicago, Illinois.

Bray, R., Hourani, L., Olmstead, K., Witt, M., Brown, J., Pemberton, M., . . . Hayden, D. (2006). *2005 department of defense survey of health related behaviors among active duty military personnel: A component of the defense lifestyle assessment program* (DLAP). Research Triangle Park, NC: Research Triangle Institute.

Bray, R. M., Spira, J. L., Olmsted, K. R., & Hout, J. J. (2010, August). Behavioral and occupational fitness. *Military Medicine, 175*(8), 39–56.

Brewin, C. Andrews, B., & Valentine, J. (2000). Meta-analysis of risk factors for posttraumatic stress disorder in trauma-exposed adults. *Journal of Consulting and Clinical Psychology,* 68, 748–766.

Burns, D. (1980). *Feeling good: The new mood therapy.* New York, NY: Avon Books.

CDC. (2007). *Suicide prevention. Scientific information: Risk and protective factors.* National Center for Injury Prevention and Control, Division of Violence Prevention. Retrieved from http://www.cdc.gov/ncipc/dvp/suicide/Suicide-risk-p-factors.htm

CDC. (2007). Centers for Disease Control and Prevention. *Web-based injury statistics query and reporting system* (WISQARS) [Online]. National Center for Injury Prevention and Control, Centers for Disease Control and Prevention (producer). Retrieved from http://www.cdc.gov/injury/wisqars/LeadingCauses.html

CDC. (2010b). *Preventing suicide: A program activities guide. National Center for Injury Prevention and Control. Division of Violence Prevention.* Retrieved from http://www.cdc.gov/ncipc/dvp/preventingsuicide.htm

Chairman of the Joint Chiefs of Staff. (2011). *CJCS guidance 2011.* Retrieved from http://www.jcs.mil/content/files/2011–01/011011165132 CJCS Annual Guidance_2011.pdf

Conn, V. S. (2010). Depressive symptom outcomes of physical activity interventions: Meta-analysis findings. *Annals of Behavioral Medicine, 39*(2), 128–138.

Coulter, I., Lester, P., & Yarvis, J. (2010). Social fitness. *Military Medicine, 175*(8S), 88–96.

Craighead, W. E., Craighead, L. W., & Ilardi, S. (1998). Psychosocial treatments for major depressive disorder. In P. E. Gorman & J. M Gorman (Eds.), *A guide to treatments that work* (pp. 226–239). New York, NY: Oxford University Press.

Defilippis, S., Erbuto, D., Gentili, F., Innamorati, M., Lester, D., Tatarelli, R., . . . Pompili, M. (2008). Mental turmoil, suicide risk, illness perception, and temperament, and their impact on quality of life in chronic daily headache. *Journal of Headache and Pain*, 9, 349–357.

Deslandes, A., Moraes, H., Ferreira, C., Veiga, H., Silveira, H., Mouta, R., . . . Laks, J. (2009). Exercise and mental health: Many reasons to move. *Neuropsychobiology*, *59*(4), 191–198.

Donnelly, J. E., Blair, S. N., Jakicic, J. M., Manore, M. M., Rankin, J. W., & Smith, B. K. (2009). Appropriate physical activity intervention strategies for weight loss and prevention of weight regain for adults. *Medicine and Science in Sports and Exercise*, *41*(2), 459–471.

Dunn, A. L., Trivedi, M. H., Kampert, J. B., Camillia, G., Clark, C. G., & Chambliss, H. (2005). Exercise treatment for depression: Efficacy and dose response. *American Journal of Preventive Medicine*, *28*(1), 1–8.

Garmezy, N. (1983). Stressors of childhood. In N. Garmezy & M. Rutter (Eds.), *Stress, coping, and development in children* (pp. 43–84). New York, NY: McGraw-Hill.

Gearon, J. S., & Coursey, R. (1996). *Defining competency among people with schizophrenia: An exploratory study*. Unpublished dissertation, University of Maryland, College Park, Maryland.

Gladwin, T. (1967). Social competence and clinical practice. *Psychiatry*, *30*, 30–34.

Goldberg, J. H., & King, A. C. (2007). Physical activity and weight management across the lifespan. *Annual Review of Public Health*, *28*, 145–170.

Grenier, S., Darte, K., Heber, A., & Richardson, D. (2007). The operational stress injury social support program: a peer support program in collaboration between the Canadian Forces and Veterans Affairs Canada. In C. Figley & W. Nash (Eds.), *Combat stress injury: Theory, research, and management* (pp. 261–293). New York, NY: Routledge.

Groh, D. R., Jason, L. A., & Keys, C. B. (2008). Social network variables in Alcoholics Anonymous: A literature review. *Clinical Psychology Review*, *28*(3), 430–459. Retrieved from http://www.ncbi.nlm.nih.gov/pmc/articles/PMC2289871/pdf/nihms43350.pdf

Hufford, D. J., Fritts, M. J., & Rhodes, J. E. (2010). Spiritual fitness. *Military Medicine*, *175*(8), 73–87.

Jahoda, M. (1958). *Current concepts of positive mental health*. New York, NY: Basic Books.

Jonas, W. B., O'Connor, F. G., Deuster, P., Peck, J., Shake, C., & Frost, S.S. (2010). Why total force fitness? *Military Medicine*, *175*(8), 6–13.

Kobasa, S. C. (1979). Stressful life events, personality and health: An enquiry into hardiness. *Journal of Personality and Social Psychology*, *37*(1), 1–11.

Koenig H. G., McCullough M.E., & Larson D.B. (2001). *Handbook of religion and health*. Oxford: Oxford University Press.

Land, B. (2010). Current department of defense guidance for total force fitness. *Military Medicine*, *175*(8), 3–5.

Luxton, D., Skopp, N., Kinn, J., Bush, N., Reger, M., & Gahm, G. (2009). *Department of Defense suicide event report (DODSER) calendar year 2009 annual report*; National Center for Telehealth & Technology (T2); Defense Centers of Excellence for Psychological Health & Traumatic Brain Injury (DCoE). Retrieved from http://t2health.org/programs-surveillance.html#dodser

MacCoun, R. J. (1993). Unit cohesion and military performance. In *National defense research institute, sexual orientation and U.S. military personnel policy: Policy options and assessment* (pp. 283–331). Santa Monica, CA: RAND.

Masten, A. S. (2001). Ordinary magic: Resilience processes in development. *American Psychologist, 56*, 227–238.

Masten, A. S. (2009). Ordinary magic: Lessons from research on resilience in human development. *Education Canada, 49*(3), 28–32.

Mazzucchelli, T. G., Kane, R. T., & Rees, C. S. (2010). Behavioral activation interventions for well-being: A meta-analysis. *Journal of Positive Psychology, 5*(2), 105–121

Montain, S. J., Carvey C.E., & Stephens, M. B. (2010). Nutritional fitness. *Military Medicine*, 8(65), 65–72.

Mullen, M. (2011). On total force fitness in war and peace. *Military Medicine, 175*(8), 1–2.

O'Connor, F. G., Deuster, P. A., DeGroot, D. W., & White, D. W. (2010). Medical and environmental fitness. *Military Medicine, 175*(8), 57–64.

Pearlin, L., & Schooler, C. (1982). The structure of coping. *Journal of Health and Social Behavior*, 9, 2–21.

PDUSD. (2008, March 3). *PDUSD P&R memo: Well-being of the force indicators*. Retrieved from http://www.tricare.mil/tma/ddrp/documents/2008.03.03%20Well%20Being%20of%20the%20Force%20Indicators.pdf

RAND. (2011). Ramchand, R., Acosta, J., Burns, R., Jaycox, L., & Pernin, C. *The war within: Preventing suicides in the U.S. military*. Santa Monica, CA: RAND.

Resick, P. A. (2001). *Stress and trauma*. Hove, United Kingdom: Psychology Press.

Robins, S. (2011, March 25). Study: Women three times as suicide-prone while deployed. *Army Stars and Stripes*. Retrieved from http://www.stripes.com/news/special-reports/suicide-in-the-military/study-women-three-times-as-suicide-prone-while-deployed-1.138885?localLinksEnabled=false

Roy, T., Springer, B. A., McNulty, V., & Butler, N. (2010). Physical fitness. *Military Medicine, 175*(8), 14–20.

Seligman, M. (1991). *Learned optimism: How to change your mind and your life*. New York, NY: Knopf.

Solomon, P. (2004). Peer support/peer provided services: Underlying process, benefits and critical ingredients. *Psychiatric Rehabilitation Journal, 27*(4), 392–401. Retrieved from www.parecovery.org/documents/solomon_peer_support.pdf

Tyler, F. (1978). Individual psychosocial competency: A personality configuration. *Education and Psychological Measurement*, 38, 209–323.

U.S. Air Force. (2002, March). *Primary behavioral health care services practice manual, version 2.0*. Retrieved from http://www.integratedprimarycare.com/Air%20Force%20Manual/primary%20care%20practice%20manual.pdf

U.S. Air Force (2004). *Guide for managing suicidal behaviors: Strategies, resources, and tools*. Washington, DC: Air Force Medical Operations Agency, Population Health Support Division. Retrieved from www.health.mil/dhb/mhtf/mhtf-report-final.pdf

U.S. Army. (2009). *2009 Army posture statement: Comprehensive soldier fitness information paper*. Retrieved from http://www.army.mil/aps/09/information_papers/comprehensive_soldier_fitness_program.html

U.S. Army. (2010). Army suicide prevention task force. *Army health promotion risk reduction suicide prevention report 2010*. Retrieved from http://usarmy.vo.llnwd.net/e1/HPRRSP/HP-RR-SPReport2010_v00.pdf

U.S. DoD. (2007). Department of Defense task force on mental health 2007. *An achievable vision: Report of the department of defense task force on mental health*. Falls Church, VA: Defense Health Board. Retrieved from http://www.health.mil/dhb/mhtf/mhtf-report-final.pdf

U.S. DoD. (2010). Department of Defense task force on the prevention of suicide by members of the armed forces, 2010. *The challenge and the promise: Strengthening the force, preventing suicide and saving lives*. Falls Church, VA: Defense Health Board. Retrieved from http://www.health.mil/dhb/downloads/Suicide%20Prevention%20Task%20Force%20final%20report%208–23–10.pdf

U.S. Marine Corps. (2010, December). *Combat and operational stress*. NTTP, 1–15M, MCRP 6–11C. Retrieved from http://www.med.navy.mil/sites/nmcsd/nccosc/coscConference/Documents/COSC%20MRCP%20NTTP%20Doctrine.pdf

U.S. Public Health Service. (1999). *The surgeon general's call to action to prevent suicide*. Washington, DC: U.S. Department of Health and Human Services. Retrieved from http://www.surgeongeneral.gov/library/calltoaction/default.htm.

U.S. Public Health Service. (2009). *National strategy for suicide prevention compendium of federal activities*. NSSP Compendium-Final 3–27–09. Washington, DC: U.S. Department of Health and Human Services.

Walter, J. A., Coulter, I., Hilton, L., Adler, A. B., Bliese, P. D., & Nicholas, R. A. (2010). Program evaluation of total force fitness programs in the military. *Military Medicine, 175*(8), 103–108.

Westphal, R. J., & Woodward, K.R. (2010). Family fitness. *Military Medicine, 175*(8), 97–102.

White, R. W. (1955). Motivation reconsidered: The concept of competence. *Psychological Review, 55*, 297–333.

PART III

Veterans and Systems of Care

CHAPTER

15

Homelessness Among Veterans

Edward V. Carrillo, Joseph J. Costello, and Caleb Yoon Ra

INTRODUCTION

This is an era of renewed hope that the United States will meet the social-political challenge to prevent and end homelessness among veterans. A renewed sense of patriotism and social awareness has mobilized the American public and its political representatives to address the issue of chronic homelessness among veterans in general, and in particular the new wave of returning Operation Iraqi Freedom (OIF), Operation New Dawn (OND), and Operation Enduring Freedom (OEF) veterans. This social contract has been bolstered empirically by evidence-based practice models such as Housing First, Assertive Community Treatment (ACT), and harm reduction, which demonstrate that ending and minimizing homelessness among veterans is possible (Cheng, Lin, Kasprow, & Rosenheck, 2007; Hurlburt, Hough, & Wood, 1996; Rosenheck, Kasprow, Frisman, & Liu-Mares, 2003; Tsemberis, Gulcur, & Nakae, 2004).

This chapter discusses empirically supported interventions and modalities for the treatment, case management, and counseling of homeless veterans. Additionally, it reviews programmatic models focused on the prevention, reduction, and eventual alleviation of homelessness among veterans. It also examines the particulars of diverse subpopulations within the homeless veteran community. Furthermore, it addresses the human realities of working with this high-risk population that may place the emotional health of homeless care providers at risk of compassion fatigue and occupational burnout.

CAUSES AND PREVALENCE OF VETERAN HOMELESSNESS

There are many reasons for the phenomenon of veteran homelessness. For instance, veterans may experience difficulty with the culture shock of transition from military to civilian life. On discharge from military service, many veterans find it difficult to reconnect with social support systems, and they may lack the self-advocacy skills necessary to facilitate a fruitful transition. As a result, veterans in general are overrepresented in the U.S. homeless population and women veterans are 3 to 4 times more likely to become homeless than their civilian counterparts (Gamache, Rosenheck, & Tessler, 2003).

According to Witte (2012), veterans comprise 11% of the homeless population and represent a rate of approximately 31 homeless veterans for every 10,000 veterans. This may not seem like a high proportion, but it is substantially higher than the rate of 21 homeless persons for every 10,000 people in the general population (p. 11). Current trends in homelessness have also deviated from past trends. For example, there is an increasing number of younger veterans experiencing homelessness. Moreover, the number of homeless women veterans has increased as a result of more women serving in the current conflicts of Iraq and Afghanistan (National Coalition for Homeless Veterans [NCHV], 2011).

Mental health problems comprise another cause of homelessness among veterans returning from Iraq and Afghanistan (Cunningham, Henry, & Lyons, 2007). The National Coalition for Homeless Veterans (2011) asserts that physical, sexual, and emotional trauma may be both a cause and a consequence of homelessness. Additional studies identify domestic violence among women as a primary cause of homelessness in the United States. Clinical research over the past century has confirmed that the psychological effects of physical violence or sexual abuse persist long after the traumatic event. Furthermore, trauma suffered by combat veterans or prisoners of war is similar, in its psychological effects, to domestic violence or other trauma inflicted during times of peace (Herman, 1992).

A supplemental report released by the Department of Housing and Urban Development (HUD) and the Department of Veterans Affairs (VA) reported that the behavior of homeless veterans is similar to the general homeless population. Each group tends to be transient, and the people often move in and out of the shelter system and medical facilities. This finding was consistent with prior comparative studies that found few differences between homeless veterans and other homeless men (Rosenheck & Koegel, 1995). Policy-changing investigations conducted in the 1990s on the patterns of homeless resource utilization found that a small group comprised of 10% of the total chronic homeless population occupied 50% of total homeless shelter capacities. Essentially, this same minority of homeless continues to cycle in and out of shelter facilities. These findings have changed the national focus on ending homelessness toward seeking out those homeless veterans who are most vulnerable through aggressive outreach and permanent housing solutions (Culhane, 2008).

The U.S. Department of Housing and Urban Department and Department of Veterans Affairs (HUD/DVA) homeless report (2010) presented substantial evidence on the severity of the problem of homeless veterans. The study cited Point in Time (PIT) statistics and 1-year estimates of the number of current homeless veterans nationally. PIT counts are annual estimates of sheltered and unsheltered homeless veterans on a single night.

The PIT estimates are submitted to HUD annually and account for homeless veterans in emergency shelters or transitional housing on the night of the PIT count. The estimates also account for homeless veterans who are living on the streets, in abandoned buildings, vehicles, or encampments. The 1-year estimates account for veterans who accessed an emergency shelter or transitional housing facility during a 12-month period (HUD/VA, 2010). For instance, on a single night in January 2010, the PIT count estimated there were 76,329 homeless veterans, both sheltered and unsheltered. More than 43,000 (57%) of the veterans were sleeping in emergency shelters or transitional housing and the remaining 32,000 (43%) were sleeping on the streets, in vehicles, in abandoned buildings, or in other places not meant for human habitation (HUD/VA, 2010).

The study's 1-year estimates included 144,842 people that self-identified as veterans who spent at least 1 night in a shelter or transitional housing program in 2010. This statistic represents 1 in every 150 veterans throughout the United States or 1 in every 10 veterans that live under the poverty threshold as defined by the United States Census Bureau. Nearly 98% of veterans in shelters were provided services as individuals and less than 4% were homeless as a part of a family. Interestingly, the proportion of veterans receiving shelter services as members of families is considerably lower than the nonveteran sheltered adult population. In the civilian population, approximately 20% of homeless adults are receiving shelter services with their families (HUD/VA, 2011).

A 2010 annual report indicated that four states—California, New York, Florida, and Texas—accounted for 50% of the total number of homeless veterans in the nation, but only 28% of the total veteran population (HUD/VA, 2010). These same states maintain 46% of the total homeless population, but only 32% of the total U.S. population, and 28% of all veterans. A number of states comprise a small fraction of the national total of homeless veterans. For instance, there are 29 states that individually account for less than 1% of the national total (HUD/VA, 2010).

Interventions

The following sections explore intervention models and techniques currently being implemented to address the issue of homelessness. Program descriptions interspersed with case examples provide illustrations of current trends used to mitigate the homeless situation.

Motivational Interviewing

Many homeless clients can benefit from counseling approaches such as motivational interviewing (MI). As discussed earlier in Chapters 12 and 13 of this book, MI is a client-centered directive treatment approach whose primary goals are to help clients increase their fundamental motivation and resolve ambivalence in an effort to affect behavioral change (Arkowitz, Westra, Miller, & Rollnick, 2008).

Empirical research points to the efficacy of motivational interviewing techniques in the reduction of alcohol consumption, increased abstinence rates, enhanced social adjustment, and successful referrals to treatment (Gold & Miller, 1993, as cited in Fisk, Sells, & Rowe, 2007). This is particularly true when matched with an individual's stage of readiness. There are six stages of treatment readiness based on the transtheoretical model of change (i.e., Stages of Change). These stages include precontemplation, contemplation, preparation, action, maintenance, and relapse (Arkowitz et al., 2008).

In the precontemplation stage, individuals are not interested in changing their behavior even if they have identified their state as a problem. In the contemplation stage, they may believe they have a problem, but are not sure about change. In the preparation stage, individuals are aware that they have a problem and are taking preliminary steps to address the problem. The action stage involves doing things to help change the problem behavior and in the maintenance stage there is active involvement in recovery. The final stage in this model is relapse, which for some is part of the recovery process (Fisk et al., 2007). However, it is important to note that relapse does not have to occur with active engagement and support. The Case Vignette: Sam (in which Sam moves from precontemplation to contemplation) illustrates how MI can be utilized with a homeless veteran.

Case Vignette: Sam

Homeless Veteran Sam (pseudonym) has been living in a homeless encampment in the San Diego River bed area located approximately 5 miles from the downtown area. His counselor has been working with him in an effort to obtain a permanent housing solution. Although his counselor was able to secure a Section 8 housing voucher (government rent subsidy that required recipient to pay only 30% of their gross income as their rent portion), Sam was surprisingly resistant. He argued, "There's a comfort level in being homeless. I don't have to worry about paying rent. I don't pay the light bills, and I don't have to hassle paying gas bills. My biggest problem staying outdoors is where to charge my cell phone." Despite his circumstances, Sam was hesitant to accept the responsibilities of receiving permanent Section 8 housing benefits. More importantly, he was seemingly unwilling to stop spending nearly half of his disability checks on alcohol and cigarettes. Sam would clearly benefit from the stability that a permanent housing solution would provide, but he was ambivalent about accepting help.

Sam's counselor recognized that he was initially in the precontemplative stage. With skillful engagement in Stages of Change dialogue and client-centered treatment planning, the counselor was able to help Sam move from the precontemplation to contemplation phase by the end of their first counseling session. The counselor motivated Sam's shift in thinking by asking him pertinent and sometimes poignant questions, such as: So do you feel safe on the streets? Do you recall your doctors' recommendations after your last liver screen? What are you chances of getting sober on the streets? By the third session, Sam was able transition from a preparatory phase and into action. Through the use of MI, Sam was able to identify and assert his desire to obtain housing. At that point, he was ready to enroll in a Housing First Program and complete his packet for a Section 8 housing choice voucher.

Assertive Community Treatment

Assertive Community Treatment (ACT) is a multidisciplinary team model that provides intensive case management services in the community to persons with serious and chronic mental and medical disabilities (Manuel, Covell, Jackson, & Essock, 2011). The VA utilizes a modified version of ACT in the HUD-VASH program.

The main features of the ACT model are:

- Consumer-driven treatment goals
- Multidisciplinary teams with daily case consultations

- Shared, not individual, case loads
- Close medication management and monitoring
- Assertive outreach
- Low client-to-staff ratios, ideally 10 to 1
- 24-hour responsibility for client care

A meta-analysis of 10 ACT studies, 6 randomized and 4 observational, concluded that homeless persons receiving ACT demonstrated a 37% greater reduction in homelessness and a 26% improvement in psychiatric symptoms over standard case management and continuum of care models (Coldwell & Bender, 2007). The Department of Veterans Affairs has adopted a modified version of ACT as a key component in the HUD-VASH Housing First program that has been empirically supported as an effective intervention in reducing homelessness among veterans (Cheng et al., 2007; Rosenheck et al., 2003) as well as among nonveteran populations (Stefanic & Tsemberis, 2007; Tsemberis et al., 2004).

Padget and Henwood have raised the question that if few services for persons with mental illness have proven as effective as ACT over the past four decades, why isn't ACT more commonly applied? As of 2009, although ACT had been adopted by only 38 states, they report that 2.3% of mental health clients were benefiting from it (Pagett & Henwood, 2011). In 2009, when Secretary of Veterans Affairs Eric Shinseki issued the challenge to end veteran homelessness by 2015, he answered the question raised by Padget and Henwood by pouring the larger portion of increased funding to end homelessness into HUD-VASH funding that is employing modified ACT tactics to permanently house homeless veterans.

Housing First Model

The Housing First model was developed in the early 1990s by Sam Tsemberis, at Pathways to Housing in New York (Senate Sub-Committee on Veterans Affairs, 2010). Its primary goal is to serve the housing needs of the chronically homeless by utilizing a consumer-driven psychosocial rehabilitation treatment model. In its formative stage, Pathways to Housing surveyed hundreds of homeless individuals and concluded that if homeless people are asked what they want most, their first answer will usually be "housing." This model represents an alternative from the traditional lock-step, Continuum of Care model that requires sobriety and medical and psychiatric medication compliance prior to qualifying for transitional and long-term housing (Senate Sub-Committee on Veterans Affairs, 2010). The effectiveness of this model has been supported by several studies (Cheng et al., 2007; Hurlburt et al., 1996; Rosenheck et al., 2003; Stefanic & Tsemberis, 2007; Tsemberis et al., 2004). The Housing First model has been adopted by the VA's HUD-VASH Program as the model of choice for ending long-term homelessness. It provides long-term (Section 8) government-supported housing, coupled with intensive case management (in the VA more than 90% provided by social workers), Assertive Community Treatment (ACT), and motivational interviewing (as described earlier in this chapter).

HOUSING AND URBAN DEVELOPMENT VA-SUPPORTIVE HOUSING (HUD-VASH) PROGRAM

The HUD-VASH program is the VA's version of Housing First and utilizes a modified version of the Assertive Community Treatment (ACT) model (Rosenheck et al., 2003). The requirements of the program include:

- Formulation of a treatment plan that reflects the goals of the veteran, in which potential strengths and barriers to maintaining housing placement are addressed.
- Establishment of a process to monitor the treatment plan, including the use of alcohol and drug screenings.
- Frequent medical and mental health appointments.
- Assistance with employment and income needs.
- Resolution of legal and financial issues.
- Provision of "wraparound" services that include services such as guidance with the benefits process and crisis counseling (United States Department of Veterans Affairs [USDVA] HUD VASH Handbook, 2011).

To be eligible for HUD-VASH veterans and their families must first meet the following criteria: (a) be eligible for VA health care services; (b) meet VA criteria for homelessness; and (c) have case management needs in the following domains: housing, mental health, health and medical, financial, family and social support systems, substance abuse, and assistance with Activities of Daily Living (ADLs) and Instrumental Activities of Daily Living (IADLs). The program goals include promoting full recovery and independence for veteran clients so they can maintain permanent independent housing in the community (USDVA *HUD VASH Handbook*, 2011). Veterans with other than honorable discharges are eligible for municipally managed HUD Section 8 housing but do not get the priority housing vouchers and case management provided in the HUD-VASH legislation.

This program is designed to address the needs of the most vulnerable and chronically homeless veterans, and it is utilizing empirically supported interventions such as motivational interviewing and Assertive Community Treatment. In a randomized controlled study on the cost effectiveness of HUD-VASH supported housing at four VA sites, Rosenheck et al. (2003) compared veterans receiving HUD-VASH Section 8 housing choice vouchers combined with intensive case management to two other types of care models: (1) VA homeless program case management as usual with no access to Section 8 housing; and (2) standard VA care (Rosenheck et al., 2003). This 3-year study concluded that HUD-VASH supported housing results in "superior housing outcomes" compared to intensive case management alone (without housing assistance) or standard outpatient care alone (Rosenheck et al., 2003, p. 940). In a reanalysis that tracked missing data from the original 2003 Rosenheck et al. study, Cheng et al. (2007) determined the improved HUD-VASH outcomes to be even more pronounced. These improvements included fewer days housed in institutions; fewer days spent using alcohol; and lower expenditures on alcohol and drugs. These studies have supported the expanded funding of the HUD-VASH program, which has become a cornerstone in the VA's ambitious 5-year plan to end veteran homelessness (Committee on Veterans Affairs, 2010). In addition, HUD-VASH vouchers are also portable, which means that veterans are allowed to transfer their housing vouchers to live in communities where VA case management services are available (Kuhn & Nakashima, 2009).

The Case Vignette: John Doe illustrates how the Housing First model has been adapted in the HUD-VASH program. The vignette shows that the program requires much flexibility, creativity, and collaboration in its approach to housing the chronically homeless veterans. With the goal to end homelessness among veterans across the nation by 2015, all VA Medical Centers and their respective Public Housing Authorities (PHA) are working on reviewing the barriers these clients have to streamline efforts to meet this goal. Also, HUD-VASH case managers are adapting to the needs of the most vulnerable chronically homeless veterans by becoming more skilled at identifying barriers to service working to create links to overcome these barriers. In addition, they are utilizing collaborative troubleshooting with local service providers to connect the veteran with vital community as well as VA resources. With the goal of helping veterans obtain and maintain independent long-term housing, motivational interviewing and the ACT models are used throughout the initial contact with the homeless individual to the end of case management needs.

Case Vignette: John Doe

Many of the homeless population in nonrural areas are able to transport themselves to a clinic or outreach location to seek assistance and treatment. However, not all homeless individuals—for reasons of pathology, medical disability, or poor transportation—are able to access the treatment and help they need. For instance, John Doe is a heterosexual male Vietnam era soldier who is more than 65 years old, has severe chronic untreated arthritic pain, is actively abusing alcohol, has no income, is chronically homeless and has been sleeping on the streets for more than 20 years. He was found in the streets under a bush and smelled of urine and was covered from head to toe with lice and various other mites.

Mr. Doe was open to receive assistance but was unable to independently present at outreach clinics throughout the main service area. He was 10 blocks from a day center and a large community program. Due to difficulties with arthritis and his alcohol use to "numb the pain," he was unable to ambulate several blocks around his sleeping area to the day center or local food shelter. He had several hospital bands around his wrist indicating several trips to the local emergency rooms. There were several programs available for this veteran to address his alcohol addiction, provide detox, and provide transitional housing. However, he was unable to present to the community services and was too unstable medically to be safely housed under the Housing First model.

Mr. Doe needed to be stabilized medically and needed to go through a medical detoxification process from alcohol. This veteran was too sick for independent housing and inappropriate for transition housing, due to continuous alcohol use. Traditional clinic models require John to present to the emergency department to be medically stabilized and to be monitored for alcohol detoxing as he has a history of seizures from alcohol withdrawals. So it took the coordinated efforts of community nonprofit agencies, VA outreach workers, VA case managers, community emergency response teams, and VA emergency department medical staff to collaborate and streamline a viable treatment plan to get Mr. Doe off the streets.

Mr. Doe needed stable housing and assistance with alcohol withdrawal. However, his underlying medical and mental health needs were unclear as his baseline was undetermined due to being under the influence of alcohol throughout the engagement process with VA outreach social workers. He also needed transportation to the medical facility.

Second, Mr. Doe needed emergency care for immediate medical needs before he would be sufficiently stable to access community programs. He also needed transportation to a community program that provides a social work case manager, on-site nursing care, 24-hour house manager, and transitional housing.

Mr. Doe was also connected to a VA outpatient/outreach case manager. This hybrid case management position allowed the flexibility for the case manager to collaborate with the emergency department (ED) social worker, ED attending provider, and Recuperative Program Liaison to streamline services for Mr. Doe. The case manager transported Mr. Doe to the ED and contacted the ED social worker and ED attending MD to alert them with the plan to discharge Mr. Doe to the Recuperative Program on being medically stabilized. After the ED attending MD cleared Mr. Doe medically, he was transported by the hybrid case manager to the recuperative program and provided the appropriate documentation to the recuperative program social worker case manager to "preapprove" Mr. Doe for a stabilization stay.

During the stabilization stay Mr. Doe revealed he had paid into the Social Security retirement system for many years. Consequently his HUD-VASH social worker assisted him in obtaining Social Security Disability Insurance (SSDI) and procuring VA service-connected disability. His social worker transported him to outpatient care at the Veterans Administration, where he was assessed for baseline ADLs and IADLs to determine needed supports. He was guided through the process of applying for a state-issued ID and Social Security card. Once his identification documents were acquired (a prerequisite for public housing) he was assisted in applying for a Section 8 voucher with the local public housing authority. He was later housed at an adult independent community and he furnished his apartment with resources provided by a local community nonprofit.

HEALTH CARE FOR HOMELESS VETERANS

The Health Care for Homeless Veterans (HCHV) program screens honorably discharged and other-than-honorably discharged (OTH) veterans at outreach sites for referral to VA transitional housing, VA Regional Office (VARO) benefits Vet Centers, and a full range of VA and non-VA social service programs. All OTH veterans are eligible to be screened for VA transitional housing, except for those veterans who received a dishonorable discharge (DD). In rare cases OTH veterans are eligible for humanitarian VA medical services. The HCHV program is the mother ship of all the VA homeless programs. Consequently, it has assumed administrative responsibility for most of the newly expanded homeless services such as the HUD-VASH program and several other special needs programs (mentioned in this chapter) serving homeless veterans. HCHV has traditionally exercised a three-pronged approach to serving homeless veterans: (1) outreach to veterans at all VA medical centers and surrounding communities; (2) linkage to VA health care services; and (3) screening and admission into various community based Grant Per Diem (GPD), 2-year, time-limited transitional housing, residential treatment facilities and HUD-VASH permanent housing (McGuire, Rosenheck, & Kasprow, 2011).

The VA both distributes and monitors funding through grants for community-based programs that provide transitional housing, known as GPD sites. The VA also deploys teams composed primarily of social workers and nurses, who act as liaisons between the community GPD programs and the VA. These VA GPD liaisons provide screening, assessment, treatment planning, referral, case monitoring, and crisis management interventions for homeless veterans who are transitionally housed at GPD community agencies. Veterans can live in these programs for up to 2 years, but the average stay is 3 to 6 months. In addition to providing housing, GPD community agencies provide direct case management, counseling, benefits assistance, social service referral, employment referral; and an array of life skills, money management, and computer skills classes. Some of the larger sites are co-located with employment-focused, Homeless Veterans Reintegration Programs (HVRP), which provide direct job placement assessment counseling, and short-term career training funds (United States Department of Veterans Affairs, [USDVA] HUD-VASH Handbook, 2011).

The VA funds GPD community agencies on a daily rate. The FY 2011 allowance was $38 for each day that a veteran is provided with housing. GPD programs compete nationally for two types of federal funding. As grant recipients they are eligible to receive brick and mortar, capital funding grants and housing and social service grants. The recipients collaborate with local VA Medical Centers to provide medical and psychiatric services. A study of 363 veterans from five geographically diverse VA medical Centers found that 81% of the veterans were still housed 12 months after discharge from the program (McGuire et al., 2011).

DOMICILIARY CARE FOR HOMELESS VETERANS

The Domiciliary Care for Homeless Veterans (DCHV) provides transitional and long-term housing for veterans who cannot live independently due to medical or psychiatric disabilities. To meet the needs of returning OEF-OIF veterans, the DCHV includes the Mental Health Residential Rehabilitation and Treatment Programs (MHRRTPs) model. This program is a transitional housing model for homeless veterans with multiple and severe medical conditions, mental illness, addictions, or psychosocial deficits. The DCHV program provides a 24/7 structured and supportive residential environment as a part of the rehabilitative treatment regimen. The model is not a long-term program; it emphasizes practices that require clinically measurable treatment gains aimed to enhance lifestyle changes, self-care, and personal responsibility. To achieve these ends the program utilizes empirically supported treatments such as eye movement desensitization reprocessing (EMDR) and cognitive behavioral therapy (CBT).

HOMELESS VETERANS REINTEGRATION PROGRAM (HVRP)

The Homeless Veterans Reintegration Program (HVRP) recruits and brokers career training and employment for homeless veterans who are motivated toward securing competitive employment. It serves homeless veterans who may be shunned by other programs due to problems like severe PTSD, long-term substance abuse, severe psychosocial problems, legal issues, or being HIV-positive. The program provides more intensive assessment, specialized job referrals, and intensive counseling and case management than is possible in other veteran specific employment programs. The HVRP also fills a gap for many homeless veterans who are not eligible for VA Vocational Rehabilitation by providing funding for career track vocational and junior college programs (http://www.dol.gov/vets/programs/hvrp/hvrp-bp.htm).

PROJECT CHALENG: THE VA'S COMMUNITY NETWORK INTERVENTION

In 1994, the VA initiated a program called Project CHALENG (Community Homelessness Assessment, Local Education and Networking Groups). This program was designed to improve the continuum of care for homeless veterans provided by the local VA by establishing a service provider (stakeholder) network of local community agencies serving the homeless population. The concept behind this effort asserted that no single agency can provide all of the services necessary to help homeless veterans become productive members of society and end their homelessness. Project CHALENG endeavors to enhance coordination of services by solidifying the network of VA and community service stakeholders, raising awareness of homeless veterans' needs and coordinating community-wide planning to address those needs (USDVA, 2011).

An important component of the CHALENG project is conducting a community-wide needs assessment. The CHALENG assessment survey elicits feedback on 42 different criteria related to the met and unmet needs of homeless veterans. Table 15.1 shows the nationwide results of the top 10 unmet needs of homeless veterans. It also displays the details of changing priorities.

Table 15.1 Top 10 Highest Unmet Needs Identified by Consumers, FY 2008–2010

2008	2009	2010
1. Welfare payments	1. Welfare payments	1. Welfare payments
2. Child care	2. Legal assistance for child support issues	2. Child care
3. Legal assistance for child support issues	3. Long-term, permanent housing	3. Legal assistance for child support issues
4. Guardianship (financial)	4. Child care	4. Family reconciliation assistance
5. Family reconciliation assistance	5. SSI/SSD process	5. Guardianship (financial)
6. Long-term, permanent housing	6. Legal assistance for outstanding warrants/fines	6. Legal assistance for outstanding warrants/fines
7. SSI/SSD process	7. Guardianship (financial)	7. SSI/SSD process
8. Legal assistance for outstanding warrants/fines	8. Family reconciliation assistance	8. Credit counseling
9. Credit counseling	9. Job training	9. Job training
10. Reentry services for incarcerated veterans	10. VA disability/pension	10. Legal assistance to help restore a driver's license

Source: Kuhn and Nakashima (2011), p. 13.

Beyond conducting community-wide consumer and stakeholder needs assessments, the efforts of CHALENG includes developing close working relationships with local governmental and community agencies with the goal of striving to inform homeless veterans about the full range of homeless veteran and nonveteran resources available in their local community. Among the many gains made through the annual CHALENG project are the creation of the Homeless Veterans Dental Initiative and support for the VA's big increases in recent years in funding for permanent supported housing through its growing VASH-HUD initiative.

NEW VA PROGRAMS DESIGNED TO PREVENT HOMELESSNESS

More recently, the VA has created five entirely new programs designed to prevent homelessness through outreach and early engagement. One is the Veterans Homelessness Prevention Demonstration Project (VHPD). It is a 3-year pilot program designed to provide both proactive prevention assistance to veterans and their families at risk of becoming homeless and rapid rehousing for newly homeless veterans. Support for VHPD is provided by collaboration between the Department of Housing and Urban Development (HUD) and the Department of Labor (DOL), with direct services provided by the Veterans Administration. The VHPD's target population includes: veterans returning from Iraq (OIF) and Afghanistan (OEF) Operation New Dawn (OND); female veterans: families with a veteran head of household; families with a veteran single parent; and National Guard and Reserve veterans being discharged from the military. Services include short-term rental assistance (not cash assistance) and emergency funds for housing vouchers (http://www.va.gov/HOMELESS/NationalCenter_VHPD.asp).

Another relatively new program is the National Call Center for Homeless Veterans, which is designed to assure that homeless veterans and veterans at risk for homelessness have access to trained homeless prevention counselors 24 hours a day, 7 days a week. The hotline is primarily intended to assist homeless and imminently homeless veterans and their families, and to support homeless outreach and comprehensive services at VA Medical Centers. It also assists federal, state, and local partners, homeless veteran service providers, and community agencies by providing them with resources and links to VA homeless services.

The VA also has two relatively new programs for incarcerated and justice involved veterans: (1) The Health Care for Reentry Veterans (HCRV); and (2) and the Veterans Justice Outreach (VJO) programs. Both of these programs are targeted at helping "justice involved" veterans to avoid homelessness and to access VA services. The HCRV program's target population is veterans leaving prison. This program is designed to prevent homelessness, decrease the likelihood of reincarceration, and reduce the impact of medical, psychiatric, and substance abuse problems in this vulnerable veteran population (www.va.gov/homeless/Reentry.asp). The VJO is a VA initiative designed to prevent the unnecessary criminalization and extended incarceration of mentally ill veterans, and to ensure that VA eligible "justice-involved" veterans have timely access to VA mental health and substance abuse services (www.va.gov).

The newest VA initiative aimed at preventing homelessness is the Supportive Services for Veteran Families (SSVF) Program, authorized by Public Law 119–387. This community-based program provides services aimed at creating housing stability for very low-income veterans and their families who are transitioning from homelessness to permanent housing, or trying to maintain their permanent housing. Through this program, the VA will award grants to private nonprofit organizations and community cooperatives that provide supportive services including transportation, legal assistance, child care, benefits assistance, temporary financial assistance, and daily living services (http://www.va.gov/homeless/ssvf.asp).

HOMELESS VETERANS STAND DOWN

In the United States, Stand Down is a community intervention that brings together homeless veterans for 1 to 3 days in a baseball field, park, or auditorium and provides them with a broad range of social and medical services. The included services are dental, optometry, urgent medical care, podiatry, psychiatry, substance abuse, emergency and transitional housing, legal, VA social work and psychological counseling, and VA benefits. Also included are needed resources such as shoes, clothing, diapers, blankets, backpacks, sleeping bags, toiletries, and first aid kits.

In military terminology, Stand Down is an operation that provides battle-weary combatants with a few days respite from the frontlines by relocating them to a relatively secure area with opportunities for needed medical and dental care, mail call, and physical needs such as resupply of gear, new equipment, and new clothing. Equally important in the war zone is the time it provides for grieving losses, chaplain services, good chow, and renewed camaraderie, which builds hope in a common mission. Since its inception in 1988, Homeless Veterans Stand Down has expanded to more than 200 nationwide cities. In the larger events as many as 1,000 homeless veterans participate for up to 3 days. To support the nationwide expansion of this highly viable community intervention, Nachison, Van Keuren, and Talbot (1995) published a step-by-step procedural manual for implementing a Homeless Veteran Stand Down. Each year substance abuse counselors, social workers and volunteers working at Stand Down will often hear veterans joyfully announce, "I got sober at Stand Down," and "I finally got off the streets for good at Stand Down."

MEDICATION COMPLIANCE AND PROGNOSIS FOR ENDING HOMELESSNESS

Homeless veterans with higher rates of medication noncompliance have a lower probability of ending their homelessness (Hurlburt et al., 1996; Rosenheck et al., 2003; Tsemberis et al., 2004). The usual reasons for medication noncompliance are distressing side effects, mistrust of providers, denial of need for medication, and the perception that little or no benefit is obtained from medication that has been prescribed. In addition, homeless veterans have numerous internal and external/environmental barriers that prevent medication compliance. These include high rates of missed appointments (Rosenheck, Frisman, & Gallup, 1995); insufficient funds for transportation to appointments or for medication co-payments; substance abuse by persons whose prescription drugs are contra-indicated for use while consuming alcohol and street drugs; medications lost due to confiscation by police or groundskeepers, or theft; and medication noncompliance typical of specific diagnoses common among homeless persons, that is, paranoid schizophrenia, disorganized schizophrenia, depression, and substance use disorders.

The fact that homeless persons are routinely subjected to losses by theft and various forms of crime victimization contributes to the cycle of chronic homelessness and presents special challenges to good medication compliance. All homeless subgroups, especially women, are vulnerable to the violent realities of street life. This is complicated by the environmental limitations of homeless lifestyles, which in urban areas relegates the homeless to living in high-crime areas. Consequently, certain aspects of the PTSD hypervigilance cluster, like scanning the environment and light sleeping, serve as functional survival skills. One veteran, Albert (a pseudonym), attested to this dynamic: "I sure as hell don't want to be knocked out on them meds when the druggies come raiding our camp. I'm sleeping with my knife and one eye open" (personal communication, 2007).

Homeless veterans like Albert, diagnosed with chronic PTSD, are especially vulnerable to symptoms of hypervigilance, which becomes a vicious cycle reinforced by the dangers of street life. The cycle begins with poor sleep at night, which leads to increased flashbacks during the day, which leads to increased hypervigilance throughout the day, which leads to poor sleep and increased nightmares at night. Then the cycle begins again with increased flashbacks during the day due to a poor night's sleep. Albert reported, "The nightmares don't let up. No way! They're a mixture of combat zone patrols and crazy firefights that end up right here in the streets and in our homeless camps. . . . That's why I drink at night, just to help me fall asleep." Albert exemplifies why, for many veterans, there is little chance of proper sleep while living outdoors and a very poor prognosis for recovery from substance use without proper sleep.

Medication noncompliance is commonly reported from hypervigilant veterans who have been prescribed sleep-enhancing medications. In addition to outright noncompliance, some report taking reduced doses of the medication, echoing Albert's "just enough to help me get to sleep." Others report taking sleep medication during the day when it is "safer to try and sleep," and staying up all night. However, this pattern of sleeping during the day creates barriers to accessing needed services such as food, showers, housing, bus tokens, and—of special concern here—medical/psychiatric treatment and case management. Because the reasons for medication noncompliance are complex and diverse, it is important that health care providers tailor treatment plans on a case-by-case basis and that empirically supported models such as Assertive Community Treatment and education on psychopharmacology are implemented aggressively to support medication compliance and enhance treatment planning aimed at ending homelessness (Nermin & Richard, 2004).

OUTREACH CONSIDERATIONS

Research indicates that lack of trust is a primary reason that many homeless persons are reluctant to access services. Often, no family or truly supportive friends have been available for emotional or financial support. This social disaffiliation generates a need for community outreach and a period of courting between the veteran and provider. This may require an extensive commitment, just to establish a trusting relationship. Once trust is established, providers are often called on to assume roles in an effort to facilitate access to health care and community services (Levy & O'Connell, 2004). Additionally, individuals who are homeless are often skeptical toward aspects of outreach, which may lead them to perceive available services as incompatible with their needs (Kryda & Compton, 2007).

In order to break through the emotional curtain of mistrust, Tsemberis et al. (2003) maintain that offering available housing options in outreach efforts is essential. Furthermore, the most effective time to offer housing is during the first contact. Yet this is not the model used by the majority of agencies serving individuals who are homeless. Many providers do not initially offer housing because of their emphasis on getting their clients "housing ready." This refers to ensuring medication compliance or abstinence from substances prior to receiving housing options (Kryda & Compton, 2007). An approach that places sobriety and medication compliance as a high priority over housing can be frustrating for both the worker and the client because it is not always a realistic or acceptable option for the client (Tsemberis et al., 2003, 2004).

Some advocates have called for an increase in unrestricted housing or full implementation of the Housing First model option in an effort to move individuals who are considered chronically homeless off the streets. However, this may not be realistic in areas where there are critical housing shortages. Also, this presents special challenges to case managers attempting to place their clients in VA Grant Per Diem Transitional Housing because these programs still operate on traditional guideless of requiring 60 to 90 days of sobriety prior to admission. Again, much creativity is required to coordinate services from a range of community nonprofits, non-VA transitional sober living, wet shelters (those allowing some use of ETOH), and sober living environments to assure that housing options be made available during initial contact. Lastly, the value of both housing services and outreach may be meaningless if clients refuse services due to mistrust, which often evolves from their needs not being heard. Consequently, a respectful client-centered approach with engaged active listening is needed to maximize the effectiveness of outreach efforts (Kryda & Compton, 2007).

In addition to employing a client-centered approach to outreach, other evidence-based applications point to the efficacy of peer counseling and outreach. Latkin, Sherman, & Knowlton (2003) conducted a study on HIV prevention in the African American community that is relevant to homeless veteran outreach. This program is a network-oriented HIV prevention intervention based on social identity theory and peer outreach and was implemented for both HIV positive and negative drug users.

Peer outreach has been a widely used strategy for HIV prevention with drug users and capitalizes on peer influence processes. Peer outreach is also a social role that fits with African Americans' historical experiences and communal values, and it has been effective in reducing injection-related risk behavior among contacts. The concept of incorporating social identity and peer outreach components present a promising approach to HIV prevention among inner-city drug users (Latkin et al., 2003). The veteran community also has a strong cultural component, which highly values peer identification with fellow veterans. Therefore, this approach may be a relevant consideration for those involved in homeless outreach work.

Also, a new emphasis for improving the quality of VA outreach services involves training social workers and outreach personnel to be "generalists." It is no longer acceptable that outreach personnel just hand out flyers and make referrals or limit their outreach to recruitment for VA homeless programs. The term "one-stop shopping" is being emphasized at VA trainings (personal communication, 2010). Outreach workers need to be knowledgeable and skilled in crisis intervention, substance abuse counseling, employment counseling and referral, grief work, medication management, VA benefits, and non-VA community resources.

Lastly, when providing community outreach, many veterans with other-than-honorable (OTH) discharges are encountered. These veterans, who are noneligible for VA health care services, are often not aware that there are some VA benefits and VA services for which they may qualify. The most common VA services that apply to most veterans with OTH discharges are: VA Transitional Housing, eligibility to apply for service connection disability for military-related medical and mental health injuries, and counseling at Vet Centers Readjustment Counseling Services for veterans diagnosed with combat-related PTSD.

CLINICAL ISSUES IN WORKING WITH THE VETERAN HOMELESS POPULATION: WITH AN EMPHASIS ON SOCIAL WORKER SELF-CARE AND SAFETY

Working with homeless veterans presents unique challenges that test clinical boundaries and pulls at human heartstrings. Values, ethics, and political and spiritual beliefs are called into the dynamic interplay of the case management relationship. Also, countertransference issues that relate to feeling unsafe in outreach settings are of concern. These issues need to be addressed proactively and frequently with supervision or in team case conferences. In addition, prior planning (as the saying goes, "an ounce of prevention") is the best procedure for providing structure and confidence for working in a potentially unsafe environment. For example, prior to conducting street outreach, case workers need to agree on contingency planning and notify their home office of their specific outreach location and estimated time of return. Also, in certain settings and circumstances, it is important to have working agreements with the police stations and the Homeless Outreach Team (HOT). When conducting street or rural outreach, it is important to go out in teams of at least two or more workers. At least one outreach team member should be highly skilled in crisis counseling and treatment of Acute Traumatic Stress (ATS). In addition, outreach personnel need to maintain a close distance, within eyesight or earshot of each other at all times. Lastly, teams need to take time to debrief any traumatic, dangerous, or strong countertransference situations.

At a congressional hearing in 2010, Tsemberis asserted that, "Someone who has served as a veteran is not going to accept services that are an insult to their dignity, their honor, or their capabilities which they have proven already and demonstrated for their country" (Committee on Veterans Affairs, 2010, p. 71). However, when veterans speak about their "dignity and honor" in past military service while requesting VA services, clinicians and counselors may characterize the veteran as "acting entitled." This assessment deserves examination as both a transference and countertransference issue. When homeless veterans present in a manner that is angry, aggressive, or overly dependent and unrealistic, clinicians may experience strong and unpredictable emotional reactions. These feelings can easily turn into quick, sometimes kneejerk responses on the clinician's behalf that then prevent objective assessment and accurate service provision.

Identifying the first blush countertransference, when it occurs, will help clinicians balance their emotional responses and focus on the task at hand. In the initial phases of counseling this task involves accurately assessing the client's specific needs, performing a mental status assessment and engaging clients in mutual treatment planning. Also, when strong emotions are being expressed, caseworkers and clinicians need to make accurate assessments of each unique veteran's presentation. For example, anger is different from loathing, hatred, fury and hostility (Hoge, 2010). Hoge suggests that each of these client presentations needs to be assessed separately. Anger is a misunderstood emotion, especially when working with homeless and combat veterans. Much attention is paid to managing anger and not enough attention is paid to understanding its deeper meaning. Moreover, experienced outreach workers during their assessments of homeless veterans understand that, in the streets and rural homeless camps, like in the combat zone, anger is often beneficial to survival. They are also mindful of the "street mentality" that may appear to be antisocial and that many chronically homeless veterans develop as survival behavior that serves as protection from others with whom they interact on streets or in the bush on a regular basis. During outreach and in the clinic limits on verbally abusive behaviors need to introduced assertively and—for safety purposes—expeditiously.

Homeless veterans, like hardened combat warriors, have difficulty trusting outsiders. They harbor much resentment that is "usually accompanied by anger/rage, depression, cynicism and mistrust." Knowing this ahead of time prepares the clinician for the initial phase of treatment. This first phase—which Hickman calls the "testing phase"—is characterized by veterans questioning the clinician's motives, withholding information, and testing knowledge of military culture (Hickman, 1987). Inexperienced clinicians are often surprised at the amount of "testing" they are subjected to, and they therefore are sometimes too quick to misdiagnose traumatized clients as having paranoid disorders (Shay, 2002).

In some situations, the labeling of homeless veterans as "entitled" may come from the service provider's feelings of helplessness due to the large gaps in resources and services available to meet the multiple needs of homeless veterans. These limitations are a constant source of frustration for both care providers and homeless clients. The disparity between resources and expectations is at times particularly pronounced in the minds of veterans who have just left the military. A benefit to which active duty service members grow accustomed is known in military lingo as "three hots and a cot"—that is, three hot meals and a bed to sleep in. Recently discharged veterans may anticipate similar benefits from the VA and other public institutions that serve them. This does not represent "entitlement." It is a socialized expectation inherent in military culture that needs to be addressed openly through psychoeducation and readjustment counseling. A veteran's "pride in service" needs to be honored in the clinic, street, or community setting through a dialogue, which involves the veteran's beliefs and expectations and the clinicians deeper understanding of military culture (Exum, Coll, & Weiss, 2011). Equally important, time needs to be taken to educate veterans on the limitations and realities of nonmilitary social services, while at the same time advocating for and empowering veterans to access the public and private services they most need and are entitled to receive.

Sometimes veterans express their "pride in service" by reminding clinicians of their "proven capabilities" as "killing machines," or by using other military metaphors that can easily be perceived as threatening. The perception of a threat may be more common among treatment providers who are not accustomed to or acculturated in military language. For example, some veterans in intake screening or emergency walk-in settings take pride in referring to themselves as *trained killers*. Then they are surprised or shocked when an emergency code is called and hospital security arrive. When clinicians experience perceived threats, it is essential that they follow safety protocols, and conduct suicide and homicide risk assessments. However, some emergency codes can be avoided through empathic and exploratory dialogue. For example, if the veteran reminds a clinician of his skills as a "trained killer," rather than immediately initiating a homicide or suicide risk assessment, the clinician should respond with a validating reflective question such as, "So you take pride in your military training and service?" Another possible reply using exploratory dialogue is to ask the veteran "Why is it important to you that I know your training and skills?" A reframe for clinicians and case managers in understanding this dynamic is to acknowledge the fact that we take pride in displaying our graduation degrees and certificates on our walls. The clinician's display of these credentials may be intimidating to some clients, especially those new to clinical settings. So, isn't it logical that some veterans will want to share their pride in their credentials in specialized military skills?

On the other hand, clinicians who have served in the armed forces and are familiar with military mannerisms of speech may minimize and/or under react to a genuine threat when it is camouflaged in military metaphor. Every verbal threat—even those expressed as cloaked metaphor or humor—needs to be explored thoroughly. To support the goal of providing objective standardized threat assessment, the VA has implemented structured protocols for suicidal and homicidal risk assessment that provide template guidelines to objectively assess all potential lethal threats. In addition, universal screening for suicide risk is required at regular intervals for all mental health clients. During these assessments it is important to educate the veteran on the legalities and clinical requirements of risk assessment. Limits of confidentiality reporting requirements, which need to be established prior to beginning clinical services, may need to be reviewed more than once and discussed openly as a part of the veteran's clinical acculturation process and treatment planning.

SELF-CARE AND BURNOUT PREVENTION

Working with homeless veterans involves indirect exposure to the brutality and tyranny of street or bush life, and direct exposure to its victims and sometimes perpetrators. Homeless veterans' heartbreaking stories of day-to-day survival can contribute to caregivers experiencing compassion fatigue (Figley, 1995) or vicarious traumatization (Pearlman & MacIan, 1995), which were discussed in Chapter 5 of this handbook.

Furthermore, working with homeless persons can be viscerally difficult for caseworkers when they encounter homeless persons who are not bathed, unlaundered, disheveled, and malodorous. Much like emergency room workers, outreach specialists need to be prepared to meet all clients who walk through the door or who they encounter on the street, and work with them without passing judgment, regardless of their appearance and their impact on one's senses. To maintain appropriate empathy, frontline service providers may need to adjust their levels of tolerance in the face of uncanny and sometimes appalling physical presentations by homeless veterans. According to C. King, former VA social work chief at the VA San Diego Health Care system, "Not all social workers are cut out for working in the trenches with street homeless veterans" (personal communication, November 2009).

In addition, frontline service providers for homeless veterans need to be prepared for critical gaps and limitations in services, especially emergency housing during peak periods of utilization. This will often result in outreach workers having to ask their clients, "Where did you sleep last night," with the understanding that they need to let the veteran know that he or she may need to return there for another night. A VA nurse, who after providing crisis counseling to the victim of a violent crime, and was not able secure her client housing for the night stated, "It feels like I'm sending him right back out there to be victimized again" (personal communication, October 2007). Similarly, when clients are assaulted (or worse, killed), counselors are subject to the same type of survivor guilt experienced by war veterans whose fellow combatants are wounded or killed in action. This supports one of the key strengths of the ACT model that practices a team approach to working with homeless persons. Outreach and case management workers need to take time off from work for their self-care needs as well as planned vacations. The team approach provides for built-in back up for frontline workers to take needed time off. One of the sure signs of compassion fatigue is workers saying "I can't take time off because my clients need me," or "I will be too worried about my clients to enjoy my vacation."

Counselors who are exposed vicariously to the suffering and traumas of chronically homeless persons need to have their own self-care plans in place (Lipskey & Burk, 2009). They need plans that include routine maintenance as well as contingency plans for their own personal crises. Employee assistance programs (EAPs) provide a highly viable resource for employee crisis counseling and stress management. In addition, support and hope for coping with the stress of working with chronic substance abusing persons is available in Nar-Anon and Al-Alon Groups. These worldwide, spiritually based, 12-step organizations provide fellowship for those affected by someone else's addiction.

Mother Teresa, who worked for more than 45 years ministering to and feeding the poor, sick, and homeless, said: "Without prayer I could not work for even half an hour" (Teresa & Vardey, 1995, p. 39). For the Missionaries of Charity, the order of nuns she founded, she instituted the practice of starting and ending the day with prayer. It is not surprising that in the new challenge to end homelessness among veterans, the VA and HUD and the Department of Labor have entered into collaborative working agreements with faith-based organizations that have long track records for serving the poor and homeless.

Research findings at the VA support the efficacy of Mantram Repetition, a manualized mindfulness treatment for managing stress and burnout among VA employees (Bormann et al., 2006). It has also been supported as a viable therapeutic spiritual support for veterans with PTSD (Bormann, Liu, Thorp, & Lang, 2011). Mantram Repetition involves mindfulness skills training in mantra (a word with a special meaning) repetition, developing one-pointed attention, slowing down, and breathing and walking meditation. Bormann's research with VA employees (2006) found that Mantrum Repetition is effective in building resilience and coping with both depression and anxiety.

COST BENEFIT OF PSYCHOSOCIAL SUPPORT AND CASE MANAGEMENT

The social and financial impact of homeless veterans has been indicated by numerous local and national statistical surveys. Homeless persons become ill more often, utilize acute medical services at higher rates and experience substantially higher rates of mortality than their nonhomeless counterparts (O'Toole et al., 2010). Most studies of the homeless population have focused on emergency room intervention. However, emergency department use was found to be less likely when care is accompanied with social work intervention (O'Toole et al., 2010). Likewise, case management efforts, substance abuse intervention, and housing support also sharply reduced emergency room contacts (Sadowski, Kee, Vanderwheele, & Buchanan, 2009).

CONCLUSION

The basic nature of chronic homelessness suggests that homeless persons lack adequate resources to meet their basic housing needs. They lack resources for simple material needs such as gas, bus fare, or a decent pair of shoes. But more poignantly, they lack psychosocial skills like mental insight, motivation, hope, and sobriety. These skills are the basic requirements to get them started at a VA clinic or community outreach facility. Consequently, VA HUD-VASH outreach workers coined the term *clinic to the streets* to describe the type of assertive community outreach, resource networking, and intensive case management interventions that need to be brought to the streets and bushes to move the veteran out of the streets or bushes and into the cycle of recovery and treatment that will lead to permanent housing.

Veterans' community organizations all share one thing in common: They began from grassroots efforts, from the ground up. These programs were conceived by frontline caseworkers, volunteers, and in some instances formerly homeless practitioners who worked "in the trenches" with homeless veterans. These pioneers practiced principles of meeting homeless veterans "where they are at"—on the street and in the community. And after engaging them, they practiced respect for their client's self-determination. It should come as no surprise that these grassroots engagement practices as they are now being applied to empirically supported treatment models—such as Housing First and Assertive Community Treatment—are now appearing to be effective in understanding the needs of homeless persons, engaging them in recovery models, and ending their homelessness.

Since the post–Civil War era, we as a nation have developed multiple approaches to address complex veteran profiles and serve the needs of our homeless population. Each generation along with each wave of wounded war veterans has presented new challenges. We as a body of social service providers are utilizing clinical and street experiences along with evolving evidence-based research to formulate increasingly effective practices to better serve those wounded veterans who served our country. We recognize that newly returning veterans, including those now serving, will present new challenges, with very specific and complex needs. We have now evolved more effective means of listening to and assessing the needs of homeless veterans through the use of the various scientific and social tools described in this chapter. While utilizing all of these tools and resources, we need to remain actively engaged in creating unique and effective means to serve homeless veterans—and, most important, to learn from them if we are to succeed in ending homelessness among veterans.

CHAPTER DISCUSSION QUESTIONS

1. What are the risk factors for veterans' becoming homeless?
2. What are some of the barriers that homeless veterans face for obtaining health care and housing?
3. Describe the Assertive Community Treatment (ACT) model as it applies to intervening with homeless veterans.
4. What are the risk factors for social workers working with this population? What can be done to mitigate the risks and stress?
5. What policy, programmatic, and practice recommendations can you offer to eliminate veteran homelessness?

REFERENCES

Arkowitz, H., Westra, H., Miller, W., & Rollnick, S. (2008). *Motivational interviewing in the treatment of psychological problems*. New York, NY: Guilford Press.

Assertive Community Treatment Association. (2011). *Origins of ACT*. Retrieved from http://www.actassociation.org/

Bormann, J., Becker, S., Gershwin, M., Kelly, A., Pada, L., Smith, T., & Allen, L. (2006). Relationship of frequent mantrum repetition to emotional and spiritual well-being of healthcare workers. *Journal of Continuing Education in Nursing*, *37*(5), 218.

Bormann, J., Liu, L., Thorp, S. R., & Lang, A. J. (2011). Spiritual wellbeing mediates PTSD change in veterans with military-related PTSD. *International Journal of Behavioral Medicine*, *19*(2), 24.

Cheng, A. L., Lin, H., Kasprow, W., & Rosenheck, R. A. (2007). Impact of supported housing on clinical outcomes: Analysis of a randomized trial using multiple imputation technique. *Journal of Nervous and Mental Disease*, *195*(1), 83–88.

Coldwell, C. M., & Bender, W. S. (2007). The effectiveness of assertive community treatment for homeless populations with severe mental illness: A meta-analysis. *American Journal of Psychiatry*, 164(3), 393–399.

Committee on Veterans Affairs: United States Senate. (2010). *Hearing on VA plan for ending homelessness among veterans*. Retrieved from http://www.access.gpo.gov/ congress/senate

County of San Diego. (2010). *Grand jury report on the homeless*. Retrieved from http://www.sdcounty.ca.gov/grandjury/reports/2009–2010/HomelessReport.pdf

Cunningham, M., Henry, M., & Lyons, W. (2007). *Vital mission: ending homelessness among veterans*. Washington, DC: National Alliance to End Homelessness, Homelessness Research Institute.

Culhane, D. P., & Metraux, S. (2008). Rearranging the deck chairs or reallocating the lifeboats?: Homelessness assistance and its alternatives. *Journal of American Planning Association*, *74*(1), 111–121.

Department of Veterans Affairs. (2006). *VA mental health intensive case management.* VHA Directive 2006–004. Retrieved from http://www.mcleague.com/mdp/pdf/MentalHealth.pdf

Exum, H. A., & Coll, J. E., & Weiss, E.L. (2011). (2nd ed.). *A civilian counselor's primer for counseling veterans*. Dear Park, NY: Linus.

Figley, C. (1995). *Compassion fatigue: Coping with secondary traumatic stress disorder in those who treat traumatized.* Bristol, PA: Brunner/Mazel.

Fisk, D., Sells, D., & Rowe, M. (2007). Sober housing and motivational interviewing: The treatment access project. *Journal of Primary Prevention*, *28*(21), 281–293. doi: 10.1007/s10935-007-0096-6

Gamache, G., Rosenheck, R., & Tessler, R. (2003). Over-representation of women veterans among homeless women. *American Journal of Public Health*, *93*(7), 1132–1136.

Gold, M. & Miller, N. (1993). Dissociation of craving and relapse in alcohol and cocaine dependence. *Biological psychiatry*, 33(6A), A155–A155.

Herman, J. (1992). *Trauma and recovery*. New York, NY: Basic Books.

Hickman, P. (1987). But You Weren't There. In Williams, T. (Ed.), *Post-Traumatic Stress Disorder: A handbook for clinicians* (pp. 93–207). Cincinnati, OH: Disabled American Veterans National Headquarters.

Hoge, C. W. (2010). *Once a Warrior Always a Warrior*. Guilford, CT: Globe Pequot Press.

HUD-VASH Handbook (2011). *Housing and Urban Development (HUD)—Department of Veterans Affairs Supported Housing (VASH) Program.* Retrieved from http://www.va.gov/vha publications/ViewPublication.asp?pub_ID=2446

Hurlburt, M. S., Hough, R. I., & Wood, P. A. (1996). Effects of substance abuse on housing stability of homeless mentally ill persons in supported housing. *Psychiatric Services*, *47*(7), 731–736.

Kryda, A. & Compton, M. (2007). Mistrust of outreach workers and lack of confidence in available services among individuals who are chronically street homeless. *Journal of Community Mental Health* *45*(1), 144–150.

Kuhn, J. H., & Nakashima, J. (2009). Community homelessness assessment, local education and networking group (CHALENG) for veterans. *The 15th annual progress report on public law 105–114: Services for homeless veterans' assessment and coordination.* Retrieved from http://www1.va.gov/fbci/docs/ProjectCHALENG

Kuhn, J. H., & Nakashima, J. (2011). *The 17th annual progress report: Community homelessness assessment, local education and networking group (CHALENG) for veterans for fiscal year (FY) 2010.* Retrieved from http://www.va.gov/homeless/chaleng.asp

Latkin, C., Sherman, S., & Knowlton, A. (2003). HIV prevention among drug users: Outcome of a network-oriented peer outreach intervention. *Health Psychology*, *22*(4), 332–339.

Levy, B., & O'Connell, J. (2004) Health care for homeless persons. *New England Journal of Medicine*, *350*(23), 2329–2332.

Lipskey, L. V., & Burk. C. (2009). *Caring for those who care for others*. San Francisco, CA: Berrett Koehler.

Manuel, J. I., Covell, H. H., Jackson, C. T., & Essock, S. M. (2011). Does assertive community treatment increase medication adherence for people with co-occurring psychotic and substance use disorders? *Journal of the American Psychiatric Nurses Association*, *7*(1), 51–56.

McGuire, J., Rosenheck, R. A., & Kasprow, W. J. (2011). Patient and program predictors of 12-month outcomes for homeless veterans following discharge from time-limited residential treatment. *Administrative Policy in Mental Health*, *38*(8), 142–154.

Nachison, J., Van Keuren, R., & Talbot, D. (1995). *Vietnam veterans of San Diego stand down: A step-by-step procedural manual*. Retrieved from http://www.vvsd.net/pdf/sdmanual.pdf

National Association of Social Workers. (2008). *Code of ethics*. Retrieved from http://www.socialworkers.org/pubs/code/code.asp

National Coalition for Homeless Veterans. (2011). *Homeless veteran fact sheet*. Retrieved from http://www.nchv.org/background.cfm#facts

Nermin W., & Richard, G. (2004). Factors affecting medication adherence among the homeless. *University of Toronto Medical Journal*, *82*(1), 6–9.

O'Toole, P., Buckel, L., Bourgault, C., Blumen, J., Redihan, S., Jiang, L., & Friedman, P. (2010). Applying the chronic care model to homeless veterans: Effect of a population approach to primary care on utilization and clinical outcomes. *American Journal of Public Health*, *100*(12), 2493–2499.

Padgett, D. K., & Henwood, B. F. (2011). Commentary: Moving into the fourth decade of ACT. *Psychiatry Service*, *62*(6), 605.

Pearlman, L. A., & MacIan, P. S. (1995). Vicarious traumatization: An empirical study of the effects of trauma work on trauma therapist. *Professional Psychology: Research and Practice*, *26*, 558–565.

Ranaivo, Y. (2010). Vet center upgrades offerings. *Amarillo globe-news*. Retrieved from http://amarillo.com/news/local-news/2010–10–22/vet-center-upgrades-offerings

Rosenheck, R., Frisman, L., & Gallup, P. (1995). Effectiveness and cost of specific treatment elements in a program for homeless mentally ill veterans. *Psychiatric Services*, *46*(11), 1131–1139.

Rosenheck, R., Kasprow, W., Frisman, L., & Liu-Mares, W. (2003). Cost effectiveness of supported housing for homeless persons with mental illness. *Archives of General Psychiatry*, *60*(9), 940–951.

Rosenheck, R. A., & Koegel, P. (1995). Characteristics of veterans and non-veterans in three samples of homeless men. *Hospital and Community Psychiatry*, *44*(9), 858–863.

Sadowski, L., Kee, R., Vanderwheele, T., & Buchanan, D. (2009). Effect of a housing and case management program on emergency department visits and hospitalizations among chronically ill homeless adults: A randomized trial. *Journal of the American Medical Association*, *301*(17), 1771–1778.

Senate Sub-Committee Hearing (2010). *The VA's plan for ending homelessness among veterans. Pane II*. Retrieved from http://veterans.senate.gov/hearings.cfm?action=release.display&release_id=bab2c127-95d9-4b58-b4d6-ccfc8cc2e0f6

Shay, J. (2002). *Odysseus in America: Combat trauma and the trials of homecoming*. New York, NY: Scribner.

Stefanic, A., & Tsemberis, S. (2007). Housing for long-term shelter dwellers with psychiatric disabilities in a suburban county: A four-year study of housing access and retention. *Journal of Primary Prevention, 28*(3–40), 265–279.

Teresa, M., & Vardey, L. (Ed.). (1995). A *simple path* (1st ed.). New York, NY: Random House.

Tsemberis, S., Gulcur, L., & Nakae, B. A. (2004). Housing first, consumer choice, and harm reduction for homeless individual with a dual diagnosis. *American Journal of Public Health, 94*(4), 651–656.

Tsemberis, S., Moran, L., Shinn, M., & Asmussen, S. (2003). Consumer preference programs for individuals who are homeless and have psychiatric disabilities: A drop-in center and a supported housing program. *American Journal of Community Psychology, 32*(3/4), 305–317.

United States Department of Housing & Urban Development & United States Department of Veterans Affairs. (2010). *The annual homeless assessment report to Congress*. Washington, DC: U.S. Government Printing Office.

United States Department of Veterans Affairs (2011). *Project CHALENG*. Retrieved from http://www.va.gov/homeless/chaleng.asp

Witte, P. (2012, January). *State of homelessness in America 2012: A research report on homelessness*. Washington, DC: National Alliance to End Homelessness/Homeless Research Institute.

CHAPTER

16

Navigating Systems of Care

Jennifer Roberts

INTRODUCTION

The U.S. Department of Veterans Affairs (VA) is a government-run military veteran benefit system. The VA reports employing nearly 280,000 people at hundreds of Veterans Affairs medical facilities, clinics, and benefit offices across the nation (2010). It is responsible for administering benefit programs for veterans, their families, and survivors. These benefits include health care, disability compensation, pension, education, and vocational rehabilitation.

Navigating the VA system can be a daunting task. This chapter offers a road map for social workers to assist their veteran clients with enrollment and accessing care and benefits. The various enrollment options are addressed, in addition to an explanation of priority groups. Service-connected disabilities are reviewed as they relate to enrollment.

Next, the chapter covers specific veteran populations, such as Operation Enduring Freedom/Operation Iraqi Freedom/Operation New Dawn (OEF/OIF/OND), homeless veterans, and women veterans. These special populations of veterans have specific needs and concerns that the VA health care system has within their purview to address. The VA has also developed programs to address suicide prevention and transition assistance, which are explored. A discussion on military sexual trauma (MST) and the various programs to assist these veterans is also reviewed. A case study illustrating how a female veteran with MST navigated the VA health care system is shown. Discussion questions conclude the chapter.

BASIC ELIGIBILITY AND ENROLLMENT

The VA operates the nation's largest integrated health care system with more than 1,400 sites of care, including hospitals, community clinics, community living centers, domiciliary, readjustment counseling centers and various other facilities (Department of Veterans Affairs, 2010a).

To be eligible, a person must have served as active duty military and enlisted after September 7, 1980, or entered active duty after October 16, 1981, where they must have served 24 continuous months or the full period for which they were called to active duty (Department of Veterans Affairs, 2010b). This minimum duty requirement may not apply to veterans discharged for hardship, early out or a disability incurred or aggravated in the line of duty (Department of Veterans Affairs, 2010b).

For most veterans, entry into the VA system begins with applying for enrollment. To apply, veterans must complete VA Form 10–10EZ, which is the "Application for Health Benefits." Veterans can enroll online or as a walk-in to an eligibility office at their nearest VA facility, or mail in their application. Once enrolled, veterans can receive health care at VA health care facilities anywhere in the country (Department of Veterans Affairs, 2010b).

Although veterans are not required to enroll, they are encouraged to do so to allow for better access to health care. Due to various conditions, the following veterans are automatically enrolled:

Veterans with a service-connected disability of 50% or more (service-connected disabilities are discussed later in this chapter).

Veterans seeking care for a disability the military determined was incurred or aggravated in the line of duty, but which the VA has not yet rated, within 12 months of military discharge.

Veterans seeking care for a service-connected disability only.

Veterans seeking registry examinations (Ionizing Radiation, Agent Orange, Gulf War/Operation Iraqi Freedom and Depleted Uranium) (Department of Veterans Affairs, 2010b).

PRIORITY GROUPS

During enrollment, each veteran is assigned to a priority group. The VA uses priority groups to balance demand for VA health care enrollment with available resources. Figure 16.1 illustrates how the VA categorizes the priority groups.

COMBAT VETERANS

Since 2001, more than 2 million U.S. military personnel have been deployed to the conflicts in Iraq and Afghanistan (Amdur et al., 2011). On January, 28, 2008, "Public Law 100–181" titled the "National Defense Authorization Act of 2008" was signed into law (Department of Veterans Affairs, 2010b, p. 3). It extended the period of eligibility for health care for veterans who served in a theater of combat operations after November 11, 1998.

Under the "Combat Veterans" authority, the Department of Veterans Affairs provides cost-free health care services for veterans for 5 years following their date of discharge. This includes nursing home care for conditions possibly related to military service and enrollment in Priority Group 6 (unless eligible for enrollment in a higher priority group, as

Group 1	Veterans with service-connected disabilities rated 50% or more and/or veterans determined by the VA to be unemployable due to service-connected disabilities.
Group 2	Veterans with service-connected disabilities rated 30% or 40%.
Group 3	Veterans with service-connected disabilities rated 10% and 20%; veterans who are former Prisoners of War (POW) or were awarded a Purple Heart medal; veterans awarded special eligibility for disabilities incurred in treatment or participation in a VA Vocational Rehabilitation program; and veterans whose discharge was for a disability incurred or aggravated in the line of duty.
Group 4	Veterans in need of the regular aid and attendance of another person to perform basic functions of everyday life, such as bathing, feeding, dressing, and so on.
Group 5	Veterans receiving VA pension benefits or eligible for Medicaid/Medicare programs, and non-service-connected veterans and non-compensable 0% service-connected veterans whose gross annual household income and/or net worth are below the VA national income threshold and geographically adjusted income threshold for their resident area.
Group 6	Veterans of World War I; veterans seeking care solely for certain conditions associated with exposure to ionizing radiation during atmospheric testing or during the occupation of Hiroshima and Nagasaki; for any illness associated with participation in tests conducted by the Department of Defense (DoD) as part of Project 112/Project SHAD; veterans with 0% service-connected disabilities who are receiving disability compensation benefits and veterans who served in a theater of combat operations after Nov. 11, 1998 as follows: Veterans discharged from active duty on or after January 28, 2003, who were enrolled as of January 28, 2008, and veterans who apply for enrollment after January 28, 2008, for 5 years postdischarge. Veterans discharged from active duty before January 28, 2003, who apply for enrollment after January 28, 2003, until January 27, 2011.
Group 7	Veterans with gross household income below the geographically adjusted income threshold for their resident location and who agree to pay co-pays.
Group 8	Veterans with gross household income and/or net worth above the VA national income threshold and the geographic income threshold (GMT) who agree to pay co-pays.

Figure 16.1 VA priority groups

displayed in Figure 16.1). The 5-year enrollment period begins on the date of discharge from active military service, or in the case of multiple call-ups, the most recent discharge date (Department of Veterans Affairs, 2010b, p. 3). To be eligible, the veteran must provide documentation that he or she served in an area determined to be an area of combat and/or the veteran received a combat service medal(s), and/or received imminent danger or hostile fire pay or tax benefits. The health benefits included are cost-free care and medications provided for conditions potentially related to combat service (Department of Veterans Affairs, 2010b, p. 3). In today's health care system, it can be expensive and difficult to secure reliable coverage; therefore, many veterans benefit from the free health care provided.

SERVICE-CONNECTED DISABILITIES AND COMPENSATION

The Department of Veterans Affairs has a disability compensation program that provides payments to service members who were injured, or whose medical conditions were aggravated, as a result of their military service (Wounded Warrior Project, 2007). These disabilities are considered to be service-connected. The amount of compensation that veterans receive depends on their disability rating. The disability rating takes into account all of the service member's disabilities and medical conditions to arrive at a combined disability rating. To receive VA disability compensation the veteran must demonstrate three elements:

1. A medical diagnosis of the current disability.
2. Medical evidence, or in some cases lay evidence, of an in-service injury.
3. A link between the in-service injury (or aggravation of a preexisting condition) and the current disability.

The VA disability payments are dependent on the severity of the veteran's disabilities. The VA disability rating is not a permanent rating and it can be adjusted as the service member's condition changes (Wounded Warrior Project, 2007).

OPERATION ENDURING FREEDOM/IRAQI FREEDOM/NEW DAWN VETERANS

Since 2001, more than 1 million (of the over 2 million U.S. military personnel) have been separated from the military and are eligible for health care and other services through the Department of Veterans Affairs (Amdur et al., 2011). Approximately 46% of these eligible Operation Enduring Freedom/Operation Iraqi Freedom (OEF/OIF) combat veterans have used VA services since 2001 based on Global War on Terrorism (GWOT) data (Amdur et al., 2011). Service in these conflict areas has exposed these individuals to a variety of risks, including physical injury, psychological trauma, environmental agent exposure, and numerous stressors impacting personal life (Amdur et al., 2011).

The VA health care system developed and implemented a veteran-centered, postcombat care program, which assists veterans and their family members with the transition to civilian life and postcombat care. They partner social work, primary care, mental health and rehabilitation services to address the full spectrum of risk exposure and complex health complications that combat veterans experience. All 152 VA medical centers in the United States have a care management team consisting of both clinicians (e.g., registered nurses and social workers) that also include OEF/OIF/OND program managers, OEF/OIF/OND case managers, and nonclinical staff led by Transition Patient Advocates (TPA). Case management provided by social workers is the core component of services rendered to assist veterans in restoring or maintaining their functioning within the context of their family and community reintegration post combat. Social work case managers use proactive case management, by maintaining regular contacts with veterans and their families to coordinate services, and address emerging needs. They support and guide veterans to appropriate resources. Additionally the TPA help veterans better navigate the VA system (Amdur et al., 2011).

VET CENTERS

In addition to case management, Vet Centers offer readjustment counseling to assist combat veterans in their transition from military to civilian life. Readjustment counseling is provided at community Vet Centers at 271 sites across all 50 states and most U.S. territories. Readjustment counseling includes the following services: individual counseling, group counseling, marital and family counseling, bereavement counseling, medical referrals, assistance in applying for VA benefits, employment counseling; substance abuse assessment and referral, and military sexual trauma counseling. Veterans who served in a combat zone and received a military service ribbon are eligible for this specific type of counseling. Family members of combat veterans are eligible for military related issues. There is no fee for readjustment counseling (Wounded Warrior Project, 2007).

HOMELESS VETERANS PROGRAM

According to the Department of Veterans Affairs the nation's homeless veterans are predominantly male, with roughly 5% being female; the majority are single; come from urban areas; and suffer from mental illness, alcohol and/or substance abuse, or co-occurring disorders. According to the National Coalition for Homeless Veterans, the VA estimates that 107,000 veterans are homeless on any given night (2011). To assist these veterans, the VA has designated the Health Care for Homeless Veterans Program (HCHV), also known as "VA Homeless Outreach," to provide varied services and programs to help homeless veterans live as self-sufficiently and independently as possible. The details of this program are addressed in Chapter 15.

MILITARY SEXUAL TRAUMA

The term *military sexual trauma* (MST) is defined in U.S. Code (1720D of Title 38) as "physical assault of a sexual nature, battery of a sexual nature, or sexual harassment [repeated, unsolicited verbal or physical contact of a sexual nature which is threatening in character] that occurred while a veteran was serving on active duty or active duty for training." From a mental health perspective, this may include any sexual activity where someone was involved against his or her will. Examples of MST include being pressured into sexual activities (e.g., with threats of consequences for refusing to be sexually cooperative or with implied faster promotions or better treatment in exchange for sex); being unable to consent to sexual activities (e.g., when intoxicated); or being physically forced into sexual activities (Department of Veterans Affairs, n.d.b, p. 1).

Other experiences that fall into the category of MST include unwanted sexual touching or grabbing; threatening offensive remarks about a person's body or sexual activities; and/or threatening and unwelcome sexual advances (Department of Veterans Affairs, n.d.b, p. 1). In 1992, Congress mandated the Department of Veterans Affairs to treat distress related to Military Sexual Trauma (MST). Following the mandate, 61% of Veterans Affairs medical centers had sexual trauma treatment teams by 1995 (Suris, Davis, Kashner, Gillaspy, & Petty, 1998). Today, every VA facility has an MST coordinator who serves as a contact person for MST-related issues. This person can help veterans find and access VA services and programs, as well as state and federal benefits and community resources (Department of Veterans Affairs, 2011b).

The VA has a universal screening program for military sexual trauma. Under this program, all veterans seen at VA facilities are asked whether they experienced sexual trauma during their military service. Veterans who respond yes are offered further information about MST-related services. According to the National Center for PTSD, about 1 in 5 women and 1 in 100 men respond yes when screened for MST. Though rates of MST are higher among women, there are almost as many men seen in the VA that have experienced MST as there are women (n.d.).

Military sexual trauma is an experience, not a diagnosis or mental health condition. MST affects each person differently, resulting in a wide range of emotional responses. Sexual assault is more likely to result in symptoms of posttraumatic stress disorder than are most other types of trauma, including combat. Symptoms of depression, anxiety, and substance abuse are also common. Sexual trauma can have severe consequences for physical health and is associated with gastrointestinal difficulties, chronic pain, chronic fatigue, and headaches. Even survivors without a formal diagnosis of PTSD may still struggle with issues related to emotional deregulation, interpersonal functioning, and meaning-making about their experiences (Department of Veterans Affairs, n.d.b, p. 1).

There are many treatment options available for veterans who are survivors of military sexual trauma. All treatment for physical and mental health problems related to MST is free for both men and women. Every VA facility has providers who are knowledgeable about treatment for MST. Many facilities have special outpatient mental health services for sexual trauma. Vet Centers also have specially trained sexual trauma counselors. Across the country, the VA also has special residential or inpatient sexual trauma treatment programs. These are programs for veterans who need more intense treatment and support. Some veterans are more comfortable in same gender treatment programs; VA offers separate support groups for men and women, as well as mixed gender groups. Some commonly used protocols include Cognitive Processing Therapy (CPT), Prolonged Exposure (PE), and other exposure-based therapies for PTSD. Other options are Acceptance and Commitment Therapy (ACT) for anxiety and depression and Dialectical Behavior Therapy (DBT) for emotional dysregulation and interpersonal deficits, particularly for patients who have experienced multiple traumas.

SUICIDE PREVENTION

The rate of suicide among veterans has been on the rise. The National Violent Death Reporting System reports 18 veterans commit suicide per day. The VA Serious Mental Illness Treatment, Research and Evaluation Center reports five deaths per day among vets receiving care from Department of Veteran Affairs (Kemp, 2010). According to the Department of Veterans Affairs, there are certain suicide risk factors specific to veterans, including frequent deployments, deployments to hostile environments, exposure to extreme stress, physical/sexual assault while in the service (both women and men), length of deployments, and service-related injury (n.d.b).

Each VA Medical Center has a Suicide Prevention Coordinator to ensure that veterans receive needed counseling and services. One of these services is the Veterans Crisis Line. It is a toll-free, confidential resource that connects veterans in crisis and their families and friends with qualified, caring VA responders. The professionals at the Veterans Crisis Line are specially trained and experienced in helping veterans of all ages and circumstances—from veterans coping with mental health issues that were never addressed to recent veterans struggling with relationships or the transition back to civilian life (Department of Veterans Affairs, n.d.b).

TRANSITION ASSISTANCE

The Transition Assistance Program (TAP) consists of comprehensive 3-day workshops at military installations designed to help service members as they transition from military to civilian life. The program includes job search, employment and training information, as well as VA benefits information, for service members who are within 12 months of separation or 24 months of retirement. A sister workshop, the Disabled Transition Assistance Program (DTAP), provides information on VA's Vocational Rehabilitation and Employment Program, as well as other programs for the disabled (Department of Veterans Affairs, 2010b).

The Vocational Rehabilitation and Employment (VR&E) program provides educational and vocational counseling to service members, veterans, and to certain dependents at no charge. These counseling services are designed to help an individual choose a vocational direction, determine the course needed to achieve the chosen goal, and evaluate the career possibilities open to them. Assistance includes aptitude testing, occupational goals, locating the right type of training program, and exploring educational or training facilities that can be utilized to achieve an occupational goal. Service members are eligible during the period in which they are on active duty and within 180 days of the estimated date of discharge from active duty (Department of Veterans Affairs, 2010b).

WOMEN VETERANS

The number of women veterans is growing rapidly with increasing demands for gender specific health care. In addition, there appears to be an influx of younger veterans entering the VA health care system. According to the Women Veterans Health Strategic Health Care Group (WVHSCG), women comprise approximately 14% of active duty military, 18% of National Guard and Reserves, and 6% of VA health care users (2010). Women veterans are one of the fastest growing subpopulations of veterans, second only to elderly veterans. The median female veteran's age is 46, for males the median age is 60. The number of women veterans enrolled in health care is expected to double in the next 5 years (Department of Veterans Affairs, 2010a).

Women who were deployed and served in the recent conflicts in Afghanistan and Iraq are enrolling in the VA at historical rates. For example, 42.6% of female OEF/OIF veterans have enrolled with VA health care, according to the WVHSCG (2010). Furthermore, almost all OEF/OIF women veterans accessing VA health care are under the age of 40 and of childbearing age, creating a significant shift in the provision of health care (Department of Veterans Affairs, 2008b).

With the growing population of women veterans discharging from the military and entering the VA health care system, the VA has recognized the need to improve their services for women. These enhancements include comprehensive primary care throughout the nation, using state-of-the-art health care equipment and technology (Department of Veterans Affairs, *VHA Handbook* 1330.01, 2010a). Women's health care is provided by proficient and interested primary care clinicians who focus on safety, dignity, and sensitivity to gender-specific needs. All VA medical centers are staffed with a Women Veterans Program Manager (WVPM), who is responsible for increased outreach to women veterans, improvement in quality of care, and the development of best practices in organizational delivery of women's health care (Department of Veterans Affairs, 2008b). The WVPM is a health care professional who serves as an advisor and advocate for women veterans. She works with the local VA staff to plan and coordinate VA health care services for women veterans at VA medical centers and outpatient clinics.

According to the Department of Veterans Affairs, health care services available to women veterans include comprehensive primary care, mental health evaluation and treatment; specialty care for chronic conditions; reproductive health care including maternity and newborn care as well as infertility evaluation; rehabilitation and long-term care. In addition, a VA health care professional is available by phone at each VA medical center to answer questions and advise on health concerns 24 hours, 7 days a week (n.d.b).

Case Vignette: Lisa Smith

Lisa Smith is a 29-year-old single, Caucasian U.S. Marine Corps (USMC) OIF/OND, female veteran. She is unmarried and has no children. Her parents divorced when she was a child and she has one sister who she rarely sees. She has a minimal support system. For approximately 8 months, Lisa has struggled with a substance abuse issue. She served 5 years active duty in the military with a 2-year (total) deployment to Iraq. Lisa served as foot patrol and was involved in convoys. She was exposed to countless dangerous missions in some of the most hostile combat zones in Iraq. While in the military, she obtained counseling and has been sober for 13 months.

Prior to military service Lisa graduated from a high school in the Midwest and worked odd jobs for a few years trying to figure out what she wanted to do with her life. Her father left when she was 8 years old and her mother remarried soon thereafter. Her stepfather physically abused Lisa for several years, but the abuse stopped once she reached adolescence. She never pursued counseling to cope with the abuse that she had suffered. Looking for direction in her life and a means to escape her hometown, she decided to join the military at age 24.

During her second deployment to Iraq, she was sexually assaulted by two of her fellow male Marines in her command. She reported the assault to her command and suffered posttraumatic stress disorder (PTSD) as a result. She also reports trauma symptoms related to gunfire exposure, improvised explosive devices, and witnessing multiple war casualties including the deaths of her colleagues. Lisa currently endorses significant symptoms of PTSD, major depressive disorder with passive suicidal ideation.

Lisa was separated from military service under a medical board as a severely ill/injured veteran with the following diagnoses: traumatic brain injury (TBI), PTSD, military sexual trauma (MST), major depression, migraines, tinnitus, lumbar sacral strain, and chronic pain to back and shoulders. Lisa spent 8 months at a Naval Transition Unit while awaiting the medical board decision.

On medical retirement from the USMC, the veteran met with the VA/DOD liaison at her local naval base, who assisted her with transition into the VA health care system. Lisa was agreeable to VA OEF/OIF/OND case management services and was connected to her case manager before her military separation. An administrative and personal transfer was completed. The OEF/OIF/OND case manager (CM) contacted and personally met with Lisa. The CM provided Lisa with further education on transition process and OEF/OIF/OND services and referrals.

The CM assisted Lisa with:

- Member Services for enrollment into the VA Healthcare System
- Appointment with OEF/OIF/OND Intake Social Worker
- Linkage to the Transition Patient Advocate (TPA)
- Scheduled Initial Medical Provider appointment for Health Assessment
- Submitted consults to specialty clinics as needed: traumatic brain injury (TBI), mental health, audiology, orthopedics, women's clinic
- Connected veteran to a 6-month inpatient/residential VA polytrauma PTSD program
- CM worked collaboratively with the TPA in obtaining ongoing services specific to finances, housing, and social support in the community
- Linked to Veteran Service Officer (VSO) to increase service-connected disability rating if needed in the future

Once a veteran like Lisa is stable and connected to all VA resources, the CM will follow the veteran and offer additional resources, referrals, and support as needed.

CONCLUSION

The Department of Veterans Affairs is a complex system. This chapter offered a road map for social workers to assist our nation's veterans with enrollment and accessing services. An in-depth explanation of the enrollment process including the difference between priority groups was reviewed as the first step to accessing care. A connection between enrollment and service-connected disabilities was also covered.

Special populations of veterans, namely OEF/OIF/OND, homeless, and women veterans were covered as a means to illustrate the various programs the VA offers for these veterans. A discussion of military sexual trauma sought to bring awareness to this sensitive, yet important topic. Suicide prevention and transition assistance were also reviewed. The case vignette featuring Lisa Smith illustrated the process a social worker can follow to access services for veteran clients through the Department of Veterans Affairs.

The goal of this chapter is to provide social workers with a practical guide for navigating a complex system such as the Department of Veterans Affairs. There are many programs and services offered, which are also evolving on a consistent basis. Social workers can use this chapter as a tool for understanding the ways to access care for their veteran clients and to locate the resources they need.

CHAPTER DISCUSSION QUESTIONS

1. What is the first step in accessing care at the VA health care system?
2. Why is it important for a veteran to apply for service-connection disability compensation?
3. Why would an MST survivor be hesitant in reaching out to the Department of Veterans Affairs for treatment for MST?

REFERENCES

Amdur, D., Batres, A., Belisle, J., Brown, J., Cornis-Pop, M., Mathewson-Chapman, M., . . . Washam, T. (2011). VA integrated post-combat care: A systemic approach to caring for returning combat veterans. *Social Work and Health Care, 50*, 564–575. doi: 10.0180/00981389.2011.554275

Department of Veterans Affairs. (n.d.a). *Combat veteran eligibility* [Brochure]. Washington, DC: Author.

Department of Veterans Affairs. (n.d.b). *A primer on military sexual trauma for mental health clinicians* [Brochure]. Washington, DC: Author.

Department of Veterans Affairs. (2008a). *Health care for homeless veterans (HCHV)*. [Brochure]. San Diego: Author.

Department of Veterans Affairs. (2008b). *Provision of primary care to women veterans*. Washington, DC: Department of Veteran Affairs.

Department of Veterans Affairs. (2010a). *VHA handbook 1330.01, health care services for women veterans*. Washington, DC: Department of Veteran Affairs.

Department of Veterans Affairs. (2010b). *Federal benefits for veterans, dependents and survivors*. Washington, DC: Department of Veteran Affairs.

Department of Veterans Affairs. (2011a). Mental Health. *How to recognize when to ask for help*. Retrieved from http://www.mentalhealth.va.gov/suicide_prevention/whentoaskfor help.asp

Department of Veterans Affairs. (2011b). National Center for PTSD. *Military sexual trauma*. Retrieved from http://www.ptsd.va.gov/public/pages/military-sexual-trauma-general.asp

Department of Veterans Affairs. (2011c). *Women veterans healthcare*. Retrieved from http://www.womenshealth.va.gov/WOMENSHEALTH /healthcare.asp

Kemp, J. (2010). *VA program for suicide prevention*. [PowerPoint slides].

National Coalition for Homeless Veterans. (2011). *Facts and media*. Retrieved from http://www.nchv.org/background.cfm

Suris, A. M., Davis, L. L., Kashner, T. M., Gillaspy, J. A. Jr., & Petty, F. (1998). A survey of sexual trauma treatment provided by VA medical centers. *Psychiatric Services, 49*, 382–384.

Women Veterans Health Strategic Health Care Group. (2010). *Key messaging*. Washington, DC: Department of Veterans Affairs. Retrieved from www.publichealth.va.gov/womens health

Wounded Warrior Project. (2007). *A handbook for injured service members and their families*. Washington, DC: Wounded Warrior Project.

CHAPTER

17

Transitioning Veterans Into Civilian Life

Jose E. Coll and Eugenia L. Weiss

INTRODUCTION

It is estimated that 30,000 to 300,000 veterans will be affected by the invisible wounds of war (i.e., PTSD and other related mental disorders, including traumatic brain injury) as a result of the U.S. engagement on the Global War on Terrorism (Tanielian & Jaycox, 2008). Many of these wounded warriors will be facing discharge or separation from military downsizing, or from being medically separated or by choosing to separate or retire from service. Even for those veterans who are not suffering from the aftermath of combat experiences (keeping in mind that many veterans do not have PTSD) there is a veteran mind-set that is influenced by military culture (Exum, Coll, & Weiss, 2011), which could present challenges in terms of reintegrating into civilian society. This chapter addresses the various transitions that veterans may experience as they move from being full-time military personnel to civilians and it also offers knowledge for social workers to understand the various military-operated transition programs such as Transition Assistance Program (TAP), Disabled Transition Assistance Program (DTAP), and Wounded Warriors as well as the systems of care through the Veteran Affairs (VA). The chapter also addresses the different kinds of veteran transitions, for instance, into higher education, and/or into civilian community and employment. Last, the chapter offers skill-building practices for clinicians in the form of veteran reintegration training and the application of a case vignette followed by discussion questions.

TRANSITION

Transition from military life to civilian life can be a daunting task, and for many people it's a confusing time. Many individuals leaving the military, both men and women, find that in the civilian world their job skills are not transferable. An individual who was an infantryperson in the service may only find those skills translatable into security, police force, border patrol, and the like, while an individual with computer technology training may have skills more easily translated into the civilian world. Additionally, the individual may not always know how to translate military terminology into civilian language for potential employers to appreciate their knowledge and skills. For some service members, separation from the military can be an overwhelming personal experience, create financial hardship, and contribute to the already challenged family system. In 2010 as many as 153,396 service members decided to reenlist and not separate (U.S. Government Accountability Office, 2011). However, for those who did receive a DD-214 (i.e., discharge) there may have been a period in which they struggled to accept the lack of cohesiveness that exists in the civilian world as opposed to the sense of camaraderie in the service. This alone may prompt individuals to seek out a recruiter and attempt to reenlist. According to the Department of Defense, 5% of those enlisting (i.e., new recruits) in 2010 met the criteria for prior service, a number that is believed to fluctuate due to the U.S. job market and the needs of the military.

In an effort to meet the needs of service members prior to separating from the military, the Department of Defense, Department of Veterans Affairs, Department of Transportation, and the Labor Department's Veterans Employment and Training Service (VETS) established a partnership to create a program known as the Transition Assistance Program (TAP) and the Disabled Transition Assistant Program (DTAP) (U.S. Department of Labor, 2011). These programs offer employment assistance and training information for service personnel within 180 days of separation from military service.

These transition assistance programs were developed with the intention of meeting the needs of service members prior to and during separation rather than waiting for the separation to occur and then addressing issues related to military separation. This proactive approach can save a significant amount of money to both the service member and to the government. According to the U.S. Department of Labor (2011) an independent evaluation of the program determined that on average, service members who have participated in TAPS find jobs 3 weeks sooner than those who do not participate in the program.

TAPS consists of a 3-day workshop at selected military installations, which offers state employment services, military family support services, Department of Labor contractors, and Veteran's Employment and Training Services (U.S. Department of Labor, 2011). The individuals who attend TAPS learn how to conduct job searches and receive assistance with regard to career decision making. Individuals are informed about current occupational and labor market conditions and are provided skills in resume writing, cover letter preparation, as well as interview techniques. Additionally, service members receive information on the veteran benefits that are available to them (granted for those who are honorably discharged). For example, veterans are eligible for the following services, most of which are free: burial in military cemeteries; home loan guarantees at lower interest rates; veterans employment and training services; and access to VA health care benefits, among other benefits (Kitchen, 2010). The VA health care system offers a variety of services, such as hospitalization; outpatient medical services; dentistry; pharmacy; prosthetic services; domiciliary; nursing home care; community-based residential care; sexual trauma counseling; PTSD treatment services; comprehensive women's health care; rehabilitation services for homeless veterans; readjustment counseling; and alcohol and drug dependency treatment. The VA provides health care at no cost for veterans who served in combat after November 11, 1998. Veterans have 5 years from the time they served to receive services at no cost for illnesses or injuries related to combat (U.S. Department of Veterans Affairs, 2009). Additional information on how a veteran can access care through the VA is provided in Chapter 16 on helping veteran clients navigate through the systems of care.

DISABLED TRANSITION ASSISTANCE

For seriously disabled service members, a joint VA and Department of Defense (DoD) program is in place that allows service members to file disability claims with the VA up to 180 days prior to separation from active duty. This can mean a significant difference in the life of an injured veteran. As most claims take 6 months or longer to be evaluated by the VA, a noteworthy hardship can be placed on a veteran if this program is not accessed before separating (U.S. Air Force, 2010). Additionally, the TAP program has a disabled transition assistance program (DTAP) for all injured and ill service members regardless of the branch of service (U.S. Air Force, 2010).

For those individuals that are separating due to a service-connected disability, it is strongly encouraged for them to attend a specialized transition assistance program called DTAP (Disabled Transition Assistance Program). DTAP offers guidance about VA services and Vocational Rehabilitation and Employment (VR&E). Under DTAP, veterans can be suitably employed through the provision of funding for technical training and education and can be eligible for a daily living subsidy (U.S. Air Force, 2010).

The program is intended to assist service members in successfully adjusting to civilian life, much like the traditional TAP, but concentrates on the services necessary to assist individuals separating due to a disability incurred while on duty. Additionally, the program covers insurance, adapted housing, and falls under the Americans with Disabilities Act (U.S. Army, 2010).

Like the TAP informational sessions, DTAP sessions are group sessions that go over a significant amount of information. For instance, they cover VA Vocational Rehabilitation and Employment programs, educational and vocational counseling, home loan benefits, educational benefits, VA health care information, and the more recently developed VA Caregiver Assistance Program. The VA Caregiver Support program addresses some of the psychosocial needs of caregivers within the VA system (U.S. Department of Veterans Affairs, 2011). Additionally, Adult Day Health Care Centers (ADHC) are available and provide supervision for veterans to participate in activities and as a means of socialization. This program allows for caregivers to have some respite from caregiving. Respite care provides the caregiver up to 30 days per year to maintain personal needs. This service can also be provided for a caregiver's unexpected hospitalization, a need to go out of town, or due to a family emergency (U.S. Department of Veterans Affairs, 2011). Home-based primary care is also available to veterans, and this program delivers routine services like primary care, nursing, medication management, nutrition, physical rehabilitation, mental health, social work, and referrals (U.S. Department of Veterans Affairs, 2011). Skilled home care is another program that offers nursing services and physical, occupational, and speech therapy in home.

Home hospice care is also available 24 hours a day, 7 days a week, along with bereavement care. The VA is also working on launching a pilot program for caregivers that offers additional services of insurance for the caregiver, including possible monetary compensation, and health care techniques training to assist the caregiver in caring for the veteran (U.S. Department of Veterans Affairs, 2011).

WOUNDED SERVICE MEMBERS AND MILITARY PROGRAMS

A wounded service member tends to have a unique transition either returning to duty after recovery from an injury or in his or her transition out of the military. Either situation presents a unique set of circumstances for each individual. For example, the Marine Corps has a battalion dedicated to recovery called Wounded Warriors while the Army has the Warrior Transition Unit (WTU). However, the Navy and Air Force take a slightly different approach due to the smaller number of seriously injured service members. In a later section, we present a brief overview of the different Wounded Warrior programs offered by each branch of the military.

U.S. Army

According to the U.S. Army (2010) the mission for the Warrior Transition Unit is simple: "to heal." The program is individualized through the development of a Comprehensive Transition Plan (CTP). This plan includes personalized goals for the soldier and the family. This plan may include a Community-Based Warrior Transition Unit (CBWTU) for those soldiers residing outside of a military installation. With the collaboration of the Department of Defense (DoD), TRICARE insurance, and the Department of Veterans Affairs (VA) the soldier is able to access health care on an outpatient basis. The program was set up to allow soldiers to seek care close to their personal support system as well as having their support system involved in the process.

Depending on the type of injury or injuries incurred, different transition options are available. Whenever possible, the military would prefer to return the service member to duty. After completing rehabilitation and with the combined input of all major health care providers that are involved in the service member's care, if the service member is deemed that he or she is fit for duty, the service member will be returned to their previous Military Occupational Specialty (MOS); granted, if the military still has a need for them. Unfortunately, not all service members are capable of returning to the previously held MOS after an injury. Another option is to return to duty with a new MOS. Those service members who are capable of choosing this option have injuries, or illnesses, that prevent them from performing their previous MOS, but their injuries are not deemed serious enough for the military to be unable to find another specialty available to them. In the Army the request for the assignment of an alternative MOS would go to the Military Assessment Retention Review (MAR2) committee to determine if the soldier is capable of continued service (U.S. Army, 2010).

Many individuals sustain injuries that preclude them from continuing military service even after some degree of rehabilitation and recuperation. The only option remaining after such an injury is incurred is to separate the service member from the military. Depending on the injury, the military may coordinate with the VA to ensure that the individual receives the benefits and services they need and are eligible for. A team is put into place to assist the service member to focus on alternative career options and educational goals, enabling the transition to civilian life to be as smooth as possible (U.S. Army, 2010).

U.S. Marine Corps

The Wounded Warrior Regiment is the unit for wounded Marines all over the world. The services offered to individuals within this unit include nonmedical case management types of services such as continuity of care; pay/benefits/charitable support; assistance with employment and vocational rehabilitation benefits; assistance with smooth transition from the Department of Defense (DoD) to the VA; and assistance with obtaining Traumatic Service member's Group Life Insurance (TSGLI).

The Marine Corps attempts to avoid a one-size-fits-all mentality and responds to the needs of the individual warrior. To accomplish this many different departments are involved in the process to ensure good retention, or successful transition into civilian life. Those involved in this process include Marine leaders; Recovery Care Coordinators (RCCs); medical departments; Warrior Athlete Reconditioning Program; Charitable Giving Office; Chaplain Services/Spiritual Care; Job Transition Cell; Family Support Staff, and Disability Evaluation System (DES) Support (Wounded Warrior Regiment, 2011).

U.S. Navy

Due to the smaller number of seriously injured service members who serve in the Navy, the Navy offers an oversight, advocacy, and case management program rather than a comprehensive care program. The Safe Harbor program assists sailors in navigating the complex systems through the VA that are already in place. The design behind this program is to follow the service member even after discharge or separation from the Navy and continue to make certain the sailors' needs are being met. This being said, when a veteran is having difficulty accessing or receiving needed care through the VA system, Safe Harbor can step in and advocate for the veteran to get the assistance that the veteran is eligible for.

U.S. Air Force

Established in 2005, the Air Force Wounded Warrior Program, takes a similar approach to the Navy in having case managers to assist the Air Force members in traversing the complex world of health care in and out of the military (Tan, 2009). Recovery care coordinators are nonmedical workers who offer personalized support to wounded, ill, or injured Air Force members. Additional support is offered by the family readiness centers, which provide liaisons to assist in early days of recovery.

The Air Force also spells out the eligibility for the Wounded Warrior program. For instance, Air Force members must have a combat or hostile-related injury or illness requiring long-term care that is severe enough to require a Medical Evaluation Board hearing or a Physical Evaluation Board hearing to determine fitness for duty (U.S. Air Force, 2010).

MILITARY TO CIVILIAN TRANSITION

Historically, individuals who experience the most success in reintegrating into civilian society have utilized some form of transitional assistance prior to separation or immediately on separation. A successful transition can be accomplished by helping the service member clarify their personal and professional goals as well as identify their plans for achieving those goals. Individuals who are undergoing separation from the military have been known to experience a variety of feelings, including; anxiety, frustration, fear, and loss. At times individuals can also question the meaning and purpose of their lives.

A strategy for combating these difficult feelings is through the provision of education and information. For instance, information on how to secure civilian jobs, including what skills are transferable from military to civilian employment, are helpful to those transitioning. Information on how to find adequate housing and ways to get back into a civilian lifestyle can also assist the service member in their transition. The military can also help pay for college, if educational advancement is what the veteran is looking for, with the Post-9/11 GI Bill and the Yellow Ribbon programs that are available to eligible service personnel. For those who are not interested in personally taking advantage of the educational benefits, as of August 1, 2009, the benefits can be transferred to a spouse or to an eligible dependent (U.S. Department of Veterans Affairs, 2009).

FACTORS RELATING TO TRANSITION

Deciding whether to separate from military service is a difficult process unless the service member is being involuntarily separated due to a Department of Defense downsize or has been medically discharged due to injuries or illnesses or is retiring from service. Those who have the opportunity to make a decision with regard to transitioning out of the military will want to keep several things in mind when determining what type of lifestyle they would like to lead postmilitary service.

For instance, one major concern is access to health care. With many civilian companies having to make drastic cutbacks due to the current economic crisis, having health care benefits through the military may be a deciding factor in the decision to stay in military service. While in the service, military personnel and their families have a unilateral form of health coverage, which includes medical, dental, vision, pharmacy, life insurance, and overseas provisions (Military.com, 2011). The military continues coverage for surviving family members after the death of a service member, as well as retirement coverage for individuals and their spouses. Additionally, health care for dependents continues for children up to age 26 (TRICARE, 2011). In contrast, many civilian companies have had to drastically reduce health coverage and other benefits, or have eliminated these completely in recent years. Medical, dental, vision, and pharmacy coverage can no longer be expected in civilian jobs, but have become an added bonus. Additionally, health insurance in the civilian sector has limitations for preexisting medical conditions, and certain other conditions may be turned down completely by these insurance carriers.

Job security is another major issue to consider in the decision-making process. Service members have a guaranteed paycheck that does not depend on hours worked (Kitchen, 2010). Although this means shorter hours worked at some times, at other times it requires longer hours. Thus, this type of job security has a downside. Unlike civilian work—in which pay is often dependent on how many hours are worked and many can get overtime pay and are free to quit if they are unsatisfied with their position—in the military longer hours worked comes without overtime, holiday, or bonus pay at the end of the day for going above and beyond the call of duty. Also, job security in the military comes with the price that the "employee" cannot simply quit the job if they do not like it.

Military service members receive other benefits, such as uniforms, training, equipment, and schooling (while in the military) at no additional expense (Kitchen, 2010). Civilians, in contrast, must often purchase appropriate attire for their particular work environment as well as work-related equipment. Many civilian jobs offer little employee training and expect the employee to bring the experience to the job. Although some jobs offer educational allowances in the civilian market, most of the employee's education and pursuit of an advanced degree is dependent on employees to accomplish on their own time and with their own finances.

Housing is another issue that service members must consider. One of the most obvious financial and structural difficulties of separation may be the absence of military on-base housing or if living off-base receiving a housing allowance. Service members who are married have an option to either live in a military dwelling or reside off the military installation. Those who prefer to live off-base receive a basic housing allowance that will differ according to rank, family size, and geographical location. An annual publication of housing per diem can be found at http://militarypay.defense.gov/Pay/BAH.html and is published in the *Marine Corps*, *Navy*, and *Army Times* for service members and families. Life on a military base is fairly uniform. Homes tend to look the same (according to rank) and military personnel dress alike as they are in uniform and even sport similar haircuts. Due to the strict housing rules, many of the yards are maintained alike and the homes should be kept clean. The family is limited in terms of what types of pets they can own, as well as how many pets they can have, and all pets must have ID chips. Even parking is designated in most areas, and this is based on rank, so individuals know where to park (Wright, 2008). Civilian life, however, is not always so clear-cut and uniform. As a civilian an individual must find a home, depending on the income level the individual can afford, and maintenance of the home is up to whatever standards individuals hold for themselves (unless a homeowners association is involved).

Moreover, military families can see the world. Military personnel can be assigned to a military installation throughout the world, depending on the service member's military occupational specialty (MOS). The military pays for moving expenses, mileage, food, displacement, and temporary housing associated with the relocation (Leyva, 2003). On the other hand, if civilians relocate they must handle all of the moving expenses on their own as most companies do not offer their employees relocation assistance. The few civilian companies that do offer assistance are far more limited than what the military coverage entails.

Yet another consideration in the decision to separate from the military involves the ready access to support systems. Support systems can be strong within the military community. For instance, military families often have other military families to rely on when things get tough (Wright, 2008). The perception is that military families have been through similar situations and that other military families within the military community will understand what a family is going through. This can also lead to military families cutting themselves off from civilian families. Civilian families, on the other hand, tend to be self-reliant or turn to their extended families, kinship, or friendship networks for support. Although military families can also be close to their own extended family members (which are often comprised of civilians), geographic distances may get in the way of maintaining the bonds between extended family members and the military family.

Separation occurring either on a voluntarily or on an involuntarily basis is never easy. Although those who serve honorably and are able to retire with full benefits after 20 years of service tend to experience both jubilation and sorrow, few reach full retirement. In fact, it is estimated that less than 5% of those who join as enlisted service personnel will reach 20 years and reap the benefits of retirement. After 20 years of service, vestment in the pension begins (Wolpert, 2000). An additional benefit available only to those retiring is the opportunity to remain enrolled in the TRICARE health plan. TRICARE Prime offers a network of treatment facilities in and out of military installations. The retired veteran is required to pay an enrollment fee to remain in TRICARE and pays a small co-pay amount for medical visits. Another benefit available exclusively to such retirees and their families is the opportunity to utilize the various resources on a military installation such as the gym, PX (i.e., post exchange; retail store on base), and hospital.

TRANSITIONING FROM MILITARY TO HIGHER EDUCATION

Since the end of World War II many veterans have utilized their education benefits to complete higher degrees as part of their transition into civilian society; however, not without challenges. It can be difficult to study calculus or English after a few years of being outside of an educational setting. It can also be frustrating for veteran students to listen to civilian peers complain about workload issues or social problems when veterans have often seen and been through so much that these issues seem trivial in relation to their life experiences. Veterans who attend colleges with younger peers may have more difficulty integrating into campus life than if they attend colleges with a demographically diverse student body (U.S. Department of Veterans Affairs, 2007c). According to the U.S. Department of Veterans Affairs (2007c), unlike nonveteran students, military service members, and veterans in undergraduate programs are also more likely to be married (48% nonveterans are married versus 75% of veteran students are married). Many colleges are developing programs to assist veterans in this transition, and when researching different colleges and universities a veteran should keep these factors in mind. More colleges and universities are beginning to realize the difficulties associated with veteran reintegration and are hiring veteran liaisons to assist in this transition into higher education.

As a means of providing institutions of higher learning assistance with the increase of veteran students, the American Council on Education (ACE) developed several working groups that have identified key areas and programs of service that colleges can institute to support veteran students. Many schools appear to be already doing many of the things that ACE has suggested, such as the need for institutions to acknowledge the importance of serving military students and to incorporate their needs into the institutional strategic plans. More specifically, it is recommended that colleges develop programs designed especially for veteran students, such as offering credits for prior service experience, training, and occupational education, which some colleges have implemented (ACE, 2009). Although many veterans will seek counseling through the VA or local Vet Centers, ACE recommends that schools become aware of their students' psychosocial needs and community resources to assist in finding appropriate counseling services as this is a critical need for schools in the rural United States (where there is less access to military and veteran resources). It is estimated that 85% of campus counseling centers tend to refer veteran students to off-campus counseling or community resources when the need arises.

EDUCATIONAL BENEFITS

The Post-9/11 GI Bill provides a substantial financial packet for veterans to attend college. However, policies need to be developed and implemented to support students who are activated and are mobilized and deployed during the course of a college semester. In fact many schools have established policies that encourage reimbursement or allow the student to take an incomplete when such instances occur (ACE, 2009). Unfortunately, the GI Bill does not always cover all of the costs associated with higher education and this can pose additional challenges for the veteran and his or her family.

However, an area of much needed improvement that colleges need to address is the transition from active duty status to college student. ACE reported that less than 22% of those institutions serving military and veteran students currently provide any form of transition assistance such as a special course or summer bridge program. An additional finding from the ACE study group was the need for professional development for faculty and staff, specifically in the area of disabilities, transition issues, and military culture. One aspect of military culture that needs to be considered is the core value of military service consisting of unit cohesion. When veterans attend college many feel disoriented or removed from the college experience. Therefore, colleges are encouraged to develop and provide the opportunity for veterans to connect with their peers through clubs and college-based veteran centers, as well as national veteran student organizations such as the Student Veterans of America (ACE, 2009).

A BRIEF HISTORY OF THE GI BILL

Ever since the original *GI Bill of Rights* or the *Servicemen's Readjustment Act of 1944* (P.L. 78–346) was passed by Congress there have been modifications made to meet the needs of an ever-changing military population. The 1944 act provided veterans who had served 90 days or more after September 16, 1940, with VA home loans and enough money to pay for school, including a $75 monthly allowance for a single veteran with a cap of $500 annually for tuition, books, and fees. Due to the success and popularity of the GI Bill, in 1947 veterans represented 49% of all college enrollments.

Unfortunately, due to institutional fraud with World War II GI Bill payments, Congress was forced to make changes to the original Act, and in 1952 the *Veterans Readjustment Assistance Act* was signed into law. The *Korean War GI Bill* (P.L. 50) cut eligibility from 48 months to 36 months and no longer paid universities directly. Instead, it required and expected veterans to make tuition payment arrangements with the college. A single veteran received a stipend of $110 monthly, which was meant to pay for tuition, books, supplies, and housing. Veterans earned 1.5 months of education allowance per month of service; therefore, only those who served at least 2 years would qualify for their full educational benefits.

Later, the *Veterans Readjustment Benefits Act of 1966* was signed by President Johnson. This was the first time that educational benefits were not directly linked to a specific war and instead retroactively included post–Korean War veterans. Unlike the previous Acts, the Veterans Readjustment Benefits Act allowed for active-duty personnel to become eligible with no combat exposure. However, veterans had to serve twice the amount as their Korean War counterparts, with a required 180 days of continuous service and/or eligibility equal to the time served. However, financial assistance for books, tuition, and living costs—totaling $100 per month for a veteran without children—was not enough to cover the required educational expenses.

The *Post-Vietnam Veterans Educational Assistance Program* (VEAP), was later enacted as part of the Veterans Education and Employment Act of 1976 as a means of attracting young recruits to a post-Vietnam all voluntary Army. Veterans who served between 1977 and 1985 and who qualified for VEAP were given the option to transfer benefits to their spouse and children. VEAP required service members to financially contribute to their education benefits similar to a current 401(k) program, where the government matched every dollar up to a maximum contribution of $5,400.

The *Montgomery GI Bill*, enacted in 1984, replaced the VEAP and authorized education benefits to Reservists. Similar to VEAP service members, veterans were also asked to contribute and were permitted to invest an additional $600 for a return of $5,400 in educational benefits. Veterans who qualified for the Montgomery GI Bill had 15 years postdischarge to utilize their benefits.

The *Post-9/11 GI Bill* began on August 1, 2009, and is available to individuals who served in the military after September 11, 2001, (U.S. Department of Veterans Affairs, 2009). The Post-9/11 GI Bill has three parts: tuition and fee assistance; monthly housing assistance; as well as book and supply stipends. Tuition assistance is paid directly to the college and is based on the highest in-state tuition according to where the veteran resides with an annual cap of $17,500. The housing allowance is based on the zip code according to the college location and other determining factors. The annual stipend for books and supplies is $1,000 paid proportionately based on enrollment.

Additionally, this program gives a one-time rural benefit payment of $500 if the veteran resides in a county with six persons or less per square mile. This extends to students under this provision that either have to physically relocate at least 500 miles to attend college, or have to travel by air to physically attend (U.S. Department of Veterans Affairs, 2009). Active duty members receive 100% tuition coverage for the college of their choosing; however, they do not receive the housing allowance or book and supply stipends. Unused benefits can be transferred to eligible family members, including spouse, children under age 26, or a combination of both spouse and children (U.S. Department of Veterans Affairs, 2009).

The Yellow Ribbon GI Education Enhancement Program (Yellow Ribbon Program; to be differentiated from the Yellow Ribbon Reintegration Program for National Guard and Reserve components) is another assistance program available to veterans (U.S. Department of Veterans Affairs, 2009). This program allows colleges and universities in the United States to voluntarily enter into an agreement with the VA to fund tuition expenses that exceed the highest public in-state undergraduate tuition fee. The institution may contribute up to 50% of the expenses for the education, and the VA will match the amount. This program is based on a first-come first-served basis.

CONNECTING TO THE COMMUNITY

One of the major hurdles service members face when transitioning out of the military into civilian life is losing a sense of camaraderie. Veterans know that when they were in the service the man or woman next to them had their back. The individual was trained to put the needs of the squad, unit, platoon, and the military above his or her own needs. The military garners a sense of cohesion that is difficult to find in the civilian world. For some, once separation from the military occurs, this sense of closeness with others is gone. However, the sense of unity can be regained in the manner of the veteran reconnecting with the community.

One way for veterans to get involved in the community is to participate in their child's education. Volunteering by joining a Parent Teacher Association, and any number of other school-related activities, can foster veterans bonds not only with their child but also with other community members (Banta, 2006). Additionally, for those veterans inclined to do so, joining a religious organization can further help to create a sense of community. In the case where a veteran does not have a child, and prefers to not become religiously affiliated, there are still other options for the veteran to build community connections. Discovering new interests, tapping into old interests, learning new hobbies, and even joining a community sports team can be extremely beneficial. These activities not only get the service member involved in the community, but the activities also serve as a way to bring meaning into an individual's life.

Volunteering with a nonprofit organization can also garner feelings of meaning and purpose (Banta, 2006). Service members could volunteer in a veteran's organization, or an organization that helps service members and their families. Those who love animals could volunteer at the local animal shelter. It does not matter what the organization is, as long as the service member feels connected to the organization in some way.

In fact, a civic-minded organization for disabled veterans called *The Mission Continues* provides veterans with a stipend to serve as volunteers in the nonprofit sector (such as social service, youth, or veteran organizations) for a period of 14 to 28 weeks. The goal of this "fellowship" program is to facilitate the veteran's career and educational development and to provide leadership and service to communities. This program is based on the notion that veterans who continue to serve in some capacity in their communities will not only demonstrate improved well-being (e.g., health, mental health, and psychosocial well-being), but will also be able to successfully transition into higher education or into the civilian workplace as well as make a positive impact on the communities that they serve (Matthieu, Smith, McBride, & Morrow-Howell, 2011). Civic organizations such as this one and others like it that offer veteran involvement in the community can restore a veteran's sense of purpose and usefulness beyond military service as well as help to build long-term relationships that can also assist in promoting a civilian career (Banta, 2006).

TRANSITIONING INTO CIVILIAN EMPLOYMENT

To improve the transition process from active duty service to civilian employment, there are several recommendations that military personnel should consider. For instance, the service member should not wait until 30 days from separation or retirement before starting the military to civilian transition process (Griffin, 2011). Seeking out the services of agencies such as the VA, county-operated veterans services, and traditional veterans service organizations can be extremely helpful to those veterans who are seeking to transition from the military. The service members should make certain prior to separation to research key certifications and go after them while they are still in the service. Also, getting assistance from a sponsor, mentor, or a job coach on how to translate the military skills into civilian language and terminology would be useful. Attending career fairs for military veterans and seeking out recruiting firms that specialize in placing military veterans is also recommended. Additionally exploring all employment options, such as federal, state, and civilian opportunities is a good idea; this includes not settling for the first job that comes along that may not be a good fit.

In terms of understanding the impact of military worldviews and the veteran navigating through the civilian workplace, Weiss and Coll (2011) suggest that veterans can follow orders very well. However, there needs to be a clear chain of command. Therefore, it would be helpful for employers to provide veteran employees with an organizational chart explaining who is in command and who they need to turn to if they are having any challenges. Veterans also work best in teams, as they are combat-trained to function as part of a unit (unit cohesion). They are loyal to their team and loyal to the organization as long as they understand their function in the team (by having clear direction). This way they can avoid feeling frustrated. In fact, the sense of loyalty to the team is so strong that often military personnel will volunteer to go on deployments to "be there" for their battle buddies. This aspect of group cohesion, in terms of belonging to a military unit, can be a strong pull toward reenlisting or remaining in the military. Thus, employers can utilize the strengths of military culture, (i.e., cohesion and mission) rather than responding to these as workplace barriers or limitations.

Lafferty, Alford, Davis, and O'Connor (2008) offer tips for employers and educators regarding engaging veteran employees or students. For example, employers/educators should learn to curb their own anxiety about working with a veteran in that although military service trains individuals for combat and in the use of weapons, there is no empirical evidence that a veteran will be more likely to resort to violence than a civilian employee or student. They (and social work professionals, as well) should not engage in political discussions with the veterans around anti-war sentiments. They should curb their curiosity and not ask insensitive questions such as "Did you kill anyone?" They should be aware of signs of emotional stress in veterans (such as trouble with extended concentration, uneasiness in large gatherings, an increase in absenteeism, and disturbances in peer relationships). Consequently, they should be familiar with community and veteran resources.

Finally, in light of the prevalence of PTSD symptoms among veterans (as discussed in earlier chapters of this book), employers may want to take a proactive and preventive stance toward all of their employees (not to single out veterans), and provide wellness seminars focusing on stress management, sleep hygiene, health, and diet as well as seminars on interpersonal and communication skill building (to help manage or prevent potentially conflict ridden relationships at the workplace).

FEMALE VETERANS

Female veterans are now twice as likely to become homeless than women who never served in the military. This is particularly problematic in that the Veteran Affairs system is not adequately set up for helping women. According to Quast (2011), many believe that the VA is unable to meet the needs of female veterans in the areas of health care and mental health. According to the Bureau of Labor Statistics (2011), unemployment rates for female veterans of the most recent wars rose to 14.7% in November 2011. With the presence of women in the military climbing over the past decade to about 1.8 million of the 23 million U.S. veterans and with more service members coming home from war, women veterans will need even more help in the near future with transition.

REINTEGRATION SKILLS TRAINING

A. Nezu and Nezu (2011) developed a pilot curriculum for assisting veterans with what they coined as "Reintegration Skills Training." This curriculum is comprised of teaching veterans and their families problem-solving and emotion-regulation skills in the form of "tools" to be utilized in easing the stress and tension associated with transitioning home from combat. These tools are helpful for both dealing with the everyday stressors and with the various maladaptive responses to major life events (e.g., combat). Clinicians deliver the curriculum, and through it they teach problem-solving skills and inform the veteran client and his partner about the neurobiology of the stress response system, including the role of adrenalin. Veterans may still be under the influence of the adrenalin-seeking rush of combat experience and associated activities. Thus, they may engage in risk-taking behaviors in the civilian world to compensate for the lack of rush in everyday life. Additionally, they may react with hypersensitivity to common situations or stressors, and their overreactions could exacerbate family problems. The first toolkit, termed the *Stop, Slow Down, Think & Act* (SSTA) method, teaches veterans to approach their problems with a "cool head." The authors describe the SSTA method in the following manner (pp. 9–13):

- (S) Stop = Notice how you are feeling and what you are thinking—recognize that a problem exists that "needs to be solved" (noticing physical reactions, negative thoughts, negative mood, change in behaviors).
- (S) Slow Down = Give your brain and body a chance to lower the intensity of any negative emotions (slow down through techniques such as deep breathing, meditating, visualizations, exercise).

- (T) Think = Think with a "cool head," use your planned problem-solving skills to deal with the problem. (Steps: First define the problem; second, brainstorm alternative solutions; third, decide which ideas are potentially effective or not and develop an action plan.)
- Act = Carry out your action plan (carry out the plan and monitor/evaluate the outcomes).

In this curriculum, the authors also present communication-building tools for couples and family members through taking turns dialoging with each other and by developing empathic listening skills. The concept of Reconnecting the Relationship, or "R&R" is for the veteran and his or her spouse or partner to spend structured quality time together as a means of becoming reacquainted with one another.

In the next section, a case study of a veteran is provided that highlights some of the elements relating to veteran transition challenges that have been discussed in this chapter. The reader is encouraged to review the case and consider the discussion questions following the case vignette.

Case Vignette: Howard

Howard is a 32-year-old Caucasian male who presents for treatment. Howard has been in the U.S. Army for 13 years, and has served two tours in the past 4 years, one to Iraq for 9 months, and one to Afghanistan for 18 months. Howard has had an exceptional career in the Army, starting at 1st Battalion 66th Armor at Fort Hood to his current position as a Non-Commissioned Officer (NCO) tanker at Fort Bragg. Howard is considering separating from the service; however, he is having financial difficulties and has decided to reenlist. This reenlistment will make him eligible for another overseas tour. His presenting issue is marital difficulties and family discord. On evaluation during intake and assessment Howard is diagnosed with posttraumatic stress disorder (PTSD) and major depression. However, Howard insists that he does not want to work on his personal problems, but would prefer to work on his family problems.

Howard has explained that although he loves his job in the military, his wife is tired of his deployments and wants him to leave the Army. He is worried that if he does separate from the Army before he is eligible for full retirement (at 20 years of service) he will not be eligible for full pension and retirement benefits and will not be able to support his family. He also fears that since military life is all he has known for most of his adult life that he will feel out of place in the civilian world. He feels he does better when he is deployed, and he understands the world better when he is part of a team. He knows what his job is while he is deployed, and he knows that the man next to him has his back. He believes that he will not have this same sense of camaraderie in the civilian world. Additionally he does not think that his Army skills will prepare him for the civilian world and is worried about the current financial crisis and the scarcity of employment opportunities in the civilian sector.

On the other hand, Howard's wife feels as if she has lost her husband. When Howard returned from his first deployment she began to notice a change in him. He went to fewer family functions, had a temper she had never seen before, and felt that he was pulling away from the family. On his return from his second deployment the marriage began to truly suffer. He completely isolated himself from the family, began eating all meals in his room alone, would not attend any family functions, started yelling at the children for making noise, and began yelling at his wife for any little problem.

Howard refuses to allow his wife to work outside of the home, because she is supposed to be at home caring for their children. After his second deployment, Howard does not participate in the care of the home or help out in the care of the children. Howard's wife feels that if he reenlists and redeploys there will be no reason for him to come home because the marriage will be over. She explains how she has lost the man she married and this "stranger" is not someone she wants to be with. He has cut himself off emotionally from her and the children and when he gets really angry she is beginning to fear for their safety.

Howard has refused to speak about his time overseas with his wife. He even has difficulty broaching the subject with the therapist and often breaks down in tears before he can get a word out. He believes he is supposed to be able to handle the things he saw, because he was trained to do so, and the problems he is currently having are his own personal problems. Thus, he believes that "a good soldier can handle anything."

Case Vignette Discussion Questions

1. What transition issues do you notice about this veteran and his family?
2. What would a social worker do to address the needs of this veteran and of his family in the decision regarding transitioning out of the military into civilian life?
3. What sort of skills would a social worker utilize in helping this veteran and his family with reintegration?
4. What resources or referrals would a social worker consider in this case?
5. What are some of the potential challenges facing the social worker in this case?

CONCLUSION

Whether the service member is separating after 4 years, retiring after 20 years, being forced to discharge, or separating due to injury or illness, transition can be a difficult time for many veterans and their families. No two individuals experience the same situation, and not all problems can be averted. Fortunately, the military has programs in place to assist the service member in preparing for this transition. After separation, the Department of Veterans Affairs and the Department of Labor also have programs set in place to help prevent major transitional problems. However, the current transition assistance programs that are in place have been under scrutiny lately as so many service personnel are not successfully transitioning into the civilian world and as some of them are joining the ranks of the unemployed or have gotten into legal troubles. At the time of this writing, the White House administration is working with military leaders to enhance the transition programs and to consider other initiatives to improve employment opportunities, such as veteran hiring incentives and new-job creation strategies. These efforts seem to recognize that in the case of separation from the military an ounce of prevention is worth a pound of cure, and the more programs the service member has access to help with transition the more likely their separation will be a success story.

CHAPTER DISCUSSION QUESTIONS

1. Discuss how communities may want to prepare for returning warriors to minimize the rate of unemployment among veterans.
2. How has the American Council on Education (ACE) responded to the increase of utilization of the Post-9/11 GI Bill?
3. How has this transition of OIF/OEF veterans differed from past wars, that is, Vietnam, Korea, or World War II?

REFERENCES

American Council on Higher Education. (ACE). (2009). *Military service members and veterans in higher education: What the new GI bill may mean for postsecondary institutions*. Retrieved from http://acenet.edu/stws

Banta, V. (2006). Five ways to make a military to civilian transition easier. *Government articles*. Retrieved from http://www.articlesfactory.com/articles/government/five-ways-to-make-a-military-to-civilian-life-transition-easier.html

Exum, H., Coll, J., & Weiss, E. L. (2011). *A civilian counselor's primer for counseling veterans* (2nd ed.). New York, NY: Linus.

Griffin, C. (2011). *10 tips for a successful military to civilian transition in corporate America*. SVP Operations: Bradley-Morris. (BMI). Retrieved from http://www.bradley-morris.com/MilitarytoCivilianTransition.html

Kitchen, R. E. (2010). *Life after the military: Transitioning back into civilian life*. Retrieved from http://www.associatedcontent.com/article/2938188/life_after_the_military_transitioning.html?cat=25

Lafferty, C. L., Alford, K. L., Davis, M. K., & O'Connor, R. (2008). "Did you shoot anyone?": A practitioner's guide to combat veteran workplace and classroom reintegration. *Advanced Management Journal, 73*(4), 4–11.

Leyva, M. (2003). *Married to the military: A survivors guide for military wives, girlfriends, and women in uniform*. New York, NY: Simon & Schuster.

Military.com. (2011). *Understanding TRICARE*. Retrieved from http://www.military.com/benefits/tricare

Matthieu, M. M., Smith, I. D., McBride, A. M., & Morrow-Howell, N. (2011). *The mission continues: Engaging post-9/11 disabled military veterans in civic service*. Research Brief, George Warren School of Social Work, Center for Social Development, CSD Publication, 11–25. Washington University in St. Louis, Missouri.

Nezu, A. M., & Nezu, C. M. (2011). *Reintegration skills training*. Reintegration partnership project presented at a workshop at the University of Southern California, Center for Innovation and Research on Veterans and Military Families.

Quast, L. (2011). The struggle for female veterans to transition into civilian jobs. *Forbes*. Retrieved from http://forbes.com/lisaquast/2011/04/11/the-struggle-for-female-veterans-to-transition-into-civilian-jobs/

Tan, M. (2009). Wounded Warrior program helps injured airmen. *Air Force Times*. Retrieved from http://www.airforcetimes.com/news/2009/10/airforce_wounded_warriors_101009/

Tanielian, T. & Jaycox, L. H. (2008). *Invisible wounds of war: Psychological and cognitive injuries, their consequences and services to assist recovery*. Santa Monica, CA: RAND.

TRICARE. (2011). *Tricare benefits at-a-glance*. Retrieved from http://tricare.mil/mybenefit/ProfileFilter.do;jsessionid=NG3bH32QBCwkTTJywh8Zd8qy6y8HS9dZfmGfNB42mDbJclv04nCW!1530652655?ref=Benefits_at_a_Glance&puri=%2Fhome%2Foverview%2FWhatIsTRICARE%2FTRICAREBenefitAtAGlance

U.S. Air Force. (2010). *Air Force: Wounded Warrior*. Retrieved from http://www.woundedwarrior.af.mil/

U.S. Army. (2010). *Disabled Transition Assistance Program (DTAP)*. Retrieved from http://myarmybenefits.us.army.mil/Home/Benefit_Library/Federal_Benefits_Page/Disabled_Transition_Assistance_Program_(DTAP).html?serv=147

U.S. Army. (2010). *Warrior transition command: Transition options*. Retrieved from http://www.wtc.army.mil/soldier/transition_options.html

U.S. Department of Labor: Bureau of Labor Statistics. (2011). *Employment situation of veterans summary*. Retrieved from www.bls.gov/news.release/vet.nr0.htm

U.S. Department of Veterans Affairs. (2007c). *Table 10L: Veterans 2000–2036 by Gulf War service, age, gender, period*. Vetpop 2007 National Tables. http://www1.va.gov/vetdata/docs/10l.xls

U.S. Department of Veterans Affairs. (2009). *2008–2009 maximum in-state tuition & fees*. http://www.giBill.va.gov/GI_Bill_Info/CH33/Tuition_and_fees.htm

U.S. Department of Veterans Affairs. (2011). *VA caregiver services and in-home care*. Retrieved from http://www.caregiver.va.gov/VA_Caregiver_Services.asp

U.S. Government Accountability Office. (2011). *Military personnel: Management and oversight of selective reenlistment bonus program needs improvement*. Retrieved from http://www.gao.gov/products/GAO-03-149

U.S. Marines. (2010). *Wounded warrior regiment mission statement*. Retrieved from http://www.marines.mil/unit/hqmc/mnra/wwr/Pages/Home.aspx

Weiss, E. L., & Coll, J. E. (2011). The influence of military culture and veteran worldviews on mental health treatment: Implications for veteran help-seeking and wellness. *International Journal of Health, Wellness & Society, 1*(2), 75–86.

Wolpert, D. S. (2000). Military retirement and the transition to civilian life. In J. A. Martin, L. N. Rosen, & L. R. Sparacino (Eds.), *The military family: A practice guide for human service providers*. Westport, CT: Praeger.

Wounded Warrior Regiment. (2011). *United States Marine Corps Wounded Warrior Regiment: Our mission*. Retrieved from http://www.woundedwarriorregiment.org/Mission.cfm

Wright, J. (2008). *Military life vs. civilian life: Advantages and disadvantages*. Retrieved from http://www.associatedcontent.com/article/730149/military_life_vs_civilian_life_advantages.htm.?cat=9

PART

IV

Families Impacted by Military Service

CHAPTER

18

A Brief History of U.S. Military Families and the Role of Social Workers

Jesse Harris

Throughout history families in every generation have dreaded the thought of their loved one being engaged in combat. The questions they ask about their member's unit scheduled for deployment are always the same: "Where are they going?" "Is it dangerous?" "When will they return?" The fact that these questions cannot be answered with any precision adds to the family's level of anxiety. Communication or the absence of communication presents another level of stress. Before the age of rapid communication one waited for days, weeks, and even months before hearing the status of the family member in the combat zone. Today, with instantaneous "real-time" hourly news, the stress is heightened by instant replays of the battle in one's living room television set.

In today's military, the importance of families is recognized both from the standpoint of stressors with which they must cope as well as their impact on the mission. Military families today also experience more national appreciation for their sacrifices than ever before. Families were not always recognized in past U.S. military conflicts, and in some instances they were even invisible in the eyes of the average citizen. Whether the returning warrior was celebrated as in World Wars I and II or ignored (Korea) or criticized by some who opposed the Vietnam War, the family, and the stressors they endured were not widely considered. In fact, families often suffer in silence as loved ones are killed or severely injured on the battlefield or return home suffering from the mental anguish associated with combat.

Depending on the diagnostic designations of the era, those veterans afflicted with psychological wounds were branded as "cowards," while others were thought to be suffering from "Soldier's Heart," "Shell Shock," or "Battle Neurosis," and more recently from "Posttraumatic Stress Disorder." In the past veterans who experienced problems with transition and reintegration back into the family were often not taken seriously by society or by the government. However, those social workers and other helping professionals, whose experience included working with military families, did recognize the stresses and strains brought on by war and separation. They also understood the impact that these challenges had on children and on marriages. These early social workers also recognized the need for family intervention as being critical in easing the veteran's transition back home and promoting family and community reintegration. Thus, the purpose of this chapter is to examine the emergence of the military family from the status of being merely tolerated to becoming a recognized partner in the military mission. Specifically, the intent is to provide a historical perspective of the external events that impacted the military family from the U.S. Revolutionary War to the current Global War on Terrorism, including the social-political movements that influenced military family policies. The chapter also examines the role of social workers in addressing the needs of the family impacted by military service.

THE REVOLUTIONARY (1775–1783) AND CIVIL WAR ERAS (1861–1865)

During the Revolutionary War soldiers from the colonial armies were expected to settle their family affairs at home and make provisions for their family's needs prior to reporting to their units. The family was the soldiers' responsibility and was not deemed the responsibility of the military. This was true during the Civil War period as well. Family members left behind were expected to carry on the family business, work the farms, and in general take over the duties of their deployed soldiers (Albano, 1984).

The Family as "Camp Followers"

Some civilian spouses (typically female) who remained at home were unable to carry out the responsibilities of the husband. These women packed up their children and followed the tradition set by families of European armies by joining their soldiers and sailors to be near them in the military camps. These families became known as *Camp Followers*. Unfortunately, this was a name that became associated with women who were considered to be prostitutes. Indeed, there were women who engaged in prostitution who accompanied the armies, but so did men who were merchants, traders, and drivers. For the most part, however, Camp Followers were the wives and family members of the soldiers who assisted with activities of daily living, such as cooking, carrying water, sewing torn uniforms, and making the living environment somewhat tolerable. Those family members who had medical skills served as physicians, nurses, and medical attendants.

Camp Followers were considered part of the militia and subject to their rules (Wickham, 1983). Provisions were made for meals and housing, and adult females were given one half of the rations allowed for soldiers. Children who accompanied their mothers were allotted one-quarter rations. The wives who accompanied their husbands were not paid from public funds. The soldiers themselves paid for whatever services the families provided. These Camp Followers caused concerns for military leaders who felt responsible for their safety as well for the safety of their regiments. Children and pregnant women were especially a source of concern to military leaders. There were times when the Camp Followers outnumbered the troops. General Grant at one time attempted to prohibit traders from being Camp Followers. Although there were restrictions on women joining the militia as soldiers, there were reports of wives dressing as men and manning the cannons, thereby relieving their husbands (Mayer, 1996).

Assistance for Families

Neither being married nor having a family was encouraged during the Revolutionary or Civil wars. Although marriage was tolerated for officers and noncommissioned officers, enlisted men had to get permission to marry from their commanders. However, the often-quoted remark, "If the military had wanted you to have a family they would have issued you one," was never entirely true. As early as 1636 veterans and their families were recognized for participating in the Indian wars and were compensated by being "privy to outdoor relief" (Compton, 1943, p. 198). The military's recognition for the need to provide medical care for family members dates back to the late 1700s, during the Revolutionary War. Although the family was considered to be the soldier's responsibility, there was a Department of the Army Regulation, which, during the Civil War, authorized allotments to families (Wickham, 1983). In 1884, Congress directed that the "medical officers of the Army and contract surgeons shall whenever possible attend the families of the officers and soldiers free of charge" (Monroe-Posey, 1999, p. 67). From the earliest period in this nation's history there has been concern for providing for the widows and orphans of soldiers who had fallen in battle. The Army Relief Society was established in 1900 to assist widows and orphans of deceased full-time Army members. The Navy Relief Society (later to be renamed the Navy-Marine Corps Relief Society) was established in 1904 for the same purpose. To fund this new organization President Theodore Roosevelt ordered 50% of the proceeds from the 1903 Army-Navy football game be used as seed money to support the Relief Society. The Air Force Aid Society was established in 1942. This would have been while the "Air Corps," as it was then called, was still part of the Army (News of Society, 2003).

WORLD WAR I ERA: (1914–1918)

The recruitment activities of World War I had the same impact as with previous wars—the impact of family disruptions. Although the Red Cross was founded in 1881 and provided services to troops and their families in previous wars, the United States Congress authorized the American Red Cross its second charter in 1905.

The American Red Cross and Services to Families

The 1905 American Red Cross charter had the effect of making the American Red Cross the primary institution serving as a liaison between the military service units and the family. The social work profession had now come of age, and many social workers worked for the American Red Cross. In 1917, when the United States entered the war, the Red Cross appointed W. Frank Persons, as its Director General of Civilian Relief. Frank Persons in his recognition of the military family wrote: "men may be the best soldiers in the world, but if things are not well with their families at home they worry and lose efficiency and the morale of the army—that all-important factor—begins to fail" (Persons, 1918, p. 171).

One of the first actions Persons took in his new role was to consult with Mary Richmond, one of the two most prominent social workers of that era (the other being Jane Addams). He asked her to write a manual for the Red Cross to help them work with families. Richmond completed the manual and also suggested that the Red Cross establish what she coined "The Home Services" Office. The Home Service Office was officially recognized by the Department of War by General Order 17 on February 13, 1917. Social workers would be given the status of officers and their aides (required to be males) would hold the status of noncommissioned officers. The emphasis of the Home Services Office would be to provide casework to families with regard to financial, social, medical, and communication assistance. Families would benefit from social workers assigned to the Home Services Office in both World War I and later in World War II. However, due to the popularity of the medical model and the increasing interest in psychiatric casework, the Home Service model would in time sadly become a "methods lost" (Beck, 1991).

FAMILIES AND WORLD WAR II ERA: (1941–1945)

During the period of 1938 to 1939, as the winds of war were blowing throughout Europe, social work agencies were being inundated by displaced families and European immigrants seeking refuge from the instability of their homelands.

The Expansion of Military Family Programs

When the United States Congress declared war in December 1941, the nations' Selective Service began the draft and the call went out for men and women to join the Armed Forces. Social workers of the Red Cross Home Services Office in locations throughout the country had mobilized to provide services to mostly young military families, many of whom had never endured separation before. Once again, families were asked to sacrifice their spouses and parents, but during this time, most of these families were still recovering from the economic losses brought on by the Great Depression. This may, in part, have accounted for the fact that the U.S. government was more generous to families in World War II than in any previous conflict. In addition to pay raises for all military personnel, family allowances were provided for what was termed *Basic Maintenance*, which covered the cost of food, housing, and home heating fuel.

President Roosevelt took further steps to assist service personnel and their families. In November 1940 he designated the administrator of the Federal Security Agency to become the Coordinator of the Office of Health, Welfare, and Related Defense Activities. This office provided services to military training camps and their civilian communities. Then in 1941, Roosevelt placed the Office of Civilian Defense under the Office of War Management in an attempt to integrate service member and family health, welfare, and recreation services with defense activities. By 1943 these services had been subsumed into the Office of Community War Services under the Federal Security Agency, which served both soldiers and their families (Day, 2009). Thus, through the development and sustainment of these programs, the government furthered its commitment to serving the needs of military families.

The Emergency Maternal and Infant Care Program (EMIC)

Most of the service members who responded to their nation's call were young men with wives of childbearing ages. Because of the war, existing military medical facilities were unable to handle the anticipated number of patients; therefore, Congress authorized the Emergency Maternal and Infant Care program (EMIC). The EMIC served more than 1.2 million military spouses and approximately 230,000 infants and young children. Additionally, inoculation programs for all children were undertaken through public health services (Day, 2009). The EMIC program was available to the wives of enlisted men in the four lower pay grades regardless of where they were living. The program was administered by the Children's Bureau through state health departments.

THE KOREAN WAR ERA: (1950–1953)

As was true in earlier conflicts, the war in Korea would require families to sacrifice its members as the nation began to rebuild its armed forces. Social workers who had been commissioned at the end of World War II joined most other military personnel, and returned to the civilian sector. There was now a need to recruit a new generation of social workers to join the Army and Air Force as well. There also was a need to recruit and train those newly enlisted personnel to serve as paraprofessionals. All would require training in the practice of social work within a military environment. Although Red Cross social workers were providing family therapy and other services within the military, the initial training manual for military psychiatric social workers made no reference to families (*Psychiatric Social Work*, 1950). Additionally, the fact that the manual was written in the masculine gender was probably a reflection of the times. However, the buildup of troops, including the activation of reserve units, resulted in an increase in families, including those with children. This change in the demographics of the military was reflected 4 years later in the next major training manual *Army Social Work* (1958). This manual not only included traditional families but unmarried mothers as well. The conflict between the United States and Korea ended in 1953, and service members returned home with all of the problems inherent in military family reintegration.

THE VIETNAM WAR: (1954–1975)

In the early 1950s the United States had already began to send advisors into a country of which few U.S. families had ever heard—Vietnam. The United States involvement in Vietnam escalated in the early 1960s.

Social Movements and the Military Family

Uniformed social workers were now firmly established in the U.S. Army and in the U.S. Air Force. With the expansion of the military came an increase in the population of military families. The services responded to this increase with several family-oriented programs. For example, as early as 1961 the Air Force introduced its Children Have a Potential program (CHAP) to assist families with children with disabilities. Fourteen years after the CHAP was introduced the U.S. Congress passed the Education for All Handicapped Children's Act (PL 94–142). This Act entitled handicapped children to a free education as well as any medically related services while in pursuit of their education. As a result of and based on this law, the Air Force expanded CHAP to include the adult-dependent disabled family members of the Air Force. This became known as the Exceptional Family Member Program (EFMP), which still exists today. Chapter 21 of this book is dedicated to describing this program.

The Army created the Army Community Services in 1965 for families and soldiers. This program consisted of a variety of services such as budget counseling, housing assistance, finding and developing resources for complex personal problems, as well as the Army Emergency Relief program. In the 1960s, another event occurred in the civilian population that had a significant impact on military policies regarding children and families. C. Henry Kempe and his colleagues (1962) shocked the nation with the publication that exposed the seriousness of child abuse in U.S. families. However, it was not until 1974 that federal laws provided for the funding of programs to eliminate child abuse and to protect and provide a safe environment for children. With the realization that child abuse was a serious problem within the military community as well, Air Force social workers in 1975 initiated the Child Advocacy Program (Mollerstrom, Patchner, & Milner, 1995).

However, children were not the only ones being maltreated. The Women's Movement of the 1970s raised awareness to the overwhelming problem of spousal abuse in the country. Again, the Air Force responded by expanding the Child Advocacy Program to include spouse abuse. The name of the program was changed to the Family Advocacy Program (FAP) to reflect the more comprehensive problem of domestic violence. The Navy's instructions establishing its Family Advocacy Program were published in 1979. In that same year the Navy Family Support Program was established and now operates throughout the world. Its overall emphasis is on prevention and education services to reduce the risk for family violence. The Army started its Family Advocacy Program in the 1980s. Each of the services has modified its programs over time, but the emphasis remains on the family.

Military spouses have complained through the years of the difficulty of finding employment, in part because of frequent moves and the challenges of establishing themselves in new communities. Therefore, there is an emphasis in assisting spouses to find employment, and each branch has an employment assistance program. Although these programs do not guarantee employment, they provide the tools and skills necessary for military spouses to compete.

Likewise, each service branch has its own family service programs (i.e., Army Community Service, Navy Family Service Center). In addition to the direct services provided to military families, these programs work closely with school administrators and faculty to provide wholesome extracurricular activities including sports. They assure that installation libraries are stocked with film and books on such topics as finance, self-improvement, and parenting. These books are all available for checkout. These services are available to single service members, as well. The value of these family services and programs was underscored by an analysis of an Air Force survey. Bowen and Orthner (1986) concluded that those support programs and services, which could be utilized by single parents, have unlimited potential and could achieve even more than they have already.

A New Recognition of Family

The unpopular war in Vietnam highlighted the widespread disdain for the Selective Service "draft." Many young men chose to flee to Canada rather than be conscripted to serve. At the end of the conflict in 1973 President Nixon signed a law that set aside conscription. The nation would now have an All-Volunteer Force (AVF). This act introduced a new set of dynamics, which would ultimately change the status of military families. There was the recognition that with an all-volunteer force the service member would enlist, but the family would play a significant role in the soldier's decision to reenlist. The World War I admonition of Frank Persons seemed to be echoing through time. As though on cue, a fascinating movement began to take place around military installations throughout the world.

The Army is a case in point. Army wives began expressing their concerns about living conditions for themselves and their families. Family symposia were held on military installations across the country and overseas between 1980 and 1982. Some of them were officially sponsored, but others were grassroots movements started by the wives themselves. Because of the urgency to retain soldiers, policy makers at the highest levels of command would have to pay attention to the family's complaints and concerns.

The symposia produced several major recommendations. Among them were to provide assistance in helping military spouses find employment and to provide a common educational model for children attending schools on military installations. The spouses also called for improved medical and dental care. They wanted recognition for the spousal volunteer service in the form of documentation showing professional development if skills were being used or taught. Another recommendation had to do with an expansion of transportation, which would include families living in the civilian community. Their demands also included improved child care services and expanded youth activities (Wickham, 1983).

Based on the results of the symposia, the Army Chief of Staff introduced his groundbreaking *White Paper: The Army Family* (Wickham, 1983). In this document the Army officially recognized the family not just as "dependents" but also as part of the Army team. The statements in this document marked a significant change in the status of the military family. Soon afterward, action plans were developed detailing the concepts that were expressed. Family members would now have a voice and be able to contribute to what would be known as the *Family Action Plan* by making suggestions at the installation level. The suggestions are reviewed on a regular basis and by every level of command. In 2008 the Army celebrated the 25th anniversary of the Family Action Plan.

One of the organizations instrumental in promoting family recognition was the Defense Department Advisory Committee on Women in the Service (DACOWITS). The then Chief of Staff, General George C. Marshall, established this Committee in 1951. The mission of DACOWITS is to provide advice and recommendations on matters and policies related to recruitment and retention, treatment, employment, integration, and well-being of highly qualified professional women in the military. In addition, beginning in 2002, the Committee was tasked to provide advice and recommendations on family issues related to recruitment and retention of highly qualified professionals (About DACOWITS, 2011).

THE PERSIAN GULF WAR: (AUGUST 1990–MARCH 1991)

Operation Desert Shield was President George H. W. Bush's response to Iraqi President Hussein's threat to Kuwait. National Guard and Reserve units throughout the nation were called to active duty, and many of those units were deployed to Southwest Asia.

The Reserve and National Guard Components

Operation Desert Storm was the response to Iraq's attack on Kuwait. The U.S. military joined with the Coalition Forces in Kuwait's Liberation. The Persian Gulf War was one of the most successful conflicts in terms of strategy and tactics in modern times. The efficiency of this 7-month-long war notwithstanding, Schneider and Martin (1994) noted that a major lesson was that the military (the Army specifically) could not fight a sustained battle without calling on the Reserve and National Guard units. However, many of these folks were not ready to deploy as a result of not having made adequate arrangements for the caregiving of their dependent children. Thus, the Family Care Plan was put into place.

The Family Care Plan

In July 1992 the DoD came out with Family Care Plans, to standardize the requirements for all of the military services. The Family Care Plan is required of all single parent–headed households and dual career families (both parents in the military) and Reserve Component families. The plan requires that a parent designate a guardian with a special power of attorney in the care of their children. It is the responsibility of the parent to assure that the guardian has everything necessary to function effectively.

Family Support Groups

Units scheduled for deployment were encouraged to form family support groups. The U.S. participation in the Multi-National Peacekeeping Force in the Sinai Peninsula in the mid-1980s witnessed the utility of family support groups (FSG). The support groups were unit-based and composed of families whose unit was scheduled for deployment. These families would not only provide support for each other and for less-experienced families, but they also served as liaisons between the deployed unit and the family members. Usually (but not always), the spouse of the commander served as the group's leader. Deployed units left behind a Rear Detachment Commander who not only carried out the day-to-day duties of the commander but to the extent possible served as the link between the unit and the families. The success of the support group was dependent on a number of factors. For example, it was dependent on volunteers who may come from the civilian sector as well as from military families. Another factor was the extent to which the unit encouraged and supported the FSG programs. The modern Family Readiness Groups (FRG) developed out of the Family Support Groups. FRGs are formally organized and officially recognized by the military to support the families of service members through the cycle of deployment.

National Guard and Reserve Families

Family support groups were encouraged and supported in active duty units scheduled for deployment. In general they were considered a success. Schneider and Martin (1994) noted that few soldiers in the Gulf War had to return home due to family problems. However, they also referred to the U.S. Army Combined Arms Command Study (1991) and noted that, "Many reservists, their spouses, and their children were not adequately prepared for this reality, and as a result, they experienced significant distress during the deployment" (Schneider & Martin, 1994, p. 26). Although there may have been many reasons for these problems, two are worth mention: lack of family support, and the deployment of military mothers.

Most Reserve and National Guard units lacked the family-support group structure found in the active duty military. Thus, for many families there was little opportunity to share the experiences and challenges resulting from a deployed head of household. As citizen soldiers, these families might live miles away from military installations, be widely dispersed from one another, and probably not even know another military family. Therefore, many had no knowledge of the resources available to them. Furthermore, chances were good that their civilian neighbors might have no knowledge of their military affiliation.

The lessons learned from the experiences of the Persian Gulf War have resulted in the National Guard and Reserve units institutionalizing the family support group to include support for single headed households. The support groups are now similar in concept to those of the active components. To provide guidance to families and soldiers, units and group leaders, *The Army Family Readiness Handbook* was developed and can be retrieved at: http://www.au.af.mil/au/awc/awcgate/army/frg_hdbk.pdf Additionally, the Yellow Ribbon program was created to meet the needs of National Guard and Reservist service members and their families (see Chapter 20 and this book's appendix for more information on this program).

THE GLOBAL WAR ON TERROR (2001–)

The devastating effects of 9/11 resulted in what President George W. Bush referred to as the Global War on Terrorism (GWOT). The primary battlegrounds were Afghanistan (Operation Enduring Freedom) and Iraq (Operation Iraqi Freedom/Operation New Dawn). As in the Persian Gulf War, the active duty components had to be augmented with National Guard and Reserve units from around the country. As with past wars, the families were affected by their loved ones being killed or injured in battle. However, by the time of the GWOT, science and medicine had become more sophisticated in dealing with PTSD and traumatic brain injury. Additionally, the advancement in body armor was such that more lives were protected but fighters suffered injuries to the more exposed parts of the body such as the limbs and head. Equally as important, the public became more aware, knowledgeable, and accepting of these injuries. There was also the recognition that the service member's family was also a victim. Family dynamics would be significantly changed. Not only would the spouse be affected, but the children as well. A major breakthrough was when the Veterans Administration began to provide some family services. For example, housing is now provided for veterans and their families who qualify, and many of the Vet Centers now include family counseling services (U.S. Department of Veterans Affairs, n.d.).

CONCLUSION

The family has played a noble and significant role throughout the history of the U.S. military. Whether families were "keeping the home fires burning" or accompanying troops as "Camp Followers," history has shown that the military family is but a microcosm of our larger society. As movements occurred in the civilian population, it sparked changes in the military community. These changes have had a profound impact on the family. By necessity, the military has adapted by modifying its policies, institutions and in some cases its traditions. The military has had to change its definition of the family—a reflection of the zeitgeist. How one defines a military family today is different than the way it would have been defined by the commanders in the colonial Army or by the commanders of World War II. The health workers in General Washington's forces, General Grant's Army, or Admiral Nimitz's Navy would be baffled by issues presented by today's family whose *mother* has deployed. The student of military history and warfare understands that each war is different than the one before for a variety of reasons. Today, although the stress of military life on the family has not significantly changed in some ways, it has changed in others—particularly regarding the impact of multiple deployments and the length of tours of duty. Nevertheless, the military family whose loved one is in Afghanistan can relate to families of past generations whose member served at Concord, Gettysburg, Verdun, Iwo Jima, Pork Chop Hill, or Saigon. In light of the stressors on families and children, there will continue to be a need for family intervention by social workers and other skilled therapists. The challenge is—as it has always been—to understand the world as the service member has witnessed it and understand the military family, their issues, and concerns.

CHAPTER DISCUSSION QUESTIONS

1. Compare the similarities and differences between the role of the family in today's United States military and its role in the past.
2. Describe the range of roles social workers perform in working with military families.

REFERENCES

About DACOWITS. (2011). Retrieved from http://www.dtic.mil/dacowits/tableabout_subpage.html

Albano, S. (1984). Military recognition of family concerns: Revolutionary War to 1993. *Armed Forces and Society*, *20*(2), 283–302.

Army Social Work. (1958). TM 8–241. Washington, DC: Department of the Army.

Beck, G. Jr. (1991). Social work in World War I: A method lost. *Social Service Review, 65*(3), 379–402.

Bowen, G. L., & Orthner, D. K. (1986). Single parents in the U.S. Air Force. *Family Relations, 35*(1), 45–52.

Compton, B. R. (1943). *Introduction to social work: Structure, foundation, and process.* Homewood, IL: Dorsey Press.

Day, P. (2009). *A new history of social welfare* (6th ed.). Boston, MA: Allyn & Bacon.

Kempe, C. H., Silverman, F. N., Steele, B. F., Droegemueller, W., & Silver, H. K. (1962). The battered child syndrome. *Journal of the American Medical Association, 181*(1), 17–24.

Mayer, H. A. (1996). *Belonging to the Army.* Columbia: University of South Carolina Press.

Mollerstrom,W. W., Patchner, M. A., & Milner, J. A. (1995). Child maltreatment in the United States Air Force response. *Child Abuse and Neglect, 19*(3), 325–334.

Monroe-Posey, C. A. (1999). *TRICARE and its impact on military social work practice.* In J. Daley (Ed.), *Military social work practice* (pp. 67–90). Binghamton, NY: Hayworth.

News of the Society. (2003). *Celebrating a century of service.* Retrieved November 2, 2011, from http://www.nmcrs.org/centennial01.html

Persons, F. W. (1918). The soldiers and sailors families. *Annals of the American Academy of Political and Social Science, 77*(1), 171–184.

Psychiatric Social Work. (1950). TM 8–241. Washington, DC: Department of the Army.

Schneider, R. J., & Martin, J. A. (1994). *Military families and combat readiness.* In R. Zajtchuk (Ed.), *Military psychiatry: Preparing in peace for war* (pp. 19–30). Washington, DC: Department of the Army.

U.S. Army Combined Arms Command. (1991). *The yellow ribbon: Army lessons learned from the home front.* Fort Leavenworth, KS: Center for Army Lessons Learned.

U.S. Department of Veterans Affairs. (n.d.). *Supportive services for veteran families.* Retrieved December 17, 2011, from www.va.gov/homeless/ssvf.asp

U.S. Department of Veterans Affairs. (2012). *Vet Center.* Retrieved from www.vetcenter .va.gov/

Wickham, J. A. (1983). *White paper: The Army family.* Washington, DC.

CHAPTER

19

Cycle of Deployment and Family Well-Being

Keita Franklin

The military as an institution of professionals is a relatively new concept. Throughout U.S. history, citizens were typically conscripted into service during times of war. After the war, the military was downsized to prewar levels or lower. Most draftees during war times did not see themselves as "military professionals," but rather patriots serving their nation during a time of war. However, downsizing following the Vietnam War left the military as a "hollow force" and policy makers decided, in the 1970s, to establish an all volunteer, professional military force (*Hearings Before the House*, 1998). With this new vision came the investment in professional education for service members and, eventually, an infrastructure of support for family members. Concepts such as "quality of life," "retention rates," and "family readiness" all became embedded in the U.S. military culture as military leaders recognized the important role of the family in meeting the mission, particularly during times of war (Segal & Wechsler-Segal, 2005).

Retention, a term historically used to describe how well the military keeps its service members on active duty after their initial enlistment, suddenly had implications for the family system. One scholar, describing the end of the draft in 1973, stated; "the need to keep older, mostly married troops happy enough to re-enlist meant that military wives became too numerous and too vocal to ignore" (Freedberg, 2005, p. 1). Today, across all service branches, more than half of personnel are married, and 40% have children (Freedberg, 2005). This compares to 1968, at the height of Vietnam, when fewer of the active duty force were married service members. Consequently, the notion of caring for or considering the impact of war on military families was less of a focus for military leaders compared to today, where it is a primary focus. This is evident across all the service branches. Service-specific examples are provided below to provide context about the important and emerging role of the family for today's military.

A simple but meaningful quote from an Army leader demonstrates the important role of families: "Recruit a soldier, retain a family" (Geren, 2007). The Air Force has also focused on the link between retention and quality of life for families. A senior Air Force leader, Chief Master Sergeant Roy at a 2009 hearing to the House Armed Service Subcommittee on Military Personnel titled "The Oversight of Family Support Programs," appropriately described the Air Force support to families and the link between family wellness and retention,

> Airmen make a decision to remain on duty based on many factors, one of which is the quality of support they and their families receive. This underscores the fact that caring for families has a direct impact on mission readiness. When we take care of Air Force families, Airmen are freer from distractions and better able to focus on the mission. (*Department of the Air Force*, 2009)

The Department of the Navy has also focused research on the changing role of families and determined "if a military member's spouse is not happy with the military lifestyle, then that member may be more likely to leave the military" (Zellman, Gates, Moini, & Suttorp, 2009). General Amos, the Commandant of the Marine Corps, in his 2010 *Commandants Planning Guidance*, shared his vision for focusing on families during and beyond the current wartime efforts: "We will keep faith with our Marines, our Sailors, and our families. Our approach to caring for Marines, families, and relatives of our fallen Marines is based on our unwavering loyalty; this will not change" (U.S. Marine Corps, 2010). Across all service branches, constructs such as military "readiness" and "organizational commitment" are consistently linked with perceived policy support for families, primarily implemented through family-support programming and practices.

Today's military professionals share a common ethos of personal sacrifice, which can be codified as "Selfless Service." During times of war and specifically the current conflicts: Operation New Dawn (OND) (formerly referred to as Operation Iraqi Freedom, OIF) and Enduring Freedom (OEF), persisting in this personal sacrifice can become particularly difficult not only for the service members but for the families that serve as well. How does maintaining this sacrifice over extended periods of time impact the psychosocial well-being of service members and their families serving in today's political climate? In other words, how does the associated stress accompanied with the "profession of arms" impact the ability of military families to function, cope, solve problems, and work together as a unit? More broadly, what are the implications for the relationships that exist within the context of the military family? The psychosocial issues impacting military families can be largely explored through the context of deployment and the subsequent spillover effects that arise as a result of (a) extended periods of parental absence and (b) parental trauma exposure (e.g., combat stress). These issues are explored throughout this chapter, with a particular emphasis on prevention and intervention programs for service members, spouses, couples, children, and families.

COMBAT STRESS

It is important to note that many service members return from both combat and noncombat deployments without mental health issues or concerns. Additionally, some service members experience initial symptoms of stress that dissipate on their own (Jaycox & Tanielian,

2008). Despite the Department of Defense efforts to reduce the length of time of deployments and to provide more predictability in terms of when and how long deployment will last, the long-term consequences of deploying and performing the duties associated with a constant state of war can include repeated exposure to trauma. This exposure at times causes combat-related stress symptoms that can become difficult to manage and, ultimately, impact family relationships and the entire family system.

Combat stress is not a new concept. Its roots can be traced back (at least) to the "shell shock" era of World War I (Mott, 1916; Southard, 1918). In World War II, the term *combat neuroses* was used to describe experiences of war returnees (Grinker & Spiegel, 1945). Within the *Diagnostic Statistical Manual* (*DSM*), in the first iteration (American Psychiatric Association, 1952), the diagnosis of "Gross Stress Reaction" was used to describe the "severe physical demands or extreme stress such as combat or in a civilian catastrophe" (p. 40) to describe problems associated with war returnees from World War II. A full 14 years later, the second edition of the *DSM* (American Psychiatric Association, 1968) transitioned from "Gross Stress Reaction" to "transient situational disturbance" in its attempt to describe or quantify the experiences of war returnees. Twelve years later, in 1980, the American Psychiatric Association's *DSM III* introduced posttraumatic stress disorder (PTSD) as it is known today. This classification system, primarily familiar to clinicians as a clinical tool, also helps researchers, government officials, policy makers, and the U.S. public better categorize the experiences of war returnees. PTSD has emerged as the most prevalent consequence of trauma exposure during war (Tanielian & Jaycox, 2008), and this consequence extends well beyond the service member to his or her family (spouse, child) and community. PTSD is discussed in more detail in other chapters, but for the purposes of this chapter it is important to highlight the connection among trauma exposure, PTSD, and implications for the functioning of the family as a unit. Trauma exposure, in the context of the current OIF/OEF/OND wars, has direct consequences for the well-being of service members. Service members often return from combat with varying degrees of mental health issues. In some sense, similar to their Vietnam counterparts, since the onset of the current wars, there has also been an increase in associated psychosocial issues, including the rates of alcohol abuse, domestic violence, and suicide (Kuehn, 2009) across all service branches. Although the diagnostic criteria for PTSD require symptoms that fall within all four of the clusters identified in the *DSM*, subclinical symptoms (not meeting the diagnostic threshold) are also of concern. However, due to constrained resources, clinicians often give little consideration to service members with fewer symptoms. Consequently, there is a need for some discussion that differentiates the degrees of combat-related posttraumatic stress symptomology. This discussion centers on the continuum approach to recognizing symptoms. At one end of the continuum, there are enough diagnostic indicators to represent a full-blown diagnosis of PTSD. At the other end, there are fewer symptoms, not enough to meet the diagnostic threshold, yet still sufficient to cause concern in a number of life domains, including within the family context.

Examining subclinical posttraumatic stress symptoms draws attention to lower levels of symptoms that do not meet diagnostic criteria yet still present as a problem for service members. The U.S. Marine Corps has appropriately captured this phenomenon within its Combat Stress Control Program through a model referred to as the Combat Operational Stress Continuum for Marines. A graphic depiction of this model is provided below (see Figure 19.1). Marine leaders and fellow Marines are trained to identify

READY	REACTING	INJURED	ILL
• Good to go • Well trained • Prepared • Fit and tough • Cohesive units, ready families	• Distress or impairment • Mild, transient • Anxious or irritable • Behavior change	• More severe or persistent distress or impairment • Leaves lasting evidence (personality change)	• Stress injuries that don't heal without intervention • Diagnosable • PTSD • Depression • Anxiety • Addictive Disorder

Figure 19.1 United States Marine Corps combat operational stress continuum

symptoms of stress across a continuum. Marines coping with symptoms that fall in subclinical thresholds (depicted in this practice model under the title "Reacting") are encouraged to seek help early. On identification, Marines are taught how to respond, by appropriate referral, and follow through with traditional peer-to-peer intervention. This model has been successful in identifying Marines in distress early and providing appropriate interventions before symptoms escalate and result in more chronic problems.

Researchers have cited the difficulties in treating PTSD: "half of those treated retain the diagnosis at post-treatment and responders often report considerable residual symptomology" (Forbes, Lewis, Rarslow, Hawthorne & Creamer, 2008, p. 142). For this reason, it becomes essential for researchers and practitioners alike to truly understand the factors that influence treatment outcomes; for example, social support or family relationships. Early intervention also becomes important, particularly if practitioners are able to intervene at the family level before the full-blown diagnostic criteria are evident. Consequently, considering these factors, it makes conceptual sense that early intervention should occur when the thresholds for PTSD are at the subclinical levels. Despite the attention drawn to PTSD as a result of the lengthy war efforts associated with OIF/OEF/OND conflicts, clinicians, fellow service members, and the community at large should focus on chronic, subclinical thresholds as components of early intervention, particularly within the context of the family. Typical individual- and family-level interventions should include short-term brief therapy models, involving problem solving, behavioral modification techniques and principles of cognitive and narrative therapies. The success of these interventions is often associated with the length of time service members or their families struggle with symptoms, with increased rates of success and swift return to duty when clients access services early. How to appropriately provide early intervention services during ongoing wars that often require service members to swiftly prepare for repeat deployments is a question that those helping professionals working with military personnel struggle with on a day-to-day basis.

DEPLOYMENT STRESSORS

Long—and at times repeat—deployments are a harsh reality for today's military members and their families. Examining a snapshot in time, in just one service branch in September 2009 there were 40,000 Air Force members deployed away from their families, with 32,000 of those serving in the direct OIF/OEF/OND deployed zones and the "vast majority have served on multiple deployments, with no doubt more in their future" (Schwartz, 2009). These same figures for both the Army and the Marine Corps are much higher. Military leaders have worked to improve the predictability of the cycle of combat tours and to stabilize the tempo of the wartime environment. Yet, even with a predictable cycle of deployment, military members and, subsequently, their families have experienced stressors associated with a wartime environment. These stressors are viewed within the context of a "cycle of deployment" that includes predeployment, deployment, sustainment, redeployment, and postdeployment stages. A graphic depiction of the cycle of deployment is shown in Figure 19.2. A description of each stage and associated intervention programming that typically follow each phase is provided.

Predeployment (mobilization and training periods), actual deployment, sustaining the deployment, redeployment, and then postdeployment (referred to by some branches of the military as reintegration or reunion) make up the cycle of deployment. Each stage can be defined in terms of a loose time frame and include both the logistical and emotional characteristics that accompany it. There are challenges for both the military members and their family members across each stage of the deployment cycle. How well those challenges are handled often depends on a number of different factors, including length of marriage, number of prior deployments, number of children, and strength of community support system. Another factor is termed *emotional outlook*, which refers to how a person views the

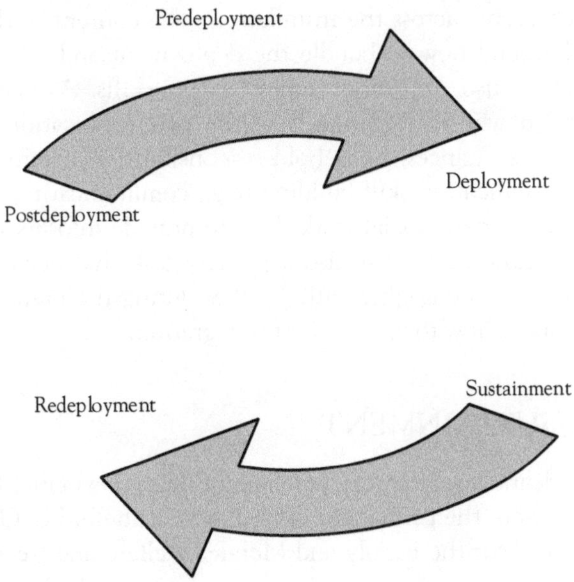

Figure 19.2 Cycle of deployment

deployment. Installation-level programs and support structures have an important role in providing interventions across each stage within the cycle of deployment. Civilian agencies also provide support to military families living in remote communities, away from day-to-day supports available on an installation.

PREDEPLOYMENT

The predeployment stage is described as the period leading up to the actual deployment itself. This stage can be a particularly stressful time for military members as there are many "predeployment" tasks that need to be completed. From a logistics standpoint, military members and their families spend the predeployment time attempting to get affairs in order and tying up loose ends, professionally and personally. From an emotional standpoint, military members often worry about how the deployment will impact their spouses and children. Complicating matters is the actual departure date. Despite the fact that military members are often given a precise date when they are likely to deploy, that date often changes with little or no notice (Waynick, Frederich, & Scheider, 2005). Concerns about the stability of marriages and the ability of spouses to handle the extended absence are commonplace (Black, 1993; Logan, 1987; Pincus & Na, 1999). Additionally, part of predeployment preparation can include service member trainings away from home for weeks or months before they are actually deployed.

Military Programs for Deployment Preparation

Military installations typically offer a host of psychoeducational interventions for military members and their families during the predeployment stage. Psychoeducation is offered in the form of large-scale briefings, small group training sessions and through handing out literature at outreach events across the installation. The content of the psychoeducation is largely structured around how to handle the deployment and subsequent family separation. Psychoeducation also consists of improving life skills. As many service members today are young and newly married, much of the psychoeducation focuses on "family readiness" issues such as finances, household responsibilities, parenting struggles, single parenthood, and communication skill building (e.g., communicating with children about deployment). Drawing on basic social work skills to provide information and referral and follow-up services to those in need is also a primary task that occurs during predeployment. The service providers engaging with families during the predeployment stage also begin to plant seeds about how to prepare for reintegration.

DEPLOYMENT/SUSTAINMENT

Deployment can be defined as "the assignment of military personnel to temporary, unaccompanied duty away from the permanent duty station" (Stafford & Grady, 2003, p. 111). Another report prepared for the Family and Morale, Welfare and Recreation Department for the U.S. Army defines deployment as "discrete events in which Soldiers are sent with their unit (or as individuals joining another unit) to a particular location to accomplish a specific military mission" (Booth et al., 2007, p. 33).

Although deployment itself is likely the highest stressor facing military members and families today, the issue is much broader than "the deployment" and extends through the sustainment stage. During sustainment, families must adjust to long-term separations that are unpredictable and difficult to manage. Much of the deployment and sustainment stages are filled with uncertainty for both military members and their families. This uncertainty is often dealt with by attempting to maintain close communication (whenever possible). Sustainment itself can be taxing for the stay-behind parent and children for a number of different reasons. During this stage, military spouses take on new responsibilities that were typically handled by the service member spouse. These responsibilities range from household maintenance and managing the family finances to becoming the sole parent for the children. This reorganization of responsibilities and routines can become particularly stressful for the remaining spouses and children. Mmari, Roche, Sudhinaraset, and Blum (2009) focused on examining this issue across all four services branches through the use of small focus groups and the qualitative collection of "word" data from the lens of adolescents in military families. Participants were recruited from middle and high school populations and were living with an active-duty parent. Eleven focus groups were conducted with a total of 39 students. The resulting data were organized according to overarching themes that shed light on both the experiences and relationship factors that are impacted by deployment. One such identified theme centered on "adolescent health and well-being." One adolescent described his anxiety over his father leaving for a deployment as:

> [L]ike for this war, you are always thinking about it because you don't want your father to be shot at or anything like that, but when my dad left, even before he left on the plane, I was crying like a little kid. I don't like it when he has to leave our family and stuff like that. (Mmari et al., 2009, p. 463)

Another theme of the Mmari et al. (2009) study centered on "changing family roles and responsibilities." An adolescent described the additional responsibilities placed on him during the deployment itself: "And when they deploy you get like . . . I know in my house, my mom started making me do all the laundry and I had to help her do the dishes, like way more than I normally had to" (Mmari et al., 2009, p. 464). This theme emerged as one of the strongest issues for the adolescents who participated in the study: the idea that there is an enormous amount of stress related to roles and responsibilities and the shifting dynamics within these constructs through the cycle of deployment. There is large variance in how families cope during deployment, with some overperforming and others struggling to meet the demands of day-to-day life stressors.

Military Support Programs During Deployment

Military families remaining at installations during a deployment are offered a wide variety of services to help ease the burden of maintaining a household on their own. Some services are aimed at the remain-behind parent, while others focus on the children. Services ranging from "give parents a break" (after hours respite care) to classes on financial stability and parenting assistance are typical. Additional psychoeducation reinforcements related to how to handle the deployment are also offered; such as communication and life-skills workshops that are generally offered at various stages during the deployment cycle. Life-skills classes typically teach the remaining spouses how to communicate with children about the deployment and how to help children prepare for the reunion. From an emotional perspective, early on in the deployment many families experience an extreme sense of uncertainty and loss (Huebner, Mancini, Wilcox, Grass, & Grass, 2007). The uncertainty can carry through the entire deployment because spouses and children are uncertain about the safety of their loved one, whether their service member will be emotionally and physically healthy when he or she returns, and whether the actual return date will occur as planned. When psychological symptoms persist, particularly surrounding uncertainty and loss, and the need presents, short-term counseling services are typically available for both spouses and children. The installation based counseling services typically utilize a general problem solving approach coupled with supportive reinforcement. Counseling services are offered both on the installation and through private providers in the community. Spouses are able to access civilian-based and community counseling services through Military OneSource. This is a 24/7 web-based and telephonic-based referral service that offers service members and their spouses referrals for short-term confidential stabilization counseling services in the civilian sector; it also provides many other support resources. Military dependents can also access community mental health services through TRICARE health insurance.

After the initial shock of the deployment occurring and the loss brought on by family separation, families tend to rebound and adjust to the new responsibilities that are associated with the deployment. Some families even report the growth of familiar bonds and abilities to overcome challenges during deployment (MacDermid, Samper, Schwarz, & Nishida, 2008). Thus far, social support is consistently identified in the literature as the primary buffer or protective factor that differentiates those who do well with the associated stressors resulting from deployment from those who struggle with challenges that occur during the deployment process. Within the military, social support is appropriately defined by Bowen, Mancini, Martin, Ware, and Nelson (2003) as "a social psychological variable that we define from a military/base perspective as reflecting the degree to which members feel positively attached to the military as an organization and view the base community as a source of support and connection to others" (p. 35).

Conceptually, it makes sense that families who feel a sense of social support are better prepared to deal with both everyday life stress as well as the unique stressors associated with being a military family (e.g., deployment). As such, military installations typically offer support group opportunities for spouses to network and share in the trials and tribulations of military life. Military installations also typically offer outreach events that provide forums for fun and friendship building for remaining spouses and children. Formal and informal spouses' groups also provide a system of support for families dealing with deployment. Just as the history of PTSD can be traced back to World War I era "shell shock," the role of military spouses can be traced back to the Revolutionary War. During that war, 39 spouses, with the help of Esther Reed (the wife of an aide to George Washington), started the first military spouses "club," referred to at the time as *the association*. Spouses were integral to the war efforts by performing such traditional duties as cooking, sewing, and nursing. These groups continued and their roles evolved over time, yet it was not until after the Gulf War that the U.S. Army formalized this process by mandating that all units have an established family-support group. The other service branches have also adopted some form of a support structure for spouses. Many of the groups still serve the function of providing support structures for families with a deployed service member. They also provide a forum for communication and support for the spouses themselves during a time of critical need.

A study conducted by the National Military Family Association (2005) examined the psychosocial stressors of spouses of service members across three "phases" of deployment: (1) notification of deployment, (2) actual departure of their spouse, and finally, (3) during the deployment itself. Sixty-two percent of those who responded reported the greatest stress occurred during the deployment itself (National Military Family Association, 2005). It quickly becomes evident that spouses of today's service members are viewed as serving "alongside their service members," and the family support groups are "beneficial during the difficult times that military spouses must face" (Di Nola, 2008, p. 5).

REDEPLOYMENT/POSTDEPLOYMENT

The redeployment stage begins when the military member prepares to return to their family from the deployment. This stage is often filled with anticipation and mixed emotions. This is followed by the postdeployment stage where the service member returns home and attempts to reintegrate into his or her family and community (sometimes referred to as *reintegration* or *reunion*). The early part of postdeployment is often referred to as the *honeymoon* period. The honeymoon is described as a time frame filled with joyous excitement by military members and their families and can last from a few days to a number of weeks. During this stage, families begin their work of renegotiating roles and responsibilities associated with family life.

After some time has passed, however, some families move into a period of struggle where they experience conflict with newly negotiated roles and responsibilities. Postdeployment can be the most difficult stage of the deployment cycle for military members and their families. This can be a tension-filled period because military members, spouses, and children have gone through various developmental milestones and have inevitably changed. Spouses have become more autonomous, and children have advanced through various life stages. Children experience deployment differently, depending on their age and developmental phase during the actual parental absence. Successfully navigating this stage of the deployment cycle requires patience, commitment, and resource navigation skills on behalf of the military members and the family. The reintegration process is unique for every family and differs with every deployment (Di Nola, 2008). Naturally, this variation has implications for service providers and policy makers aiming to understand both the nature of deployment and the appropriate support services necessary to assist during these stressful circumstances. Many service members step back into parenting roles, as mothers and as fathers, for children of all developmental ages and some with unique and special needs.

The ongoing nature of the current wars and the propensity for repeat deployments make this process particularly challenging. Besides unpredictable return dates, there are concerns about deploying again and the degree of combat-related posttraumatic stress or trauma exposure experienced by the service member. Bowling and Sherman (2008) suggest that some service members struggle with reintegration; especially if they know that they are on target to deploy again within a relatively short period of time, they will not make the effort to engage with their family at the emotional level that is necessary to allow for the full reintegration process to occur (Bowling & Sherman, 2008). The time in-between each deployment is referred to as *dwell time*. During dwell time service members and their families continue the work of reintegrating by refining roles and responsibilities and coping with the emotional aspects of deployment. The reintegration process is stressful for all families, even for those where the service member has experienced the least amount of trauma or combat exposure.

Military Programs to Support Redeployment and Postdeployment

Helping professionals provide military members and their families education on ways to manage this stage of the deployment cycle successfully. Factors—such as positive communication, gaining an understanding of appropriate expectations, and taking time to become reacquainted with one another—have all been identified in the literature as helping to ease the stressors associated with reintegration (Logan, 1987; Peeble-Klieger & Klieger, 1994; Pincus & Na, 1999). Counseling-based interventions may be necessary to help families fully reconstitute after a deployment. Helping families recognize and process the multitude of emotions that accompany redeployment and postdeployment is often the goal focused on by helping professionals working with families during this stage of the deployment cycle.

DEPLOYMENT IMPACT ON MILITARY FAMILIES

Frequent and repeat deployments have become the norm for military families serving in a post–9/11 era. Indeed, deployments are the greatest source of stress for service members and their families. Additionally, exposure to trauma during combat can result in service members returning with such "invisible wounds" as varying degrees of posttraumatic stress symptomology (Jaycox & Tanielian, 2008). Inevitably, the wartime experiences of service members affect both spouses and children and, more broadly, relationships within the context of the family. In fact, deployment-related experiences have been well documented in the literature within a number of different domains, including impact on service members, impact on spouses, and impact on children. For example, families of Vietnam veterans experienced higher rates of divorce compared to their nonveteran counterparts, and their marriages had higher rates of conflict (including in some cases, increased rates of domestic violence). In addition, there was difficulty expressing emotion between partners, which inherently led to difficulty with interpersonal skills, problems with intimacy, and caregiver burden (Forbes et al., 2008; Jordan et al., 1992; Riggs, Byrne, Weathers, & Litz, 1998).

Shifting the focus from Vietnam to the current war efforts, there are similarities with regard to family-level variables. For example, military spouses of the OIF/OEF conflicts also report problems with communication and expressing emotion, which in extreme cases can lead to instances of domestic violence. Clearly, there is an important link between trauma and interpersonal relationships. One small study that examined this issue by collecting data from 45 male Army soldiers who had recently returned from OEF or OIF/OND deployments and their spouses found a strong correlation between an increase in combat-related posttraumatic stress symptoms (e.g., sleep problems, emotional numbing) and lower marital relationship satisfaction. Like the Vietnam era researchers that studied these problems before them, the OIF/OEF researchers determined that "trauma, specifically combat or military related traumatic experience, may be particularly detrimental to the marriage" (Goff, Crow, Reisbig, & Hamilton, 2007, p. 344). If war trauma is "detrimental to the marriage," then it makes sense that these detrimental effects would extend beyond the marriage to the children. Helping families cope in both the context of marriage and parenting relationships during stressful situations brought on by high-operations tempo associated with the OIF/OEF/OND conflicts is an area that will continue to need attention, well after the current war effort comes to an end.

DEPLOYMENT IMPACT ON SPOUSES AND MARITAL RELATIONSHIPS

Deployment experiences (e.g., trauma exposure) and subsequent impact of posttraumatic stress symptomology extend beyond the service member and are said to have "spillover" effects for the family and, in particular, intimate relationships. A Vietnam era study highlights this phenomenon. Fifty male Vietnam veterans and their female partners participated in a study in which they were administered a number of relationship satisfaction type scales: the Dyadic Adjustment Scale (DAS), the Marital Status Inventory (MSI), the Relationship Problems Scale (RPS), the Fear of Intimacy Scale (FSI), and the PTSD Checklist–Military Version (PCL-M). According to this study, veterans with PTSD had higher levels of significant relationship distress and more difficulty with intimacy. More than 70% of the study participants had what the researchers referred to as "clinically significant relationship difficulties" that required clinical interventions (Riggs et al., 1998, p. 97).

Another study that also examined relationship issues with Vietnam veterans diagnosed with PTSD, using a much larger sample of 1,200 male veterans and their female partners, found similar results: "severe problems in marital and family adjustment . . . in parenting skills" (Jordan et al., 1992, p. 916). Finally, according to the Presidents Commission on Mental Heath Report (1978), a report produced as a result of the Vietnam Veterans Adjustment Study, "38% of the marriages of Vietnam veterans dissolved within 6 months of the return of the veteran" (Galovski & Lyons, 2004, p. 479).

The U.S. Army also examined these issues in the context of the current OIF/OEF/OND war efforts. Drawing on the "family context" of wellness as it applies to the current wartime environment, the Army conducted an evaluation of their "Building Healthy Families Program." The overarching goal of this program is to enhance service members relationships with their spouses and children while promoting healthy lifestyle choices and decreasing risk behaviors. The intervention consisted of a number of day-long educational sessions targeted toward service members and spouses on content that focused on adverse health behaviors (e.g., stress, exercise, communication). Ultimately, the program focused on "recognition of unhealthy behaviors and development of skills for self-wellness" (Niederhauser, Maddock, LeDoux, & Arnold, 2005, p. 228). The intervention group in this study displayed an overall reduction in stress across a number of areas, with the highest effect in the areas of stress, seatbelt use, and tobacco cessation. An interesting component of this study was that two thirds of the study participants had more than one risk behavior;

thus, the intervention had to target multiple areas (Niederhauser et al., 2005), and it became difficult to tease out which intervention helped with each specific risk factor.

From a psychosocial standpoint, military spouses, like other population groups, present with varying degrees of characteristics that predispose or buffer against the stressors of military life (Niederhauser et al., 2005). Typical risk factors for military families—such as age, length of marriage, preexisting coping abilities, and levels of social support—all impact outcomes that relate to military spouses (Rosen, Carpenter, & Moghadam, 1989). After deployment, if service members struggle with combat-related posttraumatic stress symptoms, spouses can also become at-risk of developing secondary traumatic stress (Figley, 1993). This concept, first coined by Friedman, occurs when spouses "become attuned to trauma cues in their environment and through normal learning processes, may come to mimic their service members' reactions upon exposure to these cues" (Galovski & Lyons, 2004, p. 485). This circular feedback loop of symptoms occurring between the service member and the spouse has clear implications for the family system and children in particular, in part because of the important role of spouses as systems of support for service members and communities.

Domestic Violence in the Military

A final psychosocial issue impacting military marriages and spouses is domestic violence. Domestic violence occurs within the military across all services and all military ranks. Domestic violence can be defined as a pattern of behavior resulting in emotional/psychological or physical abuse that is directed toward an intimate partner. Some military social science research points toward correlations between war trauma, the development of PTSD, and anger and subsequent domestic violence in military families. Other research points toward the stressors placed on military members and a transient life style that at times impedes the development of strong systems of support for spouses or marriages. Social scientists have well documented other issues that may lead to abusive relationship patterns, including: exposure to family violence as a child, intergenerational transmission of violence, lack of positive caring relationships, lack of attachment, and the incidence of childhood physical abuse. It is important to recognize that in situations of domestic violence, social work practitioners work with offenders that can be manipulative, controlling, and threatening in the context of their interpersonal relationships with significant others.

In 2002 there were a number of incidents of domestic violence in the military that resulted in homicide that drew national media attention. These incidents resulted in a thorough examination of domestic violence in the military. The Department of Defense issued a task force and subsequent Government Accountability Office reviews of domestic violence in the military. The findings of these reviews pointed toward the need for commanders and communities to work together to prevent domestic violence. Reports also highlighted the fact that domestic violence is predominantly an issue impacting female spouses (although males are victims as well—albeit less often) and that the military transient life style can perpetuate the geographical isolation from family and friends that is so often seen in situations of domestic violence. Finally, unique to the military is the notion that military spouses report being afraid to come forward to report the abuse because of implications for their active duty member's career (i.e., fear of punishment or discharge that will result in loss of income for the family). The Family Advocacy Program was developed for the purpose of preventing and intervening on issues of domestic violence across the military. This program is discussed in more detail later in the chapter.

CHILDREN IMPACTED BY MILITARY SERVICE

More than half of the current military forces are married with children. Furthermore, 40% of those have children under age 5. Demographically, the military is made up, in large part, of young families with young children. Although the rates of active duty women—mothers—are currently growing (in 2011 15% of the active duty forces were women, compared to 1995 when the rate hovered around 13%) and are higher than at any other time in our nation's history, the U.S. military is in large part comprised of men, that is, fathers. When examining children's reactions to the current OIF/OEF/OND wartime environment, in a broad sense, what is really being examined is the impact of "father absence" on children.

There are some unique factors associated with the phenomenon of wartime "father absence." For example, children with a deployed father have an increased level of concern related to the safe return of their family member as compared to their civilian counterparts, who are often less concerned with safety needs during times of parental absence. Available studies highlight the important interconnectedness of the health of service members and their spouses and children, as well as the importance of social support in the context of war deployments and military families. Ultimately, father absence can be perceived as a loss of social support for spouses, which can then be correlated to decreases in academic performance and increases in behavioral problems in children (Hiew, 1992).

Interestingly, some studies highlight that the actual absence of the father (the deployment itself) is the most emotionally stressful time for children. This phenomenon is interesting in the context of the current U.S. military cycle of deployment model (previously discussed in this chapter) that conceptualizes the experiences of service members and their families as a staged yet fluid model that includes experiences across each cycle of deployment: predeployment, deployment, sustainment, redeployment, and postdeployment. From a programmatic standpoint, it is important to understand that children's emotional needs are most critical during the actual deployment stage. This is also consistent with the research on spouses that cite deployment as the most stressful time for those spouses (National Military Family Association, 2005). Other outcomes for children include depression, behavioral difficulties (Jensen, Martin, & Watanabe, 1996), and higher rates of irritability and impulsiveness (Hillenbrand, 1976).

As with families, children's reactions to war are largely variable and cannot be viewed outside the context of the family and individual development. Communities and outside influences, such as peer groups and even the media, impact the experiences of today's military children. One study indicated that exposure to media and a constant state of worry about their parent's safe return is a primary issue facing military children (Ryan-Wenger, 2001). Another study examining children's reactions to wartime father absence found that the emotional aftermath of the Persian Gulf War "may constitute a significant interference with children's development" (Jensen & Shaw, 1996, p. 84). Understanding how the entire deployment process—from predeployment to deployment and reintegration—impacts the ongoing development of children is an essential feature of intervention and of overall program development. Also important is recognizing that optimal child development depends on healthy parenting and the absence of key parental mental health symptoms (emotional numbing, depressive symptoms) from both parents, but most importantly in regard to the primary care taker.

CHILD ABUSE

Some military children, like their civilian counterparts, are at-risk for child abuse. Certain demographic risk factors for child abuse exist within subgroups of the military population, including young couples, (i.e., couples that marry young after short courtships) and those that fall within the ranks of E-1 to E-4 (typically ages 18 to 24); those with multiple deployments and extended periods of single parenting; those that perform in particularly stressful positions (e.g., military police and explosive ordinance division); and those with little support systems in place to assist with the demands of parenting. The research on child abuse within the military includes a number of studies that compare military and civilian rates of child abuse. Any comparison of these rates, however, should take into account many of the differences between the populations, including the unique stressors of each community. For example, all children of active duty military personnel have health insurance, and typically have housing and immediate access to other basic necessities. The same cannot be said for their civilian counterparts. Nevertheless, child abuse continues to be a serious issue within the military, and the Department of Defense has taken great strides to ensure that military leaders, practitioners, and policy makers are engaged across all levels to promote early intervention and support services.

Within the military, child abuse can take the form of physical, emotional, neglect, or sexual abuse. According to Department of Defense Instruction, *child abuse* is defined as "The physical or sexual abuse, emotional abuse, or neglect of a child by a parent, guardian, foster parent, or by a caregiver, whether the caregiver is intrafamilial or extrafamilial, under circumstances indicating the child's welfare is harmed or threatened." Child abuse within the military can occur in the context of poor judgment, as it relates to disciplinary practices that stem from inappropriate expectations placed on children by their parents. An example of this might involve an inappropriate reaction by a parent who believes that a 2-year-old should be toilet trained and never have an "accident." When the child has an accident such a parent might perform harsh disciplinary practices toward the child, resulting in physical or emotional harm. Stress—whether from deployment, high operations tempo during nondeployment or other work-life balance issues—is associated with poor parenting practices. At times, these practices can result in abuse that leaves a permanent impact on the child. The military has invested in a number of programs aimed at helping families cope with the stressors of military life. A review of some of these programs is provided later. Part of learning how to cope involves education on how to improve parenting practices with an overall goal of improving the quality of relationships that exist between parents and children.

Additional Military Programs

There are a number of Department of Defense programs that have been developed, particularly during the course of the recent decade of war, to respond to the emerging psychosocial needs of military members and their families. There are also a number of long-standing programs that have stood the test of time, established well before the current war efforts.

The Family Advocacy Program was developed in 1982 by the Department of the Defense for the purpose of providing prevention and treatment services to families engaged in maltreatment. The Family Advocacy Program is comprised of helping professionals from military communities around the world that work as part of a coordinated community response to ensure that the needs of families are met. Central to this effort is the coordination between the medical and legal communities as well as the on-base and off-base law enforcement officials and the community-based counseling services. Within the military, small unit commanders are ultimately responsible for ensuring victim safety and offender accountability. Commanders coordinate with helping professionals who perform the day-to-day work within this program. Family Advocacy Program social workers train military members and the staff that work within community/installation helping agencies on their role in preventing family violence and in procedures for reporting abuse.

The Department of Defense established two types of reporting options for victims of domestic violence: (1) restricted reports, and (2) unrestricted reports. These reporting options were designed to empower victims by encouraging them to come forward and report abuse. Restricted reports occur when a victim reports domestic violence to one of the following professionals; a victim advocate, medical providers, or a chaplain. This avenue affords victims the opportunity to receive assistance without the notification of law enforcement or the chain of command. The primary purpose of this report is to facilitate a swift response to victim needs and safety.

On the other hand, victims can elect to make an unrestricted report. Unrestricted reports are reports that are given to victim advocates, military police officials, or to the military chain of command for action. With an unrestricted report, victims continue to receive prompt assistance with safety and advocacy, while also engaging the processes that ensure offender accountability (e.g., police reports and commander notification). If a victim elects to conduct a restricted report, he or she may then determine to change the report to unrestricted if they choose at a later date.

Military communities publish abuse hotline numbers for both child and spousal abuse and encourage all members to report suspected abuse. At the core of every family advocacy intervention is assessing for the safety of potential child or spouse abuse victims. When a victim's safety is in question, military commanders physically separate victims and offenders and issue military protective orders to potential service member offenders. Family advocacy services are "victim-centric" in that the service delivery is focused on ensuring that the immediate and long-term needs of victims are met and that offenders are held accountable. Although the program components may vary slightly across the individual service branches, generally speaking the program consists of a number of prevention and treatment-based services. These include home visits, couples counseling, psychoeducational classes (e.g., stress management, anger management, parenting education), offender accountability, and group and individual counseling services.

The success of any prevention-based intervention hinges on early identification and engagement on problem areas. Military families can self-refer for any prevention-based program on military installations. Beyond self-referrals, providers of prevention-based services also receive referrals from command level senior leadership, from collateral agencies within or the installation (e.g., child care facilities), or from the surrounding community. Some service and family members prefer to access prevention-based services in local communities near military bases. Military-based family advocacy prevention services consist of typical evidence-based practices and take into account the military environment, culture, deployment, and overall operation tempo that exist for the families that they serve. The goal of all prevention programming is to help strengthen family relationships and assist families with managing conflict before it escalates to violence.

The New Parent Support Program is a prevention-based, family-advocacy program that is offered in military communities for families of children age 3 or younger. Like many civilian-based home-visiting programs, this parent-support program provides intensive home-based services to families in an effort to improve parenting skills and prevent abuse. Home visitors (who often are social workers) provide information on parenting expectations, child development, sibling issues, and managing early childhood behaviors. As a result of the long war effort, home visitors also engage with families on issues related to parental absence, dealing with posttraumatic stress symptoms, and helping to communicate with children about deployments.

The Family Advocacy Program also provides treatment for families engaged in violence. At the core of all treatment services is effective safety planning measures. All service branches offer some form of victim-advocacy services. Victim advocates are available 24/7 to provide hands-on advocacy services that include safety planning, system navigation, legal advocacy, and case management coordination. The treatment components of the Family Advocacy Program include assessments and ongoing counseling at the individual and group level, as determined by the client needs. Military service members that have been determined to meet the criteria set forth by the Department of Defense for abuse are mandated into the treatment service delivery. Traditional empirically supported interventions are utilized by providers in their efforts to keep victims safe and help clients change destructive relationship patterns. Victims are offered safety planning and supportive counseling services aimed at breaking the cycle of violence. Helping professionals typically utilize cognitive behavioral therapy, narrative therapies, and support groups in their work with victims. Offenders are typically mandated into an offender group where they learn techniques that challenge their belief systems as well as new skills aimed at behavior change.

Military commanders engage with Family Advocacy Program helping professionals (e.g., social workers) to ensure that service members are getting the necessary help and assistance required to develop and maintain healthy relationships. Military civilian social workers collaborate with local child protective services to conduct joint assessments on child abuse cases, with a goal of minimizing the potential retraumatization on children. Since the Department of Defense maintains its own criteria for abuse, there may be times when the state and the military service department case outcomes differ. Children who have been exposed to domestic violence are also assessed and provided necessary services based on needs and development.

All branches of the military have also adopted the use of military family life consultants (MFLC). MFLCs are typically utilized as "surge capability" (i.e., not permanent staff), assisting communities in need during specific times of high deployment. The program provides behavioral health specialists to locations all around the world to provide short-term problem solving (community based, nonmedical) confidential counseling for service members and their spouses in distress. The MFLC service delivery model is unique in that the confidentiality of the counseling can reduce the stigma attached to seeking help within a military environment. This program is offered at military community counseling centers, in military units, at local schools, summer camps, and child care facilities. The family life consultants are trained to help families deal with family separation and deployment stressors using a problem-solving model.

Another program that emerged out of the need for increased community-based, family-centered services during the OIF/OEF/OND war efforts is called Families Overcoming Under Stress (Lester et al., 2011). This program provides in-home or in-community psychoeducational, resilience training for families. This program is reviewed in Chapter 24.

CASE VIGNETTES

Two case vignettes with follow-up discussion questions are provided in an effort to give readers the opportunity to more critically examine psychosocial issues impacting military service members and their families. Although these examples are hypothetical, they are grounded in real-life situations that occur on U.S. military installations around the world.

Case Vignette: Michael

Michael is an 11-year-old male child who was referred to counseling services by his mother. His mother's concerns are that he is impulsive, often breaks his toys when upset, pulls at his hair, and never sleeps. He is also frequently in trouble in school due to threatening harm to another child through use of a firearm. Michael lives in the home with his mother, older sister Kristen who is 14, half-brother Evan who is 1, and his stepfather (officer in the military). Michael's stepfather is currently assigned to Ft. Belvoir, Virginia, where he works as a military police officer.

Michael was diagnosed with ADHD on entering kindergarten. He has taken stimulant medications since that time and has always been on individualized education plans for ADHD. When he was 6 years old, his stepfather, deployed as part of Operation Iraqi Freedom and while patrolling in a dangerous area on a cliff, lost his balance and fell many feet and ultimately suffered a severe traumatic brain injury. According to the stepfather, this situation has caused his behavior to be erratic and violent at times. At times, he has taken out his anger on his children, hitting them and throwing things at them. Over the past 6 months, Michael's behavior has escalated, and he is in trouble at home and school about two to three times per week. His mother has told the children that she is leaving the stepfather, and the children appear to have little respect for him. This mother just "wants Michael to follow directions from the stepfather until they leave him several months from now and to stop acting out in school."

Case Vignette: Smith Family

Mr. Smith is a stay-at-home dad, taking care of two children ages 3 and 5, Lizzie and Jane. Mrs. Smith is a Navy seaman (a nurse, Lieutenant) currently attached to a Navy hospital in the deployed zone of Afghanistan. Mrs. Smith currently talks to her husband and children via Skype each night before bedtime.

This family arrived at a new base about 10 months ago, and shortly after arriving Mrs. Smith was selected for a no-notice deployment and told to prepare to leave within 30 days. The family lives off-base in an apartment complex that they found when they arrived at New London, Connecticut. The family located the apartment quickly and is now slowly realizing it is not in the "best part of town."

Mr. Smith was not prepared to be a single parent. He has a degree in engineering and has not been able to find a job with the economy in Connecticut. The family is struggling with finances, as they have previously been a two-parent-income household. They are saving money by not paying for child care. Lieutenant Smith is receiving hazardous duty pay, but it is not enough.

Mr. Smith is not happy that his wife tries to tell him how to parent the girls via Skype. He is contemplating moving with the girls back to his hometown of Chicago, Illinois. He is also concerned about his wife returning and further criticizing him related to his parenting when she returns. The girls appear healthy, but are very quiet, hesitant to engage in playful activity, and they present as somewhat reserved. A full assessment on the children has not been conducted.

Case Vignette Discussion Questions (for each case vignette)

1. What psychosocial issues are impacting each family?
2. What are the key elements to conducting an assessment with each family?
3. What background information would you need related to the military context of each family situation to fully understand the dynamics occurring in this situation?
4. Where might you begin an intervention with each family?
5. What types of services or programs do you think would benefit each family?

CONCLUSION

Serving today's military population is both an honor and a challenge for any provider. The military as a population group is a unique culture and as such any provider aiming to conduct interventions with service members must have a sense of cultural humility and respect for the work performed and sacrifices made by service members and their families. Additionally, due to the length and frequency of deployment, and propensity for combat exposure, an underlying focus on trauma informed care, (i.e., universal approaches) should be part of any intervention model or program. Due to the prevalence of comorbid issues (e.g., substance abuse, family violence, and posttraumatic stress) providers should be prepared to engage with service members and their families on multiple levels. Engagement may involve treatment in one area and referral and monitoring of another area. Close attention should be paid to the treatment outcomes of individual areas (e.g., substance abuse) and how those outcomes impact the successful treatment of other areas (e.g., posttraumatic stress) and the identified problem as a whole. This holistic approach of assessing and treating problems involves both the service members, their families, and the relationship with the social worker as integral parts of the treatment/helping process. Finally, comprehensive assessments that include an examination of deployment history, type of deployment, type of military occupational specialty, length of time in the military, across traditional biopsychosocial–spiritual domains provide the foundation for determining appropriate referral and intervention strategies.

REFERENCES

American Psychiatric Association. (1952). *Diagnostic and statistical manual of mental disorders* (1st ed.). Washington, DC: Author.

American Psychiatric Association. (1968). *Diagnostic and statistical manual of mental disorders* (2nd ed.). Washington, DC: Author.

American Psychiatric Association. (1980). *Diagnostic and statistical manual of mental disorders* (3rd ed.). Washington, DC: Author.

Black, W. (1993). Military induced family separation: A stress reduction intervention. *Social Work, 38*, 273–280.

Booth, B., Segal, M., Bell, B., Martin, J., Ender, M., Rohall, D., & Nelson, J. (2007). *What we know about Army families*. Fairfax, VA: Family and Morale, Welfare, and Recreation Command.

Bowen, G., Mancini, J., Martin, J., Ware, W., & Nelson, J. (2003). Promoting the adaptation of military families: An empirical test of a community practice model. *Family Relations, 52*(1), 33–44.

Bowling, U., & Sherman, M. (2008). Welcoming them home: Supporting service members and their families in navigating the tasks of reintegration. *Professional Psychology Research and Practice, 39*, 451–458.

Department of the Air Force presentation to the House Armed Services Subcommittee on military personnel on the oversight of family support programs, House of Representatives (2009). (Testimony of James A. Roy). Retrieved from http://www.af.mil/shared/media/document/AFD-090724–036.pdf

Di Nola, G. (2008). Stressors afflicting families during military deployment. *Military Medicine, 173*, v–vii.

Figley, C. R. (1993). Coping with stressors on the home front: Psychological research on the Persian Gulf War. *Journal of Social Issues, 49*(5), 51–61.

Forbes, D., Lewis, V., Parslow, R., Hawthorne, G., & Creamer, M. (2008). A naturalistic comparison of models of programmatic interventions for combat related posttraumatic stress disorder. *Australian and New Zealand Journal of Psychiatry, 42*(12), 1051–1059.

Freedberg, S. (2005). They also serve. *National Journal, 37*(3), 1–5.

Galovski, T., & Lyons, J. A. (2004). Psychological sequelae of combat violence: A review of the impact of PTSD on the veteran's family and possible interventions. *Aggression and Violent Behavior*, 9, 477–501.

Geren, P. (2007). Secretary of the Army arrival ceremony remarks, Fort Myer, Virginia.

Goff, B., Crow, J., Reisbig, A., & Hamilton, S. (2007). The impact of individual trauma symptoms of deployed soldiers on relationship satisfaction. *Journal of Family Psychology, 21*, 344–353.

Grinker, R., & Spiegel, J. (1945). War neuroses in flying personnel. *American Journal of Psychiatry*, 619–624.

Hearings before the House National Security Committee Subcommittee on military readiness. (1998). (Testimony of Lieutenant General William P. Hallin.)

Hiew, C. (1992). Separated by their work: Families with fathers living apart. *Environment and Behavior, 24*(2), 206–225.

Hillenbrand, E. (1976). Father absence in military families. *Family Coordinator, 25*, 251–258.

Huebner, A., Mancini, J., Wilcox, R., Grass, S., & Grass, G. (2007). Parental deployment and youth in military families: Exploring uncertainty and ambiguous loss. *Family Relations*, 56(4), 112–122.

Jaycox, L. H., & Tanielian, T. (2008). *Invisible wounds of war: Psychological and cognitive injuries, their consequences and services to assist recovery*. Santa Monica, CA: RAND.

Jensen, P., Martin, D., & Watanabe, H. (1996). Children's response to separation during Operation Desert Storm. *Journal of American Academy of Children and Adolescent Psychiatry, 35*, 433–441.

Jensen, P., & Shaw, J. (1996). The effects of war and parental deployment upon children and adolescents. In R. Ursano & A. Norwood (Eds.), *Emotional aftermath of the Persian Gulf War: Veterans, families, and communities, and nations* (pp. 83–109). Washington, DC: American Psychiatric Press.

Jordan, B. K., Marmar, C. R., Fairbank, J. A., Schlenger, W. E., Kulka, R. A., Hough, R. L., & Weiss, D. S. (1992). Problems in families of male Vietnam veterans with posttraumatic stress disorder. *Journal of Consulting and Clinical Psychology*, 60, 916–926.

Kuehn, B. (2009). Soldier suicide rates continue to rise: Military, scientists work to stem the tide. *Journal of the American Medical Association, 301*, 1111–1113.

Lester, P., Mogil, C., Saltzman, W., Woodward, K., Nash, W., Leskin, G., . . . Beardslee, W. (2011). Families overcoming under stress: Implementing family-centered prevention for military families facing wartime deployments and combat operational stress. *Military Medicine, 19–25*(7).

Logan, K. (1987). The emotional cycle of deployment. *Proceedings, 2*, 43–47.

MacDermid, S., Samper, R., Schwarz, R., & Nishida, J. (2008). *Understanding and promoting resilience in military families. A report prepared for the Office of Military Community and Family Policy in the Office of the Secretary of Defense*. Retrieved from http://www.mfri.purdue.edu/content/Reports/Understanding%20and%20Promoting%20Resilience.pdf

Mmari, K., Roche, K., Sudhinaraset, M., & Blum, R. (2009). When a parent goes to war: Exploring the issues faced by adolescents and their families. *Youth and Society*, 40, 455–475.

Mott, F. (1916). Special discussion on shell shock without visible signs of injury. *Journal of Royal Society of Medicine*, 9, i–xxiv.

National Military Family Association. (2005). *Cycles of deployment: An analysis of survey responses from April through September, 2005*. San Diego, CA: Defense Web Technologies.

Niederhauser, V., Maddock, J., LeDoux, F., & Arnold, M. (2005). Building strong and ready army families: A multi-risk reduction health promotion pilot study. *Military Medicine, 170*, 227–233.

Peeble-Klieger, M., & Klieger, J. (1994). Reintegration stress for Desert Storm families: Wartime deployments and family trauma. *Journal of Traumatic Stress, 7*, 173–194.

Pincus, S., & Na, T. (1999). Psychological aspects of deployment. The Bosnian experience. *Army Medical Department Journal, 1*, 38–44.

Riggs, D. S., Byrne, C. A., Weathers, F. W., & Litz, B. T. (1998). The quality of the intimate relationships of male Vietnam veterans: Problems associated with posttraumatic stress disorder. *Journal of Traumatic Stress, 11*, 87–101.

Rosen, L., Carpenter, C., & Moghadam, L. (1989). Impact of military life stress on the quality of life of military wives. *Military Medicine, 154*, 116–120.

Ryan-Wenger, N. A. (2001). Impact of the threat of war on children in military families. *American Journal of Orthopsychiatry, 71*(2), 236–244.

Schwartz, N. (2009). *Keeping the promise*. Retrieved from http://www.afa.org/events/conference/2009/scripts/AFA-090915-Schwartz.pdf

Segal, D., & Wechsler-Segal, M. (2005). America's military population. *Diversity Factor, 13*(2).

Southard, E. (1918). Shell shock and after. *Boston Journal of Medical Surgery, 179*, 73–93.

Stafford, E., & Grady, B. (2003). Military family support. *Pediatric Annals, 32*(2), 110–115.

Tanielian, T., & Jaycox, L. (2008). *Invisible wounds of war psychological and cognitive injuries, their consequences, and services to assist recovery*. Arlington, VA: RAND Study, Center for Military Health Policy Research.

United States Marine Corps, (2010). *35th Commandant of the Marine Corps Commandant's Planning Guidance*. Retrieved from http://www.marines.mil/unit/marforres/MFR_Docs/CMC_Planning_Guidance_FINAL.pdf

Waynick, T., Frederich, P., & Scheider, D. (2005, October). *Enabling military families to survive the traumas of war*. Paper presented at the 63rd meeting of the American Association of Marriage and Family Therapists, Kansas City, Missouri.

Zellman, G. L., Gates, S. M., Moini, J. S., & Suttorp, M. (2009). Meeting family and military needs through military child care. *Armed Forces & Society, 35*, 437–459.

CHAPTER

20

Supporting National Guard and Reserve Members and Their Families

Christina Harnett

Throughout U.S. history, citizens have been called on to make tremendous sacrifices in the name of freedom. In our struggle to become an independent nation, militia—or "citizen-soldiers"—were recruited to serve as forces in the American Revolution. Volunteer warriors left farms, shops, families, and homes to follow the U.S. ideal of independent rule; militia members often toiled under difficult circumstances and at great personal sacrifice. These warriors were frequently underfed, underclothed, underpaid, and underarmed. Today, their modern counterparts, the Reserve force[1] component (RC) of the U.S. military has much in common with early militia members. For example, the reservist is often termed *weekend warrior*[2] while the National Guard member is called the *citizen soldier* to denote their status as part-time military; when called, they depart from civilian jobs to serve, they suffer injuries both physical and psychological, and they leave families and communities behind to cope with their absence. By contrast, the RC, as a military culture, exhibits distinct differences when compared to the Active Components (AC) of the military. These differences are highlighted later in this chapter as a way to contextualize the Global War on Terrorism's (GWOT) far-reaching psychosocial imprint.

The author wishes to express her appreciation to members of the Reserve forces who contributed insights to this manuscript and for their service to our country. A special debt of gratitude is due my friend and mentor, LTC Michael Gafney of the Maryland National Guard, who shared many valuable military experiences and points of culture with me.

[1] Reserve Component Forces include the Army National Guard, Army Reserve, Navy Reserve, Marine Corps Reserve, Air National Guard, Air Force Reserve, and the Coast Guard Reserve.

[2] This term will be used throughout the chapter to denote members of both National Guard and Reserve services.

As in the earliest days of this country, our weekend warriors have been called to serve—and they have served well and long. They have met their war-time responsibilities, and then returned home to a civil society. Reservists have assumed instrumental roles in "the Revolutionary War, the War of 1812, the Mexican-American War, the Civil War, the Spanish-American War, World War I, World War II, the Korean War, and the Gulf War. Today, the reserves are playing an indispensable role in the Global War on Terror. . . . Reserve component personnel use has increased from 12.7 million duty days in fiscal year 2001 to 61.3 million duty days in fiscal year 2006" (Commission on the National Guard and Reserves, 2008, p. 6). In each of these scenarios, the federal government called, trained, and deployed them in service to the nation as authorized by federal law (Library of Congress, 2007).

GWOT, comprising deployments for Operation Enduring Freedom (OEF), Operation Iraqi Freedom (OIF), and Operation Noble Eagle (ONE) has resulted in Reserve forces being pressed into service for multiple deployments with extended tours of duty creating a shift in function from a strategic Reserve force to an operational one. This reliance on the state-based militia of National Guard members as well as the Federal Reserve was required to compensate for the reduced size of the active force (Korb & Segal, 2011). Bacevich (2011) maintains that throughout GWOT National Guard, especially, were regarded as "part-time regulars" by the upper echelon military decision makers. These members, as opposed to AC personnel, left loved ones and employers who were not "necessarily expecting, organized around, or supported during multiple deployments" (Erbes, 2011, p. 53).

Reserve forces constitute almost 40% of U.S. forces deployed in OEF and OIF. Not since World War II has the U.S. military relied so heavily on the RC, deploying them at higher rates with longer terms than "it knew was optimal for combat performance . . . from 2003–2009, the civilian and military leaders overstretched and abused the active and reserve components of the All Volunteer Force" (Korb & Segal, 2011, p. 81) in a perpetual rhythm of deployments and reentries.

Heavy reliance on reservists as active forces has extracted a significant toll on its members, families, civilian careers, and communities (Department of Defense [DoD], 2011). Despite the fact that stressors our warriors faced may have had direct effects on themselves, their families during deployment and during reintegration, and force readiness, scholarship around the RC remains sparse (Lomsky-Feder, Gazit, & Ben-Ari, 2008). Regardless of the strong presence of reservists represented in deployment totals for GWOT, there is scant scholarship on psychosocial health and morbidity affecting all associated with this population. For example, factors impacting coping patterns of youth across age, gender, service component, and deployment features, and the experience of the spouse or caregiver who remains stateside during the deployment of a service member remain shrouded in mystery (Esposito-Smythers et al., 2011). Our present knowledge surrounding reservist deployment issues is out of keeping with the known distress of multiple deployments, lengthier deployments, shortened respites between deployment, and a heightened sense of danger engendered in our AC military families (Flake, Davis, Johnson, & Middleton, 2009). Reservist families live in civilian communities and may not have benefit of a social support network that includes other military spouses and dependents. Perhaps it is this sense of heightened isolation that puts them most at risk for psychosocial dysfunction and for exacerbation of deployment-affiliated emotional conditions.

To fully understand the nature of the burden GWOT deployments have made on reservists' families, one must understand the world of the weekend warrior and the duality of worlds in which they live, work, and interact. The focus of this chapter is on the nature of the RC, elements of culture common to it, and the impact of these cultural rudiments on the deployment experiences of individuals, families, and communities. Although the dynamics of this military society have been a relatively neglected subject of investigation over the course of the GWOT (American Psychological Association [APA], 2007; Castaneda et al., 2008), recent research and a renewed DoD commitment to support all military families holds promise for new knowledge and subsequent strategies to mitigate the effects of deployment on them (Chandra et al., 2009; Chandra et al., 2011; DoD, 2011; Faber, Willerton, Clymer, MacDermid, & Weiss, 2008; Institute of Medicine, 2010).

Global War on Terror: The Context

The intransigence of GWOT has obligated the military to have an extended dependence on national, state, and local community partnerships to satisfy the growing behavioral health and psychosocial needs of our returning veterans and their families. In the face of the destruction resulting from the terrorist attacks of 9/11, the U.S. government retaliated through its Global War on Terror generating Operation Enduring Freedom (OEF) in Afghanistan, Operation Iraqi Freedom (OIF), Operation New Dawn (OND), and Operation Noble Eagle (ONE), which provided increased homeland security initiatives for both our country and military bases abroad (Belasco, 2009).

The conflicts addressed in GWOT are distinct from previous ones in our country's history. For example, the nature of military operations has changed, and multiple and extended deployments are common (Chandra et al., 2011; Tanielian, Jaycox, Adamson, & Metscher, 2008). The war theaters lack distinct "clear zones," and this creates not only heightened risk for injury but it also intensifies stress levels among warriors (Katz, Bloor, Cojucar, & Draper, 2007; Manderscheid, 2007). Moreover, military patrols carry out their duties under constant threat of sniper attacks and injuries due to the detonation of improvised explosive devices (IEDs), and service members may experience "grinding tension between terror and tedium" (Lafferty, Alford, Davis, & O'Connor, 2008, p. 3). For the first time in history, the number of wounded soldiers has outpaced the number of combat fatalities and this is most likely attributable to scientific advances in both medicine and military armature (Tanielian, Jaycox, Adamson, & Metscher, 2008). Also, large numbers of females as well as parents of young children have been deployed (Institute of Medicine, 2010). Last, this long-term conflict has been waged for the first time by an all-volunteer force, and the RC has been deployed at its highest level in 50 years (Sollinger, Fisher, & Metscher, 2008).

Another significant deviation from earlier conflicts lies in the military's reliance on National Guard and Reserve members as operational rather than strategic forces. For example, prior to GWOT, the National Guard was primarily engaged in domestic state issues (Commission on the National Guard and Reserve, 2008), and their initial federal utilization was in serving as a strategic reserve that could be activated under presidential authority in the event of a national emergency (National Governor's Association, 2007). The concept of the "all-volunteer force" and the protracted nature of conflicts in GWOT is responsible for both multiple and extended deployments (Korb & Segal, 2011). Moreover, according to Griffith (2009), the reliance on Reserve forces in GWOT has resulted in changes in their mission, structure, and organization as emergent threats to national security surfaced. Consequently, as a result of GWOT's operational tempo and multiple and extended deployments, many military children have endured parental absences from the home; as of 2006, the number of children with at least one deployed military parent reached almost 1.9 million for all services with 38% of those youth representing reservist families (Chandra, 2010). It has been estimated that approximately 3 million family members have been directly impacted by deployments of RC military members (House Committee on Veterans Affairs, Subcommittee on Health, 2008). Furthermore, children of military families are at increased risk for emotional and behavioral dysfunctions (Chandra et al., 2009) and for maltreatment in those families experiencing domestic violence, alcohol abuse, or heightened stress (Gibbs, Martin, Clinton-Sherrod, Walters, & Johnson, 2011).

As of 2009 more than 1.8 million service members have been deployed in GWOT; collectively, the Reserve component represented nearly one third of service members deployed. Moreover, they composed almost one third of the military force called for multiple tours of duty (DoD, 2009a). As of April 2009, service members deployed to Afghanistan and Iraq contributed 3 million deployments to GWOT efforts (Wadsworth & Southwell, 2010). To date, the Reserves continue to be deployed and play important roles in peacekeeping missions.

Although many veterans return home and successfully readjust to civilian society and deployment may be perceived as having positive benefits for some military members (e.g., financial gain, application of training, increased responsibility, additional training, and a sense of accomplishment) (Hosek, Cavanagh, & Miller, 2005); the negative consequences of it in GWOT have been well-documented in the literature (e.g., physical injury, psychological injury, domestic violence, child abuse, homelessness, unemployment) (DoD, 2011; Institute of Medicine, 2010; Tanielian & Jaycox, 2008). A release from the Defense Centers of Excellence (n.d.) reported that approximately 12% to 20% of OIF/OEF veterans have been diagnosed with traumatic brain injury (TBI); through March 2010, the total of persons across all services diagnosed with the disorder or reporting symptoms of it reached a total of 178,876. As of September 2010, 66,935 cases of posttraumatic stress disorder (PTSD) have been reported for service members deployed in OIF/OEF and Operation New Dawn (OND) (Congressional Research Service, 2010). Both TBI and PTSD are considered to be "invisible wounds of war" in that these deployment-related disorders relate to cognitive impairments and mental health conditions that impair functioning but whose presence is not readily observable to peer military service members or command, or to family members and others in the larger community (Tanielian et al., 2008). PTSD and TBI, as well as depression, are associated with comorbid psychiatric conditions and higher rates of physical health impairments and increased rates of mortality. In addition, they are related to homelessness, impaired work performance, and interpersonal difficulties that include marital problems and other familial dysfunctions (Karney, Ramchand, Osilla, Caldarone, & Burns, 2008; Monson, Taft, & Fredman, 2009).

These effects are more complex for "weekend warriors" because of their "dual citizenship"—a status that alters the concept of a traditional "yellow ribbon homecoming."

It has been argued that the citizen-soldier is more similar to active component members in acceptance of military culture, values, and attitudes than civilians in the communities in which they live and work (Goldich, 2011), and after living in a full military culture for a period of time, these similarities may indeed complicate resettlement back into the family, community, and workplace of a civilian society. In this case, the costs of war not only include the physical and psychological costs of combat that typically complicate successful reintegration, but they also include unique career and work-related issues for warriors who stop-out of a civilian workplace or career with the intention of returning to it postcombat (Harnett & DeSimone, 2011).

Homecoming to the workplace is made all the more complex by consequences of separation from the civilian community (Harnett & DeSimone, 2011) as well as by rapid changes in the nature of work influenced by 21st-century changes in social and economic forces (Blustein, 2008), and the availability of jobs. Blustein (2008) has noted that "working represents the lifeblood of people" (2008, p. 237). Unlike warriors' homecomings of yesteryear, today's homecomings are the entry point for exposure to a complex journey of adjustments around work identity, technological advances, an economic tsunami of unparalleled proportions, and a home culture that was reshaped by economic realities. According to the U.S. Department of Labor, Bureau of Labor Statistics (2010), during 2009, younger veterans (ages 18 to 24) were unemployed at a rate of 21% (65,000 persons) in 2009, while their older veteran cohort, ages 25 to 34, had more than 100,000 persons unemployed (10.6%). Reiterating a popular press report, an Institute of Medicine (2010) account observed that National Guard and Reserve service members have difficulty returning to their civilian jobs postdeployment despite protection afforded by the Uniformed Services Employment and Reemployment Rights Act of 1994 (USERRA); the latter act serves to protect veterans against the disadvantages of stepping out of their civilian careers while serving in the military. The account further notes that Pentagon sources cited that more than 10% of the National Guard and Reserve members as having "employment-related problems," and that some smaller businesses may avoid employing reservists because of the threat of potential deployments.

Although data on the number of homeless GWOT veterans are unavailable (Institute of Medicine, 2010), data do exist on the extent of homelessness among veterans of all U.S. wars. The U.S. Department of Veteran Affairs (2010) estimates that in 2009 more than 100,000 veterans were homeless on any given night with 20% of those being minority veterans; sadly, one in three homeless males is a veteran. Given the large number of deployments and persons deployed, as well as the rates of TBI, PTSD, and emotional consequences of deployment in current veterans, GWOT members may be at increased risk for homelessness. It is reasonable to assume that reservists experiencing emotional difficulties and who lack access to services live outside the confines of military communities, and/or who have challenges in workplace reintegration may be at heightened risk for this consequence of war.

A majority of Iraq and Afghanistan veterans report "exposure to multiple life-changing stressors, and their wartime experiences often challenge their ability to easily reintegrate following deployment" (APA, 2007, p. 9). Like other GWOT veterans, reservists' resilience may be compromised by intrapersonal and interpersonal changes deriving from service. Although few studies have investigated the association between deployment stress and health outcomes for the RC (LaBash, Vogt, King, & King, 2009), one longitudinal study of OIF veterans revealed that reservists reported higher rates of emotional difficulties and were referred for intervention at higher rates than their AC cohort (Milliken, Auchterlonie, & Hoge, 2007). Collectively, the physical, psychological, and psychosocial costs of war threaten not only long-term personal adjustment, they also foreshadow societal costs playing out in scenarios of homelessness, domestic violence, lowered work productivity, suicide, familial strain and disharmony, and a diminished quality of life for our veterans (Tanielian et al., 2008).

National Guard and Reserve Cultures: A World Apart

Culture has been called the *software of the mind.* This is an appropriate analogy for understanding the challenges that reservists and their families face when confronted with a deployment (G. Hofstede & Hofstede, 2005). In this meaning of culture, the software is "programmed" to provide us with adaptive functions allowing for structure, predictability, and control over our environments and our reactions to our world. It is tempting to speculate that "sudden" shifts from civilian to military identities cause issues around self and adjustment for all, and may explain deployment-related emotional issues that emerge or wax and wane across the deployment cycle.

Although each service has its unique culture, National Guard and Reserve forces have the distinction of living within a civilian culture and participating in the military world on a part-time basis until called to serve. For them, the civilian and military universes exist in parallel; the military world may not have a significant impact on members or their families—until the reality of deployment strikes. At that juncture, these individuals may have their first taste of what it means to be a "military family." Moreover, reservists have been labeled *transmigrants* in so far as they move between different spheres (military and civilian), are "outside yet inside the military system," and have socioemotional investments in both (Lomsky-Feder et al., 2008, p. 593).

Although all members of the military and their families may experience challenges in "homecoming," the demands of the reservists' world often present unique impediments to adjustment for U.S. families as they prepare their loved ones for departure and themselves for the anticipated homeland return. Such demands unfold in a culture that stands in stark contrast to one a traditional military member experiences. Weekend warriors have a primary identity of being civilians (Manderscheid, 2007), and they move between civilian and military worlds upon deployment and reintegration (McNutt, 2005). The paucity of research into the dynamics of reservist culture, especially in times of ongoing conflict (APA, 2007), and the challenges associated with choosing this career, complicate and threaten adaptive resilience capacities of military members and their families. In addition, it is generally believed that the culture of Guard and Reservists in general is little understood by the mainstream in the United States and by members of other branches of the military (Harnett & Gafney, 2011).

National Guard and Reserve forces—unlike their active military constituents—straddle both civilian and military worlds. This complicates adjustment, as families actively work to adapt to the changes deployment brings. Typically, reservists drill 1 weekend a month and serve 2 weeks active duty during the year. Both the active components and some Reserve forces function under Title 10 of the U.S. Code, meaning that they are federal employees;

for members of the traditional Reserve (e.g., Army Reserve) this carries federal Reserve status. National Guard members, however, operate under Title 32 of the U.S. Code and are a state-based military/militia Reserve force typically deployed for state emergencies. However, under presidential authority, the National Guard troops may become federalized and deployed under Title 10 to meet force needs. This is exactly what occurred in GWOT (Korb & Segal, 2011).

Another point of difference may be seen in the communities in which RC and AC members reside. Members of the AC live and work on military posts or in nearby military communities surrounded by other members and families of the same culture. By contrast, RC members and their families live and work within civilian communities either in or outside of the state in which their military organization is located. Griffith (2009) has noted that it is not exceptional for these members to live great distances from their home military posts even as far as "50–100 miles from their unit of assignment" (p. 199).

On deployment, RC service members leave families that may not have had any exposure to military culture. Moreover, they step-out of civilian careers often putting career advancement on hold, and they may withdraw from educational pursuits. By contrast, AC members pursue career advancement opportunities through deployment and leave families who have the advantage of living in military cultures as support systems; RC families may not benefit from such arrangements given their lack of familiarity with the RC community and the geographic dispersion of families. Also, the AC typically deploys as units while RC members may deploy as individuals or units to already established units in theatre. Thus, the camaraderie RC members established in their state-side military organization may dissipate and need to be reestablished among new members in new units abroad. Greene, Buckman, Dandeker, and Greenberg (2010) suggest that this immersion into a different culture (e.g., different services, different units, and foreign cultures in theaters of operation) may increase reservists' risk for mental health problems.

Prior to deployment and as private citizens, RC members seek health care through private practitioners; their insurance is privately held and may be subsidized through private employer contributions. In some cases, members and the families of the various RC components may not have the benefit of any health insurance prior to deployment. On the other hand, AC members and families receive health benefits through the military and may access services directly on bases or through allied health facilities in the community. One final point of departure around the health maintenance issue deserves note: Active members may attend health appointments on duty time, while Reserve members must use time away from civilian jobs to seek health care. The latter group experiences difficulties during reintegration when seeking health care for a deployment-related condition. Many employers may be reluctant to grant leave, and many reservists may live far from a Veterans Affairs facility (VA) or allied health facility (Harnett & Gafney, 2011).

As noted earlier, although both the RC and the AC receive social support from members of their immediate families, the AC does have the advantage of being embedded in the military culture with its shared experience of deployment and deployment-related family demands. In contrast, the RC member and families may struggle to understand and adjust to the realities of deployment. The inability to benefit from as shared military culture, in which all members understand the tasks, the language, and the norms, can create a heightened sense of isolation for RC families. Finally, civilian employers may not understand the reservist culture and experience the strain and burden of a deployment-related employee loss. This may cause tension between employer and reservists prior to and returning from deployment (Harnett & DeSimone, 2011).

After returning home, reservists find their lives again disrupted because they lack the support of peers who have common deployment experiences (Allison-Aipa, Ritter, Sikes, & Ball, 2010). When reservists return from deployment to demobilization sites in the homeland, the disparities between military and civilian cultures reemerge and directly affect reintegration tasks of all involved—the member, the family, and the employer. Unlike AC units that are discharged back to their posts and military communities, reservist veterans are released back into civilian lives and communities scattered across states, sometimes after only 3 days at the demobilization site. Regrettably, some may find themselves homeless and jobless at the point of demobilization and thus reading the "welcome home" signs as a "welcome to homelessness." "Given the systemic disparity of benefits between the Active Component and Reserve Component, including continued access to housing in active duty installation post-deployment and prevalent underemployment of lower enlisted soldiers, an increasing number of National Guard soldiers are homeless" (S. Lee, personal communication, November 5, 2011). Such innovative programs as Partners-in-Care, an initiative of the Maryland National Guard, was founded to coordinate support for Guard members and families through formal partnerships among faith communities. These partnerships provide an array of services to members and families from housing through employment and the concept has been promoted to a national best practice.[3]

On homecoming, many reservists choose to return to their civilian jobs shortly after returning or begin the search for civilian employment. Others choose to take a brief respite and engage with families. For a short period following demobilization, the member is covered under military health care and may have access (although limited) to military medical facilities; despite the access, one reservist observed that "the VA will treat you for life for a line of duty issue. The problem is, you need to live near one" (Harnett & Gafney, 2011, p. 192). On workplace reintegration, RC members typically return to private health care plans through their employers and confront the issue of requesting work leave to attend health appointments.

From demobilization to the beginning of the home side Yellow Ribbon reintegration activities, reservists may not have direct military peer support. At best, the support may be episodic and dependent on peers attending the full cycle of postdeployment support activities or future drill weekends. Lafferty et al. note (2008) that these factors may complicate reintegration tasks for the RC by disrupting the continuum of social support and raising issues around continuity of care for both behavioral health and physical health issues. By association, this makes the challenge of reintegration even more complex for families of the members.

Inherent cultural disparities between AC and RC forces, unique challenges of modern warfare, shifting economic forces in our country and in the business climate, and "invisible

[3] CH (COL) Sean Lee, JFHQ Chaplain for Maryland, is the founder of *Partners-in-Care*. http://www.md.ngb.army.mil/XHTML/GuardMembers/Joint/Chaplain/Chaplain.html A resource link for the organization is provided in Appendix A.

wounds of war" have coalesced to make postdeployment transition to family, community, and workplace a challenging endeavor. Multiple deployments and reentries only further complicate the health and psychosocial aspects of "re-enculturation" of our reservists. A 2008 report observed that "there is no reasonable alternative to the nation's continued increased reliance on reserve components as part of its operational force for missions at home and abroad. However, the Commission also concludes that this change from their Cold War posture necessitates fundamental reforms to reserve components' homeland roles and missions, personnel management systems, equipping and training policies, policies affecting families and employers, and the organizations and structures used to manage the reserves" (Commission on the National Guard and Reserves, 2008, p. ii).

To address mounting issues around the heavy reliance on Reserve component forces, the Yellow Ribbon Reintegration Program was signed into law as part of the Defense Authorization Act of 2008 (P.L. 110–118).[4] This law amended policies on Guard and Reserve affairs and mandated the establishment of a national combat veteran reintegration program to provide service members and families deployment-related information, information on services and referrals, and outreach activities across the entire deployment cycle from predeployment through reintegration. The program mandates activities and services for soldiers and their families in the form of trainings/outreach in the areas of health, behavioral health, family readiness, financial management, military benefits, and employer support provided by military, federal, state, and community partnerships. This national initiative was designed to serve all stakeholders throughout the Guard and Reserve components by heightening awareness of resource venues through federal, national, state, and community partnerships. In a directive memorandum that was issued in July 2008, the Under Secretary of Defense for Personnel and Readiness issued a further statement on the policies and procedures for specific implementation within the program and it established Joint Family Resource Centers in every state: The centers' function was to provide support services to the RC and their families including "spouses, children, parents, grandparents, siblings and/or significant others" (DoD, 2008, p. 2).

The Yellow Ribbon Program is an extremely important initiative for Guard and Reserve members, families, and communities as a form of prevention and intervention along the deployment cycle. Given their civilian status prior to and after return from deployment, these constituents are dependent on this form of outreach to adapt to challenges before, during, and after deployment. As will be seen later, this program provides direct support and intervention modalities in the forms of psychoeducational activities as well as information regarding venues for more formal sources of medical and psychotherapeutic interventions. Reservist families who do not avail themselves of these support activities are left to navigate the complexities of the journey without beneficial information and, perhaps, appropriate sources of social support. Employers are at heightened risk of violating federal regulations around the veteran's rights in returning to work as well as how to appropriately manage the workplace reintegration process.

---

[4] Although the law was originally designated for these RC forces, reintegration programs and activities for families are now core components of all of the military services.

PORTRAIT OF RESERVIST FAMILIES

In 2009, the American military was more than 3.5 million members strong; of these, approximately 1.4 million represented the active duty component, while Reserves constituted another 1.1 million members. However, for both components, family members outnumbered military members. Active duty family members accounted for 1.84 million members, while the Reserve component family members accounted for another 848,000 dependents (DoD, 2009b).

Demographics of the Reserve components tell us that reservists tend to be older compared to active duty personnel, with more than 40% being at least 36 years of age. In addition, 56.3% report family responsibilities that include a spouse, child, or other dependent (DoD, 2009b). A significant consequence of the GWOT has been that both male and female reservists have been required to spend significant time away from families (Karney & Crown, 2011) and from civilian jobs.

It is generally accepted that there is a direct link between family wellness and military force preservation and readiness. Family readiness, as a paradigm of preparedness, is a crucial component of the reservists' readiness for active military service. Thus, the Department of Defense has recognized the importance of providing deployment assistance to Reserve families as fundamentally important to mission readiness and the military's goal of sustaining mission capabilities (Castaneda et al., 2008). In fact, General Richard Myers, Chairman of the Joint Chiefs of Staff, speaking before the Senate Armed Services Committee highlighted quality-of-life issues as "inseparable from overall combat readiness" (Myers, 2004, p. 24).

Given that reservist families are relatively unfamiliar with the deployment experience, members may struggle with the "ambiguous presence/ambiguous absence" of the deployed member insofar as they experience ambiguity of who is "in or out" of the family and which roles/tasks are assigned to which members (Faber et al., 2008). Consequently, a 1-year deployment played out in relative isolation for reservists families is a world away from a 1 weekend a month and 2 weeks a year commitment (Erbes, 2011).

The construct of readiness of Guard and Reserve families has multiple layers of meaning. Readiness may apply to financial issues (e.g., bill paying, budgeting around deployment income losses), resilience/preparedness to cope with changes the family member's absence brings, arrangement of legal matters, awareness of military resources for deployment support, or one's perceived efficacy to assume additional household responsibilities in the absence of the deployed other (Castaneda et al., 2008). Using interviews with reservist experts and family members of reservists, a 2008 study of the readiness of reservist families to cope with deployment stressors (Castaneda et al., 2008) found that the uniqueness of deployment cycle stressors for this culture required different forms of psychosocial support and outreach than what might be needed by active military families. Experts identified, and family members confirmed, challenges in fiscal, health care, behavioral health, and household responsibility areas. These authors note that reservist families focus on "boots away from home and not boots on the ground" (p. 251), meaning that these reservist families perceive deployment time as including activities from predeployment trainings through reintegration activities. This perception stands in contrast to the military's definition of "deployment length." Two significant recommendations deriving from this study include limiting the average mobilization length and investigating means for networking families.

Overview of Deployment Cycle Impact on Military Families

An important caveat opens this section of the discussion around deployment stressors and coping for members and families of the National Guard and Reserve forces. Despite what is known about how military families cope with deployment, relatively little is known about how all constituencies (family, friends, co-workers, etc.) cope during the actual deployment phase of significant military operations, and the types of psychosocial impacts that conflicts such as GWOT bring to all of those impacted by these absences, especially those belonging to special populations such as National Guard and Reserves, female service members, and minorities (APA, 2007). Another factor clouding our understanding of the postdeployment mental health needs of reservist families "is that the military often loses track of the family members of National Guard and Reservists as they quickly blend back into the civilian community following deployment" (APA, 2007, p. 24). Consequently, the availability of knowledge around how war affects the service member and significant others is extrapolated from research on earlier conflicts. This is a limitation in addressing the role reservist culture plays in our understanding of behavioral health issues and social needs of this group. The following section addresses literature findings regarding service members and families as they adjust to the realities of deployment of a loved one. Much of the information presented is drawn from literature not specific to reservist culture; while much of it may apply to the specific circumstances of the population of interest here, some of it may have limited generalizability and must be interpreted and applied within a framework of military cultural competence and sensitivity to the uniqueness of reservist services.

Emotional Cycle of Deployment

Across the landscape of GWOT, military families have confronted deployment challenges to family functioning and individual coping. Deployment creates tensions around the competing demands of the military and the family, often leading to strain in family relations (Hosek et al., 2005). It has been noted that families often exhibit "risk factors" related to deployment vulnerabilities, and that early identification and deployment cycle support through prescribed interventions help mitigate potential dysfunctions. Younger families may lack the required life skills for proactive stress management while families experiencing their first deployment may be unfamiliar with navigating the complexity of military systems to have needs met. Families or members with poor skills for adapting to change have a heightened risk for deployment-related difficulties as they confront changes in daily routines. Preexisting family stressors are often exacerbated during periods of parental wartime absence and may have a cumulative effect on its members and may include anything from special needs children to an impending birth (Weinstock, n.d.). These stressors have also been shown to have specific effects. For example, children's adjustment to the many challenges of having a deployed parent or to the deployment cycle has been found to be related to maternal well-being in the case of a father's deployment (Andres & Moelker, 2011), related to behavioral problems and/or attachment-related issues (Barker & Berry, 2009), as well as to parental stress (Flake et al., 2009). Finally, these vulnerabilities are made all the more threatening for all involved given the fact that today's armed forces' families live in communities scattered throughout the country—often at great distances from military installations (DoD, 2009b).

In addition to vulnerabilities during deployment, families also may experience a predictable sequence of emotions as the cycle of deployment unfolds. As early as 1987, it was recognized that a predictable pattern of emotions emerged along the deployment cycle. Although initially developed as a model for Navy wives, the paradigm has been applied to all military family members across services with varying modifications and has been extended from 5 to 7 stages grounded in the deployment cycle (Logan, 1987; Morse, 2006; Pincus, House, Christenson, & Alder, 2005).

The 5-stage model proposed by Pincus, House, Christenson, and Alder (2005) was developed in an effort to identify new challenges for military families resulting from multiple deployments and extended tours of duty with briefer respites in-between for military members. As described by the authors, the 5-stage model identifies time frames and emotional challenges that must be addressed and mastered. They propose that knowledge of these stages and their challenges help families to "normalize" and more effectively cope with the deployment experience. The 5 stages are: Predeployment, Deployment, Sustainment, Redeployment, and Postdeployment. They are briefly described in Table 20.1.

As may be seen, each of the stages carries with it specific tasks and challenges for the warrior and family members. The demands of "training-up" for the mission apply not only from a military perspective but also from a family systems perspective in that each member is confronted with challenges in adjusting to new roles and routines. The degree to which each member is successful in mastering adjustment tasks directly impacts individual, spousal, and familial functioning. The military also recognizes that familial functioning may impact mission success.

An additional challenge for reservist families is to learn about or increase awareness of this cycle and its influence on deployment adjustment. While the warrior may develop insights into it through briefings and trainings as part of predeployment readiness, the family is dependent on psychoeducational activities offered through "family readiness" activities in "training-up" for the mission. These activities are a rich source of information, social support, outreach, and referral for families, moreover, they help to "normalize" the experience for military families. As observed earlier, families who do not avail themselves of such services may experience a more difficult adjustment to the deployment experience than families who take advantage of these outreach efforts.

As in any stage model, an individual's success in mastering the challenges of a given stage is dependent on resolving issues/conflicts contained within the stage; this is somewhat dependent on the unresolved issues one carries into the stage. In the case of children, adjustment and behavioral reactions are also dependent on developmental considerations. Across all stages, Pincus et al. (2005) note that open family communication helps family members identify, address, and resolve issues. Despite challenges of the emotional cycle of deployment, most families successfully meet the obstacles and look to the future when the absent member returns (Pincus et al., 2005).[5]

---

[5] For a more thorough discussion of children's developmental issues in deployment see Pincus, S. H., House, R., Christensen, J., & Adler, L. E. (2005). *The emotional cycle of deployment: A military family perspective*. Retrieved from http://www.hooah4health.com/deployment/familymatters/emotionalcycle.htm

Table 20.1 5-Stage Emotional Cycle of Deployment Model

Stage	Time Period	Challenges/Tasks	Emotional Reactions
Predeployment	Begins with warning orders, ends with warrior leaving home station (Time range = few weeks >12 months)	Warrior trains-up for mission with extended hours away from family; set family affairs in order; confront separation fears	Denial alternating with anticipation of loss; verbal conflicts between spouse and warrior resulting from psychological distance
Deployment	Begins with point of home departure, through first month of deployment	Roller-coaster period of emotions; security issues may surface; adjustment to new demands/roles; appropriate use of new communication technology	Mixed emotions; feelings of disorientation, feelings of being overwhelmed; feelings of abandonment, anger, sadness, anxiety
Sustainment	Begins Month 2 extends through Month 5	New routines develop; family seeks new sources of social support	Confidence in ability to cope; "hot topics" or unresolved issues may fuel anger/resentment; children's negative behaviors and moods as stress reactions may appear
Redeployment	Begins month before homecoming	Prepare emotionally for homecoming	Anticipation and excitement of homecoming; spouse may experience conflicting emotions around role challenges and/or threats to independence
Postdeployment	Begins when warrior arrives home extends from 3 to 6 months	Celebration through frustration experiences; "honeymoon" period possible where couples reconnect physically but not necessarily psychologically; renegotiation of roles and routines; returning member attempts to reassert former role; warrior reintegration into family, workplace, and community	Anger/resentment on part of family member who remained at home; children's reactions vary along developmental dimensions in meeting reintegration challenges

Source: Adapted from *The emotional cycle of deployment: A military family perspective*, by S. H. Pincus, R. House, J. Christensen, & L. E. Adler, 2005. Retrieved from http://www.hooah4health.com/deployment/familymatters/emotionalcycle.htm

> His being away from the family has been difficult in different ways mostly for the kids . . . our 8-year-old daughter has been very patient with the situation, she understands that this is her daddy's job and he would not be away if the Army didn't need him. Prior to him leaving, she and I would battle for his attention, which created conflict in our relationship; since he has been away, we have become much closer and understand one another. Our 10-year-old son has had the most difficulty especially when sports are going on. This past 6 months has been a difficult transition for our son to handle. For myself, I continue to work and try to keep everything as normal as possible. I have my emotions intact as long as the kids don't get upset about Dad not being home. When they do have their breakdowns that's when I seem to have my own reality check and have my own emotional breakdown after reassuring them he will be home soon and we have to stay strong because that's what daddy would want us to be. The kids and I are very proud of him and know that he is our Hero. We are comforted to know that everyone who has come in contact with him in the past 10 months will be a better person because of it.[6]

Although this model allows us to anticipate how families might function as they move across the deployment cycle, unfortunately there is little empirical evidence for its support. Also, it is not known if these experiences vary by gender, family demographics, service branch, or deployment frequency and lengths of deployment (Chandra et al., 2008). Consequently, the paradigm is best regarded as a working model.

Military Family Issues

As service members return from combat, they face a host of intrapersonal and interpersonal stressors that complicate reintegration back into traditional family roles and routines. Mental health issues and dynamics involving interpersonal conflict may undermine reunification efforts with families and partners (Erbes, 2011).

Chandra et al. (2011) have noted the quality of communication between children and caregivers is related to level of adjustment in youth, and that caregiver emotional well-being is inversely related to perception of deployment-related stressors. These stressors include increased household responsibilities, parenting and maintaining a relationship with the deployed service member, and adjusting to the deployed member's return and resettlement into family routines and responsibilities. These stressors may be significant sources of stress for military spouses and families.

In a study of both caregivers and military children targeting the relationship between deployment length and academic, social, and familial functioning for 11- to 17-year-olds, Chandra et al. (2009) found that both groups reported higher levels of emotional difficulties than what might be expected in the normal population. Also, there was a positive association between the length of deployment and children's difficulties as reported by caregivers, and a relationship between caretakers' mental health and academic involvement and functioning. Most importantly, living on military bases was related to fewer

[6] Reservist wife commenting on impact of deployment on family.

challenges around deployment. In a follow-up study, Chandra et al. (2011) refined and extended their previous findings. In this later study it was found that Guard and Reserve caregivers reported more emotional difficulties during and after deployment and "less community understanding of their deployment experience" (p. 52), and this may be due in part to problems around accessing services. Last, across all services, deployment lengths of 13 months or more were associated with more emotional difficulties in youth.

INTERVENTIONS TO MITIGATE DEPLOYMENT IMPACT ON FAMILIES

GWOT has resulted in a surge in the number of military as well as national community partnerships designed to mitigate deployment-related issues involving military members, veterans, and their families. Many of these initiatives predate the present conflict, while others derived from a lack of capacity in meeting existing needs. Nevertheless, what is most noteworthy in this evolution of aid is the degree of responsibility taken by community organizations to aid the military and their families.

Additional Military Initiatives and Community Partnerships

As family dynamics of deployed service members began to draw national attention, services initiated resources for families and developed programs whose structure, content, and focus paralleled that designed for warriors. For example, the Department of Defense, Defense Centers of Excellence (DCOE) launched service-specific resources to aid military families in boosting resilience and "family fitness." "Family fitness is every military family's ability to use physical, psychological, social and spiritual resources to prepare for, adapt to and grow from military lifestyle demands" (Defense Centers for Excellence [DCOE], n.d.). The rationale for such an approach rests on the assumption that developing support systems for military families leads to better coping, better psychological health in children, and ultimately results in greater support for the service member and greater force readiness. Although each service provides deployment cycle support resources for its member families, the Department of Defense (2009b) has also responded to the needs of military families.

In 2009, the Department of Defense acknowledged the "unprecedented demands" placed on military families since its earlier 2004 report; as part of that recognition, the geographic dispersion of, and novelty of military culture to reservists' families was observed. In response, it developed programs of educational awareness and quality of life programs to fill "gaps" in service; primary among those initiatives was the implementation of MilitaryOneSource Center. It was designed to provide commanders of all forces a vehicle for support during the deployment cycle in helping troops and families. MilitaryOneSource.com serves as the main pipeline for information and support for all military families throughout the world (DoD, 2009b). An additional outreach effort specifically geared toward reservist families was the development of a web link for disseminating information on benefits and entitlements.[7]

---

[7] www.defenselink.mil/ra/familyreadiness.html

As an expansion of these outreach avenues for "institutionalizing family readiness," the Department of Defense has sought to expand its influence through alliances of varying kinds. In addition to direct support for families, the Department of Defense also partners with the RC and community organizations that serve youth. For example, relationships with the Boys & Girls Clubs of America, National Military Family Association, U.S. Department of Agriculture 4-H Programs, and Armed Services YMCA have been forged. Through a collaborative effort of community partnerships the DoD also sponsors Operation: Military Kids providing youth programming and support resources (DoD, 2009b). In response to GWOT's impact on service members and their families, the national and civilian communities responded with a host of initiatives to mitigate the effects of deployment. SOFAR, the Military Child Education Coalition, the Military Child Initiative, Sesame Street, and UCLA' Focus Project for Military Families are a few examples of such outreach efforts. Today, an impressive host of resources are available via the web for all military families.

Case Vignette: Josh

As discussed throughout this chapter, the dynamics of the deployment cycle are complex and may be challenging for veterans and their families. By its very nature, the Reserve culture may present additional barriers to successful adaptation for all parties involved. After reading this chapter, you have an increased sensibility and cultural competence around Reserve culture issues in the GWOT era. Apply those new understandings to the case that follows as you consider points for clinical and psychosocial intervention.

Josh hated being called "a citizen soldier." He knew he was a real warrior. He proved that during his two duty tours in Iraq and Afghanistan as part of the National Guard. Now back home only 40 days after his second deployment, he felt a bit alone in his thoughts and in his experience.

At the demobilization site, he remembered being anxious to return home to his wife and 3-month-old little girl, Molly. But the actual homecoming was different than he had imagined. Molly was not the child he remembered. She was taller than he recalled and had grown into a free spirit, moving around the apartment at a pretty good clip. It seemed to him she might be someone else's child when she began to speak in short fragments of sentences. The Molly he looked forward to seeing was the one in his arms he kissed good-bye a year ago. While Josh's wife, Marni, had sent him pictures of the baby throughout the year, the mental picture of her remained as he had left her that day at the airport. Yet, Molly pulled away from him when he approached her and cried hysterically when Marni left her in his care. Although Marni explained that she was just a "baby," this child was not the baby that he knew. Josh wondered if all veterans had the same experience of their children and homecoming: reconciling the year away with what was missed at home.

Marni was a supportive wife and she appreciated the increased income the deployments had garnered. However, Josh began to suspect that she did not need him as she once did. Before deployment, he handled the household finances. Now, she was in charge of banking and paying bills. Although his job was to take care of routine household repairs before deployment, lately Marni resented his interference in trying to help in this way.

She had compiled a list of specialists that was posted on the fridge. To Josh the message was clear; she had things firmly under control. Indeed, she seemed changed in some ways, he thought.

Although the reunion had been "bumpy," and returning combat veterans had been warned by commanders to expect it, Josh began to suspect his situation was out of the ordinary. Although he had fantasized about intimacy with Marni many, many nights in Baghdad, he no longer had the enthusiasm, interest, or energy to respond to her advances or initiate his own. As surprised as he was, sex was the furthest thing from his mind. Getting back to work was the most pressing concern for him.

Josh loved his job and the camaraderie it provided him. Being a car mechanic always held intrigue for him. He likened it to solving a puzzle, and he prided himself on being very good at unraveling mysteries. One aspect Josh was not prepared to handle was the changes he found in his workplace. Will, his former supervisor, had retired and been replaced by a new guy from the next town. Josh was a bit angry because Will had groomed him for that job. Josh also thought it a bit odd the way some of his co-workers seemed to have changed toward him. After his "welcome back" luncheon, they seemed to distance themselves from him. He had not been invited to the regular Friday gatherings at the bar nor was he included in monthly poker games. He reflected on changes in his workplace and the faded camaraderie and realized he no longer liked his job.

As the weeks passed, Marni observed that Josh had become more sullen and quick-tempered. He appeared exhausted and often spent the weekend milling about the house without helping with family chores. She spoke to him about his inability to fall asleep most nights, and his growing habit of drinking beer while watching television until the early hours of the morning. What worried her most was his sad demeanor, which seemed out-of-keeping with all of the good wishes and goodwill that marked his deployment and his return. Everyone seemed excited to have him safely home but Josh appeared to "live in a bubble" where none of this warmth and love touched him.

More time passed and Marni could no longer rationalize Josh's behavior as the "new normal" she had read about in the newspaper. When she suggested contacting the Reserve Chaplain, Josh became enraged and threw his coffee mug against the wall. Although these fits of anger were frightening and increasing in frequency, Josh was never violent toward his family. He just "flew off the handle" and threw things. Marni could tell by his behavior that he was contrite following the episodes, but she was beginning to worry about these spur-of-the-moment rages. She wondered what triggered them.

Since joining the Reserves, Josh prided himself in showing "true warrior strength." Not once had he complained about any military order, and he did what he needed to do for mission success when in theater. Moreover, Josh didn't go for the whole idea of having his family involved in his military career. Like some of his buddies, Josh would not let his family attend Yellow Ribbon events, and he forbade Molly's joining the Family Readiness group, which he regarded as a bunch of chatty women passing gossip and checking up on their husbands. No, Josh made sure his military career was his alone.

Sunday, when Marni arrived home from her mother's house, she found Josh sitting motionless in the dark family room. Although he acknowledged her entry, he remained expressionless and seemed deaf to the questions she asked of him. Frightened, Marni called Josh's parents to the house. Together, they transported him to St. Michael's Hospital Emergency Room. As he sat there with the sound of an ambulance alarm piercing the ER atmosphere, he wondered if this were Baghdad.

Case Vignette Discussion Questions

1. What particular aspects of the reservist culture make reintegration a more difficult process for Josh and his family than for members of active military services?
2. Describe the individual, marital, and family dynamics in this case.
3. What types of resources might you recommend for the couple as an adjunct to formal psychological intervention?
4. What aspects of Josh's case seem typical for a returning reservist? Which factors are of most concern to you? Explain.
5. Using this chapter, identify elements of the case that signal the unique challenges reservists face in reintegration into family, workplace, and community.
6. How might this story be different if Josh were a member of the active services? How might your intervention be different?

CONCLUSION

Although President Barack Obama announced the beginning of our withdrawal of troops from Iraq on October 22, 2011, this is not the end of our engagement in the GWOT. Troops remain in Afghanistan and other areas throughout the world. Moreover, serious challenges confront us as the impact of this military campaign plays out across the next several decades after almost a 10-year "odyssey" in which reservist members and their families lived their lives by a calendar of deployment cycles. Parents missed the developmental milestones of their children, and in some cases their births, spouses served as single parents, and children grew to maturity in a single-parent household bathed in the light of a significant others' "ambiguous absence, ambiguous presence" (Faber et al., 2008).

A new paradigm of war demands a new paradigm of understanding around the cultural implications of military service for reservists, their families, and the community. In this era of "modern warfare," stakeholders deploy actually or virtually. As families, friends, and communities settle into their "new normal," it is incumbent on the behavioral health sciences and the U.S. community to work collaboratively for the welfare of all military families—especially those members of the Reserve forces. Significant gains in our understanding of the ramifications of deployment as well as improvements in our programs of prevention and intervention and continuum of care may be made through a more systematic program of research around deployment issues. Although some strides have been made in deployment psychology within recent years and within specific service branches (Willerton, Wadsworth, & Riggs, 2011), we have yet to fully understand how GWOT deployments will impact the long-term functioning of service members and their families. This is true of the active component and it is especially true of our reservist community. Nevertheless, "the effects of deployment of parent-soldiers on children and families need to be understood in the context of military culture" (Lincoln, Swift, & Shorteno-Fraser, 2008, p. 984) unique to each of the two components.

It has been said that in times of war we deploy families, not only warriors. Therefore, our reservists and their families deserve the honors and services to which they are entitled as heroes for having served our country nobly.

REFERENCES

Allison-Aipa, T. S., Ritter, C., Sikes, P., & Ball, S. (2010). The impact of deployment on the psychological health status, level of alcohol consumption, and use of psychological health resources of postdeployed U.S. Army Reserve soldiers. *Military Medicine, 175*(9), 630–637.

American Psychological Association. (2007). Presidential Task Force on Military Deployment Services for Youth, Service Members and Families. *The psychological needs of U.S. military service members and their families*. Retrieved from http://www.apa.org/about/governance/council/policy/military-deployment-services.pdf

Andres, M. D., & Moelker, R. (2011). There and back again: How parental experiences affect children's adjustments in the course of military deployments. *Armed Forces and Society, 37*(3), 418–447.

Bacevich, A. J. (2011) Whose Army? *Daedalus, 140*(3), 122–134.

Barker, L. H., & Berry, K. D. (2009). Developmental issues impacting military families with young children during single and multiple deployments. *Military Medicine, 174*(10), 1033–1040.

Belasco, A. (2009). *The cost of Iraq, Afghanistan, and other Global War on Terrorism operations since 9/11*. Washington, DC: Congressional Research Service.

Blustein, D. L. (2008). The role of work in psychological health and well-being: A conceptual, historical, and public policy perspective. *American Psychologist, 63*(4), 228–240.

Castaneda, L. W., Harrell, M. C., Varda, D. M., Hall, K. C., Beckett, M. K., & Stern, S. (2008). *Deployment experiences of Guard and Reserve families: Implications for support and retention*. Santa Monica, CA: RAND National Defense Research Institute. Retrieved from http://www.rand.org/content/dam/rand/pubs/monographs/2008/RAND_MG645.pdf

Chandra, A. (2010). *Children on the homefront: The experiences of children from military families*. Testimony presented before the House Armed Services Committee, Subcommittee on Military Personnel, March 9, 2010. Retrieved from http://www.rand.org/content/dam/rand/pubs/testimonies/2010/RAND_CT341.pdf

Chandra, A., Burns, R. M., Taniellian, T., Jaycox, L. H., & Scott, M. M. (2008). *Understanding the impact of deployment on children and families: Findings from a pilot study of operation purple camp participants*. (Working Paper.) Santa Monica, CA: RAND Corporation. Retrieved from http://www.rand.org/pubs/working_papers/WR566.html

Chandra, A., Lara-Cinisomo, S., Jaycox, L. H., Tanielian, T., Burns, R. M., Ruder, T., & Han, B. (2009). Children on the homefront: The experience of children from military families. *Pediatrics, 125*(1), 13–22. doi: 10,1542/peds.2009–1180

Chandra A., Lara-Cinisom, S., Jaycox, L. H., Tanielian, T., Han, B., Burns, R. M., & Ruder, T. (2011). *Views from the homefront: The experiences of youth and spouses from military families*. Santa Monica, CA: RAND Corporation. Retrieved from http://www.rand.org/pubs/technical_reports/TR913.html

Commission on the National Guard and Reserves. (2008). *Transforming the National Guard and Reserves into a 21st century operational force*. Final Report. Washington, DC: U.S. Congress. Retrieved from http://www.loc.gov/rr/frd/pdf-files/CNGR_final-report.pdf

Congressional Research Service. (2010). *U.S. military casualty statistics: Operation New Dawn, Operation Iraqi Freedom, and Operation Enduring Freedom.* Retrieved from http://www.fas.org/sgp/crs/natsec/RS22452.pdf

Defense Centers of Excellence for Psychological Health and Traumatic Brain Injury. (n.d.). *An executive level overview of psychological health and traumatic brain injury in the defense department: Understanding the facts and recognizing the misconceptions.* Retrieved from http://www.dcoe.health.mil/Content/navigation/documents/An%20Executive%20Level%20Overview%20of%20Psychological%20Health%20and%20Traumatic%20Brain%20Injury%20in%20the%20DoD.pdf

Defense Centers of Excellence for Psychological Health and Traumatic Brain Injury. (n.d.). *Boosting family resilience.* Retrieved from http://www.realwarriors.net/family/change/family resilience.php

Department of Defense, Office of the Undersecretary of Defense for Personnel and Readiness. (2008). Directive-Type Memorandum (DTM) 08–029. *Implementation of the yellow ribbon reintegration program* (pp. 1–15). Retrieved from www.dtic.mil/whs/directives/corres/dir3.html

Department of Defense, Office of Public Communication, Defense Data Manpower Center. (2009a, February). *CTS deployment file baseline report.* (Contingency tracking system.)

Department of Defense. (2009b). *Report of the second quadrennial quality of life review.* Office of the Deputy Under Secretary of Defense, (Military Community and Family Policy). Retrieved from http://cs.mhf.dod.mil/content/dav/mhf/QOL-library/PDF/MHF/QOL%20Resources /Reports/Quadrennial%20Quality%20of%20Life %20Review%202009.pdf

Department of Defense. (2011). *Strengthening our military families: Meeting America's commitment.* Retrieved from http://www.defense.gov/home/features /2011/0111_initiative/strengthening_our_military_january_2011.pdf

Erbes, C. R. (2011). Couple functioning and PRSD in returning OIF soldiers: Preliminary findings from the readiness and resilience in National Guard soldiers project. In S. M. Wadsworth & D. Riggs (Eds.), *Risk and resilience in military families* (pages 47–68). New York, NY: Springer.

Esposito-Smythers, C., Wolff, J., Lemmon, K. M., Bodzy, M., Swenson, R. R., & Spirito, A. (2011). Military youth and the deployment cycle: Emotional health consequences and recommendations for intervention. *Journal of Family Psychology, 25*(4), 497–507.

Faber, A. J., Willerton, E., Clymer, S. R., MacDermind, S. M., & Weiss, H. M. (2008). Ambiguous absence, ambiguous presence: A qualitative study of military reserve families in wartime. *Journal of Family Psychology, 22*(2), 222–230.

Flake, E. M., Davis, B. E., Johnson, P. L., & Middleton, L. S. (2009). The psychosocial effects of deployment on military children. *Journal of Developmental and Behavioral Pediatrics, 30*(4), 271–278.

Gibbs, D. A., Martin, S. L., Clinton-Sherrod, M., Walters, J. L., & Johnson, R. E. (2011). Child maltreatment within military families. In S. M. Wadsworth & D. Riggs (Eds.), *Risk and resilience in U.S. military families* (pp. 111–130). New York, NY: Springer.

Goldich, R. L. (2011). American military culture from colony to empire. *Daedalus, 140*(3), 58–74.

Greene, T., Buckman, J., Dandeker, C. &, Greeneberg, N. (2010). The impact of culture clash on deployed troops. *Military Medicine*, *175*(12), 958–963.

Griffith, J. H. (2009). Contradictory and complementary identities of U.S. Army reservists: A historical perspective. *Armed Forces and Society*, *20*(10), 1–23.

Harnett, C., & DeSimone, J. (2011). Managing the return to the workplace: Reservists navigating the stormy seas of the homeland. In D. Kelly, S. Barksdale, & D. Gitelson (Eds.), *Treating young veterans: Promoting resilience through practice and advocacy* (pp. 219–257). New York, NY: Springer.

Harnett, C., & Gafney, M. (2011). Ensuring equality after the war for National Guard and Reserve forces: Revisiting the yellow ribbon initiative. In D. Kelly, S. Barksdale, & D. Gitelson, (Eds.), *Treating young veterans: Promoting resilience through practice and advocacy* (pp. 175–217). New York, NY: Springer.

Hofstede, G., & Hofstede, G. J. (2005). *Cultures and organizations: Software of the mind*. New York, NY: McGraw-Hill.

Hosek, J., Kavanagh, J., & Miller, L. (2005). *How deployments affect service members*. Santa Monica, CA: RAND. Retrieved from http://www.rand.org/content/dam/rand/pubs/monographs/2005/RAND_MG432.sum.pdf

House Committee on Veterans' Affairs, Subcommittee on Health. (2008). *Statement of mental health America*. Retrieved from http://veterans.house.gov/hearings/Testimony.aspx?TID=42018&Newsid=177&Name=Mental Health America

Institute of Medicine. (2010). *Returning home from Iraq and Afghanistan: Preliminary assessment of readjustment needs of veterans, service members, and their families*. Washington, DC: National Academies Press.

Karney, B. R., & Crown, J. S. (2011). *Families under stress: An assessment of data, theory and research on marriage and divorce in the military*. Santa Monica, CA: RAND.

Karney, B. R., Ramchand, R., Osilla, K. C., Caldarone, L. B., & Burns, R. M. (2008). Predicting the immediate and long-term consequences of post-traumatic stress disorder, depression, and traumatic brain injury in veterans of Operation Enduring Freedom and Operation Iraqi Freedom. In T. Tanielian & L. Jaycox (Eds.), *Invisible wounds of war: Psychological and cognitive injuries, their consequences, and services to assist recover* (pp. 117–176). Washington, DC: RAND.

Katz, L. S., Bloor, L. E., Cojucar, G., & Draper, T. (2007). Women who served in Iraq seeking mental health services: Relationship between military sexual trauma, symptoms, and readjustment. *Psychological Services*, *4*(4), 239–249.

Korb, L. J., & Segal, D. R. (2011). Manning and financing the twenty-first century all volunteer force. *Daedalus*, *140*(3), 75–87.

LaBash, H. A., Vogt, D. S., King, L. A., & King, D. W. (2009). Deployment stressors of the Iraq war: Insights from the mainstream media. *Journal of Interpersonal Violence*, *24*(2), 231–258.

Lafferty, C. L., Alford, K. L., Davis, M. K., & O'Connor, R. (2008). "Did you shoot anyone?": A practitioner's guide to combat veteran workplace and classroom reintegration. *Advanced Management Journal*, *73*(4), 4–11.

Library of Congress, Federal Research Division. (2007). *Historical attempts to reorganize the Reserve components*. Washington, DC: Author. Retrieved from http://www.loc.gov/rr/frd/pdf-files/CNGR_Reorganization-Reserve-Components.pdf

Lincoln, A., Swift, E., & Shorteno-Fraser, M. (2008). The effects of military deployment of parent-soldiers on children and families need to be understood in the context of military culture. *Journal of Clinical Psychology, 64*(8), 984–992.

Logan, K. V. (1987). The emotional deployment cycle. *Proceedings Magazine, 113*(2/1). Retrieved from http://www.usni.org/magazines/proceedings/1987–02/emotional-cycle-deployment

Lomsky-Feder, E., Gazit, N., & Ben-Ari, E. (2008). Reserve soldiers as transmigrants: Moving between the civilian and military worlds. *Armed Forces & Society, 34*(4), 593–614.

Manderscheid , R. W. (2007). Helping veterans return: Community, family, and job. *Archives of Psychiatric Nursing, 21*(2), 122–124.

McNutt, J. M. (2005, October). Work adjustment of returning Army reservists: The effect of deployment and organizational support. *Dissertation Abstracts International-B 66/04* (p. 2293). Retrieved from http://proquest.umi.com/pqdlink?did=913530251&Fmt=2&clintid=79356&RQT=309&VName=PQD

Milliken, C. S., Auchterlonie, J. L., & Hoge, C. W. (2007). Longitudinal assessment of mental health problems among active and reserve component soldiers returning from the Iraq war. *Journal of the American Medical Association, 298*(18), 2141–2148.

Monson, C. M., Taft, C. T., & Fredman, S. J. (2009). Military-related PTSD and intimate relationships: From description to theory-driven research and intervention development. *Clinical Psychology Review, 29*(8), 707–714.

Morse, J., (2006). *The new emotional cycles of deployment*. U.S. Department of Defense: Deployment Health and Family Readiness Library, San Diego, California. Retrieved from http://www.hooah4health.com/deployment/familymatters/Emotional_Cycle_Support.pdf

Myers, R. B. (2004, February 3). *Posture statement of general Richard B. Meyers, USAF, Chairman of the Joint Chiefs of Staff, before the 108th Congress Senate Armed Services Committee, Joint Chiefs of Staff*. Washington, DC. Retrieved from http://www.au.af.mil/au/awc/awcgate/dod/posture_3feb04myers.pdf

National Governor's Association, Center for Best Practices, Social, Economic and Workforce Programs Division. (2007, October). *State programs to facilitate the reintegration of national guard troops returning from deployment* (pp. 1–29). Retrieved from www.nga.org/portal/site/nga

Pincus, S. H., House, R., Christensen, J., & Adler, L. E. (2005). *The emotional cycle of deployment: A military family perspective*. Retrieved from http://www.hooah4health.com/deployment/familymatters/emotionalcycle.htm

Sollinger, J. M., Fisher, G., & Metscher, K. N. (2008). The wars in Afghanistan and Iraq: An overview. In T. Tanielian & L. Jaycox (Eds.), *Invisible wounds of war* (pp. 19–31). Santa Monica, CA: RAND.

Tanielian, T., & Jaycox, L. (2008). Preface. In T. Tanielian & L. Jaycox (Eds.), *Invisible wounds of war: Psychological and cognitive injuries, their consequences, and services to assist recover* (pp. iii–iv). Washington, DC: RAND.

Tanielian, T., Jaycox, L. H., Adamson, D. M., & Metscher, K. N. (2008). Introduction. In T. Tanielian & L. Jaycox (Eds.), *Invisible wounds of war: Psychological and cognitive injuries, their consequences, and services to assist recovery* (pp. 3–18). Washington, DC: RAND.

U.S. Department of Labor, Bureau of Labor Statistics. (2010). *Employment situation of veterans—2009*. (USDL-10–0285). Washington, DC: Government Printing Service. Retrieved from http://www.bls.gov/

U.S. Department of Veteran Affairs. (2010). *Strategic plan refresh: Fiscal year 2011–2015*. Retrieved from http://www.va.gov/VA_2011–2015_Strategic_Plan_Refresh_wv.pdf

Wadsworth, S. M., & Southwell, K. (2010). Military families: Extreme work and extreme "work-family." Workplace flexibility. *Public policy platform on flexible work arrangements*. Washington, DC: Georgetown University Law Center. Retrieved from http://workplaceflexibility.org/images/uploads/program_papers/wadsworth_military_families.pdf

Weinstock, M. (n.d.) *Military families and deployment*. Center for Deployment Psychology. Retrieved from http://deploymentpsych.org/topics-disorders/military-families-and-deployment

Willerton, E., Wadsworth, S. M., & Riggs, D. (2011). Introduction: Military families under stress, what we know and what we need to know. In S. M. Wadsworth & D. Riggs (Eds.), *Risk and resilience in U.S. military families* (pp. 1–20). New York, NY: Springer.

CHAPTER

21

The Exceptional Family Member Program: Helping Special Needs Children in Military Families

Barbara Yoshioka Wheeler, Deborah McGough, and Fran Goldfarb

INTRODUCTION

Martin and McClure (2000) remind us that, "military service has always produced widows and orphans" (p. 3). Warriors and soldiers have always had families—spouses, children, siblings, parents, and grandparents. The families of individuals serving in the military would be the first to acknowledge the unique culture in which they live and for most, thrive. Military families with children with disabilities have less of a history, partially because of the tendency of society to institutionalize children with disabilities and early in history, to euthanize these children. As societal norms regarding disability have changed, more and more people with disabilities live, work, and play in communities like any other citizen. Omnibus civil rights laws such as the Americans with Disabilities Act of 1990 (as amended, P.L. 110–325) guarantee the rights of people with disabilities to the same liberties as any U.S. citizen. With medical advances, survival rates for premature births, catastrophic illnesses, and injuries have increased significantly. Consequently, there are greater numbers of child survivors with long-term residual disabilities or specialized health care needs.

At the same time, the military's view of families has changed over time. Historically families were sometimes seen as distracting service members from their mission or military service, that is, "If they wanted you to have a family, they [the military] would have issued you one" (Martin & McClure, 2000, p. 5). Today public officials and military leaders alike recognize that the retention of service members requires attention to the quality of their

The views presented are those of the authors and do not necessarily represent those of the Department of Defense or its components.

personal lives, resulting in a greater emphasis on "profamily" values and "family well-being" and in the proliferation of programs and services for families.

Parenting a child with special needs can change the architecture of parenting for any family. Depending on the severity of the disability and the nature and number of functional deficits, the need for prolonged (and in some cases, lifelong) assistance with activities of daily living, such as feeding, bathing, grooming, moving, and protection from harm. Although one should not assume these heightened needs have a negative impact on families, there can be greater physical and/or psychological stress on caregivers (Skok, Harvey, & Reddihough, 2006). Unlike civilian families, parenting a child with special needs in a military family is additionally influenced by the military life course of the service member—a series of recurring events that prepare service members for deployment, reintegration at the end of their tour, and back to training and mobilization for the following deployment (Bowen & Zipper, 2010). For the family of a service member, the family's life is characterized by a cycle of absences for one parent (sometimes both parents), the recurring series of homecomings and farewells, and the unremitting threat that the spouse/parent may not return or will return injured.

All of these aspects of military life may be altered or experienced differently (in some cases, exacerbated) when there is a child with a disability in the family. Understanding the dynamic interaction of military life and parenting a child with a disability is critical to the social worker's effectiveness in working with EFMP families.

MILITARY AND DISABILITY CULTURE—TWO WORLDS

Military life has distinct characteristics that are not typical of civilian life. These characteristics shape the social, political, and economic context in which service members operate and in which their families must live and thrive. It is also this context that contributes to the lens with which children with developmental disabilities and other special needs are seen, served, and supported. In describing military culture, Martin and McClure (2000) noted that service, sacrifice, and mission characterize service members' daily lives and careers. Their commitment is unlimited and constant. In much the same way, parents of children with special needs have their day-to-day lives characterized by meeting the child's needs as the first priority, and their commitment to do so is unlimited and constant. Just as the service member has to be available at all times and prepared for deployment on short notice, the parents of children with special needs must be prepared to deal with on short notice unexpected changes regarding their child's well-being.

Thus, the level of passion for a military career can be comparable in power and force to the passion service members and/or spouse has for their child with a disability. Underlying both situations is an unquestionable quest to protect and serve, a willingness to sacrifice personal ambitions for a larger mission or goal, and what could be seen as an inordinate requirement for time and dedication, which leaves little room for other commitments. Martin and McClure (2000) note that both the military and the family are "greedy institutions" often requiring enormous amounts of time and energy from its members. Areas of potential tension may surface as a result.

Families at the nexus of military and disability life may experience unique challenges not experienced by families in either culture alone. For example, studies report that civilian families with children with disabilities will forego career opportunities to stay near an effective service program or provider for their child and to be near family and friends who are part of their informal social support network. Yet, the life of a service member includes frequent relocations and/or deployments. Geographic relocations frequently take military families away from their informal social networks and require resettling in new communities with new providers every few years. Although military families can and do adjust to routine relocations, the social worker will need to be cognizant of the pull that military parents may experience when attempting to meet the needs of their child with a disability without jeopardizing their military status.

Military Conduct and Ethics

Not only does the military community define the social norms for service members and their families around social responsibility, the military also provides reinforcements and structures to assure compliance with social norms. The military family experience is influenced by a stringent code of military ethics and conduct. Service members and their families are expected to behave in a manner that does not bring embarrassment to the military. In the eyes of the military, service members are always in uniform, regardless of whether they are on-duty or off-duty because their behavior reflects directly on their unit. Violations of this code of conduct may lead to administrative consequences and punishments under the Uniform Code of Military Justice (UCMJ, 2000). What may seem like mild violations in civilian life, for example, bouncing a check or failing to adequately maintain base family housing, can result in formal reprimands and a continuum of consequences for the service member, typically delivered by the service member's commander. Service members are considered "military sponsors" of their family members and as such are held accountable for the "misconduct" of their family members. The behaviors of family members may challenge usual norms of appropriate military conduct to the point of resulting in administrative actions taken against the military sponsor including penalties as severe as being forced to move from base housing or having one's family returned early from an overseas assignment "for the good of the government." As described earlier in the chapter, a child's disability-related behaviors may manifest in what may seem as inappropriate or disruptive using military norms. Attempting to explain that the atypical behavior is due to the child's disability and not fully under the child's control should be helpful, but the question that may remain for a military family is whether such behaviors are beyond the limits of what can be accommodated within the military environment.

For these reasons, parenting a child with special needs in a military family has historically been thought to detract a service member from military duty. However, research shows that when families have the information and supports they need, parenting a child with a disability should not be a significant deterrent to fulfilling the total commitment demanded by military service.

THE EXCEPTIONAL FAMILY MEMBER PROGRAM (EFMP)

Consistent with the military's commitment to families, the Department of Defense (DoD) established the Exceptional Family Member Program (EFMP), as a mandatory enrollment program for active duty service members who have family members with *special medical and educational needs*, to assure that the needs of the exceptional family member are considered when service members are reassigned duty stations. General DoD policy allows each branch of service to determine the extent and exact nature of installation-specific systems for EFMP to operate, including requirements for EFMP enrollment for active duty reservists and National Guard. Although each branch of service may use slightly different terms for the activities and functions of the EFMP program, DoD policy assures that the same practices are implemented when a service member has an exceptional family member. Throughout this chapter, we refer to the policies of all branches of service to provide the reader with a notion of the variation in language and processes characterizing how EFMP is operationalized at the field level where social workers would be working.

The Army was the first to implement the EFMP in 1979 (Exceptional Family Member Program: Army, 2011) and since that time, the Navy (Exceptional Family Member Program: Navy, 2005), Air Force (Exceptional Family Member Family Program: Air Force, 2011), and Marine Corps have incorporated EFMP into their assignment process. Regardless of branch of service, EFMP has four core components: (1) EFMP identification and enrollment, (2) EFMP services, (3) personnel assignment, and (4) family support services. The following section describes the first three components. Family support services are discussed at the end of this chapter because of its special relevance to social work practice.

EFMP Identification and Enrollment

Enrollment in the EFMP program is mandatory for the service member who has a dependent family member with special needs. Only military personnel with Exceptional Family Members (EFMs) who are active duty status (Reserve or National Guard requirements vary by branch of service) are eligible and required to enroll in the EFMP. To qualify for EFMP services, EFMs are limited to the member's spouse, child, or other person (e.g., elderly parents of the service member) actually residing in the member's household who is dependent on the member for more than half of his or her financial support, and who meets DoD criteria for enrollment in the EFMP. In this chapter we focus in particular on EFMs who are children with disabilities or special needs because of the significant size of this subpopulation within EFMP.

Although accurate numbers of children with developmental disabilities in military families are not available, the closest estimates are provided by the number of families enrolled in the DoD Exceptional Family Member Program (EFMP). In 2006, there were approximately 102,596 exceptional family members enrolled in EFMP across all branches of service. Because EFMP also includes spouses and parents of service members who have medical, psychiatric, and other special needs, it is not clear what percentage of those enrolled in EFMP are due to one or more children with developmental disabilities and/or other special needs, but we suspect this is a large subpopulation due to epidemiological trends. We utilize the Air Force EFMP regulations below to describe how EFMP operates at the base level.

Within the Air Force, the Special Needs Identification and Coordination (SNIAC, 2008) process is governed by Instructions from Medical Command. The Commander of each Major Command (MAJCOM) assigns the Command Surgeon to manage and monitor the SNIAC process. The command surgeon designates a clinical officer or civilian officer-equivalent as the Special Needs Coordinator for the MAJCOM. The Special Needs (or EFMP) coordinator at a base is responsible for (1) ensuring the quality of the special needs identification process, conducts annual training for staff, recommends and disseminates additional policy or guidance; (2) reviews facility determination packages from gaining bases (the prospective base for relocation) when medical or educational services are not available to support active duty assignment; and (3) maintains cooperative working relationships with staff responsible for DoD educational activities. Command points of contact and EFMP coordinators can assist service and family members with the enrollment process.

EFMP Personnel and Services

EFMP personnel and services are typically identified at bases to implement the functions of the EFMP program. For example, a Special Needs Coordinator (SNC) is typically a medical officer assigned to the medical treatment facility (MTF) appointed by the MTF Commander. Services identified within EFMP that may be required by eligible service members include (1) Family Member Relocation Clearance (FMRC); (2) General Medical Services (GMS) (which encompasses physiological, psychological, or social conditions of a chronic nature that have been medically diagnosed and that require specialized treatment); (3) Special Educational Services (DODI 1342.12, 2005), which refers to specially designed instruction to meet the unique educational needs of a child with a disability, including education provided in school, at home, in a hospital, or in an institution, physical education programs, and vocational education programs; (4) Early Intervention (EI) Services (DODI 1342.12, 2005) which address the needs of children 0 to 3 years with or at risk for disabilities; and (5) Related Services (RS) (DODI 1342.12, 2005), which refers to transportation, developmental, corrective, and other supportive services as required to assist a child, from birth to 21 years of age with a disability to benefit from special education under the child's Individualized Family Service Plan (IFSP) or Individualized Education Plan (IEP). Early intervention and related services can include early identification and assessment of disabilities in children; speech-language pathology and audiology; psychological services and counseling; physical, occupational, and recreational therapies; rehabilitation counseling; orientation and mobility services (for the visually impaired); and medical services for diagnostic or evaluative purposes. Special education services can also include school health services, social work services, parent counseling, and training.

These descriptions of special education, early intervention, and related services in military policy mirror components of civilian special education laws (Individuals with Disabilities Education Act, Part C and Part B, 2004), but may be delivered and organized differently for military families. Modeled on federal special education law, these services are provided for military families through DoD schools, when available. However, with recent base closures, military children are increasingly receiving educational services in civilian schools (a factor considered in base assignments). Other components of services under EFMP include structural accessibility, which encompasses design modification and enhancements that permit safe access to or from military housing in accordance with the provisions of the Architectural Barriers Act of 1968 (42 U.S.C. 4151). The immediate non-availability of military housing that meets structural accessibility requirements at a projected gaining location will not be a limiting factor for assignment purposes.

Bowen and Martin (1998) state that military community resources are designed to assist families in fulfilling their needs and meeting duty, career, and citizenship requirements. Children with disabilities need the same services as any other military child such as primary health care, education, child care and youth services, recreational opportunities, supervision and guidance, transportation, a supportive family and home environment, friends and a sense of community, as well as opportunities to learn, grow, and become independent functioning adults. Many of the services available to military families in general can and should be used by EFMP families. Not only are military services frequently convenient and cost-effective, utilization of base resources is an important mechanism for families to connect to formal and informal social networks within their primary family, the military. For children with mild disabilities or with medically managed special health care needs, base services for military families described later can provide for most of their needs.

Housing

Although the military provides housing for its service members, growing numbers of married service members and their families (70%) must find housing in the surrounding civilian community, for which a housing allowance is provided. For children who use wheelchairs and other mobility devices, home searches may need to focus on single-level dwellings, which may limit the family's choices of neighborhood and proximate amenities. Simple home modifications to eliminate architectural barriers (such as building a ramp) are frequently not costly. The cost of these modifications (with permission from the landlord) would be covered by the base housing office, up to a certain point. For families who have children with special needs, there may be a competing desire to be close to needed civilian services (such as occupational, speech, or behavioral therapy) for their child, which may be in higher-cost areas and at a distance that does not meet the military alert requirements for service members to be within a 15-minute travel time of the base. For families who have only one car, the service member must have first priority for duty demands. This can isolate the spouse if public transportation is poor and if the family's housing is far from the base. Low pay for families of young enlisted service members paired with the costs of civilian housing exceeding their housing allowance may result in EFMP families living in marginal but affordable neighborhoods, living in better neighborhoods that require out-of-pocket payments, or necessitating some parents living in separate residences—base and civilian community. The consequences of such living arrangements include unsafe home environments, financial stress, or social isolation for the parenting spouse and limited access to the military community that provides the social network and supports for most families.

Child Care

Like civilians, quality affordable child care is an important resource for families where both parents are employed. Child care within a military installation is available to families on a sliding scale based on service member rank. For the young enlisted, the costs of child care can be a large percentage of their household budget. Paradoxically for individuals who are unskilled or semi-skilled (which may be the case for the young enlisted), the income earned from a second job may push the family into a higher income bracket, which increases the cost for child care, making the economic gains of a second job negligible. Not only does base child care make it possible for both parents of a military family to work, it is a way for military families to meet other families and develop informal social networks.

There is a preference by military families to utilize base services whenever possible due to convenience factors and the desire to be part of the military community. However, the capacity of generic types of military services to accommodate a child with a disability can be a barrier for EFMP families. As with civilian child care services, providers may not have the necessary training or experience to work effectively and comfortably with infants and children with developmental disabilities and/or special health care needs. Child care providers may have concerns in three areas: (1) that the infant/child with a disability will take a disproportionate amount of the child care provider's time, taking away from the needs of the other children being served; (2) that children with behavior problems may increase their liability because of potentially heightened risk of injury to self or injury to others; and (3) potential resistance from the families of other children being served. Of the three reasons, the most common concern is the first, that is, perceptions of the need for excessively high staff to child ratios for children with disabilities. Consulting with local disability organizations or special education teachers who are experienced in inclusion will be helpful in sorting out whether the concerns stem from a lack of familiarity and therefore discomfort with various types of disabilities (which can be resolved through training and support), and the need to identify accommodations in the program to allow a child with a disability to participate without requiring increased staffing or specially trained staff.

Special Needs Evaluation and Review Team (SNERT). All installation child-care facilities have a review team to address the needs of EFMP children. The Army uses the Special Needs Accommodation Process (SNAP) and other branches use the Special Needs Evaluation and Review Team (SNERT). SNAP and SNERT both utilize a multidisciplinary team established to ensure that children with special needs have access to the most appropriate placement and accommodations at any military installation child care facility. Additional training of military child care staff is usually provided by EFMP managers, occupational nurses, new parent support managers, and/or other qualified personnel. In instances where personnel with training in accommodations and modifications are not available on base, trainings by civilian disability specialists may be available.

Youth Services

Military bases also operate excellent youth services programs for military families, providing after-school recreational and other services. As with military child care, base staff in youth programs may not have the knowledge and skills to provide the necessary accommodations to serve youth with developmental disabilities, inadvertently leaving EFMP families to find alternative civilian services or to care for their children with disabilities at home, which isolates them from the military community.

Medical Services—TRICARE

TRICARE, the military medical insurer, provides a basic level of medical and mental health care for service members and their family. Specialty health care may be provided by health care providers who are civilian contractors of TRICARE. However, depending on the location of the military installation, certain medical services may be difficult to obtain because of a limited number of specialists available in DoD's health care system in these communities. A DoD Health Survey (Williams, Schone, Archibald, & Thompson, 2004) found that 23% of children in military families had special health-care needs, that is, prescription drugs, medical services, special therapies, or counseling; 6% had emotional, developmental, or behavioral problems that required treatment or counseling from an array of interdisciplinary professionals. The majority of these therapies or interventions can be provided by civilian TRICARE contractors, if they are available. Depending on the complexity and severity of their disability, a child with a developmental disability may need specialized medical services (e.g., a developmental-behavioral pediatrician); surgical interventions; physical, occupational, and/or speech therapy; behavioral intervention; social skills training; special education; assistive technology; durable medical equipment; personal assistance services, and recreation services. Referrals are made first to military services, and when needed services are not available on base, referrals are made to state and local civilian medical, family support, and educational services in the community (Williams et al., 2004). For beneficiaries with qualifying mental or physical disabilities the TRICARE Extended Health Care Option (ECHO) is the next level of care.

Extended Care Health Option (ECHO) is a supplementary military program that provides in-home and respite care to individuals with certain physical disabilities, or physical/psychological conditions that result in the EFMP member being homebound. Qualifying conditions include children with moderate or severe mental retardation, motor impairments, behavior disorders, and some cases of Autism Spectrum Disorders. Most families with children with disabilities need occasional respite from continuous caregiving. However, because ECHO's eligibility criteria focuses on individuals who are homebound and need nursing care and/or personal assistance services, a number of children with developmental disabilities whose parents have a legitimate need for intermittent respite do not qualify because they are not homebound and do not need nursing care or personal assistance services. The recourse for these families is to pay for child care out of pocket or seek civilian services that will fund occasional respite. TRICARE Respite Care and EFMP Respite Care can be provided to the family concurrently. ECHO provides assistance with integrated services, supplies, and case management, and will pay for Applied Behavioral Analysis (ABA) therapy, and specific services for individuals with autism through the Autism Demonstration Program, respite care, wheelchairs, hospital beds, and so on. EFMP enrollment may be required to receive ECHO services.

PERSONNEL ASSIGNMENT

The intent of the EFMP assignment policy is to assign the service member, based on current or projected manning requirements, to locations where required medical, educational, early intervention, or related services are available either through the military medical system, through civilian resources, utilizing TRICARE, or a combination thereof and local resources. EFMP enrollment results in the flagging of the service member's personnel and medical files and those of the exceptional family member (EFM), so that once the reassignment process is initiated, the "losing" base (the base where the EFMP service member is currently based) communicates with the "gaining" base to complete a "facility determination" to evaluate whether the services currently being provided at the losing base are comparably available at the gaining base. This process involves timely and precise communication between the losing base and the gaining base to assure a smooth transfer process.

A problem identified by the Government Accountability Office (GAO) Report (U.S. GAO, 2007) was the inherent bias in DoD policy toward seeing exceptional needs in terms of medical conditions. Consequently, facility determinations have historically focused on the availability of medical specialists at the gaining base or through TRICARE contractors. Facility determination for EFMP families who had children with behavioral, developmental, psychiatric, and significant educational needs more frequently led to poor matches for EFMP service members, although this has improved as behavior specialists and autism services are now allowable TRICARE contractor categories. Manpower shortages of specialists continue to be a significant issue, especially in rural areas. EFMP parents whose children have Individualized Educational Programs (IEPs) can be helpful in this process, as the IEPs children have from the losing base can be forwarded to possible school districts within the community surrounding the gaining base. Important questions to be asked of the gaining base include: Are the services in the child's IEP available in the school district in the local area? What are the qualifications of the individuals providing the service? And if more than one school district is available surrounding the gaining base, what is the distance from the military base to the various schools where the child may be served? Parents can make these inquiries independently, but educational consultants at both the losing and gaining bases can play an important role by communicating with the family support personnel at the gaining base regarding names of key contact persons at schools or school districts where the child might be served. Frequently, early and direct communication between EFMP parents and civilian resources can address this gap in the facility determination process.

CIVILIAN SERVICES FOR EFMP FAMILIES

As a result of base closures, military families are increasingly living in the civilian community and there may be a greater reliance on civilian services by EFMP families for their child with a disability. As noted earlier in this chapter, the social norms, values, and principles of civilian disability services differ somewhat from those of the military community. These differences come from a strong disability advocacy movement that has its origins in many years of societal discrimination and exclusion of individuals with disabilities from community life leading to the evolution of a cadre of disability laws, statutes, and regulations that redress these instances of prejudice and discrimination. This legal framework defines the civil rights of people with disabilities to participate in community activities available to any citizen, and shape how disability services are organized and delivered.

Civilian Norms, Values, and Principles

Several core values and philosophical approaches underlie the civilian disability service system. These core values and philosophical approaches may at times clash with military values and process. The following section will help social workers to understand how to support military families to effectively access civilian services and to recognize where there may be conflicts between military and civilian values.

Family-Centered Care/Person-Centered Planning

Goldfarb et al. (2010), note that family-centered care (FCC) initially emerged in the maternity nursing literature in the 1970s and rapidly progressed in 1987 with former Surgeon General C. Everett Koop's national initiative to promote family-centered, community-based, coordinated care for children with special health care needs and their families. Although this concept has many different names such as "family-driven" in mental health and "relationship-based" in social work, the following core principles are operant: Professionals (a) intentionally partner with families in the delivery of services, (b) seek family input, (c) view the family as the primary expert on the child, and (d) respond to family concerns using a strengths-based individualized approach. Although the field still struggles with penetrating practice in service systems to reflect these values, EFMP families will encounter this partnership approach when applying for and using civilian services. When children with developmental disabilities reach age of majority, the concept is called *person-centered planning* (other terms include self-determination and self-directed services), which recognizes that individuals being served should be actively involved in identifying and assessing their needs as well as have their preferences for services considered when negotiating the configuration of services which will be provided (Field, Martin, Miller, Ward, & Wehmeyer, 1998). These concepts are among the core values contained in federal law (e.g., the Developmental Disabilities Assistance and Bill of Rights Act, 2000, and the Individuals with Disabilities Education Act, 2004), state law, and regulations that govern maternal child health programs, developmental disability services, and special education. Some military families who are new to civilian developmental disabilities (DD) and special education services may find this interactive style of service delivery new.

Least Restrictive Environment and Inclusion

"Least restrictive environment" (LRE) in education law refers to the right of students with disabilities to be educated with nondisabled peers to the greatest extent appropriate. They should have equal access to the general education curriculum, extra-curricular activities, or any other program that nondisabled peers are able to access, with appropriate special education supports and related services. LRE was introduced in special education law back in the 1970s to address historical trends to segregate students with disabilities from students in general education. Over time this principle has been used to guide how individuals with disabilities are served in DD service systems, within institutions, and other environments where mainstream citizens are served (e.g., housing, child care, higher education). *Inclusion* is the term that describes including infants, children, and adults with disabilities in activities with their peers without disabilities. When EFMP families attempt to enroll their children with disabilities in child care or youth services on base, these services are considered the "least restrictive environment."

Accommodations and Modifications

The impact of a disability on a child or adult can frequently be mediated by what are called *accommodations* and *modifications*. An accommodation is a *change in the environment that helps a student/individual to overcome or work around the disability*. For example, allowing a student who has trouble writing to give his answers orally is an example of an accommodation. This student is still expected to know the same material and answer the same questions as fully as the other students, but he doesn't have to write his answers to show that he knows the information. Using a child care enrollment example, a child with autism who has difficulty with a new setting and loud noises may be allowed to visit the child care center (possibly several times) when other children aren't present to get familiar with the surroundings and then, during the first week of child care may be allowed to come early (before the other students arrive) to allow the child to acclimate. When noises get too loud, the child may be allowed to move to a quieter area or possibly wear headphones for a short time. Consulting with a disability expert can help to fine-tune accommodations to maximize the inclusion of the child in the child care setting.

A modification refers to *a change in what is being taught to or expected of the student* to allow that student to make progress and/or to be in a classroom with general education students (the least restrictive environment). Making an assignment easier for a student with a disability is an example of a modification. The student isn't doing exactly what other students are doing, but is able to participate with his or her peers by broadly doing the task but at a level closer to his or her ability. What is most important to know about modifications and accommodations is that both are meant to help a child to learn and participate in learning, social, and developmental activities side by side with their general education peers. Typically students have an aide assisting them in the general education classroom when modifications are needed.

Formal Dispute Resolution Procedures—Due Process

Because people with disabilities have a long history of discrimination, segregation, and exclusion from activities, services, and community, enforcement of the legal rights of individuals with disabilities is guaranteed by stringent dispute resolution procedures (due process). How the due process works will depend on the law. In general, these protections require service systems to notify the individual or his family that an assessment is being planned, or a service is being changed in a timely manner. In addition, if parents do not agree to what is being proposed, they are allowed to enter into a hearing and to bring legal representation to resolve the dispute. EFMP policy directives describe the staff judge advocate's responsibility to provide legal assistance to active duty sponsors regarding the legal rights of family members with special medical and/or educational conditions. It is not clear to what degree military attorneys engage in civil litigation, and if so, to what degree they do so on behalf of the special education and/or disability rights of exceptional family members. Special education law is a specialization that most attorneys do not have, so it may be necessary to engage a civilian representative—see section on

"Legal Foundations" later in this chapter. Because special education law can be influenced by state special education law, families should seek assistance from someone in the state where they are residing. There is a national trade organization of special education attorneys and advocates (the Council of Parent Attorneys and Advocates [COPAA]) that posts lists of special education attorneys and advocates by state on their website. For reasons of liability, COPAA does not recommend any individual, so families need to interview potential advocates and attorneys to assess their credentials. If there is a dispute around a potential violation of disability rights in general, individuals and families should seek the assistance of an attorney who understands the Americans with Disabilities Act (Americans with Disabilities Act of 1990), civil rights law, and Section 504 of the Rehabilitation Act (U.S. Department of Health and Human Services [DHHS] Office of Civil Rights, 2006).

Legal Foundations to Protect the Rights of People With Disabilities

There are several categories of laws that protect the rights of people with disabilities. First, **Civil Rights** laws prohibit discrimination of groups of individuals based on a trait or characteristic. Beginning with the Civil Rights Act of 1964 (Dirksen Congressional Center, n.d.), which responded to denying black Americans access to public accommodations available to whites, other disenfranchised or marginalized groups (women, gays, lesbians, bisexual, and transgender) have invoked these same protections and guarantees for individuals with disabilities. **Disability laws** specifically articulate protections for individuals with disabilities. Section 504 of the Rehabilitation Act of 1973 (Section 504) (U.S. DHHS, 2006) and the Americans with Disabilities Act (ADA, 1990) are examples of disability laws that are based on anti-discrimination protections for individuals with disabilities. Section 504 applies to equal access to federally conducted and federally funded programs and specifically mandates making programs and activities accessible to people with disabilities. Unlike Section 504 of the Rehabilitation Act, the ADA is an omnibus civil rights law for people with disabilities that has multiple titles that require any entity available to the general public (not just those receiving federal funds) be made available to people with disabilities. Second, certain laws focus on specific arenas of community life, such as **education laws**—for example, Individuals with Disabilities Education Improvement Act (IDEA, 2004), and the No Child Left Behind Act (NCLB, 2001) now embedded in the Elementary and Secondary Education Act (ESEA, 2010). The latter two laws define expectations for learning and achievement of all school-age children, and therefore, must include students with disabilities. IDEA defines specific requirements of public schools to educate children with disabilities. Finally, people with disabilities are protected by **privacy laws** that are designed to protect the rights of individuals to access information about themselves *and* to keep personal information confidential. Key laws include the Family Educational Rights to Privacy Act (FERPA, 2011) and the Health Insurance Portability and Accountability Act (HIPAA, 1996).

Federal and state laws provide a powerful legal framework for a free and appropriate public education for all families that have children with disabilities. For EFMP families, military life can present unique challenges to meeting the special education needs of an exceptional family member. First, because each individual school district is charged with developing a child's Individualized Education Program (IEP), frequent transfers and relocations may interfere with the continuity of the child's educational program, because there is no national educational curriculum to assure uniformity of practice across states (Booth & Kelly, 2004). This also places additional burdens on EFMP parents to constantly learn new special education systems and to develop and maintain strong relationships with school personnel. Second, military families have reported feelings that public schools aren't attuned to the special circumstances of being a child in a military family (Ender, 2006), which requires intervention by both parents and military support personnel. Third, the power of special education law accords parents with legal rights, which are exercised through a due process legal mechanism. When there is a dispute with an educational system, parents may engage in negotiations that could become adversarial, and result in legal action. Such action may challenge the military's code of ethics and conduct described earlier in this chapter—"Service members and their families are expected to behave in a manner that does not bring embarrassment on the military." Torn between their child's needs and their commitment to duty, EFMP families may need the support of family support personnel to navigate these dilemmas.

Civilian DD Services, Education, Support, Advocacy, and Monitoring

State Developmental Disabilities Services. Each state provides services to individuals with developmental disabilities using a combination of state and federal monies. These services may be under a stand-alone agency such as the California Department of Developmental Services or they may be combined with services for individuals with mental health needs or services for the aging. Who is served and exactly what is provided is determined on a state-by-state basis (National Association of State Directors of Developmental Disabilities Services, n.d.).

***Civilian Parent Training and Information Center* (PTIs)** are part of a national system of parent run organizations to provide training and information to parents of children birth to age 22, about how to access special education and related services (Alliance National Parent Technical Assistance Center, n.d.). The PTI for military families is called Specialized Training of Military Parents (STOMP). All PTIs are staffed by parents who have experience with the special education system locally. Military families may utilize both STOMP and civilian PTIs as appropriate.

Other civilian resources for parent education, advocacy and support organizations exist in states and locally such as **Family Resource Centers**, which focus on information, training, advocacy, and parent support around early intervention and disability issues; **Family Voices**, which is a national network of parent-run chapters that advocate for more effective maternal child health services for children with special health care needs; **disability-specific parent organizations** such as United Cerebral Palsy, the National Down Syndrome Association, Autism Speaks, the Fragile X Association of Southern California, CHADD (for people with attention deficit disorder), and the National Organization for Rare Disorders (NORD), which targets people with rare diseases. As individuals with DD become adults, there may be an interest in joining a **self-advocacy group**, such as People First (people with disabilities helping people with disabilities through peer support, education, and advocacy), Self-Advocates Becoming Empowered (SABE), and the National Youth Leadership Network (NYLN).

Each state also has an array of disability education, support, and advocacy organizations. Although it is beyond this chapter to include all of these, we refer the reader to national networks of agencies that can be helpful for finding and understanding resources in states. 'Every state has three agencies authorized by the Developmental Disabilities Assistance and Bill of Rights Act and funded by the Administration on Developmental Disabilities, which represent three mechanisms for promoting systemic change in states on behalf of people with DD: (1) a **Governor's Developmental Disabilities Planning Council** (DD Council), which develops a state plan for DD under the Governor's office (National Association of Councils on DD); (2) a **Disability Rights Organizations** (National Disability Rights Network), which uses a team of attorneys and advocates to assure that the rights of people with DD are not being violated (through education, advocacy, individual and class action law suits); and (3) **University Centers for Excellence in DD Research, Education, and Service** (Association of University Centers on Disability)—federally funded centers within universities that provide interdisciplinary training to future leaders in the DD field, conduct evaluation and research, disseminate information which can be used by individuals, their families, service systems and policy makers, and/or provides clinical and community services to meet emerging needs. In addition, the Administration on Developmental Disabilities began funding **Family Support 360 for Military Families** (U.S. DHHS, ACF, n.d.) in response to its recognition that children with DD in military families needed similar 360-degree integrated services as civilian families. All of these programs are required to work with a specific military base (some work with several) and focus on achieving the intent of the DD Act for military families. These organizations are excellent state and national resources for information, training, advocacy, and capacity building for EFMP program administrators, providers, and families. Finally, the Maternal Child Health Bureau funds approximately 47 **Leadership Education in Neurodevelopmental Disorders (LEND)** (Association of University Centers on Disability [AUCD] or University Centers for Excellence in Developmental Disabilities Education [UCEDD]) Interdisciplinary Training Programs in the nation, which prepare future leaders in health care and related fields to work effectively with children with special health care needs, including those with neurodevelopmental disorders. A number of LEND/UCEDD programs operate clinics for children and youth with DD and do community training, conduct community education activities, and develop useful informational products for EFMP coordinators and EFMP families (AUCD).

FAMILY SUPPORT SERVICES FOR EFMP FAMILIES—MILITARY AND CIVILIAN

DoD policy *allows, but does not require* military services to provide family support services. The GAO Report on EFMP (2007) noted that this permissive approach to family support services typically results in a minimum amount and breadth of family support services available to military families. Although evidence on the effectiveness of alternative models for military family support is in its seminal stages, we borrow liberally from the work of Bowen and Martin (1998) and Mancini, Bowen, and Martin (2005) in proposing a model, which argues that family-support services for EFMP families should be developed, delivered, and evaluated within the social context in which these families live and work. A deep understanding of the formal and informal community networks of EFMP families is critical to the family support mandate of EFMP.

Formal communities refer to those social networks that are defined by authoritative law, procedural guidelines, and policies that serve to structure the delivery of services (who is eligible, what and how much they get and under what circumstance, who is responsible for the service delivery). *Informal communities* refer to voluntary associations and less formal networks that are based on mutual exchanges and reciprocal responsibility, such as relationships with friends, work associates, and neighbors (Bowen & Martin, 1998). Compliance is not the primary goal of informal networks but the provision of tangible, informational, and social-emotional supports provided by individuals who have life experience is primary—more of a "consumer" perspective, than a regulatory perspective. These supports provide practical information on how to effectively navigate formal networks. Together, an EFMP family's formal *and* informal community networks create the infrastructure for the following eight goals of community: (1) develop a sense of community identity and pride, (2) meet individual and family needs and goals, (3) participate meaningfully in community life, (4) secure instrumental and expressive support, (5) solve problems and manage conflicts, (6) affirm and enforce pro-social norms, (7) cope with internal and external threats, and (8) maintain stability and order in personal and family relationships (Bowen & Martin, 1998). When these networks are not robust, service members and family units will not be able to achieve the eight implicit goals of community. It is through this lens that social workers should assess an EFMP family's support needs and provide meaningful interventions.

Although programs vary across branches of service, delivery of reimbursable and non-reimbursable services is based on legislative and DoD authority. In theory, the EFMP, working in concert with other military and civilian agencies, should provide a comprehensive, coordinated, multiagency approach for community support, housing, medical, educational, and personnel services to families with special needs. Examples of such services include Family Centers and Military Treatment Facilities on base delivering information about specialized services (including day care, recreational opportunities) that can accommodate the exceptional family member, the provision of information about support groups, available advocacy services, and housing to accommodate special needs; working with the school to provide additional support for a child with a behavioral disorder; supporting a military family that gave birth to a 20-week-old premature infant during 3 months of extra-uterine life and the decision to discontinue life supports; or creating a special needs section to the post library. In addition the following excellent resources for military families have special information for EFMP families.

Military Homefront **(2011)** is the official Military Community and Family Policy (MC&FP) website designed to provide program information, policy, and guidance to troops and their families, leaders, and service providers. It is a resource covering all branches of the military that contains valuable tools for military families in general and contains some information for families of children with disabilities. The website is divided into three sections: *Troops and Families*, *Leadership*, and *Service Providers*, which contains information of use to social workers and other practitioners. Within the *Troops and Families* section is a subsection entitled ***Special Needs/EFMP,*** which provides information on military supports and services available to families of children with special needs including links to **EFMP Enrollment, EFMP Toolbox** (a downloadable manual to help families navigate the military and generic systems that serve children with special needs and their families), **EFMP Family Support** (a list of possible EFMP support services, links to EFMP programs in each branch of the military and a link to the **Military Installations Directory**, which contains a list of services and resources for each Military installation), and **Benefits, Allowances & Eligibility** (information on child care, education, federal programs, financial, legal [guardianship], medical care, and respite care). Additionally, families can access **Plan My Move**, which is a searchable directory of services, including but not specific to services for children with special needs, that provides information on programs within an up to 200-mile radius of any base. Because of the national focus of this resource, much of the information, while excellent, is by necessity general and provides address and phone numbers of local resources, but cannot help families to actually navigate local systems and supports when they meet resistance (which can happen often). This reinforces the critical need for highly trained EFMP staff and other family support personnel.

***Specialized Training of Military Parents* (STOMP, 2003)** is a project of Washington PAVE (Partnerships for Action, Voices for Empowerment), the statewide Parent Training and Information Center (PTI) for Washington state. It provides "information about parent rights and responsibilities to access appropriate special education services for military children." They also help military families with children with special needs to navigate the military and generic special education and health systems through (a) workshops and presentations, (b) direct one-on-one consultation with families, and (c) provision of a 3½ day training and technical assistance for parent professional teams (consisting of EFMP personnel, a military parent of a child with a disability, and a PTI member) to serve families in their local area. STOMP has four locations across the country and is a valuable resource because its staff bridges both the military and generic service systems and resources. STOMP is familiar with challenges that military families face and also can link families to local mentors who know what is available at and around local installations.

Parent to Parent Support. EFMP families can frequently benefit from meeting and participating in activities with other EFMP families on base or in the civilian community. Although formal parent support groups may not be as readily available on military installations, military families can take advantage of the following common military venues:

- Family Team Building or Family Readiness Groups—These groups are designed to educate and support military spouses with the requirements of the military culture. Spouses often communicate among themselves when trying to resolve issues and find resources. By knowing about EFMP, members of these groups could guide potential EFMP families for resources or assistance before a situation becomes too daunting. Every branch has a version of these groups but they are named differently. Family Team Building is usually coordinated through Morale, Welfare, and Recreation (MWR). Family Readiness Groups are a part of the unit command structure.
- Play morning—Organized play date for children under the age of 3 years. Often organized through the New Parent Support Program. These groups allow EFMP to be a part of the community, meet families, and understand the needs of that community. The focus is to connect families to resources early in the child's development.

- Any and all Morale, Welfare, and Recreation (MWR) events/community activities—The presence of EFMP families in these "all military family events" is critical to creating an environment in which EFMP is a natural part of the base community, to meet other families to create informal natural supports and for EFMP families to be seen as a resource to other families.

Service Member Support—Utilizing Military Command Structure

The unit chain of command often provides the first line of support for military families and serves as an intermediary social structure that links the two worlds of formal and informal services and support (Bowen & Martin, 1998). As such, the military unit to which the service member is assigned can represent a quasi-family for some service members in the rendering of support and friendship and opportunities for social relationships. The military unit structure has historically been underutilized as a resource for EFMP-eligible service members and their families. If harnessed appropriately, the military unit has the capacity to promote an informal support system within the unit for EFMP service members and their families, through sponsorship of new members, social activities, family support groups, and, if needed, connecting families to formal systems of care. In addition, the military's command structure can address problems faced by EFMP service members and their families. The following are common venues where EFMP and family support personnel can raise awareness of EFMP and to help EFMP service members within their military unit.

- First Sergeant and Commander's courses—These are training courses for military personnel moving up the ranks to take on more responsibility. It is important that these future leaders understand how they can work as a team with EFMP to improve the quality of life of EFMP service members and their families while ensuring that the requirements of duty are met and the mission is accomplished.
- In-processing or newcomers briefs—This is the venue for disseminating initial information on EFMP at the gaining base for all newly arriving military personnel.
- Out-processing briefs—This is the venue for providing information on special concerns of EFMP families who are relocating to another duty station.
- Training days or deployment briefs—These are 1-day or a specific time frame dedicated to increasing information and resources to an entire group of military personnel. It is a rich forum to ensure that military personnel understand what EFMP is, who is eligible, who to contact for enrollment, and so on. Well-deployed information about EFMP will increase more timely enrollment, dispel myths about stigma, and create an environment where the service member can be proactive rather than reactive.

Training for Military and Civilian Service Providers

Many military service providers for families may feel they cannot accommodate exceptional family members with disabilities, and some community service agencies may not be knowledgeable about how military life can impact accessing needed services for the child with a disability. An important function for the EFMP coordinators and social workers working with them is cross-training of military and civilian service providers. Below are examples of audiences for training:

- Family child care providers are military spouses providing child care in their homes as a business. These homes are regulated under the installation child development centers. The children enrolled in these programs can be reviewed through the Special Needs Evaluation and Review Process (SNERT). EFMP may coordinate resources or training of staff as appropriate.
- Medical providers training—Each medical facility has a scheduled training day in which medical providers can receive information about EFMP. These physicians are responsible for completing the EFMP enrollment packet (DD Form 2792) and treating EFMP families.
- County agencies—Temporary Assistance for Needy Families (TANF), children service agencies and law enforcement—EFMP can work to assist military families involved in these systems and/or are eligible for these services.
- Mental health providers (both military and civilian)—Military mental health professionals who are responsible for completing the EFMP enrollment packet (DD Form 2792) for a mental health diagnosis, could benefit from EFMP training. Civilian MH professionals could benefit from learning about EFMP services and military culture.
- Chaplains (both military and civilian)—As spiritual leaders, chaplains counsel individuals and families in crisis, but may not be familiar with EFMP. As they are an important resource for EFMP eligible families, EFMP staff should work collaboratively with chaplains to coordinate the provision of supportive services and resources to EFMP families, as appropriate.
- Schools and the school district administration—Civilian schools and military families belong to two separate cultures. EFMP is the natural bridge for military families who must navigate both cultures. EFMP can also help professionals in both cultures to understand the dual "citizenship" of EFMP families and is also a referral resource for both entities.

Case Management Services

Because of the voluntary nature and limited funding for family support services under EFMP, the minimum family support service provided is information and referral, that is, a list of possible programs/services to which the EFMP member may be eligible. EFMP families are then on their own to explore, apply for, and navigate multiple systems of service on behalf of their child. Although some resources are available to prepare families for their new location (e.g., Military Homefront and STOMP), the national scope of these resources requires additional work at the local level to identify and access needed services.

Because EFMP families must coordinate both civilian and military services when they have a child with a disability and many service systems are not transparent in their policies and procedures, this can be a daunting task for EFMP families. As a proactive advocate, social workers can work with EFMP coordinators to assist families to access needed information and resources, navigate complex systems to which they are entitled, and to provide sustained support for families who may feel they are constantly in flux.

Advocacy Services

Although not common, there is a great need for EFMP advocacy services. Advocacy can look very different from one case to the next because it is case-directed or goal-directed. In some branches of the service, EFMP coordinators engage in active advocacy work by attending Individualized Educational Plan (IEP) meetings for military children in special education, going to doctor appointments with family members, and working with child care and recreational programs to include children with disabilities in these generic programs. The success of advocacy services depends on the relationship the EFMP coordinator has with base and civilian personnel. Where this is not a universal function of the EFMP coordinator, the social worker can focus on providing some of these resources for EFMP families, and/or working collaboratively with EFMP personnel to build their skills in this area.

A Case Example

The case vignette, "Darcy," that will be presented in the next section contains several major learning points of this chapter. First, it is a good example of how the Special Needs Evaluation and Review Team (SNERT) and client advocacy on the part of EFMP can help families in need, and why these should be essential components of EFMP family support services. As noted earlier, EFMP families are expected to participate in services on base for all military families, that is, to be "included." As with inclusion efforts in generic civilian services, a child with a disability may have needs that challenge the comfort level of the staff of generic base services. Frequently staff of base child care centers, youth services, and so on respond positively to the inclusion of children with special needs if EFMP or related family support personnel can provide them with practical concrete methods to address the needs of the child with special needs. As noted earlier, service providers are concerned about accommodations or strategies that will require excessive changes in their current procedures, manpower needs, and practices. The social worker should be sensitive to this underlying concern when working with base providers.

The solution in the case vignette involved the development of a Behavioral Support Plan by the EFMP coordinator. This may not be a skill set of all EFMP staff nor part of their scope of practice. When this is the case, there are other avenues for assisting Darcy's parents. School personnel may be helpful as every school district has special education services, and behavior management is a key component of special education services. Because this child is currently not identified by the school district for special education services, the school will likely utilize a student success team or some other similar mechanism for students in general education who are at risk for academic failure or requiring special education services. Another strategy is to discuss the possible need for an assessment for special education eligibility with the parent, who can request such an evaluation of the child by the school district. An assessment for special education includes an assessment of behavior as a possible eligible condition for special education, which would provide the SNERT team with a formal evaluation of Darcy's behavior. Even if it is not severe enough to qualify for special education, the assessment can still be very useful to the SNERT team to develop solutions on base. Finally, a referral to a developmental-behavioral pediatrician could be made to rule out underlying medical conditions such as ADHD, a medical/genetic condition with behavioral symptoms, and/or potential environmental causes (e.g., neglect, abuse). Such a referral would be covered under TRICARE.

Case Vignette: Darcy

The parents of Darcy, a 5-year-old female with no medical or mental health conditions, came to the EFMP office seeking assistance. They reported that she seemed angry all the time, and physically acted out with little provocation. She frequently would throw things at adults and other children. Her military child care provider had tried everything in their training tool box to assist this child. The parents were frustrated with staff of the child care center; the child care center staff was frustrated with the parents.

A Special Needs Evaluation and Review Team (SNERT) meeting, which included the daycare providers and parents, was called by the EFMP coordinator. Prior to the meeting, the EFMP coordinator asked Darcy's parents to get permission to talk to Darcy's teacher and found out that the school was having the same problem but had not reported anything to the parents. At the SNERT meeting, information was gathered and a plan compiled. A Behavioral Support Plan was developed that would be used at both the child care facility and at home. In addition, it was decided that Darcy's parents and the EFMP coordinator would request a meeting with the school principal and Darcy's kindergarten teacher to discuss implementation of the Behavior Support Plan at school. A follow-up Special Needs Evaluation and Review Team (SNERT) meeting was scheduled in 4 weeks to review Darcy's progress.

When Darcy's parents and the EFMP coordinator met with the school to request that they implement the Behavior Support Plan, there were a few questions/concerns. After discussion and a modification to the plan, Darcy's school agreed to implement the plan. At the follow-up meeting of the SNERT, Darcy's behaviors had improved and the tension between the child care center staff and Darcy's parents was significantly reduced. Darcy's parents were pleased that she was participating more with her peers and seemed to be benefiting from her experience at school and in the child care center.

CONCLUSION

Earlier in this chapter we briefly discussed what accommodations and modifications are and resources for ideas on how to modify service space and program characteristics to allow a child with a disability to participate in an activity or a setting. Information on military and civilian websites can help the social worker create practical solutions to help military service providers to make small, incremental changes, which will increase their competence and comfort in serving children with disabilities in base resources. Sharing these websites and other resources with military service providers can also be helpful to raise their awareness of the needs of this population and to more independently explore possible solutions to problems experienced by EFMP families. Once base service providers accumulate a series of positive experiences making reasonable accommodations to children with disabilities, they will, over time, be open to including children with more severe disabilities in their programs.

The deliberate inclusion of the civilian service provider (local school) in the SNERT process is an example of the substantial benefits of integrating military and civilian services to achieve the best outcomes for EFMP children. Military and civilian services each contribute unique assets and value to EFMP children and their families. The social worker has a key role in implementing meaningful interventions to increase the awareness of both the military and civilian community of how to best support EFMP families. The social worker has a key role in helping to maximize the formal and informal communities to which EFMP service members and their family units belong. When these networks are robust, current concerns of service member retention in the volunteer military will no longer be an issue.

CHAPTER DISCUSSION QUESTIONS

1. What are the differences between accommodations and modifications? Please provide examples of each.
2. Which are the categories of laws that protect the rights of individuals with disabilities? Describe each.
3. Based on the case vignette presented in this chapter (Darcy) please provide a comprehensive treatment plan. What information would you need to have as part of a psychosocial assessment? And how would you utilize resources for the client and her family?

REFERENCES

Alliance National Parent Technical Assistance Center. http://www.parentcenternetwork.org/national/aboutus.html

Americans with Disabilities Act of 1990. (Amended, 2008, P.L. 110–325). Retrieved from http://www.ada.gov/pubs/ada.htm

Architectural Barriers Act of 1968. (Amended 42 U.S.C. §§ 4151 et seq.). Retrieved from http://www.access-board.gov/about/laws/aba.htm

Association of University Center on Disabilities. (AUCD). www.aucd.org

Booth, C. L., & Kelly, J. F. (2004). Child care patterns and issues for families of preschool children with disabilities. *Infants and Young Children, 17*(1), 5–16.

Bowen, G. L., & Martin, J. A. (1998). Community capacity: A core component of the 21st century military community. *Military Family Issues: The Research Digest, 2*, 1–4.

Bowen, G. L., & Zipper, I. N. (2010, August 19). *Strengthening military families with children who have special needs: OneStop for family support.* Presentation to the Eastern Area Health Education Center.

Council of Parent Attorneys and Advocates (COPAA). www.copaa.org

Department of Defense Directive (DODD) 1342.17. (1988, Certified 2003). Retrieved from http://www.dtic.mil/whs/directives/ corres/pdf/134217p.pdf

Department of Defense Instruction DODI 1342.12. (2005). *Provision of early intervention and special education services to eligible DoD dependents.* Retrieved from http://www.dod.mil/dodgc/doha/134212p.pdf

Developmental Disabilities Assistance and Bill of Rights Act of 2000—Public Law 106–402, 114 Stat. 1677. (2010, July). Administration on Developmental Disabilities, Administration on Children and Families, Department of Health and Human Services. Retrieved from http://www.acf.hhs.gov/opa/fact_sheets/add_factsheet.html

Dirksen Congressional Center, Major Features of the Civil Rights Act of 1964 (Public Law 88–352). Retrieved from http://www.congresslink.org/print_basics_histmats_civilrights64text.htm

Elementary and Secondary Education Act. (2010). Retrieved from http://www2.ed.gov/policy/elsec/leg/esea02/index.html

Ender, M. G. (2006). Voices from the backseat: Demands of growing up in military families. In C. A. Castro, A. B. Adler, & T. W. Britt (Eds.), *Military life: The psychology of serving in peace and combat: Vol. 3. The military family* (pp. 138–166). Westport, CT: Praeger Security International.

Exceptional Family Member Family Program: Air Force. (2011, July). AFI36–2110_AFGM2. Retrieved from http://www.e-publishing.af.mil/shared/media/epubs/AFI36–2110.pdf

Exceptional Family Member Program: Army. (2011, February). *AR608–75, Rapid action revision (RAR) issue.* Retrieved from http://www.apd.army.mil/pdffiles/r608_75.pdf

Exceptional Family Member Program: Navy. (2005, December). SECNAV Instruction 1754.5B. *Department of the Navy.* Retrieved from http://www.cnic.navy.mil/navycni/groups/public/@hq/@ffr/documents/document/cnicp_a193511.pdf

Family Educational Rights to Privacy Act (FERPA). (2011). Retrieved from http://www2.ed.gov/policy/gen/guid/fpco/ferpa/index.html

Field, S., Martin, J. E., Miller, R., Ward, M. J, & Wehmeyer, M. L. (1998). Self-determination for persons with disabilities: A position statement of the Division on Career Development and Transition. *Career Development for Exceptional Individuals, 21*, 113–128.

Goldfarb, F., Devine, K., Hill, A., Moss, J., Ogburn, E., Roberts, R., . . . Yingling, J. (2010). Family centered care from the parent perspective. *Journal of Family Social Work, 13*(2), 91–99.

Health Insurance Portability and Accountability Act (HIPAA). (1996). https://www.cms.gov/HIPAAGenInfo/Downloads/HIPAALaw.pdf

Individuals with Disabilities Education Act. (2004). U.S. Department of Education. Retrieved from http://idea.ed.gov/

Mancini, J. A., Bowen, G. L., & Martin, J. A. (2005). Community social organization: A conceptual linchpin in examining families in the context of communities. *Family Relations, 54*, 570–582.

Martin, J., & McClure, P. (2000). Today's active duty family. In J. Martin, L. Rosen, & L. Sparacino (Eds.), *The military family: Guide for human service providers* (pp. 4–23). Westport, CT: Praeger.

Military Homefront. (2011). Department of Defense. Retrieved from http://apps.mhf.dod.mil/pls/psgprod/f?p=MHF:RELO:0

National Association of Councils on Developmental Disabilities. http://www.nacdd.org/site/home.aspx

National Association of State Directors of Developmental Disabilities Services. http://www.nasddds.org/AboutNASDDDS/index.shtml

National Association of University Centers on Disability. http://aucd.org/template/index.cfm

National Disability Rights Network. http://www.ndrn.org/

National Organization of Rare Disorders. http://www.rarediseases.org/info/about.html

No Child Left Behind Act. (2001). PL 107–110. Retrieved from http://www2.ed.gov/policy/elsec/leg/esea02/107–110.pdf

Skok, A., Harvey, D., & Reddihough, D. (2006). Perceived stress, perceived social support, and well-being among mothers of school-aged children with cerebral palsy. *Journal of Intellectual and Developmental Disability*, *31*, 53–57.

SNIAC (2008). Special needs identification and assignment coordination (SNIAC) Air Force instruction 40–701. Retrieved from http://www.e-publishing.af.mil/shared/media/epubs/afi40–701.pdf

STOMP. (2003). Specialized training of military parents. Retrieved from www.stompproject.org/services.asp

Uniform Code of Military Justice. (2000). *Index and legislative history: Uniform code of military justice*. UCMJ 50th anniversary edition, 1950–2000. Buffalo, NY: Hein.

U.S. Department of Health and Human Services, ACF. (n.d.). Family Support 360 for Military Families. http://www.acf.hhs.gov/programs/add/pns/fs360_militaryfactsheet.html

U.S. Department of Health and Human Services, Office of Civil Rights. (2006). *Your Rights under Section 504 of the Rehabilitation Act*. Retrieved from http://www.hhs.gov/ocr/civilrights/resources/factsheets/504.pdf

U.S. Government Accountability Office. (2007, March). *Military personnel: Medical, family support, and educational services are available for exceptional family members*. Washington, DC. Publication GAO-07–317R DOD Exceptional Family Member Program.

Williams, T. V., Schone, E. M., Archibald, N. D., & Thompson, J. W. (2004). A national assessment of children with special health care needs: Prevalence of special needs and use of health care services among children in the military health system. *Pediatrics*, *114*, 384–393.

CHAPTER

22

Grief, Loss, and Bereavement in Military Families

Jill Harrington-LaMorie

The loss of a loved one to death is recognized as one of life's most difficult stressors. However, when a loved one dies by suicide, the common observation generally supported by anecdotal evidence is that suicide presents one of the most burdensome and complicated forms of bereavement for survivors. Surprisingly, empirical evidence has provided scant support for this belief and furthermore, "the question of how best to help survivors of suicide remains pressing" (American Foundation for Suicide Prevention, 2010, p. 2). Survivors of suicide loss are a poorly understood and understudied population (Cerel, Jordan, & Duberstein, 2008; B. Feigelman & Feigelman, 2008; McMenamy, Jordan, & Mitchell, 2008; Parker & McNally, 2008). Little is known about the impact of suicide loss, risk factors for suicide survivors, and therapeutic treatments. Our knowledge of suicide loss survivors is largely anecdotal from clinical observation and first-person accounts of survivors. However, there is a growing body of research literature emerging on bereavement after suicide and how to best support survivors.

Similar to the civilian population, the U.S. military has placed its emphasis on prevention of suicide in service members, leaving an obvious and unattended gap to the postvention crisis and care needs of survivors of a military suicide death, whether the survivors are family members or fellow service members.

Given the increasing rates of suicide among U.S. military service members, the rise in the military suicide loss survivor population continues to mount. With more than 2,000 reported suicide deaths in the active duty armed services since 2001 (Department of Defense [DoD], 2010) and 20% of the 30,000 suicide deaths each year in the United States completed by veterans (Congressional Quarterly, 2010), conservative estimates of suicide loss survivors that are associated with veteran and military personnel reaches into the hundred-thousands.

The goal of this chapter is to provide clinicians working with survivors of a military/veteran suicide death a better understanding of: (a) suicide bereavement and the corresponding complexities of a military related death; and (b) clinician issues that may surface as a result of working with those bereaved by suicide. Suggested resources and interventions for care are provided.

SUICIDE BEREAVEMENT

Not everyone who is exposed to a suicide death—such as that of a friend, family member, or co-worker—will be significantly impacted or extremely harmed by the death. However, for most who have had a meaningful attachment to the deceased, the effects of this mode of death can be profound and devastating. The death of a loved one, friend, or significant other is consistently considered one of life's most stressful events (M. Stroebe & Stroebe, 1993), and bereavement and grief following suicide has its own particular challenges for those left in its wake (McIntosh, 1987).

Grief and bereavement following a loss through death is a normative human process (Worden, 2009). How each individual responds to loss is a highly personalized and subjective experience. There is no definitive, prognostic response to death; loss and bereavement reactions vary among individuals in their meaning, presence, intensity, frequency, and duration (Bonanno, 2004). Common intense emotions during the first few weeks and months of grieving include sadness, anger, longing, guilt, fear, and sorrow. These are frequently accompanied by somatic sensations in the stomach, shortness of breath, profound fatigue, agitation, difficulties in swallowing, and perceived helplessness. Bereaved individuals also commonly experience loss of interest, lack of motivation, and social withdrawal. However, distress is often followed by an adaptive course of adjustment, and most survivors are able to integrate the loss into their lives and accommodate with resilience (Bonanno, 2004; Neimeyer, Burke, MacKay, & van Dyke Stringer, 2010). Conversely, research suggests that 10% to 20% of bereaved persons suffer from more complicated grief reactions (Holland, Neimeyer, Boelen, & Prigerson, 2008). Those bereaved by suicide are more vulnerable to the cumulative effects of completed suicide, predisposing them to a higher risk of complicated grief and heightened states of distress (Aguirre & Slater, 2010).

Anecdotal evidence suggests that bereavement following suicide is different than mourning other types of deaths (Jordan, 2001, 2008). However, there is mixed scientific evidence in the field when comparing suicide bereavement to bereavement subsequent to other modes of death (Mitchell, Sakraida, Kim, Bullian, & Chiappetta, 2009). Over the past 20 years, a large number of studies, using rigorous research methods—such as large group sizes, comparison groups, and control for socioeconomic variables—have found little difference between groups bereaved through different modes of death (Barrett & Scott, 1990; Cleiren, 1993; Demi, 1984; Farberow, Gallagher-Thompson, Gilewski, & Thompson, 1992; Grad & Zavasnik, 1996; Seguin, Lesage, & Kiely, 1995). On the other hand, research has also indicated that suicide loss survivors experience longer grief-related symptoms as well as increased intensity of symptoms over time (Kovarsky, 1989; Thompson, Futterman, Farberow, Thompson, & Peterson, 1993). Some have argued that suicide bereavement is a combination of grief and posttraumatic stress (Callahan, 2000).

Given the mixed data and dearth of research, it is critical to note that our understanding about long-term effects of suicide on this population is limited (B. Feigelman & Feigelman, 2008; Jordan, 2001). However, we do know that those bereaved by suicide have a greater prevalence of risk factors (Clark, 2001). We know that suicide loss survivors demonstrate higher levels of distress in several areas of functioning at some point in their grieving process (McMenamy et al., 2008) and are prone to complications in mourning as well as being at higher risk for negative psychological, affective, social, behavioral, and physiological consequences (Latham & Prigerson, 2004; McMenamy et al., 2008; Mitchell et al., 2009). This distress associated with suicide bereavement can lead to an increased risk of depressive symptoms, anxiety disorders, posttraumatic stress symptoms and poor self-reported physical health (Mitchell et al., 2009). Not being prepared for the death of a loved one predisposes the survivor to a higher likelihood of experiencing a complicated grief reaction (Rando, 1993). Furthermore, if violence was associated with the suicide and the suicide death, this could result in the development of posttraumatic stress disorder and major depression for survivors (Kaltman & Bonnano, 2003). Suicide survivors also are at an increased likelihood of completing suicide themselves (Jordan, 2008).

ISSUES THAT INFLUENCE SUICIDE BEREAVEMENT

When a suicide happens unexpectedly and/or traumatically, survivors are exposed to the synergistic influences of both loss and trauma. This can severely disrupt the survivor's sense of control; shatter their assumptive view of the world; alter their foundational beliefs; impair their ability to function, and contribute to emotional numbing (Jordan, 2008; Mitchell et al., 2009).

The suicide of a friend, loved one, or close relationship can unleash upon survivors an "emotional tsunami" (Jordan, 2008, p. 681). Edwin Shneidman, known to be the father of the suicide prevention movement in the United States, believed that "the person who commits suicide puts his psychological skeletons in the survivor's emotional closet—he sentences the survivors to deal with many negative feelings . . . it can be a heavy load" (Cain, 1972, p. x).

Jordan (2001, 2008) contends that suicide bereavement is a different experience for the bereaved than any other type of loss and that there are certain accompanying themes that survivors tend to commonly report. For example, when a death is from suicide, the pain of the loss for the survivor is often compounded by overwhelming and intense feelings of blame, guilt, anger, and incomprehension. If the suicide is experienced as a sudden, unexpected loss, this will add the element of shock to the survivor's suffering. Survivors are also confronted with the additional burden of stigma that still surrounds suicide (Feigelman, Gorman, & Jordan, 2009; Houck, 2007).

Suicide loss survivors often compare the distress they experience as being trapped on an endless roller coaster of emotions, inhibiting their ability to cope with the death and interfering in their grief and healing. The roller coaster of emotions can sometimes include simultaneous paradoxical feelings leading to an often conflicted and confusing state for survivors struggling to cope in the aftermath.

The compound effect of these themes and issues can result in a stigmatizing grief and a state of heightened distress for survivors, which increases their vulnerability to mental health impairments, complicated grief, and attempting and completing suicide (Aguirre & Slater, 2010).

Recurrent themes and issues that contribute to the subjective experience of suicide loss and differentiate survivors' bereavement process and experience from survivors of other modes of death include:

- The overwhelming need to answer the question, "Why?"
- Guilt/responsibility/self-blame
- Perceived rejection/abandonment by the deceased
- A sense of betrayal
- Feelings of anger, confusion, and despair
- A sense of relief
- Shame, stigma, and social isolation
- Family disturbances
- Spiritual/religious/existential crisis
- Exposure to trauma; and risk of developing complicated grief, depression, and PTSD (Jordan, 2008; Jordan & McIntosh, 2010).

Comparatively described as living in a canyon of "why" (Campbell, 2001), suicide loss survivors often struggle more with questions of meaning-making around the death. Because suicide is an act of self-destruction, which violates the fundamental norms of self-preservation, survivors are often encapsulated in trying to answer the question, "Why did he or she do it?" The need to make sense of the motives and frame of mind of the deceased are major preoccupations for survivors, which can severely inhibit their ability to connect with and work on their grief.

This haunting question of "Why" often includes questions of responsibility, which can lead to blame, self-blame, guilt, and self-reproach. Compared to survivors of other types of death, suicide loss survivors demonstrate higher levels of guilt, blame, and responsibility for the death (Feigelman et al., 2009; Jordan 2001, 2008; Wilson & Marshall, 2010). The survivor's role and responsibility in the death is often self-exaggerated, and as Jordan (2008) argues, most survivors overestimate their own role in contributing to or preventing the suicide. The ensuing guilt is often the result of survivors feeling as if they may have directly caused the suicide through ill treatment, neglect, or abandonment of the deceased. Self-blame in suicide survivors results in their perceived inability to anticipate or prevent the suicide; furthermore, guilt and self-blame are particularly difficult if the suicide occurred within the context of an interpersonal conflict between the deceased and the survivor (Worden, 2009).

There are many factors that may contribute to a death by suicide. Some data suggest that 90% of people who die by suicide meet the criteria for a psychiatric disorder (Robins, 1981). However, survivors are often unaware of these factors or may minimize them.

The intensity of a survivor's guilt may lead them to have the need to feel punished, further influencing self-punishing behaviors, which may lead to societal rejection and isolation. Guilt can also be one of the underlying forces in the need to place blame for the death on oneself or on others. Blame can be an effort by survivors to establish control in a very uncontrollable and incomprehensible situation.

Anger is an intense and sometimes confusing emotion for survivors. It may often be the precipitating emotion in the emergence and manifestation of blame for the suicide. A survivor's anger can have many moving targets. It can be directed toward other family members, friends, co-workers, occupation (e.g., the military), health care professionals, the clergy, God, oneself, and even the person who died. This need to blame, often driven by an intense anger, can cause severe disturbances in familial and social relationships. Blame only further fragments and isolates the survivors.

Survivors often grapple with guilt and confusion over their anger toward the deceased and the role that mental illness may have played in their loved one's demise. The uncertainty over why the deceased completed suicide can be perceived as a willful rejection, abandonment, and act of betrayal to the survivor. This may contribute to intense feelings of anger ("How could they do this to me?") and tremendous feelings of low self-worth ("I wasn't good enough to live for").

Additionally, feelings of anger at the deceased are often considered taboo by survivors, so appropriate anger can be coupled with guilt, which leads to confusion (Worden, 2009). Feelings of anger toward the deceased are often the most difficult feelings for survivors to reach or become aware of, which sometimes provoke a parallel process of idealizing the deceased (Wertheimer, 2001).

Sometimes for the survivor, an existential crisis may develop in the aftermath of a suicide. This kind of crisis can lead the survivors to question the very foundations of their way of life and whether their life has any meaning, purpose, or value. It can also result in a sense of being alone in the world and contribute to even further isolation. Survivors can also find additional pain or solace around their religion and the suicide death of a loved one. Certain religious stigma associated with sin and suicide can further isolate survivors in their grief, limit their support systems, and leave them hyperfocused on the perception that their loved one may be doomed to an eternal life in hell (Early, 1992). Conversely, some survivors find support within their religious communities and develop an even stronger resolve in their new or strengthened faith and spirituality.

The feeling of relief may come as a surprise to some suicide loss survivors, which may be helpful or hurtful in their healing process as they try to make meaning of the death. Families in which there has been a long disruption in functioning due to a member's mental illness, addiction, self-destructiveness, and suicidality may afterward feel a certain sense of relief once the disruption to the family system is over. These families may have already experienced an emotional distance and sense of separation from this person, who they watched slowly "die" over time. The relief may stem from the survivor's prolonged agony and helplessness as bearing witness to a loved one's suffering. This may result in feelings of relief that both their sufferings have ended. This type of anticipatory grief and sense of relief is not so different from feelings experienced by families bereaved by cancer, dementia, or other long-term illnesses (Clark, 2001). The following case scenario demonstrates a Navy spouse's sense of helplessness at bearing witness to her husband's emotional suffering and yet also highlights the type of psychological relief that she experienced from her husband's eventual self-destruction.

> He was a man who always had the angel on one shoulder and the devil on another. He struggled with a very dark past—abusive parents, domestic violence, sexual trauma, addiction in the family. He tried to run from that and genuinely tried to seek a better life. He thought the military would help him form an identity, make friends, give him purpose, start anew. And it did, but it also did not erase the memories of his past and further complicated and stigmatized his mental health concerns he needed to address. Living with him was like living with two different people and at a point in our marriage I came to realize he was a time bomb waiting to explode, but I loved him (not always his behavior) and practicing "tough love" was one of the hardest things in my life I ever had to do. Until you have lived with someone who is mentally ill and works in a system that punishes help seeking you will never understand what it is like to lose someone who is chronically self-destructive. It is heartbreaking, but at times I am relieved to know that he and we are at peace.
>
> Surviving Spouse of a U.S. Navy Chief, Norfolk, Virginia, died by asphyxiation at 36 years old, February 2006

Suicide loss survivors tend to be highly stigmatized (Feigelman et al., 2009). Both real and perceived feelings of stigma and shame seriously interfere with the survivor's ability to heal from the emotional pain associated with suicide and can contribute to problems in the mourning process. Informal social disapproval, blame, beliefs/morals/values with regard to suicide—on top of lack of understanding and failed attempts to gain empathy from expected others—combine to create greater grief difficulties for suicide loss survivors (Jordan, 2008). Fear of this stigmatization and shame associated with the suicide may influence survivors to keep the death by suicide a secret. This veil of secrecy can be a heavy burden for survivors to carry and may impact their ability to heal. It can also cause great tension and stress within families (Jordan & McIntosh, 2010).

Finally, stigmatizing reactions only add to the burdens suicide survivors already bear. Many individuals do not know how to respond to a suicide death nor understand how to support those affected. Survivors may often have to educate people in their social networks on how to interact and support them in their grief (Feigelman et al., 2009). The quality, measure, and type of social supports survivors receive are instrumental in buffering distress. When supportive responses are missing, this can compound a survivor's difficulties with grieving. Survivors must navigate a new path, discovering which relationships and support networks are helpful and which are toxic. And if no helpful relationships exist, survivors are often left alone in a vacuum of self-blame, isolation, and shame. This can contribute to what Joiner (2005) calls a sense of "thwarted belongingness" and "perceived burdensomeness," which are considered risk factors for suicide. Aguirre and Slater (2010) contend that trained senior peer survivors, who have shared the tragedy of suicide, can foster a sense of belonging and begin to help increase self-efficacy to those newly bereaved survivors through active postvention outreach programs. Creating a sense of belongingness can act as a protective factor in suicide prevention (Aguirre & Slater, 2010) and serve as a mechanism to link new survivors with suicide support services. With a heightened risk of suffering from PTS/PTSD, complicated grief, familial stress, depression, and suicidal thinking, peer-support postvention can act as critical short-term and long-term preventative and healing services for suicide loss survivors.

SURVIVORS OF A MILITARY SUICIDE LOSS AND THE ASSOCIATED COMPLEXITIES

In the aftermath of a military suicide, as is true with any suicide, it is the survivors who are left to cope with the haunting veil of death by suicide. Coupled with complex factors surrounding a death in the U.S. Armed Services, in addition to the emotional distress and feelings of guilt that generally consume survivors following a suicide, other distinctive issues are often faced by military suicide loss survivors. These multiple layers of compounding complexities, as well as the exposure to the dual burden of grief and trauma, may predispose survivors to a prolonged, distressing, and complicated grief process as well as contribute to enduring impairments in their physical, psychological, social, and spiritual health.

Based on these factors associated with a death in the U.S. Armed Services and distinctive issues faced by suicide loss survivors—which are discussed later in this chapter—this population should be considered at a high risk for the development of PTSD, depression, anxiety-related disorders, complicated grief, and suicide (Harrington-LaMorie & Ruocco, 2010). To help understand some of the prominent factors and differences affecting military suicide loss survivors, several areas need explication. The observations of associated issues and complexities surrounding a military death and further, a military suicide loss, have yet to be fully noted in the literature. Therefore, these observations are based on the clinical experience of the author, who has worked closely with this population.

The death of a loved one in the U.S. Armed Services involves complexities unlike those typically experienced in the civilian world (Carroll, 2001; Steen & Asaro, 2006), leading to a potentially prolonged, distressing, and complicated grief process for many survivors.

Acutely grief-stricken and often traumatized survivors—especially if they are the primary next of kin (PNOK), secondary next of kin (SNOK), and/or person authorized to direct disposition (PADD)—are instantly confronted with the task of making difficult decisions in the face of complex loss and trauma. They must navigate through the intricate bureaucratic process involved with the disposition of the remains of a service member; deal with personal effects of the service member; and attend to a substantial amount of paperwork associated with entitlements for survivor benefits. These tasks often involve multiple systems within the larger macro systems of the Department of Defense (DoD) and Department of Veterans Affairs (VA).

Interpersonally, survivors are coping with their own response to the service member's death. Often, they must negotiate a roller coaster of emotions and complex factors within the context of multiple, intrapersonal, familial, military, and organizational interactions. The aftermath of a military death does not exist in a vacuum, nor does the survivor. The death of a loved one in the U.S. military also confronts surviving family members with a coexisting series of crises as well as primary and secondary losses. This is especially relevant for dependent spouses and children who not only lose a family member, but a way of life. The social changes that death may bring to the survivor may come very unexpectedly (Harrington-LaMorie & Ruocco, 2010). Factors surrounding a death in the U.S. military that may compound the loss experience and predispose survivors to complications in their grief process will be elaborated next.

CIRCUMSTANCES OF THE DEATH AND CONDITION OF BODILY REMAINS

The manner in which someone dies can have a deeply profound and enduring impact on survivors. Since the majority of deaths in the U.S. Armed Services are sudden and/or violent in nature, the psychological and emotional impact of violent death to the survivor is a synergistic experience of both grief and trauma (Neria & Litz, 2004). Bereavement following death by sudden and/or violent means—such as accident, suicide, or homicide—increases the survivor's risk for complications in grieving and challenges their fundamental beliefs about themselves and the world in which they live (Currier, Holland, Coleman, & Neimeyer, 2007; Doka, 1996; Rynearson, 2006; Worden, 2009).

With military deaths, bodily remains may be fragmented, retrieved bit by bit, never found, or due to circumstance, not viewable. If not viewable or not received by the survivor, this can further complicate the survivor's grief as the survivor can deny or delay the reality of the death. Recent evidence suggests that there may be benefits to being allowed to view a loved one's body after a sudden death (Chapple & Ziebland, 2010). The ability for the survivor to get up close to the deceased affords them the opportunity to orient themselves to the reality of the death and recognize the loss. When bodily remains are not viewable, the survivor is robbed of this opportunity.

Clearly, the circumstance of a service member's death has a long-term impact on a survivor's grief and bereavement experience. How a service member dies can bring with it a community of support from others who honor their loss throughout the years at memorial events or an intense sense of disenfranchisement from the micro to the macro level, which may be real or perceived as a result of a death that is considered less than honorable. As is discussed shortly, military suicides may also be perceived as dishonorable deaths.

GEOGRAPHY OF THE DEATH/GEOGRAPHY OF THE SURVIVOR

The location of the service member's death can play an important role as to the impact and effect it has on the survivor/s. Service members die in varied conditions and in varied parts of the world. Many die in the United States, close to their base/post, or close to home, while others die in foreign lands, sometimes never to be found. One exceptional challenge faced by military families is that service members spend an extraordinary amount of time away from their families, both primary and extended families, due to training, deployments, and other operational demands.

When the death occurs overseas or when the family is geographically separated, for married service members, spouses and children are often living on or around the base/post from which their service member was deployed. They may need to rely on the military community as their primary support system, as most live far away from their families of origin (with the exception of some National Guard service members and Reserve members). The service member was also most likely far away from his or her parents, siblings, family, and friends for extended periods of time. Last words and last moments spent together may have been few and far between. Otherwise known as "deployment-delayed" grief, survivors can employ high levels of defense mechanisms to cope and create a subconscious denial that their loved one has died, and instead at some level of consciousness the survivors think they are still "away" on deployment even if they have been informed of the death by the military. The reality often hits the survivor, with acute-grief reactions, when the unit returns and the service member is not with his or her unit. This delay can often interfere with survivor's ability to accept the reality of their loss and impede their healing (Steen & Asaro, 2006).

AGE OF DECEDENTS/AGE OF SURVIVORS

The majority of service member deaths involve those between the ages of 18 and 40 (Harrington-LaMorie & Ruocco, 2010). Their survivors are often young adults themselves, including young adult spouses/significant others, parents, siblings, and other family and friends. Their surviving children can range from being young adults to adolescents to younger children, some yet to be born.

The unexpected, tragic, and untimely death of a young adult places the survivor in a position that is out of sync with their developmental phase. Young adult loss presents unique challenges to survivors. Various factors contributing to this are: (a) a lack of similar others who are experiencing the same loss, (b) an inexperience with previous deaths, especially that of a spouse or child at a young age, and (c) a limited peer group who can serve as role models to demonstrate how to cope and live with such a traumatic and untimely loss (Walter & McCoyd, 2009).

Distinctive problems plague families who experience the loss of a young adult. Children may need to be raised by single parents or custodians, family roles may change, identity within the family may change and familial developmental tasks are challenged as they grieve this loss through the life span (Walter & McCoyd, 2009). The grief and loss consequent to the death of a young adult can involve grieving the past, the present, as well as the hopes and dreams of a future.

COMMITMENT TO SERVICE

Today's U.S. military is an all-volunteer force of men and women who are making the choice to enter into the armed services during a time of war. There are multiple reasons why individuals join the military. A predominant theme among many is a driving force to commit themselves and their skills to a purpose-driven, mission-oriented life in protection, support, and defense of the United States.

The reasons for the service member's commitment to serve may present as an additional risk factor for how survivors cope with grief, or they may serve as a protective factor. The survivor's viewpoint of the service member's military career is an essential determining factor. For example, a surviving mother may have been very supportive of her son or daughter's decision to join the military, or the mother might have been completely and diametrically opposed to it. In addition, the survivor's grief process can also be impacted by the way in which a survivor views the military's potential responsibility for the service member's death and how the decedent and the survivor have been treated by the military in the aftermath of the loss.

DEATH NOTIFICATION

For many survivors, especially the next of kin, their lives are indelibly altered by a knock at the door. The U.S. military formally notifies the primary and secondary next of kin that their service member has died by an official death notification process. The military usually arrives by an official government vehicle, wearing sharply cleaned and decorated uniforms and come in pairs—a "notifier" and a chaplain. For each service branch, there are differences with the death notification process. For example, the Army assigns a Casualty Notification Officer (CNO) who notifies the family with a chaplain. They strictly provide notification and are separate individuals from the Casualty Affairs Officer. In the Navy and Marine Corps, the Casualty Assistance Call Officer (CACO) provides both notification and casualty assistance. Casualty personnel are equal or higher rank than the deceased. For example, in the Army the service member must be an E7 or above to serve as a CNO or CAO.

Receiving and delivering this news is painful and difficult for both the survivor and notification team. However, even with the best training and sensitivity, notifying a family that a service member has suddenly died can be a "primary" traumatic event. When the death is sudden, traumatic, and/or violent, the shock of the news can overwhelm the internal resources of the survivor, triggering a variety of individual responses.

The Casualty Officer

The military assigns a casualty officer to be the point of contact for the PNOK for weeks or months after the death. The core duties and responsibilities for casualty officers in each branch is essentially the same. They are there to meet the immediate needs of the next of kin; assist the family with the return home of the service member's remains; make funeral and interment arrangements; help the family handle the media; navigate the bureaucratic process; educate the family about benefit entitlements; process benefits claims; and assist with applying for requests for investigation reports (Steen & Asaro, 2006). Once these requests or benefits/entitlements are submitted and the last benefit is claimed, the job of the casualty officer is over.

The casualty officer is assigned to a family for guidance and support during one of the most difficult and challenging times of their lives. Many military widows, who are far away from their families of origin and without support, rely heavily on their casualty officers for practical and emotional support. The officers assist the primary next of kin in making complex, major life decisions during a time of intense trauma, grief, and confusion. When the officers' role and job is over, sometimes the survivor may experience this as an additional loss and an undeniable finality.

THE IMMEDIATE IMPACT TO SURVIVORS

The practical and emotional demands on the individual survivor and family who are suddenly notified of a service member's death are extraordinary. From the moment the casualty officer walks in the door, the complex decisions regarding the service member's death begin.

Designated survivors must often deal with the transfer of bodily remains (this can have another layer of distress if the service member dies overseas or far away from home); funerals/memorials/burials (including the military rites and rituals that accompany these); and media involvement (military deaths are often deaths of high public interest).

When dealing with young children regarding the death of a parent, "what to tell the children" is a struggle for the surviving parent or guardian/s. Because of the circumstances of the death, the condition or lack of bodily remains and parent's own coping skills, some parents may delay relating detailed information to their children and may need assistance in the next few days, weeks, months, or years after the death. This problem is illustrated in the following quote:

> How do you tell an 8-year-old and a 10-year-old that their dad has made it safely back from Iraq and has taken his own life?
>
> Surviving Spouse of Major, USMC, AH-1W Super Cobra gunship pilot, died by suicide at 40 years of age

If the circumstance of the death involves an unattended body (e.g., a soldier's dead body is found in the house and appears to be a suicide) or the cause of death warrants further examination, survivors are also subjected to the burden of a death investigation, which involves more layers of military bureaucracy that the family has to contend with. Death investigations can be prolonged (extended over a year or more), chronically retraumatizing to the survivor and performed by criminal investigators who may not often work in tandem with victim assistance providers. Part of the death investigation process is also to determine whether the service member died in the line of duty, and line of duty determinations affect benefits and entitlements to survivors.

Immediate complex, life-altering decisions need to be made within hours, days, and short weeks following a service member's death. Grief experts suggest that you refrain from making any life-altering decisions within the first 6 months after the death of a loved one or significant relationship (Creagan, 2009). The military is beginning to recognize this best practice suggestion, but often survivors, especially spouses, are faced with relatively immediate, life-altering decisions on where to move, financial considerations/monetary benefits, handling personal effects and household goods and schooling for children all within the first 3 to 12 months after a service member has died, depending on where they are stationed.

SECONDARY AND MULTIPLE LOSSES

The death of a loved one in active duty military service confronts the family member with a series of other types of losses, thus the term *secondary losses*. These losses include not only the actual death (or the primary loss), but also a loss of their way of life and identity associated with this life (e.g., military spouse, military mom, military child), loss of their housing (if on base/post), and loss of their greater military community. For spouses and children, it is an "involuntary transition" from military family to civilian family life. These often sudden, multiple, and compounding losses may bring with them a profound sense of isolation, loneliness, and disenfranchisement for the surviving family.

ADDITIONAL CHALLENGES FACING MILITARY SUICIDE LOSS SURVIVORS

As previously mentioned, for the survivor of a military suicide death, a profound sense of isolation, loneliness, and disfranchisement is often experienced in the immediate aftermath of the death. Although the military has recently made efforts to confront institutional policies surrounding suicide, there is still stigma attached to suicide that is both real and perceived. In addition to the complexities faced by survivors of a military death, suicide loss survivors must contend with additional challenges.

A "Dishonorable" Death: Shame and Stigma

Similar to the culture of police departments, who "subscribe to a myth of indestructibility," (Violanti, 1995, p. 2), military suicide may be viewed as a disgrace to the victim and to the profession. In addition to the prevailing societal stigma associated with a death by suicide, military suicides are often perceived as "dishonorable deaths." Supported by military institutional policies, suicide deaths may be handled inequitably different in terms of memorials, condolences, recognition of service, death investigations, finances, pension rights, and entitlements. Although the military has recently begun to make institutional changes regarding these policies, these stigmatizing differences may exacerbate the myriad feelings unleashed in the aftermath of a suicide. These feelings include shame, guilt, blame, self-reproach, rejection, abandonment, anger, powerlessness, vulnerability, and confusion. Thus, the stigma heightens the family survivors' distress, isolates them in their grief, and complicates their struggle to comprehend a self-inflicted death (Jordan, 2001).

Social support for survivors may be limited due to the perception of a suicide death in the military as less than honorable or dishonorable. Perceived feelings of shame on behalf of survivors may cause them to self-isolate. Existing cultural stigma may bring with it withdrawal of military community support. Or, like many survivors of a suicide loss in Western civilian society, military survivors often face "a wall of silence" by family, friends, and the community (Feigelman et al., 2009). Family relationships may be strained or broken in the aftermath of suicide, sometimes due to anger and blame-seeking behaviors. Friends, neighbors, and coworkers may naively struggle with how to be supportive, feel uncomfortable with what to say, or have a limited capacity to offer comfort when a death is by suicide. Communally and individually, there are also those who willfully withdraw support as an act of disapproval of this dishonorable type of death.

In addition to immediate family and friends, another group of survivors who are often overlooked and suffer in the wake of a service member's suicide are their military peers. Much like police units, where strong familial bonds may be created among service members, military suicides can leave enduring emotional hardship and critically impact surviving peers. Institutional policies and cultural attitudes further perpetuate the stigma surrounding suicide and deter help-seeking behavior in the military. Additionally, due to a lack of access to effective postvention services, military peer survivors can be at risk for heightened distress, suicide, and the contagion effect. The theory of the contagion effect is that one suicide, if not treated through postvention, can spread like a virus and trigger other suicides in the unit (Loo, 1986; Violanti, 1995).

Empirical evidence suggests that stigmatization with an ensuing lack of social support by expected others is a detrimental influence in the healing process of suicide survivors and often intensifies grief difficulties and leaves them at risk for depression and suicide (Feigelman et al., 2009). Research also suggests that survivors who experience greater stigma and complications in their grief will benefit from increased participation in peer support systems (Feigelman et al., 2009).

The Violence of the Death

Whether in a war zone, on a ship at sea, in a basic training camp or at home, suicide deaths in the military can happen anywhere. Use of firearms and asphyxiation are the two most common current methods of self-inflicted death among military service members (Kang & Bullman, 2008).

Often, survivors are exposed to the trauma of finding their loved ones' bodies and/or witnessing the death. These deaths can be violent and can leave indications of trauma, mutilation, or result in disfigurement to the body. Families are often covictimized as they become witnesses to the self-inflicted violent death of a family member or are exposed to finding their bodies. Grief and trauma reactions after a violent suicide, especially for those who find the person, can be more intense and complicated. The horror and shock on discovering the victim can be overwhelming and imprint a permanent image that can remain with the survivor, accompanied by flashbacks, nightmares, and intrusive thoughts. Those who witness the suicide or find the body are more likely to develop symptoms of acute traumatic stress, PTSD, and complications in their grief (Jordan, 2008). The following quote alludes to the family's horror of finding a loved one's body following an act of suicide:

> The kids and I had a great day at Disneyland. When we returned home that evening, we opened up the garage door and found my husband hanging from the ceiling. My daughters actually saw their father first. I couldn't protect them from that.
>
> Surviving Spouse of U.S. Marine Gunnery Sergeant,
> died by suicide at 39 years old

Media

Military deaths are often highly publicized in the media, and families are frequently further victimized, as the circumstances of their service member's death is quickly thrust into public view and taking away their choice to disclose the death as a suicide (Steen & Asaro, 2006). Thus, survivors' lives and the life and death of their service member become fair game for public scrutiny and consumption.

The media can be an intrusive, unwelcomed, and uninvited guest during an extremely traumatizing time for survivors. From the death scene, to the funeral and beyond, the media may not exercise objectivity or sensitivity while attempting to cover a story about military suicide. Survivors may not be ready or willing to share their stories, and may be directly confronted by the media at a time of immense vulnerability and pain. Media coverage of a military service member's suicide can be exploitative and sensationalistic, further contributing to a survivor's sense of stigmatization and shame. Thus, regardless of whether military suicide loss survivors are willing to expose themselves, they will need help in learning how to handle the attention and how and what to share with the public.

Memorials and Recognitions

As of this moment, the U.S. military has not instituted any policies on how units or commands should memorialize service members who die by suicide, especially those who die by suicide on the battlefield. Memorial services are handled on a case-by-case basis and by command directives.

The military does make distinctions between suicides that are service-connected to combat and/or occur in a combat zone. The families of those who die in a war zone, under honorable circumstances (e.g., accident, KIA, suicide), receive letters of condolence from the U.S. president. Interestingly, two thirds of military suicides occur outside of a war-zone (Defense Health Board (DHB), 2010). Units or commands may choose to inscribe the names of the suicide fallen on their unit war memorials; however, many do not include them. Recent controversy has been provoked among some commanders in the U.S. Army who contend that suicide is dishonorable, while the Vice Chief of Staff of the U.S. Army has ordered that memorial services for battlefield suicides should be the same as any battlefield death (*Washington Post*, 2010).

This type of nonrecognition of service adds to the stigmatization that is felt by survivors, and it is referred to as going from "hero to zero." The perpetuation of the reinforcement of suicide in the military as being a dishonorable death reaches far beyond the U.S. Armed Services. State, local, and federal war memorials may not list combat-related suicides. Organizational or community programs for veterans for families of fallen service members may not include outreach to military suicide loss survivors. Additionally, veterans or military-related membership organizations may not offer membership privileges to military suicide loss survivors. Recognition pins or other medallions of recognition may not be provided to family survivors of military suicide. Survivors must be confronted on a yearly basis with the effects of this dishonorable death stigmatization with the passing of each U.S. national holiday which honors veterans, service members, and fallen service members.

Line of Duty and Death Investigations

A Line of Duty (LOD) determination is an administrative tool used by the military commanders to determine a service member's duty status at the time of injury, illness, disability, or death. On the basis of the LOD determination, the service member may be entitled to benefits administered by their service branch or exposed to liabilities. The key link is between the injury, illness, disability, or death and the service member's duty status.

One way to determine this link is through the death investigation process. Suicides in the military typically involve an extensive investigation; to determine and confirm the cause of death and to identify the circumstances, methods, and contributing factors. These investigations are performed by agents of the designated criminal investigative divisions of each of the military service branches. Some are active duty military personnel, and some are civilian. Criminal investigators often treat the scene and those involved as part of a criminal process. Investigators are not known to work in tandem with victim assistance providers, who are skilled in working with victims of trauma.

Death investigations can take months or years to complete. The investigations can involve the use of crime scene photos; crime scene descriptions; extensive interviews with those involved or affected; search and/or seizure of personal effects and property; seizure of personnel effects and property; review of service records; autopsy photos; multiple interviews with survivors over extended periods of time; and other chronically invasive measures. Families are often subjected to continually having to reopen the wound for the death investigation process as they struggle to make sense of their own grief and loss in the aftermath of their service member's suicide.

Family members may experience feelings of intense anxiety centered on waiting for the final report and the outcome of the death investigation that then assists the command in determining the LOD. If the death is not considered to be LOD, then benefits may be negatively affected, causing hardship.

Pensions/Insurance/Entitlements

Suicide deaths in the line of duty receive the same burial rites as all military deaths. Pensions and entitlements are affected when deaths are deemed as a willful act of misconduct. Designated survivors may not receive the service member's survivor benefit plan, dependent's indemnity compensation, or other entitlements. However, service members' group life insurance (SGLI) is payable to the designated beneficiary, regardless of the circumstance of death, with some exclusions. When it comes to private life insurance, policies are often subject to the 2-year suicide clause, which will not pay out a life insurance premium to designated beneficiaries if the policyholder dies by suicide in the first 2 years of obtaining the policy.

For service members who die by a combat-connected suicide death, families often struggle to find information and receive extra entitlements and tax benefits on the local, state, and federal level designated specifically for war-related deaths.

Mental Illness/Help-Seeking/Blame

The military represents a highly cohesive subculture whose members tend to "take care of their own" (Hall, 2008). "The whole culture of the military is that you don't talk about feelings or emotions" (Marshall, 2006, p. 32). Given a culture whose norm is to resist seeking mental health help, coupled with research that suggests that 90% of people who die by suicide meet the criteria for a psychiatric disorder (Robins, 1981), this can be a fatal combination.

There still exists a stigma both within the institution of the military and within the culture of the military regarding help seeking and mental health care. In a dominant culture whose ethos revolves around stoicism and invincibility, there are both real and perceived barriers to seeking help with personal problems (Hall, 2008). In a culture that promotes strength, service members often struggle with identifying and seeking help for their psychological, emotional, practical, and personal problems. Concerns center on being perceived as weak, losing the confidence of others, and being treated differently, resulting in a direct correlation to one's ability to perform, affecting their reputation and career (Hall, 2008).

A big concern for service members and their families is whether seeking help for mental health related issues will be documented on a service member's record and threaten their career and/or ability to be promoted (Hall, 2008). Many times service members and their families will subvert the system and seek care outside of the military. Families also fear that disclosing concerns about their service member to their command may come with reprisal as well as create a betrayal of trust between the service member and their family. In some cases, service members and their families have sought help within the system and have been challenged with multiple barriers that impede care.

Even with the increased efforts in suicide prevention by the DoD, many military families suffer in silence, fearful of the stigma of mental illness and seeking help (Hall, 2008). The stigma of mental illness, fear of help seeking, frustration with barriers to care, and feelings of helplessness are factors that contribute to families withdrawing from support systems prior to the suicide (Harrington-LaMorie & Ruocco, 2010). The added stigmatization of a completed suicide can further isolate survivors, cutting them off from support systems, both in the military and civilian communities. This can contribute to a severe interference of a healthy grieving process, which can lead to complications in grief and add to the risk for biopsychosocial problems, including a higher risk for suicide.

In the aftermath of suicide, familial disturbances can be created or exacerbated over feelings of anger and the need to ascribe blame. Suicides can leave a division in families, with members spinning off from one another with their own anger, guilt, blame, and sorrow (Harrington-LaMorie & Ruocco, 2010). In the aftermath of a suicide death in the military, a common observance of survivors, friends, and extended family is the displacement of real and perceived anger and blame (Harrington-LaMorie & Ruocco, 2010). Finding someone to blame enables survivors to direct anger toward the person who died (anger they may feel is inappropriate to directly address to someone else). Blame helps survivors feel a sense of control, instead of searching for answers that may never be answered. The media, the military, and the community also can contribute to the circle of blame that gets created in the aftermath of a military suicide.

Survivors are often blamed by others for the suicide and frequently perceive that others blame them, even if the others do not (Cerel et al., 2008). Often survivors are not free to mourn because they encounter reactions from others who assign blame to the deceased for causing the survivor's suffering.

These additional challenges and risk factors faced by military suicide loss survivors may result in an unwillingness to gain social support and involve others in the grief process. This will reduce the likelihood that survivors will seek help (McIntosh, 1993). It is estimated that only one in four suicide survivors seek help (Aguirre & Slater, 2010). However, when survivors do seek help, individual counseling coupled with peer-facilitated groups are considered the preferred model of treatment (B. Feigelman & Feigelman, 2008; Jordan, 2008).

Case Vignette: Rob

Rob is a 62-year-old father of five whose 25-year-old son, Ted, an OIF/OEF combat veteran and sergeant in the U.S. Marine Corps took his life by a public, self-inflicted gunshot wound to the head at Camp LeJuene, North Carolina. Ted enlisted in the Marine Corps at 19 years of age. His father Rob had served in combat in Vietnam, and his grandfather served in World War II; making Ted, the third-generation U.S. Marine in his family—himself, his father, and his paternal grandfather.

Ted had served in a reconnaissance unit in the Marine Corps, which is considered a Special Forces Unit and had completed two combat tours in both Iraq and Afghanistan. During each of these deployments, Ted had been exposed to multiple blasts. On returning from his last tour in Afghanistan, he began to exhibit symptoms of traumatic brain injury (TBI) and posttraumatic stress disorder (PTSD). He was being treated as an outpatient and allowed to continue working with his unit, however, as his symptoms began to worsen, his father pleaded with him to seek inpatient care. On a spring afternoon, after an ensuing argument with his spouse, Ted brought himself to the base medical clinic. He told the nurses on duty he could no longer deal with the pain of the "confusing and jumbling" emotions running through his mind. After consultation, the medical team was going to admit him for inpatient care, but left him alone in the consultation room to begin the admission process. A few moments later Ted fled the clinic and was chased by several Marines who followed him to his truck. Before they could catch up to him, Ted reached inside his truck and pulled out a personal pistol—waving it at them. He fled the scene in his truck and was chased by the military police (MP), who stopped him on base. In front of other cars and bystanders they drew their weapons on him and asked him to step out of the truck. According to a bystander who was in her car stopped next to him, Ted sat in the truck for a while as the MPs continued to yell for him to step out of his truck. He sat there in silence, looking up and down. She said right before he stepped out of his truck his eyes changed. Finally when Ted stepped out, he had his pistol in his hand, did an immediate about-face, placed the pistol to his head, and fatally shot himself in front of everyone.

His father was driving through the mountains of Tennessee when he received the life-changing call that no parent ever wants to receive. His youngest of five children had died and he had died by suicide. Rob was in an immediate state of disbelief. He yelled at the Casualty Assistance Call Officer (CACO) on the phone stating that he must be mistaken! His son was in the hospital receiving treatment for his TBI and PTSD. When the CACO repeated that he was not and that he had killed himself, Rob pulled over. He was numb, confused, and conflicted as he knew he was a father and needed to get home to his family to take care of them. When Rob got home, he immediately compartmentalized his feelings of profound grief to assume his roles and responsibilities as head of the family. He had been designated by his son as the caretaker of all his funeral arrangements and made sure that everything was well taken care of—including all the rites and rituals that accompany a military funeral. Rob was particularly hyperfocused on making sure that his son's uniform, including his ribbons and medals, were perfect. The care and compassion he received from the Marine CACO, the Marines, and the casualty personnel was comforting in the midst of all the shock and trauma that he and his family were feeling. Rob struggled with his own feelings of shame that his son's death may be one under less than honorable circumstances; however, he never perceived any of these feelings or attitudes from his CACO or the Marines that served and cared for his son.

Ted was buried in Arlington National Cemetery almost 3 months after his death. From the time of his death to his funeral and burial, Rob had difficulty feeling any emotions. The main priorities of taking care of his son's personal affairs, worrying about his other children and spouse, and shifting into the role of detective to try and piece together the events that led up to his son's suicide allowed Rob to compartmentalize his role—feeding his ability to sustain feelings of shock and numbness. After Ted was buried, the support of the military and community lessened, and most of the practical matters associated with

Ted's death were attended to, Rob began feeling a roller coaster of emotions on a daily basis. It was around the fifth or sixth month after Ted's death when Rob "felt the iceberg of his numbness thaw" and the waves of emotions come crashing down. He struggled to keep a sense of normalcy, returning back to work and back to old routines. His wife was dealing with her grief in her own way—one very different than his and this was causing many problems with their communication and relationship. Rob was spending less time with friends. He was afraid of his lack of control over his emotions and feared the waves of mini "emotional tsunamis." Crying out of the blue, uncontrollably, with no warning, at any time of the day was something he had never experienced before. This caused him great anxiety and he began to isolate himself—which was very painful to him, as he was a social person by nature. Being a retired police officer from Philadelphia, Rob had been through many "on-scene" deaths and investigations, even those of suicides of fellow policemen. He thought he had seen it all and was capable of handling death. He became very hard on himself and had fits of anger and rage. This pushed him even further away from his friends and family. Rob had difficulty sleeping and often had intrusive thoughts both at night and during the day. The image of his son taking his own life and what he could have done to prevent that moment played over and over again in his mind.

Rob blamed himself for encouraging Ted to enlist in the Marine Corps, feeling that if his son had he never joined the Corps he would have never gotten TBI and PTSD and taken his own life. He blamed himself for giving Ted the gun that was a family heirloom and a gift for his 25th birthday. Rob believed that if he had never had the gun, Ted wouldn't have had the means to kill himself. Rob blamed himself for not protecting Ted. He promised Ted when he deployed to both Iraq and Afghanistan that if anything ever happened to him, Rob would find him and take him home. Rob felt he let Ted down—something did happen to Ted, except it was an invisible wound that was not easy to see. Rob felt that he should have been there to rescue Ted. That was his promise. Rob felt guilty for not speaking with Ted on the day of his death, as he was on a business trip and thought he was getting help. Rob laid awake at night thinking, "if only," and "why?"

Rob is having trouble sleeping, having intrusive nightmares, experiencing a roller coaster of emotions on a daily (if not minute-by-minute) basis and has become obsessed with figuring out the piece of the puzzles as to "why" his son took his own life that day. He has isolated himself from his friends and family. His work performance is suffering. Although he is still performing, it is at a minimal level. He lacks any motivation. Rob has lost weight and has no desire to engage in any activities. Most days he comes from home from work and either falls asleep at 6:30 in the evening, or can't fall asleep and stays awake the whole night, frantically cleaning the house. Because Rob perceives that his wife doesn't want to talk about Ted's death, he feels he has no one close to the situation to talk to about his son and his suicide. Rob has reached a point where he feels that the pain of what he is going through is intolerable and has decided to seek counseling. He is referred by his insurance company to a social worker in the community who is part of a group private practice.

Case Vignette Discussion

Rob can be any survivor who has lost a loved one to suicide in the military. Whether he walks through your door for his first mental health counseling session, or you meet him as part of a suicide loss group or part of a community program, there are a few key issues clinicians need to keep in mind when working with suicide loss survivors.

First, it is important to understand why suicide loss survivors seek counseling services. When survivors seek mental health services they often do so on their own or through the encouragement of family or friends. They may be seeking help for several reasons, such as survivors often come to a point where they are unable to tolerate the mental anguish and pain they are living with each day; they believe getting help is what they are "supposed to" do; important family or close relationships begin to become severely impacted; their friends encourage them to; and/or they just recognize that they need support.

Because it may take several months or more for military suicide loss survivors to deal with the practical matters of a service member's death (including burial and paperwork), along with the emotional numbness and shock that may accompany a sudden, unexpected death, when survivors come to counseling they might have a feeling that they should be "doing better by now." The belief that grief has a certain timeline and ought to be "over" after a certain period of time is common in Western society. Survivors may hold that belief themselves but they may also be receiving that message from those in their social network that something is "not normal" about them and their grieving process. However, what may appear abnormal to the outsider or even to the survivor is actually a "normal" grief process. Grief after suicide can be complex, complicated, prolonged, and difficult to bear. Assessing the client's bereavement is the job of the clinician, and how these complications impact the client's emotional, psychological, physical, and spiritual health should also be considered.

Jordan (2008) suggests that practitioners should resist the urge to try and "fix" a survivor's grief, but rather adapt to an "expert companion" model with survivors who often may take years, navigating through a lengthy complex bereavement process. Bereavement caregivers should steer away from any model that seeks to quickly "resolve" a survivor's grief, which can truly be a soul-based journey. This can be especially true of suicide grief in which survivors live and struggle in the face of existing guilt, abandonment, shame, and responsibility. The long-term healing process for survivors is often underscored.

Wolfet (2006, 2009) has proposed the grief companioning model, which postulates that companioning the bereaved is not about fixing or resolving their grief. Instead, it is about being totally present for those who are grieving, even so far as being a temporary guardian of their soul. The caregiver creates a safe place to embrace another's profound loss. As being a companion, caregivers observe and learn, becoming familiar with the survivor's story, their experiences, and their needs. Sometimes this involves companioning the survivor on their story many, many times, for them to make sense of their loss as they define and redefine their needs. Wolfelt believes that to "bear witness" is the essence of true companioning. Listening to the stories of those who have been bereaved by suicide is in itself healing. Creating and telling stories helps humans to order our experience, to make meaning, as well as to make community. It also allows the professional companioning practitioner the opportunity to provide helpful support along points of the journey as they assess and reassess survivor needs along the way.

Wolfelt includes the following 11 principles or tenets set forth for grief companioning:

1. Companioning is about being present to another person's pain; it is not about taking away the pain.
2. Companioning is about going to the wilderness of the soul with another human being; it is not about thinking you are responsible for finding the way out.

3. Companioning is about honoring the spirit; it is not about focusing on the intellect.
4. Companioning is about listening with the heart; it is not about analyzing with the head.
5. Companioning is about bearing witness to the struggles of others; it is not about judging or directing these struggles.
6. Companioning is about walking along side; it is not about leading or being led.
7. Companioning means discovering the gifts of sacred silence; it does not mean filling up every moment with words.
8. Companioning the bereaved is about being still; it is not about frantic movement forward.
9. Companioning is about respecting disorder and confusion; it is not about imposing order and logic.
10. Companioning is about learning from others; it is not about teaching them.
11. Companioning is about curiosity; it is not about expertise.

To learn more in depth about these principles and the grief companioning model you can refer to Wolfelt's two books, *Companioning the Bereaved* (2006) and *The Handbook for Companioning the Mourner* (2009).

Suicide is a difficult situation for anyone to confront—not only for the survivor, but for clinicians as well. Suicide is an intensely emotional subject and clinicians are human beings who may have their own reactions to it. They may have their own personal experience with suicide, or their own professional experiences as a clinician where they may have had a client die by suicide, or someone who made suicide attempts. Clinicians are also humans who may have their feelings and attitudes about the military, military service, and war. It is vital for the practitioner to check in with themselves about their own feelings surrounding the current wars and military service. An examination of one's own attitudes about suicide is essential, including a clinician's viewpoints about the morality of suicide, the causation of the deceased's suicide, and who is responsible for the suicide. Being self-aware about your own feelings and thoughts about suicide as well as your own judgments is part of providing competent care. These thoughts, experiences, and feelings are going to influence how you may react to a survivor who has lost someone to suicide. These issues of countertransference will likely be triggered in working with survivors. Therefore, it is helpful to get consultation and supervision. Moreover, if you are vastly ill-experienced in working with suicide loss survivors, lack the proper supervision, or you cannot overcome these issues, it is imperative that you remember that you should first "do no harm!" This ethical stance suggests that you provide the appropriate referral to another clinician who is better equipped to treat the survivor.

Referrals to grief therapists can be found through the Association for Death Education and Counseling (www.adec.org), the American Association of Suicidology (www.aas.org), and the Tragedy Assistance Program for Survivors (www.taps.org).

Identifying a survivor's view of the military may be very important in their healing. For a dependent family member, such as a spouse, the secondary loss of identity and connection with the military may add to the compounding effect of dealing with multiple losses associated with a service member's death. It can be especially difficult if there are feelings of shame and stigma—real or perceived. For surviving parents who may also be veterans of military service, their view of their own service and the military can become affected—depending on the wide range and variation in circumstances surrounding a suicide death. Gaining a survivor's view of how to repair that impact can assist in their healing. Some survivors find a continued connection to the military or to veteran organizations helpful and healing. Some volunteer their experience and stories in trainings as case examples in suicide prevention efforts with the military. Some want nothing to do with the military. If desired, a clinician can help encourage a healthy amount of connections and boundaries with the military and veteran community.

Psychoeducation is also an important part of the process. Education about suicide, the role of psychiatric disorders, and realistic expectations of the suicide bereavement process can be invaluable for survivors. Education should also include information the family's development of trauma symptoms, complicated grief, family disturbances in the aftermath of suicide, and a survivor's own suicidality. Books on personal accounts from suicide loss survivors and how they have coped in the face of such tragedy or professional books can also be of assistance to survivors in their healing.

Given the emotional pain of suicide loss, survivors of suicide loss are also at increased risk for life-threatening behaviors and suicide. Those at acute risk may talk about killing themselves or are actively seeking access to a method of taking their life. Other indicators for suicide risk are past attempt; overwhelming hopelessness; profound mood changes; extreme anxiety/agitation; reckless and risky behaviors; extreme anger, rage, or revenge seeking; isolation; feelings of being trapped; access to firearms and a history of mental illness; and/or addiction/substance abuse. The National Suicide Prevention Lifeline can be contacted at 1–800–273–TALK or www.suicidepreventionlifeline.org

If a survivor is a parent, spouse, or child of a U.S. Armed Service member, reservist, or National Guard member who died in the line of duty, they are eligible for bereavement counseling through the Department of Veterans Affairs Vet Centers (www.vetcenter.va.gov). Finally, clinicians should be aware of compassion fatigue in working with suicide loss survivors and their need for self-care. If clinicians lose a patient to suicide or family member, they should seek the appropriate support and/or mental health care to help work through the clinician's own reactions to the death. The American Association of Suicidology has specific resources for clinician-survivors at www.suicidology.org

CHAPTER DISCUSSION QUESTIONS

1. What recurrent themes and issues that contribute to the subjective experience of suicide loss differentiate the suicide bereavement process from survivors of other modes of death? Did you see any of these themes in the Case Vignette: Rob?
2. Can you name and describe some complexities associated with a military death. Which ones can you find with Rob's story?
3. What are the additional challenges faced by military suicide loss survivors? Can you see any for Rob?
4. Describe indicators that a suicide loss survivor is at risk for suicide. Would you assess Rob for suicide? Why? How do you assess this risk and what do you do?

5. List some interventions and resources of care for suicide loss survivors.
6. What are your feelings, attitudes, and beliefs about the military, suicide, and suicide loss?
7. As a clinician, what do you do to monitor your own compassion fatigue? How do you practice self-care?

REFERENCES

Aguirre, R. T. P., & Slater, H. (2010). Suicide postvention as suicide prevention: Improvement and expansion in the United States. *Death Studies*, *34*, 529–540.

American Foundation for Suicide Prevention. (2010). *Survivor research: AFSP and NIMH propose research agenda*. Retrieved from http://www.afsp.org/index.cfm?fuseaction=home.viewpage&page_id=2D9DF73E-BB25–0132–3AD7715D74BFF585

Barrett, T. W., & Scott, T. B. (1990). Suicide bereavement and recovery patterns compared with non-suicide bereavement patterns. *Suicide and Life-Threatening Behavior*, *20*, 1–15.

Bonanno, G. A. (2004). Loss, trauma, and human resilience: Have we underestimated the human capacity to thrive after extremely aversive events? *American Psychologist*, *59*(1), 20–28.

Cain, A. C. (Ed.). (1972). *Survivors of suicide*. Springfield, IL: Thomas.

Callahan, J. (2000). Predictors and correlates of bereavement in suicide support group participants. *Suicide & Life-Threatening Behavior*, *30*, 104–124.

Campbell, F. R. (2001). Living and working in the canyon of why. *Proceeding of the Irish Association of Suicidology*, 6, 96–97.

Carroll, B. (2001). How the military family copes with a death. In O. D. Weeks & C. Johnson (Eds.), *When all the friends have gone: A guide for aftercare providers* (pp. 173–183). Amityville, NY: Baywood.

Cerel, J., Jordan, J. R., & Duberstein, P. R. (2008). The impact of suicide on the family. *Crisis*, *29*(1), 38–44.

Chapple, A., & Ziebland, S. (2010). Viewing the body after bereavement due to a traumatic death: Qualitative study in the UK. *British Medical Journal*, *340*, c2032.

Clark, S. (2001). Bereavement after suicide: How far have we come and where do we go from here? *Crisis*, *22*(3), 102–108.

Cleiren, M. (1993). *Bereavement and adaptation: A comparative study of the aftermath of death*. Washington, DC: Hemisphere.

Congressional Quarterly. (2010). *Rising military suicides: The pace is faster than combat deaths in Iraq or Afghanistan*. Retrieved from http://www.congress.org/news/2009/11/25/rising_military_suicides

Creagan, E. T. (2009, December 15). Grief: A Mayo Clinic doctor confronts painful emotions. *Mayo Clinic online*. Retrieved from http://www.mayoclinic.com/health/grief/HQ00771

Currier, J. M., Holland, J. M., Coleman, R. A., & Neimeyer, R. A. (2007). Bereavement following violent death: An assault on life and meaning. In R. Stevenson & G. Cox (Eds.), *Perspectives on violence and violent death* (pp. 175–200). Amityville, NY: Baywood.

Defense Health Board (2010). *Final report of the Department of Defense task force on the prevention of suicide by members of the armed forces*. Retrieved from http://www.health.mil/dhb/downloads/Suicide%20Prevention%20Task%20Force%20report%2008-21-10_V4_RLN.pdf

Demi, A. S. (1984). Social adjustment of widows after a sudden death: Suicide and non-suicide survivors compared. *Death Education*, 8, 91–111.

Department of Defense. (2010). *Military casualty information*. Retrieved from http://siadapp.dmdc.osd.mil/personnel/CASUALTY/castop.htm

Doka, K. (Ed.). (1996). *Living with grief after sudden loss: Suicide, homicide, accident, heart attack, stroke*. New York, NY: Routledge.

Early, K. (1992). *Religion and suicide in the African-American community*. Westport, CT: Greenwood Press.

Farberow, N., Gallagher-Thompson, D., Gilewski, M., & Thompson, L. (1992). The role of social support in the bereavement process of surviving spouses of suicide and natural deaths. *Suicide and Life-Threatening Behavior, 22*, 107–124.

Feigelman, B., & Feigelman, W. (2008). Surviving after suicide loss: The healing potential of suicide survivor support groups. *Illness, Crisis & Loss, 16*(4), 285–304.

Feigelman, W., Gorman, B. S., & Jordan, J. R. (2009). Stigmatization and suicide bereavement. *Death Studies, 33*(7), 591–608.

Grad, O., & Zavasnik, A. (1996). Similarities and differences in the process of bereavement after suicide and after traffic fatalities in Slovenia. *Omega, 33*, 243–251.

Hall, L. K. (2008). *Counseling military families: What mental health professionals need to know*. New York, NY: Routledge.

Harrington-LaMorie, J., & Ruocco, K. (2010). The tragedy assistance program for survivors (TAPS). In J. R. Jordan & J. L. McIntosh (Eds.), *Grief after suicide: Understanding the consequences and caring for the survivors* (pp. 403–411). New York: NY: Routledge.

Holland, J. M., Neimeyer, R. A., Boelen, P. A., & Prigerson, H. G. (2008). The underlying structure of grief: A taxometric investigation of prolonged and normal reactions to loss. *Journal of Psychopathology and Behavioral Assessment, 31*(3), 190–201.

Houck, J. (2007). A comparison of grief reactions in cancer, HIV/AIDS, and suicide bereavement. *Journal of HIV/AIDS & Social Services*, 6, 97–112.

Joiner, T. (2005). *Why people die by suicide*. Cambridge, MA: Harvard University Press.

Jordan, J. R. (2001). Is suicide bereavement different? A reassessment of the literature. *Suicide and Life-Threatening Behavior, 31*(1), 91–102.

Jordan, J. R. (2008). Bereavement after suicide. *PscyhiatricAnnalsOnline.com, 38*(10), 679–685.

Jordan, J. R., & McIntosh, J. L. (2010). Is suicide bereavement different? A framework for rethinking the question. In J. R. Jordan & J. L. McIntosh (Eds.), *Grief after suicide: Understanding the consequences and caring for the survivors* (pp. 403–411). New York, NY: Routledge.

Kaltman, S., & Bonanno, G. A. (2003). Trauma and bereavement: Examining the impact of sudden and violent deaths. *Journal of Anxiety Disorders, 17*, 131–147.

Kang, H. K., & Bullman, T. A. (2008). Risk of suicide among US veterans after returning from the Iraq and Afghanistan war zones. *Journal of the American Medical Association, 300*(6), 652–653.

Kovarsky, R. S. (1989). Loneliness and disturbed grief: A comparison of parents who lost a child to suicide or accidental death. *Archives of Psychiatric Nursing, 3*, 86–96.

Latham, A., & Prigerson, H. (2004). Suicidality and bereavement: Complicated grief as a psychiatric disorder presenting greatest risk for suicidality. *Suicide and Life-Threatening Behavior, 34*(4), 350–362.

Loo, R. (1986). Suicide among police in a federal force. *Suicide and Life-Threatening Behavior, 16*, 379–388.

Marshall, J. (2006). Counseling on the front line: Providing a safe refuge for military personnel to discuss emotional wounds. *Counseling Today, 48*(8), 1, 32–33.

McIntosh, J. L. (1993). Control group studies of suicide survivors: A review and critique. *Suicide and Life-Threatening Behavior, 23*, 146–161.

McIntosh, J. L. (1987). *Suicide and its aftermath*. New York, NY: Norton.

McMenamy, J. M., Jordan, J. R., & Mitchell, A. M. (2008). What do suicide survivors tell us they need? Results of a pilot study. *Suicide and Life-Threatening Behavior, 38*(4), 375–389.

Mitchell, A. M., Sakraida, T. J., Kim, Y., Bullian, L., & Chiappetta, L. (2009). Depression, anxiety and quality of life in suicide survivors: A comparison of close and distant relationships. *Archives of Psychiatric Nursing, 23*(1), 2–10.

Neimeyer, R. A., Burke, L. A., Mackay, M. M., & van Dyke Stringer, J. G. (2010). Grief therapy and the reconstruction of meaning: From principles to practice. *Journal of Contemporary Psychotherapy, 40*(2), 73–83.

Neria, Y., & Litz, B. T. (2004). Bereavement by traumatic means: The complex synergy of trauma and grief. *Journal of Loss and Trauma, 9*, 73–87.

Parker, H. A., & McNally, R. J. (2008). Repressive coping, emotional adjustment, and cognition in people who have lost loved ones to suicide. *Suicide and Life-Threatening Behavior, 38*(6), 676–687.

Rando, T. A. (1993). *Treatment of complicated mourning*. Champaign, IL: Research Press.

Robins, E. (1981). *The final months: A study of the lives of 134 persons who committed suicide*. New York, NY: Oxford University Press.

Rynearson, E. K. (Ed.). (2006). *Violent death: Resilience and intervention beyond crisis*. New York, NY: Routledge.

Seguin, M., Lesage, A., & Kiely, M. C. (1995). Parental bereavement after suicide and accident: A comparative study. *Suicide and Life-Threatening Behavior, 25*, 489–498.

Steen, J. M., & Asaro, M. R. (2006). *Military widow: A survival guide*. Annapolis, MD: Naval Institute Press.

Stroebe, M. S., & Stroebe, W. (1993). The mortality of bereavement. In M. S. Stroebe, W. Stroebe, & R. O. Hansson (Eds.), *Handbook of bereavement: Theory, research, and intervention* (pp. 175–195). New York, NY: Cambridge University Press.

Thompson, D. G., Futterman, A., Farberow, N., Thompson, L. W., & Peterson, J. (1993). The impact of spousal bereavement on older widows and widowers. In M. S. Stroebe, W. Stroebe, & R. O. Hansson (Eds.), *Handbook of bereavement research: Consequences, coping, and care* (pp. 227–239). New York, NY: Cambridge University Press.

Violanti, J. M. (1995, February). The mystery within: Understanding police suicide. *FBI Law Enforcement Bulletin*, 19–23. Retrieved from http://www.graphlete.com/IACP/Reference%20Material/Select%20Publications/Handout-%20Mystery%20Within-Police%20Suicide%20-%20FBI%20LEB.PDF

Walter, C. A., & McCoyd, J. L. M. (2009). *Grief and loss across the lifespan: A biopsychosocial perspective*. New York, NY: Springer.

Washington Post. (2010). Retrieved from http://www.washingtonpost.com/wpdyn/content/article/2010/07/17/AR2010071702692.html?sid=ST2010071801227

Wertheimer, A. (2001). *A special scar: The experiences of people bereaved by suicide*. Philadelphia, PA: Taylor & Francis.

Wilson, A., & Marshall, A. (2010). The support needs and experiences of suicidally bereaved family and friends. *Death Studies*, *34*, 625–640.

Wolfelt, A. D. (2006). *Companioning the bereaved: A soulful guide for caregivers*. Fort Collins, CO: Companion Press.

Wolfelt, A. D. (2009). *Understanding your suicide grief: Ten essential touchstones for finding hope and healing your heart*. Fort Collins, CO: Companion Press.

Worden, J. W. (2009). *Grief counseling and grief therapy: A handbook for the mental health practitioner* (4th ed.). New York, NY: Springer.

CHAPTER

23

The Stress Process Model for Supporting Long-Term Family Caregiving

Monica M. Matthieu and Angela B. Swensen

INTRODUCTION

Across all medical, psychological, and psychiatric settings, clinical practitioners commonly encounter military service members, veterans, their families, and their caregivers who are experiencing health, illness, and disability issues across the life course. These issues impart a significant psychological, physical, and financial impact. Clinical practitioners—representing a variety of professionals from disciplines such as medicine, nursing, psychology, rehabilitation, counseling, and social work—are uniquely positioned to attend to the various health, mental health, and psychosocial needs of these individuals and their families.

Clinical practitioners who work with veterans are often provided with guidelines to direct care, which now encompass support services necessary to assist caregivers. In 2010, with the passing of the Caregivers and Veterans Omnibus Health Services Act (Public Law 111–163), attention now includes an important and often overlooked focus on the needs of caregivers, particularly family members providing long-term care to military service members and veterans. This timely law aids in mandating a range of services for the caregivers of our military service members and veterans, specifically defined here as individuals who have experienced nonmortal injuries through military service to the United States. Herein, wounded military service members and veterans are referred to as *Wounded Warriors*. Further, clinical practitioners who provide services to family caregivers of Wounded Warriors will find it important to understand theory and assessment models. With these foundational models, clinicians can expand the range of their competencies and add new practice behaviors to their delivery of quality caregiver services.

The aims of this chapter are to describe theoretical approaches and models designed to inform practitioners who perform assessments on the myriad of challenges facing family caregivers of Wounded Warriors. In particular, the stress process model (Pearlin, Mullan, Semple, & Skaff, 1990) provides a framework for understanding the intersection of stress, appraisal, and coping that are often a result of ongoing stressful life events, such as caregiving. Theoretical concepts that make up this framework can be utilized in the assessment, intervention, and evaluation of the stress response and the coping processes used to mitigate increased caregiver burden and strain. Understanding the stress process model allows the clinician to comprehend the unique nature of stress experienced by caregivers, its physiological and psychological effects, and provides a mechanism to view the stress response more holistically, as an interaction of the mind and the body, therefore informing appropriate clinical treatment and intervention strategies (Everly & Lating, 2002).

SCOPE OF THE ISSUES

Due to medical and technological advances over the past 100 years, more military service members are surviving traumatic injuries from their service and combat exposure than ever before. As the incidence of nonmortal wounds increases, more and more military service members are returning home in need of long-term care and rehabilitation. Prominent injuries experienced by the current generation of post–9/11 Wounded Warriors include amputations, traumatic brain injury (TBI), and combat-related stress, often referred to as *posttraumatic stress disorder* (PTSD). A new term framing an array of physical and mental injuries is referred to by the medical profession as *polytrauma*. Most polytraumatic injuries result in permanent disability and thus require long-term care. Compounding these injuries, military service members and veterans are apt to struggle with issues common to the U.S. population: sedentary lifestyle, obesity, diabetes, hypertension, cancer, depression, and alcohol and tobacco use.

In addition to health and mental health challenges, Wounded Warriors and their families experience other stressful life events uniquely related to military service. Particularly today, military families face frequent and repeated relocations and deployments. Further, the need for ongoing medical care for Wounded Warriors in the postacute phases of traumatic injuries disrupts family life and often results in significant stress on family relationships, increasing the need for social support, professional support, and community resources in various geographic areas. Moreover, there are unique grief and loss issues associated with military related traumatic injuries. The impact of a disability most likely ends a service member's military career. Such disabilities change relationships and responsibilities within the family; for example, the spouses or parents of wounded veterans find themselves thrust into new caregiving roles. More so, Wounded Warriors, their families, and their caregivers must adjust to disabling physical and mental health conditions in the veteran, which necessitate long-term rehabilitation and may result in significant financial impact for the family.

Prudence by clinical practitioners is therefore required in working with these families. Copious physical, psychological, occupational, social, and financial challenges become a part of the everyday existence or the "new normal" for Wounded Warriors, their families, and their caregivers. Thus clinical practitioners need to be aware of the full range of issues impacting the wounded veteran and their caregivers. Furthermore, clinicians need to be savvy with respect to the mental health consequences of combat operations, repeated deployments, and chronically stressful downrange experiences. Such experiences are known to exacerbate symptoms of PTSD, or in some cases, result in the development of PTSD along with co-occurring disorders of depression, generalized anxiety, and substance abuse. What is more, adverse outcomes such as suicide and interpersonal violence have been associated with combat PTSD. Clinical practitioners who work with Wounded Warriors, their families, and their caregivers must also be skilled in assessing risk-taking behaviors; marital and family conflict; intimate partner violence; the effects of sexual and combat trauma; as well as child maltreatment and neglect. Clinicians are on the front lines of prevention and intervention, charged with the task of intervening when merited, and are uniquely positioned to provide access to necessary resources and supports.

Occupationally, Wounded Warriors, their families, and their caregivers face significant employment readjustments. Wounded Warriors often find themselves training for a new vocation and career path that may include returning to school or pursuing a higher education. Some Wounded Warriors face barriers to employment due to their debilitating circumstances, which for some may result in homelessness. For others, dramatic changes in the family structure, roles, and time spent caring experienced by family caregivers who provide long-term care often affect their availability for outside employment. Clinicians who understand how Wounded Warriors, their families, and their caregivers are affected by occupational and financial instability are positioned to most effectively help their clients move through taxing situations in a resourceful manner. An important aspect for the clinician in appreciating these notable needs is to first understand the caregiver.

WHO ARE THE CAREGIVERS OF MILITARY SERVICE MEMBERS AND VETERANS TODAY?

Research stemming back to 1905 indicates that caregiving in the early 20th century was primarily the responsibility of women. Recipients of caregiving were members of an older generation and disabled children. It was common practice for women to care for more than one individual at a time, as well as to experience multiple caregiving episodes during their life span. In the late 20th century, women continued being the central caregivers, regardless of the competing role of employment outside of the home (Robison, Moen, & Dempster-McClain, 1995).

However, women's employment outside the home has had a substantive effect on care recipients, particularly if the woman caregiver works full time. In such instances, "care recipients of caregivers employed full time were less likely to receive large amounts of care from their caregivers, more likely to receive personal care from paid care providers, more likely to use community services, and more likely to experience service problems than were care recipients of non-employed caregivers. Employed caregivers were more likely to use caregiver support services than were non-employed caregivers" (Scharlach, Gustavson, & Dal Santo, 2007, p. 752).

Caregivers are most often family members, generally speaking, spouses. Family caregivers who are the wives of the care recipients report experiencing high levels of stress. For example, Beckham, Lytle, and Feldman (1996) found that the caregiving spouses of

Vietnam-era veteran care recipients with combat-related PTSD indicated "high levels of nonspecific distress," with nearly 50% reporting that they felt "on the verge of a nervous breakdown" (p. 1068). Beckham et al. (1996) noted that these experiences are similar to those reported by caregivers who provide long-term care for individuals with chronic illnesses. Furthermore, they found that spouses who provide care to their veteran with PTSD "report problems with burden and financial stress, and a significant number report at least moderate levels of psychological distress, dysphoria, and anxiety" (p. 1070).

In the early 21st century, policy is attempting to catch up with the changing times. As baby-boomers age, and more veterans than ever before are returning home with nonmortal wounds, both physical and psychological, the burden of care continues to increase exponentially.

Families play an important role in veterans' recovery and readjustment, with spouses often taking on the role of primary caregiver. Thus, identifying how exposure to trauma and other disabling conditions affects families, especially spouses, becomes a critical component in closing the gap of our understanding.

Additionally, it is more likely than ever before that spouses and mothers who are the primary family caregivers are also employed full time outside the home. Current trends indicate that once care work begins, working women are highly prone to depart from their employment. However, when employers provide necessary time provisions to caregiver employees, these caregivers are more likely to continue working (Pavalko & Henderson, 2006). Nevertheless, such changes in policy and employment benefits are not found to lessen family caregiver burden or experiences of financial stress. In summary, understanding the history related to who provides care and the impact on spouses of veterans with PTSD provides clinical practitioners with a lens to view the issues that precipitate the onset of caregiver stress, which is a hallmark of the stress process model.

WHAT IS THE STRESS PROCESS MODEL?

The aim of this section is to explore more closely the intersection of stress, appraisal, and coping theories, as these theories comprise the foundation of the stress process model.

Historical Background

Walter Bradford Cannon (1871–1945) was an American physiologist, professor, and chairman of the Department of Physiology at Harvard Medical School. He coined the phrase *fight or flight* to describe an animal's reaction to stress in his book *Bodily Changes in Pain, Hunger, Fear and Rage: An Account of Recent Researches into the Function of Emotional Excitement* (1927). During his celebrated career, he set out four propositions related to the concept of *homeostasis*, which are found in his later book, *Wisdom of the Body*(1932). What ensued is an entire field of study dedicated to the nature of, and responses to, stress among humans.

Stress Theory

Selye (1956), the father of modern stress research, extended Cannon's revolutionary work with clinical observations and laboratory research resulting in a widely accepted stress theory, General Adaptation Syndrome (GAS), which posits that stressful events are linked to the onset of distress or disorders. The human body's response to stress begins with a *stressor*, which is defined as any real or imagined event, condition, situation, or stimulus that instigates the onset of the stress response process within an individual (Everly & Lating, 2002). Selye (1956) also noted that human beings have nonspecific reactions to these stressors. The reactions occur in three stages, beginning with alarm as the initial response to the stressor, followed by resistance to the ongoing demands of the stressor, and finally exhaustion. These reactions produce both physiological and psychological effects within the individual, which ultimately results in deterioration of the body and mind.

Everly and Lating (2002) further define stressors as being comprised of two types: psychosocial and biogenic. A *psychosocial stressor* occurs when the individual reacts to a situation, event, or condition based on the attributed perception of that stressor as a threat. The psychosocial stressor is cognitively interpreted by an individual along a continuum ranging from no harm to threat of personal security (Lazarus & Folkman, 1984). In other words, a stressful event becomes a psychosocial stressor when individuals react based on their thoughts that the event will adversely affect their personal well-being. Stressors can also be *biogenic*, where thoughts, cognitions, or appraisals of a situation or event are not needed to produce a physiological stress reaction. Biogenic responses can occur in instances where stress arises in the body as it reacts to the external environment (e.g., temperature changes in a room) or within an individual's internal environment (e.g., ingesting substances such as caffeine). Although physiological response to stress is a fundamental concept in stress theory (Selye, 1956), our inability to determine which particular events are psychologically stressful—and to whom and in what ways—has been a challenge for researchers and practitioners alike (Lazarus, 1999).

Over time, the strain of an individual's response to stressful situations, whether mentally or physically, can be cumulatively detrimental. The result of the stress process on the mind and body may contribute to the occurrence of eventual disease (Everly & Lating, 2002). Thus, a basic scientific understanding of the stressful effects of excessive psychological and physiological arousal enables clinical practitioners to assess clients' presenting problems from the vantage point of mind-body interactions. Further, this knowledge will inform the most effective place within the stress response process to intervene: (a) in the environment where the stressful event presents; (b) with individuals and their thoughts about the event; (c) with individuals and the physical responses within their bodies; or (d) with individuals and their cognitive or behavioral coping strategies used to mitigate the stressful event.

Appraisal Theory

In addition to stress theory, one of the cornerstones of the stress process model is appraisal theory. Lazarus and Folkman (1984) define appraisals as the individual cognitions about a specific event or stressor. Appraisal theory refers to the significance of the individual's cognitive analysis, or subjective appraisal, of the stressful events that occur within his or her environment. Any event, irrespective of its importance, may or may not be perceived as stressful or harmful by an individual (Regehr & Bober, 2005). Appraisal theory posits that there are two types of appraisal: primary appraisal and secondary appraisal (Lazarus & Folkman, 1984).

Primary appraisal is the individual's evaluation of an event or situation that may present as a potential hazard to their well-being. According to Lazarus and Folkman (1984) there are three types of primary appraisal: (1) *irrelevant*, where the individual has no vested interest in the event or in the results of the situation; (2) *benign-positive*, in which the individual assumes that the situation is positive with no potential negative results to their well-being; and (3) *stressful*, where the individual only perceives negative results or that the circumstances of the situation are detrimental to their well-being. To determine the magnitude of an event or situation, an individual focuses on one of three perceptions: harm or loss; threat; or challenge (Lewis & Roberts 2001):

- *Harm or loss*: The belief that one has endured a physical or emotional loss with the temporal nature of the loss as having occurred in the past.
- *Threat*: An anticipation of future harm or loss.
- *Challenge*: The potential for positive personal growth by applying coping skills to mitigate the stressful event or encounter (Lazarus & Folkman, 1984; Lewis & Roberts 2001).

Secondary appraisal is the individual's evaluation of her or his ability to handle the event or situation before or after it has happened. This estimation of the range of coping skills in the person's repertoire occurs in relation to a primary appraisal of a situation (Lazarus, 1999). Thus, the cognitive evaluation is dependent on the subjective interpretation of whether the event poses a threat to the individual (i.e., primary appraisal) and whether the individual perceives that they have the resources (inner and outer) to cope with it (i.e., secondary appraisal) (Regehr & Bober, 2005). Since secondary appraisal is purely a cognitive process, coping efforts have not been instituted at this point.

Coping Theory

Depending on the nature of the primary appraisal, the secondary appraisal can be influenced by contextual-level factors such as demands, constraints, and opportunities. The resulting appraisal then generates an emotion or meaning to attribute to the event or situation; where the individual is now able to move from thoughts to action (Lazarus, 1999). After the event has been appraised by the individual as stressful, meaning and emotions are generated. Then a behavior called *coping* ensues. Coping involves the decision of which behaviors to utilize to handle the event and this is an interaction between the person's internal resources and external environmental demands (Lazarus & Folkman, 1984). Coping is also defined as constantly changing cognitive and behavioral efforts to manage specific demands that are appraised as potentially taxing or exceeding a person's resources. This also includes attempts to reduce the perceived discrepancy between situational demands and personal resources. Coping is firmly rooted in the person and environment because appraisals are often influenced by cues either in the person, in the environment or in both (Lazarus, 1993).

According to coping theory, under stressful conditions an individual employs coping strategies to deal with the stressor in one of two ways; *problem-focused coping* or *emotion-focused coping*. Problem-focused coping involves actively altering the external person-environment relationship. It is defined as channeling efforts to behaviorally handle distressing situations by gathering information, decision making, conflict resolution, resource acquisition (knowledge, skills, and abilities) and instrumental situation-specific or task-oriented actions (Folkman & Moskowitz, 2000). Problem-focused coping allows the individual to focus attention on situation-specific goals and allows for sense of mastery and control in working toward attaining that specific goal. Alternatively, emotion-focused coping involves altering the personal or internal meaning or relationships, including positive reappraising or making meaning of the stressful events (Lazarus, 1999). This process of cognitively reframing typically difficult thoughts in a positive manner impacts deeply held values that become apparent when certain conditions occur that instigate coping (Lazarus, 1999). In summary, coping is an active effort to deal with stressors by either changing the situation (e.g., problem-focused coping) or changing one's feelings about the situation (e.g., emotion-focused coping).

Integration of Stress, Appraisal, and Coping Theories

The stress process model provides a structure for understanding the multitude of challenges facing Wounded Warriors and their family caregivers. For example, thinking about the stressful events occurring in one's life when facing caregiving demands and deciding if one has the personal resources to handle those demands is a familiar presenting problem for caregivers. Given the range of stressors faced by Wounded Warriors, their families, and their caregivers, these theories merge at the point when appraisals and coping can impact the overall stress response an individual experiences within one's mind and body. Clinical interventions can ultimately avert illness and disease in the caregiver.

Clinical practitioners need to understand theoretical concepts related to stress, appraisal, and coping to apply this knowledge in practice when working with a Wounded Warrior and their family members who are providing long-term care. This understanding can help clinicians provide psychoeducation programs on stress and coping with diverse client groups to enhance their clients' understanding of the physical and psychological implications of stress. Likewise, it can help guide clinicians toward other interventions that buffer stress (e.g., social support) or manage stress (e.g., biofeedback, relaxation training, visual imagery, cognitive behavioral therapy). Ultimately, the health benefits of reducing stress by applying effective coping strategies can include improved emotional well-being, greater ability to function, as well as mitigating disease progression for both Wounded Warriors and their caregivers. Building on this theoretical foundation, the next section in this chapter applies these concepts to an assessment model specifically applicable to the caregivers of Wounded Warriors.

USING THE STRESS PROCESS MODEL TO GUIDE ASSESSMENTS OF CAREGIVERS OF WOUNDED WARRIORS

The stress process model intersects stress, appraisal, and coping theories by organizing the fundamental elements of these theories into a temporal sequence that leads from the stressor to specific health outcomes or disease states. In recent years, a number of caregiver stress researchers (e.g., Goode, Haley, Roth, & Ford, 1998; Pearlin et al., 1990) have applied the stress process model to the specific needs and experiences of caregivers to examine the long-term health and psychosocial impacts of family caregiving. According to Pearlin et al. (1990), there are four domains in the stress process model that are pertinent to assessing caregivers: (1) background and context of stress, (2) stressors, (3) mediators of stress, and (4) outcomes or manifestations of stress. Understanding the details of the four domains can help clinical practitioners to provide a traditional biopsychosocial assessment of the health and well-being of family members providing long term care for Wounded Warriors.

BACKGROUND AND CONTEXT OF STRESS

The first domain in the caregiver stress process model is the *background and context of the stress*. This domain is vital for any assessment because it entails understanding the totality of the caregiver experience. Although this may seem obvious to most clinical practitioners, knowing the sociodemographic characteristics of age, gender, ethnicity, education, occupation—and in particular, the social and economic status of caregivers—provides a wealth of information with regard to the background and context of stress. For example, the unequal distribution of rewards, privileges, opportunities, and responsibilities affects the kind and intensity of stressors to which people are exposed, the personal and social resources available to deal with these stressors, and the way stress is expressed (Pearlin et al., 1990).

In addition to these individual characteristics, the caregiving history also provides critical background information on both the caregiver and the health challenges facing the veteran. With regard to the Wounded Warrior, information should be gathered about the onset, duration, and nature of the health challenge, illness, or disabling condition—providing clinical practitioners with an introduction to the scope of the health challenge. A detailed military history should be taken, which chronicles the service members' entry into the military, any positive or negative incidents, or injuries incurred during training or as part of deployments, and the events leading up to and including the episode of the injury, wound, or accident. This history can provide a timeline to determine the duration of injuries and of caregiving.

The relationship of the caregiver to the Wounded Warrior, whether that be a spouse, child, or parent—as well as the nature and duration of the relationship—are important to assess. With the family structure, roles and responsibilities may shift as a new normal takes shape, which affects nearly all family relationships. A more balanced relationship and sharing of roles and responsibilities in the family between spouses may now also become husband as a Wounded Warrior and spouse as caregiver. As roles shift, so do power differentials, time allocated to family members, resources, and money. Further, any other stressful life events, such as health problems in the caregiver or other family member health care concerns, and family separations due to military life or due to relationship conflict, should be queried. Finally, the length of time spent in caregiving activities is one of the most important indicators of chronic stress experienced by the caregivers (Pearlin et al., 1990) and thus this requires careful attention and exploration by the clinical practitioner when gathering background information.

Another contextual issue is the access to and use of resources (Pearlin et al., 1990). There are two types of resources. The first type is the composition of networks, both family and social networks, which provide the caregiver with attachments to family members, friends, and others outside of the caregiving relationship. The sum total of these networks as well as the nature and frequency of contacts with network members are seen as a tangible resource that can offer aid and assistance to the caregiver as needed. A second type of resource is formal community-based programs. Although a variety of caregiver programs may exist, access to these programs—due to geographic distance, eligibility, and cost—may hinder availability for caregivers of Wounded Warriors. However, new legislation is making Family Caregiver Programs available at medical facilities across the country, operated by the Department of Veterans Affairs (VA), for caregivers of eligible post–9/11 veterans. These new programs, started in 2011, support the needs of Wounded Warriors, their caregivers and their families, and provide services such as in-home and community-based care, respite care, comprehensive caregiver education and training, caregiver support groups, and other services.

STRESSORS

The second domain in the stress process model that is pertinent to assessing caregivers involves the *stressors* they face as part of providing care to Wounded Warriors. "These are the conditions, experiences, and activities that are problematic for people; that is, that threaten them, thwart their efforts, fatigue them, and defeat their dreams" (Pearlin et al., 1990, p. 586). Stressors in this model are comprised of two types: primary and secondary stressors. Primary stressors emanate from actual caregiving duties. Secondary stressors emerge from the perception of challenge or adversity arising from the demands of caregiving.

Primary stressors. Clinical practitioners should focus on both objective and subjective indicators of the nature, course, and actual needs of the Wounded Warrior for assessing the type of attention and care that is required from caregivers (Pearlin et al., 1990). The functional dependence of the Wounded Warrior on the caregiver can be assessed by using a variety of objective standardized measures regarding the Wounded Warrior's activities of daily living (ADL) and instrumental activities of daily living (IADL). According to Goode et al. (1998), these include "the performance of direct patient care such as providing assistance with tasks that the care recipient is no longer able to perform independently . . . such as bathing and feeding, as well as more complex duties such as managing finances" (p. 190).

After determining the nature and amount of activities the caregiver performs and supervises for the Wounded Warrior, the cognitive status of the *caregiver* using a mental status exam would be important information to gather to assess for cognitive impairments. Following this, an enumeration of and a description of any problematic behaviors of the Wounded Warrior is necessary. Research has found that the amount of caregiving activities are not nearly as mentally and physically taxing on the caregiver as the constant attentiveness needed from the caregiver for damage control (i.e., managing unwanted behaviors by the patient). As noted by Goode et al. (1998), "patient behavioral problems (e.g., angry, dangerous, or embarrassing behavior) and memory impairments (e.g., disorientation and asking repetitive questions) are another source of stress to the caregiver" (p. 190). In addition, the integration of the assessment information gathered on all of these primary stressors provides clinicians with a benchmark to evaluate how much the Wounded Warrior and the caregiver have changed since the injuries and to anticipate future changes for the caregiver as a result of long-term family caregiving.

Although these *objective* indicators of primary stressors on the caregiver focus on the physical and mental health, well-being, and functioning of the Wounded Warrior, the *subjective* indicators involve the assessment of feelings of overload and relational deprivation in the caregiver. Pearlin et al. (1990) define overload as the amount of energy and time that is needed to complete caregiving activities—noting that the feelings of fatigue, exhaustion, and burnout are paramount in the assessment. Feelings of overload signify that the caregiver is weighed down by the chronic nature of providing care. Relational deprivation, however, pertains to the emotional distance that may result from the drastic changes in roles and dynamics within the caregiver–Wounded Warrior relationship. Said another way, the relational balance of emotional intimacy and goals and activities that used to be shared between the couple has been altered. This transformation, and the need to restructure the relationship, offers a significant challenge to both the caregiver and the Wounded Warrior to develop a "new normal" for the important things that will sustain their personal relationship over good times and bad.

Secondary stressor. According to Pearlin et al. (1990), the secondary stressors for caregivers include role strains and intrapsychic strains. **Role strains** are those activities and roles that are external to the needs and demands of providing care to the Wounded Warrior. In the assessment of secondary stressors related to caregiving roles, clinical practitioners need to inquire about role strains that lead to family conflicts, job–caregiving conflicts, economic tensions, and finally, the social strains that result in a marked constriction of the social life of the caregiver. When assessing family conflicts, a broad definition of family is needed to include the disagreements between caregivers and any family member or friend that expresses differences of opinions related to the level of impairment and severity of the Wounded Warrior's condition and the amount and quality of the care provided by the family and other care providers. Last, clinicians should inquire about the attitudes and actions of all involved family members and friends toward the patient and toward the caregiver. These various role strains encompass a large part of the burden felt by caregivers.

Occupationally, the amount of time devoted to caregiving is immense, yet employment outside the home provides a host of social, economic, and personal benefits for the caregiver. However, pressures from the conflicting roles of work and caregiving typically mount into irresolvable job-caregiver conflicts. If the caregivers do work outside of the home, their quality and satisfaction with their job may be impacted by near constant worries about the Wounded Warrior and interruptions at work to coordinate and to manage care performed by others in their absence.

Economically speaking, the strains are also evident. Typically, caregiving involves a reduction in total household income with a corresponding increase in health care, travel, and housing costs related to care and treatment for the Wounded Warrior at various specialty care and polytrauma Department of Defense medical treatment facilities and

Department of Veterans Affairs facilities. Inquiring about and comparing the standard of living postinjury to earlier times before the injuries, provides clinicians with information on the life transitions and financial struggles the family has faced over time. In addition, clinicians can obtain in-depth information related to specific financial details on how the family are making ends meet, the status of military and VA disability benefits related to service connected injuries, and applications for new caregiver programs, supports, and services is critical to ensure accurate and timely care planning for the Wounded Warrior and their caregiver.

Last, there are **social strains.** These strains often result in the noticeable restrictions around social, recreational, and respite time for the caregiver. Therefore, assessments focusing on activities caregivers previously engaged in and ones they currently miss due to caregiving responsibilities are important to evaluate. Over time, the amount of contact caregivers have with other family members, friends, and others in their professional network will decrease as the demands of caregiving constrict the amount of time and energy available for outside relationships.

Intrapsychic strains are secondary stressors that impact the self-concepts held by caregivers. These strains are particularly important and represent the near final step in the stress process model, just prior to caregiver health outcomes or manifestations of stress. Clinical practitioners should initially assess the global aspects of self-esteem and mastery using well-established standardized instruments, as these will provide an objective indicator of how caregivers regard their sense of self within their world and the control they feel over their lives. Other intrapsychic assessment areas that Pearlin et al. (1990) outline that are more situation-specific to caregiving include role captivity, loss of self, caregiving competence, and personal gain. *Role captivity* refers to the caregivers' feelings of being trapped in the unremitting demands of caregiving that were thrust on them in addition to having fantasies of running away and escaping. *Loss of self* involves the caregivers' feeling that they do not know who they are anymore and that an important part of their sense of self is missing. Conversely, *caregiving competence* reflects the positive beliefs held by caregivers about their ability to rise to the challenge of caregiving and the corresponding belief that they have developed into good caregivers. *Personal gain* also represents an area of positive growth in the caregiver that provides an awareness of new strengths, talents, and improved confidence as a result of caregiving.

The intrapsychic and role strains that comprise the secondary stressors, combined with the primary stressors, encompass nearly all of the concepts outlined in the stress process model specific to the earlier discussion of stress and appraisal theories. Other concepts, however, related to coping theory are included in the third domain of the stress process model, referred to as the *mediators of stress.*

MEDIATORS OF STRESS

In stress research, mediators are typically defined as concepts that intervene or change the pathway from a negative to a more positive health outcome for an individual. Traditionally, coping has been the most important concept that mitigates the long-term effects of stress. In the stress process, assessing coping strategies specific to caregiving relate to the management of the situation. Specifically, this includes directing the behavior and activities of the Wounded Warrior and the caregivers' own self-directed education on the prognosis, course, and treatment options for the specific health challenges they face. Next, management of meaning examines the emotion-focused, cognitive strategies caregivers use to reduce expectations of the Wounded Warriors, and of their future. In addition, caregivers make positive comparisons to others less fortunate to derive meaning from their experience. Finally, caregivers begin to construct a larger sense of the health challenge, for instance, some may pray for strength and resolve for the future. Equally important is managing distress, which is another coping strategy similar to the action-oriented nature of problem-focused coping, where the clinical practitioner should focus the assessment on the behavioral things that caregivers can do to relieve stress. For some caregivers, desirable activities might include taking a nap to cope, whereas other caregivers may utilize maladaptive ways of coping such as drinking alcohol to mitigate stress.

Social support is another mediator of stress. Social support is known to buffer the impact of stress on the individual, thus lessening the ultimate impact of stress on the individual's health outcomes. Social support is defined as the help and support that caregivers attain in tangible and emotional ways from family and friends within their support network. In the stress process model put forth by Pearlin et al. (1990), social support can be assessed using a measure of expressive support specifically designed and tailored to caregivers. Other standardized measures of social support, for example, the Social Network List (Stokes, 1983); Inventory of Social Supportative Behaviors (Barrera, Sandler, & Ramsey, 1981); Reactions to Social Situations (Sarason, 1986); Interpersonal Support Evaluation List (Cohn, Mermelstein, Kamarck, & Hoberman, 1985); Perceived Social Supports, Friend and Family Measure (Procidano & Heller, 1983); Social Support Questionnaire (Sarason, Sarason, Shearin, & Pierce, 1987) can be used to gather objective assessments with regard to the amount and types of social support a caregiver has available to reduce stress in their lives (see references at the end of the chapter).

OUTCOMES OR MANIFESTATIONS OF STRESS

The fourth and final domain in the stress process model (Pearlin et al., 1990) that is pertinent to assessing caregivers of Wounded Warriors is the *outcomes* or *manifestations of stress*. The outcomes, whether positive or negative, are a cumulative result of the impact of primary and secondary stressors on the lives of caregivers. The manifestations of stress include impacts on caregiver psychological security, mental health, and physical health. Psychological security is defined as a person having positive affect about life; having a sense of competence in managing one's own environment; a sense of development and realizing one's potential for personal growth; a sense of meaning and purpose in one's life; and a sense of positive attitude toward oneself and self-acceptance. Mental health issues that are negative health outcomes for caregivers include depression and anxiety. Additionally, caregivers can experience physical health deterioration, vulnerabilities, and injuries in a variety of bodily systems.

Other outcomes include disengaging from caregiving activities, by death or replacement with another caregiver. In this first scenario, the death of the client (i.e., in this case, the

Wounded Warrior) can occur, releasing the caregiver from this role forever. Replacement as an alternative outcome includes the ability to engage in usual activities by yielding the role of caregiver to other helpers, whether they are professionals or not.

Most research focuses on the impact of caregiver stress on caregivers outcomes in relation to health and mental health. For example, a study of long-term impacts of caregiving (Goode et al., 1998) found that "psychosocial resource variables (appraisals, coping responses, and social support) predict longitudinal changes in caregiver mental and physical health, whereas objective changes in the severity of patient impairment do not predict caregiver changes over time" (p. 196). In essence, caregivers who utilize positive psychosocial resources available improve their lives to a greater extent than caregivers who have a loved one whose condition significantly improves.

APPLYING THE STRESS PROCESS MODEL TO GUIDE ASSESSMENTS OF CAREGIVERS

As displayed in Figure 23.1, clinical practitioners using the biopsychosocial assessment framework integrated with the stress process model concepts typically begin the assessment with the presenting problem from the perspective of the caregiver. In the Case Vignette: "LeeAnn and Dan" (which follows), as in real-life clinical practice, many of the major assessment sections would need to focus on taking a history of the caregiver, LeeAnn (e.g., family, employment, legal, physical/medical, substance use, mental status exam, strengths/resources, social support, community resources, and obstacles and motivations for change). Other assessment sections would focus on Dan, the veteran who is experiencing health challenges and limitations that require caregiving by his wife, LeeAnn. The information on Dan's military history and a description of his injuries are critical to obtain from the veteran and/or the caregiver to have a fuller understanding of the caregiver demands that LeeAnn experiences.

Prior to making any diagnostic impressions or treatment recommendations to LeeAnn, an in-depth assessment is needed on all of her primary and secondary stressors. From assessing the history and current status of her actual caregiving duties, the clinical practitioner can begin to identify the primary stressors and problematic behaviors that are a result of caregiving (e.g., the impact of Dan's appointments on her absences from work) as well as issues of caregiver overload and how caregiving has over time taxed LeeAnn's individual strengths and resources. LeeAnn faces a number of secondary stressors in the form of role strains that lead to a variety of conflicts: at home with the family, between her work and caregiving, financially, and socially. Assessing the intrapsychic strains is also important, including determining the impact of caregiving on LeeAnn's self-concept and self-esteem. Next, the mediators of stress, that is how LeeAnn manages to handle stress, would need to be assessed to provide a balance to the assessment, which ensures that strengths, resources, and other positive coping strategies used to decrease distress are included. Finally, the assessment of the physical and mental impacts of caregiving on LeeAnn cannot be underestimated; thus, on completion of the full biopsychosocial assessment, a number of referrals for screenings, physicals, and annual examinations should accompany the treatment recommendations.

	Stress Process Model Concepts														
Biopsychosocial Assessment Framework	Cognitive Status	Problematic Behavior	Overload	Relational Deprivation	Family Conflict	Job-Caregiving Conflict	Economic Strain	Role Captivity	Loss of Self	Caregiving Competence	Personal Gain	Management of Situation	Management of Meaning	Management of Distress	Expressive Support
Presenting Problem		✓													
Description of the Veteran's Health Status and Injuries								✓							
Family History					✓										
Employment History						✓	✓								
Military History		✓													
Legal History							✓								
Physical/Medical History	✓		✓										✓		
Substance Use History														✓	
Mental Status Exam	✓								✓						
Diagnostic Impressions															
Individual Strengths and Resources			✓						✓	✓	✓				
Social Support and Resources				✓								✓		✓	✓
Community Resources												✓			
Obstacles and Motivation to Change										✓	✓		✓		
Treatment Recommendations															

Figure 23.1 Integrating concepts and measures from the stress process model

Source: Adapted from Pearlin, Mullan, Semple, & Skaff, 1990.

Case Vignette: LeeAnn and Dan

LeeAnn, age 32, is the primary caregiver and spouse of an OEF/OIF Wounded Warrior, Dan. They are the parents of two children; Dylan, age 8 and Brittani, age 10. LeeAnn and Dan were high school sweethearts. She remembers the first time she saw Dan, as it was love at first sight. She described him as rugged, yet being a gentle giant. She recalls how his large stature and calm mannerisms made her feel safe from the moment they met. She loved how they could talk about anything and everything for hours on end. He enlisted in the Army right out of high school and left for boot camp about a month after they got married.

Dan recently returned from his second tour, this time to Afghanistan. He served as a combat engineer with the 510 Route Clearance Companies, 20th Engineer Battalion working to clear the roads of Improvised Explosive Devices (IEDs). About 14 months ago on a Route Clearance Patrol (RCP), his company came under attack when a Vehicle Borne Improvised Explosive Devices (VBIEDs) exploded blowing up the Humvee he was in. Dan sustained injuries to both of his legs and compression fractures to his lower back. His right hand and arm were broken and the impact knocked him unconscious. He has had multiple surgeries over the past year to save his legs, and is now a bilateral below-knee amputee, with limited functioning in his right hand. He has been through 12 surgeries.

He is currently in treatment at the VA Medical Center, which is located about an hour from his home. His rehabilitation and treatment for his wounds and a moderate traumatic brain injury (TBI) is primarily centered at the VA's Polytrauma Network Site. He also has appointments with his psychologist and psychiatrist at the OEF/OIF PTSD Clinical Team for posttraumatic stress disorder and his issues with anger and need for medication to sleep and regulate his emotions. As a result of his disability, he was medically discharged from the military and has had a hard time dealing with the end of his military career.

LeeAnn is a payroll supervisor at the local grocery store chain, working full time again now that Dan's care has been moved closer to home. She has been at his side for the past year assisting with his care and coordinating the various medical appointments he has at the VA and before that at the Department of Defense Medical Treatment Facility. She feels that it is good that the whole family is finally back home and together again.

At the beginning of the school year, their son Dylan was diagnosed with a learning disability in reading comprehension, thus requiring a lot more school meetings and evaluation appointments and work on the Individualized Education Plan (IEP). Brittani, their daughter, is on the youth soccer team with frequent weekend tournaments, and has tryouts for the elite team coming up. With LeeAnn's work schedule, the kids back in school, their activities, and all of Dan's appointments, life is busy. At times, LeeAnn just feels more like a taxi driver than a wife and mother.

LeeAnn has been thinking of taking on extra hours at the store as a cashier to earn some extra money, but just can't seem to find an hour to spare, much less have time to go to happy hour with her girlfriends whom she never sees. She always has to make up hours at work from having to drive Dan to his appointments, so getting extra hours at work just never seems to happen.

Since Dan's separation from the military, he and LeeAnn have been struggling to pay the bills and keep up with the kids' activities. Dan applied for his VA disability rating and benefits immediately on discharge, but he has been told it may take several months to 2 years before he receives a check. In the meantime, many bills have become overdue, and LeeAnn has to make and field multiple telephone calls each day to request forbearances from their creditors until Dan's disability benefits come through.

Hoping to be able to continue in his role as provider, Dan was persuaded to incorporate his own small business for the purpose of securing government contract work reserved for disabled veterans, and passing that work along (for a fee) to a large regional construction company. A government auditor recently conducted a site visit to review Dan's contract bid, and discovered that he is not the full-time operator of the company that would perform the work. The auditor has advised Dan to retain a lawyer, in the event that the government elects to prosecute or fine him for fraud. LeeAnn is furious that Dan would put himself and their family through such an ordeal. She has contacted several attorneys and they cannot afford the retainer fees. She does not know where they will turn if legal action is taken against Dan.

LeeAnn has always done the family finances, and taken care of the kids and the house. But now, when things have gotten so tight financially, it seems that Dan's angry outbursts are out of control. She knows he is just frustrated that he can't help out more financially, but his outbursts are getting to her. He wants to do more around the house, but he just does not remember what to do for very long. She makes lists, but he loses them or needs to review them with her over and over again on the phone while she is at work. She's even tried to limit the household chores he does to the things he can't mess up, because for most things, she has to go behind him and do it over again anyway. It's just easier if she does everything herself. She's just so tired of arguing with him all the time about what he can or can't do. She's exhausted all the time and, of late, has been feeling more and more trapped and alone.

She and Dan have had their share of ups and downs with their marriage, and since he's been home, intimacy has been a real problem. Dan has experienced erectile dysfunction, and his physicians have tried to adjust his medications to allow him to take Viagra, but intercourse is a challenge and it is difficult for them to talk about it. Things used to be good between them, but now LeeAnn just wants to be left alone and Dan just wants to have sex all the time. The fights usually end in sullen silences.

LeeAnn has been referred to the VA's new Caregiver Support Program by their couple's counselor at the VA and she has an appointment to see the Caregiver Support Coordinator next week. All she really wants is more hours in the day to get everything done and not another appointment. If someone could just drive Dan to the appointments, that would make life so much easier on her.

CONCLUSION

Assessment is the bedrock of clinical practice, yet is often overlooked in its importance. This chapter outlines the framework of the stress process model—which is informed by the theories of stress, appraisal, and coping—for clinical practitioners who provide services to family caregivers of Wounded Warriors. In addition, this chapter reviews the historical origins of caregiving for military service members and veterans and recent policy and program initiatives in the VA to support long-term family caregivers of eligible post–9/11 veterans. Although advances in caregiver research using assessment models are ongoing, clinical practitioners can use this chapter to develop their competencies in assessment models and ultimately sharpen their skills in the delivery of quality caregiver services for Wounded Warriors and their families.

CHAPTER DISCUSSION QUESTIONS

1. What are some of the caregiver stressors that LeeAnn is facing? Which are the primary stressors and which are secondary?
2. List and describe LeeAnn's strategies to decrease distress. What other questions or topics would provide additional information as to how LeeAnn deals positively or negatively with the stress of caregiving?
3. Both appraisal theory and intraspychic strains suggest that the cognitions, thoughts, and the meaning that caregivers derive from caring is critically important to determine within the biopsychosocial assessment. Compare and contrast the outcomes (or manifestations of stress) if caregiving was perceived to be a challenge that provided LeeAnn with feelings of personal competence and mastery versus the perception that caregiving has become a burden.

REFERENCES

Barrera, M. J., Sandler, I. N., & Ramsey, T. B. (1981). Preliminary development of a scale of social support: Studies of college students. *Journal of Community Psychology*, *9*, 435–437.

Beckham, J. C., Lytle, B. L., & Feldman, M. E. (1996). Caregiver burden in partners of Vietnam war veterans with posttraumatic stress disorder. *Journal of Consulting and Clinical Psychology*, *64*(5), 1068–1072.

Cannon, W. B. (1927). *Bodily changes in pain, hunger, fear and rage: An account of recent researches into the function of emotional excitement*. New York, NY: Appleton.

Cannon, W. B. (1932). *Wisdom of the body*. New York, NY: Norton.

Cohn, S., Mermelstein, R., Kamarck, T., & Hoberman, H. M. (1985). Measuring the functional components of social support. In I. G. Sarason & B. R. Sarason (Eds.), *Social support: Theory, research and application*. Dordrecht, The Netherlands: Martinus Nijhoff.

Everly, G. S., & Lating, J. M. (2002). *A clinical guide to the treatment of the human stress response* (2nd. ed.). New York, NY: Kluwer/Plenum.

Folkman, S., & Moskowitz, J. T. (2000). Positive affect and the other side of coping. *American Psychologist*, *55*(6), 647–654.

Goode, K. T., Haley, W. E., Roth, D. L., & Ford, G. R. (1998). Predicting longitudinal changes in caregiver physical and mental health: A stress process model. *Health Psychology*, *17*, 190–198.

Lazarus, R. S. (1993). Why we should think of stress as a subset of emotion? In L. Goldberger & S. Breznitz (Eds.), *Handbook of stress: Theoretical and empirical aspects* (2nd ed., pp. 21–39). New York, NY: Free Press.

Lazarus, R. S. (1999). *Stress and emotion: A new synthesis*. New York, NY: Springer.

Lazarus, R. S., & Folkman, S. (1984). *Stress, appraisal, and coping*. New York, NY: Springer.

Lewis, S. J., & Roberts, A. R. (2001). Crisis assessment tools: The good, the bad, the available. *Brief Treatment and Crisis Intervention*, *1*(1), 17–28.

Pavalko, E. K., & Henderson, K. A. (2006). Combining care work and paid work do workplace policies make a difference? *Research on Aging*, *28*(3), 359–374. doi: 10.1177/01640275 05285848

Pearlin, L. I., Mullan, J. T., Semple, S. J., & Skaff, M. M. (1990). Caregiving and the stress process: An overview of concepts and their measures. *Gerontologist, 30*(5), 583–594.

Procidano, M. E., & Heller, K. (1983). Measures of perceived social support from friends and freom family: Three validation studies. *American Journal of Community Psychology*, 11, 1–24.

Regehr, C., & Bober, T. (2005). *In the line of fire: Trauma in the emergency services*. New York, NY: Oxford University Press.

Robison, J., Moen, P., & Dempster-McClain, D. (1995). Women's caregiving: Changing profiles. *Journals of Gerontology*, *50B*(6), S362–S373. doi: 10.1093/geronb/50B.6.S362

Sarason, B. R. (1986). Social behavior and cognitive processes. R. Schwarrer (Ed.), *Self-related cognitions in anxiety and motivation* (pp. 77–86). Hillsdale, NJ: Erlbaum.

Sarason, I. G., Sarason, B. R., Shearin, E. N., & Pierce, G. R. (1987). A brief measurement of social support: Practical and theoretical implications. *Journal of Social and Personal Relationships*, 4, 497–510.

Scharlach, A. E., Gustavson, K., & Dal Santo, T. S. (2007). Assistance received by employed caregivers and their care recipients: Who helps care recipients when caregivers work full time? *Gerontologist*, *47*(6), 752–762.

Selye, H. (1956). *The stress of life*. New York, NY: McGraw-Hill.

Stokes, J. P. (1983). Predicting satisfaction with social support from social network structure. *American Journal of Community Psychology*, *11*, 141–152.

CHAPTER

24

Family-Centered Programs and Interventions for Military Children and Youth

Gregory A. Leskin, Ediza Garcia, Julie D'Amico,
Catherine E. Mogil, and Patricia E. Lester

BACKGROUND AND OVERVIEW

Military children, similar to their service member parents and caretakers, demonstrate tremendous strength and resilience as they contend with the many challenges that are inherently part of growing up in a military family. Although many military children thrive, recent research has shown that the ongoing cycles of deployment of service members to Iraq and Afghanistan during the past decade has taken its toll on family members. To increase support for these children and their families, the military, universities, and community-based agencies have developed behavioral health programs, interventions, and resources aimed toward supporting military families, with specific emphasis on supporting children impacted by military service. This chapter describes the ways in which military life experiences may positively shape, as well as negatively impact, a child's emotional and developmental growth. To begin with, we present a brief overview of the current demographics of military families. We examine the typical aspects of military life, such as frequent relocations and prolonged separations, which can affect the lives of military families and children as they adapt to shifting social situations and physical environments. We explore how deployment-related stressors extend beyond the service member to affect the children's emotional and behavioral functioning, academic performance, interpersonal relationships and physical health. Finally, we underscore the importance of utilizing a family-centered approach and describe several programs, interventions, and resources that provide targeted assistance for these families within the military and civilian systems of care.

COMPOSITION OF FAMILIES IN THE MILITARY

Since 2001, more than 1.6 million Active and Ready Reserve Component forces, including the National Guard, have deployed to combat missions as part of Operation Iraqi Freedom (OIF), Operation Enduring Freedom (OEF), and/or Operation New Dawn (OND). This section describes the current demographics of the U.S. military according to statistics provided by the Department of Defense Manpower Data Center for 2009 (Office of the Deputy Under Secretary of Defense, 2009). It also provides the composition of the U.S. Military Active Duty and National Guard and Reserve units as well as providing actual counts for the number of families and children. These numbers suggest a large population of family members across the active components.

Active Duty

In 2009, the total population of the U.S. Active Duty and Reserve Components equaled 3.6 million, with the largest segment comprised of active duty service members. The Department of Defense branches with the most active duty members are the Army, followed by the Air Force, Navy, and Marine Corps. Women comprise 14.3% of the total active duty force. The average age for the active duty force is 28.4 years (average age for active duty officer is 34.7, and enlisted personnel is 27.2 years). More than half of active duty personnel are married (55.8%). A greater number of officers (70.1%) report being married compared with enlisted personnel (53.1%). Further, approximately 6.6% of marriages are dual-military (both partners are in same or different branch of service). More than one third (38.4%) of active duty families are married with children, and 5.3% are single parents with children. There are 1,175,055 military children of active duty personnel. The largest age group is those between the age of birth to 5 years (43%), followed by those 6 years to 11 years (32%), and then those 12 to 18 (24%).

Reserve and Guard

The average age for Selected Reserve and Guard members is 32.2 years (average age for Reserve and Guard officer is 40.2, and enlisted personnel is 30.9 years). Women comprise 17.8% of the total selected Reserve personnel force. More than one third (33.7%) are married with children and 9% are single parents with children. There are 650,549 military children from reservist families. The largest age group for the children of reservists is the 12- to 18-year (35%) group, followed by 6 to 11 years (34%), and then the younger children from birth to 5 years (31%).

THE IMPACT OF MILITARY CULTURE ON FAMILIES

As noted, there are a large number of service members with spouses and children who accompany them into military service. The children in these families are often born into and grow up under the auspices of military culture. This section provides a context of the family's experiences of life in the military.

Military Culture

Military culture is defined as a core set of traditions, values, beliefs, and worldviews that structure how military members communicate, interact, and understand their experiences (Coll, Weiss, & Yarvis, 2011; Weiss & Coll, 2011). Common threads transcend all military branches and commands despite the numerous units designed with a specific military purpose, physical location, and historical perspective. These commonalities include the presence of hierarchical rank order, command structure, and judicial and legal codes. Furthermore, every service member is expected to train for and perform a multitude of tasks and occupations, as well as follow orders issued by military command. Though not in uniform, the family member's experiences of the military will often parallel those of the service member. For example, military spouses are expected to demonstrate a sustained commitment to the military mission via support for the service member and the larger military community (Knox & Price, 1995). Likewise, military children are indoctrinated in the customs of the service branch including patriotism and pride for the parent's duty. There may also be pressure to conform and to display disciplined behavior.

Geographic Mobility

Another common feature of military life that may influence families and children is the potential for a more transient lifestyle with frequent physical relocations (i.e., moving from one installation to another or to an overseas duty station). Military families change residence, on average, every 2 to 3 years (U.S. Department of Defense, 1998). Studies that examined the effect of this sort of military geographic mobility report a potential for negative impact on the child's psychological functioning. For example, Brett (1982) found that military children who experience frequent moves report difficulties establishing and maintaining sustained friendships and social networks. Still others have found geographic mobility related to reduction in academic success (Temple & Reynolds, 1999) and difficulties with emotional/behavioral adjustment (Simpson & Fowler, 1993). Further, adult children of military parents report that geographic mobility is the single most stressful aspect of growing up within the military culture (Ender, 2000).

PARENTAL SEPARATION AND DEPLOYMENT

Spending time apart from the service member is another common aspect of military life. Below we describe the effects of general separation from the family and then focus on the impact of war-time deployment on the at-home caretaking parent and the child. Developmental and gender differences in response to deployment are also described. The section ends with a review of service member parent reintegration.

Parental Separation

Frequent separations from a parent are also a fact of life for most military children. A service member parent may be physically separated from their spouse and children during peacetime and wartime for a variety of reasons, besides a formal deployment: prolonged unaccompanied tours (e.g., 12-month overseas), temporary duty assignments (TDY), field training, certification, or education. The specifics associated with the separations a family experiences vary depending on branch and position. Members of special or elite forces and security details, for example, might experience more frequent yet briefer separations from families. Even during peacetime, these separations from a military parent have been found to be related to increases in child anxiety and depression compared with children in nondeployed families (Jensen, Grogan, Xenakis, & Bain, 1989). Other studies have found that parental separations can be stressful for the at-home caretaking parent and for the children including difficulties with depression, loneliness, and shifts in roles and responsibilities (Coolbaugh & Rosenthal, 1992).

Parental Deployment

Although peacetime parental separations can be difficult, deployment during wartime represents one of the most potentially stressful experiences military families face. Wartime deployments require the family to not only adapt to the difficulties that normally accompany parental separation, but also to grapple with the additional fears and concerns about potential losses due to injury, fatigue, stress, or even death of the service member. In many situations, the stressors experienced by the family go through a cyclical process (White, de Burgh, Fear, & Iversen, 2011). These stages of deployment include predeployment, deployment, postdeployment, reintegration, and redeployment (Lagrone, 1978; Pincus, House, Christensen, & Adler, 2005).

Impact On the Nondeployed Parent

The at-home caretaking parent may experience clinically significant levels of anxiety and other mental health challenges (Lester et al., 2010; Mansfield, Kaufman, Engel, & Gaynes, 2011). These psychological symptoms may be due to the expectation of adequately running a household as a single parent while managing feelings of concern for the partner's safety. Furthermore, families living away from their family of origin may feel isolated and may have a little to no social support system. The combination of increased anxiety and worry coupled with the diminished support system can create increased risk for child maltreatment on the part of the caretaking parents (Gibbs, Martin, Kupper, & Johnson, 2007; Rentz et al., 2007). Similar to their civilian counterparts, caretaker functioning in military families is influential in predicting child adjustment because children generally look toward their parent for cues of safety and security (Cox & Paley, 1997; Lester et al., 2012).

Impact of Deployment on the Child

Military children may experience numerous stressors associated with each phase of deployment. For example, the predeployment phases might feature a sense of anticipatory anxiety or distancing from the deploying parent as a means to cope with their concerns about separation and fears of war (Burrell, Adams, Durand, & Castro, 2006; Huebner, Mancini, Wilcox, Grass, & Grass, 2007; Kelley et al., 2001; Orthner & Rose, 2005).

While the parent is deployed, the roles of the children might change with older children taking more active roles in caring for the younger children (Bowling & Sherman, 2008). Furthermore, one of the most common child reactions to parental deployment is increased anxiety (Lester et al., 2010). Children with a deployed parent may worry about the deployed parent's safety as well as express concerns for the caretaking (i.e., nondeployed) parent's well-being. One potential reason for this increase in anxiety is the high level of media coverage of the war and the fact that children may be exposed to television and radio broadcasts that describe loss of lives or the inherent danger in a battlefield.

Military communities are cohesive units that provide significant support for each other. When there is a loss in the community, children are often aware of this information and it can potentially exacerbate their fears. In addition to increased anxiety, military children have shown an increase in feelings of sadness and uncertainty, with significant increases in mental health diagnoses and outpatient visits (Gorman, Eide, & Hisle-Gorman, 2010; Mansfield et al., 2011; Williams, Schone, Archibald, & Thompson, 2004).

Although anxiety is an effect of deployment that is seen across children of a variety of ages, there are other significant developmental differences in children's response to deployment. As previously mentioned, approximately 75% of children of U.S. service members are under age 11 (Office of the Deputy Under Secretary of Defense, 2009). This period has wide developmental variability; thus, it is important to consider the distinctive behaviors that may be observed depending on the child's developmental stage.

Infants may express their feelings through crying more frequently or refusing to separate from their caregiver (Williams, in press). Toddlers may display an increase in temper tantrums or regressive behaviors. For instance, a 2-year-old who was toilet-trained may begin regular bed wetting as a way to communicate his or her ambivalent feelings about the missing parent. These children may also demonstrate a change in their eating and sleeping habits. Young children ages 3 to 5 may also respond to the transition in family roles with confusion, disruptive behaviors, and behaviors they had previously mastered. Maintaining a connection with the military parent via photographs, audio and video recordings, and other personal items, such as dolls, is important and often serves as a source of comfort for the child (Williams, in press).

Six- to 11-year-olds typically have a better understanding of time and the impact of the separation from the parent; however, they require proper guidance about the reason for the parent's absence from the home. Without an explanation, some school-age children develop their own interpretation of the situation and may feel responsible for the parent's departure. These children also demonstrate somatic complaints, such as stomachaches, and express feelings of loneliness and sadness (Johnson et al., 2007). Additionally, there may be more frequent attention-seeking behaviors to increase the amount of time spent with the at-home parent. Aside from these responses, children also evidence pride in their parent's career and in the military service branch. They may also begin to develop a sense of duty to serve their community.

Adolescents may be at particularly heightened risk during deployment. Teenagers may experience a range of behavioral and emotional problems, including acting out behaviors, depression, and anxiety (Chandra et al., 2010). Adolescents often acquire caretaking responsibilities, and assume a leadership role in their family, particularly if there are younger siblings in the home. Given their cognitive development, teenagers generally recognize the danger the service member parent may experience during a combat deployment. During adolescence, teenagers are often interested in spending more time with their peers than their family. This can be a protective factor as it's often helpful for teens to associate with other military teens who can relate to their unique life experience.

In addition to the developmental differences, research demonstrates certain gender differences in adolescent's response to the various phases of deployment, such as males exhibiting more maladaptive behaviors than females (Reed, Bell, & Edwards, 2011).

Boys may also demonstrate higher levels of acute stress, behavioral problems, depression, and adjustment disorders during their parent's deployment (Mansfield et al., 2011). However, Chandra et al. (2010) reported that teenage females reported greater problems during the family's reintegration phase following deployment. Several explanations have been provided to support this finding, including the family role that girls may take during the deployment. Specifically, girls may occupy additional caretaking functions when the service member is deployed. On the service member's return, girls are often expected to relinquish their heightened role in the family, which can lead to tension between the teen and their service member parent. Also, problems may arise due to difficulties establishing emotional connections with the service member parent, especially among female adolescents (Chandra et al., 2010). The gender difference has important clinical implications when developing and implementing effective interventions; however, additional research is required to understand the exact nature of gender differences among military youth as a response to military deployments (White et al., 2011).

Reintegration Challenges Following Deployment

The challenges for a military family do not disappear when the deployment ends. Once the service member returns home, family members may contend with renegotiating family roles and responsibilities. Additionally, the service member is readjusting to family life and may be dealing with physical and/or mental health injuries and stressors. At the time of a parent's return from deployment, children may be relieved and excited, as well as challenged and conflicted with the task of reintegrating the separated parent back into the family unit. Further complicating the families' reintegration tasks is the potential for the occurrence of additional future combat deployments. The National Military Families Association (2005) describes the reintegration challenges, multiplied by concerns over future deployment, as a "spiral of deployment" (p. 14), rather than a cycle of deployment, to reflect the many changes that occur within the family across the phases of multiple deployments.

Reestablishment of effective co-parenting can be an important task, especially during the reintegration phase. For example, problems in the co-parenting relationship have been linked with behavior problems, attachment insecurity, and emotional dysregulation in children, as well as less positive parent-child interactions (Bonds & Gondoli, 2007; Feinberg, 2002; Feinberg & Kan, 2008; Schoppe-Sullivan, Weldon, Claire, Davis, & Buckley, 2009). Multiple and/or prolonged deployments can challenge the co-parenting relationship in significant ways. For example, the caretaking parent who has assumed all parenting responsibilities may become accustomed to performing tasks in a particular way and thus may have difficulty relinquishing some of his or her parenting duties when the service member parent returns. Alternatively, the service member may feel thrust back into the parenting role before he or she is ready, especially if the caretaking parent is eager to resume the sharing of parenting responsibilities. On reunion, parents may find it difficult to reestablish themselves as a team. This challenge is especially true for families in which the service member returns with physical and/or mental health injuries.

THE FAMILY-CENTERED APPROACH

The recognition of the difficulties and challenges faced by the whole family has led to the development of family-centered approaches that provide behavioral health support across the phases of deployment. Several randomized controlled studies have demonstrated how resilience-enhancing family programs that deliver specific parent and family-level skill-based interventions improve a broad range of child psychological outcomes, including reductions in depression, anxiety, and acting out behavior (Beardslee et al., 2007; Layne et al., 2008; Rotheram-Borus et al., 2006).

Key goals of many family-centered programs are enhancing resilience and increasing opportunities for positive outcomes following stressful life events (Cicchetti & Hinshaw, 2002; Luthar, 2006). As described by Saltzman et al. (2011), family-centered, resiliency enhancing interventions are theorized to bolster positive family support processes. Further, Saltzman et al. (2011) describe the main mechanisms related to strengthening family resilience as part of family-centered interventions for military families. These include:

- Providing psychoeducation and developmental guidance to family members and children about the impact of parental deployment and distress.
- Developing a shared family narrative about each family member's experience through the deployment.
- Enhancing family awareness and understanding of each other's experiences.
- Improving family empathy and communication, and highlighting the family's strengths and instilling a sense of hope.

One of the benefits of family-centered programs is that they are structured to offer flexibility in implementation and can be conducted in a variety of different settings. Moreover, the "family-friendly" service philosophy includes working in settings where families and children might naturally feel more comfortable, and they may be more accessible for busy family members. This is especially beneficial when the target population is military families, as there continues to be some lingering stigma against traditional mental health settings; and even where stigma has been erased it can be difficult for these busy families to get to a mental health facility. Three settings (i.e., school, medical, and telemedicine) are considered when offering services to military families.

School Settings

Military schools and community-based schools with military children may represent particularly important settings in which to intervene with military children (Fitzsimons & Krause-Parello, 2009). Bradshaw et al. (2010) suggest that some children experience challenges with their academic performance when a parent deploys. Additionally, most children and adolescents spend a large majority of their time within a school setting making it a practical location for service provision.

Medical Settings

Many military families access health care during parental deployment (Eide, Gorman, & Hisle-Gorman, 2010), which makes it an important access point of care. Mental health clinicians can work with medical professionals to evaluate psychological functioning and provide tools to build the child's skills. The challenge of connecting with children and families in a medical setting is that children respond to environments that are stimulating and inviting, which is often an atmosphere that is difficult to achieve in a medical facility. Ideally, an office should be set apart for mental health purposes. It should have toys and games appealing to children and should have little to no medical equipment. There should also be space to draw and to play on the floor depending on the age and interests of the child. Facilitating sessions in the late afternoon and early evening is also a key consideration to minimize the time spent away from school.

Telemedicine

A unique type of mental health delivery using Internet and digital technology remotely linking family members with health services is called *telemedicine*. The American Telemedicine Association (2011) defines telemedicine as the "delivery of any healthcare service or transmission of wellness information using telecommunications technology" (http://www.atmeda.org/i4a/pages). Telemedicine in the military is implemented across services branches to treat psychological and medical disorders such as posttraumatic stress, depression, traumatic brain injury, suicide risk, and diabetes. Furthermore, the geographic dispersal of military families suggests the importance of using technology in the provision of health care services. For further reading, see the National Center for Telehealth and Technology guidebook that provides specific considerations for using this technique with military-related individuals (Kramer, Ayers, Mishkind, & Norem, 2011).

PROGRAMS, INTERVENTIONS, AND RESOURCES

Programs that aid military families have waxed and waned throughout the history of the military. Since the early years of U.S. warfare, the military has made efforts to provide at least some assistance to military families and to promote services that allow families to better adapt to the stressors of military life and war (Bowen, 1989). Over time, however, it has become apparent that additional programs are necessary to support families as they face increasing challenges. The modern U.S. military offers many high-quality, evidence-based family programs that support child and adolescent behavioral health for a wide range of deployment related concerns (Weinick et al., 2011). The number and quality of programs reflect, in part, appreciation from military and political leadership that a well-adjusted military family can easily equate to higher levels of military member reenlistment, more satisfied personnel, and greater overall military community cohesion (Bourg & Segal, 1999). In another sense, the number of programs reflects how military service, for service members and their families, represents a courageous commitment to one's country that is often accompanied by challenges, risks, and stressors. Not all families, however, will be informed or sufficiently aware of these programs, interventions, and resources designed to provide services, information, and education to military families with children. Social workers, therefore, should know about these resources and be able to refer families to them. The web-based initiatives may be especially applicable to military families who live in rural or less populated settings. Additionally, web-based programs provide lower cost services that families can access on-demand at times that are convenient for them. This service delivery type also connects family members who are at a distance from each other by providing information and increased family closeness (Ritterband et al., 2003). Some of the online programs listed in the appendix offer assistance to military children and seek to help military children through the use of interactive activities that teach and build resiliency skills.

One approach that merits attention here is the Family-Based Resilience Enhancing Model, or Families OverComing Under Stress (FOCUS). The FOCUS intervention is based on a conceptual framework of evidence-based interventions with the primary goal of lessening the family's stress while simultaneously increasing psychological resilience and family support (Beardslee et al., 2011; Lester et al., 2010). The family's resiliency is enhanced through active involvement in learning and practicing communication, emotion regulation, goal setting, problem solving, and managing reminders associated with deployment and loss. The skill-training programs can be delivered by a Resiliency Trainer (RT) to an individual family (called Individual Family Resiliency Training or IFRT), or to skill-building groups, workshops, and through consultations with individual family members. Several outcome studies (Beardslee et al., 2011; Lester et al., 2012) demonstrate the FOCUS program's effectiveness in reducing child and parent distress, and increasing military families' sense of cohesion and support for one another.

Additionally, military families have accessed FOCUS services across different physical settings (e.g., clinics and schools) as well as through telemedicine and Internet-based instruction. In the section that follows, several fictional vignettes illustrate the implementation of the "family-centered approach" that teaches the FOCUS core skills as a means to enhance resilience in the face of deployment related challenges and stress.

The Case Vignette: Charlie explains key considerations for building a child's skills through the FOCUS approach.

Case Vignette: Charlie

Charlie is a 7-year-old whose father deployed 2 months ago. Since Charlie's birth, his father has been home for approximately 3½ years. Charlie performed well in the first grade, but his transition to second grade has been a challenge. His teacher reports that Charlie has difficulty sustaining attention, staying in his seat, and turning in homework assignments. Furthermore, Charlie exhibits aggressive behavior toward peers accompanied by frequent tearfulness. These behaviors in particular have resulted in limited peer interaction and social isolation.

The course of intervention with Charlie involved building his emotional awareness. The session began with establishing a vocabulary of feelings to help Charlie label his experience. The clinician then assisted Charlie with tying his feelings to their physical manifestation on his body. Developing the connection between emotions and one's bodily reactions provides a signal to the child about the feelings of discomfort. He also learned new coping tools to help him relax when his feelings become elevated. Sharing the techniques learned by Charlie with his teacher helped translate the skill to the classroom setting. For instance, when Charlie became upset, he was able to tell his teacher how he was feeling. This notification allowed Charlie's teacher to help him implement his coping strategies and calm down.

The child of a deployed parent is filled with mixed emotions and it can be challenging to sort through them all, especially at a young age. Emotional regulation is a key tool for helping children develop an understanding of what they are experiencing as well as giving their experience a voice. In the case vignette involving Charlie, his feelings were impacting his school performance both academically and socially. Emotional awareness skills were crucial to supporting his academic success. The Case Vignette: Sophia highlights key considerations for working with an adolescent utilizing the FOCUS model.

Case Vignette: Sophia

Sophia, a 15-year-old girl, was referred by her pediatrician to the mental health practitioner working out of her pediatrician's office, due to noncompliance with taking her medication. She was diagnosed with diabetes a few years earlier and was reportedly functioning well. On her mother's deployment, Sophia's father noted a change in her behavior. For instance, she appeared less concerned with the food she ate, often consuming foods that she knew she should not eat, and she would forget to take her insulin. During Sophia's regular checkup with her pediatrician, she was dismissive about the effects of not taking her medication and stated that she was responsible for caring for her younger brothers so she could also take care of herself.

While working with Sophia, the clinician validated her quest for independence from her family and normalized her desire to fit in with her peers. These are both typical behaviors observed in adolescence. As a result of her medical illness, Sophia felt different from her friends. Psychoeducation about diabetes helped Sophia understand the gravity of her situation, but she was still hesitant to commit to the regimented dosage of insulin.

The clinician utilized the FOCUS model, including a narrative timeline activity to engage Sophia in telling the story of her major life events. Sophia verbalized many positive experiences such as making the basketball team and taking a family vacation. The timeline also included her medical appointments, obtaining the diagnosis, and her medication noncompliance. While talking through the events, Sophia shared that many of her memories related to her medical condition included her mom, who served as a supportive and nurturing presence. She also noted missing her mom and wishing her mom could help remind her about taking the medication. Creation of a narrative helped Sophia to recognize that her behaviors were partially due to wishing her mom was around to care for her. The clinician provided psychoeducation about deployment and helped Sophia develop effective coping strategies. Equally important, Sophia created ways to incorporate thoughts of her mother into her daily routine in order to maintain the connection.

Treatments for Traumatized Children and Families

Several interventions have been developed for PTSD and traumatic grief in children. For example, trauma-focused cognitive behavioral therapy (TF-CBT: Cohen & Mannarino, 2011) is a treatment for children who have been exposed to traumatic experiences and might be experiencing stress reactions. A related adaptation, traumatic grief-cognitive behavioral therapy (TG-CBT) may be appropriate for bereaved military children who may experience traumatic grief interconnected with trauma symptoms as a result of familial loss. TF-CBT is an evidenced-based treatment well suited for work with military children and their parents or caregivers. Treatment components include psychoeducation about the process of grieving and recovery from exposure to traumatic stress, learning effective communication and relaxation skills, emotion modulation, and cognitive coping. Through TF-CBT children learn to develop and share their trauma narrative with other family members.

An additional intervention that has been adapted for treating the specific issues faced by military families is Parent-Child Interaction Therapy (PCIT: Hembree-Kigin & McNeil, 1995). Developed specifically for parents who tend to use more corporally based types of discipline (Chaffin et al., 2004), PCIT has been adapted for use within military settings for younger children and their parents. In PCIT, a military parent is taught appropriate communication skills to improve their relationships with their children. The goal of PCIT is to improve children's behavior and reduce parental stress through practice of efficacious parenting and communication skills.

CONCLUSION

Military families face unique and potentially complex challenges as a result of parental separations, frequent relocations, combat-related deployments, and parental injury or even death. To support family members and children, the military and community-based organizations have created programs, interventions, and resources across a variety of settings and through Internet-based platforms. The goals of these programs are to offer support, education, treatment, and prevention for parents and children to adapt and cope through cyclical nature of deployment and military life. Most military children respond to the stressors of military life with resilience and strength, while other children might require additional assistance to cope with the difficulties and challenges. All children and families can take advantage of these helpful supportive programs to anticipate and plan for the unique issues that can accompany their parent's separation for prolonged periods of time into combat situations.

CHAPTER DISCUSSION QUESTIONS

1. Describe how military children might respond differently across the cycle of deployment. How might these reactions differ by age group? How might they differ according to gender?
2. Describe the theories underlying the development of family-centered interventions. How might a family-centered approach specifically address issues that impact military families and children (e.g., deployment related stress reactions in children)?
3. How do the authors define military culture? Compare and contrast the unique military cultures of active duty Army, National Guard, and U.S. Coast Guard. How might these qualities impact the family and children?
4. Discuss different ways that web-based interventions might assist military families. How can web-based interventions assist families that frequently need to change their living arrangements? How about those with a parent deployed into a combat zone?

REFERENCES

American Telemedicine Association. (2011). Retrieved from http://www.atmeda.org/i4a/pages

Beardslee, W., Lester, P., Klosinski, L., Saltzman, W., Woodward, K., Nash, W., . . . Leskin, G. A. (2011). Family-centered preventive intervention for military families: Implications for implementation science. *Prevention Science, 12*, 339–348.

Beardslee, W. R., Wright, E. J., Gladstone, T. R. G., & Forbes, P. (2007). Long-term effects from a randomized trial of two public health preventive interventions for parental depression. *Journal of Family Psychology, 21*(4), 703–713.

Bonds, D. D., & Gondoli, D. M. (2007). Examining the process by which marital adjustment affects maternal warmth: The role of co-parenting support as a mediator. *Journal of Family Psychology, 21*, 288–296.

Bourg, C., & Segal, M. W. (1999). The impact of family supportive policies on organizational commitment to the Army. *Armed Forces & Society, 25*, 633–652.

Bowen, G. L. (1989). Satisfaction with family life in the military. *Armed Forces & Society, 15*, 571–592.

Bowling, U. B., & Sherman, M. D. (2008). Welcoming them home: Supporting service members and their families in navigating the tasks of reintegration. *Professional Psychology: Research and Practice, 39*, 451–458.

Bradshaw, C., Sudhinaraset, M., Mmari, K., & Blum, R. (2010). School transitions among military adolescents: A qualitative study of stress and coping. *School Psychology Review, 39(1)*, 84–105.

Brett, J. (1982). Job transfer and well-being. *Journal of Applied Psychology, 67*, 450–463.

Burrell, L. M., Adams, G. A., Durand, D. B., & Castro, C. A. (2006). The impact of military lifestyle demands on well-being, Army, and family outcomes. *Armed Forces & Society, 33*, 43–58.

Chaffin, M. Silovsky, J. F., Funderburk, B., Valle, L. A., Brestan, E. V. Balchova, T., . . . Bonner, B. L. (2004). Parent–child interaction therapy with physically abusive parents: Efficacy for reducing future abuse reports. *Journal of Consulting and Clinical Psychology, 72*, 500–510.

Chandra, A., Lara-Cinisomo, S., Jaycox, L. H., Tanielian, T., Burns, R. M., Ruder, T., & Han, B. (2010). Children on the homefront: The experience of children from military families. *Pediatrics, 125*, 16–25.

Cicchetti, D., & Hinshaw, S. (2002). Development and psychopathology: Editorial: Prevention and intervention science: Contributions to developmental theory. *Development and Psychopathology, 14*, 667–671.

Cohen, J. A., & Mannarion, A. P. (2011). Trauma-focused CBT for traumatic grief in military children. *Journal of Contemporary Psychotherapy, 41*, 219–227.

Coll, J. E., Weiss, E. L., & Yarvis, J. S. (2011). No one leaves unchanged: Insights for civilian mental health care professionals into the military experience and culture. *Social Work in Health Care*, 50, 487–500.

Coolbaugh, K. W., & Rosenthal, A. (1992). *Family Separations in the Army*. Research Triangle Park, NC: Research Triangle Institute.

Cox, M. J., & Paley, B. (1997). Families as systems. *Annual Review of Psychology*, 48, 243–67.

Eide, M., Gorman, G., & Hisle-Gorman, E., (2010). Effects of parental military deployment on ediatric outpatient and well-child visit rates. *Pediatrics, 126*, 22–27.

Ender, M. G. (2000). The experiences of adult children of military parents. In M. J. Rosen & L. Sporacino (Eds.), *The military family: A practice guide for human service providers* (pp. 241–255). Westport, CT: Praeger.

Feinberg, M. E. (2002). Coparenting and the transition to parenthood: A framework for prevention. *Clinical Child and Family Psychology Review, 5*, 173–195.

Feinberg, M. E., & Kan, M. L. (2008). Establishing family foundations: Intervention effects on coparenting, parent/infant well-being, and parent-child relations. *Journal of Family Psychology, 22*, 253–263.

Fitzsimons, V. M., & Krause-Parello, C. A. (2009). Military children: When parents are deployed overseas. *Journal of School Nursing, 25*(1), 40–47.

Gibbs, D. A., Martin, S. L., Kupper, L. L., & Johnson, R. E. (2007). Child maltreatment in enlisted soldiers' families during combat-related deployments. *Journal of the American Medical Association, 298*, 528–535.

Gorman, G. H., Eide, M., & Hisle-Gorman, E. (2010). Wartime military deployment and increased pediatric mental and behavioral health complaints. *Pediatrics, 126*, 1058–1066.

Hembree-Kigin, T. L., & McNeil, C. B. (1995). *Parent–child interaction therapy*. New York, NY: Plenum Press.

Huebner, A. J., Mancini, J. A., Wilcox, R. M., Grass, S. R., & Grass, G. A. (2007). Parental deployment and youth in military families: Exploring uncertainty and ambiguous loss. *Family Relations, 56*, 112–122.

Jensen, P. S., Grogan, D., Xenakis, S. N., & Bain, M. W. (1989). Father absence: Effects on child and maternal psychopathology. *Journal of the American Academy of Child & Adolescent Psychiatry, 28*, 171–175.

Johnson S. J., Sherman M. D., Hoffman J. S., James, L. C., Johnson, P. L., Lochman, J. E., . . . Riggs, D. (2007). *The psychological needs of US military service members and their families: A preliminary report*. Washington, DC: American Psychological Association.

Kelley, M. L., Hock, E., Smith, K. M., Jarvis, M. S., Bonney, J. F., & Gaffney, M. A., (2001). Internalizing and externalizing behavior of children with enlisted navy mothers experiencing military-induced separation. *Journal of the American Academy of Child & Adolescent Psychiatry, 40*, 464–471.

Knox, J., & Price, D. H. (1995). The changing American military family: Opportunities for social work. *Social Service Review, 69*, 479–497.

Kramer, G., Ayers, T., Mishkind, M., & Norem, A. (2011). *DoD telemental health guidebook: Version 1*. Retrieved from http://t2health.org/sites/default/files/cth/guidebook/tmh-guidebook_06-11.pdf

LaGrone, D. M. (1978). The military family syndrome. *American Journal of Psychiatry, 135*, 1040–1043.

Layne, C. M., Saltzman, W. R., Poppleton, L., Burlingame, G. M., Pasalić, A., & Duraković-Belko, E. (2008). Effectiveness of a school-based group psychotherapy program for war-exposed adolescents: A randomized controlled trial. *Journal of the American Academy of Child and Adolescent Psychiatry, 47*, 1048–1062.

Lester, P., Peterson, K., Reeves, J., Knauss, L., Glover, D., Mogil, C., . . . Beardslee, M. (2010). The long war and parental combat deployment: Effects on military children and at-home spouses. *Journal of the American Academy of Child and Adolescent Psychiatry, 49*, 310–320.

Lester, P., Saltzman, W. R., Woodward, K., Glover, D., Leskin, G., Bursch, B., . . . Beardslee, W. (2012). Evaluation of a family-centered prevention intervention for military children and families facing wartime deployments. *American Journal of Public Health, 102* (S1), S48–S54.

Luthar, S. S. (2006). Resilience in development: A synthesis of research across five decades. In D. Cicchetti & D. J. Cohen (Eds.), *Developmental psychopathology: Vol. 3. Risk, disorder, and adaptation* (2nd ed., pp. 739–795). Hoboken, NJ: Wiley.

Mansfield, A. J., Kaufman, J. S., Engel, C. C., & Gaynes, B. N. (2011). Deployment and mental health diagnoses among children of U.S. Army personnel. *Archives of Pediatrics and Adolescent Medicine, 165*, 999–1005.

National Military Families Association. (2005). *Report on the cycles of deployment.* Washington, DC: Author.

Office of the Deputy Under Secretary of Defense. (2009). *Demographics profile of the military community*. Washington, DC: Author.

Orthner, D. K., & Rose, R. (2005). *Adjustment among army children to deployment separations.* Washington, DC: Army Research Institute for the Behavioral and Social Sciences.

Pincus, S. H., House, R., Christensen, J., & Adler, L. E. (2005). The emotional cycle of deployment: A military family perspective. *Journal of the Army Medical Department*, 615–623.

Reed, S. C., Bell, J. F., & Edwards, T., C. (2011). Adolescent well-being in Washington state military families. *American Journal of Public Health, 101*, 1676–1682.

Rentz E. D., Marshall S. W., Loomis D., Casteel C., Martin S. L., & Gibbs D. A. (2007). Effects of deployment on the occurrence of child maltreatment in military and nonmilitary families. *American Journal of Epidemiology, 165*, 1199–1206.

Ritterband, L. M., Cox, D. J., Walker, L. S., Kovatchev, B., McKnight, L., Patel, K., . . . Sutphen, J. (2003) An internet intervention as adjunctive therapy for pediatric encopresis. *Journal of Consulting and Clinical Psychology, 71*, 910–917.

Rotheram-Borus, M. J., Lester, P., Song, J., Lin, Y., Leonard, N. R., Beckwith, L., . . . Lord, L. (2006). Intergenerational benefits of family-based HIV interventions. *Journal of Consulting and Clinical Psychology, 74*, 622–627.

Saltzman, W., Lester, P., Beardslee, W., Layne, C., Woodward, K., & Nash, W. (2011). Mechanisms of risk and resilience in military families: Theoretical and empirical basis of a family-focused resilience enhancement program. *Clinical Child and Family Psychology Review, 14*, 213–230.

Schoppe-Sullivan, S. J., Weldon, A. H., Claire Cook, J., Davis, E. F., & Buckley, C. K. (2009). Coparenting behavior moderates longitudinal relations between effortful control and preschool children's externalizing behavior. *Journal of Child Psychology and Psychiatry, 50*, 698–706.

Simpson, G., & Fowler, M. (1993). Geographic mobility and children's emotional/behavioral adjustment and school functioning. *Pediatrics, 37*, 303–309.

Temple, J. A., & Reynolds, A. J. (1999). School mobility and achievement: Longitudinal findings from an urban cohort. *Journal of School Psychology*, *37*, 355–377.

U.S. Department of Defense. (1998). *Selected manpower statistics, MO1 (the directorate for information, operations, and reports)*. Washington, DC: U.S. Government Printing Office.

Weinick, R. M., Beckjord, E. B., Farmer, C. M., Martin, L. T., Gillen, E. M., Acosta, J., Fisher, M. P., . . . Scharf, D.M. (2011). *Programs addressing psychological health and traumatic brain injury among U.S. military service members and their families*. Santa Monica, CA: RAND.

Weiss, E. L., & Coll, J. E. (2011). The influence of military culture and veteran worldviews on mental health treatment: Practice implications for combat veteran help-seeking and wellness. *International Journal of Health, Wellness and Society*, *1*, 75–86.

White, C. J., de Burgh, H. T., Fear, N. T., & Iversen, A. C. (2011). The impact of deployment to Iraq or Afghanistan on military children: A review of the literature. *International Review of Psychiatry*, *23*, 210–217.

Williams, D. S. (in press). Research and resilience: Young children and military combat deployments. *Zero to Three*.

Williams, T. V., Schone, E. M., Archibald, N. D., & Thompson, J. W. (2004). A national assessment of children with special health care needs: Prevalence of special needs and use of health care services among children in the military health system. *Pediatrics*, *114*(2), 384–393.

CHAPTER

25

Couple Therapy for Redeployed Military and Veteran Couples

KATHRYN BASHAM

INTRODUCTION

Military couples face unique challenges and rewards in navigating ordinary moves, separations, and reunions throughout their lives in the military. Adding the complexity of deployment, or multiple deployments, contributes layers of stressors facing these families. Given the high number of service members who returned from Iraq at the end of 2011 and the increasing number of service members who will be returning home from Afghanistan in the ensuing months, clinicians must be adequately prepared to address their needs. We need to support these service members and their partners as they renew attachments with each other, their children, and other family members and renegotiate family roles.

Everyone must address the reality that each family member has changed and is different as a result of the time apart and the impact of deployment. Understandably, it is unrealistic to return to a previous status quo. Instead, change is the dominant theme. Issues of gender, as well as other diversity themes, often remain invisible during the psychosocial transitions facing service members and their families following deployment. Yet, they play a central role, albeit implicit, in shaping different responses to combat and deployment stressors and in seeking help for physical and mental health problems. They also influence access and receptivity toward or avoidance of contemporary evidence-based mental health interventions, including psychotherapy and recovery models. In this chapter, the intersections of various diversity themes are addressed, foregrounding the role of gender in relation to the ways that service members and their partners adapt to post-deployment challenges. A phase-oriented trauma-informed couple therapy model is introduced that attends to the complexity of individual and interactional issues that affect the process of reuniting during a post-deployment period. After presenting research data and a theoretical scaffolding grounded in attachment and trauma theories to provide a rationale for this focus, the chapter summarizes key principles and interventions in couple therapy, with specific attention focused on the role of gender. Finally, these processes are illustrated with a disguised composite clinical case vignette featuring Staff Sergeant Maria Sanchez and her husband Carlos Sanchez.

RATIONALE

War by definition is horrific. Service members often respond to combat with normal responses to abnormal events. Even with sound resilience fortifying service members and their families, many still face a full range of adjustments and transitions. The Operation Iraqi Freedom (OIF), Operation Enduring Freedom (OEF), and Operation New Dawn (OND) troops are presenting with a constellation of what is referred to as the *signature injuries* of these conflicts. Each war produces a different set of signature injuries. For our current troops, research data support a high incidence of a constellation of co-occurring conditions including posttraumatic stress (PTSD), depression and suicidal thinking, traumatic brain injury, substance abuse, and intimate partner violence (Institute of Medicine [IOM], 2010; Mental Health Advisory Team 7 [MHAT VII], 2011; Tanielian & Jaycox, 2008). Theoretical practice and research literature supports the knowledge base that provides the scholarly scaffolding for this chapter. Given the increasing need for mental health and psychosocial services for returning service members, their partners, children and families, clinicians need to advance their knowledge base and clinical skills related to the most effective ways to help these couples (IOM, 2010; Weinick et al., 2011). Stigma remains a powerful negative force that prevents many at-risk service members and their partners from seeking and engaging in necessary services. Gendered roles play a significant role in understanding and coping with various stressors throughout the deployment cycle.

KEY PRINCIPLES OF CLINICAL SOCIAL WORK PRACTICE

An obvious question arises: How can we as clinical social workers be most useful in assisting these couples with their transitions? What values, knowledge, and clinical skills are important in our work? Throughout the years, I have distilled central principles and have arrived at a working mantra that guides my clinical social work practice. Optimally, I aim to provide "relationship-based, culturally responsive, research informed, and theoretically grounded" practice (Basham, 2009, p. 264). As clinicians, you may or may not agree with all of these principles of practice. However, as clinical social workers, we are obligated to abide by our code of ethics to engage with clients in a respectful, nonjudgmental alliance, while drawing from theoretically grounded and research informed knowledge. Cultural responsiveness is central as well.

Relationship-Based

Many clinicians recognize the importance of a relationship-based treatment model, especially in light of the disruptions to attachment caused by exposure to traumatic stressors during deployment. Establishing effective engagement with military and veteran couples requires that a clinician conveys respect for the couple's resilience and values the notion of empowerment. Most service members and veterans express a wish for their treatment to be customized to them as individuals, rather than following prescribed, manualized protocols, exclusively. A one-size-fits-all treatment approach often alienates returning service members, by reinforcing the objectifying of people and reinforcing the tendency to detach or disengage. Whether a clinician holds military or civilian status, he or she needs to recognize how each service member makes meaning out of her or his military experience and identity.

SYNTHESIS OF THEORY MODELS

Because most of the current psychotherapy models for our returning troops and their families are based on cognitive-behavioral models, less attention has been paid to how deployment stressors may shake the very foundation of intimate partnerships and other family relationships (Basham, 2008; Weinick et al., 2011). I propose a flexible, collaborative, integrative couple therapy approach that draws on a synthesis of social and psychologically based theory models. Although this clinical social work model draws from a broad range of theory models, this chapter focuses primarily on the role of attachment and trauma theories. I address certain key constructs that are relevant from both of these theoretical perspectives and draw your attention to the usefulness of attachment theory in practice with military couples.

Attachment Theory

Relationships and attachments for military couples and families are challenged not only by the inevitable physical separations. They are also affected by the shifts in roles required during deployment. To understand the complexity of these challenges, attachment theory provides a useful psychological theory lens to explain the most effective ways to navigate these shifts in attachments. The central notion of a "secure base of attachment" and insecure or secure working models of attachment guide our understanding (Ainsworth, 1989; Basham, 2008; Bowlby, 1982; Clulow, 2001; Fisher & Crandall, 2001; Hazan, Gur-Yaish, & Campa, 2004; Schore, 2003).

Contemporary attachment theory also recognizes that there are different functions involved in attachments (i.e., caregiving or offering a safe haven; care seeking or proximity seeking; and exploration [venturing out with curiosity]). The notion of a circle of security (Marvin, Cooper, Hoffman, & Powell, 2002) suggests that an attachment figure provides a secure base of support and comfort in times of distress and facilitates a child's exploration of the wider world. This attachment working model sets the stage for ways that adults operate in relationships in adult life as well. Similarly, when there is distress, adults often seek the comfort of their primary attachment figure. During and following deployment, this predictable reliance on one another (i.e., each partner) for support is more difficult and requires effort to renegotiate new ways of relating.

In the wake of experiencing traumatic events during deployment, a returning service member may have experienced a dismantling of attachment, with a reactivation of an earlier insecure or unresolved working model of attachment. Dysregulation of affect commonly occurs, characterized by lability of moods and difficulties balancing emotions. The capacity for mentalization, a construct originally developed by Fonagy, Gergely, Jurist, and Target (2002) refers to the capacity for self-reflection and the regulation of affect. Another aspect of mentalization, one that resembles empathy, is the ability to anticipate another person's affect and behaviors. Such capacities provide a foundation for secure-autonomous attachment. Military couples who engage in therapy need to assess the nature of their attachments toward each other, children and other key family members.

Trauma Theory

While briefly turning to trauma theory for the moment, the role of secondary trauma warrants attention. This concept was originally understood as a typical response for caregivers and first-responders based on their exposure to traumatized persons (Bride & Figley, 2009). Although many service members and their partners reunite with a harmonious sense of shared accomplishment, others return with heightened anxiety, panic attacks, and rage eruptions, which set the stage for secondary trauma. Similar processes of experiencing PTSD-like symptoms of hyperarousal, avoidance, and numbing may affect family members as well. Another relational construct that bears attention is the "victim-victimizer-bystander" dynamic originally described by social psychologist Staub (1989), who explored the concept of the bystander as associated with violence and the roots of evil in his groundbreaking work on the effects of relational trauma.

To explain this construct, let me describe the processes involved. Some children who have suffered traumatic abuse understand experientially what it was like to be victimized by a victimizer. They may have experienced the absence of protection or attunement from unhelpful bystanders. Not only do the children experience the traumatic events in their external lives, they may also internalize this relationship template. While growing up, a traumatized child may begin to perceive, interact with, and experience the world through the lens of the "victim-victimizer-bystander" scenario. The question often arises if this construct is useful to returning troops. When a solider fights and kills others, he or she may identify as a victimizer, victim, and/or a bystander. Some question why this process of identification would occur when killing and capture have been sanctioned by society as part of preparedness for combat and a wartime code of ethics. Even so, paradoxically, the internalization of these new disturbing combat experiences can disrupt earlier relationship templates that provide safety and security. When a service member enters combat with a preexisting secure or insecure internal working model of attachment, the vagaries of war can alter those existing attachment patterns, especially if she felt betrayed (relational trauma) by her command or fellow service members. In fact, the service members may experience family members as victims, victimizers, and bystanders, a phenomenon that leads to dissension, polarized beliefs, and conflicts around power and control. This pattern is vitally important as we grasp to understand the complexity of issues facing traumatized couples and families as their attachments shift and change.

As noted earlier, this clinical work can be psychologically challenging for clinicians in relation to secondary trauma (as discussed in Chapter 5) as well as stimulated by potential enactments of the "victim-victimizer-bystander" relationship scenario. As a result, it is important for us to be mindful of the pull to become an overly zealous rescuer or a detached bystander. Yielding either to a passive, futile victim stance or an aggressive and victimizing condemnation of clients remain ongoing risks for the clinician as well (Basham & Miehls, 2004). Now that I have established the groundwork for the relationship-based and theoretical-grounding for clinical practice with military couples, let us turn our attention to the guideline of cultural responsiveness.

Cultural Responsiveness

What is the rationale for using the term *culturally responsive* rather than *culturally competent*, which is our clear mandate required by our professional practice guidelines (Basham, 2008)? Cultural responsiveness moves beyond and enhances definitions of cultural competence. It implies a dynamic interchange between the client and clinician to explore the meanings and the meaning-making processes that are attached to issues such as ethnicity, race, and gender. Rather than assuming a static model of competence, which relies on the building of knowledge, values, and skills, a culturally responsive approach presumes that an individual defines himself or herself with a complex intersection of meanings related to themes of race, ethnicity, religion, sexual identity, socioeconomic status, ability, gender, and language of origin. When clinical social workers engage early on with a client, they need to acquire the knowledge, values, and skills defined as cultural competence and also explore a shared understanding of how cultural themes have shaped the client's place in the world. Efforts should be made to avoid imposing stereotypical assumptions about sociocultural influences.

What does cultural responsiveness have to do with issues of diversity, in particular the role of gender with postdeployed military couples? First, to practice effectively with military couples, it is important to understand the values, customs, procedures, and hierarchy of the military. Values of responsibility, duty, courage, self-sacrifice, loyalty, and an "esprit-de-corps" guide the lives of these couples. They commit to a set of rules and responsibility to the well-being and safety of others. As the military privileges the universality of such values, there is a deliberate focus on "oneness" aimed to foster a worldview of homogeneity—the antithesis of heterogeneity or diversity. As service members bond with each other and stress their common goals, they often experience a sense of sustaining and comforting brotherhood and sisterhood, and for many, patriotic allegiance. This unit cohesion also has a strong positive influence on one's effectiveness in theater. During a mission, this is not the time to amplify differences because a sense of harmony and commonality of objectives are essential to safety and effectiveness. Yet what occurs at the end of the day when service members share meals and return to their sleeping quarters? Is the same degree of "sameness" operative? Often, the uniqueness of an individual service member is minimized or overlooked with a universalistic perspective.

Research-Based and Research-Informed

Primary treatment models for individual service members are often focused on symptom relief and grounded in evidence supported by randomized controlled research trials (often considered the gold standard for evaluation of efficacy). When we shift to the world of couple and family therapy models, there are few approaches that have been evaluated with randomized controlled trial methods. As a result, we need to shift our focus to the emerging evidence that is surfacing with a number of innovative models in work with military families. At present, one cognitive-behavioral model that helps service members and their partners learn about PTSD and find ways to renegotiate roles and functions is titled *Cognitive-Behavioral Conjoint Therapy* (Fredman, Monson, & Adair, 2011). Although participants report improvement in knowledge and symptom relief, it is unclear if any relationship shifts have occurred. A limitation of the model is the lack of suitability for many service members who suffer mild to moderate traumatic brain injury that affects their cognitive abilities and concentration. Several attachment theory–based models have been proposed that focus on repairing attachment injuries, although they have not yet been evaluated with military couples (Johnson, 2002; Sneath & Rheem, 2010). Although emerging evidence suggests usefulness in fostering renewed connections, not all clients can benefit from affectively charged work if they lack adequate affect regulation.

ROLE OF GENDER

To engage in culturally responsive treatment, we, as clinicians, need to recognize the complex issues related to the role of gender in shaping worldviews, gendered stereotypes, and family roles, including caregiving; responses to stress; physical and mental health conditions; and engagement with treatment. Although there have been major shifts in the training and preparedness of our troops that address inclusion of women, many service members still report a "masculinized" culture that values self-sufficiency, emotional containment, and physical and psychological strength (MHAT, 2011). These values are vitally important to completing a mission as long as there is also room, with proper timing, to validate the expression of feelings and a reliance on others to provide support and comfort and seek assistance, when needed.

Women represent a minority cohort in the Armed Forces with a majority of male service members, so we start with a brief review of demographics.

Demographics

Women now comprise more than 14% of the active duty force, with 17% in the National Guard and Reserve and 20% of new recruits (IOM, 2010). In 2008, U.S. women veterans reached 1.8 million, translating into 7.7% of the U.S. veteran population (Yano et al., 2010). Younger, on average, compared with male veterans (48 versus 61 years), women veterans are less likely to seek health care at the Veterans Administration (VA) settings as compared with male veterans (15% versus 22% in 2007) (Washington et al., 2007). Interestingly, VA enrollment has reached twice the national level among OIF and OEF veterans. Despite this shift in participation, most of today's women veterans obtain most of their medical care outside the VA (IOM, 2010; Murdoch et al., 2006). Their mental health issues and chronic diseases are similar to male VA users including PTSD, hypertension, depression, hyperlipidia (excess lipids), and chronic low back pain. In response to the apparent reluctance of women service members to seek necessary treatment, research needs to proactively attend to the needs of women as well as male service members (Gilliss et al., 2001).

Although women are technically barred from serving in combat specialties, such as armor or infantry, a growing and unprecedented number of female service members are deployed to combat areas where their lives are at risk. This is a relatively new phenomenon

(Hoge, Auchterlonie, & Milliken, 2006; IOM, 2010). They serve in a range of support positions (such as pilots, intelligence agents, transportation specialists, and mechanics) that involve traveling outside military bases, coming under direct fire and working alongside combat service members.

Mental Health and Health Issues

All deployed service members are exposed to exceptionally high levels of workplace stress, but women in the military often face some unique stressors that may affect their mental health and physical health. In general, women veterans have a higher burden of medical illness, worse quality-of-life outcomes, and earlier psychological morbidity than do men who are exposed to the same level of trauma (IOM, 2010; Kimerling et al., 2010; Tolin & Foa, 2006). Disturbing rates of military-related sexual harassment and assault are higher than the general population (Gradus, Street, Kelly, & Stafford, 2008; Suris, Lind, Kashner, Borman, & Petty, 2004). Kimerling et al. (2010) conducted a research study of Army reservists that revealed rates of 60% sexual harassment among women and 27% among men along with rates of physical and/or sexual assault of 23% among women and 3% among men. Military sexual assault presents some unique features. The victim usually knows the perpetrator, often someone the victim depends on. The risk to the victim often involves continuing exposure to the perpetrator and victimization. The same positive values promoted in the military of self-sufficiency, loyalty, and protection of the group can sometimes interfere with a victim's capacities to report an assault.

In general, rates of PTSD, depression, and substance abuse are higher for women who were assaulted as compared with those who were not assaulted (IOM, 2010). Himmelfarb, Yarger, and Mintz (2006) examined relationships between military sexual trauma and non-military sexual trauma (before and after military service) and PTSD in female veterans. They discovered that military sexual trauma was more strongly associated with PTSD as compared with premilitary trauma or postmilitary trauma. Rates of premilitary trauma (i.e., childhood sexual, physical, and emotional abuse) for both men and women are higher than the general population. Yet, women veterans are more likely than male veterans to have experienced interpersonal trauma prior to military service (Caulfield, et al., 2005; IOM, 2010; Merrill et al., 1999). For example, Rosen and Martin (1996) reported that 35% of active duty Army soldiers and 58% active duty female soldiers reported childhood abuses. In general, women are more likely to have experienced chronic trauma. Although preexisting childhood trauma is considered a risk factor for vulnerability to mental health problems, an interesting study conducted by Yehuda et al. (2006) revealed that those service members who had successfully resolved trauma-related symptoms, and attachment and relationship issues related to their childhood experiences navigated better in combat situations without suffering negative mental health outcomes.

There are significant gaps in the study of women and PTSD, yet as noted earlier, there seems to be a direct association with incidence of PTSD among deployed women and military sexual assault (IOM, 2010). Although there are new programs that specifically address military sexual assault, attention is still needed to expand such services and to address co-varying conditions of substance abuse, depression, traumatic brain injury, and intimate partner violence.

Health Care Needs

Wartime conditions impose unique challenges in relation to physical health and well-being for both male and female service members. Women service members also frequently report a range of physical health problems (e.g., lower back pain, headaches, pelvic pain, GI pain/symptoms, sexual dysfunction, gynecological symptoms, and chronic fatigue). Although the majority of women service members are childbearing age, several reports note the barriers to accessing appropriate gynecological visits and prenatal care, when indicated (IOM, 2010).

Additional issues facing female service members include differential gendered responses to trauma, heightened rates of intimate partner violence during post-deployment, and the central role as caregivers (MacDermid & Riggs, 2010).

Gendered Responses to Trauma

Although earlier research data support the notion of universality in relation to gendered responses to stress, including traumatic stress, a study launched at UCLA by Taylor et al. (2006) revealed that part of the stress response for women is a release of the hormone oxytocin. It is known to induce desires for connection, tenderness, and prosocial behavior. This process correlates with bonding, an enhanced sense of trust and reduction in fear and anxiety. As a neuromodulator that affects brain function, oxytocin also reduces cortisol and is associated with increased estrogen. Rather than assuming that the only responses to traumatic events are the options of "flight-fight-freeze" as elaborated by many contemporary researchers in neurobiology (Schore, 2003; Siegel, 2007; van der Kolk, 2003), other studies offered by Taylor (2006) suggest an alternative of "tend and befriend." Additional research data related to the role of ethnicity in shaping a response to stress yield similar findings. For example, cultural mores that view the self as interconnected with family and community are introduced as different from an independent, and individualistic self (i.e., the "we" self as distinguished from the "I" self) (Mattei, 2011). Individuals reared in collectivist "we-self" cultures often react to stress with "tend and befriend" or "pause and collect" patterns. As a result, they are inclined to reach out to others to provide care and connection in times of duress, including combat situations.

Intimate Partner Violence

Recent research data reveal high rates of intimate partner violence reported by returning OIF, OEF, and OND service members and the veterans of these and other conflict zones (Fonagy, 1999; Jakupcak et al., 2007; Taft, Vogt, Marshall, Panuzio, & Niles, 2007; West & Tinney, 2011). An extensive study exploring the prevalence of intimate partner violence in a representative U.S. Air Force sample revealed widespread prevalence of partner maltreatment as compared with civilian samples with lower rank considered a risk factor for perpetration and victimization (Foran, Slep, Heyman, & United States Air Force Family Advocacy Research Program, 2011). Several explanations are offered to explain this heightened volatility. The hyperarousal cluster of the PTSD diagnosis is characterized by affect dysregulation, alternating numbness and hyperarousal, and occasional rage outbursts. A physiological traumatic stress response can be triggered by stimuli that are associated with the original traumatic event, stored in an iconic memory (Schore, 2003). When the biological determinants of a flashback intersect with a full range of intense emotions for the service member and family members, an incendiary milieu activates. Fear, threats of abandonment, anxiety, anger, and hurt emerge with intensity. As a result, all family members are challenged to arrive at some semblance of equilibrium and working together once again to carry on with the tasks of family life.

Caregivers

Women in the military may have unique stressors related to the multiple roles as service member, mother, spouse, and caregiver with aging parents. To provide some context for this topic, 55% of the troops are married and 1.0 million have at least one parent who serves in the military (IOM, 2010). A survey of deployed service members noted that 50% felt that deployment negatively affected their partners and children (Patten & Parker, 2011). In fact, several research projects have revealed that children are affected by parental deployment with heightened behavioral and emotional difficulties (Chandra et al. 2011; Chandra, Hawkins, Martin, & Richardson, 2010; Rentz et al., 2007). Sixty-five percent of service members have the direct responsibility to care for children and/or parents. Although many men assume a caretaker role, more women than men still tend to be the primary caretakers of children and senior citizens and providers of housework (Wain & Gabriel, 2007). As some of our wounded warriors return home, the parents of the younger injured veterans often step in as the primary caregivers and can benefit from a full range of supports to help them provide the optimal caregiving for their adult child.

Deployment often involves separation from children and families for months at a time and leaving children behind with spouses or alternative caregivers. Many single mothers experience more stress given the absence of additional supports during and following deployment. Deployment affects marital stability of men and women soldiers differently. Several reports demonstrated a statistically significant increase in divorce rates in women in the army but not men (IOM, 2010; Sayers, Farrow, Ross, & Oslin, 2009). Military wives on bases receive more support from their communities as compared with military husbands (men married to a service member) who have fewer resources available, especially for members of the National Guard and Reserve. As gay, bisexual, and lesbian service members return to their husbands, wives, and partners, their needs for psychosocial and mental health support require exploration as well.

PHASE-ORIENTED COUPLE THERAPY WITH MILITARY AND VETERAN COUPLES

I argue for a flexible, collaborative, trauma-informed, phase-oriented couple therapy model (Basham, 2008; Basham & Miehls, 2004). The principles of relationship, cultural responsiveness, theoretical-grounding and research-base provide scaffolding for the approach. Before proceeding to define goals and interventions, a complete biopsychosocial-spiritual assessment needs to be completed first (see Figure 25.1). Serving as both an anchor and compass for directing the couple therapy plan, the following themes need to be addressed. Similar to assessment models that focus on the person in context, this approach reviews the client's presenting issues through three domains: the institutional/sociocultural; the

I. INSTITUTIONAL/SOCIOCULTURAL (grounded in social constructionist, feminist, and critical race theories)

1. Clinicians' attitudes and responses (e.g., countertransference and secondary trauma)
2. Social supports (e.g., family, community, faith-based organization, unit, command)
3. Military and VA context: (e.g., branch, rank, status, era of service and MOS)
4. Service delivery context (e.g., social policies, finances, and political context)
5. Previous and current health and mental health treatment
6. Intersecting diversity factors (e.g., race, ethnicity, religion, socioeconomic, ability, sexual orientation, and gender)

II. INTERACTIONAL (grounded in intergenerational and narrative family theories)

1. Relational dynamics (including "victim-victimizer-bystander" themes)
2. Power and control struggles
3. Distancing and distrust
4. Sexuality and physical touch
5. Boundaries
6. Communication
7. Dearth of rituals
8. Intergenerational patterns

III. INDIVIDUAL/INTRAPERSONAL

A. Individual, cognitive, affective, and behavioral functioning (grounded in trauma and cognitive-behavioral theories)
   - Indicators of resilience
   - Complex PTSD symptomatology and FEARS (Goodwin, 1990, p. 62)

     Fears (nightmares, flashbacks, intrusive thoughts)
     Ego fragmentation (dissociation, identity distortion)
     Affective changes (hyperarousal/numbness, compulsive/addictive/ antisocial behaviors
     Reenactment
     Suicidality/**s**omatization (insomnia, hypervigilance, startle response, bodily complaints)

B. Intrapersonal/intrapsychic (grounded in attachment, object relations, and relational theories)
   - Working model of attachment, affect regulation, and capacity for mentalization
   - Capacity for whole? part? Or merged object relations?
   - Role of projective identification
   - Internalized "victim-victimizer-bystander" dynamic

Figure 25.1 Phase-oriented therapy with military couples: Biopsychosocial-spiritual assessment
Adapted from *Transforming the Legacy: Couple Therapy with Survivors of Childhood Trauma*, by K. K. Basham & D. Miehls, 2004, New York, NY: Columbia University Press. Revised by Kathryn Basham, PhD, January, 2012.

interactional; and the individual/intrapersonal. In each of these domains, the clinician should assess both strengths and vulnerabilities in each area and compose a complete summary at the end of the assessment-in process.

In the institutional/sociocultural realm, the following six topics are covered: (1) social supports (e.g., family, community, faith-based-organizations, unit command); (2) military or VA context (e.g., branch, rank, status, era of service, and MOS); (3) service delivery context (e.g., social policies, finances, and political contexts; (4) previous and current health and mental health treatment; (5) intersecting diversity factors (e.g., race, ethnicity, age, religion, socioeconomic status; ability; sexual orientation and gender); and (6) clinician's attitudes, responses and world views (e.g., cultural countertransference and secondary trauma).

In the interactional realm, the following eight topics are explored: (1) relational patterns (including the "victim-victimizer-bystander" scenario); (2) power and control issues; (3) distancing/intimacy; (4) sexuality and physical touch; (5) communication skills; (6) boundaries; (7) presence or absence of healing rituals; and (8) intergenerational relational patterns.

Finally, the individual/intrapersonal realm covers the area of physical and mental health for each individual in the couple, including possibly posttraumatic stress-related symptoms and disorders and internal relational patterns. In the latter, exploration of internal working models of attachment, capacities for affect regulation and mentalization are explored along with other internalized relational templates that influence how a partner sees her or his world from the inside out. The summary of the strengths and vulnerabilities in each of these areas sets the stage for a coherent treatment plan attuned to the client's needs and meaning-making. The in-depth nature of this evaluation creates problems in settings where there are unrealistic expectations to arrive at a thorough differential assessment within one or two meetings

Couple Therapy Phases

Following the completion of the biopsychosocial-spiritual assessment, a treatment plan is crafted and specific goals and interventions are identified (see Figure 25.2). In the following brief overview of the phases, I highlight the major themes, elaborated more fully in the upcoming clinical vignette.

Phase I focuses on safety, self-care, and stabilization for the couple. As couples enter therapy, each partner may approach the work with long-standing secure or insecure attachment patterns of relating. Combat exposure can often destabilize a service member's working model of attachment, so entry into therapy can be experienced as stressful. While conveying knowledge, cultural responsiveness, and benign authority, a clinician forges a workable therapeutic alliance with the military or veteran couple. A major focus during this phase is basic safety and affect-regulation, often disrupted for one or both partners during a post-deployment transition. Cultural relativity (in particular attention to themes of the military and gender) must be considered here since different cultural worldviews shape responses to stress in many different ways. Exploration of the full range of social supports is crucial to evaluate and strengthen the sources of resilience within the family and community.

Once a stable scaffolding has been reestablished, Phase II of the couple therapy model addresses the long-term effects and relational disruptions brought about by earlier

Phase I. Safety, Self-Care, Stabilization, and Establishing a Context for Change

1. Assessing and establishing safety
2. Strengthening self-care
   - Physical health
   - Mental health
   - Sleep, nutrition, and fitness
   - Substance use, abuse, medications
   - Communication skills
   - Biobehavioral strategies for stress reduction/affect regulation
   - Knowledge of deployment-related stressors
3. Exploring relevant sociocultural influences (i.e., military culture, gender, race, religion, ethnicity, sexual orientation, socioeconomic status, ability, age, and primary language)
4. Strengthen support systems (e.g., family, community, and religion/spirituality)
5. Determining partnership status (e.g., continuation? stasis? dissolution?)

Phase II. Reflection on Trauma Narratives and Grieving

1. Exploring and reflecting on the meaning of traumatic experiences
2. Grieving of multiple losses and bereavement
3. Exploring the intergenerational legacy of the "victim-victimizer-bystander" pattern
4. Developing shared empathy
5. Developing mentalization
6. Creating bereavement and healing rituals

Phase III. Consolidation of New Perspectives, Attitudes, Behaviors, and Social Vindication

1. Remediating presenting concerns and symptoms
2. Reestablishing connections (e.g., family, faith-based community)
3. Enhancing sexual relationship
4. Strengthening co-parenting
5. Developing complex social identities (e.g., gender, military, ethnicity)
6. Developing opportunities for social vindication

Figure 25.2 Phase-oriented couple therapy with military and veteran couples
Adapted from *Transforming the Legacy: Couple Therapy with Survivors of Childhood Trauma*, by K. K. Basham & D. Miehls, 2004, New York, NY: Columbia University Press. Revised by Kathryn Basham, PhD, January, 2012.

traumatic events that have been experienced by one or both partners. Exploration of the "victim-victimizer-bystander" pattern is pursued as it plays out in the couple's day-to-day relationships with each other, children, their friends and other family members. For example, distrust, persistent battles related to power and control and oscillating patterns of hyperarousal and distancing besiege many traumatized couples. Grieving major losses often occurs within this phase as well. Narrating and reflecting on trauma narratives allow each partner to address their feelings associated with these traumatic events as well as any attachment injuries and losses. Each partner also benefits from witnessing the partner's narrative, developing enhanced empathy and deepening a shared understanding of each other's experiences.

From an attachment theory perspective, Bowlby (1982) anticipated stages of grief, including intermittent protest, despair, detachment, and reorganization following a disrupted attachment. Addressing attachment injuries facilitates the reemergence of the "circle of security" (Basham, 2008; Marvin et al., 2002).

Finally, Phase III of the couple therapy model involves tasks that focus on consolidating new perspectives, attitudes, and behaviors. In attachment theory language, this is the territory of "exploration." As both partners experience greater empathy toward each other and increased capacities for mentalization, they report feeling more joy, a sense of connection, and enhanced sexual exchanges (Basham, 2008). As they move into consolidating the gains of the therapy in Phase III, many couples use this opportunity to discuss their values and worldviews and reshape their complex social identities (e.g., gender and ethnicity). New ways to reconnect within the community are also discussed and moves toward social vindication are explored.

Now that the research and the conceptual base for this chapter has been articulated and followed by a brief overview of the phase-oriented trauma-informed couple therapy model, I introduce a disguised composite clinical Case Vignette: Staff Sergeant Maria Sanchez. The case vignette illustrates the complexity of intersecting physical, psychological, and psychosocial issues affecting a postdeployment couple with specific attention paid to the invisibility or visibility of gender, race, and ethnicity in the treatment process.

Case Vignette: Staff Sergeant Maria Sanchez-Background and Assessment

Staff Sergeant Maria Sanchez, a 36-year-old Army Reservist, IOF veteran of Puerto Rican descent, married for 14 years to Carlos Sanchez, returned from her 12-month tour of duty in Iraq 11 months ago with second- and third-degree burns to her right arm and a broken pelvis as a result of an improvised explosive device (IED) blast that killed two of her soldiers. In theater, she worked as a communications specialist (MOS) in charge of alerting convoys of transports to potential danger and received a medical discharge with a diagnosis of PTSD and physical injuries. At home, in her civilian occupation, she typically worked full time as a troubleshooter technician overseeing the medical record-keeping system at a local hospital. On return to the United States from deployment, she was reunited with her husband, a physical therapist, and her three young children, Antonio, age 13, Delia age 8, and Ana age 2. During deployment, Sgt. Sanchez's mother-in-law (i.e., "abuela") moved into the family home to care for her grandchildren and her son. Both parents are bilingual and rely on their Catholic spiritual community as a source of hope, healing, and social support. The family maintains a middle-income socioeconomic status in a small city in New England.

Presenting Issues

Although the initial reunion brought great relief and pride to the family, within 6 weeks Sgt. Sanchez started to experience pervasive anxiety, insomnia, nightmares, poor concentration, limited attention span, generalized pain, persistent headaches, and tingling from her skin grafts on her right arm. She feared going to her office at the hospital where she had worked previously, finding the bright fluorescent lights distressing and the long hallways terrifying.

Although previously an avid reader, Sgt. Sanchez was unable to sit still to read or concentrate for more than a few minutes. Most of the time, she felt alternately "tense, nauseated, agitated, irritable, enraged, and numb." She experienced trouble falling asleep, awakened fitfully throughout the night and suffered nightmares and grogginess in the mornings. When touched by her husband, Sgt. Sanchez bristled and described the complete absence of any sexual desire. She started to drink several glasses of wine at night after the children went to bed to "knock herself out and blot out her pain."

Sgt. Sanchez also struggles with obsessive thoughts related to her guilt of surviving an IED blast that killed her fellow soldiers. She described hearing sexually harassing comments about her being female and culturally bigoted remarks from her commanding officer (e.g., "Why don't you go back to the country you came from?" And "Your English sounds weird."). Four months ago marked the last time she cried after her daughter, Ana, screamed hysterically when Sgt. Sanchez approached her to give her a kiss. The toddler shunned her and flapped her hands until her mother left the room in tears. She has not cried since then.

Sgt. Sanchez reports flashbacks of horrific combat memories, such as smells of burning rubber, sights of men and women cloaked in heavily layered garments, sounds of cars backfiring, and visions of a vast expanse of sand blowing on the beach. Such events stimulated an intense traumatic stress response that activated alternating hyperarousal followed by numbness and detachment, consistent with a posttraumatic stress response. One example of a flashback occurred while Sgt. Sanchez was shopping for groceries in a huge chain store with her husband and children. As she anxiously pushed the shopping cart through the aisles, she quickly tried to stuff produce and cans into the cart as she became increasingly bothered by the crowds of people and glaring overhead lights. Suddenly, she heard a car backfiring in the parking lot, and immediately grabbed her toddler, Ana, and dove to the floor, trying to crawl under a display table. She was trembling and hyperventilating. Her husband came rushing to her and told her that she was embarrassing him and the children with her weird behavior. He yelled for her to get up and "Stop it!"

Sgt. Sanchez was mortified and apologized profusely, then moved away from her husband, children, and the gawking customers. No one understood that this flashback was triggered by the loud explosive sound of the backfiring and the blinding lights reminiscent of the intense sun in Iraq. Nor did they understand that these visual and auditory stimuli were also reminiscent of her encoded traumatic memory of the blaring sounds and blinding light from the IED explosion that killed her fellow soldiers in Iraq. Mr. Sanchez feared that his wife was having a "breakdown" and resented her abdication of mothering since she had returned home. This seemed so counterintuitive to their shared understanding of her primary role as a caring mother. Although Mr. Sanchez wanted the marriage to work, he threatened Maria with divorce if she did not "shape up."

When Mr. Sanchez experienced anger and confusion following one of her flashbacks, he criticized her for "going crazy on him" and being irrational. In contrast, the children were frightened and anxious and retreated to the safety of the distant rooms throughout the house. Fighting ensued between the couple with Mr. Sanchez yelling and criticizing his wife in a condemning fashion and Sgt. Sanchez detaching.

Unable to return to her usual job, Sgt. Sanchez felt useless as a worker, a mother, and a marital partner. In her words, she felt "dead to the world" and "worthless." In contrast, her husband continued to thrive in his primary role as the wage earner. Yet Sgt. Sanchez expressed that her involvement in the Army Reserves and her nontraditional career choice in technology challenged stereotypical gendered notions. When she returned home to assume her full-time mothering job and her anticipated full-time job in the work force, she felt displaced by her mother-in-law who had settled in comfortably during the 11 months of deployment. The children adored their abuela (i.e., grandmother) yet felt intermittently angry and confused about their mother's absence and the uncertainty of her return. Although reserving primary mothering to the women in the family is culturally congruent with this family's experience of their Puerto Rican ethnicity, the drastic replacement of Sgt. Sanchez by her mother-in-law felt devastating to Sgt. Sanchez. On one occasion, when Antonio, the couple's oldest son, was communicating through the web (i.e., Skyping) with his mother in Iraq, the visual image of his mother on the screen disappeared as he heard a loud explosion emerging from the screen. Only after a lapse of 4 hours, was Sgt. Sanchez able to call back and reconnect with the family to let them know she was injured but safe. Antonio cried hysterically and remained acutely anxious for his mother's safety. Although valiantly trying to sustain her connection with her son and daughters, the horrors of war continued to interrupt Sgt. Sanchez's ability to care for her son and for him to feel a sense of secure connection with his mother while she was deployed. Sgt. Sanchez continued to have a difficult time connecting emotionally with her family on her return.

Developmental and Family Factors

Sgt. Sanchez met normal developmental milestones while growing up with her family in a poor neighborhood in San Juan, Puerto Rico. Her father struck her regularly, ostensibly as discipline for "naughty" behavior from ages 2 to 8. She thrived in school, both academically and socially, until her mother died from a sudden septic infection when she was 8 years old. Sgt. Sanchez was protective of her two younger siblings when her dad remarried and moved the family to New York City. Although innately very bright, she developed an insecure-disorganized internal working model of attachment related to the abuse she suffered from her dad and the major early loss of her mother.

Her husband was reared in a second-generation middle-income urban Puerto Rican family that valued school and financial achievements. He works as a physical therapist in a major rehabilitation center. Both partners and their children are bilingual and speak Spanish and English interchangeably at home. The parents and children rely on their Catholic spiritual community as a source of hope, healing, and social support. Essentially, Mr. Sanchez experienced a loving and protected childhood, leading to the emergence of a secure internal working model of attachment. During the early years of their marriage, Sgt. Sanchez benefited from the predictable, safe, caring environment of their marriage and family and "earned security," in the language of attachment theory. She functioned with greater capacities for secure attachment although her primary working model remained disorganized when suffering distress.

Assessment in Process

To complete a thorough biopsychosocial-spiritual assessment, a clinician needs to identify both the strengths and vulnerabilities within the institutional/sociocultural, interactional, and intrapersonal domains noted in the assessment guide (see Figure 25.1). The following is a preliminary summary of the strengths and vulnerabilities in these various arenas.

Within the institutional/sociocultural domain, Sgt. and Mr. Sanchez, as a couple, revealed distinct resilience (e.g., strong shared commitment to family; bilingualism; successful careers; solid finances; college-level education; and earlier commitment to their faith-based community). Vulnerabilities for the couple include socioeconomic differences in their families of origin; conflicts with their extended families and spiritual community; and exposure to racial and cultural trauma.

On an interactional level, the couple experienced harsh verbal exchanges, reminiscent of the "victim-victimizer-bystander" pattern; poor communication; lack of physical and sexual intimacy; struggles over control in decision making; and conflicts around co-parenting. Although the family environment during pre-deployment was characterized by stability, mutual sharing, and companionship, the current home environment was racked by fear, uncertainty, and detachment inflamed by pervasive anxiety for everyone involved.

Within the individual/intrapersonal domain Sgt. Sanchez experienced a range of physical and mental health issues. Sadness overwhelmed Sgt. Sanchez as she grappled with traumatic grief over the losses of her battle buddies and the loss of multiple social/occupational identities. Her plaguing guilt and sense of profound loss reactivated earlier unresolved grief related to the untimely death her mother from a virulent infection. In her words, she felt "inconsolable, dead and empty." Her symptoms not only signaled a diagnosis of PTSD but also syndromes of depression, and intense marital and family conflict. Possible traumatic brain injury and substance abuse needed to be assessed and ruled out as well. Clearly, the emerging differential assessment led to a complex nexus of severe mental health concerns, physical injuries, and psychosocial stressors. Mr. Sanchez complained of stress and gastrointestinal upset. He expressed deep sadness about having "lost the wife he remembered."

Case Vignette Discussion Questions

1. What aspects of culture (i.e., military, gender, and ethnicity) shape the responses of Sgt. Sanchez and her family as she reintegrates back home following deployment?
2. What are the gendered expectations for caregiving for Sgt. Sanchez and her husband?
3. In what ways can they address the shifts in gendered roles during and post-deployment?

Case Vignette: Staff Sergeant Maria Sanchez—First Treatment Plan

When Sgt. Sanchez agreed to meet with her family practitioner, she was prescribed medications to help with her nightmares and referred to a licensed mental health civilian provider in the community. Although she expressed deep worry about her marriage and her children, the clinician invited her to come in for an individual session. What ensued was a rapid one-session assessment and a recommendation to pursue prolonged exposure therapy to remediate symptoms of combat-related posttraumatic stress disorder (PTSD). Goals included a reduction in nightmares and flashbacks and increased capacity to shop at the local chain store and drive her car. This clinician also recommended weekly cognitive behavioral therapy that involved journaling and tracking of moods. When Sgt. Sanchez was unable to concentrate on her writing assignments, feeling deeply ashamed of her incapacity, she tried to invest herself in the exposure therapy but experienced a flooding of emotion. After feeling overwhelmed and actively suicidal, she terminated treatment.

Case Vignette Discussion Questions

1. Was Sgt. Sanchez herself a failure, or were there unintended iatrogenic effects based on the absence of a thorough biopsychosocial-spiritual assessment and differential diagnosis?
2. Was there a failure on the part of the civilian clinician to engage in conducting a thorough biopsychosocial-spiritual assessment with Sanchez couple?
3. While ignoring cultural responsiveness, did this clinician ignore the sociocultural meanings and stigma related to mental health problems for Sgt. Sanchez and her husband?
4. What did the clinician need to do in terms of conducting a risk assessment to determine safety or lack of safety in the home?
5. Are there signs of possible intimate partner violence that should be considered by the clinician?
6. Were the children expressing symptoms of secondary trauma evidenced by heightened insecurity?

The treatment protocol for Sgt. Sanchez and her family revealed five problems, including (1) an incomplete biopsychosocial-spiritual assessment; (2) inattention to safety risks; (3) lack of attunement to sociocultural factors in terms of the central role of the extended family and faith-based community in providing social supports; (4) lack of attention to family roles that were changed during deployment and now disrupted upon homecoming; and (5) absence of attention to Sgt. Sanchez's sense of loss and grief related to the caretaking of her soldiers, her children, her husband, colleagues, and family members.

After a suicide attempt with an overdose of prescribed medications, Sgt. Sanchez decided to seek treatment once again, this time in relation to problems expressed by the principals in the schools for all three of her children. Each of the children had been expressing words and behavioral signs of anxiety and worry in their classrooms. At this time, Sgt. Sanchez and her husband were invited to participate in an extended biopsychosocial-spiritual assessment with a new civilian clinician. An assessment of the strengths and vulnerabilities were documented for each individual family member, the couple relationship, and the children before crafting a treatment plan. At the time, a phase-oriented multimodality treatment plan was instituted in conjunction with other providers.

Case Vignette: Couple Therapy for Sgt. and Mr. Sanchez

Initially, in Phase I of the couple therapy, Sgt. and Mr. Sanchez talked about issues of safety, ways that they address conflicts, and their attunement to issues of potential abuse. Self-care plans were implemented for each partner to find ways to modulate affect regulation (e.g., neural relaxation, stress reduction, grounding exercises, and yoga). Referrals for extended evaluation for Sgt. Sanchez were offered to assess for traumatic brain injury, substance abuse, and psychopharmacological interventions. In couple therapy, they discussed their adjustments back home, discussing family roles and finding ways to understand the causes of PTSD-related symptoms and patterns. They talked about new ways to co-parent and coordinate efforts to collaborate with the principals and counselors at their children's schools. They also reviewed the strengths and vulnerabilities in their network of extended family, workplace, and church.

Phase I couple therapy included 10 goals: (1) demonstrate capacities to identify and balance emotions; (2) ensure safety for couple and with children; (3) apply stress reduction, anger management, and grounding techniques; (4) demonstrate effective communication and conflict resolution skills; (5) recognize triggers and responses associated with the traumatic stress response; (6) recognize effects of alcohol in coping and family life; (7) reengage partners and restore stable attachments; (8) renegotiate gendered power and family roles and reestablish circle of security; (9) develop plans to pursue extended referrals for assessment to rule out traumatic brain injury and substance abuse; and (10) identify and expand social supports in family, church, work, and community.

After basic criteria for establishing safety, adequate self-care, scaffolding of supports and stabilization, the Sanchez couple was able to move along to four Phase II couple therapy goals: (1) grieving the multiple losses (e.g., Sgt. Sanchez—deaths of fellow soldiers, loss of military identity, identity as worker, mother, wife, family member, and "able-bodied" citizen and Mr. Sanchez's loss of his beloved wife prior to deployment and family harmony); (2) altering destructive trauma-related relational patterns ("victim-victimizer-bystander"); (3) demonstrating ability to visit large stores and shopping centers without flashbacks (through a prolonged exposure method); and (4) narrating and reflecting on combat-related traumatic events (with attachment-theory based practice and cognitive-processing treatment).

As she grieved these major losses, Sgt. Sanchez realized that she identified her son, Antonio, with the deceased soldiers in her unit. Her unresolved grief prevented her from fully reconnecting with her son until her profound sadness and guilt abated. As each partner grieved his or her respective losses and created new ways to create healing rituals for the family, they were able to move along in their psychotherapeutic work.

Finally, Phase III for the couple included five goals: (1) consolidating changes in gendered family roles and strengthening of family and social supports; (2) demonstrating enhanced emotional and sexual intimacy; (3) exploring creative solutions for co-parenting with parents and grandmothers; (4) demonstrating new and reshaped nexus of social identities (e.g., gender, race, ethnicity, ability, religion); and (5) demonstrating avenues for social vindication.

Case Vignette Discussion Questions

1. In what ways does the couple therapy case vignette address the potential derailment issues that were ignored in the earlier two vignettes?
2. Do you note any ethical dilemmas in any of the case vignettes? If so, what are they, and how would you address them?

CONCLUSION

The clinical case vignettes in this chapter vividly revealed the depth of pain suffered by Sgt. Sanchez, her husband, children, and extended family along with their distinct resilience that enabled them to reclaim healthy, more positive and productive lives together. Such progress is noteworthy and can serve as an exemplar for many other service members, veterans, and their families who may also need and deserve a similar nexus of sound evidence-based and research-informed mental and behavioral health approaches. Although the first treatment plan missed important dimensions of Sergeant and Mr. Sanchez's presenting issues, the second integrative course of treatment proved far more successful. Both of the clinicians were Euro-American, nonmedical female civilian clinicians, so the challenge of intercultural practice was present in both situations. Although the issues of similarities and differences in gender and ethnicity remained invisible in the first culture-blind treatment, in the second course of treatment the clinician and client couple openly explored the meaning of gender, military culture, race, and ethnicity in terms of how these issues surface in their day-to-day lives, their histories along with their worldviews in the context of the therapeutic alliance. A phase-oriented treatment plan stressed six central features: (1) attunement to the therapeutic alliance; (2) cultural responsiveness; (3) knowledge and skills based in research-informed and evidence-based practice models; (4) ongoing attention to a thorough biopsychosocial-spiritual assessment; (5) collaboration and consultation; and (6) flexibility to assess and treat a complex, multidimensioned set of conditions and challenges. To promote similar positive outcomes in practice with service members and their families, each clinician needs to be prepared with satisfactory education from an accredited academic institution. In addition, actual preparedness should involve documentation of supervised clinical experiences with a diverse range of military clients and their families as well as certification, licensure and privileging within a clearly defined scope of practice. Given the serious negative consequences of unsuccessful treatment, we should be all the more vigilant in our efforts to provide optimally effective, culturally responsive behavioral health and psychosocial services.

CHAPTER DISCUSSION QUESTIONS

1. How do the sociocultural factors of gender and ethnicity shape responses to traumatic stress?
2. How do cultural mores influence gendered roles for parenting? Work? And family life?
3. How do ethnicity and culture influence the losses of identity as a soldier? A temporarily able-bodied citizen? Mother? Worker? Wife? And daughter-in-law?
4. What are some of the mental health outcomes that service members might expect to experience in response to deployment and combat stressors?
5. What are the key features in completing a biopsychosocial-spiritual assessment of a military couple?
6. What are the central guiding principles in crafting a phase-oriented, collaborative couple therapy treatment plan that ensures safety, adequate pacing, and integrates evidence-based treatment models in context?

REFERENCES

Ainsworth, M. (1989). Attachments beyond infancy. *American Psychologist*, *44*, 709–716.

Basham, K. (2008). Homecoming as safe haven or the new front: Attachments and detachment in military couples. *Clinical Social Work Journal*, *36*(1), 83–96.

Basham, K. (2009). Commentary on keynote lecture presented by Dr. Jonathan Shay 6/27/09. The trials of war: Odysseus returning from Afghanistan and reflections. *Smith College Studies in Social Work, 3/4,* 283–286.

Basham, K., & Miehls, D. (2004). *Transforming the legacy: Couple therapy with survivors of childhood trauma.* New York, NY: Columbia University Press.

Bowlby, J. (1969/1982). *Attachment and loss: Vol. 1. Attachment* (2nd ed.). New York, NY: Basic Books.

Bride, B., & Figley, C. R. (2009). Secondary trauma and military veteran caregivers. *Smith College Studies in Social Work, 79*(3/4), 314–329.

Caulfield, M., Wolfe, J., Turner, K., Newton, T. C., Melia, K., Martin, J., & Goldieri, J. (2005). Gender and trauma as predictors of military attrition: A study of Marine Corps recruits. *Military Medicine, 170*(12), 1037–1043.

Chandra, A., Hawkins, S. A., Martin, L. T., & Richardson, A. (2010). The impact of parental deployment on child social and emotional functioning: Perspectives of school staff, *Journal of Adolescent Health, 46*(3), 218–223.

Chandra, A., Lara-Cinisomo, S., Jaycox, L. H., Tanilien, T., Han, B., Burns, R. M., & Ruder, T. (2011). *Views from the homefront: The experiences of youth and spouses from military families.* Santa Monica, CA: RAND, TR-913-NMFA.

Clulow, C. (Ed.). (2001). *Adult attachment and couple psychotherapy: The "secure base" in practice and research.* Philadelphia, PA: Taylor & Francis.

Fisher, J. V., & Crandell, L. E. (2001). Patterns of relating in the couple. In C. Clulow (Ed.), *Adult attachment and couple psychotherapy: The secure base in practice and research* (pp. 15–27). Philadelphia, PA: Taylor & Francis.

Fonagy, P. (1999). Male perpetrators of violence against women: An attachment theory perspective. *Journal of Applied Psychoanalytic Studies, 1*(1), 7–27.

Fonagy, P., Gergely, G., Jurist, E., & Target, M. (2002). *Affect regulation, mentalization, and the development of the self.* New York, NY: Other Press.

Foran, H. M., Slep, A. M., Heyman, R., E., & United States Air Force Advocacy Research Program. (2011). Prevalences of intimate partner violence in a representative Air Force sample. *Journal of Consulting and Clinical Psychology, 79*(3), 391–397.

Fredman, S. J., Monson, C., & Adair, K. C. (2011). Implementing cognitive-behavioral conjoint therapy with the recent generation of veterans and their partners. *Journal of Clinical Psychology, 18*(1), 120–135.

Gilliss, C. L., Lee, K. A., & Gutierrez, Y., Taylor, D., Beyene, Y., Neuhaus, J., & Murrell, N. (2001). Recruitment and retention of healthy minority women into community-based longitudinal research. *Journal Womens Health Gender Based Medicine, 10*(1), 77–85.

Goodwin, J. M. (1990). Applying to adult incest victims what we have learned from victimized children. In R. Kluft (Ed.), *Incest-related syndromes of adult psychopathology* (pp. 55–74). Arlington, VA: American Psychiatric.

Gradus., J. L., Street, A. E., Kelly, K., & Stafford, J. (2008). Sexual harassment experiences and harmful alcohol use in a military sample: Differences in gender and mediating role of depression. *Journal of Study of Alcohol and Drugs, 69*(3), 348–351.

Hazan, C., Gur-Yaish, N., & Campa, M. (2004). What does it mean to be attached? In S. Rhodes & J. Simpson (Eds.), *Adult attachment: Theory, research and clinical implications* (pp. 55–85). New York, NY: Guilford Press.

Himmelfarb, N., Yarger, D., & Mintz, J. (2006). PTSD in female veterans with military and civilian sexual trauma. *Journal of Traumatic Stress, 19*(6), 837–846.

Hoge, C. W., Auchterlonie, J. L., & Milliken, C. J. (2006). Mental health problems, use of mental health services and attrition from military service after returning from deployment from Iraq or Afghanistan. *New England Journal of Medicine, 295*(9), 1023–1032.

IOM (Institute of Medicine). (2010). *Preliminary assessment of readjustment needs of veterans, service members and their families*. Washington, DC: National Academies Press.

Jakupcak, M., Coneybeare, D., Phelps, L, Hunt, S., Holmes, H. A., Felker, B., . . . McFall, M. (2007). Anger, hostility, and aggression among Iraq and Afghanistan war veterans reporting PTSD and subthreshold PTSD. *Journal of Traumatic Stress, 20*, 945–954. doi: 10.1002/jts.20258

Johnson, S. M. (2002). *Emotionally focused couple therapy with trauma survivors: Strengthening attachment bonds*. New York, NY: Guilford Press.

Kimerling, R., Street, A., Pavaro, J., Smith, M. W., Cronkite, R. C., Holmes, T. H., & Froyne, S. M. (2010). Military-related sexual trauma among veteran health administration patients returning from Iraq and Afghanistan. *American Journal of Public Health, 100*(8), 1409–1412.

MacDermid, S. M., & Riggs, D. (Eds.). (2010). *Risk and resilience in military families*. New York, NY: Springer.

Marvin, R., Cooper, G., Hoffman, K., & Powell, B. (2002). The circle of security project: Attachment-based intervention with care pre-school child dyads. *Attachment & Human Development, 4*, 107–124.

Mattei, L. (2011). Coloring development: Race and culture in psychodynamic theory. In J. Berzoff, L. M. Flanagan, & P. Hertz (Eds.), *Inside out and outside in: Psychodynamic clinical theory and psychopathology* (pp. 258–283). Lanham, MD: Rowman & Littlefield.

Mental Health Advisory Team 7 (MHAT). (2011). *Mental Health Advisory Team (MHAT) Iraqi freedom*. Washington, DC: Office of the Surgeon Multinational Force–Iraq, Office of the Surgeon General United States Army Medical Command, Mental Health Advisory Team.

Merrill, L. L., Newell, C. E., Thomsen, C. J., Gold, S. R., Milner, J. S., Koss, M. P., & Rosswork, S. G. (1999). Childhood abuse and sexual re-victimization in a female Navy recruit sample. *Journal of Traumatic Stress, 12*(2), 211–225.

Murdoch, M., Bradley, A., Mather, S. H., Klein, R. E., Turner, C. L., & Yano, E. M. (2006). Women and war: What physicians should know. *Journal General Internal Medicine, 22*(3), 5–10.

Patten, E., & Parker, K. (2011). *Women in the U.S. military: Growing share; distinctive profile*. Washington, DC: Pew Research Center.

Rentz, D. E., Marshall, S. W., Loomis, D., Casteel, C., Martin, S. L., & Gibbs, D. A. (2007). Effect of deployment on the occurrence of child maltreatment in military and non-military families. *American Journal of Epidemiology, 16*, 1199–1206. doi: 0.1093/aje/kwm008

Rosen, L. M., & Martin, L. (1996). The measurement of childhood trauma among male and female soldiers in the U.S. Army. *Military Medicine, 161*(6), 342–345.

Sayers, S. L., Farrow, V. A., Ross, J., & Oslin, D. W. (2009). Family problems among recently returned military Veterans referred for a mental health evaluation. *Journal of Clinical Psychiatry, 2*, 163–170.

Schore, A. N. (2003). Early relational trauma, disorganized attachment, and the development of a predisposition to violence. In M. F. Solomon & D. J. Siegel (Eds.), *Healing trauma: Attachment, mind, body and brain* (pp. 107–167). New York, NY: Norton.

Siegel, D. (2007). *Mindful brain: Regulation and attunement in the cultivation of well-being.* New York, NY: Norton.

Sneath, L., & Rheem, K. (2010). Use of emotionally focused couple therapy with military couples and families. In R. Blair Everson & C. R. Figley (Eds.), *Families under fire: Systemic therapy with military families.* New York, NY: Taylor & Francis.

Staub, E. (1989). *The roots of evil: The origins of genocide and other group violence.* New York, NY: Cambridge University Press.

Suris, A., Lind, L., Kashner, M., Borman, P. D., & Petty, F. (2004). Sexual assault in women veterans: An examination of PTSD risk, health care utilization and cost care. *Psychosomatic Medicine, 66*, 749–756.

Taft, C. T., Vogt, D. S., Marshall, A. D., Panuzio, J., & Niles, B. L. (2007). Aggression among combat veterans: Relationships with combat exposure and symptoms of posttraumatic stress disorder, dysphoria, and anxiety. *Journal of Traumatic Stress, 20*, 135–145.

Tanielian, T., & Jaycox, L. H. (2008). (Eds.). *Invisible wounds of war: Psychological and cognitive injuries, their consequences, and services to assist recovery.* Santa Monica, CA: RAND, MG-720-CCF. http://www.rand.org/pubs/monographs/MG721.html

Taylor, S. F. (2006). Tend and befriend: Biobehavioral bases of affiliation under stress. *Current Directions in Psychological Science, 15*(6), 273–277.

Tolin, D. C., & Foa, E. R. (2006). Sex differences in trauma and PTSD diagnosis: A quantitative review of 25 years of research. *Psychological Bulletin, 132*(6), 959–992.

Van der Kolk, B. (2003). Posttraumatic stress disorder and the nature of trauma. In M. F. Solomon & D. J. Siegel (Eds.), *Healing trauma: Attachment, mind, body and brain* (pp. 168–195). New York, NY: Norton.

Wain, H. J., & Gabriel, G. M. (2007). Psychodynamic concepts inherent in a biopsychosocial model of care of traumatic injuries. *Journal of the American Academy and of Psychoanalysis Dynamic Psychiatry, 35*(4), 555–573.

Washington, D. L., Kleimann, S., Michelini, A. N., & Canning, M. Women veterans' perceptions and decision-making about VA health care. *Military Medicine, 172*(8), 812–817.

Weinick, R., Beckjord, E. B., Farmer, C. M., Martin, L. T., Gillen, E. M., Acosta, J. D., . . . Scharf, D. M. (2011). *Programs addressing psychological health and traumatic brain injury among U.S. military service members and their families.* Santa Monica, CA: RAND.

West, K. M., & Tinney, G. (2011). *Safety on the homefront: Adequately addressing violence in families impacted by military service.* Los Angeles, CA: USC Center for Innovation and Research on Veterans and Military Families.

Yano, E. M., Hayes, P., Wright, S., Schnurr, P. P., Lipson, L., Bean-Mayberry, B., & Washington, D. L. (2010). Integration of women veterans into VA quality improvement research efforts: What researchers need to know. *Journal General Internal Medicine*, *25*(1), 55–61.

Yehuda, R., Flory, J. D., Southwick, S., & Charney, D. (2006). Developing an agenda for translational studies of resilience vulnerability following trauma exposure. *Annals of New York Academy of Science*, *1071*, 379–396.

CHAPTER

26

Theory and Practice With Military Couples and Families

EUGENIA L. WEISS, TARA DEBRABER, ALLISON SANTOYO, AND TODD CREAGER

Military families experience considerable demands that are unique to the military lifestyle. This chapter provides a review of the many challenges and strengths that are inherent in the military family's experience; with a particular emphasis on our military's involvement in the Global War on Terrorism (GWOT). The chapter begins with outlining the stressors and the theoretical models that provide the foundation to our understanding and intervening with families under stress. The chapter then shifts to a focus on assessment and intervention strategies with families that have been impacted with "signature wounds" (i.e., posttraumatic stress disorder [PTSD], traumatic brain injury [TBI]) associated with veterans from GWOT.

STRESSORS

As discussed in various chapters throughout this book, the demands associated with military service include periods of long separation, changing family member roles during cycles of deployment (including reintegration), and frequent geographic relocations (Laser & Stephens, 2011; Savitsky, Illingsworth, & DuLaney, 2009). Families must often cope with service member trauma/injury and provide caregiving. Family members may also experience secondary traumatization as a result of the service member having PTSD or experience traumatic grief as a result of the death of a service member (Johnson & Williams-Keeler, 1988; Rosenheck & Fontana, 1999; Savitsky et al., 2009).

Hardaway (2004) posited that although military family life can be a "broadening" experience for many families, therapists also need to understand the nature and severity of stressors associated with military family life. Hardaway (2004) distinguished between types of military stressors as follows (p. 260):

- *Routine stressors* (e.g., geographic relocation, separations)
- *Acute or severe stressors* (e.g., wartime deployments, injury or death of the service member)
- *Chronic, recurring, and severe stressors* (e.g., overseas assignments in hostile areas, threats of terrorism)
- *Complicating factors* (e.g., mental health problems, developmental delays, health issues in family members)

We would add that service member serious injury, disability, or chronic illness that requires long-term family caregiving would also fall under the chronic, recurring and severe stressor dimension. Hardaway's (2004) notion of the "complicating factors," such as when a dependent family member is disabled or has special needs, presents a unique set of challenges for the service member and for the military. Often this situation (e.g., caring for a disabled child and working for the military) can imply competing demands for the service member. For example, a service member's military life-cycle events and priorities (such as job success, reassignments, deployments) can coincide and conflict with family life-cycle needs and events (such as becoming a couple, child birth, entry into school, adolescent angst). The conflict can be exacerbated if there are any "trajectory" events (e.g., unexpected stressors or unusually demanding family circumstances, such as an illness or disability in a family member).

Hardaway (2004) noted that military family life stressors can get in the way of quality of life issues, and are often mediated by some of the following factors (risk or protective factors) that also need to be part of the clinician's assessment:

- Service member's military occupational specialty (MOS)
- Family's income level
- The locations of assignments
- The schools that the child attends (include the number of schools)
- Degree of civilian and military support systems
- Geopolitical times and circumstances
- Degree of flexibility in the family members
- Preexisting medical, mental health, or other family problems
- The length and number of separations between the service member and his or her family. (We would include the type of separation; i.e., combat deployment versus noncombat.)
- How the remaining parent manages the family
- Whether the family resides in a military installation
- Individual personality factors and response to novel situations
- The role of religion

We would also add to this list of factors dual-career military families (i.e., where both parents are in the military), single-parent households, and families were there are several adult children in the service. Finally, National Guard and Reserve Component families should also be considered, as they often do not have ready access to military support systems because they reside in rural areas of the United States or live outside or nowhere near a military installation. These "citizen soldiers," or "weekend warriors," may have been activated to serve as part of the Total Force in the GWOT. However, they eventually return to civilian jobs and communities without the benefit of a transition or without the built-in support systems that living on a military base provides. (Chapter 19 provides more information on this topic.)

In light of the foregoing stressors, support for families (whether through various military and/or community support systems or through professional behavioral-health services), is a key element in three areas:

1. Helping families manage the aforementioned demands associated with military service and build resilience. Family resilience, according to Walsh (2006) is the "coping and adaptational processes in the family as a functional unit" (p. 15).
2. Assisting with retention of the service member in the military, through reenlistment (and successful performance while in the service) (Bourg & Segal, 1999).
3. Ensuring that a service member is able to transition home to his or her family, eventually separate from the military and successfully reintegrate into civilian life (Riggs, 2000; Sherman, Zanotti, & Jones, 2005).

Various theoretical models have been developed pertaining to understanding and intervening with families under stress. These models lay the foundation for considering later sections of this chapter, and are examined next, beginning with the family systems approach.

THEORETICAL MODELS

In the following section, we delineate various models for understanding and intervening with families.

The Family Systems Approach

Riggs (2000) found that the family systems approach is appropriate for addressing any disruptions in the family. The term *family systems*, as utilized in this context, refers to the inclusion of the family as part of a comprehensive paradigm used to address the demands and stressors associated with military lifestyle, rather than as a specific model of intervention. The notion of family systems stems from general social systems theory, which focuses on environmental factors, emphasizing the community as a whole, and analyzing how subsystems interact with each other (Zastrow & Kirst-Ashman, 2010). Family systems also address the interrelated elements and structure of a family where each member of the family is an "element" of the system and each element has unique characteristics as well as interdependent characteristics. The sum total of the interrelationships among the elements creates a structure with boundaries, which can be open or closed to outside systems and contain subsystems, which have their own rules, boundaries, and unique characteristics (Morgaine, 2001). A systemic perspective is thought to be particularly useful when addressing military families because the two systems (i.e., military and family) are intertwined and create a larger system that is "mutually influential across contextual boundaries" (Everson & Camp, 2011, p. 4).

The family's affiliation with the military needs to be understood from the perspective of the military being a social institution that requires adherence to military values and culture (Everson & Camp, 2011). Yet, in a reciprocal manner, the family has historically influenced the development of military programs and policies. The military, as an organization, recognizes that the family plays a major role in the success of the mission and as a result, different military family-friendly programs have come to fruition, propelled by the combination of family needs, national security concerns, and the zeitgeist of each American era. The Department of Defense (DoD) designed a "social contract" with service members and their families. The contract was initiated in 2002 as a partnership between the DoD, service members, and their families, with the notion that for those individuals who commit to supporting the nation's defense the military in turn commits to improving service member and military family quality of life (Office of the Deputy Assistant Secretary of Defense, 2002; as cited in Schwerin, 2006). (Chapter 17 provides a review of the sociopolitical evolution of the military family and military related programs.)

Coping and Resilience Models

Coping under stress is another area often examined in military families. There are several noteworthy foundational models that address the promotion of coping and resilience in families under stress or crisis. These models have laid the framework for many of the theories and interventions that are being implemented with military families today. For instance, Hill's (1949) ABC-X model—developed to illustrate the interactive forces of family stress and resilience on World War II military families—posited that a life event or transition stressor (A) interacts with the extent to which the family has internal or community support resources (B), which influences how the family perceives the stressor (C), which then influences the extent of the crisis (X) and the family's ability or inability to maintain balance or homeostasis.

Later, the Double ABC-X model by McCubbin and colleagues, pertaining to Vietnam military families, introduced the "pile-up" of demands and the concept of adaptation, either in a positive or a negative direction (Lavee, McCubbin, & Olson, 1987; McCubbin & Patterson, 1983). This model posited that cumulative stressors interact with existing resources to influence the family's perception of the stressor, which then affect whether the family moves toward a new balance or toward maladaptation.

The Circumplex Model (Olson, Russell, & Sprenkle, 1989), although not specific to military families, nevertheless was influential in light of its research-driven family prototypes. In this model, family balance is conceptualized on a continuum of three dimensions:

1. Adaptability (or flexibility in terms of role relationships, rules and power structure in relation to stress)
2. Cohesion (how separated or connected family members are to each other)
3. Communication among family members

Communication and Skills Training

More recently, communication and social skills training was advocated based on the research findings of Gottman and associates. Gottman, Gottman, and Atkins (2011) stated that communication is an essential part of any couples or family based therapy. They noted that with military families in particular combat experiences can make simple communications distorted and strained. Gottman et al. (2011) developed the family component of the Army's Comprehensive Soldier Fitness Program, a resilience-building model that was recently launched and is being piloted by the Army. The family aspect of the program is based on Gottman and Silver's (1999) book, *The Seven Principles for Making Marriage Work.*

Community Capacity Model

For those who are active duty, the service member's unit is often the first line of support for military families and can help the family to establish positive connections with both military and community resources. Bowen, Martin, Marsini, and Nelson (2001) devised the Community Capacity Model as part of a family violence prevention program for U.S. Air Force families. The rationale behind the model is that both formal and informal support networks within the military and within the community collaborate to provide a "supportive context" for military families.

> The model focuses on the production of social capital in formal and informal networks and the relationship between social capital and community results. Emphasis is placed on how military unit leaders and military community human services agencies, which are both formal networks, can work independently and collectively to strengthen informal networks in the community as a supportive context for family life.
>
> (Bowen, Martin, Marsini, & Nelson, 2001, p. 2)

AN INTRODUCTION TO VETERAN INJURY AND IMPACT ON THE FAMILY

In January 2010 the U.S. Department of Defense (DoD) reported that more than 42,000 soldiers, sailors, marines, and airmen had been injured in Operation Iraqi Freedom (OIF) and Operation Enduring Freedom (OEF) (U.S. Department of Defense, 2010). Families with injured or ill service members face significant challenges that may require more intensive individual or family treatment (Laser & Stephens, 2011). The range of experiences for these families vary depending on the specific type of injury and severity, as well as the composition of the family (e.g., the developmental age of the children and the preexisting parent, child and family characteristics) (Cozza & Guimond, 2011). Cozza and Guimond (2011) recommend that interventions with combat-injured families should focus on reducing distress, supporting healthy child and parent functioning, and encouraging constructive communication about the injury with the family. Since the ability of the parent to maintain effective parenting relies on his or her ability to cope, it is essential that therapeutic interventions focus on helping both the injured and the non-injured parent learn positive coping skills. As parents learn these skills, they model them for their children, which can have a positive impact on the children, since children often respond negatively to parental stress (Cozza & Guimond, 2011).

RATIONALE FOR FAMILY-BASED INTERVENTIONS

There are several rationales for providing family therapy for those families that are coping with injured veterans. One such rationale is the recognition that family members can serve as important sources of social support for injured service members (Riggs, 2000). Family functioning can be significantly impacted when combat veterans return home to their families with issues such as posttraumatic stress disorder (PTSD) or posttraumatic stress symptoms (PTSS); traumatic brain injury (TBI); polytraumatic injuries (e.g., injuries to multiple body systems); and/or substance use disorders (SUD). These issues can destabilize the entire family system and impact its ability to be a source of support for the service member as well as for one another (Makin-Byrd, Gifford, McCutcheon, & Glynn, 2011). Research shows that families who are attempting to cope with stressful events tend to draw together for mutual comfort and assistance; however, in cases of extreme stress, family members tend to separate and avoid interactions with each other (McKenry & Price, 2000). Another rationale for the provision of family therapy services is based on an assertion by Bowling, Doerman, and Sherman (2011) that it is useful to include family members in treatment because veteran reintegration into family life is one of the major challenges that veterans and their families face postdeployments, and even more so in combat-related deployments.

Thus, the objective of this segment of the chapter is to bring to light the importance of the family as part of a comprehensive approach in treating injured veteran clients, specifically those who are suffering from combat PTSD and TBI. We will begin by examining the impact of veteran TBI and PTSD on the family. Next, a section on family assessment is provided, including content on the use of genograms and ecomaps that are particularly relevant to this population. The remainder of the chapter focuses on providing the reader with several couples and family-based treatments that are specific to combat PTSD and TBI. The models highlighted are drawn mostly from the evidence-based literature, with a focus on psychoeducational and cognitive-behavioral therapeutic perspectives. We also offer a military family case vignette and associated discussion questions.

The Effects of TBI on the Family

Survivors of TBI and their family members must often confront and learn to cope with the long-lasting changes to family life resulting from a TBI injury (Perlick et al., 2011). Much of the caregiving responsibility for injured persons during their recovery falls on the family. Even when there are formal rehabilitation services in place the family is usually continuously involved and often plays a vital role in the recovery process (Oddy & Herbert, 2003).

TBI-associated symptoms of aggression, irritability, and emotional instability will frequently contribute to family turmoil (Savitsky et al., 2009). TBI often leads to diminished libido, as well, which can result in intimacy and sexual functioning problems in couples (Cameron et al., 2011; Melby, 2008; Pensford, 2003). Additionally, physical impairments (e.g., spasticity, poor balance, ataxia, speech difficulties, decreased or heightened sensitivities) and cognitive impairments (e.g., inattention, poor concentration, memory deficits, poor planning, and problem solving) associated with TBI can also impact individual and family functioning (Cameron et al., 2011).

When a service member has TBI (as well as other co-occurring polytraumatic injuries), families experience stress not only from the challenges associated with the injury but also from being propelled into numerous hospitals and rehabilitation settings. Bishop, Degeneffe, and Mast (2006) found that understanding the needs of family members and knowing how to help families have their needs met is an important component when providing effective family support services. In fact, Savitsky et al. (2009) found that family turmoil may even interfere with service member recovery.

Research has shown that the family's coping ability in addressing TBI-associated challenges is likely to have a direct impact on the brain injured person (Oddy & Herbert, 2003). As TBI patients are discharged home following hospitalization and/or rehabilitation, relatives often assume caregiver roles (Kreutzer et al., 2009). Family member caregivers often face multiple responsibilities depending on the severity of the TBI, including helping to manage the patient's activities of daily living; following up with medical appointments; monitoring medications; arranging for socialization and recreational activities; and serving as sources of emotional support for the injured individual and for other family members (Kreutzer et al., 2009).

Interventions with family members of those suffering from TBI or other polytraumatic injuries require care considerations at all stages of the rehabilitation process. Cozza and Guimond (2011) proposed an injury recovery trajectory model where the veteran rehabilitation process is broken up into four phases. The first phase is the acute phase, followed by a medical stabilization phase; a transition to outpatient care phase; and finally the long-term rehabilitation and recovery phase. Cozza and Guimond (2011) suggest that the recovery trajectory is not always linear, in that it may involve alternating periods of medical stability and instability depending on the type of injury and the severity. Thus, family members may need to continuously readapt to the demands of the different phases. However, regardless of the phase, Oddy and Herbert (2003) suggested that family members be kept informed and be part of the decision-making process regarding the injured individual's ongoing care.

The Effects of Posttraumatic Stress Disorder on the Family

PTSD occurs when an individual has been exposed to an event that involved actual or threatened death or serious injury, or the threat to the physical integrity of self or others. The person's response involves intense fear, helplessness, or horror (American Psychiatric Association, 2000). As a result of combat-related trauma in service members, families may be impacted by the veteran's symptoms in a number of ways (Galovski & Lyons, 2003). For instance, the avoidance/numbing cluster of symptoms associated with PTSD has been implicated in relationship discord as well as in intimacy problems, both emotionally and sexually (Matsakis, 2007; Monson, Guthrie, & Stevens, 2003). There are several areas of sexual concern related to the veteran's combat trauma experience. These include sexual disinterest; problems in sexual performance; insistence in sex on demand; the separation of affection and romance from sexual activity; the need to stay in control; and various forms of sexual obsession (Brown & Hall, 2009; Cameron et al., 2011; Garte, 1989; Matsakis, 2007).

There is also evidence of an association between hyperarousal symptoms and physical and psychological aggression in male veterans (Monson et al., 2003). Spouses and family members of traumatized combat veterans sometimes cope with the veteran's hypersensitivity and arousal by emotionally withdrawing or by becoming verbally and/or physically aggressive (Dekel & Monson, 2010). Johnson and Williams-Keeler (1998) pointed out that even the most positive relationships can be engulfed by the aftereffects of trauma and that once a trauma victim's marriage becomes stressed, these couples tend to engage in self-perpetuating cycles of distancing, defensiveness, and mistrust. Moreover, marital distress often evokes, maintains, and exacerbates trauma symptoms. McDevitt-Murphy (2011) posited that although social support is often a necessary component in being able to successfully cope with PTSD, many PTSD symptoms deleteriously impact interpersonal relationships and diminish social support for the individual who was originally traumatized.

Secondary Traumatization and the Family

The literature shows that when one partner in a relationship has experienced trauma, the likelihood that the other partner will be traumatized is higher than in couples where neither partner has experienced trauma (Monson et al., 2003). Dekel and Goldblatt (2008) noted that the consequences of traumatic events often affect the individual's family, friends, and caregivers. In fact, secondary, or vicarious traumatization often results from strong emotional connections with the trauma victim (Monson et al., 2003). Nelson and Wright (1996) defined secondary traumatization as the instance when those who closely interact with a trauma victim experience similar symptoms. In the case of the parent-child relationship, the traumatic experiences of the parent can be transmitted to the child in several ways. The child can be directly traumatized by the parent's behavior; the transmission may occur as the child identifies with the parent; or the impact of parental trauma on the child may occur indirectly as a result of nonspecific dysfunction within the family system (Rosenheck & Fontana, 1999).

Monson and colleagues (2003) pointed out that partners of traumatized individuals may have experienced previous traumatization prior to or during their intimate relationship. It is imperative when working with military couples and/or families that the therapist take into account the possibility that multiple individuals in the family system may have experienced previous trauma.

ASSESSMENT

As part of a comprehensive assessment, a clinician would need to take into account all of the aforementioned considerations (e.g., impact of veteran injury on the family, the use of support systems, and prior trauma in family members). As previously mentioned, based on Hill's (1949) original War World II study on family stress and resilience, McCubbin and Patterson (1983), working with Vietnam era military families, found that the three most critical family factors that influence adaptation and resilience in the face of serious disability include: the family's social support network, the family's appraisal of the disability, and its coping and problem-solving strategies.

McCubbin (1987) devised the *Family Index of Regenerativity-Adaptation-Military* (FIRA-M) scale, which is an instrument that can be used by clinicians to assess the military family on the dimensions of stress, resilience and adaptation. More recently, Cozza et al. (2009; as cited in Cozza & Guimond, 2011) found that injured veterans and their families tend to engage in risk-taking behaviors. Although the behaviors are mostly observed in veterans, other family members might also engage in risk taking. The high-risk behaviors noted in their study included excessive alcohol use, prescription drug abuse, reckless driving and compulsive spending. Excessive drinking and drug use could also play a role in increasing the risk for domestic violence, aggression, and suicide. Thus, all risk factors should be assessed when working with this population. The Case Vignette: The O'Reilly Family illustrates some of the risk and protective factors and assessment issues discussed above. It also provides a basis for considering two important assessment tools that are discussed: a family genogram and an ecomap.

Case Vignette: The O'Reilly Family

Thomas O'Reilly is a 32-year-old Irish Catholic originally from New York City. He is third-generation military—his grandfather fought in the Irish Republican Army from 1919 to 1921 and possibly suffered from combat trauma; his father fought in Vietnam, and Thomas currently serves in the U.S. Army. Thomas was born while his father was deployed in Vietnam and he grew up with his mother in New York. Thomas has two younger brothers and the brothers are all 2 years apart. His youngest brother currently serves in the Navy and his middle brother is in jail on drug-related charges. While Thomas lived at home, he witnessed domestic violence between his mother and father. His father drank excessively, isolated himself from the family, and was easily startled as a result of his untreated PTSD. Thomas enlisted in the U.S. Army when he finished high school and married Sue, his high school sweetheart.

Thomas is a Battalion First Sergeant (E-8) in the Army. He has been combat deployed 3 times, twice to Operation Iraqi Freedom (OIF) and the other time to Afghanistan, Operation Enduring Freedom (OEF). On his last deployment, he lost his battle buddy to an improvised explosive device (IED). Thomas also suffered a mild TBI as a result of the IED. Thomas is currently reporting having nightmares, flashbacks, difficulty sleeping, and short-term memory loss. He is also distancing himself from his family and binge drinking and abusing prescribed painkillers. Thomas also reports sexual dysfunction (impotence), which is affecting his relationship with his wife. After work, Thomas spends the majority of his time surfing the Internet or playing video games.

Sue, his wife, is a 31-year-old female of Filipino heritage. Her grandfather served in World War II from 1941 to 1943 and possibly suffered from combat trauma, and other than Thomas's service, she has no other connection with the military. Sue's family suffered from natural disasters while living in the Philippines. Her grandmother lived through the volcanic eruption in 1911. Sue's parents experienced a large earthquake in 1976. Sue is an only child whose parents divorced when she was 7 years old. After the divorce, Sue lived with her mother and maternal grandparents in New York City. Sue reported that she was molested by her paternal uncle between the ages of 5 and 6. She met Thomas while she was in high school, got pregnant, and married Thomas. She wanted to be a nurse but she is currently a homemaker. Sue currently reports feeling down and stressed. Sue believes Thomas is having an affair because they have not had sex in more than 8 months. She often feels irritable toward the children and feels isolated as she lives on a military base in Texas with Thomas and their children. Although she feels that the military installation and her Army neighbors have been very welcoming, she misses her extended family, as they now live in upstate New York. Sue reports feeling frustrated that she never went to college. Sue attended a spousal support group 3 years ago at their last duty station and felt it was helpful. She reports enjoying cooking and learning new things.

Thomas and Sue have three children: Daisy age 11, Lily age 9, and Rose age 7. Daisy is an outstanding student and earns straight As in school. All of her teachers love her and she helps her mother take care of her younger siblings Lily and Rose. When Daisy is not in school, she spends a lot of time at the neighbor's house or upstairs in her room. Daisy enjoys taking singing classes and is closer to her mother.

Lily is 9 years old and is currently having some difficulties in school. She enjoys art. During recess and lunch she seeks out her teachers and isolates from her peers. Lily has gotten into fights with kids who make fun of her.

Rose is 7 years old and is currently experiencing enuresis (bed wetting) even though she was successfully toilet trained when she was 2 years old. Rose occasionally sleepwalks at night. Twice she has run into her father in the middle of the night as he was walking around the house, holding a knife and talking about the "enemy." Both times her mother woke up and intervened. Rose has temper tantrums at home and cries easily. At school, she is sociable with other children.

Thomas is currently seeking marital therapy with Sue because she has threatened to leave him if he didn't attend counseling. Thomas and Sue are also concerned over their children's behaviors.

Family Genograms

A practical tool that can be used when assessing families is the family genogram (McGoldrick & Gerson, 1985). The genogram is a widely used and comprehensive systemic assessment device that is useful for gathering large amounts of information in a relatively concise and time-effective manner that allows both the client and the therapist to view the "big picture" (i.e., in a diagrammatic form) with regard to the family system (Jordan, 2004).

Genograms can assist in assessing the interactional and intergenerational structure, function and relationship patterns of the family as well as family resources, history, and predisposing factors. Weiss, Coll, Gebauer, Smiley, and Carrillo (2010) proposed a military-specific genogram to be used as an assessment tool. In this type of genogram, military family intergenerational patterns, strengths, and barriers are examined through a solution-focused perspective. Also, by delineating combat-related trauma and aspects of military culture, the therapist can conduct a culturally informed assessment. The military-specific genogram identifies family risk and protective factors, which could mitigate distress or even reduce secondary traumatization within the family (Weiss et al., 2010). Figure 26.1 provides a basic illustration of a military-specific genogram based on the O'Reilly case vignette. For further instructions on conducting a military-specific genogram with a family to obtain the content as well as the solution-focused prompts the reader is referred to Weiss et al. (2010).

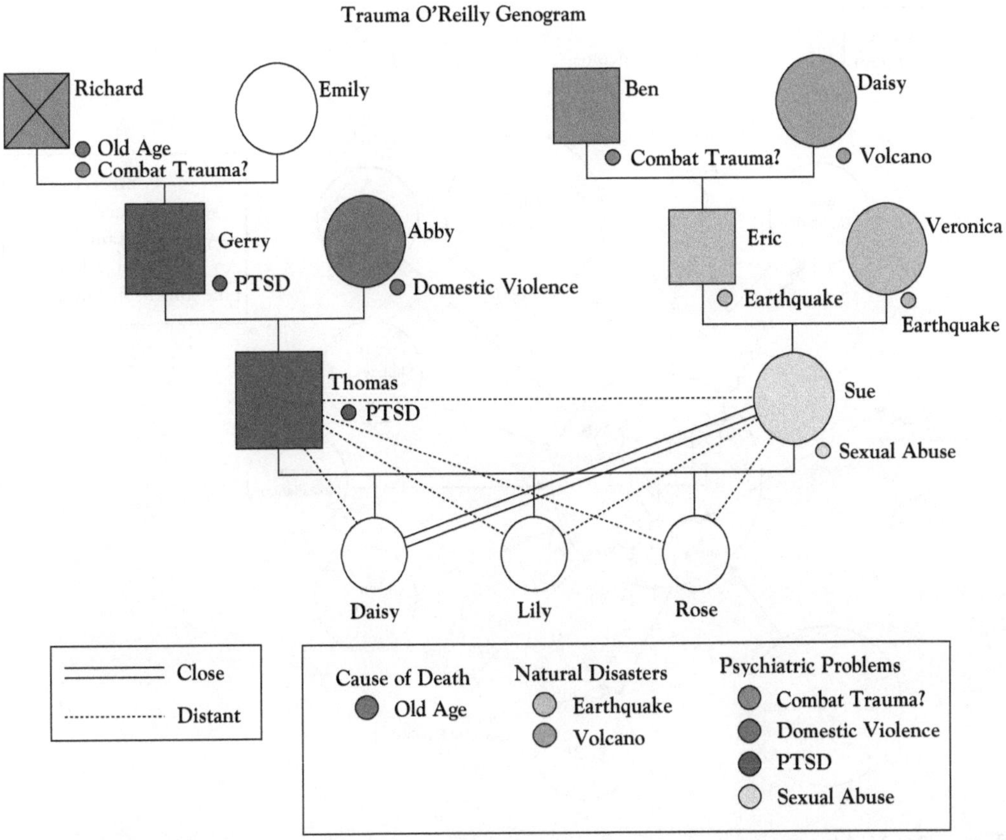

Figure 26.1 Military-specific genogram
Source: Adapted from McGoldrick and Gerson, 1985; Weiss et al., 2010.

Family Ecomap

Finally, the application of an ecomap with military families has been recommended by Everson and Camp (2011) as an added tool in addressing the family context within a larger environmental network. An ecomap, like the genogram, is a symbolic illustration that denotes the family's participation (or lack thereof) in work, school, community, civic, and religious organizations and can include military life. Ecomaps are an especially helpful technique in assisting families to re-create their supportive networks that occur with military geographic relocation. This includes the relocation that sometimes occurs in cases of injury, where the family must move to another city or state to receive services for the injured veteran. Ecomaps often place the identified individual or his or her family in a center circle, with lines drawn to outer circles that represent other individuals and communities, or organizations with which the individual interacts. Solid lines depict strong, positive relationships while broken lines represent a tenuous relationship (Hartman, 1995). Ecomaps provide information about the family's size, diversity, stability, and available resources, as well as helping the family and the clinician to evaluate the strengths and challenges of the social environment and identifying where additional supports may be needed. Figure 26.2 presents an example of an ecomap diagram as applied to the O'Reilly case vignette.

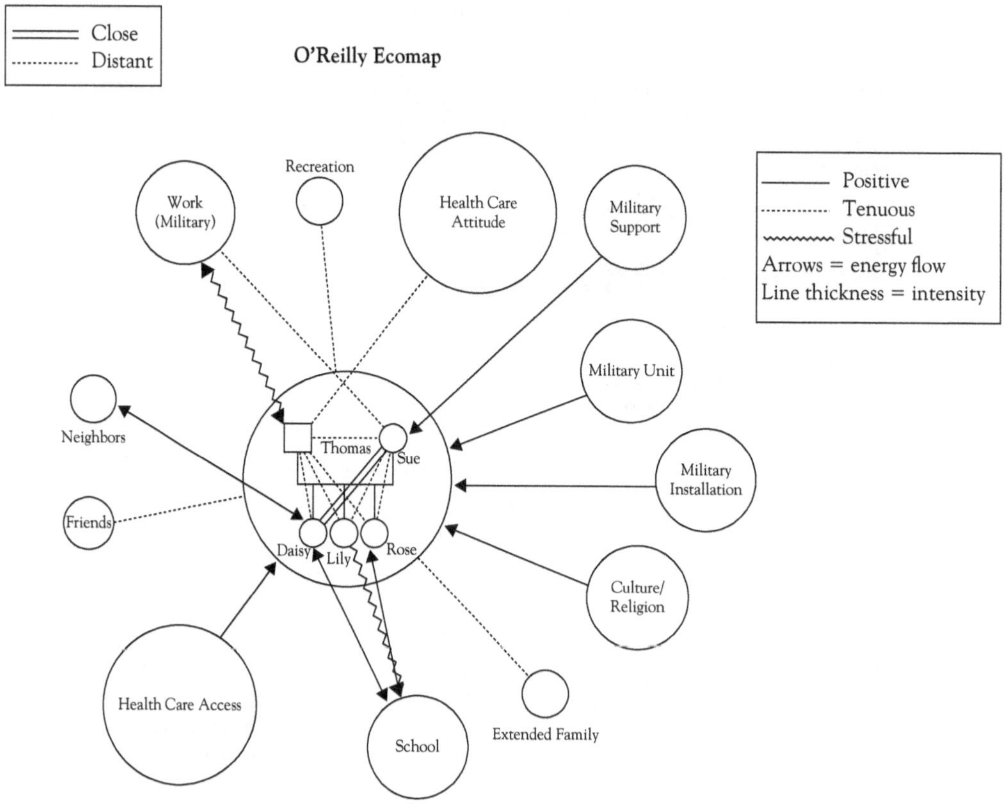

Figure 26.2 Military-specific ecomap

EMPIRICALLY INFORMED THERAPIES

After the assessment is conducted by a clinician an intervention and corresponding treatment plan can be devised. The rest of this chapter is devoted to the delineation of several models of empirically informed couples' and family therapies that are currently being implemented with service members, veterans, and their families. Five types of models are described. The first three, which address PTSD in the context of military couples and family based interventions include: Integrative Behavioral Couples Therapy; Cognitive-Behavioral Couples and Family Therapy; and Psychoeducational Models (i.e., the SAFE program and Operation Enduring Families). Two additional models are provided that address interventions used to support families that are coping with veteran TBI: The Multifamily Group Treatment for TBI and the Brain Injury Family Intervention.

Integrative Behavioral Couples Therapy

Integrative Behavioral Couples Therapy (IBCT) is an approach that is aimed at helping couples use their problems as vehicles to establish greater closeness and intimacy (Jacobson, Christensen, Prince, Cordova, & Eldridge, 2000). IBCT focuses on increasing emotional acceptance between partners and assumes that relationship problems lie in the actions (i.e., behaviors) carried out by each partner and in his or her emotional reactivity to those corresponding behaviors. Therefore, IBCT attempts to alter the emotional context and interaction between partners to achieve intimacy as well as to make concrete changes in their target problems (Christensen, Atkins, Yi, Baucom, & George, 2006). Additionally, IBCT integrates the twin goals of acceptance and change as positive outcomes for couples, with the premise that couples who succeed in therapy are those who can make behavioral changes to accommodate each other's needs while demonstrating greater acceptance of one another.

IBCT consists of two major phases: an evaluation/feedback phase and an active treatment phase. During the evaluation phase, the first session is comprised of the therapist having a joint session with both partners present. The therapist learns what brings the couple to therapy and obtains a brief history of the relationship. In the second and third sessions, each partner has an individual session where the therapist explores each partner's relationship concerns and individual history. The fourth session is considered the "feedback session," where the couple receives feedback from the therapist. The couple's problems are formulated, the major themes and reasons for their struggles are conceptualized, and the therapist discusses how therapy can be beneficial. The couple actively participates in this feedback and then privately discusses whether they would like to continue with treatment. If they agree to participate in treatment, the subsequent sessions are considered part of the active treatment phase. Therapy is then conducted jointly with a focus on recent incidents in their relationship that reflect major problematic themes. The therapist helps the couple communicate more openly, directly, and clearly, while also helping them to identify patterns that they struggle with and explore alternative ways of interacting (Integrative Behavioral Couple Therapy, 2010).

Erbes, Polusny, Macdermid, and Compton (2008) stated that IBCT may be particularly relevant when working with veterans with PTSD and their partners. IBCT reduces conflict and increases intimacy between service members and their partners by fostering acceptance, tolerance, and expression of emotions, which are often minimized by service members suffering from PTSD. Additionally, IBCT's emphasis on intimacy and increased positive activities fosters relational exposure that may encourage service members to confront situations, feelings, and conversations that they have avoided having with their partner (Erbes et al., 2008). These authors proposed an adaptation of IBCT for the military population, where intimacy is encouraged through acceptance and skill-building strategies. Erbes and colleagues (2008) posited that the balance between acceptance and change strategies emphasized in IBCT serves as an ideal platform to target both the relationship and the individual problems faced by couples when one partner has PTSD.

In the adapted version of IBCT, clinicians focus on the assessment of the following relational areas: level of distress; level of commitment to the relationship; types of conflict and what makes the conflict problematic; individual and the relationship strengths that keep the couple together; deployment related issues; and PTSD-related problems. As part of treatment, the therapist incorporates basic education about PTSD symptoms while facilitating acceptance and change of PTSD related behaviors within the couple (Erbes et al., 2008). Furthermore, Erbes and colleagues suggested that when working with veterans and their partners' therapists should: shorten the length of treatment (due to therapy dropout rates and continuous deployments); include motivational interviewing (Miller & Rollnick, 2002); and use values clarification (Hayes, Strosahl, & Wilson, 1999). Their treatment approach includes education about trauma and trauma reactions, emphasizing behavioral exchange and activity schedules to increase involvement with shared and individual activities, and identifying ways to block experiential avoidance as it manifests in the couple's interactions (Erbes et al., 2008).

Cognitive Behavioral Couples Therapy (CBCT)

Cognitive behavior therapy emphasizes both cognitive interventions and behavioral change. The therapist working with couples must focus equally on each partner's expectations about the nature of their relationship and use behavioral interventions such as assertiveness training, behavior-exchange procedures, communication training, and problem-solving techniques (Dattilio, 1993). The primary tenets of this type of therapy as applied to couples involve: the modification of unrealistic expectations in the relationship; the correction of faulty attributions in relationship interactions; and the use of self-instructional procedures to decrease destructive interactions. The application of cognitive behavioral couples therapy (CBCT) has been found to produce a variety of positive outcomes for couples, including an increase in relationship satisfaction, a decrease in intimate aggression, and lower rates of attrition during treatment (Monson et al., 2003).

An important aspect of CBCT is the cognitive restructuring of automatic thoughts. Automatic thoughts are typically negative thoughts held by individuals that occur spontaneously in their minds about life circumstances or about others. Restructuring these thoughts involves clients considering alternative explanations to their negative thoughts and adopting the alternatives as part of their daily routines (Dattilio, 1993). Cognitive distortions may be evident in an individual's automatic thoughts and are believed to have developed from faulty information processing. Essential to the restructuring process is that each partner accepts responsibility for the distress in the relationship, which requires both discussion and evaluation of causes and attributions that each partner places on their perceived relationship problems (Dattilio, 1993).

Dattilio and Epstein (2003) recommended that the therapist working within a CBCT frame conduct an initial joint interview. During the interview, couples are asked about their reasons for seeking assistance and information is gathered on each partner's perspectives about his or her concerns and what would enable their life together to be more satisfying. The therapist should also ask about the couple's family history, individual family histories, and family resources and strengths. Throughout the interview, the therapist gathers information about the couple's cognitions, emotional responses, and behaviors toward each other (Dattilio & Epstein, 2003).

The therapist should also conduct an interview with each partner individually in order to gather information about past and current functioning, including life stresses, psychopathology, overall health, and coping strategies. Dattilio and Epstein (2003) suggested that after collecting information from interviews, questionnaires, and behavioral observations, the therapist should meet with the couple and provide a summary of:

- Relational patterns that have emerged
- Individual and couples' strengths
- Major presenting problems

- Life demands or stressors that have produced adjustment problems
- Constructive and destructive patterns in their interactions that seem to be influencing their presenting problems

Next, the therapist and the couple should identify the couple's top priority for change, as well as review interventions that might have the potential to alleviate their problems (Dattilio & Epstein, 2003).

To improve the skill of identifying one's automatic thoughts, clients are typically asked to keep a small notebook between sessions to record a brief description of the circumstances in which they felt distressed about the relationship or became engaged in conflict. Through this assignment the therapist demonstrates to couples how their automatic thoughts are linked to emotional and behavioral responses and helps them understand the themes that upset them in their relationship. This also increases the individual's understanding that their negative emotional and behavioral responses to each other are manageable (Dattilio, 2005; Dattilio & Epstein, 2003).

CBCT and Posttraumatic Stress

Cognitive-behavioral couples' therapy is considered by some authors as a useful framework for addressing reintegration tasks faced by couples that have experienced a wartime military deployment. This includes assisting the couple in understanding each other's experiences during the deployment; renegotiating spousal and/or parental roles; reestablishing intimacy within the relationship; and developing or adapting family routines and rituals (Sayers, 2011). Several studies have noted the applicability of CBCT for couples in which one or both partners have been diagnosed with PTSD (Glynn et al., 1999; Monson et al., 2003; Monson, Fredman, & Adair, 2008; Monson, Schnurr, Stevens, & Guthrie, 2004). CBCT for posttraumatic stress was developed to address the need for conjoint treatment that targets both PTSD and relationship distress with the simultaneous goals of improving PTSD symptoms and improving intimate relationship functioning (Fredman, Monson, & Adair, 2011; Monson et al., 2008). Additionally, Monson et al. (2004) posited that through CBCT a couple can recognize how their behaviors and belief systems interact and how the couple reciprocally maintains both relationship discord and PTSD symptoms. PTSD symptoms are considered to contribute to couple distress, which in turn exacerbates and reinforces PTSD symptomatology (Monson et al., 2008). While participating in this type of treatment couples are encouraged to explore how the partner who has been diagnosed with PTSD understands the effects of the trauma on him- or herself and on their relationship. They also examine how PTSD symptoms contribute to their emotions and behaviors, and how they and their partner relate to each other as a result of the trauma (Monson et al., 2008).

In CBCT for posttraumatic stress, the avoidance symptoms associated with this disorder are targeted both early on and throughout treatment because these symptoms are considered to be a primary behavioral mechanism that contributes to perpetuating PTSD and intimate relationship problems (Cozza & Guimond, 2011; Monson et al., 2003). Conflict-management skills are also introduced by the therapist to improve the handling of anger and irritability, which have been linked to the hyperarousal symptoms of PTSD (Monson et al., 2003). The couple is also encouraged to explore and gently challenge or support their thoughts and beliefs about the communication skills used by both partners in the relationship in a non-judgmental way (Monson et al., 2003), while also paying attention to the identification of emotions. Partners are to express their negative feelings about the loss of their old routines and patterns, as well as work together to find new ways that fit their current circumstances (Sayers, 2011).

Monson and colleagues (2004) suggested the following format for this type of therapy that usually consists of 15 sessions in 3 treatment phases. The three phases are: (1) treatment orientation and psychoeducation about PTSD and its related intimate relationship problems and safety building; (2) behavioral communication and skills training; and (3) cognitive interventions. Monson and colleagues (2008) offered a revised version of this treatment that differs slightly on the emphasis of each phase. The revised phases can be remembered using the acronym "RESUME" Living, which is designed to convey a recovery orientation and a hopeful philosophy. Monson et al. (2008, p. 962) described the acronym in the following manner:

R—Rationale for treatment (Stage 1)
E—Education about PTSD and relationship issues (Stage 1)
S—Satisfaction enhancement (Stage 2)
U—Undermining avoidance (Stage 2)
M—Making meaning out of the trauma(s) (Stage 3)
E—End of therapy (Stage 3)

The three stages are sequenced such that psychoeducation and conflict-management strategies are provided first to increase both partners' commitment to treatment and ensure that conjoint therapy sessions will be a "safe place," both physically and emotionally. Fredman and colleagues (2011) pointed out that safety should be secured prior to engaging in further treatment. Sayers (2011) added that a psychoeducational approach combined with behavioral couples therapy can serve as a framework for identifying how the veteran's behaviors may be adaptive in combat but maladaptive in family life.

Fredman et al. (2011) suggested that when using CBCT for posttraumatic stress, the therapist teaches the couple a process that they can use together to challenge cognitions that are maintaining PTSD symptoms and relationship problems. This strategy is described in the acronym UNSTUCK (p. 122):

U—Unified and curious as a couple as they join together in collaborative empiricism
N—Notice and share thoughts and feelings
S—(Brain) Storm alternative thoughts or interpretations, even if they seem implausible
T—Test the thoughts (consider the evidence for each alternative thought)
U—Use the most balanced thoughts
C—Changes in emotions and behaviors that ensue as a result of the new thoughts
K—Keep practicing

Monson et al. (2003) noted that when using CBCT with traumatized couples there is no requirement that either partner disclose specific information about his or her trauma history. In fact, explicit renditions of trauma should be discouraged (Fredman et al., 2011). If either partner wishes to speak of past trauma with his or her partner the therapist should encourage the trauma disclosure to be in relation to the couple's here-and-now thoughts and feelings rather than an in-depth retelling of his or her individual experiences (Monson et al., 2003).

Despite the fact that clients may not share details of their individual traumatic experiences, beliefs and emotions that are linked to their traumas are likely to be evoked. These moments will provide opportunities for the couple to engage in cognitive and emotional processing and to improve their mastery and tolerance of associated emotions (Monson et al., 2003). CBCT strategies work well to facilitate shifts in the couple's thinking about the trauma and its consequences, while simultaneously decreasing the likelihood that either partner might become emotionally distressed due to explicit retelling of the other's trauma (Fredman et al., 2011).

CBT With Families

Cognitive behavioral therapy can be used with families by applying many of the same strategies that are used with couples; however, these strategies must be expanded in order to address family schemata (i.e., member's beliefs about each other) (Dattilio, 1993). Additionally, emphasis must be placed on encouraging family members to become conscientious observers of their own interpretations and evaluations of family transactions. Dattilio (1993) portrayed the focus of this approach as being twofold. The first focus is to explain family member expectations of one another and how through these expectations interactions are affected within the family context. The second focus considers how member expectations and interactions impact the family's ability to cope with crises, change, and other unexpected life events.

When working with families, it is also important to identify the types of cognitive distortions that are involved in each individual's automatic thoughts. This is accomplished by identifying thought distortions and finding alternative ways to view relationship events that contribute to different emotional and behavioral responses towards other family members. As members of the family identify their automatic thoughts, they are better able to modify their distorted or extreme cognitions about themselves and others (Dattilio & Epstein, 2003). It is also important to explore potential barriers to family therapy, such as member's fears about changes that they anticipate will be stressful and difficult for them, and to problem-solve with the family regarding steps that could be taken to reduce the stress (Dattilio & Epstein, 2003).

Psychoeducation

Psychoeducation has been demonstrated to aid the therapeutic approach (Fisher, 2008), and elements of psychoeducation exist in nearly every form of treatment (Wessely et al., 2008). In fact, all of the interventions discussed in this chapter include psychoeducation. Kreutzer (2002) recommended that teaching couples and families about the course of recovery and methods to promote recovery are key elements in any intervention. Erbes and colleagues (2008) recommended providing education of symptoms in IBCT to enhance the couple's retention of and comprehension of the information, as well as to facilitate acceptance and change behaviors. Monson et al. (2004) suggested that psychoeducation about

PTSD and related relationship problems should be discussed at the beginning of CBT treatment (Monson et al., 2004).

Psychoeducation can also be used with families. Family psychoeducation includes educating family members about an illness or injury in a family member (Fisher, 2008) and describing new ways of responding to the illness or injury (Rabin & Nardi, 1991). Sherman and colleagues (2009) posited that the family desire for information about a diagnosed illness in a family member is a universal need. In fact, marital or family conflict can be exacerbated if family members lack sufficient information about a family member's injury or illness. This conflict can lead to psychological distress and social isolation for both the injured member (e.g., the veteran) and his or her family, as well as result in suboptimal illness management (Perlick et al., 2011). Psychoeducation can be particularly useful when working with a couple or family in which one or more members have been diagnosed with PTSD, because many family members do not fully understand the issues associated with this diagnosis and its impact on the family.

Additionally, Riggs (2000) reported that educating and supporting family members of trauma survivors may help them to provide more useful support to the survivor, which then fosters recovery. Wessely and colleagues (2008) suggested that if people are provided information about trauma symptoms, their experience of these symptoms may be less disturbing and this may promote a sense of empowerment.

Psychoeducation for Military Families: The SAFE Program and Operation Enduring Families

The Support and Family Education (SAFE) Program—Mental Health Facts for Families—is a psychoeducation curriculum that was created by Michelle D. Sherman in a Veteran Affairs (VA) setting. It is not specific to any one psychiatric diagnosis, and most of the sessions deal with general mental illness (Sherman, 2003). Multifamily group sessions address numerous issues surrounding mental health and include such topics as causes of mental illness; PTSD and its impact on the family; problem-solving skills for family members (including problem-solving strategies for dealing with angry or violent members); skills for managing stress; empowerment of the individual suffering from mental illness; and dealing with the stigma surrounding mental illness (Sherman, 2008).

Based on the SAFE Program, Operation Enduring Families is a five-session family education and support program for veterans who have recently returned from combat and their families (Bowling et al., 2011). Operation Enduring Families attempts to integrate and welcome family members into the VA system and provides them with helpful resources in supporting their military family member. The goals of the Operation Enduring Families Program include:

- Providing information to veterans and their family members about the common experiences of veterans returning from combat and to help normalize their experiences
- Providing resources and coping tools for veterans and their families who are adjusting to life after deployment

- Assisting veterans and families with the common challenges that arise when reintegrating into the civilian community
- Providing an atmosphere where veterans and their families can support and encourage each other
- Linking veterans and their families with other opportunities for support both within the VA and with community resources (Bowling et al., 2011, p. 12).

Multifamily Group Treatment for TBI

MacFarlane described a Multifamily Group treatment for TBI (MFG-TBI) that emphasizes an education and problem-solving approach that was adapted from an evidence-based family model used in supporting family members of individual's suffering from schizophrenia (cited in Perlick et al., 2011). Perlick and colleagues (2011) believe that veterans with TBI and their families have many needs that can be addressed with a similar problem-solving approach. In MFG-TBI the clinician first meets with each individual family for several sessions to determine the issues that need to be addressed. Then the clinician provides an educational workshop for all families in which information is provided regarding TBI and the format of the multifamily group treatment model is presented. The clinician then holds biweekly group meetings with all families for 12 months. Throughout the duration of treatment, the families and clinician work together using an interactive, structured approach centered on solving everyday problems. MFG-TBI is currently being implemented and evaluated at two VA Medical Centers in the United States (Perlick et al., 2011).

Perlick and colleagues (2011) observed several challenges to working with the OEF/OIF veterans with TBI and their families. One challenge is that families are often too overwhelmed to seek out mental health care, as they are coping with acute psychosocial difficulties such as the loss of housing or legal complications. Additionally, TBI often compromises a veteran's organizational abilities and memory, which makes the veteran's attendance in MFG-TBI sporadic. Due to these concerns—as well as the fact that participation in mental health services may be stigmatizing—Perlick and colleagues (2011) proposed further adaptations to the MFG-TBI model for this population. The recommended adaptations include using motivational interviewing (MI) (Miller & Rollnick, 2002) to address stigma concerns and elicit "change talk." Using MI may help to emphasize that MFG-TBI is a problem-solving intervention rather than a trauma-focused therapy, which can reduce the anxiety faced by the veteran. Perlick and colleagues (2011) also suggested that presenting problems be clustered into three areas: family and relationship issues; veterans problems related to cognitive deficits or mental disorders; and veteran self-identity and community interface. They also noted that some group members may require additional support between multifamily group sessions, which may be in the form of individual- or couples-based sessions.

Brain Injury Family Intervention

Kreutzer and colleagues (2009) described the Brain Injury Family Intervention (BIFI) as a structured treatment that is designed to meet the needs that are most commonly identified by family members and survivors of TBI. Although it is not specific to combat veterans,

BIFI was developed to improve the psychological well-being of TBI survivors and enhance family functioning through the use of family systems theory and techniques. BIFI relies heavily on techniques such as the therapist use of empathic reflections; validation; reframing; and the normalization of common concerns. The primary tenet of BIFI is that families are interconnected systems and the actions, communications, and feelings of each family member influence those of other family members, which in turn influence the entire family system (Kreutzer et al., 2009).

BIFI uses collaborative self-examination to facilitate each family member in sharing their perspectives about events and how they interpret one another's behavior and interactions between members (Kreutzer & Taylor, 2004). These methods provide opportunities for each person to understand how others perceive them. BIFI also encourages perspective talking, self-monitoring, and enhanced awareness, while family members are encouraged to recognize and stop using approaches that do not work. CBT techniques can be incorporated into BIFI to improve cognitive, emotional, and behavioral functioning. Additionally, psychoeducation can be used to inform participants about common injury sequelae and recovery, while skills-training techniques are used to improve problem-solving, communication, and emotional control (Kreutzer et al., 2009). Topics covered in BIFI include:

- Understanding the typical consequences of brain injury
- Recognizing ambivalent feelings and developing strategies for positive coping
- Recognizing that brain injury happens to the entire family
- Recognizing the detrimental effect of guilt and the need to care for one's self
- Appreciating the natural limits of rehabilitation and helping to extend improvements well beyond the first 6 months
- Avoiding giving inconsistent or contradictory advice
- Understanding the differences between physical and emotional recovery
- Managing stress more effectively
- Learning effective ways to judge success
- Avoiding working on too many things at one time
- Expanding support systems
- Recognizing and addressing gaps in the system of care
- Encouraging communication and asking questions
- Politely addressing disagreements
- Resolving conflicting advice and information

(Kreutzer, 2002)

CONCLUSION

It is essential that social workers be able to identify the signs of distress among military personnel and their families as well as be versed with the common stressors associated with military service. Efforts to support military families have direct value for each family member as well as for the family unit, and ultimately for the success of the military. Appropriate couples- and family-based interventions, such as those described in this chapter, may enhance family resilience and increase the likelihood of creating positive and enduring change, while also decreasing the negative effects of PTSD symptoms (Sherman et al., 2009) and supporting healthy functioning in the veteran and in his or her family (Cozza & Guimond, 2011).

Addressing Barriers for Care and the Role of Social Work

There are many reasons why service personnel and their families are not receiving services. One such reason has to do with stigma (Bowling et al., 2011) or fear of negative work repercussions for those in active duty. Another reason is the therapist's lack of knowledge about this population (Coll, Weiss, Draves, & Dyer, 2012). It is essential that clinicians be able to understand military culture, identify the signs of distress among military personnel and their families, and be familiar with the common stressors that are encountered when one or more family members are in the military. This knowledge will help them to establish and maintain a therapeutic alliance, as well as to provide optimal interventions (Exum, Coll, & Weiss, 2011).

There are also barriers for community outreach to military families, for reasons such as assumptions regarding the self-sufficiency of the military, ideological ambivalence toward war, or lack of knowledge regarding military culture (Hoshmand & Hoshmand, 2007). The Department of Defense (DoD) and Department of Veterans Affairs (VA) along with state and community partnerships (schools, religious organizations, primary health organizations) are attempting to provide outreach services to reduce stigma and provide appropriate referrals (Kudler & Straits-Troster, 2009). Thus, they should keep in mind that the best way to intervene is through a Community Capacity model like the one presented earlier in this chapter.

Military personnel, veterans, and their families will be accessing care in local communities (Chapin, 2011); thus, civilian social workers and other mental health and family practitioners will need to be versed in the many areas that pertain to practicing with this population, including education, child welfare, domestic violence, mental health, health care, and substance abuse among others (Savitsky et al., 2009).

CHAPTER DISCUSSION QUESTIONS: BASED ON THE O'REILLY FAMILY CASE EXAMPLE

1. What are the risk factors in this family?
2. What additional information is needed?
3. What are the individual and family strengths?
4. Which assessment tool(s) would you use and why?
5. What do you notice about the family patterns in the genograms and the strength of the systemic connections in the ecomap?
6. What are the primary intervention issues to focus on?
7. Which treatment approach do you think would be most effective for this couple and/or family? (Provide a rationale.)
8. What are the family dynamics? (Also consider intergenerational transmission of trauma.)
9. What additional resources would you use or referrals would you make for this case?

REFERENCES

American Psychiatric Association. (2000). *Diagnostic and statistical manual of mental disorders* (4th ed., text rev.). Washington, DC: Author.

Bishop, M., Degeneffe, C. E., & Mast, M. (2006). Family needs after traumatic brain injury: Implications for rehabilitation counseling. *Australian Journal of Rehabilitation Counseling, 12*(2), 73–87.

Bourg, C., & Segal, M. W. (1999). The impact of family supportive policies and practices on organizational commitment to the army. *Armed Forces and Society, 25*(4), 633–652. doi: 10.1177/0095327X9902500406

Bowen, G. L., Martin, J. A., Mancini, J. A., & Nelson, J. P. (2001). Civic engagement and sense of community in the military. *Journal of Community Practice*, 9, 71–93.

Bowling, U., Doerman, A., & Sherman, M. (2011). *Operation enduring families: Information and support for Iraq and Afghanistan veterans and their families*. Oklahoma City, OK: Oklahoma City VA Medical Center. Retrieved from http://www.ouhsc.edu/oef/pdf/OEFManual122107.pdf

Brown, J., & Hall, B. (2009). Exploring intimate partner communication in military couples: Implications for counselors. In G. R. Walz, J. C. Bleuer, & R. K. Yep (Eds.), *Compelling counseling interventions: VISTAS 2009* (pp. 55–65). Alexandria, VA: American Counseling Association.

Cameron, R. P., Syme, M. L., Fraley, S. S., Chen, S. S., Welsh, E., Mona, L. R., . . . Lemos, L. (2011). Sexuality among wounded veterans of operation enduring freedom (OEF), operation Iraqi freedom (OIF), and operation new dawn (OND): Implications for rehabilitation psychologists. *Rehabilitation Psychology, 56*(4), 289–301.

Chapin, M. (2011). Family resilience and the fortunes of war. *Social Work in Health Care, 50*, 527–542.

Christensen, A., Atkins, D. C., Yi, J., Baucom, D. H., & George, W. H. (2006). Couple and individual adjustment for 2 years following a randomized clinical trial comparing traditional versus integrative behavioral couple therapy. *Journal of Consulting and Clinical Psychology, 74*(6), 1180–1191.

Coll, J. E., Weiss, E. L., Draves, P., & Dyer, D. (2012). The impact of military cultural awareness, experience, attitudes, and education on clinician self-efficacy in the treatment of veterans. *Professional Development: The International Journal of Continuing Social Work Education, 15*(1), 39–48.

Cozza, S. J., & Guimond, J. M. (2011). Working with combat-injured families through the recovery trajectory. In S. MacDermid Wadsworth & D. Riggs (Eds.), *Risk and resilience in U.S. military families* (pp. 259–277). New York, NY: Springer.

Dattilio, F. M. (1993). Cognitive techniques with couples and families. *Family Journal, 1*(1), 51–65.

Dattilio, F. M. (2005). Cognitive-behavioral couple therapy. In G. Gabbard, J. Beck, & J. Holmes (Eds.), *Concise Oxford textbook of psychotherapy* (pp. 21–33). Oxford, UK: Oxford University Press.

Dattilio, F. M., & Epstein, N. B. (2003). Cognitive-behavioral couple and family therapy. In T. L. Sexton, G. R. Weekes, & M. S. Robbins (Eds.), *The family therapy handbook* (pp. 147–175). New York, NY: Routledge.

Dekel, R., & Goldblatt, H. (2008). Is there intergenerational transmission of trauma? The case of combat veteran's children. *American Journal of Orthopsychiatry, 78*(3), 281–289.

Dekel, R., & Monson, C. M. (2010). Military-related post-traumatic stress disorder and family relations: Current knowledge and future directions. *Aggression and Violent Behavior, 15*, 303–309.

Erbes, C. R., Polusny, M. A., Macdermid, S., & Compton, J. S. (2008). Couple therapy with combat veterans and their partners. *Journal of Clinical Psychology, 64*(8), 972–983.

Everson, R. B., & Camp, T. C. (2011). Seeing systems: An introduction to systemic approaches with military families. In R. Blaine Everson & C. Figley (Eds.), *Families under fire: Systemic therapy with military families* (pp. 4–29). New York, NY: Routledge.

Exum, H. A., Coll, J. E., & Weiss, E. L. (2011). *A civilian counselor's primer for counseling veterans* (2nd ed.). Deer Park, NY: Linus.

Fisher, M. E. (2008). *The use of psychoeducation in the treatment of PTSD with military personnel and their family members: An exploratory study from a clinician's perspective* (unpublished master's thesis). Smith College, Northampton, MA.

Fredman, S. J., Monson, C. M., & Adair, K. C. (2011). Implementing cognitive-behavioral conjoint therapy for PTSD with the newest generation of veterans and their partners. *Cognitive and Behavioral Practice, 18*(1), 120–130.

Galovski, T., & Lyons, J. A. (2003). Psychological sequelae of combat violence: A review of the impact of PTSD on the veteran's family and possible interventions. *Aggression and Violent Behavior*, 9(5), 477–501. doi: 10.1016/S1359-1789(03)00045-4

Garte, S. H. (1989). Sexuality and intimacy in Vietnam veterans with post traumatic stress disorder (PTSD). *Psychotherapy in Private Practice, 7*(2), 103–109.

Glynn, S. M., Eth, S., Randolph, E. T., Foy, D. W., Urbaitis, M., Boxer, L., . . . Crothers, J. (1999). A test of behavioral family therapy to augment exposure for combat-related posttraumatic stress disorder. *Journal of Consulting and Clinical Psychology, 67*(2), 243–251.

Gottman, J. M., Gottman, J. S., & Atkins, C. L. (2011). The comprehensive soldier fitness program: Family skills component. *American Psychologist, 66*(1), 52–57. doi: 10.1037/a0021706

Gottman, J. M., & Silver, N. (1999). *The seven principles for making marriage work: A practical guide from the country's foremost relationship expert*. New York, NY: Three Rivers Press.

Hardaway, T. (2004). Treatment of psychological trauma in children of military families. In N. Webb (Ed.), *Mass trauma and violence: Helping families and children cope* (pp. 259–282). New York, NY: Guilford Press.

Hartman, A. (1995). Diagrammatic assessment of family relationships. *Families in Society, 76*(2), 111.

Hayes, S. C., Strosahl, K., & Wilson, K. (1999). *Acceptance and commitment therapy: Understanding and treating human suffering*. New York, NY: Guilford Press.

Hill, R. (1949). *Families, under stress: Adjustment to the crises of war separation and reunion*. New York, NY: Harper.

Hoshmand, L. T., & Hoshmand, A. L. (2007). Support for military families and communities. *Journal of Community Psychology, 35*(2), 171–180. doi: 10.1002/jcop.20141

Integrative Behavioral Couple Therapy. (2010). *What is IBCT?* Retrieved from http://ibct.psych.ucla.edu

Jacobson, N. S., Christensen, A., Prince, S. E., Cordova, J., & Eldridge, K. (2000). Integrative behavioral couple therapy: An acceptance-based, promising new treatment for couple discord. *Journal of Consulting and Clinical Psychology, 68*(2), 351–355.

Johnson, S. M., & Williams-Keeler, L. (1998). Creating healing relationships for couples dealing with trauma: The use of emotionally-focused marital therapy. *Journal of Marital and Family Therapy, 24*(1), 25–40.

Jordan, K. (2004). The color-coded timeline trauma genogram. *Brief Treatment and Crisis Intervention, 4*(1), 57–70.

Kreutzer, J. S. (2002). A structured approach to family intervention after brain injury: A quantitative analysis. *Journal of Head Trauma Rehabilitation*, 9(3), 104–115.

Kreutzer, J. S., Stejskal, T. M., Ketchum, J. M., Marwitz, J. H., Taylor, L. A., & Menzel, J. C. (2009). A preliminary investigation of the brain injury family intervention: Impact on family members. *Brain Injury, 23*(6), 535–547.

Kreutzer, J. S., & Taylor, L. A. (2004). *Brain injury family intervention manual*. Richmond, VA: National Resource Center for Traumatic Brain Injury.

Kudler, H., & Straits-Troster, K. (2009). Partnering in support of war zone veterans and their families. *Psychiatric Annals, 39*(2), 64–70.

Laser, J. A., & Stephens, P. M. (2011). Working with military families through deployment and beyond. *Clinical Social Work Journal, 39*(1), 28–38.

Lavee, Y., McCubbin, H. I., & Olson, D. H. (1987). The effect of stressful life events and transitions on family functioning and well-being. *Journal of Marriage and Family, 49*(4), 857–873.

Makin-Byrd, K., Gifford, E., McCutcheon, S., & Glynn, S. (2011). Family and couples treatment for newly returning veterans. *Professional Psychology: Research and Practice, 42*(1), 56–62.

Matsakis, A. (2007). *Back from the front*. Baltimore, MD: Sidran Institute Press.

McCubbin, H. I. (1987). Family index of regenerativity and adaptation-military (FIRA-M). In H. I. McCubbin, A. I. Thompson, & M. A. McCubbin. *Family assessment: Resiliency, coping and adaptation—Inventories for research and practice* (pp. 843–864). Madison: University of Wisconsin Press.

McCubbin, H. I., & Patterson, J. M (1983). The family stress process: The double ABCX model of adjustment and adaptation. *Marriage and Family Review*, 6 (7), 7–37.

McDevitt-Murphy, M. E. (2011). Significant other enhanced cognitive-behavioral therapy for PTSD and alcohol misuse in OEF/OIF veterans. *Professional Psychology: Research and Practice*, 42(1), 40–46.

McGoldrick, M., & Gerson, R. (1985). *Genograms in family assessment*. New York, NY: Norton.

McKenry, P. C., & Price, S. J. (2000). Families coping with problems and change: A conceptual overview. In P. McKenry & S. Price (Eds.), *Families and change: Coping with stressful events and transitions* (pp. 1–17). Thousand Oaks, CA: Sage.

Melby, T. (2008). Regaining intimacy after war. *Contemporary Sexuality, 42*(10), 1.

Miller, W. R., & Rollnick, S. (2002). *Motivational interviewing: Preparing people for change.* (2nd ed.). New York, NY: Guilford Press.

Monson, C. M., Fredman, S. J., & Adair, K. C. (2008). Cognitive-behavioral conjoint therapy for posttraumatic stress disorder: Application to operation enduring and Iraqi Freedom veterans. *Journal of Clinical Psychology, 64*(8), 958–971.

Monson, C. M., Guthrie, K. A., & Stevens, S. P. (2003). Cognitive-behavioral couples treatment for posttraumatic stress disorder. *Behavior Therapist, 26*(8), 393–402.

Monson, C. M., Schnurr, P. P., Stevens, S. P., & Guthrie, K. A. (2004). Cognitive-behavioral couples treatment for posttraumatic stress disorder: Initial findings. *Journal of Traumatic Stress, 17*(4), 341–364.

Morgaine, C. (2001). *Family systems theory*. Retrieved from http://web.pdx.edu/~cbcm/CFS410U/FamilySystemsTheory.pdf

Nelson, B. S., & Wright, D. W. (1996). Understanding and treating post-traumatic stress disorder in female partners of veterans with PTSD. *Journal of Marital and Family Therapy, 22*(4), 455–467.

Oddy, M., & Herbert, C. (2003). Intervention with families following brain injury: Evidence-based practice. *Neuropsychological Rehabilitation, 13*(1/2), 258–273.

Olson, D. H., Russell, C. S., & Sprenkle, D. H. (1989). *Circumplex model: Systemic assessment and treatment of families*. Binghamton, NY: Haworth Press.

Pensford, J. (2003). Sexual changes associated with traumatic brain injury. *Neuropsychological Rehabilitation, 13*(1/2), 275–289.

Perlick, D. A., Straits-Troster, K., Dyck, D. G., Norell, D. M., Strauss, J. L., Henderson, C., & Cristinan, A. (2011). Multifamily group treatment for veterans with traumatic brain injury. *Professional Psychology: Research and Practice, 42*(1), 70–78.

Rabin, C., & Nardi, C. (1991). Treating post traumatic stress disorder couples: A psychoeducational program. *Community Mental Health Journal, 27*(3), 209–224.

Riggs, D. S. (2000). Marital and family therapy. In E. B. Foa, T. M. Keane, & M. J. Freidman (Eds.), *Effective treatments for PTSD: Practice guidelines from the traumatic stress studies* (pp. 280–301). New York, NY: Guilford Press.

Rosenheck, R., & Fontana, A. (1999). Changing patterns of care for war-related post traumatic stress disorder at department of veterans affairs medical centers: The use of performance data to guide program development. *Military Medicine, 164*(11), 795–802.

Savitsky, L., Illingsworth, M., & DuLaney, M. (2009). Civilian social work: Serving the military and veteran population. *Social Work, 54*(4), 327–339.

Sayers, S. L. (2011). Family reintegration difficulties and couples therapy for military veterans and their spouses. *Cognitive and Behavioral Practice, 18*(1), 108–119.

Schwerin, M. J. (2006). Quality of life and subjective wellbeing among military personnel: An organizational response to the challenges of military life. In T. W. Britt, A. B. Adler, &

C. A. Andrew (Eds.), *Military life: The psychology of serving in peace and combat* (pp. 145–179). Westport, CT: Praeger.

Sherman, M. D. (2003). The safe program: A family psychoeducational curriculum developed in a veterans affairs medical center. *Professional Psychology: Research and Practice, 34*(1), 42–48. doi: 10.1037/0735-7028.34.1.42

Sherman, M. D., Zanotti, D. K., & Jones, D. E. (2005). Key elements in couples therapy with veterans with combat-related posttraumatic stress disorder. *Professional Psychology: Research and Practice, 36*(6), 626–633. doi: 10.1037/0735-7028.36.6.626

Sherman, M. D. (2008). *SAFE program: Mental health facts for families* (3rd ed.). Retrieved from http://www.ouhsc.edu/safeprogram/

Sherman, M. D., Fischer, E., Bowling, U. B., Dixon, L., Ridener, L., & Harrison, D. (2009). A new engagement strategy in a VA-based family psychoeducation program. *Psychiatric Service, 60*(2), 254–257.

Stratton, P. (2005). *Report on the evidence base of systemic family therapy*. Clovis, CA: Association for Family Therapy.

Substance Abuse and Mental Health Services Administration. (2006). *Psychoeducational multi-family groups*. Washington, DC: Author. Retrieved from http://nrepp.samhsa.gov/View Intervention.aspx?id=120

U.S. Department of Defense. (2010). *Military casualty information*. Retrieved from http://siadapp.dmdc.osd.mil/personnel/CASUALTY/castop.htm

Walsh, F. (2006). *Strengthening family resilience* (2nd ed.). New York, NY: Guilford Press.

Weiss, E. L., Coll, J. E., Gebauer, J., Smiley, K., & Carrillo, E. (2010). The military genogram: A solution-focused approach for resiliency building in service members and their families. *Family Journal, 18*, 395–406.

Wessely, S., Bryant, R. A., Greenberg, N., Earnshaw, M., Sharpley, J., & Hacker Hughes, J. (2008). Does psychoeducation help prevent post traumatic psychological distress? *Psychiatry, 71*(4), 287–307.

Zastrow, C. H., & Kirst-Ashman, K. K. (2010). *Understanding human behavior and the social environment* (8th ed.). Belmont, CA: Thomson Learning.

Appendix
Veteran Organizations and Military Family Resources

Prepared by James A. Martin, Keita Franklin, Jeffrey S. Yarvis, Jose E. Coll, and Eugenia L. Weiss

Disclaimer: The references and the hyperlinks provided in this document do not constitute an endorsement of the information, products, or services contained therein. The authors remind the reader that it is always necessary to evaluate websites you are using to access practice information. The Duke University Library provides a useful general guide for evaluating information from the Internet: http://library.duke.edu/services/instruction/libraryguide/evalwebpages.html

There are now thousands of Internet sites and individual web pages that provide a range of information related to the behavioral health needs of military members, veterans, and their family members. The information in these gateway Internet sites is intended to provide the civilian behavioral health provider a starting point for identifying information and resources that will (a) inform practice and (b) provide valuable resource information for patients/clients and loved ones whose lives have been either directly or indirectly impacted by military service—while on active duty or serving as a member of the National Guard or a member of one of the other Reserve Components.

Most of this appendix is organized according to the alphabetical order of general topic headings. Relevant resources are listed under each topic heading. Not in alphabetical order are the headings pertaining to books and videos, which appear at the end of this appendix.

ARMED FORCES TREATMENT PROGRAM WEBSITES

Air Force: www.af.mil/shared/medical/epubs/AFI44–121.pdf
Army: http://armypubs.army.mil/epubs/pdf/R
Navy: www.public.navy.mil/bupers-npc/support/nadap/Pages/default2aspx

CHILD TRAUMA

The Trauma Institute and Child Trauma Institute: This website provides a host of resources for clinicians working with children who have been exposed to trauma. The website provides information and research on assessment, treatment for trauma related disorders. http://www.childtrauma.com/

The National Child Traumatic Stress Network (NCTSN) www.nctsnet.org is a unique collaboration of academic and community-based service centers whose mission is to raise the standard of care and increase access to services for traumatized children and their families across the United States. Combining knowledge of child development, expertise in the full range of child traumatic experiences, and attention to cultural perspectives, the NCTSN serves as a national resource for developing and disseminating evidence-based interventions, trauma-informed services, and public and professional education. The NCTSN has a special section of their program/website focused on military families and children, including resources for behavioral health professionals: www.nctsnet.org/nccts/nav.do?pid=ctr_top_military

UCLA National Center for Child Traumatic Stress: FOCUS Project for Military Families: http://www.focusproject.org/

CHILDREN RESOURCES

The Child Welfare League of America: This organization consists of a group of public and private agencies that have joined forces for the purposes of advocating for policies and best practices that produce positive outcomes for children and families impacted by abuse and neglect. http://www.cwla.org/

Military Families Knowledge Bank: The Military Families Knowledge Bank (MFKB) is an online database of resources for and about members of the military, veterans, and their families. MFKB provides access to a wealth of web resources on family functioning and support, social and government services, PTSD and traumatic stress, traumatic brain injury, and other issues. (http://mfkb.nctsn.org)

Defense Centers of Excellence: Helping Children Cope with Deployments and Reunions: http://www.realwarriors.net/family/children

Military Child Education Coalition: http://www.militarychild.org/

Military Child Initiative: http://www.jhsph.edu/mci/training_course

Zero to Three: Military Projects at Zero to Three Information for parents and mental health providers on the needs of very young children of military families. (http://www.zerotothree.org/about-us/funded-projects/military-families/)

CRISIS HOTLINES

DSTRESSline is a by-Marine-for-Marine 24/7 crisis line that is offered to Marines and their family members. The line affords Marines the opportunity receive professional anonymous counseling related to the everyday stressors of life. This line has incorporated a website that allows for Marines or family members to chat or look up local resources. http://www.dstressline.com/

Deployment Health Clinical Center 800-796-9699

Marine for Life-Injured Support 866-645-8762
Military Severely Injured Center 800-774-1361
National Sexual Assault Hotline 800-799-7233
National Suicide Prevention Hotline 800-SUICIDE (784-2433)
Navy Safe Harbor-Severely Injured Support 877-746-8563
Rape, Abuse & Incest National Network (RAINN) 800-656-4673
U.S. Army Wounded Soldier & Family Hotline 800-984-8523
Veterans Suicide Prevention Hotline 800273-TALK (8255)
Wounded Warrior Regiment Call Center 877-487-6299

CULTURE IN THE MILITARY

Understanding Military Culture When Treating PTSD: http://www.ptsd.va.gov/professional/ptsd101/flash-files/Military_Culture/player.html

Army Community Services http://www.armycommunityservice.org/home.asp

Uniform Code of Military Justice: www.4.law.cornell.edu/uscode/10/stApllch47.html

Military Acceptance Project is evolving to include broader educational information and support resources in the areas of gender, sexual orientation, race/ethnicity, faith and trauma survivor status. Originally designed with input from service members seeking more information on the DADT repeal progress. www.militaryacceptanceproject.org

Officers: http://www.defenselink.mil/specials/insignias/officers.html

Enlisted: http://www.defenselink.mil/specials/insignias/enlisted.html

For a discussion about military ranks: http://www.ask.com/questions-about/Military-Ranks

EDUCATION/EMPLOYMENT AND TRANSITION

Post– 9/11 GI Bill: The Post–9/11 GI Bill provides financial support for education and housing to individuals with at least 90 days of aggregate service on or after September 11, 2001, or individuals discharged with a service-connected disability after 30 days. You must have received an honorable discharge to be eligible for the Post–9/11 GI Bill. http://www.gibill.va.gov/

Marine Corps Scholarship Foundation: The privately funded, 501(c)(3) nonprofit organization provides scholarships for post–high school education to deserving sons and daughters of Marines with particular attention given to children whose parent has been killed or wounded in action. Additionally, the Scholarship Foundation's Heroes Tribute fund provides up to $30,000 over 4 years to every child of a Marine, or Navy Corpsman serving with the Marines, who has been killed in combat since September 11, 2001. www.mcsf.org

Yellow Ribbon Program: The Yellow Ribbon GI Education Enhancement Program (Yellow Ribbon Program) is a provision of the Post–9/11 Veterans Educational Assistance Act of 2008. This program allows institutions of higher learning (degree granting institutions) in the United States to voluntarily enter into an agreement with the VA to fund tuition expenses that exceed the highest public in-state undergraduate tuition rate. The institution can contribute up to 50% of those expenses and the VA will match the same amount as the institution. http://www.gibill.va.gov/post-911/post-911-gi-bill-summary/yellow-ribbon-program.html

Veterans Employment Coordination Service (VECS): The Veterans Employment Coordination Service (VECS) provides employment services for veterans, particularly severely injured veterans, who have an interest in pursuing career opportunities within the Department of Veterans Affairs (VA) http://www.va.gov/vecs/ or 866–606–6206

National Resource Directory (NRD): The Department of Veterans Affairs, along with the Department of Defense, and the Labor Department relaunched a new and improved website for wounded warriors. This directory provides access to thousands of services and resources at the national, state, and local levels to support recovery, rehabilitation, and community integration. The NRD is a comprehensive online tool available nationwide for wounded, ill, and injured service members, veterans, and their families. It is easy to navigate and intended to meet the needs of a broad spectrum of users within the military, veteran, and caregiver communities. www.nationalresourcedirectory.gov

The eBenefits portal is a joint VA and Department of Defense project that provides veterans, service members, their families, and caregivers with self-service access to online benefits-related tools and information. eBenefits is a "one-stop shop" for benefit applications, benefits information, and access to personal information, such as official military personnel documents. The portal provides two main services. It is a catalog of links to information on other websites about military and veterans benefits, and it provides a personalized workspace called "My eBenefits," which gives quick access to all the online tools currently integrated into eBenefits (Department of Veteran Affairs, 2010). www.ebenefits.va.gov

FAMILY RESOURCES

The Deployment Health and Family Readiness Library: This library was established by DoD to provide service members, families, leaders, health care providers, and veterans an easy way to find deployment health and family readiness information. http://deploymenthealthlibrary.fhp.osd.mil/home.jsp

The National Military Family Association (NMFA) provides a comprehensive listing of links to sites containing valuable information for service members and their families. Additional information about the subjects listed on the site is available under "Family Topics" on the sites left navigation bar.

National Guard Bureau, Office of the Chaplain: Partners-in-Care: http://chaplain.ng.mil/resources/Pages/WarriorCareNational.aspx

National Guard Family Program: http://www.jointservicessupport.org/FP/Default.aspx

Our Military Kids: Information on Grants for Children of National Guard and Reserve Forces: http://www.ourmilitarykids.org/

SOFAR: Guide for helping children and youth cope with the deployment and return of a parent in the National Guard and other Reserve Components: http://www.sofarusa.org/downloads/SOFAR_2008_Final.pdf

Uniformed Services University: Center for the Study of Traumatic Stress, Podcast/Children and Families of Combat: http://www.cstsonline.org/resources/resource-103_children_families_combat_vets

Operation R.O.S.E. (Faith-Based): Ministry resource provided by military wives for other military spouses to support and encourage the military lifestyle. http://www.operationrose.com

Readjustment Counseling Centers: Information, programs, services, and readjustment counseling for veterans. http://www.vetcenter.va.gov

Strategic Outreach to Families of All Reservists: www.sofarusa.org

USO: Provides support and help to combat troops (their families), wounded warriors (and their families), and families of the fallen. http://www.uso.org

U.S. Department of Defense: Information for Reserve Families on Benefits and Entitlements: www.defenselink.mil/ra/familyreadiness.html

Armed Services YMCA: Offers national and local programs to benefit families of the U.S. military. http://www.asymca.org

CinCHouse: Provides information, resources, and a community of friends for military spouses to survive the challenges and adventures of military life. http://www.cinchouse.com

Congressional Military Family Caucus: Educates Congress and their staff on resources for military families as well as providing support and advocating on the behalf of military families. http://www.facebook.com/militaryfamilycaucus

Family Life (Faith-Based): Resources and support for military marriages and families. http://www.familylife.com (Enter "military" in search box)

Fleet and Family Services: Provides programs and resources to help Navy families be resilient and informed. http://cnic.navy.mil/CNIC_HQ_Site/WhatWeDo/FleetAndFamilyReadiness/FamilyReadiness/FleetAndFamilySupportProgram/index.htm

Give an Hour Foundation: Provides free mental health counseling by private practitioners to U.S. military personnel and their families affected by the Iraq/Afghanistan conflicts. http://www.giveanhour.org

The Soldier's Project: Provides free mental health counseling by private practitioners to U.S. military personnel and their families affected by the Iraq/Afghanistan conflicts. http://www.thesoldiersproject.org

Military Family: Support and resources for military families provided by family resources. http://www.militaryfamily.org

GATEWAY SITES

Military OneSource (sponsored by the Department of Defense) is the principal source of assistance for military members and military family members (active duty, National Guard, or other Reserve components). This site also provides a full array of specific websites for the different service components and branches, as well as a full menu of topic-specific sites. For immediate assistance from OneSource call 800–342–9647 or go to www.militaryonesource.com

The (DCoE) Resources Section offers a central list of products and resources produced by DCoE, organized by topic. We encourage you to explore the broad range of resources we have available and to share with all who may find them useful. http://www.dcoe.health.mil/Resources.aspx

Military Homefront: The official Department of Defense website for reliable quality-of-life information designed to help military members and their families, leaders, and service providers. This is a great "one-stop" site. For access go to http://www.militaryhomefront.dod.mil/

HEALTH

MedLinePlus: A service of the National Library of Medicine, MedlinePlus is a trusted source of health and mental health information. To access this site go to www.nlm.nih.gov/medlineplus/medlineplus.html

(**Note:** MedlinePlus has a specific collection of information on military and veterans issues. To access this site go to www.nlm.nih.gov/medlineplus/veteransandmilitaryhealth.html)

Special Environment Health Registry Evaluation Programs for Veterans http://www.publichealth.va.gov/docs/exposures/registry-evaluation-brochure.pdf

Gulf War (including Operation Iraqi Freedom) Health Registry Program Handbook http://www1.va.gov/vhapublications/ViewPublication.asp?pub_ID=1574

Department of Defense *Military Health System* (MHS) is a unique partnership of medical educators, medical researchers, and health care providers and their support personnel worldwide. This DoD site is sponsored by the Office of the Assistant Secretary of Defense for Health Affairs; the medical departments of the Army, Navy, Marine Corps, Air Force, Coast Guard, and the Joint Chiefs of Staff highlights health care resources for military members and their families. The site is a source of innovative information on education, medical training, research, technology, and policy information. For access go to www.health.mil

The Office of the Deputy Secretary of Defense for Health Affairs supports two useful sites with training and resource materials for working with military members and/or family members who may have health and mental health questions. For access to the training page go to http://fhp.osd.mil/pdhrainfo/training.jsp and for access to the resource page go to http://fhp.osd.mil/pdhrainfo/resources.jsp

Courage to Care is a new, electronic health campaign for military and civilian professionals serving the military community, as well as for military men, women, and families. Courage to Care consists of electronic fact sheets on timely health topics relevant to military life that provide actionable information. Courage to Care is in the public domain, designed to be or fit into health outreach; customized with local contact information and sent to the provider or support group network, even put on websites or sent to friends and family. Courage to Care content is developed by leading military health experts from Uniformed Services University of the Health Sciences, the nation's federal medical school. http://www.usuhs.mil/psy/courage.html

NC Health Info is a resource of the University of North Carolina at Chapel Hill Medical Library System (with support from the Center for Citizen Soldier Support). This site contains information on services for military children, as well as an array of health and mental health topics for military members, veterans, and their loved ones. http://nchealthinfo.org/

The Behavioral Health Information Network (BHIN) is a web-based clearing house for the latest information and tools for commanders, Marines, families, and professionals on prevention as well as other resources concerning behavioral health. Individuals can go onto this website and order free educational materials (tools) on how to recognize Marines in distress, how to intervene, and how to build resilience. Items include brochures, wallet cards, posters, graphic novels, pocket guides, and training DVDs.

HOMELESS VETERANS RESOURCES

Department of Veterans Affairs: Department of Veterans Affairs website for the Homeless Veterans Program offering prevention services, housing support, treatment, employment/job training, and other resources. http://www.va.gov/homeless/ or call 877-424-3838

National Center on Homelessness among Veterans: *The center's mission is to promote recovery oriented care for veterans who are homeless or at-risk for homelessness.* The goal is to establish a national forum to exchange new ideas; provide education and consultation to improve the delivery of services; and disseminate the knowledge gained through the efforts of the center's Research and Model Development Cores to VA, other federal agencies, and community provider programs that assist homeless populations. http://www.va.gov/HOMELESS/NationalCenter.asp

Project CHALENG: Project CHALENG enhances coordinated services by bringing the VA together with community agencies and other federal, state, and local governments that provide services to the homeless to raise awareness of homeless veterans needs and to plan to meet those needs. http://www.va.gov/HOMELESS/chaleng.asp

Non-VA Homeless Resources: This is a series of links to other federal and community resources that could be helpful to those who are homeless, or are at risk for homelessness, and their families. http://www.va.gov/HOMELESS/NonVAResources.asp

National Coalition for Homeless Veterans: http://www.nchv.org/index.cfm

LEGAL SERVICES FOR VETERANS

The National Veterans Legal Services Program (NVLSP) is an independent, nonprofit veterans service organization that has been assisting veterans and their advocates for more than 25 years. NVLSP achieves its mission through education, advocacy, litigation, training advocates who represent veterans, and publications. http://www.nvlsp.org/

MENTAL HEALTH

NAMI is the ***National Alliance on Mental Illness***, the nation's largest grassroots organization for people with mental illness and their families. NAMI has affiliates in every state and in more than 1,100 local communities across the country. NAMI provides an extensive array of information and resources for veterans and active duty military members, as well as their families, friends, and advocates. Go to: http://www.nami.org/template.cfm?template=/contentManagement/contentDisplay.cfm&contentID=53586

PRISONERS OF WAR

The American Ex-Prisoners of War http://www.axpow.org/ is an organization of former POWs (military and civilian), their spouses, families, and civilian internees who help those affected by their capture deal with the trauma through friendship of those who share a common experience.

PTSD

The National Center for PTSD (NCPTSD) is part of the Department of Veterans Affairs and is dedicated to advance the clinical care and social welfare of U.S. veterans through research, education, and training on PTSD and stress-related disorders. It is a primary source of information for clinicians, human service providers, as well as service members, veterans, and their loved ones. To access this site go to www.ncptsd.va.gov/ncmain/index.jsp

NAMI (see earlier) has a new PTSD brochure—"Transmission of trauma" is a 14-page brochure on posttraumatic stress disorder (PTSD), treatment, and recovery. It is available online at www.nami.org/PTSD and is intended to help individuals experiencing symptoms or diagnosed with the illness, along with their families and caregivers.

PTSD Check List—Military Version (PCL-M) available at the Deployment Health Clinical Center at: www.pdhealth.mil/guidelines/appendices.asp

PTSD Support Services: http://www.ptsdsupport.net/index.html

Uniformed Services University: Center for the Study of Traumatic Stress, Military Topic Resources: http://www.cstsonline.org/resources/category-3_military

SEXUAL ASSAULT

United States Department of Defense: Sexual Assault Prevention and Response. www.sapr.mil

National Center on Domestic and Sexual Violence (NCDSV): Works with local and state officials to provide information and resources to victims of violence. www.ncdsv.org/ncd_about.html

Women Veterans of America: Unites women veterans, provides advocacy, and education services. www.wvanational.org

Vet Center: Contact a Vet Center near you. http://www.vetcenter.va.gov/

MyDuty.mil: Provides information and guidance on your reporting options and rights. http://myduty.mil/

SUBSTANCE ABUSE

The Substance Abuse and Mental Health Services Administration (SAMHSA) vision and mission is focused on building resilience and facilitating recovery for people with or at risk for mental or substance use disorders. SAMHSA is gearing all of its resources—programs, policies, and grants—toward that outcome. SAMHSA has a comprehensive resource list for returning vets and families. Go to http://www.samhsa.gov/vets/

Seeking Safety website: Available at this site (some free/some have a cost) are the Seeking Safety Manual, training videos/DVDs, and other useful materials. www.seekingsafety.org

Motivational Interviewing (MI) website: Available at this site is information about MI trainings, Internet links to MI-related information, and information about the network of MI trainers. www.motivationalinterview.org/

SUICIDE PREVENTION

The Suicide Prevention and Risk Reduction Committee (SPaRRC) is a multiagency committee that was established in 1999. This collaborative effort includes members from the Defense Center of Excellence (DCoE) for Psychological Health and Traumatic Brain Injury, the Department of Veterans Affairs, military service suicide prevention managers, representatives from the National Guard Bureau and Reserve Affairs, and other key agencies. The SPaRRC focuses on consolidating and disseminating information about suicide risk factors, prevention efforts, and resources to military members, social workers and other providers who work with suicidal military members, the key goals of the committee. Much of the information SPaRRC consolidates is available on its website. www.suicideoutreach.org

The Yellow Ribbon Reintegration Program provides suicide prevention information, services, referrals, and proactive outreach programs to National Guard and Reserve members. More than 2,000 events have been held for about 300,000 service members in the program launched (http://www.dodyrrp.mil/).

The DoD Suicide Event Report (DoDSER) Program: The primary goal of the DoDSER is to serve as a centralized data collection point for suicide event data across all military services. Although there are notable flaws with the DoDSER reporting and suicide death confirmation process, it represents the first-ever DoD-level collaborative effort among the military suicide prevention programs. Suicide surveillance efforts prior to 2008 were not standardized, and each of the services used service-specific tracking and reporting criteria. The DoDSER now tracks more than 250 suicide-related variables (including attempts), and the website provides online training, covering suicide death categorization criteria and reporting guidelines (https://dodser.t2.health.mil/).

TERMINOLOGY IN THE MILITARY

Air Force Slang: http://www.slangsearch.com/airforce.html

Appendix: Glossary of U.S. Navy Slang: http://en.wiktionary.org/wiki/Appendix:U.S._Navy_slang

Coast Guard Definitions and Acronyms: http://www.coastguardfamily.org/acronyms.htm

DoOD Dictionary of Military Terms: http://www.dtic.mil/doctrine/jel/doddict/

List of U.S. Marine Corps Acronyms and Expressions: http://en.wikipedia.org/wiki/List_of_U.S._Marine_Corps_acronyms_and_expressions

Milterms: http://www.milterms.com/

Slang from Operation Iraqi Freedom: http://www.globalsecurity.org/military/ops/iraq-slang.htm

U.S. Army Acronyms and Expressions: http://www.goarmyparents.com/armyacro.htm

TRAUMATIC BRAIN INJURY (TBI)

The single best starting point for TBI information is the **DoD Post Deployment Health** website. Go to: http://www.pdhealth.mil/TBI.asp

For DOD TBI Information and Resource go to: http://www.pdhealth.mil/TBI.asp

The Defense Centers of Excellence for Psychological Health & Traumatic Brain Injury leads a collaborative effort toward optimizing psychological health and traumatic brain injury (TBI) treatment for the Department of Defense (DoD). The DCoE establishes quality standards for clinical care; education and training; prevention; patient, family and community outreach; and program excellence. The DCoE mission is to maximize opportunities for warriors and families to thrive through a collaborative global network promoting resilience, recovery, and reintegration for PH and TBI. Go to http://www.dcoe.health.mil/

Real Warriors campaign is an initiative launched by the Defense Centers of Excellence for Psychological Health and Traumatic Brain Injury (DCoE) to promote the processes of building resilience, facilitating recovery, and supporting reintegration of returning service members, veterans, and their families. The Real Warriors Campaign combats the stigma associated with seeking psychological health care and treatment and encourages service members to increase their awareness and use of these resources. To reach the broadest audience possible, the campaign features a variety of strategies including outreach and partnerships, print materials, media outreach, an interactive website and social media. The campaign features stories of real service members who have sought treatment and are continuing to maintain successful military or civilian careers. In addition, DCoE established the DCoE Outreach Center, a 24/7 call center staffed by health resource consultants to provide confidential answers, tools, tips, and resources about psychological health and traumatic brain injury. http://www.realwarriors.net/

VETERANS RESOURCES

The Returning Veterans is designed to welcome home veterans of the Iraq and Afghanistan conflicts with a social, veteran-centric website focusing on their needs and questions. The website features videos, veteran stories, and a blog where veterans are encouraged to post feedback. The site also restructures the traditional index-of-benefits format found on other VA pages into question-based, categorized, and easily navigated links by topic. This will allow veterans to find benefits of interest easily and discover related benefits as they explore. www.oefoif.va.gov

The Department of Veterans Affairs also has a website intended to strengthen the connection between college and university mental health professionals and veterans of the Iraq and Afghanistan conflicts studying on their campuses. This initiative is designed to ensure that colleges and universities are able to assist with any special mental health needs they may have." The website features recommended training for college and university counselors, with online modules including "Operation SAVE" for suicide prevention, "PTSD 101" and "Helping Students Who Drink Too Much." It also will feature a resource list that will be updated regularly. Although the website is designed primarily for counselors, it also serves as a resource for veteran-students who wish to learn more about the challenges they may face in adjusting to their lives after leaving the military. http://www.mentalhealth.va.gov/College

After Deployment, as stated on the site, was designed by many behavioral health experts in the Department of Defense and the Veterans Administration. The content is directed at service members, their families, veterans, and providers. After Deployment provides information and exercises to assist the entire military community with common postdeployment problems, such as stress, anger, depression, and relationship issues. Although the site does contain a wide variety of reading materials, the developers have strived to build a fully interactive site. There are quizzes, activity vignettes, testimonials, and workshops. http://www.afterdeployment.org/

Iraq Afghanistan Veterans of America (IAVA): IAVA provides assistance to veterans in the areas of health, education, employment, and community, and promote awareness around the challenges and opportunities facing veterans of Iraq and Afghanistan, while influencing public policy so veterans and their families have increased access to health, education, employment, and community. 212-982-9699, http://iava.org/

American Combat Veterans of War (ACVOW) is a nonprofit organization that enables combat veteran volunteers to mentor, coach, and assist our warriors in the transition from combat, allowing them and their families to lead productive and fulfilling lives in the wake of combat. 760-696-0460, http://www.acvow.org/

Coalition for Iraq and Afghanistan Veterans (CIAV) is a partnership of organizations working to provide services and support to Global War on Terrorism military, veterans, families, and survivors. http://coalitionforveterans.org/ciav/home/

Coming Home Project offers a continuum of services, from retreats and psychological counseling to training and self-care for service providers and community education and consultation. http://www.cominghomeproject.net/

Air Compassion for Veterans (air transportation) ACV provides needed transportation resources to our Wounded Warriors seeking care. Air Compassion for Veterans serves to ensure that no financially stressed wounded warrior, veteran, or adversely affected family member is denied access to: distant, specialized medical evaluation, diagnosis, treatment, counseling, rehabilitation, healing and restorative programs, programs assisting with reintegration into a productive life http://www.aircompassionforveterans.org/

Operation Homefront, Inc. provides emergency financial and other assistance to the families of our service members and wounded warriors. www.operationhomefront.net

Wounded Warrior Project Wounded Warrior Project (WWP) exists to honor and empower Wounded Warriors who incurred service-connected injures on or after September 11, 2001. Offering a variety of programs and services, WWP is equipped to serve warriors with every type of injury—from the physical to the invisible wounds of war. The programs are uniquely structured to nurture the mind and body, and encourage economic empowerment and engagement http://www.woundedwarriorproject.org/content/view/1007/1119/

Vets4Vets is a nonpartisan organization dedicated to helping Iraq and Afghanistan-era veterans to heal from the psychological injuries of war through the use of peer support. http://www.vets4vets.us/

National Resources Directory: This directory connects wounded warriors, service members, veterans, their family, and caregivers with various resources. https://www.nationalresourcedirectory.gov/other_services_and_resources/oef_oif_veterans

Vet Centers: Vet Centers provide readjustment counseling, which is a wide range of psycho social services offered to eligible veterans and their families in the effort to make a successful transition from military to civilian life. To contact your local Vet Center, call 877-WAR-VETS (927-8387) or go to http://www.vetcenter.va.gov/

The National Gulf War Resource Center (NGWRC) is an international coalition of advocates and organizations providing a resource for information, support, and referrals for all those concerned with the complexities of Persian Gulf War issues, especially Gulf War illnesses and those held prisoner or missing in action. http://www.ngwrc.org/

Veterans for America offers outreach and assistance to all veterans needing help, and to those in the community when local VFA determines it to be in the best interest of the public good. http://www.veteransforamerica.org/home/vfa/

The Veterans of Foreign Wars (VFW) assists any veteran or their dependents seeking disability compensation, discharge upgrades, record corrections, education benefits, and pension eligibility. In addition, service officers regularly inspect VA health care facilities and national cemeteries, and employment specialists monitor laws concerning veterans preference in federal employment. The VFW also monitors medical and health issues affecting veterans as well as providing veterans with up-to-date information on diabetes, posttraumatic stress, Agent Orange exposure, and Persian Gulf Syndrome. A recent addition to the Washington, DC, office is the Tactical Assessment Center, a 24-hour help line for veterans with questions or concerns about VA entitlements. 800–vfw–1899, http://www.vfw.org/

VETERANS ORGANIZATIONS

There are more than 200 different organizations in the United States that are devoted to veterans' affairs. Some of these groups sponsor particular branches of the Armed Forces, while others serve all veterans from all eras. The following list of veterans organizations are national in scope, and represent a variety of the types of veterans service organizations that currently exists. The list is not intended to be exhaustive because new organizations are formed routinely to meet specific or emerging needs. Readers are encouraged to discover the veterans' organizations that are active in their local areas as well.

Asterisked Veteran Organizations are Chartered by Congress and Recognized by the Veterans Administration for Claim Representation under laws administered by the Department of Veterans Affairs.

American Ex-Prisoners of War
American Red Cross
American Veterans of WWII, Korea and Vietnam (AMVETS)
Army & Navy Union, USA, Inc.
Blinded Veterans Association
Catholic War Veterans, USA, Inc.*
Congressional Medal of Honor Society of the USA

Disabled American Veterans*
Gold Star Wives of America, Inc.
Jewish War Veterans of the USA*
Legion of Valor of the USA, Inc.
Marine Corps League
Military Order of the Purple Heart of the USA, Inc. (MOPH)*
Non Commissioned Officers Association (NCOA)*
Paralyzed Veterans of America
Polish Legion of American Veterans, USA
The American Legion *
United Spanish War Veterans
Veterans of Foreign Wars of the United States (VFW)*
Veterans of World War I of the USA, Inc.
Vietnam Veterans of America, Inc.

OTHER VETERAN ORGANIZATIONS RECOGNIZED FOR CLAIM REPRESENTATION

American Defenders of Bataan and Corregidor
American G.I. Forum of the U.S.
American Veterans Committee
Army and Air Force Mutual Aid Association
Fleet Reserve Association
National Amputation Foundations, Inc.
Navy Mutual Aid Association
Regular Veterans Association
Seattle Veterans Action Center
Swords to Plowshares: Veterans Rights Organization
The Forty and Eight
The Retired Enlisted Association
Vietnam Era Veterans Association of Rhode Island

OTHER NATIONAL ORGANIZATIONS THAT SERVE VETERANS OR FAMILIES OF VETERANS

Air Force Association
Air Force Sergeants Association
Alliance of Women Veterans
American Military Members Association
American Military Retirees Association
American Veterans for Equal Rights
American War Mothers
Army Gold Star Mothers, Inc.
Association of Ex-POW of the Korean War, Inc.

Association of the U.S. Army
Blinded American Veterans Foundation
Blue Star Mothers of America, Inc.
Brotherhood Rally of All Veterans Organization (BRAVO)
China-Burma-India Veterans Association, Inc.
Combined National Veterans Association of America
Destroyer-Escort Sailors Association
Italian American War Veterans Association
Korean War Veterans Association, Inc.
Korean War Veterans Memorial Advisory Board
Military Chaplains Association
Military Justice Clinic, Inc.
Military Order of the Purple Heart: http://www.purpleheart.org/
Military Order of the World Wars
Military Services Community Network
NAM-POWS, Inc.
National American Military Retirees Association
National Association for Black Veterans, Inc.*
National Association for Uniformed Services
National Association of Atomic Veterans
National Association of Concerned Veterans
National Association of Military Widows
National Association of Radiation Survivors
National Association of State Directors of Veterans Affairs
National Association of State Veteran Homes
National Association of Veterans Program Administrators
National Coalition for Homeless Veterans*
National Congress of Puerto Rican Veterans, Inc.
National Gulf War Resource Center, Inc.*
National Incarcerated Veterans Network
National League of Families of American Prisoners and Missing in Southeast Asia
National Veterans Legal Services Programs, Inc.*
National Vietnam Veterans Coalition
National World War II Glider Pilots Association
Navy Reserve Association
Navy League of the United States
Ninth Infantry Division Association
OSS-101 Association
Past National Commanders Organization
Pearl Harbor Survivors Association, Inc.
Red River Valley Fighter Pilots Association
Reserve Officers Association of the U.S.
Service Members Legal Defense Network
Society of Military Widows
The Retired Officers Association

Tuskegee Airmen, Inc.
U.S. Army Warrant Officers Association
U.S. Merchant Marine Veterans of World War II
Veterans of the Vietnam War, Inc.
Veterans United for Strong America
Vietnam Veterans Institute
WAVES National
Women Air Force Service Pilots, WWII
Women's Army Corps Veterans Association
Women Marines Association
In addition, each state and territory in America has an Office of Veterans Affairs.

WOMEN VETERANS

The Department of Veterans Affairs implemented a center for women veterans. As noted on its site, the primary mission of the Center for Women Veterans is to review VA programs and services for women veterans, and assure that women veterans receive benefits and services on a par with male veterans, encounter no discrimination in their attempt to access them, and are treated with the respect, dignity, and understanding by VA service providers. For further information about specialty programs and services please visit: http://www.va.gov/womenvet/

Women Marines Association: Open to women who served honorably or are serving in the U.S. Marine Corps. http://www.womenmarines.org

Women's Army Corps Veterans Association: Current, former, or retired women members of the Army who have served honorably on active duty in the Army of the United States (AUS), Regular Army (RA), Army National Guard (ANG), and the United States Army Reserve (USAR) the Army Nurse Corps (ANC), the Women's Army Auxiliary Corps (WAAC), or the Women's Army Corps (WAC) in commissioned, warrant, noncommissioned or enlisted status for 90 days or more, after May 14, 1942. http://www.armywomen.org

Navy Nurse Corps Association: Navy Nurse Corps Association is a non-profit, national organization dedicated to bringing Navy Nurses together. Membership is open to women who were or are currently serving as a Navy Nurse. Any Navy Nurse Corps Officer, whether Active Duty, Reserves, retired, or honorably discharged, may join the NNCA. http://www.nnca.org

WAVES National: WAVES National is a Sea Service women's organization for women who have served or are currently serving in one of the sea services; U.S. Navy, U.S. Marine Corps, U.S. Coast Guard or Reserves. http://www.womenofthewaves.com

Army Nurse Corps Association: ANCA is a voluntary organization of, by, and for United States Army Nurse Corps officers. Membership is open to members of the U.S. Army Nurse Corps who are currently serving or formerly served on active duty or in active service in a reserve component, or have retired from active or reserve component service. http://e-anca.org

Air Force Women Officer: AFWOA was formed in 1975 by a group of retired Air Force women officers who wished to preserve the friendships that they had made while on active service. Membership has now grown to more than 1,000, including many active duty women. Active duty, retired, and separated women officers of the regular Air Force and its reserve components are invited to join AFWOA. http://www.afwoa.org

All Navy Women's National Alliance: The All Navy Women's National Alliance, Inc. is a nonprofit organization that is dedicated to the interests of active duty, reserve, retired, and veteran Navy, Coast Guard, and Marine women. The organization is devoted to honoring the accomplishments and rich history of the women of the sea services and to sharing the Legacy. http://www.anwna.com/

MilitaryWoman.org: This website is a meeting place for military women to exchange information unique to their military experience and to offer first-hand information to women thinking about a military career. This is a site where military women can share their views and experiences; enjoy the camaraderie with other military women; meet military women from other services to broaden their perspective and knowledge; dispel stereotypes; change paradigms. www.militarywoman.org

Women's Health Issues and Prevention: www.hooah4health.com/prevention/whealth

Register with the Women in Military Service for America Memorial: The Women's Memorial is a unique, living memorial honoring all military women—past, present, and future—and is the only major national memorial honoring women who have served in our nation's defense during all eras and in all services. www.womensmemorial.org or call 1–800–222–2294

National Association of State Women Veteran Coordinators: The purpose of this organization is to exchange ideas, information and training to facilitate reciprocal service for women veterans and to secure uniformity, equality, and effectiveness in providing these services to women veterans. http://www.naswvc.com/

SELECTED BOOKS

Moving a Nation to Care: Post-Traumatic Stress Disorder and America's Returning Troops. Author Ilona Meagher (2007) urges a grassroots call to action designed to put the issue of PTSD in our returning troops front and center before the U.S. public. In addition to presenting interviews with Iraq and Afghanistan veterans suffering with PTSD, this book is the most comprehensive resource to date for concerned citizens who want to understand the complex political, social, and health-related issues of PTSD, with an eye toward moving our nation to care to do what is necessary to help our fighting men and women.

Souls Under Siege: The Effects of Multiple Troop Deployments and How to Weather the Storm. (2009). Bridget C. Cantrell, PhD, brings you a useful guide to be used over and over again. It is a book that helps find ways to support and tend to those living with the pressures of multiple deployments. Its thrust is to not only expand awareness of the issues involved, but to also outline sensible tools for finding relief in these trying times.

Down Range: To Iraq and Back. Bridget C. Cantrell, PhD, and Vietnam veteran Chuck Dean (2005) have joined forces to present this vital information and resource manual for both returning troops and their loved ones. Here you can find answers, explanations, and insights as to why so many combat veterans suffer from flashbacks, depression, fits of rage, nightmares, anxiety, emotional numbing, and other troubling aspects of posttraumatic stress disorder (PTSD).

Once a Warrior: Wired for Life. Dr. Bridget Cantrell and Vietnam Veteran Chuck Dean (2007) have teamed up once again to take you on the next step in the process of coming home when your tour of duty is over. As stated in the book description, as a caring society we cannot afford to neglect the fact that "welcome home, go back to work and forget the war" is not as easy as it sounds. Helping our military men and women transition from an adrenaline-fueled, tactically disciplined life, to conventional life in a civilian environment is a critical endeavor both for the individual and the nation.

After the War Zone: A Practical Guide for Returning Troops and Their Families. (2008). By Friedman and Slone, as stated on Amazon site, this is a highly practical, user-friendly guide to homecoming—including common aftereffects of war-zone exposure and how to cope—for returning troops and their families. Two experts from the VA National Center for PTSD provide an essential resource for service members, their spouses, families, and communities, sharing what troops really experience during deployment and back home. Pinpointing the most common aftereffects of war and offering strategies for troop reintegration to daily life, Drs. Friedman and Slone cover the myths and realities of homecoming; reconnecting with spouse and family; anger and adrenaline; guilt and moral dilemmas; and PTSD and other mental health concerns. With a wealth of community and government resources, tips, and suggestions, *After the War Zone* is a practical guide to helping troops and their families prevent war-zone stresses from having a lasting negative impact.

Back From the Front: Combat Trauma, Love, and the Family. (2007). Author, Aphrodite Matsakis, helps to explain combat trauma so that friends and family can better understand combat trauma and its possible effects on intimate relationships and family life and to guide readers to resources that can help strengthen every member of their family. The beginning chapters provide basic information about combat trauma and how it can lead to depression, posttraumatic stress disorder, and other forms of emotional pain. The remaining chapters focus on some of the most common problems confronting families of combat veterans: emotional numbing, sexual difficulties, anger, and guilt. There are also chapters on family violence, children, women veterans, and military couples and sections on how to cope with anger and depression, how to find helpful organizations and books, and how to communicate effectively on difficult issues. In addition to describing the tensions that can result from combat trauma, this book emphasizes the many ways a veteran's war experiences can help enrich individual family members and the family as a whole.

The Warrior's Guide to Insanity (2008) is written by Sgt. Brandi, a Marine, Combat Rifleman from Vietnam. This book can be ordered from Amazon. As stated on-site, Sgt. Brandi's writing is brutally honest. His work describes the traumatic effects of war, and brings hope to the young men and women who are fighting it. As warriors, they have the strength to improvise, overcome, and adapt to every problem they face in the civilian world. Each of our Young Warriors may have a productive and joyful life if they face the realities and the difficulties in their paths. The audio version of this book can be downloaded for free at http://www.warriorsguidetoinsanity.com/Audio-streaming.html

OTHER TITLES OF INTEREST

Armstrong, K., Best, S. & Domenici, P. (2006). *Courage after fire: Coping strategies for troops returning from Iraq and Afghanistan and their families*. Berkeley, CA: Ulysses Press.

Beder, J. (Ed.). (2012). *Advances in social work practice with the military*. New York, NY: Routledge.

Britt, T. W., Adler, A. B., & Castro, C. A. *Military life: The psychology of serving in peace and combat*. Wesport, CT: Praeger. (Edited series with several volumes)

Browder, L. (2010). *When Janey comes marching home*. Chapel Hill: University of North Carolina Press.

Exum, H. A., Coll, J. E., & Weiss, E. L. (2011). *A civilian counselor's guide to counseling veterans* (2nd edition). Deerpark, NY: Linus Publications.

Finley, J.R. & Moore, B.A. (2011). *Veterans and active duty military psychotherapy: Homework planner*. Hoboken, NJ: Wiley.

Grossman, D. (1996). *On killing: The psychological consequences of learning to kill in war and society*. New York, NY: Little, Brown. (classic)

Kelly, D.C., Howe-Barksdale, S., & Gitelson, D. (2011). *Treating young veterans: Promoting resilience through practice and advocacy*. New York, NY: Springer.

Martin, J. A., Rosen, L. N., & Sparacino, L. R. (2000). (Eds.) *The military family: A practice guide for human service providers*. Westport, CT: Praeger.

Moore, B.A. & Jongsma, A.E. (2009). *The veterans and active duty military psychotherapy treatment planner*. Hoboken, NJ:.

Scurfield, R. (2003) *War trauma: Lessons unlearned from Vietnam to Iraq* New York, NY: Algora. (trilogy, classic)

Shading, B. (2007). *A civilian's guide to the U.S. military: A comprehensive reference to customs, language, and structure of the armed forces*. Cincinnati, OH: Writer's Digest Books.

Shay, J. (1994) *Achilles in Vietnam: Combat trauma and the undoing of character.* New York, NY: Scribner.

Tick, E. (2005). *War and the soul: Healing our nation's veterans from post-traumatic stress disorder.* Wheaton, IL: Quest Books.

FROM THE *NEW YORK TIMES* BEST SELLER LIST

Junger, S. (2010). *War.* New York, NY: Twelve.

Luttrell, M. (2007). *Lone survivor: The eyewitness account of operation redwing and the lost heroes of seal team 10.* New York, NY: Little, Brown.

NOVELIZATION OF A MOTION PICTURE

Clancy, T. (2012). *Act of Valor.* New York, NY: Berkeley Books.

BOOKS ON TRAUMA

Figley, C. R. (Ed.). (in press). *Encyclopedia of trauma: An interdisciplinary guide.* New York, NY: Sage.

Herman, J. (1992). *Trauma and recovery: The aftermath of violence—From domestic abuse to political terror.* New York, NY: Basic Books.

Rubin, A., & Springer, D. (2009). *Treatment of traumatized adults and children: Clinicians guide to evidence-based practice.* Hoboken, NJ: Wiley.

Solomon, M. F., & Siegel, D. J. (2003). *Healing trauma: Attachment, mind, body and brain.* New York, NY: Norton.

van der Kolk, B. A., McFarlane, A. C., & Weisaeth, L. (Eds.). (1996). *Traumatic stress: The effects of overwhelming experience on mind, body, and society.* New York, NY: Guilford Press.

Yarvis, J. (2008). *Subthreshold PTSD in veterans with different levels of traumatic stress: Implications for prevention and treatment with populations with PTSD.* Saarbrucken, Germany: VDM Verlag.

VIDEOS

HBO Documentaries has produced an extraordinary set of programs related to our returning veterans. These include outstanding programming, such as "Taking Chance," "Alive Day Memories-Home from Iraq," "Section 60: Arlington National Cemetery" and "Bagdad ER." The latest HBO documentary captures the realities that our military men and women and their families face every day. "War-torn 1861–2010" offers a glimpse of the other battle that so many veterans have faced in every war: the struggle against posttraumatic stress. These videos are highlighted on the Internet and available for commercial purchase.

Where Soldiers Come From (http://www.pbs.org/pov/wheresoldierscomefrom/) is a documentary film that offers an intimate look at the young men who fight our wars and the families and town they come from. Returning to her hometown, Director Heather Courtney gains extraordinary access following these young men as they grow and change from teenagers stuck in their town, to 23-year-old veterans facing the struggles of returning home. In addition to the Independent Spirit Award, ***Where Soldiers Come From*** won awards at festivals around the country, including a jury award for editing at the SXSW Film Festival, Best Documentary Feature at the Philadelphia Film Festival, and the Founders Award for Best U.S. Documentary at the Traverse City Film Festival. The film received rave reviews in the *New York Times*, the *Washington Post* and others during its theatrical release in fall 2011, and was broadcast nationally on the PBS program POV. It made several top 10 films of 2011 lists, including *Salon* and the *Austin American-Statesman*.

Restrepo is a feature-length documentary that chronicles the deployment of a platoon of U.S. soldiers in Afghanistan's Korengal Valley. The movie focuses on a remote 15-man outpost, "Restrepo," named after a platoon medic who was killed in action. It was considered one of the most dangerous postings in the U.S. military. This is an entirely experiential film: the cameras never leave the valley; there are no interviews with generals or diplomats. The only goal is to make viewers feel as if they have just been through a 90-minute deployment. This is war, full stop. The conclusions are up to you.

This Is War: Memories of Iraq—"This Is War" tells the story of what it means to be in combat in Iraq through the eyes of the soldiers who were there. This documentary follows nine National Guard soldiers from Oregon who ended up in some of the heaviest fighting of the war.

Lioness The Film is a documentary on women in combat who have suffered from PTSD subsequent to their deployments. (http://www.pbs.org/independentlens/lioness/film.html)

Joining Forces provides a collection of video materials useful for military family life education. http://www.joiningforcesonline.org/RelatedLinks.shtml

Cover Me. Producer Norman Lloyd directs the film, which features interviews with service members who have experienced combat operational stress and medical experts experienced in treating it. The message centers on the need to encourage service members to seek medical help for combat operational stress. To view the video online please visit http://www.semperfifund.org/resources.html

MTV True Life: I Have Posttraumatic Stress Disorder. This hour-long MTV documentary chronicles the lives of three young veterans of the Iraq War who have posttraumatic stress disorder. The film crew follows them for approximately 5 months as they attempt to treat or live with the disorder. http://www.mtv.com/videos/true-life-full-episode-i-have-post-traumatic-stress-disorder-veterans-cope-with-the-horrors-of-war/1601333/playlist.jhtml

Half of Us, mtvU and the Jed Foundation desire to initiate a public dialogue to raise awareness about the prevalence of mental health issues on campus and connect students to the appropriate resources to get help. View a video of stories of veterans who have made the transition from the battlefield to the classroom. Filmed by MTV, and featuring four veteran students, this clip highlights the emotional challenges faced by these individuals in their adjustment to life back home and the importance of finding support. http://www.halfofus.com/pop/halfvidplayer.swf?videoID=47&chapterID=1

Never Leave a Marine Behind. This bystander intervention training was developed by the Marine Corps for the purposes of training Marines of all ranks on how to identify and respond to Marines in distress. Marines (and family members) are generally the first to know when a fellow Marine is struggling with a behavioral health issue. This small group, Marine-led discussion, scenario-based video training provides Marines with the necessary skills to save a life. http://www.usmc-mccs.org/suicideprevent/nlambtraining.cfm

VIDEO RESOURCES FOR FAMILIES

Talk, Listen, Connect: Deployments, Homecomings, Changes. In recognition of the contributions made by the U.S. Armed Forces–Sesame Workshop presents this bilingual video for educational outreach initiative designed for military families and their young children to share. To view website material please visit http://www.sesameworkshop.org/our-impact/our-stories/military-families.html

This site offers video clips that help to educate families on how to cope with predeployments and deployments; make homecomings go as smoothly as possible; and how to reach a "new normal" after a parent returns with an injury. Additionally, this site offers family resources and downloadable "Talk, Listen, Connect" materials.

YouTube Videos of Service Members and Veterans Discussing Their Experiences With PTSD and the VRE System

ABC Nightline: Reservist profiled on his PTSD treatment using Virtual Iraq: http://www.youtube.com/watch?v=CqB28tyrBNY

CBC: "The National" Virtual Iraq with Patient discussing treatment: http://www.youtube.com/watch?v=Ltl9zbDRZWY

CBS Evening News: A real close-up on a patient and his family and a focus on the Emory U. group that treated him with Virtual Iraq/Afghanistan. http://www.cbsnews.com/stories/2011/06/21/eveningnews/main20073100.shtml?tag=contentMain;contentAux

CNN: Marine Corp Vet Battles PTSD with Virtual Reality: http://www.youtube.com/watch?v=hjyRu1e-Jmo&feature=channel_video_title

CNN: Sanjay Gupta Tries Virtual Iraq: http://www.youtube.com/watch?v=M1orx97sFGc

HD Net: Dan Rather Tries Virtual Iraq: http://www.youtube.com/watch?v=Er4Kzx3L0iQ

PBS: Active Duty Marine (Camp Pendleton) Interview: http://www.youtube.com/watch?v=FUl6E76XPs4

PBS Frontline: Army Reservist Vet Discusses PTSD Treatment with Virtual Iraq Part 1: http://www.youtube.com/watch?v=smrespIIJmI

PBS Frontline: Army Reservist Vet Disusses PTSD Treatment with Virtual Iraq Part 2: http://www.youtube.com/watch?v=4Da5Pn42ovA

PBS Frontline: PTSD Therapy Session at VA using Virtual Iraq.mpg: http://www.youtube.com/watch?v=4F4i6vEZ-H4

Therapeutic War Game Helps Iraq Vets: http://www.youtube.com/watch?v=lNpmaKcf6PI&feature=fvsr

Virtual Iraq/Afghanistan Jeopardy Question 10–2011: http://www.youtube.com/watch?v=OKOyjutfn04&feature=channel_video_title

Virtual Iraq: The Video Game as Therapy: http://www.youtube.com/watch?v=mUXLqsGzPEM

Virtual Mojave VR Exposure Therapy PTSD Scenario: http://www.youtube.com/watch?v=8hTEqNk6vk4

Glossary of Military Terms[1]

Jose E. Coll

81 Mike-Mike 81-millimeter mortar.

A-10 A twin-engine subsonic turbofan tactical fighter bomber; fires a variety of surface-to-air weapons in a close air support role; also known as the "tank buster."

Abaya The full-body cloak worn by women in Saudi Arabia and other Muslim countries.

Abeam replenishment The transfer of personnel and/or supplies by rigs between two or more ships moving side by side while at sea.

Abort To terminate a mission for any reason other than enemy action.

ACOG Advanced combat optical gun-sight; low power, very rugged rifle scope.

Active duty Continuous duty on a daily basis; comparable to the civil term "full-time employment."

AD Accidental discharge of a weapon. (This is a serious military offense.)

Agent Orange An herbicide and defoliant containing dioxin, a potent carcinogen sprayed from airplanes to clear extensive areas of vegetation in Vietnam that provided cover for enemy troops.

Airborne Troops trained primarily to effect an assault debarkation especially by parachuting to the site.

AK Kalishnikov-designed assault rifle used by Russian and Chinese soldiers (also known as an AK-47).

Al-Jazeera Middle Eastern television station operating uncensored 24 hours each day from Qatar.

Al-Jihad Militant group of Islamic extremists also known as the Egyptian Islamic Jihad. This group was blamed for the assassination of Egyptian President Anwar Sadat in 1981 in response for his attempts to make peace with Israel. Al-Jihad leaders later joined forces with Osama bin Laden to create Al-Qaeda.

[1] Exum, H., Coll, J. E., & Weiss, E. L. (2011). *A civilian counselor's primer for counseling veterans* (2nd ed.). Deerpark, NY: Linus.

Al-Qaeda The multinational militant Islamic organization headed by Osama bin Laden responsible for the 9/11 attacks in the United States. Current Al-Qaeda members are primarily from Egypt and Saudi Arabia but other Arab and Muslim countries are represented in the membership.

Angel A soldier killed in combat, used among some U.S. medical personnel.

Ao-Dai (oh-die) Long traditional Vietnamese women's dress.

AO Area of operations or aerial observer.

APC Armored personnel carrier.

Arc-light B-52 bomber air strike (also, "rolling thunder").

Article 5, NATO The clause in the charter of the North American Treaty Organization that states that in the case of an attack on a member nation, other members will treat the attack as an attack on themselves. It was invoked for the first time after the 9/11 attacks.

Army The largest unit in the organizational chain of command. An "Army" is comprised of 50,000-plus soldiers under the command of a lieutenant general or higher officer. Army groups have not been employed since WWII; also one of the major service branches.

ARTY Artillery.

ARVN (ar-vin) Army of the Republic of South Vietnam, a South Vietnamese Soldier.

AT-4 Replacement for the M-72 LAAW; much bigger and more powerful weapon.

Auto get'em Automatic weapons fire set to "fully auto" (also, "rock and roll").

Axis of Evil Term used by President George W. Bush during the 2002 State of the Union address to describe "rogue" nations possessing or actively seeking to acquire weapons of mass destruction; specific references were made to North Korea, Iraq, and Iran.

Ayatollah Title meaning "miraculous sign of Allah" used to describe high status Shia (Islamic) scholars.

B-52 Very large long-range jet-propelled bomber capable of intercontinental flight, also large marijuana cigarette (Vietnam era).

Battalion A unit of from 300 to 1,000 soldiers under the command of a lieutenant colonel.

Battle rattle Full battle rattle is close to 50 pounds' worth of gear, including a flak vest, Kevlar helmet, gas mask, ammunition, weapons, and other basic military equipment. One component is the soft vest that covers the torso, the shoulders, and the back. It's made of soft material, a mixture of Kevlar and Twaron.

Battlefield Airmen Air Force Special Operations Command [AFSOC] pararescue, combat control, and weather troops. The term battlefield Air Force members may be new, though AFSOC troops have been filling those combat jobs for many years.

Baby-San Vietnamese child.

Balkans, The Eastern European countries that lie between the Black Sea and the Adriatic Sea. They also include countries that were part of the former Yugoslavia as well as countries that were part of the former Soviet Union. These countries include Albania, Bosnia-Herezegovinia, Bulgaria, Croatia, Greece, Macedonia, Moldova, Montenegro, Romania, and Serbia (including the autonomous region of Kosovo).

Beanies Special forces personnel (Vietnam era).

Bear hunting with a switch Undermanned, lightly armed, reconnaissance patrol.

Beaucoup (boo-koo) Many or big (Vietnamese slang).

Beef and rocks Beef and potatoes.

Beehive Anti-personnel flachette round.

BIAP Baghdad International Airport.

Bird-shit Paratroopers or scrambled eggs (Vietnam era).

Blue line Stream or river as depicted on military maps.

Body count Number of enemy dead, used to determine the success of a mission.

Bombaconda Nickname for LSA Anaconda, a major base near Balad, reflecting the frequent mortar attacks.

Boom-boom girl Whore (Vietnam era).

Boonies Jungle or in the field (also bush).

Bouncing Betty A land mind that propels itself upward and explodes at waist-level when triggered.

Brigade A unit of 3,000 to 5,000 soldiers under the command of a colonel.

Bringing smoke Outgoing artillery fire.

Bronco (OV-10) Small twin propeller airplane (Vietnam era).

Burka A full-body cloak or veil worn by women in the Middle East having only a space for the woman's eyes. This garment was mandated by the Taliban in Afghanistan.

Butt-fucked Attacked from the rear.

Butter-bar Second lieutenant (also known as Goonie-Looie).

C-4 Composition-4, a highly destructive plastic high-explosive substance.

CA Combat assault.

CC Coalition Country—The coalition of the willing allies.

C & C Command and control helicopter.

CAP team Combined-action platoon.

Can of worms Spaghetti.

Care package A package sent from home containing food and/or personal items.

"C" Grease C-rations.

Chain of command The succession of commanding officers from a superior to a subordinate through which command is executed; also the following organizational structure of a branch of the armed forces: squad, platoon, company, battalion, brigade, division, corps, and army.

Chairborne rangers Clerks (Vietnam era).

Charlie Term for Viet Cong soldiers; also VC, Victor Charlie, and Sir Charles (Vietnam era).

Cartridge trap Booby trap using a live round set to discharge when stepped on.

Cherry juice Hydraulic fluid.

Chi-com Chinese Communist.

Chieu Hoi (chew-loi) Surrendered or defected enemy soldier (Vietnam era).

Chinook CH-47 Helicopter (also, Shit-hook).

CHU Containerized Housing Unit (pronounced "choo"). Aluminum boxes slightly larger [22′ × 8′] than a commercial shipping container, with linoleum floors and cots or beds inside. This insulated CONEX shipping container has a door, window, top vent, power cabling, and an air conditioner.

CHUville A base consisting of a large number of CHUs.

Claymore Anti-personnel mine.

Click Kilometer.

Cluster fuck Anything that is disorganized; also grunts that gather in small groups.

Clyde Enemy troops (Vietnam era).

CO Commanding officer; also conscientious objector.

Cocksuckers Leeches (Vietnam era).

Cold LZ Landing zone not under enemy fire.

Collateral damage Unintended or accidental injury or damage to persons or objects that would not be lawful military targets in the circumstances ruling at that time. Such damage is not considered to be unlawful as long as it is not excessive in light of the overall military advantage anticipated from the attack.

Company A unit of 62 to 190 soldiers led by a captain.

Contact Action with the enemy force.

Corps The Marine Corps; also a unit of 20,000 to 45,000 soldiers under the command of a lieutenant general.

CP Command post.

Crispy critters Burned bodies, usually resulting from a napalm strike.

Crotch Self-depreciating or derogatory term for the Marine Corps (also Jar Heads).

CUNT Civilian Under Naval Training.

Dai-uy (dai-wee) Captain (Vietnamese).

Death blossom The tendency of Iraqi security forces, in response to receiving a little fire from the enemy, to either run away or do the "death blossom" spraying fire indiscriminately in all directions.

Delta tango Defensive target (also, DT).

Daisy cutter A 15,000 pound bomb designed to clear landing zones.

Depleted uranium The name for the element U-238 used to make very dense armor-piercing munitions. These munitions are controversial because they leave ground water and air radioactive and have reportedly been linked to increased rates of cancer among the children of soldiers who used DU munitions. The U.S. Department of Defense denies that this is a health risk.

Deployment To systematically station military persons or forces over an area or the movement of forces within an area of military operation; also, the positioning of forces into a formation for battle. The term refers to military personnel being on temporary assignment away for their home base over an extended period of time.

Desert Storm Name for the 1991 Gulf War that resulted when Iraq invaded Kuwait.

DEROS Date of Expected Return from Overseas (Vietnam era).

Deuce and a half Two and one half–ton truck.

DFAC [Dining Facility]: A DFAC is where you eat. Soldiers eat in a dining facility, or DFAC (pronounced dee-Fak). When old soldiers show their age they call it a "chow hall," and if you say "mess hall" it dates you.

Di di Fast or quick (Vietnamese).

Dien Cai Dau (dinky-dow) Vietnamese term for "crazy" or "mentally disturbed."

Ditty bag Shower kit, or "do-it-yourself" bag for short duration move.

Division A unit of 10,000 to 15,000 soldiers under the command of a major general.

Dirt sailor A member of the Navy's construction battalions (Seabees). In Iraq, a sailor playing a part that is not a normal Navy role.

Djellaba Term for the flowing gown worn by men in Saudi Arabia and other Muslim countries.

"Doc" squid Any sailor; especially a medic (Vietnam era).

Donut dollies Civilian women volunteers from the Red Cross who served coffee and doughnuts.

Drag Rear security.

Dump, The Mortuary.

Dung-lai To stop or halt.

Dust-off Medical evacuation helicopter or that mission (also Med-Evac and Buzz-Off).

DUSTWUN "Duty status-whereabouts unknown." A transitory casualty status used when a military commander suspects that a service member may be a casualty but lacks sufficient evidence to make a determination of missing or killed.

DZ Drop zone.

E&E "Escape and Evasion," avoiding a hazardous assignment.

Eagle flight Large helicopter combat assault.

El Cid U.S. Central Intelligence Division or a generic term for spies.

FAC Forward air controller.

Family advocacy A military social service program that focuses on prevention.

(FAP) Program Identification and treatment of spouse abuse as well as child abuse and neglect. Generally, military family advocacy programs provide families with direct services and they conduct various prevention, training, and data-collection activities.

Fedayeen Arabic term or guerilla fighters; applied especially to anti-Israeli Palestinian groups such as Hamas and the PLO.

Firefight Violent battle of short duration.

Fire mission Artillery or mortar fire.

Flakey Term describing a bad soldier; one making mistakes.

Flying lesson Disposing of prisoners by throwing them out of a helicopter.

FNG Fuckin' new guy.

FO Forward observer (artillery spotter).

FOB Forward operating base.

Fobbit Service member who never goes outside the wire of the forward operating base.

FOB taxi Any vehicle that never leaves the FOB.

Four deuce 4.2-inch mortar.

Frag Fragmentation ammunition, especially hand grenades.

Fragging Personal attacks on military personnel, especially officers, by other military personnel with hand grenades.

FRAGO Fragmentary order. Fragmentary order is an abbreviated form of an operation order, usually issued on a day-to-day basis, which eliminates the need for restating information contained in a basic operation order.

Frankenstein A Marine Corps monster truck, bulging and rippling with spot-welded seams of add on armor. "We scrounge around for what we need and 'Frankenstein' it together." As of December 2004, of the 30,000 estimated wheeled vehicles in Iraq and Afghanistan, about 8,000 of the older models did not have armor protection. Of those that were protected, about 6,000 had full protection, while about 10,000 vehicles had received add-on kits, many improvised in theater.

Friendlies Term used to describe allied or American units or soldiers.

Frisbees Crackers (Vietnam era).

Fruit salad Military award ribbons worn on the uniform of military personnel.

FTA Fuck the Army.

Fucked up To be troubled or seriously wounded.

Gimp Incompetent grunt and/or poor soldier (also, nonhacker).

Golf ball and bullets Meatballs and beans (Vietnam era).

Green Zone Heavily guarded area with several former presidential palaces in central Baghdad where United States, coalition, and Iraqi authorities live and work. Much of the rest of Iraq is the "red zone." An attempt was made to rename it the International Zone (IZ), but this seems not to have stuck.

Genocide Intentional attempted annihilation of a specific ethnic group.

Gone on a walk 30-day contact patrol (Vietnam era).

Gook Derogatory term for any North Vietnamese or Viet Cong soldier (also slope, dink, zip, and zipper head).

Gook sore Any skin sore or infection (also called "crud").

Grease Rations or "to kill someone."

Green Authentic U.S. currency.

Green weenie Army commendation medal (also the military in general) (Vietnam era).

Grunt Infantry soldier or Marine.

Gulf War Syndrome A constellation of debilitating symptoms of unknown etiology experienced by veterans of the Person Gulf conflict that includes headaches, muscular and joint pains, memory loss, agitation, and personality change.

Gunship Heavily armed helicopter (also Cobra gunship).

Gun run Path aircraft take when expending ordnance.

Gun truck An armored and heavily armed vehicle used for convoy security.

GWOT Global War on Terrorism.

Haji (1) Arabic word for someone who has made the pilgrimage to Mecca; (2) used by the U.S. military for an Iraqi, anyone of Arab descent, or even of a brownish skin tone, be they Afghanis, or even Bangladeshis; (3) the word many soldiers use derogatorily for the enemy.

Haji armor Improvised armor, installed by troops hiring Iraqis to update the vehicles by welding any available metal to the sides of Humvees.

Haji mart Any small store operated by Iraqis to sell small items to Americans.

Haji patrol (1) Escort detail; (2) local national unit is also referred to as the Haji patrol, with all the projects that are being performed by the local nationals.

Haji shop Even the smallest base has some form of what soldiers call a "Haji shop," or, in more politically correct terms, a shop run by locals. Frequently near the PX, the "Haji" shop would sell everything from cigarettes to knockoff sunglasses to pirated DVDs.

Hamas Islamic resistance movement dedicated to the total destruction of Israel.

Ham and mother fuckers Ham and lima beans (Vietnam era).

Ham and son-of-a-bitches Ham and eggs (Vietnam era).

Hardshell A transferred soldier.

Head Drug user (Vietnam era) (also, smacker and popper).

Heat tabs Fuel tablets used to heat water and rations.

Hezbollah (Hizbolla) An anti-Israeli resistance group comprised of Lebanese Shiites. This group operates TV and radio stations as well as health care clinics, and also holds seats in the Lebanese parliament.

Hillbilly armor Improvised vehicle armor, salvaged from digging through local landfills for pieces of scrap metal to bolster armor on their vehicles. Typically a half inch of scrap steel hastily cut in the shape of the door and welded or riveted on.

Ho Chi Mhins Rubber sandals made form tire carcasses (Vietnam era).

Honcho Leader or boss.

Hootch Residence, including tent or other temporary shelter (Vietnam era).

Hot Lz Landing zone under enemy fire.

Huey Standard Bell helicopter.

Hump To walk or carry.

I&I Intoxication and intercourse.

ICDC Iraqi Civil Defense Corps.

IED Improvised explosive device.

Inactive reserve duty Affiliation with the military in a nontraining, nonpaying status after completing the minimum obligation of active duty service.

Incoming Received enemy fire, especially artillery.

Infantry Units of the military that are trained, armed, and equipped to fight on foot.

Inside the wire Inside an enemy combatant detention facility. Working "inside the wire" of the enemy combatant detention facility can lead to stress for the U.S. troops working here. Vietnam-era phrase for the perimeter of any U.S. base in Vietnam.

Insurgency An armed rebellion by any irregular armed force that rises up against an established authority or government.

Intifada Arabic term for "uprising"; typically refers to Palestinian insurrections against Israel.

ITGA Interim Transitional Government of Afghanistan.

"J" Marijuana cigarette (also, joint) (Vietnam era).

Jihad Arabic word meaning "struggles" and referring to Muslims' individual attempts to improve themselves and grow closer to Allah. The contemporary meaning, however, refers to "holy war" between Muslims and non-Muslims. Although "holy war" is one meaning of jihad, the tactics of Al Qaeda do not warrant the term jihad. The tenets of Islam forbid harming noncombatants (such as women and children) and also forbid taking one's own life as in the case of so-called suicide bombers.

Jingle trucks [Afghanistan] (transport trucks with a narrow wheel base that are usually adorned with colorful stickers and chimes), the military contracted for host nation delivery trucks, known as "jingle trucks" because of the decorative metal tassels hanging from the bottom of the truck frames that jingled when the trucks moved.

Jody Civilian men (Vietnam era).

John Wayne'n Displaying reckless heroic behavior in combat.

Jolly Green Giant Large cargo helicopter (Vietnam era).

Joy pop Flying fast and close to the ground in a helicopter (Vietnam era).

KAF Stands for Kandahar Air Field. That is the main base of operations for the Southern part of Afghanistan. The main post is big and has lots of people. It is a main transportation hub—both Helo and Fixed Wing—also convoys of Humvees going in and out.

KBR Kellogg, Brown & Root—The biggest contractor serving the Coalition Forces.

Khalifa Term for the head scarf worn by men in Saudi Arabia and other Muslim countries.

KIA Killed in action.

Killing zone An area in which a commander plans to force the enemy to concentrate so as to be destroyed with conventional weapons or the tactical employment of nuclear weapons.

Kurds Ethnically distinct non-Arab inhabitants of northern Iraq and parts of Turkey. Thousands of Kurds were massacred by the Iraqi army when they were encouraged to rebel against Saddam Hussein in 1991 by the United States but the United States failed to support them militarily.

LAAW Light anti-tank assault weapon operated by one soldier.

Land of the big PX Reference to the United States (Vietnam era).

LBJ Long bing jail (Vietnam era).

LEG Nonairborne soldier, an infantry person.

LGH Large green helicopter.

Lifer Career military personnel.

LN Local national. A citizen of Iraq, if you're in Iraq, Afghanistan, if you're in Afghanistan, and so on. Usually encountered as labor brought on post to do construction or other labor.

LOH Light observation helicopter (also LOACH).

"Lonely Eagles" Name for African American fighter pilots during WWII.

Long rats Dehydrated rations used by LRRPs.

LRRP Long-range reconnaissance patrol.

M-240G Replacement for the M-60 series of infantry and aircraft-mounted machine guns.

M-249 Squad automatic weapon; a light machine gun carried by selected infantry.

Mad minute A 60-second expenditure of ordnance, heavy defensive fire.

Mama-San Vietnamese woman.

MEPS Military entrance processing station. Military bases at various locations in the United States that receive and train new enlisted personnel.

MGH Medium green helicopter.

MIA Missing in action.

Mk-19 A 40mm belt-fed grenade launcher.

Mk-153 SMAW (shoulder-launched multipurpose assault weapon).

Mog, The Mogadishu, Somalia.

MOS Military occupational specialty.

Mortaritaville Nickname for LSA Anaconda, a major base near Balad, reflecting the frequent mortar attacks.

MP Military police officer.

MPC Military pay certificate (also, script).

MRE Meals ready to eat; military field rations.

Mujahideen Arabic word meaning "holy warrior."

Muy Huy Duc (me-hoy duck) "Kiss my ass." (Vietnamese)

NATO North Atlantic Treaty Organization.

NCO Noncommissioned officer; an enlisted person in pay grade E-4 or higher.

NDP Night defense position.

New puppy Ensign; 2nd Lt.

Ngyeun (n-win) Enemy soldier (Vietnamese).

Nouc (nook) Water.

Nuoc Mam Fermented fish sauce.

Number–One The best or first (Vietnam era).

Number–Ten The worst or last (Vietnam era).

NVA North Vietnamese Army (also, PAVN).

Obligation The period of time an individual agrees to serve on active duty, in the reserves, or a combination of both.

OCS Officer candidate school. A program for college graduates with no prior military training that wish to become military officers. The program also accepts qualified enlisted personnel who wish to become officers; also, "On Civilian Streets."

OEF Operation Enduring Freedom.

OGA Other Government Agency—CIA.

Off To kill someone (Vietnam era).

OIF Operation Iraqi Freedom.

OPEC Organization of Petroleum Exporting Countries. A cartel formed by Saudi Arabia, Iran, Iraq, Kuwait, and Venezuela in 1960 to control the world's petroleum prices. Current members also include Algeria, Gabon, Indonesia, Libya, Nigeria, Qatar, and the United Arab Emirates.

OPCON Operational control.

Outgoing Friendly fire, especially artillery, directed toward the enemy.

Oversexed weekly Newspaper (Vietnam era).

Ps Piasters. Vietnamese currency.

Papa-San Vietnamese male adult.

Paste Peanut butter (Vietnam era).

Pay grade Newcomers, without previous military experience and without a college education, normally entering the military as recruits in pay grade E-1. The enlisted pay grades range from E-1 through E-9 with increasing responsibility and salary as the pay grade increases. Officer pay grades range from O-1 through O-9.

Pecker-checker Medic.

PFC Private first class or proud fucking civilian.

Play dough Bread (Vietnam era).

Point man First soldier in a column or on patrol.

POG People other than grunts [pronounced "pogue"] rear-echelon support troops.

Potato masher Chinese communist hand grenade.

PRC-25 or -77 Portable radio communication Model 25 or Model 77 (also, prick).

PRT This stands for provincial reconstruction team. These are military, government departments, and civilian aid organizations from our country and many others that come to a town and help to rebuild. The PRT coordinates construction projects and provide humanitarian assistance.

PRU Provincial reconnaissance unit.

PSD Personal security detail—Private security contractors.

PSYOPS Psychological operations.

Punji sticks Sharpened bamboo stakes used as bobby traps.

QCS Vietnamese military police.

Quad-50 Four .50 caliber machine guns mounted together as one unit.

Ranger Rapidly deployable airborne light infantry armed and trained to conduct highly complex joint direct actions in coordination with or in support of other special operations units of all service branches.

RCH Red cunt hair (one half kilometer).

RECON Reconnaissance. A mission undertaken to obtain information about the activities and resources of an enemy or potential enemy or to secure data concerning the metrological, hydrographic, or geographic characteristics of a particular area.

Redleg Artillery.

Red Ball Express Army service and supply unit in Europe composed primarily of African American truckers during WWII.

Red on red Enemy-on-enemy fire.

REMF Rear echelon mother fucker (Vietnam era).

Remfland The rear-echelon areas where support personnel live and work in relative safety.

Remington raiders Clerks; also called Smith-Corona Raiders.

Reserves The military forces comprised of individuals who are not presently on full-time active duty but who may be called to active duty if needed.

RF/PF, Ruff-Puffs Regional or popular forces.

Roach coach Mobile mess (food serving) vehicle.

Rocket City Da Nang (in Vietnam).

Rocket pocket Location from which the enemy fires (especially 122mm) rockets.

ROE Rules of engagement. Directives issued by military authority that delineate the circumstances and limitations under which U.S. forces will initiate and/or continue combat engagement with other forces encountered (aka Law of War).

Rogue state Term first used during the Clinton administration to describe those countries believed to sponsor terrorism. The current list includes Cuba, Iraq, Iran, Libya, North Korea, Sudan, and Syria.

ROK Republic of Korea (South Korea); also a Marine from that country.

ROK Rats Korean "C" rations (Vietnam era).

ROTC Reserve Officer's Training Corps. Refers to a program on college campuses designed to train undergraduate students who wish to become officers in the military upon graduation. Incentives for participation in the program include scholarships for tuition, books, and fees; uniforms; and a monthly allowance.

Root, The Beirut, Lebanon. Term used by service members assigned peacekeeping duty in the 1983 time frame.

RPG Rocket-propelled grenade.

R&R Rest and relaxation.

RPG Soviet-style, rocket-propelled grenade launcher.

RTC Radio telephone communicator.

Saigon tea Orange sodas or cold tea drank by bar girls (Vietnam era).

Sandbox or sandpit Iraq.

Sea duty An assignment (generally for 3 years) to any ship whether or not scheduled for deployment, or to any aircraft squadron that may or may not be deployable; the term typically refers to Navy personnel.

SGH Small green helicopter.

Shah Title used to describe high status leaders in Iran.

Shake and bake First used during the Vietnam War, and revived in Iraq, to refer to attacks using a combination of conventional bombs, cluster bombs (CBU), and napalm. In the battle of Fallujah in 2004 it was used in reference to a combination barrage of white phosphorus and explosive artillery shells.

Shariah Term meaning "the path that leads to God" and referring to Islamic law. Shariah law is based on the Koran, the sunna (other writings of Muhammad) and the hadith (outside observations of Muhammad's life). Strict interpretations of Shariah have resulted in amputations and beheadings for violations of the law.

Shiite Those who follow the Shia branch of Islam; Shiites believe that the only legitimate leaders of Islam must be blood relatives of the prophet Muhammad. Most Arabs are Sunni Muslims and relations between Sunnis and Shiites are poor.

Shore duty All duty performed within the 48 contiguous states where Navy personnel are reassigned to land-based activities and commands. Navy personnel assigned to shore duty are not required to be absent from the corporate limits of the duty station for more than 99 days per year.

Short Having less than 3 months left in Vietnam (also short-timer).

Shrine Latrine (also, shitter).

Sit Rep Situation report.

"SIX," "6" Commander's radio call-sign.

Six-By, 6 BY 6 Military truck with 6-wheel drive.

"Skinny" Enemy combatant during the conflict in Somalia; also "Skines."

Sky pilot Chaplain.

Slick UH-1 helicopter, generic term for helicopter (also, Huey, chopper, or bird).

Sneaky Petes Special forces personnel (Vietnam era).

Soul brother African American soldier or Marine (Vietnam era).

Souvenir To give without cost (Vietnam era).

Spooky and Puff the Magic Dragon C-47 aircraft armed with flares and several chain guns.

Stand down A 3-day rest period for units coming out of the field; also used to describe an occasion when VA and civilian medical personnel provide health care services for homeless veterans in the United States.

Steam and clean Steam bath and massage parlors.

Stiffs Dead bodies.

Sunni The largest branch of Islam. Unlike the Shiites, this branch does not require that religious leaders have to be blood descendants of the prophet Muhammad.

Super-chicken Army military rank, Spec 5 or over.

Super-striper Army military rank, E-6 or over.

SWAG Scientific, wild-ass guess.

TCN Third country national: A citizen of a neutral country who is in the theater of operations as a contractor.

TCP Traffic control point.

"There it is" Expression used by grunts to agree or confirm (Vietnam era).

Thieu-Uy (to-wee) Second lieutenant (Vietnamese).

Titi (tee-tee) Small or little (Vietnamese slang).

Toe popper Small plastic land mine.

Toi-le bac-si (toe-lee-bac-ci) "I'm a doctor" (Vietnamese).

Top dog First sergeant, master sergeant (also, top kick, and first shirt).

Torch To set on fire.

Tour of Duty A specified period of service obligation; also used to describe the location of a duty tour, for example, "Mediterranean tour of duty."

Track Tracked vehicle.

Trade school One of the military academies, for example, West Point, or Annapolis.

Travel bureau Graves registration (Vietnam era).

Triple nickels, The The 555th Parachute Infantry Company; the first all-African American Paratrooper companies in the U.S. military formed during WWII.

Tunnel rat Soldiers of small stature used to enter and clear enemy tunnels.

Turtle Replacement.

Unit one kit Medical bad use by corps people or medics.

VBIED Vehicle borne improvised explosive device. Also, car bomb.

Vill Village or hamlet (Vietnam era).

Wasted To be killed (also, zapped, greased, stitched, blown away, bought the farm, and ruined his whole day).

Weapons of mass destruction Term used to describe nuclear, chemical, and/or biological weapons possessed by enemy states.

White mice Saigon police (Vietnam era).

Willy Pete, WP White phosphorous; also called "Wilson Pickett."

WIA Wounded in action.

World, in the Referring to the United States of America.

Xin Loi (sin-loy) "Sorry about that."

Yards Indigenous tribal people of Vietnam; Hmong.

Zippo squad A squad that is designated to burn a village (Vietnam era).

ZOT Loser, zero, nothing.

Author Index

Subject Index